W9-ANJ-686

CAPE COD, MARTHA'S VINEYARD & NANTUCKET

EXPLORER'S GUIDE

CAPE COD, MARTHA'S VINEYARD & NANTUCKET

TWELFTH EDITION

KIM GRANT & KATY WARD

THE COUNTRYMAN PRESS
A Division of W. W. Norton & Company
Independent Publishers Since 1923

Copyright © 2021, 2017, 2014, 2011, 2009, 2007, 2005, 2003, 2001, 1999, 1997, 1995 by Kim Grant

For information about permission to reproduce selections from this book, write to
Permissions, The Countryman Press, 500 Fifth Avenue, New York, NY 10110

For information about special discounts for bulk purchases, please contact
W. W. Norton Special Sales at specialsales@wwnorton.com or 800-233-4830

Manufacturing by Versa Press
Book series design by Chris Welch

The Countryman Press
www.countrymanpress.com

A Division of W. W. Norton & Company, Inc.
500 Fifth Avenue, New York, NY 10110
www.wwnorton.com

978-1-68268-600-3 (pbk.)

10 9 8 7 6 5 4 3 2 1

To Catherine Direen "and whatever she's having." —Kim Grant

To my parents, for raising me in this beautiful place. —Katy Ward

EXPLORE WITH US!

Welcome to the 12th edition of the most comprehensive guide to Cape Cod, Martha's Vineyard, and Nantucket. I have been highly selective but broadly inclusive, based on years of repeated visits, cumulative research, and ongoing conversations with locals. All entries—attractions, inns, and restaurants—are chosen on the basis of personal experience.

I hope that the organization of this guide makes it easy to read and use. The layout has been kept simple; the following pointers will help you get started.

WHAT'S WHERE In the beginning of the book you'll find an alphabetical listing of special highlights and important information that you can reference quickly. You'll find advice on everything from where to find the best art galleries and lighthouses to where to take a whale-watching excursion.

LODGING Because prices, seasons, and specials are so variable, I have used "abstract" pricing to give you a general idea of the relative rates between lodging places. Please also see Lodging in "What's Where on Cape Cod, Martha's Vineyard, and Nantucket." Double room rate designations for high season are as follows:

$ = $1–199
$$ = $200–299
$$$ = $300–399
$$$$ = $400–499
$$$$$ = $500–599
$$$$$+ = $600+

RESTAURANTS In most sections, I make a distinction between Dining Out and Eating Out. Restaurants listed under Eating Out are generally inexpensive and more casual; reservations are often suggested for restaurants in Dining Out. A range of prices for main dishes is included with each entry. Main dish designations are as follows:

$ = $1–9
$$ = $10–19
$$$ = $20–29
$$$$ = $30+

THINGS TO SEE & DO The internet is much better suited to offering up-to-the-minute pricing than print. To give you a general idea about how much things cost per person:

$ = $1–9
$$ = $10–19
$$$ = $20–29
$$$$ = $30–39
$$$$$+ = $40+

COVID-19 Due to the COVID-19 pandemic, travel in Cape Cod, Martha's Vineyard, and Nantucket (as everywhere else) requires more planning for every activity to ensure current availability and appropriate social distancing. This means that you should call or check a venue's website to confirm, among other things, if reservations are required where walk-in activity was once the norm. It also means that providers of services from hotels to restaurants or ferries and fishing charters are likely to be running their businesses differently from in the past, with fewer visitors engaged at any one time. If you are a family group, be sure to mention that, because it may make a difference in the business owner's risk calculations. Ask if there is outdoor seating available at restaurants—many venues have changed their layouts to include more outside dining while they reduce the numbers of tables inside. Meals to go, food service delivery, and curbside pick-up options have expanded dramatically in the spring and summer of 2020; check to see if those options are still available. Annual events, including festivals, parades, and tours, have shifted their dates and ticketing procedures. You'll have a more rewarding travel experience if you arrive prepared and flexible.

GREEN SPACE In addition to trails and walks, "green space" also includes white and blue spaces, that is, beaches and ponds.

WHERE TO START Start with the aptly named "What's Where." Seriously. It gives a big-picture, contextual overview of everything on the Cape and the islands.

KEY TO SYMBOLS

❄ The "off-season" icon appears next to appealing year-round lodging or attractions.

🍴 The "special-value" icon appears next to lodging entries, restaurants, and activities that combine exceptional quality with moderate prices.

🐾 The "pet-friendly" icon appears next to lodgings where pets are welcome.

✐ The "child and family interest" icon appears next to lodging entries, restaurants, activities, and shops of special appeal to youngsters and families.

☂ The "rainy-day" icon appears next to things to do and places of interest that are appropriate for foul-weather days.

🍸 The "martini glass" icon appears next to restaurants and entertainment venues with good bars.

♿ The "handicap" symbol indicates lodging and dining establishments that are truly wheelchair-accessible.

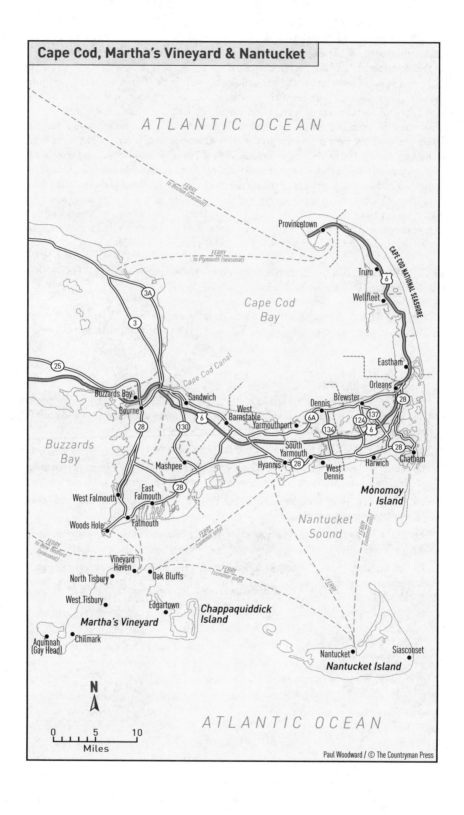

Cape Cod, Martha's Vineyard & Nantucket

ATLANTIC OCEAN

FERRY to Boston (seasonal)

Provincetown

FERRY to Plymouth (seasonal)

Truro

CAPE COD NATIONAL SEASHORE

6

Cape Cod Bay

Wellfleet

3A

3

Eastham

25

Cape Cod Canal

Orleans

Buzzards Bay

Sandwich

Dennis

Brewster

28

Bourne

West Barnstable

6A

137

124

28

130

6

Yarmouthport

134

6

Buzzards Bay

28

South Yarmouth

Mashpee

Hyannis

28

West Dennis

Harwich

Chatham

West Falmouth

East Falmouth

28

Monomoy Island

Woods Hole

Falmouth

FERRY (summer only)

Nantucket Sound

FERRY (summer only)

FERRY to New Bedford (seasonal)

FERRY (summer only)

FERRY

Vineyard Haven

Oak Bluffs

North Tisbury

West Tisbury

Edgartown

Chappaquiddick Island

Aquinnah (Gay Head)

Chilmark

Martha's Vineyard

Nantucket

Siasconset

Nantucket Island

N

0   5   10
Miles

ATLANTIC OCEAN

Paul Woodward / © The Countryman Press

CONTENTS

INTRODUCTION | 12
A TRUE LOCAL PERSPECTIVE | 14
SUGGESTED ITINERARIES | 16
WHAT'S WHERE ON CAPE COD, MARTHA'S VINEYARD & NANTUCKET | 18

THE UPPER CAPE | 31

BOURNE | 33
SANDWICH | 47
FALMOUTH & WOODS HOLE | 65
MASHPEE | 91

MID-CAPE | 101

BARNSTABLE | 103
HYANNIS | 119
YARMOUTH | 135
DENNIS | 151

THE LOWER CAPE | 171

BREWSTER | 173
HARWICH | 191
CHATHAM | 206
ORLEANS | 233

THE OUTER CAPE | 255

EASTHAM | 257
WELLFLEET | 275
TRURO | 297

PROVINCETOWN | 317

MARTHA'S VINEYARD | 371

NANTUCKET | 431

INDEX | 481

MAPS

CAPE COD, MARTHA'S VINEYARD & NANTUCKET | 8
BOURNE | 32
SANDWICH | 48
FALMOUTH & WOODS HOLE | 64
MASHPEE | 92
BARNSTABLE | 102
HYANNIS | 118
YARMOUTH | 136
DENNIS | 152
BREWSTER | 172
HARWICH | 192
CHATHAM | 207
ORLEANS | 234
EASTHAM | 256
WELLFLEET | 274
TRURO | 298
PROVINCETOWN | 318
MARTHA'S VINEYARD | 372
EDGARTOWN | 375
VINEYARD HAVEN | 378
OAK BLUFFS | 382
NANTUCKET | 432

INTRODUCTION

The Greek philosopher Heraclitus wrote, "Change is the only constant in life." After writing this guide since 1995, it's still true: just when I think I've seen it all, a ray of sunlight hits the Provincetown dune shacks to make them new again. Walk a trail with a naturalist or your own keen eye, and you will notice different birds and plants from your last walk on the same trail.

That said, the mission of this 12th edition of *Explorer's Guide Cape Cod, Martha's Vineyard & Nantucket* has not changed. Its highest objective has always been to save you time and money by helping you make the best decisions for your trip. Having trustworthy content all in one place is integral to that goal.

Did you know that the average traveler visits 38 websites while planning a trip? You can cut that number down considerably by dipping into this book first. The death of print is highly exaggerated. Curation—and having a consistent perspective—is key.

MY GO-TO SPOT FOR MAXIMUM TRANQUILITY: FORT HILL, EASTHAM, OUTER CAPE KIM GRANT

Information without context or comparison is mere commodity. This guide provides a reasoned assessment of all the possible choices to be found on the Internet. Its pages are devoted to reasons why you should visit one place over another, why one place is right for you and not for your sister. What is not reviewed here is just as important as what's included.

For the first time ever, though, this edition differs in one profound way. Katy Ward, an exceptional journalist who turned the craft of prose writing into art at the *Province-town Banner*, brings her considerable talents to these pages. Growing up on the Outer Cape, Katy ended up being the only full-time reporter responsible for covering Provincetown, Truro, and Wellfleet for *The Banner*. Katy received second place accolades in history reporting at the "Best Weekly Newspaper of the Year" (two years in a row) awards held by the New England Newspaper & Press Association. Her local news and human-interest feature stories sing with color, wit, and purpose.

Katy has witnessed, experienced, and described (so we feel as present as she was) more on Cape Cod than most would in a lifetime of visits. She rallied while on-call 24/7 covering breaking news for *The Banner*: unexpected emergency flooding following a winter Nor'easter; a four-alarm fire that engulfed a popular restaurant in the center of town on Memorial Day weekend; assisting volunteers from the International Fund for Animal Welfare in efforts to save stranded dolphins or rehabilitate cold-stunned turtles.

In an age that reveres the niche, we strongly believe that this guidebook can be many things to many people: those fortunate enough to visit often throughout the year; year-rounders who offer advice to a steady stream of summer guests; residents who live on the Upper Cape but don't know the Lower Cape; and people whose only trip to the Cape or the islands is their annual summer holiday—people who have always vacationed in Wellfleet, let's say, but are ready to explore other places.

We also aim to introduce the other Cape and islands to that segment of the traveling public that assumes traffic jams, crowded beaches, and tacky souvenir shops define the region. Nothing could be further from the truth, as you will see here.

I'm grateful for every reader who emailed, every innkeeper who shared her encyclopedic insights, and every guest who gave up a favorite place or tip over breakfast so others could enjoy the same. The book simply wouldn't have been possible without them. I'm excited to experience the changes unfolding in this edition. You will be, too.

—Kim Grant

A TRUE LOCAL PERSPECTIVE

When Kim Grant pitched the idea of being coauthor for this extremely thorough and resourceful guidebook, I thought, "How hard can it be? I know Cape Cod like the back of my hand."

It turns out—that's not exactly the case.

Born and raised in North Truro, my childhood was mostly spent at the beach—playing in the sand, exploring, swimming, making forts—you know, kid stuff. My teens were spent hanging around town, working summer retail jobs and skipping sailing school to jump off MacMillan Wharf with the older kids. I've stayed in several dune shacks, reeled in giant tunas, and successfully landed stripers shore casting on the backside. I've been to countless bonfires, surfed Wellfleet's famous waves, kayaked through Truro's Pamet Harbor, and biked the Bourne Canal.

Additionally, my previous job as reporter at the *Provincetown Banner* strengthened my knowledge for this special spit of sandy land. I became obsessed and intrigued by the Cape's rich history, and I also developed close relationships within the community that continues to flourish today. From interviews with local famed figures such as the feisty artist Ilona Royce-Smithkin to eating lunch with the locals at the Soup Kitchen in the dead of winter, I've run the gamut when it comes to Cape experiences.

MY DAD TEACHING ME HOW TO PUMP FRESH GROUNDWATER DURING ONE OF OUR MANY MEMORABLE DUNE SHACK GETAWAYS KATY WARD

I'm not trying to glamorize my life on the Cape. It's not always a day at the beach. The point I'm trying to make is: my love for the Cape bleeds deep. Which is why I thought I would be the perfect gal to rewrite and update the 12th edition of Kim's guidebook. But it wasn't until I delved into each town that I realized I didn't know everything—and yes, that was a bit hard to swallow. Even though I've spent 30-plus years living on the Cape, there were (and still are) countless beaches, ponds, hiking trails, restaurants, and museums to explore.

Read any chapter and I dare you *not* to find at least one activity, shop, resource, or event that you would not have known about otherwise. I know I was surely surprised! Don't worry, Kim's diligent research still flows heavily through this edition, but now it's meshed with an extra dose of local insight. I want to give a special thanks to Kim for taking a chance on me. Her support and encouragement through this process has been invaluable.

If you have decided to buy this book—thank you. I hope you enjoy the new revisions, personal anecdotes, historical accounts, and beautiful imagery.

This guidebook remains *the* go-to source for the most comprehensive guidance to Cape and island travel. For a real-time, on-the-ground *supplement*, please dip into the guidebook's highlights on my website, CapeCodExplorersGuide .com, or visit Kim's website, BinduTrips.com/destination/cape-cod. Be sure to also like and follow us on Facebook.

Happy reading and exploring!

—Katy Ward

FUN FACT

My dad and I both graduated from the former Provincetown High School and also had the same math teacher. The high school closed in 2013 from lack of attendance. I had just over 20 classmates in my graduating class.

SUGGESTED ITINERARIES

IF YOU HAVE 3 DAYS Special thanks for buying this book. It contains far more information than you'll ever be able to use. We hope you will pass this book along to a friend after it serves you well. For sure, as a starting point, check out the "Where to Start In..." for each town.

IF YOU HAVE 5 DAYS You'll need to be efficient. Visit the village of Sandwich, poke around antiques and artisan shops on Route 6A, and drive down scenic bayside roads north of Route 6A, spending two nights mid-Cape. On the third morning, pop down to Main Street and the lighthouse in Chatham, and then head to the Outer Cape and the famed Cape Cod National Seashore beaches, stopping at the Salt Pond Visitor Center in Eastham. Spend two nights on the Outer Cape (or in Orleans): visit galleries in Wellfleet, walk the Atlantic beaches and short nature trails, and take a day trip to Provincetown.

IF YOU HAVE 7 DAYS You'll end up with a very enjoyable trip. Spend three nights mid-Cape and three on the Outer Cape. Do all of the above, plus linger longer in Sandwich, visiting the Glass Museum and/or Heritage Museums & Gardens. Add a beach walk at Barnstable's Sandy Neck Beach and/or Nauset Beach in Orleans. Visit the Cape Cod Museum of Natural History in Brewster and/or the Wellfleet Bay Wildlife Sanctuary. Spend a day and a half in Provincetown—watching people, walking Commercial Street, ducking into art museums and the informative Provincetown Museum, taking

MARTHA'S VINEYARD KIM GRANT

in a sunset from Race Point or Herring Cove, or heading out on a whale-watching excursion.

IF YOU HAVE 10 DAYS You'll be very happy. Allot the entire three additional days (from the above plan) to Martha's Vineyard. (Trying to see the Vineyard in a day borders on silliness.) Or add a night or two in the diverse Falmouth and Woods Hole area and a day trip to Nantucket. Back on the Cape, get out on the water with a trip to Monomoy Island in Chatham or some other boat tour. Add a couple of whistle-stops at the Cape's small, sweet, historic museums.

IF YOU HAVE 2 WEEKS You're really lucky. Allot three days to one of the islands. Add a quiet canoe or kayak paddle somewhere. Take a leisurely bike ride or an aerial sight-seeing flight. Get tickets to summer stock and cheer on the home team at a free baseball game. Slip into a parking space at the Wellfleet Drive-In. Investigate an old cemetery. Take an art class. Visit Mashpee's South Cape Beach State Park.

IF YOU LIVE ON THE CAPE & ISLANDS You're the luckiest of all. Scribble comments in the margins of this book and lend it to visiting friends so you don't have to keep repeating yourself. Explore something new at least once a week. Isn't that one reason you live here?

WHERE TO START IN . . . While thorough, this guidebook can also be overwhelming. Start with these suggested town-by-town daily itineraries. These are loose suggestions, but it will get you started on how best to dip into a town. Use this as merely a guide.

WHAT'S WHERE ON CAPE COD, MARTHA'S VINEYARD & NANTUCKET

General Information

AREA CODE The area code for the region of Cape Cod, Martha's Vineyard, and Nantucket is **508**.

AIRPORTS & AIRLINES There is regularly scheduled air service from Boston to Provincetown. Hyannis is reached by air from Boston, Providence, and New York. Nantucket and Martha's Vineyard enjoy regularly scheduled year-round service; **Cape Air** (508-771-6944; capeair .com) offers the most flights. Sight-seeing by air is best done in Chatham, Barnstable, Provincetown, and Martha's Vineyard.

ATTIRE The Cape and the islands are casual for the most part; a jacket is required at only one or two places. At the other end of the spectrum, you'll always need shoes and shirts at beachfront restaurants.

CHILDREN, ESPECIALLY FOR Within this guide a number of activities and sites that have special "child appeal" are identified by the crayon symbol ✎.

EMERGENCIES Call **911** from anywhere on Cape Cod. Contact information for each town's police department is also listed in this category. Major hospitals are located in Falmouth (508-548-5300) and Hyannis (508-771-1800). And of course the Vineyard (508-693-0410) and Nantucket (508-825-8100).

EVENTS The largest annual events are listed within each chapter of this book. Otherwise, invest in the *Cape Cod Times* (capecodonline.com). It features a special section about the day's events and a Friday calendar supplement.

FERRIES There are fast and slow ferries to Provincetown from Boston and a day-tripper from Plymouth. To reach Martha's Vineyard, the car ferry departs from Woods Hole, and passenger ferries depart from Woods Hole, Falmouth, Hyannis, and New Bedford. There is a seasonal interisland ferry. There are high-speed and regular ferries to Nantucket from Hyannis (car and passenger) and Harwich (passenger). See the appropriate chapter for details on schedules.

HIGH SEASON Memorial Day weekend in late May kicks things off, then there is a slight lull until school lets out in late June. From then on, the Cape is in full swing through Labor Day (early September). There are two exceptions to this, though, and they're the best-kept secrets for planning a Cape Cod vacation: the Cape is relatively quiet during the week following the July Fourth weekend and the week prior to Labor Day weekend. You will find bed-and-breakfast vacancies and no lines at your favorite restaurant. As a rule, traveling to the Cape or the islands without reservations in high season is not recommended. Accommodations—especially cottages, efficiencies, and apartments—are often

KIM GRANT

booked by January for the upcoming summer. The Cape and islands are also quite busy from Labor Day to Columbus Day (mid-October). It's fairly common for bed-and-breakfasts to be booked solid every autumn weekend.

HIGHWAYS Route 6, also called the Mid-Cape Highway, is a speedy, four-lane, divided highway until Exit 9 1/2, when it becomes an undivided two-laner. After the Orleans rotary (Exit 13), it becomes an undivided four-lane highway most of the way to Provincetown.

Scenic Route 6A, also known as Old King's Highway and Main Street, runs from the Sagamore Bridge to Orleans. It is lined with sea captains' houses, antiques shops, bed-and-breakfasts, and huge old trees. Development along Route 6A is strictly regulated by the Historical Commission. Route 6A links up with Route 6 in Orleans. Without stopping, it takes an extra 30 minutes or so to take Route 6A instead of Route 6 from Sandwich to Orleans.

Route 28 can be confusing. It's an elongated, U-shaped highway that runs from the Bourne Bridge south to Falmouth, then east to Hyannis and Chatham, then north to Orleans. The problem lies with the Route 28 directional signs. Although you're actually heading north when you travel from Chatham to Orleans, the signs will say

ROUTE 28 SOUTH. When you drive from Hyannis to Falmouth, you're actually heading west, but the signs will say ROUTE 28 NORTH. Ignore the north and south indicators and look for towns that are in the direction you want to go.

INFORMATION For those coming from the Boston area, Cape-wide information can be obtained at the tourist office on Route 3 (Exit 5) in Plymouth. There is also a year-round **Cape Cod Chamber of Commerce Welcome Center** at Exit 6 off Route 6 (CapeCodChamber.org).

INTERNET Free wireless Internet is readily available at most lodging places, libraries, and chambers of commerce. In addition, many towns are experimenting with service that blankets part of their downtowns. You should have little trouble getting online for free almost everywhere.

LODGING There are many choices— from inns and bed-and-breakfasts to cottages, apartments, and efficiencies. Rates quoted are for two people sharing one room in the inn's definition of high season. $ means $1–199, $$ means $200–299, $$$ means $300–399, and $$$$ means $400+. Cottages are generally rented from Saturday to Saturday. Most inns and bed-and-breakfasts don't accept children under 10 to 12 years of age. All

GENERAL INFORMATION

accept credit cards unless otherwise noted. None allows smoking unless otherwise noted. Pets are not accepted unless otherwise noted by our 🐾 icon in the margin. So many places require a two-night minimum stay during the high season that I have not included that information unless it deviates significantly. Holiday weekends often require a 3-night minimum stay. And then there are a whole host of options on airbnb .com and TripAdvisor's equivalent, flipkey.com. Good youth hostels (usahostels.org/cape) are located on **Martha's Vineyard** and **Nantucket** and in **Eastham** and **Truro**.

KATY WARD

MAPS I love the out-of-print *Cape Cod Street Atlas (Includes Martha's Vineyard and Nantucket)* (DeLorme). I'm forever searching out bodies of water or shorelines that look interesting on the map and always finding scenic roads that I didn't expect.

MEDIA Print publications are charming on the Cape and really give you insight into the local scenes. The *Cape Cod Times* (capecodonline.com), with Cape- and islandwide coverage, is published daily. Also look for these local weeklies: the *The Provincetown Independent* (focusing on the Lower and Outer Cape), *Falmouth Enterprise*, and the *Provincetown Banner* (provincetown.wickedlocal .com). And on the islands: the *Vineyard Gazette* (mvgazette.com), the *Martha's Vineyard Times* (mvtimes.com), and Nantucket's the *Inquirer and Mirror* (ack .net).

In addition to its bimonthly magazine, *Cape Cod Life* publishes an annual guide and a "Best of the Cape & Islands" within its June edition.

OFF-SEASON In an attempt to get people thinking about visiting the Cape and the islands off-season, I have put the ❄ symbol next to activities, lodging, and restaurants that are open and appealing in the off-season.

PETS Look for the 🐾 icon to find lodgings where your pet is welcome. But always call ahead; there may be additional fees associated with bringing your pet, and there may be special rooms reserved for pets and their owners.

PHOTOGRAPHY For tips about how and where to take perfect photos, pick up a copy of *The Photographer's Guide to Cape Cod & the Islands* by Chris Linder. As you'll see, it *is* possible to shoot in places that are not overrun with tourists in the summertime. Special thanks to several photographers who helped make this edition bright and lively: Marcia Duggan/ CapeCodSoul, Kayla Robertson/ Do Art Photography, Leesa Burke, Anne Greenbaum, Paul Benson, and Paul Schulenburg.

POPULATION More than 220,000 people live year-round on the Cape and the islands. No one has a truly accurate count of how many people visit in summer, but it is well into the millions.

RADIO WOMR (92.1 FM) in Provincetown has diverse and great programming. Tune in to National Public Radio with WCCT (90.3 FM). On the Vineyard tune to WMVY (92.7 FM); on Nantucket, WNAN (91.1 FM); and on the Cape try

WCOD (106.1 FM), WFCC (107.5 FM), and WQRC (99.9 FM).

RAINY-DAY ACTIVITIES Chances are that if it were sunny every day, we would start taking the sunshine for granted. So when the clouds move in and the raindrops start falling on your head, be appreciative of the sun and look for the ☂ icon in this book, which tells you where to head indoors.

ROTARIES When you're approaching a rotary, cars already within the rotary have the right-of-way.

SMOKING Smoking in bars and restaurants is not permitted in the state of Massachusetts.

SWIMMING POOLS For a fee, you can swim at **Willy's Gym** in Eastham, the **Nantucket Community Pool,** and at the **Mansion House** in Vineyard Haven on the Vineyard. Swimming at the **Provincetown Inn** is free.

TRAFFIC It's bad in July and August no matter how you cut it. It's bumper-to-bumper on Friday afternoon and evening, when cars arrive for the weekend. It's grueling on Sunday afternoon and evening when they return home. And there's no respite on Saturday, when all the weekly cottage renters have to vacate their units and a new set of renters arrives to take their places.

TRAINS The **Cape Cod Central Railroad** runs between Sandwich and Hyannis, alongside cranberry bogs and the Sandy Neck Great Salt Marsh.

TRANSPORTATION *By bus:* The **Plymouth & Brockton bus line** (508-746-0378; p-b.com) serves some points along Route 6A and the Outer Cape from Hyannis and Boston's Logan Airport. The **Peter Pan bus line** (800-343-9999; peterpanbus.com) offers daily service to all Cape Cod points, including the

Barnstable Municipal Airport and both the Barnstable and Sagamore Park & Ride lots, which offer free commuter parking. If you're heading to Nantucket or Martha's Vineyard, convenient connections to the **Steamship Authority ferry** are available.

By shuttle: The **Provincetown "Shuttle" and Flex** (508-385-1430; capecodtransit .org) operates on weekends only starting in late May through June, then switches to 7 days a week with stops every 30 minutes until early September. The Flex offers trips to and from Provincetown to Harwich with reserved stops.

VALUE The ✿ symbol appears next to entries that represent an exceptional value.

WEATHER You really can't trust Boston weather reports to provide accurate forecasts for all the microclimates between Routes 28 and 6A, from the canal to Provincetown. If you really want to go to the Cape, just go. There'll be plenty to do even if it's cloudy or rainy. When in doubt, or when it really matters, consult capecodweather.net.

WEBSITES Web addresses are listed throughout.

Arts & Culture

ANTIQUARIAN BOOKS Among the many shops on Route 6A, two are great: **Titcomb's Book Shop** in Sandwich and **Parnassus Book Service** in Yarmouth Port. I also highly recommend **Isaiah Thomas Books & Prints** in Cotuit.

ANTIQUES Antiques shops are located all along **Route 6A,** on the 32-mile stretch from Sandwich to Orleans, but there is an especially dense concentration in **Brewster,** often called Antique Alley. You'll also find a good concentration of antiques shops in **Barnstable, Dennis Port, Chatham,** and **Nantucket.** (It's never made sense to me to buy antiques on an island, but folks do!)

AQUARIUMS The **Woods Hole Science Aquarium** is small, but it's an excellent introduction to marine life. There is also the small **Maria Mitchell Association Aquarium** on Nantucket.

ART GALLERIES **Wellfleet** and **Provincetown** are the centers of fine art on the Cape. Both established and emerging artists are well represented in dozens of diverse galleries. Artists began flocking to Provincetown at the turn of the 20th century, and the vibrant community continues to nurture creativity. (Special thanks to Howard Karren for his input and advice on the best Outer Cape galleries.)

Pick up a copy of the annual **Provincetown Arts Guide** for an in-depth list of exhibits, shows, and notable galleries worth visiting. The islands also attract

MARCIA DUGGAN/CAPECODSOUL

large numbers of artists, some of whom stay to open their own studios and galleries. **Chatham**, **Nantucket**, and **Martha's Vineyard** also have many fine galleries. Look for the outstanding color booklet **"Arts & Artisans Trails of Cape Cod, Martha's Vineyard, and Nantucket"**—and then don't leave home without it.

AUCTIONS Estate auctions are held throughout the year. Great benefit auctions include the **Fine Arts Work Center Annual Benefit Auction**, the **AIDS Support Group's Annual Silent and Live Auction** in Provincetown, and the celebrity-studded **Possible Dreams Auction** on Martha's Vineyard.

BASEBALL The 10-team **Cape Cod Baseball League** (capecodbaseball.org) was established in 1946. Only players with at least one year of collegiate experience are allowed to participate. Wooden bats are supplied by the major leagues. In exchange for the opportunity to play, team members work part time in the community, live with a community host, and pay rent. Carlton Fisk and the late Thurman Munson are just two alumni of the Cape Cod League who succeeded in the majors. Currently, about 250 major-league players are former league players. A whopping 13 Cape League players were in the 2016 World Series between the Cubs and Indians. Games are free and played from mid-June to mid-August; it's great fun. In relevant chapters, baseball venues are listed under *To Do*.

CLASSES & WORKSHOPS Want to "improve" yourself on vacation or brush up on some long-lost creative artistic urges? There are more programs in **Provincetown**, the **Vineyard**, and **Nantucket** than I can list here; see *To Do* under each town or region. The **Truro Center for the Arts at Castle Hill**, on page 302, offers a range of artistic expression, from day to weeks-long classes. In Wellfleet, "Trails, Birds, Seals & Classes" on page 284

KIM GRANT

discusses the **Wellfleet Bay Wildlife Sanctuary Adult Field School.**

COUNTRY STORES Old-fashioned country stores still exist on Cape Cod and the islands. Aficionados can seek out **The Brewster Store** in Brewster and **Alley's General Store** in West Tisbury on the **Vineyard.**

CRAFTS Craftspeople have made a living on the Cape and the islands since they began making baskets, ships, and furniture 300 years ago. The tradition continues as artists emphasize the aesthetic as well as the functional. Today's craftspeople are potters, jewelers (particularly in Dennis), scrimshaw and bird carvers, weavers, glassblowers, clothing designers, and barrel makers. Look for the highly coveted (and pricey) lightship baskets in Nantucket and glass objects in Sandwich, Bourne, and Brewster. There are too many artisans in Provincetown, Chatham, Nantucket, and Martha's Vineyard to detail here. Look for the outstanding color booklet, **"Arts & Artisans Trails of Cape Cod, Martha's Vineyard and Nantucket"**—and then don't leave home without it.

FLEA MARKETS **Wellfleet Flea Market** (at the Wellfleet Drive-In) is the biggie.

GOLF There are about 50 courses on the Cape and the islands, and because of relatively mild winters, many stay open all year (although perhaps not every day). **Highland Golf Links** in **Truro** is the Cape's oldest course; it's also very dramatic.

HISTORIC HOUSES Every town has its own historical museum or house, but some are more interesting than others. Among the best are **Hoxie House** in **Sandwich; Centerville Historical Museum** and **Osterville Historical Society Museum**, both in **Barnstable**; and the **Truro Historical Museum**. The center of **Nantucket** has been designated a historic district, so there are notable houses everywhere you turn; the oldest is the **Jethro Coffin House**. The **Nantucket Historical Association** publishes a walking guide to its properties. Don't miss the **Martha's Vineyard Museum** on Martha's Vineyard.

LIBRARIES The Cape and the islands boast a few libraries with world-class maritime collections and works pertaining to the history of the area: **Sturgis Library** in **Barnstable; William Brewster Nickerson Memorial Room** at Cape Cod Community College in **West Barnstable**; the **Atheneum** and **Nantucket Historical**

Association Research Library, both in Nantucket; and the **Martha's Vineyard Museum** in Edgartown on Martha's Vineyard. In addition to being great community resources, libraries also make great rainy-day ⛱ destinations.

LIGHTHOUSES It's a toss-up as to whether the most picturesque lighthouse is **Nobska Light** in **Woods Hole** or **Great Point Light** on **Nantucket**. (Nobska is certainly more accessible.) I'm partial to **Provincetown's Long Point, Race Point,** and **Wood End Lighthouses** (but I'm biased). For a really unusual trip, the lighthouse at **Race Point** is available for overnight stays by advance reservation. Truro, Eastham, Chatham, and both islands have working lighthouses, too.

MOVIES In addition to the standard multiplex cinemas located across the Cape, the **Wellfleet Drive-In** remains a much-loved institution. The **Cape Cinema** in **Dennis** is also a special venue; check it out. The **Nantucket Film Festival** and the **International Film Festival** in **Provincetown,** both held in mid-June, are relatively new "must-see" events for independent-film buffs. And not to be outdone is the **Martha's Vineyard Film Festival**, since 2001. Because moviegoing is a popular vacation activity, I have listed mainstream movie theaters under *Entertainment.*

MUSEUMS People who have never uttered the words *museum* and *Cape Cod* in the same breath don't know what they're missing. Don't skip the **Glass Museum** and **Heritage Museums & Gardens**, both in Sandwich; **Museums on the Green** in Falmouth; **Aptucxet Trading Post and Museum** in Bourne Village; **Cahoon Museum of American Art** in Cotuit; **John F. Kennedy Hyannis Museum; Cape Cod Museum of Art** in Dennis; **Cape Cod Museum of Natural History** in Brewster; **Provincetown Art Association & Museum**, the **Pilgrim Monument & Provincetown Museum,**

and the **Old Harbor Lifesaving Station**, all in Provincetown; **Martha's Vineyard Museum** in Edgartown on Martha's Vineyard; and the **Nantucket Whaling Museum** and **Shipwreck and Lifesaving Museum** on Nantucket.

Children will particularly enjoy the **Railroad Museum** in Chatham.

MUSIC Outdoor summertime band concerts are now offered by most towns, but the biggest and oldest is held in Chatham at **Kate Gould Park**. Sandwich offers a variety of outdoor summer concerts at **Heritage Museums & Gardens**.

The **Nantucket Musical Arts Society** and the **Vineyard's Chamber Music Society** are also excellent, albeit with much shorter seasons.

The 85-member **Cape Symphony Orchestra** (508-362-1111; capesymphony .org) performs classical, children's, and pops concerts year-round.

There are a couple of regular venues for folk music, including the **Woods Hole Folk Music Society** and the **First Encounter Coffee House** in Eastham.

This edition lists many more venues with live music; see the *Entertainment* headings under each town.

SHOPPING **Chatham** and **Falmouth's** Main Streets are well suited to walking and shopping. Commercial Street in **Provincetown** has the trendiest shops. **Mashpee Commons** features a very dense and increasingly fine selection of shops. Shopping on the **Vineyard** and **Nantucket** is a prime activity.

THEATER Among the summer-stock and performing arts venues are **Cape Playhouse** in Dennis; **Cape Repertory Theatre** in Brewster; **Monomoy Theatre** in Chatham; **Academy Playhouse** in Orleans; **Wellfleet Harbor Actors Theater; Provincetown Repertory Theatre** and **Provincetown Theatre Co.; College Light Opera Company** in Falmouth; **Barnstable Comedy Club; Harwich Junior Theatre;** the **Theatre Workshop**

KAYLA ROBERTSON/DO ART PHOTOGRAPHY

of Nantucket; and the **Vineyard Playhouse** on Martha's Vineyard.

Food & Drink

BARS Look for the Υ symbol next to restaurants and entertainment venues that have more than a few bar stools.

CRANBERRIES The cranberry is one of only three major native North American fruits (the other two are Concord grapes and blueberries). Harvesting began in **Dennis** in 1816 and evolved into a lucrative industry in Harwich Port. Harvesting generally runs from mid-September to mid-October, when the bogs are flooded and ripe red berries float to the water's surface. Before the berries are ripe, the bogs look like a dense green carpet, separated by 2- to 3-foot dikes. **Nantucket** has two bogs, but most of her bog acreage lies fallow due to a glut in supply. Harwich, which lays claim to having the first commercial cranberry

bog, celebrates with a **Cranberry Harvest Festival** (harwichcranberryfestival.org) in mid-September. Most on-Cape bogs are located on the Mid- and Lower Cape.

DINING Perhaps the biggest surprise to visitors is the high quality of cuisine on the Cape these days. Modernity and urbane sophistication are no longer rare breeds once you cross the canal bridges. Indeed, locals are so supportive that many fine restaurants stay open through the winter. During the off-season, many chefs experiment with creative new dishes and offer them at moderate prices.

With the exception of July and August (when *practically* all places are open nightly), restaurants are rarely open every night of the week. The major problem for a travel writer (and a reader relying on the book) is that this schedule is subject to the whims of weather and foot traffic.

Restaurants reviewed are listed in order by the type of vibe you are looking for, starting with upscale restaurants, teetering down to the best beach bars and live music spots, and ending with my favorite hole-in-the-wall eateries and fried seafood joints—all equally deserving of a shout-out regardless of price. (Also see **Sweet Treats & Coffee** and **Markets**.)

Expect to wait for a table in July and August. Remember that many restaurants are staffed by college students who are just learning the ropes in June and who may depart before Labor Day

weekend, leaving the owners short-handed. Smaller seasonal establishments don't take credit cards.

Main dish price designations are $ ($1–9), $$ ($10–19), $$$ ($20–29), and $$$$ ($30+).

WINERIES The Cape and islands are not Napa and Sonoma, but you could drop in for tastings at **Truro Vineyards of Cape Cod** in Truro and the **Cape Cod Winery** in East Falmouth. The **Nantucket Vineyard** (are you confused?) imports grapes to make wine.

Nature & Outdoors

BEACHES **Cape Cod National Seashore** (CCNS; nps.gov/caco) beaches are the stuff of dreams: long expanses of dune-backed sand. In fact, you could walk with only a few natural interruptions (breaks in the beach), as Henry David Thoreau did, from Chatham to the tip of Province-town. My favorites on the Cape include **Sandy Neck Beach** in West Barnstable; **Nauset Beach** in Orleans; **Old Silver Beach** in North Falmouth; **Chapin Memorial Beach** in Dennis; **West Dennis Beach**; **Craigville Beach** near Hyannis; and all the **Outer Cape** ocean beaches. Practically all of **Nantucket's** beaches are public, and although the same cannot be said for **Martha's Vineyard**, there are plenty of places to lay your towel.

A daily parking fee ($–$$) is enforced from mid-June to early September; many of the smaller beaches are open only to residents and weekly cottage renters. CCNS offers a seasonal parking pass for its beaches. There is no overnight parking at beaches. Four-wheel-drive vehicles require a permit, and their use is limited. Open beach fires require a permit. Greenhead biting flies plague non–Outer Cape beaches in mid- to late July; they disappear with the first high tide at the new or full moon in August, when the water level rises, killing the eggs.

Generally, beaches on **Nantucket Sound** have warmer waters than the **Outer Cape Atlantic Ocean** beaches, which are also pounded by surf. **Cape Cod Bay** beaches are shallower than **Nantucket Sound** beaches, and the bay waters are a bit cooler. Because of the proximity of the warm Gulf Stream, you can swim in Nantucket Sound waters well into September.

BICYCLING The Cape is generally flat, and there are many paved, off-road bike trails. The 26-mile **Cape Cod Rail Trail** runs along the bed of the Old Colony Railroad from Route 134 in **Dennis** to **Wellfleet**; bike trails can be found along both sides of the **Cape Cod Canal**; the **Shining Sea Bike Path** runs from **Falmouth** to **Woods Hole**; and bike trails can be found within the **CCNS** in **Provincetown** and **Truro**. **Nantucket** is ideal for cycling, with six routes emanating from the center of town and then circling the island. Bicycling is also great on the **Vineyard**, but stamina is required for a trip up-island to Aquinnah. For super specifics, consult *Backroad Bicycling on Cape Cod, Martha's Vineyard, and Nantucket* by Susan Milton and Kevin and Nan Jeffrey.

Rubel Bike Maps (bikemaps.com) are the most detailed maps available for the Cape and islands. Rubel produces a combination Nantucket and Vineyard map, as well as another that includes the islands, Cape Cod, and the North Shore.

BIRD-WATCHING The **Bird Watcher's General Store** in Orleans is on every birder's list of stops. Natural areas that are known for bird-watching include **Monomoy National Wildlife Refuge** off the coast of Chatham; **Wellfleet Bay Wildlife Sanctuary** (massaudubon.org); **Felix Neck Wildlife Sanctuary** in Vineyard Haven; **Ashumet Holly and Wildlife Sanctuary** in East Falmouth; and on Nantucket, Coskata-**Coatue Wildlife Refuge.** The **Maria Mitchell Association** and **Eco Guides**, both in Nantucket, offer bird-watching expeditions, as do **Wellfleet Bay Wildlife**

Sanctuary and **Monomoy National Wildlife Refuge**. Scheduled bird walks are also offered from both CCNS visitors centers: **Salt Pond Visitor Center** in Eastham and **Province Lands Visitor Center** in Provincetown. The **Cape Cod Museum of Natural History** in Brewster is always an excellent source of information about all creatures within the animal kingdom residing on the Cape.

CAMPING No camping is permitted on **Nantucket**, but there is still one campground on **Martha's Vineyard**. The Cape offers dozens of private campgrounds, but only those in natural areas are listed; the best camping is in **Nickerson State Park** in Brewster.

CANOEING & KAYAKING For guided naturalist trips and lessons there is no better outfitter than **Goose Hummock** in Orleans (508-255-0455; goose.com). Also look for the book *Paddling Cape Cod: A Coastal Explorer's Guide* by Shirley and Fred Bull. There are also very good venues and outfitters in **Falmouth** and **Wellfleet**, and on **Martha's Vineyard** and **Nantucket**.

CAPE COD NATIONAL SEASHORE
Established on August 7, 1961, through the efforts of President John F. Kennedy, the CCNS (nps.gov/caco) stretches more than 40 miles through Eastham, Wellfleet, Truro, and Provincetown. It encompasses more than 43,500 acres of land and seashore. Sites within the CCNS that are listed in this guide have been identified with "CCNS" at the beginning of the entry. The **Salt Pond Visitor Center** in **Eastham** and **Province Lands Visitor Center** in **Provincetown** are excellent resources and offer a variety of exhibits, films, and ranger-led walks and talks. The CCNS is accessible every day of the year, although you must pay to park at the beaches in summer.

ECOSYSTEM This narrow peninsula and these isolated islands have a delicate ecosystem. Remember that dunes are fragile, and beaches serve as nesting grounds for the endangered piping plover. Avoid the nesting areas when you see signs directing you to do so. Residents conserve water and recycle, and they hope you will do likewise.

LEESA BURKE

FISHING Procure freshwater and saltwater fishing licenses and regulations online, or try your luck at various town halls or bait and tackle shops.

Charter boats generally take up to six people on 4- or 8-hour trips. Boats leave from the following harbors on Cape Cod Bay: Barnstable Harbor in **West Barnstable**; Sesuit Harbor in **Dennis**; Rock Harbor in **Orleans**; **Wellfleet Harbor**; and **Provincetown**. On Nantucket Sound, head to Hyannis Harbor, Saquatucket Harbor in **Harwich Port**, and **Chatham**. You can also fish from the banks of the Cape Cod Canal and surf-fish on the Outer Cape. There are also plenty of opportunities for fishing off the shores of **Nantucket** and the **Vineyard**. **Goose Hummock** (goose .com) in Orleans offers lots of very good trips, as does **Chatham Family Charters** (chathamfamilycharters.com).

HORSEBACK RIDING There are a surprising number of riding facilities and

KATY WARD

trails on the Cape. Look for them in **Falmouth**, **Brewster**, and on **Martha's Vineyard**.

NATURE PRESERVES There are walking trails—around salt marshes, across beaches, through ancient swamps and hardwood stands—in every town on the Cape and the islands, but some traverse larger areas and are more "developed" than others. For a complete guide, look for the excellent *Walks and Rambles on Cape Cod and the Islands* by Ned Friary and Glenda Bendure. Watch for poison ivy and deer ticks; the latter carry Lyme disease. And pick up a copy of *Wildflowers of Cape Cod and the Islands* by Kate Carter to help make the most of any walk. For up-to-date information on fishing, visit newenglandboating.com.

To find some Upper Cape green space, head to **Green Briar Nature Center & Jam Kitchen** in Sandwich; **Lowell Holly Reservation** in Mashpee; and **Ashumet Holly and Wildlife Sanctuary** and **Waquoit Bay National Estuarine Research Reserve**, both in East Falmouth. In the mid-Cape area, you'll find **Sandy Neck Great Salt Marsh Conservation Area** in West Barnstable. The Lower Cape offers **Nickerson State Park** in Brewster and **Monomoy National Wildlife Refuge** off the coast of Chatham. The CCNS has a number of short interpretive trails on the Outer Cape, while Wellfleet has the **Wellfleet Bay Wildlife Sanctuary** and **Great Island Trail**.

On Martha's Vineyard you can escape the crowds at **Felix Neck Wildlife Sanctuary** in Vineyard Haven; **Cedar Tree Neck Sanctuary** and **Long Point Wildlife Refuge**, both in West Tisbury; and **Cape Pogue Wildlife Refuge** and **Wasque Reservation** on Chappaquiddick.

Nantucket boasts conservation initiatives that have protected 45 percent of the land from development, including the areas of **Coskata-Coatue**, **Eel Point**, **Sanford Farm**, **Ram Pasture**, and the **Woods**.

PONDS Supposedly there are 365 fresh-water ponds on Cape Cod, one for every day of the year. As glaciers retreated 15,000 years ago and left huge chunks of ice behind, depressions in the earth were created. When the ice melted, "kettle ponds" were born. The ponds are a refreshing treat, especially in August, when salty winds kick up beach sand.

SEAL CRUISES A colony of seals lounges around Monomoy, and there is no shortage of outfits willing to take you out to see them. See listings in **Chatham** and **Wellfleet** for detailed information.

SHELLFISHING Procure licenses and regulations online, or try your luck at local town halls. Sometimes certain areas are closed to shellfishing due to contamination; it's always best to ask.

SURFING & SAILBOARDING Surfers should head to **Nauset Beach** in **Orleans**, **Coast Guard** and **Nauset Light** beaches in **Eastham**, and **Marconi Beach** in **Well-fleet**. Sailboarders flock to **Falmouth**. **Vineyard** beaches are also good for sailboarding.

TIDES Tides come in and go out twice daily; times differ from day to day and from town to town. At low tide, the sandy shore is hard and easier to walk on; at high tide, what little sand is visible is more difficult to walk on. Because tides vary considerably from one spot to another, it's best to stop in at a local bait-and-tackle shop for a tide chart. For **Cape Cod Canal** tide information, log on to boatma.com/tides/Cape-Cod.html.

WALKING **Cape Cod Pathways** (cape codcommission.org/pathways/) is a growing network of trails linking open space in all 15 Cape Cod towns from Falmouth to Provincetown. Also consult cctrails.org.

And pick up *Walks & Rambles on Cape Cod and the Islands* by Ned Friary and Glenda Bendure.

WHALE-WATCHING Whale-watching trips leave from **Provincetown**, including the excellent **Dolphin Fleet Whale Watch** (508-240-3636), but you can also catch the **Hyannis *Whale Watcher* Cruises** (508-362-6088) out of **Barnstable Harbor**.

Recommended Reading

ABOUT CAPE COD Henry Beston's classic *The Outermost House: A Year of Life on the Great Beach of Cape Cod* recounts his solitary year in a cabin on the ocean's edge. Cynthia Huntington's marvelous *The Salt House* updates Beston's work with a woman's perspective in the late 20th century. Also look for *The House on Nauset Marsh* by Wyman Richardson (The Countryman Press). Henry David Thoreau's naturalist classic *Cape Cod* meticulously details his mid-1800s walking tours. Josef Berger's 1937 Works Progress Administration (WPA) guide, *Cape Cod Pilot*, is filled with good stories and still-useful information. I devoured the excellent *Nature of Cape Cod* by Beth Schwarzman, as well as everything by poet Mary Oliver. Pick up anything by modern-day naturalists Robert Finch (including *The Primal Place*) and John Hay. Finch also edited a volume of writings by others about the Cape, *A Place Apart* (with a black-and-white cover photo by yours truly). Another collection of writings

KATY WARD

KAYLA ROBERTSON/DO ART PHOTOGRAPHY

about Cape Cod is *Sand in Their Shoes*, compiled by Edith and Frank Shay. Look for *Cape Cod, Its People & Their History* by Henry Kittredge (alias Jeremiah Digges) and *The Wampanoags of Mashpee* by Russell Peters. Mary Heaton Vorse, a founder of the Provincetown Players, describes life in Provincetown from the 1900s to the 1950s in *Time and the Town: A Provincetown Chronicle*. And for children, Kevin Shortsleeve has written an illustrated history book, *The Story of Cape Cod*. Look also for Admont Clark's *Lighthouses of Cape Cod, Martha's Vineyard, and Nantucket: Their History and Lore* and photographer Joel Meyerowitz's *A Summer's Day* and *Cape Light*.

ABOUT MARTHA'S VINEYARD

Start with the *Vineyard Gazette Reader*, a marvelous "best-of" collection edited by Richard Reston and Tom Dunlop; it will give you an immediate sense of the island. *On the Vineyard II* contains essays by celebrity island residents, including Walter Cronkite, William Styron, and Carly Simon, with photographs by Peter Simon (Carly's brother). *Martha's Vineyard* and *Martha's Vineyard, Summer Resort*, are both by Henry Beetle Hough, Pulitzer Prize–winning editor of the *Vineyard Gazette*. Photographer Alfred Eisenstaedt, a longtime summer resident of the Vineyard, photographed the island for years. Contemporary *Vineyard Gazette* photographer Alison Shaw

has two Vineyard books to her credit: the black-and-white *Remembrance and Light* and the color collection *Vineyard Summer*. Also look for her new *Photographer's Guide to Martha's Vineyard*.

ABOUT NANTUCKET

Edwin P. Hoyt's *Nantucket: The Life of an Island* is a popular history, and Robert Gambee's *Nantucket* is just plain popular. Architecture buffs will want to take a gander at *Nantucket Style* by Leslie Linsley and Jon Aron, and the classic *Early Nantucket and Its Whale Houses* by Henry Chandler Forman. Photography lovers will enjoy *On Nantucket*, with photos by Gregory Spaid.

KIM GRANT

THE UPPER CAPE

BOURNE

SANDWICH

FALMOUTH & WOODS HOLE

MASHPEE

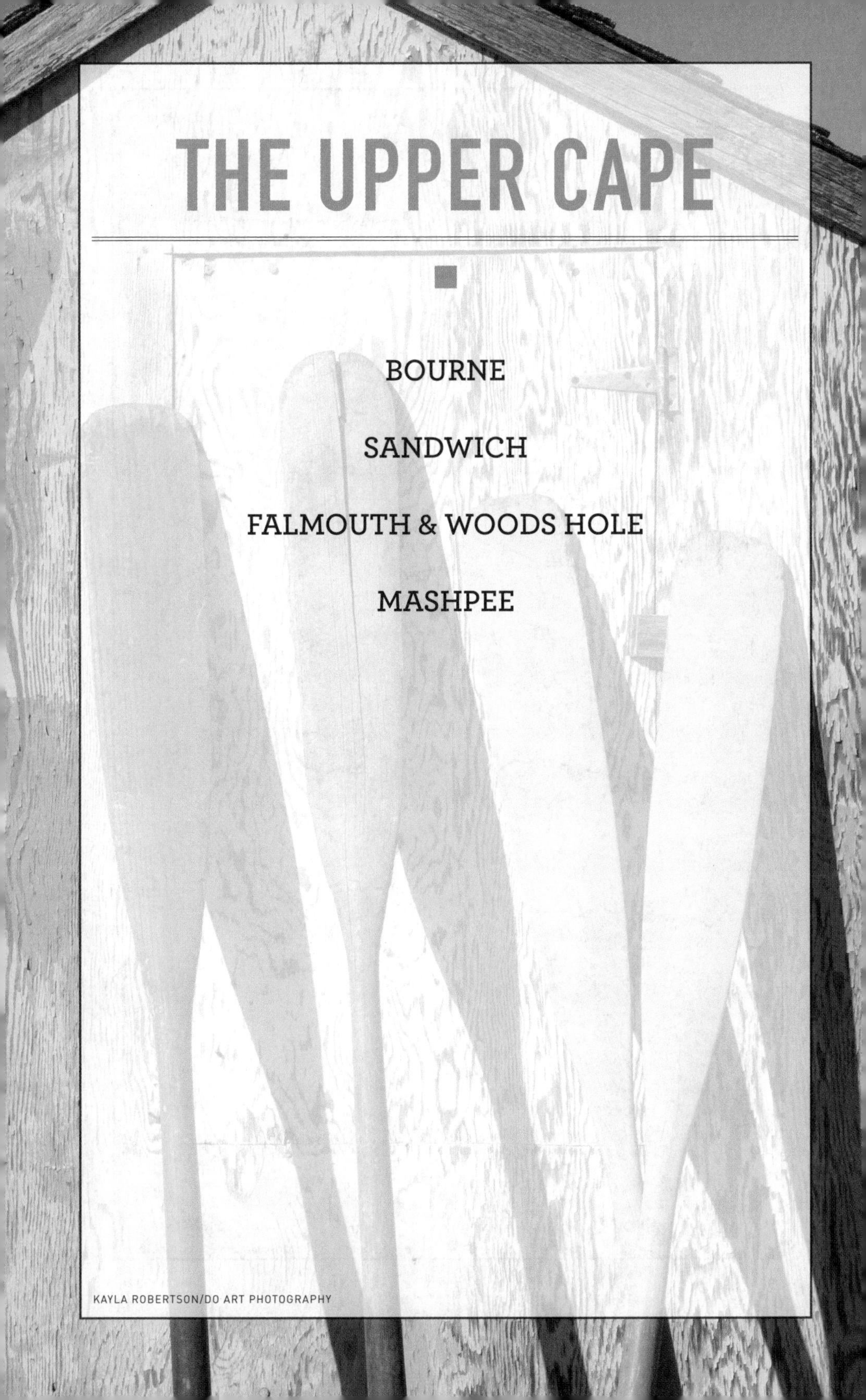

KAYLA ROBERTSON/DO ART PHOTOGRAPHY

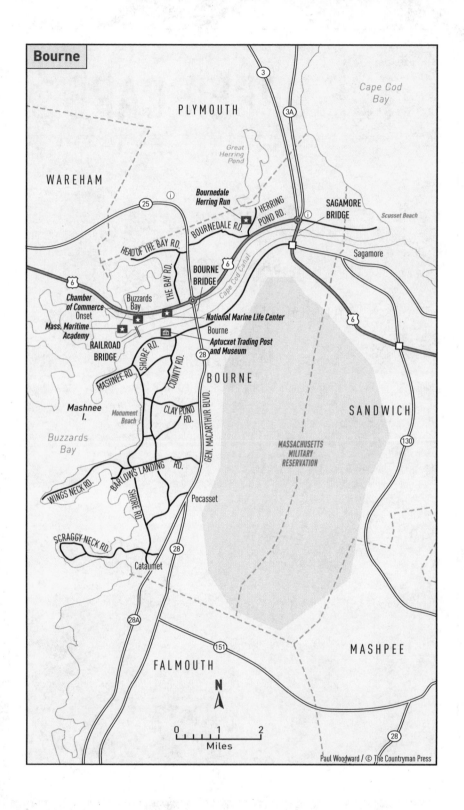

Bourne

PLYMOUTH

WAREHAM

Cape Cod Bay

Great Herring Pond

25

Bournedale Herring Run

HERRING POND RD.

BOURNEDALE RD.

SAGAMORE BRIDGE

Scusset Beach

HEAD OF THE BAY RD.

THE BAY RD.

Sagamore

BOURNE BRIDGE

Cape Cod Canal

6

Chamber of Commerce Onset

Buzzards Bay

National Marine Life Center

Bourne

Mass. Maritime Academy

Aptucxet Trading Post and Museum

6

RAILROAD BRIDGE

SHORE RD.

COUNTY RD.

BOURNE

SANDWICH

MASHNEE RD.

Mashnee I.

Monument Beach

CLAY POND RD.

GEN. MACARTHUR BLVD.

28

MASSACHUSETTS MILITARY RESERVATION

130

Buzzards Bay

BARLOWS LANDING RD.

WINGS NECK RD.

SHORE RD.

Pocasset

SCRAGGY NECK RD.

28

Cataumet

28A

151

MASHPEE

FALMOUTH

N

0   1   2
Miles

Paul Woodward / © The Countryman Press

BOURNE

Despite summertime traffic tie-ups approaching the Sagamore and Bourne Bridges, there's something magical about the first glimpse of them, a sure sign that you're entering a place separate from where you've been. All travelers, except those arriving by plane or boat, must pass through Bourne, over the bridges and the Cape Cod Canal.

Bourne straddles the canal, nips at the heels of Sandwich on the Cape Cod Bay side, and follows the coastline south toward Falmouth along Route 28, a.k.a. Cranberry Highway. (All the land to the immediate east of Route 28 belongs to the Massachusetts Military Reservation.) Bourne is often completely bypassed as travelers head south to catch the Vineyard ferry from Falmouth or Woods Hole. Indeed, there is some justification for not spending a monthlong holiday here.

Bourne is predominantly inhabited by year-rounders, enjoying a quiet, rural, unhurried existence and tending their gardens and lives. But perhaps of all the places on the Cape, Bourne remains the most unexplored area. The back roads off County and Shore Roads are lovely for bicycling, as are the peninsulas reached by Scraggy Neck Road and Wings Neck Road. Fishing, walking, and bicycling are prime activities along the Cape Cod Canal. In fact, there are more than 1,700 acres of protected land along the canal for your enjoyment.

When Sandwich refused to grant Bourne its independence, the state legislature incorporated it in 1884. Originally known for its fishing wharves, shipbuilding, and factories, Bourne quickly attracted prominent vacationers to its sandy shores. Named for an affluent resident who made his fortune during the whaling heyday, Bourne encompasses 40 square miles and consists of many tiny villages.

Sagamore, on both sides of the canal and on Cape Cod Bay, has more in common with Sandwich; it even has a renowned glassmaking factory. **Bournedale**, on the "mainland" and wedged between the two bridges, has a diminutive old red schoolhouse and a picturesque herring pond. And although **Buzzards Bay**, north and west of the Bourne Bridge, is the region's commercial center, it also offers some lovely glimpses of Buttermilk Bay. (Buzzards Bay, by the way, was misnamed by inexperienced birders. If the original settlers had gotten it right, it would be called Osprey Bay today.) On the western end of the canal, the Massachusetts Maritime Academy affords nice views of the canal and handsome summer homes on the other side.

Across the 2,384-foot Bourne Bridge (almost twice as long as the Sagamore Bridge), the Cape villages of **Monument Beach, Bourne Village, Gray Gables, Pocasset**, and **Cataumet** are tranquil in summer and downright sleepy in winter. In total, about 19,000 people live in these villages year-round.

The first "Summer White House" was in Gray Gables, where President Grover Cleveland spent the season fishing during the 1890s. Monument Beach, Cataumet, and Pocasset are pleasant, residential, seaside towns with old houses, just west of Route 28. Residents don't take much notice of visitors; they just go about their business, fishing, shopping, raising children, and commuting to work. Cataumet Pier was the site of the nation's first labor strike, when dockworkers demanded a 100 percent pay raise in 1864, from 15¢ per hour to 30¢.

GUIDANCE ❋ **Cape Cod Canal Region Chamber of Commerce** (508-759-6000; cape codcanalchamber.org), 70 Main Street, Buzzards Bay. Office open year-round. On-site information center open late May to mid-October. Another center, the Cape Cod Canal Visitor Center (774-413-7475), 1 Meetinghouse Lane, Sagamore Beach, is open late April to mid-November.

   Herring Run Visitor Center, a.k.a. **Cape Cod Canal Visitor Center** (508-833-9678), Route 6 on the mainland side of the canal, about a mile south of the Sagamore Bridge. Open late April to early October.

GETTING THERE *By car:* To reach Sagamore, take Exit 1 onto Route 6A from the Sagamore Bridge. To reach Bournedale and Buzzards Bay, take Route 6 West at the Sagamore Bridge. To reach the other villages, take the Bourne Bridge across the canal, and at the rotary take Shore Road. You can also whiz down Route 28 and head west to Pocasset, Cataumet, and Monument Beach.

   By bus: **Bonanza/Peter Pan** (888-751-8800; peterpanbus.com) operates buses from Bourne to Boston as well as Providence, New York City, and other points south and west of the Cape. The bus stops at the convenience store (105 Trowbridge Road) at the Bourne Bridge rotary.

GETTING AROUND Bourne is quite spread out, so you'll need a car.

   By shuttle: The **Bourne Route** travels Route 28A and Route 151 from the Cranberry Plaza in Wareham through Bourne to Mashpee Commons. Riders can hop on and off as they like by flagging it down when they see it or by pulling the inside rope. This route also connects with the **Sealine** at Mashpee Commons, which travels to and from Hyannis and Falmouth/Woods Hole.

PUBLIC RESTROOMS Located at the chamber office and at the Herring Run Visitor Center/Cape Cod Canal Visitor Center.

PUBLIC LIBRARY ❋ ✎ ☂ **Jonathan Bourne Public Library** (508-759-0644; bourne library.org), 19 Sandwich Road, Bourne. Book clubs, art displays, story hour, and children's programs.

EMERGENCIES **Bourne Police Department** (508-759-4453; bournepolice.com), 175 Main Street, or call **911**.

Medical: While it's not an "emergency" (the kind you'd expect under this category, anyway), many area water wells have been contaminated by years of training with grenades and other live munitions at the Massachusetts Military Reservation. I drink bottled water on the Upper Cape.

✳ To See

Massachusetts Maritime Academy (508-830-5000; maritime.edu), 101 Academy Drive, Taylors Point, off Main Street, Buzzards Bay. The academy's presence explains why you'll see so many young men with close-cropped hair jogging along the canal bicycle trail. Call ahead for a campus tour, or arrange to tag along on a weekday tour for prospective merchant mariners. Not only will you see the oldest continuously operating maritime academy in the country (established in 1891) from an insider's perspective, but, if you're lucky, you'll also get to tour the cadets' training ship and eat in the cadets' dining hall overlooking the canal.

    Aptucxet Trading Post and Museum (508-759-8167; bournehistoricalsociety.org), 6 Aptucxet Road, Bourne. From the Cape-side Bourne Bridge, follow signs for Mashnee Village, then Shore Road and Aptucxet Road. Open late May to mid-October. English settlers thought this location, near two rivers, was perfect for a post to promote trade with their neighbors, the Wampanoag and the Dutch from New Amsterdam. Furs, sugar and other staples, tools, glass, tobacco, and cloth were bought and sold; wampum (carved quahog shells made into beads) served as currency. Cape Cod commerce was born.

    The trading post you see today was built in 1927 by the Bourne Historical Society on the foundations of the original; a few bricks from the fireplace date to the Pilgrims. The hand-hewn beams and wide floor planks came from a 1600s house in Rochester, Massachusetts. On the grounds a small Victorian railroad station was used solely by President Grover Cleveland when he summered at his Gray Gables mansion in Monument Beach. You'll also find a Dutch-style windmill (which was intended merely "to add interest and beauty to the estate"), an 18th-century saltworks, an herb garden, a gift shop, and a shaded picnic area. Admission $.

    🐟 **Bournedale Herring Run** (508-759-4431), Route 6, about a mile south of the Sagamore Bridge. Open late May to early June. After the canal destroyed the natural herring run into Great Herring Pond, local engineers created an elaborate artificial watercourse to allow mature herring

APTUCXET TRADING POST AND MUSEUM KAYLA ROBERTSON/DO ART PHOTOGRAPHY

OUR VERY OWN PANAMA CANAL

The Cape Cod Canal (7.5 miles long) separates the mainland from Cape Cod. The canal, between 480 and 700 feet wide at various points, is the world's widest ocean-level canal. In 1623 Captain Myles Standish, eager to facilitate trade between New Amsterdam (New York City) and Plymouth Colony, was the first to consider creating a canal, which also would eliminate the treacherous 135-nautical-mile voyage around the tip of the Cape. George Washington brought up the idea again in the late 18th century as a means to protect naval ships and commercial vessels during war, but the first serious effort at digging a canal was not attempted until 1880 by the Cape Cod Canal Company.

For a few months, the company's crew of 500 immigrants dug with hand shovels and carted away the dirt in wheelbarrows. Then, in 1899, New York financier Augustus Belmont's Boston, Cape Cod, and New York Canal Company took over the project with more resolve. They began digging in 1909, and the canal opened to shipping five years later, on July 30, 1914. (It beat the Panama Canal opening by a scant 17 days.) On hand at the opening was then Assistant Secretary of the Navy Franklin D. Roosevelt. But the enterprise wasn't a financial success because the canal was too narrow (it could handle only one-way traffic) and early drawbridges caused too many accidents. In 1928 the federal government purchased the canal, and the US Army Corps of Engineers (USACE) built the canal we know today. The USACE has overseen the canal ever since. The canal provides a north–south shortcut for some 30,000 vessels each year, hundreds daily in summer. Water currents in the 32-foot-deep canal change direction every six hours.

The Cape Cod Canal Vertical Lift Railroad Bridge (western end of the canal at the Buzzards Bay Recreation Area) is the third-longest vertical railway bridge in the world. It stands 270 feet high and 540 feet long, but those in Chicago, Illinois, and on Long Island, New York, beat it. The railroad bridge was completed the same year as the Sagamore and Bourne Bridges. When trains approach, it takes two or three minutes for the bridge to lower and connect with the tracks on either side of it. The most reliable times (read: it's not so reliable) to witness this event are at 9:30 a.m. and 5 p.m. (more or less), when trains haul trash off-Cape. You might see the morning lowering at 7 a.m. too. Free parking.

This is a good place to start the bicycle trail on this side of the canal.

There is great bicycling, fishing, boating, and walking from the canal shores. See the appropriate sections under *To Do*.

KATY WARD

to migrate back to their birthplace. Each twice-daily tide brings thousands of the bony fish slithering upstream, navigating the pools created by wooden planks. In total, hundreds of thousands of herring pass through the Bournedale run annually. Kids really get a kick out of this spring ritual.

🐟 **National Marine Life Center** (508-743-9888; nmlc.org), 120 Main Street, Buzzards Bay. Open late May to early September. In late 2008, a marine-animal rehabilitation hospital opened to aid whales, dolphins, sea turtles, and seals that wash ashore on Cape Cod and require medical attention before they can be set free again. There are several interactive exhibits, various kids' programs in July and August, and a small science museum where young people can learn about the impact of humankind on the ocean.

Briggs McDermott House & Blacksmith Shop (508-759-8167; bournehistorical society.org), 22 Sandwich Road, Bourne. Generally open mid-June to late September. This early-19th-century Greek Revival home—complete with period gardens, a carriage house with quite a collection of carriages, and a granite-walled barn—is maintained by the Bourne Society for Historic Preservation. Inquire about guided tours, on which docents might discuss local architecture or former neighbor Grover Cleveland. Blacksmiths operate a restored forge on-site—complete with artifacts, tools, and a wagon—where President Cleveland's horses were shod.

Massachusetts Military Reservation (Otis Air National Guard Base) (508-968-4003), off the rotary at Routes 28 and 28A. The 21,000 acres east of Route 28 are a closed installation that contains Camp Edwards Army National Guard Training Site, Otis Air National Guard Base, the US Coast Guard Air Station, the State Army Aviation complex, and the PAVE PAWS radar station. The last detects nuclear missiles and tracks satellites (it was established during the Cold War).

Although you won't read about it in most guidebooks, the MMR has been designated by the Pentagon as a federal environmental Superfund site since 1989. Most experts agreed that it would take decades to clean up the toxic Cold War–era pollutants that are contaminating the groundwater. Others suggested it may be impossible to clean up all the underground chemical plumes that resulted from various training exercises, landfill leaks, and oil spills.

✳ To Do

BICYCLING & RENTALS 🚲 The **Cape Cod Canal Bikeway** is one of my most favorite routes to cycle on Cape Cod. This pair of wide, paved paths (actually US Army Corps of Engineers service roads) runs about 7 miles on either side of the canal. The level and well-maintained

BOURNEDALE HERRING RUN KIM GRANT

A GLASSY VIEW OF THE CANAL KAYLA ROBERTSON/DO ART PHOTOGRAPHY

roads are great for casual bikers, walkers, runners, rollerbladers, and families with children and strollers. A bright yellow line painted down the center designates two-lane traffic. The trail offers some of the best views of ships, barges, and tugs chugging between Buzzards Bay and Cape Cod Bay (I've successfully requested a few toot toots from my bike seat). If your timing is right, you might see the Cape Cod Central Railroad train passing through or spot a blue heron or loon near the rocky shoreline. Lush greenery with a few quaint homes tucked along the way completes the package. The trail also provides access to great fishing hotspots in the spring and fall (see *Fishing* under **To Do**). Access points on the mainland side include Scusset State Park, off Scusset Beach Road, and the Sagamore Recreation Area, off Canal Road at the Sagamore Bridge. You can also hop on near the Bournedale Herring Run (read about under **To See**). On the Cape side of the canal, there are access points at the Sandcatcher Recreation Area, off Tupper Road in Sandwich; from Pleasant Street in Sagamore; and from the Bourne Bridge. You can rent bicycles and equipment at **Canal Cruisers** (774-404-1118), 199 Main Street, Buzzard's Bay; or **Buzzard's Bay Bikes** a.k.a. **Sailworld** (508-759-6559; sailworld.com), 139 Main Street, Buzzards Bay.

BOAT EXCURSIONS & RENTALS The Department of Natural Resources (508-759-2512; townofbourne.com/natural-resources) manages the three town-owned marinas: **Taylor Point Marina**, 4 Wright Lane, Buzzards Bay; the **Monument Beach Marina** (508-759-3105), off Emmons Road at Monument Beach; and the **Pocasset River Marina.** If you're interested in renting watercraft during your stay, head over to **Stonebridge Marina** (508-295-8003; atlanticboats.com), 5 East Boulevard, Onset (a few miles west of the mainland-side of the Bourne Bridge rotary). Choose from a variety of boats and half- or full-day rentals.

✍ **Cape Cod Canal Cruises** (508-295-3883; hylinecanalcruise.com), 184 Onset Avenue at the Onset Bay Town Pier. Trips from May to mid-October. Explore the underbelly of the canal bridges via a 2- or 3-hour narrated tour. There are also sunset cocktail cruises, live music, and jazz nights, as well as discounted family trips. These tours fill up, so book in advance. $$. (See also "Our Very Own Panama Canal" on page 36.)

FLIP YOUR PERSPECTIVE

As someone who has traveled over the Sagamore and Bourne bridges more times than I can count, the Cape Cod Canal Bikeway is very special to me. Standing beneath the bridge with the rushing canal waters and massive cargo ships passing by, breathing the salty air, and hearing the echo of cars zipping overhead: it's quite the extraordinary flip in perspective. I normally access the trail from the Bourne Scenic Park (see more about this other favorite in *Camping* under *Lodging*) and bike toward Scusset Beach for a quick dip in the Bay before peddling back. In the early evening, head the opposite direction toward Buzzards Bay and watch the drawbridge go up and down. A fiery sunset is the cherry on top. There are plenty of benches to take breaks and shady spots to cool down, as well as a few surprisingly clean portable toilets dotted along the trail. Bring water, a hat, and your camera.

KATY WARD

FISHING The waters off Bourne are a bit of a fish-haven and you'll have no trouble finding that sought-for catch. But if you've never fished the canal, I recommend carving out a few hours with rod and reel. Striped bass on their migration north in the spring, and on their return south in the fall, take a short cut through the canal rather than swimming all around the cape, making it one of the best places to shore cast for trophy bass. Quick note: There is no fishing, lobstering, or boat trolling permitted in the canal. Procure freshwater and saltwater fishing licenses and regulations online (mass.gov/eea/agencies/dfg/licensing).

Big game: **Cape Cod Charter Guys** (508-566; 4723; capecodcharterguys.com), 220 Main Street, Bourne. Captain Ross and Mate Jayden cater to all kinds of fishermen "from pro to average Joe." Book a half- or full-day charter trolling around Cape Cod Bay, Buzzards Bay, Provincetown, and Vineyard Sound (depending on season). Fish the canal for giant bass on a guided bike outing (tackle and bike included). $$$$+.

Lincoln Brothers Fishing (508-564-1632 or 281-667-7680; lincolnbrothersfishing .com), 802 Shore Road, Pocasset. Trips mid-May to October. Brothers Sam and Josh Lincoln have been fishing the waters off Cape Cod since they were young boys. The two could probably navigate the area with their eyes closed; after all, they've been doing it for over 20 years. With their combined wealth of knowledge and their passion for the game, you are surely guaranteed a successful charter experience. They also offer some of the best prices when it comes to this expensive sport. Check online or give them a ring for details on discounts and specials. $$$$+.

On shore: The banks of the canal provide plenty of opportunities for landing trophy-sized bass and blues thanks to its ripping currents, formed by the exchange of water between Cape Cod Bay and Buzzards Bay. Easy access and abundant fish make the canal one of the most popular surfcasting destinations on the East Coast. But if you've never done it before, this man-made waterway can be a bit intimidating, with its strong current, big tides, big fish, and big crowds. Don't let that stop you, though. The best way to get-in-the-know when it comes to fishing the canal is by asking and observing the locals (but most fishermen are tight-lipped when it comes to sharing information) or by visiting the local bait and tackle shop. The staff will surely know what's biting. Wear comfortable shoes because the trek to the shoreline can be rocky and unstable in some areas, and bring extra equipment (I've lost several lures to the jagged bottom of the canal). (For access points, see *Bicycling & Rentals* under **To Do**; and *Fishing* in Sandwich.)

Freshwater: **Four Ponds Conservation Area,** 140 Barlows Landing Road, Pocasset. This is a great spot for teaching kids how to cast a line, or for someone seeking a quiet morning of catch-and-release fly-fishing. Explore the water by kayak or boat, too.

Supplies: **Maco's Bait and Tackle** (508-759-9836; macosbaitandtackle.com), 3173 Cranberry Highway, Wareham. Open April through October.

Canal Bait and Tackle (508-833-2996; canalbaitandtackle.com), 101 Cranberry Highway, Sagamore.

FOR FAMILIES ✍ **Water Wizz Park** (508-295-3255; waterwizz.com), 3031 Cranberry Highway, Routes 6 and 28, a few miles west of the Bourne Bridge, Wareham. Open mid-June to early September. Enjoy a waterlogged day at Southern New England's largest water park. There's plenty to do: a 50-foot-high water slide with tunnels, dozens of tube rides, a hanging rope bridge, a wave pool, three kiddie water areas, and a river ride. You can let kids run around without too much worry because the park is well staffed with lifeguards. $$$ (if under 48 inches), otherwise $$$$+.

✍ **Cartland of Cape Cod** (508-295-8360; cartlandofcapecod.com), 3022 Routes 6 and 28, East Wareham. Open daily in summer, weekends in spring and fall. Bumper

THE CANAL IS A PRIME SURFCASTING SPOT KAYLA ROBERTSON/DO ART PHOTOGRAPHY

boats, go-carts, boxing robots, batting cages, mini-golf, and an obvious place for birthday parties, especially given its ice cream menu.

❋ ✆ **Ryan Family Amusements** (508-759-9892; ryanfamily.com), 200 Main Street, Buzzards Bay. Bowling, a game room, and facilities for birthday parties.

See also **Cataumet Arts Center** under *Selective Shopping*.

HORSEBACK RIDING ❋ **Grazing Fields Farm** (508-759-3763; grazingfields.com), 201 Bournedale Road, off Head of the Bay Road, Buzzards Bay. Private and semiprivate lessons are offered. $$$$+.

ICE-SKATING **John Gallo Ice Arena** (508-759-8904; galloarena.com), 231 Sandwich Road, Buzzards Bay. The public skating schedule is highly variable.

JUNIOR RANGER PROGRAMS ✆ **The Cape Cod Canal Visitor Center (US Army Corps of Engineers**; 508-833-9678), 60 Ed Moffitt Drive, Sandwich. Free programs for kiddos in July and August; no preregistration is required.

MASHNEE ISLAND KIM GRANT

KAYAKS & PADDLEBOARDS **Cape Cod Kayak** (508-563-9377; capecodkayak .com), 802 MacArthur Boulevard, Pocasset. This place offers a little bit of everything when it comes to kayaks and paddleboards, including tours, fishing trips, tandem adventures, and more.

SCENIC DRIVE **Mashnee Island**. From the Cape side of the Bourne Bridge, take Shore Road and follow signs for Mashnee Island. From the 2-mile-long causeway, there are lovely views of summer homes dotting the shoreline, sailboats on the still waters, and the distant railroad bridge and Bourne Bridge. Parking is nonexistent in summer, and because the island is private, you'll have to turn around at the end of the causeway.

TENNIS Public courts are located at the old schoolhouse, County Road in Cataumet; at Chester Park, across from the old railroad station in Monument Beach; behind the Town Hall on Perry Avenue in Buzzards Bay; at the community center off Main Street in Buzzards Bay; and behind the fire station on Barlows Landing Road in Pocasset Village.

WINDSURFING **Cape Cod Windsurfing** (508-801-3329; capecodwindsurfing.com), 30 MacArthur Boulevard, Pocasset. Take a 2-hour windsurfing lesson or rent stand-up paddleboards for the day or the week. Call Eddie for delivery and pickup services.

CATAUMET MARINA KIM GRANT

ZOO **Butterflies of Cape Cod** (774-413-9310; butterfliesofcapecod.com), 26 Herring Pond Road. Open July to September, but call ahead because it operates based on weather conditions. Okay, so it doesn't meet the traditional definition of a zoo, but nonetheless it's similar, but for butterflies. Stop here for a quick tour of the indoor greenhouse habitat (it doesn't take long and I don't recommend wasting too much time here). Staff will provide information on these native beauties, how people can work toward protecting them, and the best ways to attract and enjoy them in our gardens. Butterflies are livelier during warm sunny days, so don't bother if it's cloudy and overcast. Located conveniently off the highway, it's a great place to stretch your legs and take a breather from a long car drive. The gift shop offers cute gift items, too.

✳ Green Space

The canal moderates considerable differences in tides between Buzzards Bay (4 feet) and Cape Cod Bay (9½ feet on average). Because of heavy boat traffic and the swift currents caused by tides, swimming is prohibited in Cape Cod Canal.

BEACHES **Scusset** and **Sagamore beaches**, Cape Cod Bay, Sagamore. Both beaches are located near the Sagamore Bridge via Scusset Beach Road. Facilities include changing areas, restrooms, and a snack bar. (Note that in season, Sagamore parking is reserved for residents.) Scusset is a state-run beach and has floating beach wheelchairs available at no charge, although reservations are recommended. Scusset does not require a town-issued parking sticker.

Monument Beach, Buzzards Bay, on Emmons Road, Bourne. The warm waters of Buzzards Bay usually hover around 75 degrees in summer. This small beach has restrooms, a snack bar, and a lifeguard. Nonresident beach sticker $$$$+/week.

WALKS ❧ **Cape Cod Canal**. The US Army Corps of Engineers (508-833-9678 or 508-759-4431, ext. 622; nae.usace.army.mil), 60 Ed Moffitt Drive, Sandwich, offers numerous and excellent 1- and 2-hour guided walks and talks from early July to mid-October. There is also biking and hiking along the canal. Call for meeting place.

Red Brook Pond (Bourne Conservation Trust; 508-563-2884; bourneconservation trust.org), Thaxter Road off Shore Road, Cataumet. With 40 acres of wooded conservation land, Red Brook Pond offers a number of hiking trails that traverse pine woods and hug a cranberry bog. The Bourne Conservation Trust offers a well-marked 0.75-mile trail.

See also **Cape Cod Canal** under *To Do*.

❋ Lodging

There really aren't many places to stay in this quiet corner.

CAMPGROUNDS 🐾 **Bourne Scenic Park Campground** (508-759-7873; bourne scenicpark.com), 370 Scenic Highway, Route 6 on the mainland side of the canal, Buzzards Bay. Open late March to late October. Personally, I love this campground, but not for the common camping experience one might expect. Camping is practically underneath the pylons of the Bourne Bridge and steps from the canal bikeway. There are over 450 sites, most of which are filled by RVs and some better situated than others (the C area is by-far superior than others). My parents spend a week here each year (they book annually because sites fill quickly), and I always pencil in a visit. The grounds are well manicured with weekly lawn mowing, and the facilities are kept tidy and clean thanks to the Bourne Recreation Authority (who leases the land from the US Army Corps of Engineers). But it's the location and laid-back atmosphere that leave the biggest impression. Regardless of your campsite, the canal and its adjoining bikeway are only a minute's walk (or steps if you're lucky) from each site. I love watching kids and curious adults run to catch a glimpse of a big barge or cruise ship passing through the canal. It's quite the show, and everyone gets excited. The staff is friendly and dogs are okay, but not allowed in the rustic rentals, such as the lodge or the five cabins, which are cozy but far from canal access. I recommend bringing or renting a bike to get around the campground and for exploring the area. Quick note: Most people who stay here set up for the entire season, so it feels a bit like a residential

CAMPING WITH A VIEW KATY WARD

neighborhood. Other on-site facilities include a playground, a basketball court, and a pool (great for kids, not so great for adults trying to relax poolside). Campfires allowed. Reservations accepted starting late March.

🐾 **Bay View Campgrounds** (508-759-7610; bayviewcampground.com), 260 MacArthur Boulevard, Route 28 (1 mile south of the Bourne Bridge). Open May to mid-October. RVers make up the majority of guests in these 325-plus sites. Services include a dog park, pools, baseball, volleyball, an ice cream parlor, and more.

CHART ROOM KIM GRANT

✳ Where to Eat

Despite the region's drive-through feel, there are a number of places to sit down.

DINING OUT ♈ **Chart Room** (508-563-5350; chartroomcataumet.com), 1 Shipyard Lane off Shore Road at the Cataumet Marina. Open L, D May to October. It's bustling and boisterous and the wait is long, but the Chart Room epitomizes summertime dining on the Cape to many (despite rising prices), with a great salty atmosphere and a cast of regulars. For the best sunset views from picturesque Red Brook Harbor, get a table on the edge of the outer dining room. The Chart Room serves killer mudslides and reliable sandwiches and seafood standards, including lobster salad and lobster rolls (ask for it even if it's not on the menu), broiled scallops, and swordfish. You won't find any fried seafood on the menu here. Live piano and bass duo nightly in summer. L $$–$$$, D $$–$$$$.

🐾 ✐ ✳ **Sagamore Inn** (508-888-9707; sagamoreinncapecod.com), 1131 Route 6A, Sagamore. Open B, L, D, mid-April to mid-December. This iconic institution, resurrected under the watchful eyes of Michael and Suzanne, successfully walks that tightrope of drawing in new patrons while not alienating longtime ones like previous longtime owner Shirley

Pagliarani, who still drops in for dinner. Inside the shuttered green-and-white building are signs of "old Cape Cod": shiny wooden floors, captain's chairs at round tables, and a white tin ceiling. I recommend skipping the Italian dishes and heading straight to the seafood choices: jumbo lump crabcake, broiled seafood platter, baked stuffed shrimp, or lobster casserole. A side order of homemade, thin-cut fries is big enough to share. Shirley's pot roast remains a classic! L $–$$, D $$$.

✳ **Stir Crazy** (508-564-6464; stircrazyrestaurant.com), 570 MacArthur Boulevard, Route 28, Pocasset. Open D. This small, welcoming Asian restaurant gets consistently good reviews and features homemade Cambodian noodle dishes with fresh spices and vegetables. Everything is prepared from scratch here, and the veggies are fresh, thanks to owner Bopha Samms. L $, D $$.

✳ ✐ **Lobster Trap** (508-759-7600; lobstertrap.net), 290 Shore Road, Bourne. Open L, D. Every town has one restaurant that overlooks water and has the requisite nautical paraphernalia; this is Bourne's. The menu (take-out or sit-down) features daily specials, fried seafood, seafood rolls, and seafood plates. There's a fish market attached, so you're pretty sure it's all going to be fresh! $–$$$.

EATING OUT **Courtyard Restaurant & Pub** (508-563-1818; courtyardcapecod .com), 1337 County Road, Cataumet. Owned and operated by former Boston Bruin and LA King Jay Miller and his wife, Paula Perini-Miller, this lively pub offers contemporary American fare with a focus on seafood dishes. It's pretty basic food, but also elevated. At night the pub puts on a different outfit, becoming one of the best nightlife hotspots in Bourne, with live music and rowdy game nights. With the owner's celebrity status, you never know who might make an appearance at the bar. $–$$$.

Lindsey's Restaurant (508-759-5544; lindseysrestaurant.com), 3138 Cranberry Highway, East Wareham on the mainland side. This eatery is not really in Bourne, per se, but it's close enough and one of my favorites, so I feel it deserves a shout-out. Since 1948 this casual seafood restaurant has been serving home-style comfort food that continues to bring back a loyal following of customers, including me. It's nothing fancy, but it's butter-doused and sure to hit the spot. I've stopped here on several occasions solely for the crab-stuffed mushrooms before crossing the bridge, or while staying at the Bourne Scenic Campground. It's worth the 5-minute-ish drive. $–$$$.

MARKETS **American Lobster Mart** (508-759-7844), 2 MacArthur Boulevard, Bourne. I'll admit I've never ordered seafood from here, but I've had several local foodie friends attest to the quality, quantity, and pleasant service.

Gray Gables Market (508-743-5587), 185 Shore Road. This family-owned market offers all the basics: groceries, meats, cheese, produce, prepared foods, baked goods, beer, wine, and liquor. (See also *Farms* under **Selective Shopping**.)

SWEET TREATS & COFFEE **Daily Brew Coffee House** (508-564-4755; thedaily brewcoffeehouse.com), 1370 Route 28A, Cataumet. This neighborhood coffee shop serves strong organic java (and a box o' brew if you're waking up a large crew); yogurt and fruit smoothies; and breakfast goodies like muffins, bagels, and breakfast burritos. They also offer filling lunch sandwiches and salads. $–$$.

Corner Café (508-563-6944), 369 Barlows Landing Road, Pocasset. Most locals living in nearby towns will make the trip here simply because the breakfast is that good. After a late night, I'm a big fan of their loaded hash browns topped with over easy eggs, or the super fluffy pancakes. Come hungry because the portions are large. $–$$.

✳ Entertainment

NIGHTLIFE 🍸 **Trading Post Lounge** (508-759-9584), 12 Trowbridge Road, Buzzards Bay. Locally known as "Gerts," this local watering hole has been referred to as the Cheers of Bourne, but I tend to disagree. Come here for a game of pool and pint of cheap beer, but dine else-

PAIRPOINT GLASS AND CRYSTAL KIM GRANT

where. (See also **Courtyard Restaurant and Pub** under **Where to Eat**.)

✳ Selective Shopping

❋ Unless otherwise noted, all shops are open year-round.

ARTISANS **Pairpoint Glass and Crystal** (800-888-2344; pairpoint.com), 851 Sandwich Road, Route 6A, Sagamore. "America's oldest glassworks," this place has existed under one name or another since 1837. Many Pairpoint pieces are found in Boston's MFA and New York City's Metropolitan Museum of Art. Thomas Pairpoint, a glass designer in the 1880s, used techniques created by Deming Jarves, and master craftspeople still employ these techniques here today. Clear or richly colored glass is hand-blown, hand-sculpted, or hand-pressed on a 19th-century press. Through large picture windows, you can watch the master glassblowers working on faithful period reproductions and candlesticks or more modern lamps, paperweights, and vases.

Interested in testing your glassblowing skills? You're in luck: they offer a series of classes such as 8-hour (2-day) intros; intermediate sessions; and 2-hour classes creating items like ornaments, paperweights, and flower bouquets. There are even classes with wine and beer, and special date night themes.

FARMS **Buzzards Bay Farmers' Market** (508-982-8612), 70 Main Street, Bourne. Open select hours on Fridays from July to September, but call to confirm.

Bay End Farm (617-212-8315; bayend farm.com), 200 Bournedale Road, Buzzards Bay. Open mid-June to mid-October. Founded in 1906, this quaint farm offers fresh produce from local,

sustainable, and organic farms. Bay End is also a member of CSA (Community Supported Agriculture).

GALLERIES ♪ **Cataumet Arts Center** (508-563-5434; cataumetartscenter.org), 76 Scraggy Neck Road, off County Road and Route 28A, Cataumet. This community arts center has ever-changing exhibits, classes, and galleries. It's a beloved resource.

SPECIALTY ♣ **Christmas Tree Shop** (508-888-7010; christmastreeshops.com), on the Cape side of the Sagamore Bridge, Exit 1 off Route 6. This may be the first Christmas Tree Shop you see, but it won't be the last—there are five more on the Cape. This is the place where "everyone loves a bargain," and they've gone all out to get your attention: you can't miss the revolving windmill and thatched roof—made from Canadian marsh grass and so authentic that thatchers come from England and Ireland every other year to make repairs. As for the merchandise, it has little to do with Christmas. It revolves around inexpensive housewares, random gourmet food items, or miscellaneous clothing accessories. By the way, it's been owned by Bed Bath & Beyond since 2003.

Pocasset Naturals (508-648-5046; pocassetnaturals.com) offers all-natural bath and body care products that are made in small handcrafted batches using only pure essential oils, high-quality plants, natural pigments, and natural additives. Two of my favorites include the mint and green zeolite clay soap and the Dead Sea salt body scrub (which truly does wonders after that mistaken sunburn starts to peel). Founded in 2017 by Steph Brandt, you can find her products at Gray Gables Market, 185 Shore Road, Bourne, as well as at various farmers' markets throughout the Cape.

SANDWICH

Sandwich is calm, even in the height of summer. Many visitors whiz right by it (which is a shame), eager to get farther away from the "mainland." Even people who know about delightful Sandwich Village often hop back onto Route 6 without poking around the rest of Sandwich—the back roads and historic houses off the beaten path. Those who take the time to explore will find that Sandwich is a real gem.

You could spend a day wandering the half-mile radius around the village center, a virtual time capsule spanning the centuries. Antiques shops, attractive homes, and quiet, shady lanes are perfect for strolling. **Shawme Duck Pond**, as idyllic as they come, is surrounded by **historic houses** (including one of the Cape's oldest), an **old cemetery** on the opposite shore, a **working gristmill**, swans and ducks, and plenty of vantage points from which to take it all in.

Sandwich's greatest attraction lies just beyond the town center: **Heritage Museums & Gardens**, a 76-acre horticulturist's delight with superb collections of Americana and antique automobiles.

Beyond the town center, the **Benjamin Nye Homestead** is worth a visit; have a look-see, even if it's closed, because it sits in a picturesque spot. East of town on Route 6A, past densely carpeted cranberry bogs (harvested in autumn), you'll find a few farm stands, antiques shops, artisans' studios, and the **Green Briar Nature Center & Jam Kitchen**, paying homage to naturalist Thornton W. Burgess, a town resident and the creator of Peter Cottontail.

At the town line with Barnstable, you'll find one of the Cape's best beaches and protected areas: **Sandy Neck Beach** (see "Barrier Beach Beauty" on page 110) and **Sandy Neck Great Salt Marsh Conservation Area** (see **Green Space** in Barnstable).

The **marina**, off Tupper Road, borders the Cape Cod Canal with a recreation area. The often-overlooked town beach is nothing to sneeze at, either, and there are numerous conservation areas and ponds for walking and swimming.

Although a surprising number of Sandwich's 20,675 year-round residents commute to Boston every morning, their community dedication isn't diminished. A perfect example took place after fierce storms in August and October 1991 destroyed the town boardwalk, which had served the community since 1875. To replace it, townspeople purchased more than 1,700 individual boards, each personally inscribed, and a new boardwalk was built within eight months.

The oldest town on the Cape, Sandwich was founded in 1637 by the Cape's first permanent group of English settlers. The governor of Plymouth Colony had given permission to "tenn men from Saugust" (now Lynn, Massachusetts) to settle the area with 60 families. Sandwich was probably chosen for its close proximity to the Manomet (now Aptucxet) Trading Post (see **To See** in Bourne) and for its abundant salt-marsh hay, which provided ready fodder for the settlers' cows. Agriculture supported the community until the 1820s, when Deming Jarves, a Boston glass merchant, decided to open a glassmaking factory. The location couldn't have been better: there was a good source of sand (although more was shipped in from New Jersey), sea salt was plentiful, salt-marsh hay provided packaging for the fragile goods, and forests were thick with scrub pines to fuel the furnaces. But by the 1880s, midwestern coal-fueled glassmaking factories and a labor strike shut down Sandwich's factories. The story is told in great

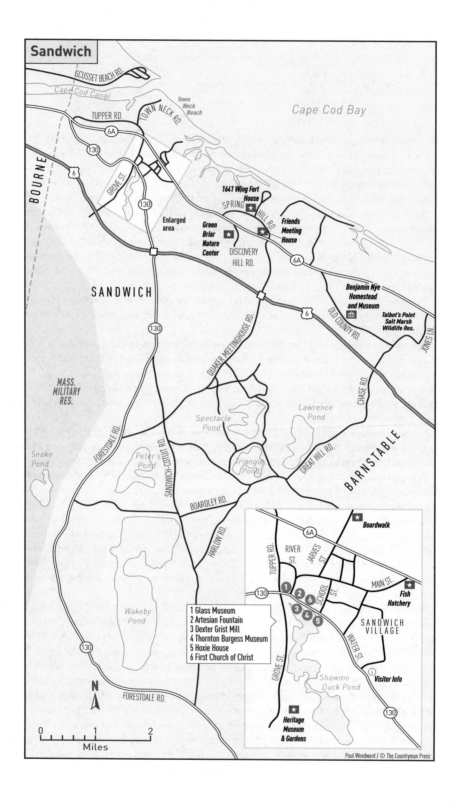

Sandwich

SCUSSET BEACH RD.

Cape Cod Canal

TUPPER RD.

TOWN NECK RD.

Town Neck Beach

Cape Cod Bay

6A

130

BOURNE

6

GROVE ST.

130

Enlarged area

1641 Wing Fort House ★

SPRING HILL RD.

Green Briar Nature Center ★

Friends Meeting House ★

DISCOVERY HILL RD.

6A

SANDWICH

130

QUAKER MEETINGHOUSE RD.

6

OLD COUNTY RD.

Benjamin Nye Homestead and Museum 🏛

Talbot's Point Salt Marsh Wildlife Res.

JONES LN.

CHASE RD.

Lawrence Pond

MASS. MILITARY RES.

Spectacle Pond

FORESTDALE RD.

Peter's Pond

SANDWICH-COTUIT RD.

Triangle Pond

GREAT HILL RD.

BARNSTABLE

Snake Pond

BOARDLEY RD.

HARLOW RD.

Wakeby Pond

130

N

FORESTDALE RD.

0   1   2
Miles

6A

TUPPER RD.

RIVER ST.

JARVES ST.

SCHOOL ST.

★ **Boardwalk**

MAIN ST.

130

① ② ⑥
③ ④ ⑤

Fish Hatchery ★

SANDWICH VILLAGE

1 Glass Museum
2 Artesian Fountain
3 Dexter Grist Mill
4 Thornton Burgess Museum
5 Hoxie House
6 First Church of Christ

WATER ST.

GROVE ST.

Shawme Duck Pond

ⓘ *Visitor Info*

130

★ **Heritage Museum & Gardens**

Paul Woodward / © The Countryman Press

detail at the excellent Sandwich Glass Museum. Today, glassblowers work in a few studios in town.

Sandwich was named, by the way, for the English town, not for the sandwich-creator earl, as many think. (That Earl of Sandwich was born 81 years after this town was founded.)

GUIDANCE ✻ **Sandwich Chamber of Commerce** (508-681-0918; sandwich chamber.com), 520 Route 130. Open May to October. Pick up the good village walking guide at this booth (and at many shops in town).

Cape Cod Canal Visitor Center (508-833-9678; capecodcanal.us), 60 Ed Moffit Drive, east of the Sandwich Marina. Open mid-May to late October. This office dispenses information about boating, fishing, camping, and other canal activities. Highlights of the center include historic photos, interactive monitors, and a small theater showing films on canal history, critters, and wildflowers. Inquire about their hikes, lectures, and other programs.

GETTING THERE *By car:* Take the Sagamore Bridge to Route 6 east to Exit 2 (Route 130 North) and travel 2 miles to Main Street. From Exit 1 and Route 6A, you can take Tupper Road or Main Street into the village center.

By bus: There is no bus service to Sandwich proper, but **Plymouth & Brockton** (508-778-9767; p-b.com) buses bound for Boston stop at the Sagamore Bridge, behind the McDonald's in the commuter parking lot.

GETTING AROUND *By shuttle:* The **Sandwich Route** (800-352-7155; capecodtransit .org) travels Route 28 from the Sagamore Park & Ride, through downtown Sandwich, to the Hyannis Transportation Center. This route also connects passengers with the **Sealine, H2O, the Hyannis Crosstown,** and **Barnstable Villager.**

PUBLIC RESTROOMS Seasonal restrooms are located across from Town Hall and at Russell's Corner.

PUBLIC LIBRARY ✻ 𝄞 ⚲ **Sandwich Public Library** (508-888-0625; sandwichpublic library.com), 142 Main Street.

EMERGENCIES **Sandwich Police Department** (508-888-1212; sandwichpd.com), 255 Cotuit Road, or call **911.**

Medical: It's not an "emergency" (the kind you'd expect under this category, anyway), but many area water wells are closed due to contamination caused by years of training with grenades and other live munitions at the Massachusetts Military Reservation. I drink bottled water on the Upper Cape.

✻ To See

IN SANDWICH VILLAGE

𝄞 **Dexter Grist Mill** (508-888-3461; sandwichmass.org), on Shawme Duck Pond, Water Street. Open mid-June to mid-October. The circa-1640 mill has had a multiuse past, and the site wasn't always as quaint as it is now. The mill was turbine powered during Sandwich's glassmaking heyday; it then sat idle until 1920, when it was converted into a tearoom. After adjacent mills were torn down in the late 1950s, it was opened to tourists in 1961, with the cypress waterwheel you see today. You can also purchase stone-ground cornmeal here—great for muffins, Indian pudding, and polenta. $.

DEXTER GRIST MILL

🔖 **Hoxie House** (508-888-4361; sandwichmass.org), 18 Water Street. Open mid-June to mid-October. For a long time, this circa-1640 structure was thought to be the Cape's oldest saltbox, but it's impossible to know definitively, because the Barnstable County Courthouse deeds were lost in a fire. Nonetheless, the house has a rare saltbox roofline, small diamond-shaped leaded windows, and a fine vantage above Shawme Duck Pond. Thanks to loaner furniture from Boston's Museum of Fine Arts, the restored interior looks much as it did during colonial times. One of the most remarkable facts about this house is that it was occupied without electricity or indoor plumbing until the 1950s. The house was named for Abraham Hoxie, who purchased it in 1860 for $400. The Reverend John Smith lived here in 1675, when he came to be minister of the First Parish Church. The rather fun tours include more of a social historical view rather than emphasizing dates.

HOXIE HOUSE WINDOWS

First Church of Christ (508-888-0434; firstchurchsandwich.org), 136 Main Street. This Christopher Wren–inspired church with a tall white spire was built in 1847, but its brass bell, cast in 1675, is thought to be the country's oldest.

Town Hall (508-888-5144; sandwich mass.org), 130 Main Street. Sandwich has certainly gotten its money's worth out of this Greek Revival building. It was constructed at a cost of little more than $4,000 in 1834 and still serves as the center for town government.

Old Town Cemetery, Grove Street, on the shore opposite the Hoxie House. You'll recognize the names on many gravestones (including those of Burgess, Bodfish, and Bourne) from historic houses and street signs around town.

WHERE TO START IN SANDWICH

Morning: Grab a great bite at Café Chew. Venture over to the Blueberry Bog and fill your bags with juicy berries before the afternoon heat cranks up.

Afternoon: Spend a few hours at the Heritage Museums and Gardens and follow up with a visit at the Sandwich Glass Museum. Fill up on pizza and wine at the Brown Jug or grab a hearty burger from Next Door Burger Bar. Then, rent kayaks from Rideaway and enjoy an afternoon paddle through Popponesset Bay, or grab your rod and reel and try your luck casting off the Scusset Beach Fish Pier.

Evening: Enjoy a fine dinner at the Belfry Inn & Bistro, or head over to the Drunken Seal for cocktails and light fare on their waterfront deck.

Although the oldest marker dates to 1683, most are from the 1700s; many are marked with a winged skull, a common Puritan design.

ELSEWHERE AROUND TOWN

❊ ❀ **Heritage Museums & Gardens** (508-888-3300; heritagemuseumsandgardens .org), 67 Grove Street. Open early April to late October. Established in 1969 by Josiah K. Lilly III, a descendant of the founder of the pharmaceutical firm Eli Lilly and Company, this place is an oasis for garden lovers, antiques and vintage-car buffs, and Americana enthusiasts. These 100 acres are planted with outstanding collections of rhododendrons, including the famous Dexter variety, which blooms from late May to early June. (Charles O. Dexter was the estate's original owner, and he experimented with hybridizing here.) There are also impressive collections of holly bushes, heathers, hostas, hydrangeas, and more than 1,000 daylilies, which bloom from mid-July to early August. Don't miss the **labyrinth** or the Hart family **maze garden**. The estate is equally pleasant for an autumn walk. Or have a go at their zip line (see **To Do**).

The **American History Museum** features an extensive collection of bird carvings by Elmer Crowell in addition to a large array of hand-painted miniatures, while the J. K. Lilly III **Antique Automobile Museum**, in the replica **Shaker Round Barn**, houses the museum's outstanding vintage-car collection. A 1930 Duesenberg built for Gary Cooper and President Taft's White Steamer (the first official auto of the White House) are two of the mint-condition classics.

The **Art Museum** features folk art, scrimshaw, cigar-store figures, weather vanes, and Currier & Ives lithographs. Also on the grounds you'll find an 1800 windmill, an operational Coney Island–style 1912 carousel, and a **café**. The alfresco café has a menu of overstuffed sandwiches, salads, and desserts. There is golf cart transportation for those who may need assistance. Keep your eyes

HERITAGE MUSEUMS & GARDENS KAYLA ROBERTSON/DO ART PHOTOGRAPHY

SAND TRANSFORMED

Sandwich Glass Museum (508-888-0251; sandwichglassmuseum.org), 129 Main Street. Open year-round except January. If you're in the habit of skipping town historical museums, break the habit this time; you won't be disappointed. During the 19th century, Sandwich glassmaking flourished at Deming Jarves's Boston & Sandwich Glass Company (1825–1888) and the Cape Cod Glass Works (1859–1869). Today, this internationally known museum, operated by the Sandwich Historical Society, chronologically displays more than 6,000 pieces of decorative and functional glass objects, which became increasingly more elaborate and richly colored as the years progressed. Many displays are dramatically backlit by natural light streaming through banks of windows. Check out the elaborate table setting featuring Hannah Rebecca Burgess's late-1800s collection; a 20-minute multimedia presentation that describes the first 200 years of Sandwich's history; and lots of changing seasonal exhibits. You'll also enjoy glassblowing demonstrations and the contemporary gallery with changing exhibits. $. ♦ ✐ ⛱

Inquire about the museum's excellent 90-minute village walking tours (mid-June through October).

peeled for museum special events, including plant sales, a rhododendron festival (see **Special Events**), concerts, and car shows. Gift and garden shop at the entrance. $$.

Benjamin Nye Homestead and Museum (508-888-4213; nyefamily.org), 85 Old County Road, East Sandwich. Open mid-June to mid-October. Off Route 6A, this 1685 homestead belonged to one of Sandwich's first settlers and has undergone many structural changes over the years. Although it began life as a small, narrow house with a central chimney, an addition turned it into a saltbox. A second floor created the full Colonial you see today. Although the interior is hardly a purist restoration, you'll see some of the original construction, early paneling, 18th-century wallpaper, a rosewood melodeon built by the Nye family in the 1850s, a spinning wheel, and handwoven sheets. $.

1641 Wing Fort House (508-833-1540; wingfamily.org), 63 Spring Hill Road (off Route 6A), East Sandwich. Open mid-June to mid-September. The Wing house is the country's oldest home continuously inhabited by the same family. This circa-1646 house began as a one-room cottage when Stephen Wing, descendant of the Reverend John Wing, arrived with his new bride. In the mid-1800s, a second house was added to it to create the current three-quarter Colonial. $.

Friends Meeting House (508-398-3773), 6 Quaker Road, off Spring Hill Road (from Route 6A), East Sandwich. Meetings every Sunday. The building standing today was built in 1810, the third Quaker meetinghouse on this site. The congregation has been meeting since 1657, which makes it the oldest continuously used meeting house in North America. The interior is simple, with pews and a wood-burning stove stoked in winter for 25 or so congregants.

❄ ✐ **Sandwich Fish Hatchery** (508-888-0008; masswildlife.org), 164 Route 6A at Old Main Street. Open daily. More than 200,000 trout at various stages of development are raised to stock the state's ponds. Throw in pellets of food (bring quarters for the vending machines) and watch 'em swarm.

✐ **Boardwalk**, Harbor Street off Factory Street. The boardwalk crosses marshland, Mill Creek, and low dunes to connect to Town Neck Beach (see **Green Space**). Depending on the season, you might see teens jumping into the creek (1½ hours before and after high tide, when the water is theoretically deep enough) or blue heron poking

FRIENDS MEETING HOUSE KIM GRANT

around the tidal pools and tall grasses. There are expansive views at the end of the 1,350-foot walkway.

✳ To Do

BLUEBERRY PICKING **The Blueberry Bog** (508-888-1560), 92 Spring Hill Road, off Route 6A, East Sandwich. In the 1940s, this former cranberry bog was turned into a blueberry farm. Today there are about 400 bushes on more than 4 acres. Pick your own from late-July to August. A few side notes: The blueberry bushes are in a heavily wooded area, so I recommend wearing long pants, long sleeves, and a hat to protect yourself from mosquitoes, ticks, and poison ivy. If you think you may have come in contact with the shiny three-leaf ivy, pick up Tec-Nu from a local drugstore and apply it to any areas of concern. The bog is pretty easy to find, and there's truly nothing better than freshly picked blueberries.

BICYCLING & RENTALS The **Cape Cod Canal Bikeway** stretches nearly 14 scenic miles alongside the canal and under the Bourne and Sagamore bridges. You can access the trail at the Cape Cod Canal Visitor Center (see *Guidance*). Rent bicycles and equipment at **Ecotourz** (508-888-1627; ecotourz.net), 20 Jarves Street; or **Rideaway Adventures** (508-247-0827; rideawaykayak.com), 449 Route 6A, East Sandwich. (See also *Kayaks & Paddleboards*.)

BOAT EXCURSIONS & RENTALS **Sandwich Marina** (508-833-0808 for **harbormaster**; sandwichmarina.com), 12 Freezer Road. This first-class marina has 140 seasonal slip holders, 42 commercial slips, and 24 transient slips available. Boaters will enjoy the marina's neutral location—head east to enjoy the plentiful fishing grounds of Cape Cod Bay, or head west for a pleasant ride through the Cape Cod Canal into Buzzard's

Bay. Frequent visitors will be quick to praise the boat-launching ramp, which some consider to be the best on Cape Cod.

FISHING The town of Sandwich has a lot to offer fishermen. Procure freshwater and saltwater fishing licenses and regulations online at (mass.gov/eea/agencies/dfg/licensing).

Big game: **Laura Jay Charters** (508-888-4033; laurajay.com), 25 Ed Moffitt Drive. Trips offered April through December. Laura Jay offers half-day in-shore charters, as well as extended offshore trips for giant tuna and hard-fighting blues.

Captain Joe P Charters (617-756-8666; captainjoecharters.com), 12 Freezer Road. This highly reviewed charter is "strictly about fishing." Whatever your pleasure—hungry to land that coveted trophy tuna, or a newbie looking for a relaxing experience on the water—Captain Joe P will do his best to make it happen.

On shore: To the north of the jetty at **Scusset Beach** is an expansive strip of beach that is great for surfcasting and bait fishing.

By bridge or jetty: Bait fishermen do well fishing off the **Scusset Beach Fish Pier**, but those who prefer casting jigs and other lures will enjoy fishing along the rocks and the long jetty marking the eastern entrance to the canal. A shallow sandbar known as Pip's Rip (just off the farthest parking lot) is one of the only areas in the canal where an angler can wade out a short distance. You will often see surface feeding fish here, especially in the fall when the striper migration is in full swing.

Supplies: **Canal Bait and Tackle** (508-833-2996; canalbaitandtackle.com), 101 Cranberry Highway, Sagamore. Though this bait shop is not in Sandwich, it's still pretty close-by and best in the area.

GOLF ❄ **Holly Ridge Golf Club** (508-428-5577; hollyridgegolf.com), off Route 130, South Sandwich. An award-winning, 18-hole, 3,000-yard, par-54 course.

❄ **Sandwich Hollows Golf Club** (508-888-3384; sandwichhollows.com), Exit 3 off Route 6, East Sandwich. An 18-hole, par-71 course.

KAYAKS & PADDLEBOARDS **Rideaway Adventures** (508-247-0827; rideawaykayak.com), 449 Route 6A, East Sandwich. Rent kayaks, paddleboards, and bikes from Rideaway and have them delivered to your vacation rental, or book a guided tour on Popponesset Bay.

Ecotourz (508-888-1627; ecotourz.net), 20 Jarves Street. Enjoy a two-hour guided tour kayaking through the estuaries of Sandwich. You can also rent kayaks and paddleboards by the hour.

MINI-GOLF ✿ **Sandwich Mini Golf** (508-833-1905; sandwichminigolf.net), 159 Route 6A. Open mid-May to mid-October and daily in summer. This course is set on a cranberry bog and boasts a floating raft for a green. An honest-to-goodness stream winds around many of the 35 holes. $–$$.

SCENIC RAILROAD ✿ **Cape Cod Central Railroad** (888-797-7245 for tickets; capetrain.com), 70 Main Street, Buzzards Bay. Late May through late October. The relaxing 48-mile trip takes 2 hours, passing alongside cranberry bogs and the Sandy Neck Great Salt Marsh. (I always try to have "beginner's eyes" on this trip, seeing it as a first-timer would, but honestly, the scenery is a tad . . . shall we say, uneventful.) On certain days in July and August, when there are two trains daily, you can take the first one from Hyannis, hop off in Sandwich, walk around Sandwich center for 3 hours, and then catch the next train back to Hyannis. The best part of this trip is the local narration—unless you've never been on a train before, in which case the simple act of taking a train will tickle you more. Oh, and the dinner part of the dinner train? They serve a pretty decent meal. $$$.

TENNIS Public courts are located at **Wing Elementary School** on Route 130; **Oak Ridge School** and **Sandwich High School**, both off Quaker Meetinghouse Road; and **Forestdale School** off Route 130.

ZIP LINE *✎* **The Adventure Park at Heritage Museums and Gardens** (508-866-0199), 67 Grove Street. This aerial obstacle course and zip line has been fun for the whole family since it opened in 2015. Open daily in summer, weekends in fall. $$$–$$$$.

✳ Green Space

✎ **Shawme Duck Pond**, Water Street (Route 130), in the village center. Flocks of ducks, geese, and swans know a good thing when they find it. And even though this idyllic spot is one of the most easily accessible on the Cape, it remains a tranquil place for humans and waterfowl alike. Formerly a marshy brook, the willow-lined pond was dammed prior to the gristmill's operation in the 1640s. It's a nice spot to canoe.

✳ ☙ *✎* **Shawme-Crowell State Forest** (877-422-6762 reservations; reserveamerica .com), Route 130. You can walk, bicycle, and camp at almost 300 sites on almost 750 acres. When the popular Nickerson State Park (see "A Supreme State Park" on page 179) is full of campers, there are often dozens of good sites still available here. There are also a few yurts; reservations required.

✳ ☙ *✎* **Scusset Beach State Reservation** (877-422-6762 reservations; reserveam erica.com), on Cape Cod Bay, off Scusset Beach Road from the mainland side of the

SHAWME POND KIM GRANT

IT IS A WONDERFUL THING TO SWEETEN THE WORLD

Green Briar Nature Center & Jam Kitchen (508-888-6870; thorntonburgess.org), 6 Discovery Hill Road off Route 6A, East Sandwich. Trails open year-round. Jam-cooking demonstrations most days April to December. Even in an area with so many tranquil spots, Green Briar rises to the top. It's run by the Thornton W. Burgess Society "to reestablish and maintain nature's fine balance among all living things and to hold as a sacred trust the obligation to make only the best use of natural resources." Located on Smiling Pond and adjacent to the famous Briar Patch of Burgess's stories, this big patch of conservation land has many short interpretive nature trails (less than a mile long), a lovely wildflower garden, and a veritable Noah's Ark of resident animals. The society hosts natural history classes, lectures, nature walks, and other programs for children and adults.

The Jam Kitchen was established in 1903 by Ida Putnam, who used her friend Fanny Farmer's recipes to make jams, jellies, and fruit preserves. Step inside the old-fashioned, aromatic, and homey place to see mason jars filled with apricots and strawberries, and watch fruit simmering on vintage-1920 Glenwood gas stoves. Two-hour workshops (sign up in advance) on preserving fruit and making jams and jellies are also held. About this place, Burgess said to Putnam in 1939, "It is a wonderful thing to sweeten the world which is in a jam and needs preserving." Berry festivals are held throughout summer: look for strawberries in June, blueberries in August, and cranberries in September.

GREEN BRIAR JAM KITCHEN KIM GRANT

GREEN BRIAR JAM TRAILS KIM GRANT

canal. The 380-acre reservation offers about 100 campsites (primarily used by RVers) in-season (early May to mid-October), bicycling, picnicking, and walking opportunities. Facilities include camping, in-season lifeguard, restrooms, changing rooms, and a snack bar. Parking $.

See also **Giving Tree Gallery and Sculpture Gardens** under *Selective Shopping*.

BEACHES **Town Neck Beach**, on Cape Cod Bay, off Town Neck Road and Route 6A. This pebble beach extends 1.5 miles from the Cape Cod Canal to Dock Creek. Visit at high tide if you want to swim; at low tide, it's great for walking. $. The lot rarely fills up.

See also **Scusset Beach State Reservation**, above.

PONDS **Wakeby Pond** (off Cotuit Road), South Sandwich, offers freshwater swimming and picnicking.

WALKS **Talbot's Point Salt Marsh Wildlife Reservation**, off Old County Road from Route 6A. This little-used, 1.5-mile (round-trip) hiking trail winds past red pines, beeches, and a large salt marsh.

See also **Green Briar Nature Center & Jam Kitchen** and **Shawme-Crowell State Forest**.

✳ Lodging

🦞 Sandwich's historic hostelries provide great diversity and something for everyone—from an incredibly impressive church conversion to a large motor inn.

RESORTS & INNS ✳ 🎐 **Dan'l Webster Inn & Spa** (508-888-3622; danlwebster inn.com), 149 Main Street. Modeled after an 18th-century hostelry where Revolutionary patriots met, today's inn has a certain colonial charm that's vigilantly maintained by the Catanias, owners since 1980. Most of the 48 traditionally decorated rooms and suites are of the top-notch motel/hotel variety. The minority is more distinctively inn-like and found in two separate older houses. Touring motor coaches are part of the parking lot landscape. $$–$$$. (See also **Where To Eat**.)

✳ **Belfry Inn & Bistro** (508-888-8550; belfryinn.com), 6 Jarves Street. Innkeeper Chris Wilson presides over the center of town (and the town's wedding business) with the circa-1900 **Abbey**, the circa-1879 **Painted Lady**, and the 1830s Federal-style **Village House**. Between the three locations, there are 23 guest rooms appointed with fine antiques and tasteful furnishings. Abbey rooms are downright spectacular: outfitted with stained glass, flying buttresses, fancy linens, bold colors, beds made from pews, gas fireplaces, Jacuzzis, and balconies. Chris and his architect deserve awards for this spectacular conversion, which consistently wins rave reviews. Most Painted Lady rooms have whirlpools, while Village House rooms are relatively modest with hardwood floors (some bleached) and down comforters. The Belfry also offers dining for the public as well as a full breakfast. $–$$$. (See also **Where To Eat**.)

BED-AND-BREAKFASTS ✳ **Isaiah Jones Homestead** (508-888-9115; isaiahjones.com), 165 Main Street. This Victorian gem in the middle of the village deserves your full attention. Filled with killer antiques and showing lots of elegant decorating prowess (they're not as fussy as the website photos suggest), there isn't one single room I'd hesitate to recommend. For more privacy, though, choose the adjacent carriage house with whirlpool tubs, robes, and upscale amenities. Presiding since 2007, the delightful innkeepers Katherine and Donnie Sanderson (he grew up in Chatham) serve a three-course breakfast (think French toast that's more akin to soufflé) and wonderful special-occasion dinners. They've also outfitted each of their seven rooms with either a fireplace or gas stove. $$.

❇ **1750 Inn at Sandwich Center** (508-888-6958; innatsandwich.com), 118 Tupper Road. Expert hospitality is a watchword at this five-room inn operated by lovely innkeepers Jan and Charlie Preus. They serve delicious breakfasts (like macadamia nut French toast or quichettes served in individual ramekins) in the keeping room—complete with a beehive oven—or on the patio. And they set out brandy and chocolates in the evening. Guests gather in

ISAIAH JONES HOMESTEAD KIM GRANT

the living room surrounded by period architectural details and are regaled with vivid stories about the inn's history. The two choice guest rooms, painted in soothing colors, are the upper floor front rooms. Come off-season to best enjoy the fireplaces (in most rooms). $–$$.

CAMPGROUND 🐾 **Peters Pond Park** (508-477-1775; peterspond.com), 185 Cotuit Road. Open mid-April to mid-October. Call for current status. At last look the RV resort offered more than 450 well-groomed campsites, cottages, yurts, walking trails, summertime children's activities, a ball field, two beaches, a campfire ring, and a popular spring-fed lake for trout and bass fishing, boating, and swimming. Rental rowboats, paddleboats, and kayaks were also available. $.

See also **Shawme-Crowell State Forest** and **Scusset Beach State Reservation** under *Green Space*.

❇ Where to Eat

Sandwich eateries run the gamut, from fine dining in a former church to casual eating in a tiny tea shop.

DINING OUT ❇ 🍷 ♿ **Belfry Bistro** (508-888-8550; belfryinn.com), 8 Jarves Street. Open L, D. The quiet setting (inside a converted church) is divinely dramatic—with soaring beadboard ceilings, stained glass, interior flying buttresses, a confessional converted into a tasteful bar, and a former altar set with tables. It's also elegant—with candlelight, damask-covered tables, high-backed leather chairs, and a wood-burning fireplace. Tasteful alfresco terrace dining is available, but it seems a waste not to sit indoors here. Chef Toby offers a menu ranging from simple (like clam chowder or fish-and-chips) to sophisticated (like tuna carpaccio nicoise or brioche-crusted codfish). The experience is as much about the food as the setting. L $$, D $$–$$$$.

1750 INN AT SANDWICH CENTER KIM GRANT

❄ ☺ ✎ ⌁ **Amari** (508-375-0011; amari restaurant.com), 674 Route 6A, East Sandwich. Open D. On the town line with Barnstable and near Sandy Neck Beach, Bob and Maureen Hixon's upscale but comfortable eatery has a little something—with big portions—for everyone. Dine within sight of an open kitchen, surrounded by lots of mahogany, on Italian cooking with a contemporary flair. Best bets include wood oven pizza and fried calamari. $$.

❄ ✎ **Dan'l Webster Inn** (508-888-3622; danlwebsterinn.com), 149 Main Street. Open B, L, D. Just so you're not wondering, this kitchen serves classic American dishes (think prime rib and filet mignon) in comfortable dining rooms. The sunlit Conservatory resembles a greenhouse; the Music Room is more traditional; and the casual Tavern has lighter fare. B $, L $–$$, D $$–$$$.

EATING OUT **Next Door Burger Bar** (508-888-3746; nextdoorburgerbar.com), 8 Jarves Street. Open L, D. As the name suggests, this gourmet fast-food joint offers upscale burgers like the signature

Upper Cape, with local goat cheese, arugula, ground chili aioli, and beefsteak tomato, or the Banh Mi Burger with organic pork, spicy kewpie mayo, cilantro, ginger, and pickled cucumber and

BELFRY BISTRO KIM GRANT

carrot. Vegetarians will enjoy their meat-less options like the Alternative Burger, with basmati rice, curry veggies, and fire roasted sweet peppers, or the plant-based Beyond Burger. All meals come with waffle fries (sub for veggie fries, sweet potato fries, or onion rings), and are served on locally made everything brioche buns. They also have wraps, salads, and delicious ice cream shakes. $–$$.

❄ ❢ **The Brown Jug** (508-888-4669; thebrownjug.com), 155 Main Street. Open L, D. Proprietors Michael and Erick continue to elevate their offerings at this specialty café and full vino bar. Stop here for a slice of gourmet pizza from their wood-fired oven, or savor a sandwich and cheese plate on their European-style patio. Wash it down with a pitcher of beer or sangria, wine, or frothy cappuccino. Their jazz afternoons are delightful. $$–$$$.

❢ **The Seal** (508-888-0060; theseal capecod.com), 98 Town Neck Road. Open L, D. Formerly known as The Drunken Seal, this beach bar restaurant was recently purchased by Christopher Wilson (who also owns the Belfry Inn & Bistro and the Next Door Burger Bar). This is a nice place for an afternoon drink on the deck; the panoramic views of Cape Cod Bay are spectacular. Tempt yourself with something off the new menu, too. $$

SWEET TREATS & COFFEE ❄ **Beth's Bakery & Cafe** (508-888-7716; beths bakery.net), 16 Jarves Street. Open B, L. Beth and Joe, lifetime residents of Sandwich, offer light breakfasts, scones and such, soups, salads, and sandwiches. Enjoy a cup of Beanstock coffee on the patio or inside on one of their marble tabletops. $.

❄ **Café Chew** (508-888-7717; cafechew .com), 4 Merchant's Road. Open B, L. Dubbed "Sandwich's Sandwichery," the Chew offers sandwiches from a blackboard menu, a full line of fair trade organic coffees, and artsy tables at which to dine. There are plenty of reasons owners Tobin and Bob win tons of awards: their renowned German breakfast sandwich features eggs with melted Gruyère cheese and ham encased in a

CAFÉ CHEW KIM GRANT

Bavarian pretzel roll. The Midwestern lunch sandwich boasts homemade meat loaf with Cheddar, bacon, and tomato relish on ciabatta bread. And don't even get me started about their mint chocolate brownie. For kids, the peanut butter is paired with all-natural preserves. Soups, specialty salads, and daily specials, too. $.

❋ **Dunbar House Restaurant & Tea Room** (508-833-2485; dunbarteashop .com), 1 Water Street. Open L and for afternoon tea. I always want to love this tiny English tearoom, set in a slightly rustic, American-style country setting. But in my experience, service can be "relaxed" and less than friendly, and the portions small. Still, if you want, try the authentic ploughman's lunch or scones and Scottish shortbread. Afternoon English tea includes scones, finger sandwiches, and desserts. In summer, garden tables are an oasis; in winter, the fireplace makes it cozy indoors. $–$$.

✐ **Twin Acres Ice Cream Shoppe** (508-888-0566; twinacresicecreamshoppe .com), 21 Route 6A. Open April to mid-October. A favorite among locals and visitors alike, this sweet spot offers some of the best homemade ice cream in the area. Unlike most seasonal ice cream places, this one boasts a lush lawn, a little oak grove, plenty of tables and chairs, and is lit up at night. My only complaint: there's so much colorful signage describing the offerings that it's overwhelming. To compensate, I've returned often enough to memorize the menu. $.

MARKETS **Lambert's Farm Market** (508-477-0655; lambertsfarmmarket .com), 271 Cotuit Road. A one-stop-shop for groceries, deli takeout, catered meals, butcher shop, freshly baked goods, wine, beer, cheese, etc.

Fishermen's View (508-591-0088; fishermensview.com), 20 Freezer Road. Local fishermen, Bob and Denny Colbert, run this boat-to-table seafood market. Choose from a selection of fresh, locally sourced seafood, or dine on the

BROWN JUG   KIM GRANT

waterfront deck and enjoy stunning views of the canal and marina. (See also *Farms* under **Selective Shopping**.)

❋ Entertainment

✐ **Band concerts**, at the Wing School off Route 130, are given by the Sandwich Town Band on Thursday evenings at 7:30 in July and August. (See also **The Brown Jug** and the **Drunken Seal** under **Where to Eat**.)

❋ Selective Shopping

❋ Unless otherwise noted, all shops are open year-round. (Still, don't expect many to be open midweek during the winter.)

ANTIQUES **Sandwich Antiques Center** (508-833-3600), 131 Route 6A. If you treasure the hunt, this multidealer shop is worth your time.

Sandwich Auction House (508-888-1926; sandwichauction.com), 15 Tupper

Road. Consignment estate sales are held once a week. Call about their monthly super-duper Oriental rug auction.

ARTISANS **The Glass Studio on Cape Cod** (508-888-6681; capecodglass.net), 470 Route 6A, East Sandwich. Open April through December. Artist Michael Magyar offers a wide selection of glass made with modern and centuries-old techniques. He's been glassblowing since 1980, and you can watch him work most weekends in season. Choose from graceful Venetian goblets, square vases, bud vases, hand-blown ornaments, and "sea bubbles" glassware, influenced by the water around him.

BOOKSTORE 🦀 🐚 🦑 **Titcomb's Book Shop** (508-888-2331; titcombsbookshop .com), 432 Route 6A, East Sandwich. Book enthusiasts won't be disappointed; rare-book lovers will be even happier; and online shoppers in heaven. This three-story barn is filled with more than 30,000 new, used, and rare books for adults and children; a good selection of Cape and maritime books, educational toys and puzzles; and cards by Tasha Tudor. Personalized service is exceptional: The Titcombs have owned and staffed the shop since 1969 and, with the help of their eight children, have made hundreds of yards of shelves. It's a charming place, encouraging browsing. By the way, owner Nancy Titcomb helped resurrect interest in Thornton W. Burgess, and, as you might imagine, she offers a great selection of his work. Titcomb's was recently selected by the International Booksellers Federation as one of 50 unique bookshops around the world. Check the website for book signings and other special events.

FARMS **Crow Farm** (508-888-0690; crowfarmcapecod.com), 192 Old King's Highway. Open May to December. In addition to jams, jellies, corn, summer squash, native peaches, and bread, Paul Crowell's farm stand also offers

cornmeal ground at the local gristmill. (See also "It Is a Wonderful Thing to Sweeten the World" on page 56.)

Sandwich Farmers' Market (339-227-0686; sandwichfarmersmarket.com), 164 Route 6A at the Village Green, every Tuesday from mid-June to mid-October.

GALLERIES **Black Crow Gallery** (401-209-9630; blackcrowartgallery.word press.com), 679 Route 6A, East Sandwich. Definitely not your average gallery, but still worth poking around because it's run by an eclectic group of artists: glass blowers, knitters, silversmiths, wood carvers, painters, soap makers, jewelers, seamstresses, print-makers, and others.

Collections Unlimited (508-833-0039; collectionsgallery.com), 23a Jarves Street. Handcrafted items—wood objects,

TITCOMBS BOOK SHOP KIM GRANT

pottery, baskets, stained glass, and the like—from members of the Cape's longest-running cooperative (since 1990).

SPECIALTY **Home for the Holidays** (508-888-4388; yourhomefortheholidays .com), 154 Main Street. Each room of this 1850 house is filled with decorations and gifts geared to specific holidays or special occasions. Items in one room are changed every month, so there's always a room devoted to the current holiday.

Modern Vintage Design Studio (774-413-5737; modernvintagedesignstudio .com), 157 Main Street. Designers Kristen and Cara mesh their unique styles together to create rustic-meets-glamour-meets-modern-but-vintage-inspired furniture, fabrics, signs, invitations, and other paper goods. These ladies are quirky and fun, with an eye for architectural salvage.

Mrs. Mugs (508-362-6462), 680 Route 6A, East Sandwich. Reader Janet Grant (no relation) and my mother (relation) write enthusiastically about this place, which has mugs (of course) but also funky T-shirts, unique watches, locally made jewelry, and what has to be the largest selection of Crocs on the Cape. The beloved owner, Lori Simon, offers gifts for all price ranges.

The Weather Store (800-646-1203; theweatherstore.com), 146 Main Street. If it relates to measuring or predicting weather, it's here: weather vanes, sundials, and weather sticks to indicate when a storm is headed your way.

Wish Gift Co. (888-978-9474), 4 Merchants Road. If you are in need of a gift for a baby shower, birthday, wedding, or just because, you will surely find something here.

✳ Special Events

Late June: **Sandwich Fest** (sandwichfest .com). This sandwich contest was hugely popular when it debuted in 2009.

Mid- to late May: **Annual Rhododendron Festival** (508-888-3300; heritage museumsandgardens.org). Includes a rhododendron canopy walk, photography and other workshops, on-site flower experts, and more. And for families: scavenger hunts, nature detectives, and other games.

Late November through December: **Holly Days** (508-833-9755; sandwich hollydays.com). A chamber-sponsored festival with caroling, hot cider served at open houses, trolley tours, and crafts sales. The full calendar is listed on the chamber's website.

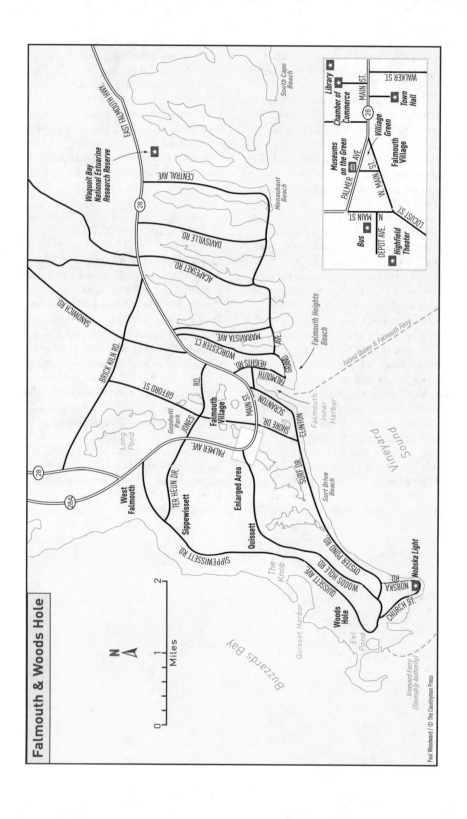

Falmouth & Woods Hole

South Cape Beach

Waquoit Bay National Estuarine Research Reserve

EAST FALMOUTH HWY.

CENTRAL AVE.

28

Menauhant Beach

DAVISVILLE RD.

ACAPESKET RD.

SANDWICH RD.

BRICK KILN RD.

MARAVISTA AVE.

Falmouth Heights Beach

WORCESTER CT.

FALMOUTH HEIGHTS RD.

GRAND AVE.

Island Queen & Falmouth Ferry

GIFFORD ST.

JONES RD.

Goodwill Park

Falmouth Village

MAIN ST.

SCRANTON

CLINTON

SHORE DR.

Falmouth Inner Harbor

Long Pond

PALMER AVE.

Enlarged Area

SURF DR.

Surf Drive Beach

28

West Falmouth

TER HEUN DR.

Sippewissett

28A

Quissett

Vineyard Sound

SIPPEWISSETT RD.

The Knob

QUISSETT AVE.

WOODS HOLE RD.

OYSTER POND RD.

Quisset Harbor

Buzzards Bay

Woods Hole

Eel Pond

NOBSKA RD.

Nobska Light

CHURCH ST.

Vineyard Ferry (Steamship Authority)

N

0   1   2

Miles

Paul Woodward / © The Countryman Press

Inset: Falmouth Village

Library

Chamber of Commerce

MAIN ST.

WALKER ST.

Town Hall

28

Museums

Palmer on the Green

PALMER AVE.

W. MAIN ST.

Village Green

Falmouth Village

N. MAIN ST.

LOCUST ST.

Bus

DEPOT AVE.

Highfield Theater

FALMOUTH &
WOODS HOLE

The Cape's second largest town, Falmouth has more shore and coastline than any other town on the Cape. In fact, it has 14 harbors, 12 miles of public beaches, and more than 30 ponds. Saltwater inlets reach deep into the southern coastline, like fjords—only without the mountains. Buzzards Bay laps at the western shores of quiet North and West Falmouth and bustling **Woods Hole**. Falmouth's eight distinctive villages accommodate about 101,000 summer people, which roughly triples the year-round population of 33,000.

The villages differ widely in character. Quiet, restful lanes and residents who keep to themselves characterize **Sippewissett** and both **North** and **West Falmouth**. The **West Falmouth Harbor** (off wooded, scenic Route 28A) is tranquil and placid, particularly at sunset. Although **Falmouth Heights** is known for its opulent, turn-of-the-20th-century shingled houses on Vineyard Sound, its beach is a popular gathering spot for 20-somethings—playing volleyball, sunbathing, flying kites, and enjoying the relatively warm water and seaside condos that line Grand Avenue and Menauhant Road. Falmouth Heights has early ties to the Kennedys: Rose Fitzgerald was vacationing here with her family when Joe Kennedy came calling.

East Falmouth is a largely residential area. There are several motels and grand year-round and summer homes lining the inlets of Green Pond, Bourne's Pond, and Waquoit Bay. Historic **Danville** was once home to whaling-ship captains and has a strong Portuguese and Cape Verdean fishing community and farming heritage.

The **center of Falmouth**, with plentiful shops and eateries, is busy year-round. And the village common, picture-perfect with historic houses (converted to beautiful bed-and-breakfasts) encircling the tidy green space, is well worth a stroll. Falmouth's Inner Harbor is awash with restaurants, boatyards, a colorful marina, and moderate nightlife. Two passenger ferries to Martha's Vineyard operate from here.

Four miles south of Falmouth, **Woods Hole** is more than just a terminus for the **Steamship Authority** auto and passenger ferries to the Vineyard. It is also home to three major scientific institutions: the **National Marine Fisheries Service** ("the Fisheries"), **Woods Hole Oceanographic Institution** (or WHOI, pronounced *hooey*), and the **Marine Biological Laboratory** (MBL).

Woods Hole, named for the "hole" or passage between Penzance Point and Nonamesset Island, was the site of the first documented European landing in the New World. Bartholomew Gosnold arrived here from Falmouth, England, in 1602.

GUIDANCE ❄ **Falmouth Chamber of Commerce** (508-548-8500; falmouthchamber .com and woodshole.com), 20 Academy Lane, Falmouth. This knowledgeable office also has Woods Hole information, good foldout street maps, and a historical walking-tour brochure.

GETTING THERE *By car:* Via Route 28 South, Falmouth is 15 miles from the Bourne Bridge and 20 miles from the Sagamore Bridge. Route 28 turns into Main Street. In

FALMOUTH PUBLIC LIBRARY KIM GRANT

northern Falmouth, Route 28A parallels Route 28 and is much more scenic. Route 28 leads directly to Locust Street and Woods Hole Road for Woods Hole.

The directional signposts for Route 28 are a tad confusing from this point on. Although Hyannis and Chatham are east of Falmouth, the signpost from Falmouth to Chatham says Route 28 South. This is because Route 28 originates in Bourne and does indeed head south to Falmouth before jogging east.

By bus: **Bonanza/Peter Pan** (888-751-8800; peterpanbus.com) has service to Falmouth (Peter Pan bus terminal) and Woods Hole (Steamship Authority) from New York, Providence, Connecticut, western Massachusetts, and Boston. Some Logan Airport buses connect with Vineyard ferries, although the ferry won't wait for a late bus. The round-trip fare from Boston to Woods Hole is $$$$$.

GETTING AROUND *By shuttle:* Take a ride on the **WHOOSH Trolley** (800-352-7155; capecodtransit.org) to popular destinations like the library, village green, and Shining Sea Bike Path. The trolley is equipped with bike racks and travels between Falmouth and Woods Hole. Tourists can hop on and off as they like by flagging it down when they see it or by pulling the inside rope.

GETTING TO MARTHA'S VINEYARD While there are a lot of seasonal ferry options from May to October, there is only one ferry service that is year-round and carries vehicles. **Steamship Authority** (508-477-8600 for reservations; 508-548-5011 for general office; steamshipauthority.com), 1 Cowdry Road, Woods Hole.

The Island Queen (508-548-4800; islandqueen.com), 75 Falmouth Heights Road, Falmouth. Open late May to mid-October. Take a quick 40-minute ride across the harbor to Martha's Vineyard for the day. (See also Martha's Vineyard.)

Morning:	Down a double espresso at Coffee O. Take a morning dip in the punch bowl kettle pond at Beebe Woods.
Afternoon:	Learn something at the Museums on the Green or kayak around Waquoit Bay and over to Washburn Island. Enjoy a seafood feast at the Clam Shack afterward. Stop at Soul to Sole for a new outfit.
Evening:	Take a leisure sunset sail on the *Liberté*. Top off the day with a fabulous meal at the Glass Onion. Check out live music at Liam Maguire's Irish Pub or something more soothing like the College Light Opera Company.

MEDIA *The Falmouth Enterprise* (508-548-4700; capenews.net), 50 Depot Avenue, Falmouth, published every Tuesday and Friday, has local news and gossip.

The Falmouth Visitor (508-548-3047; falmouthvisitor.com), geared toward repeat and long-term visitors, is a great and free publication that gets beneath Falmouth's outer shell.

PUBLIC RESTROOMS *In Falmouth:* Chamber of Commerce on Academy Lane; Peg Noonan Park on Main Street; and the library.

In Woods Hole: At the Steamship Authority.

PUBLIC LIBRARIES ✳ ✎ ☂ The area has multiple branches (falmouthpubliclibrary .org), but the biggest and downright greatest is **Falmouth Public Library** (508-457-2555), 300 Main Street, Falmouth.

Woods Hole Public Library (508-548-8961; woodsholepubliclibrary.org), 581 Woods Hole Road, Woods Hole. As you might imagine, there are lots of scientists and NPR *Science Friday* types at this branch.

EMERGENCIES **Falmouth Police Department** (774-255-4527; falmouthpolice.com), 750 Main Street, or call **911**.

Medical: **Falmouth Hospital** (508-548-5300; capecodhealth.org), 100 Ter Heun Drive (off Route 28), Falmouth.

✳ To See

IN FALMOUTH

Village Green. The green is bordered by Colonial, Federal, Italianate, and Greek Revival homes, many built for wealthy ship captains and then converted to bed-and-breakfasts. Designated as public land in 1749 and now on the National Register of Historic Places, this large triangle of grass is enclosed by a white fence, surely as pastoral a sight today as it was more than 250 years ago. It's not difficult to imagine local militiamen practicing marches and drills, and townspeople grazing horses—in fact, a local militia reenacts maneuvers on July Fourth. Walking tours around the green and old cemetery depart June through October on Tuesday and Thursday mornings from the Hallett Barn Visitor Center at the **Falmouth Historical Society**. The tour returns by a secret back route. Call 508-548-4857 to make the recommended reservations. $.

WHERE TO START IN WOODS HOLE

Morning: Enjoy pastry and java from Pie in the Sky. Watch the Eel Pond drawbridge go up and down. Meander around town and check out local artists at Woods Hole Handworks.

Afternoon: Reserve a tour of Nobska Light or take a walking tour through Spohr Gardens. Contemplate quietude from St. Mary's Garden after climbing to the top of St. Joseph's Bell Tower.

Evening: Ride the Shining Sea Bike Path out to the Knob. Enjoy a waterfront picnic here, or head back to Falmouth for dinner.

KIM GRANT

First Congregational Church, 68 Main Street, on the green. This quintessential New England church—with its high steeple and crisp white lines—is graced by a bell (which still rings) commissioned by Paul Revere. The receipt for the bell—from 1796—is on display; the inscription on the bell reads: THE LIVING TO THE CHURCH I CALL, AND TO THE GRAVE I SUMMON ALL. Today's church was built on the foundations of the 1796 church.

🍴 🖉 **Museums on the Green** (508-548-4857; falmouthhistoricalsociety.org), 55–65 Palmer Avenue, just off the village green. Open mid-May to early October; archives open by appointment year-round. Operated by the Falmouth Historical Society. **The Conant House** (a circa-1760 structure) contains sailors' valentines, scrimshaw, and old tools. One room honors Katharine Lee Bates, a Wellesley College professor and author of the lyrics for "America the Beautiful," who was born nearby in 1859 at 16 Main Street (not open to the public). I suspect most Falmouth residents would lend support to the grassroots movement in the United States to change the national anthem from "The Star-Spangled Banner" to Bates's easier-to-sing, less militaristic song.

Next door, look for a formal Colonial-style garden and a cannon from HMS *Nimrod*; the replicated 100-year-old **Hallett Barn**, with an educational center with hands-on exhibits; and the late-18th-century **Julia Wood House**, home to Dr. Francis Wicks, known for his work with smallpox inoculations. $. If it's a Friday during July and August and your pod constitutes a family, head here for tailor-made, well-done, hands-on history activities.

Cape Cod Winery (508-457-5592; capecodwinery.com), 4 Oxbow Road, East Falmouth. Open early May to mid-December. Weekend tours in July and August. Come for tastings of fruity wines, a blanc de blancs blend, cabernet, pinot grigio, merlot, and more. During harvest time in late September and early October, visitors may pick grapes in exchange for a gift certificate redeemable for that particular vintage. Once the wine is bottled, it includes a custom label that indicates the names of the harvesters.

See also **Highfield Hall** and **Bourne Farm**, both under *Green Space*.

IN WOODS HOLE

❊ ☙ ♪ **Woods Hole Science Aquarium** (508-495-2001; nefsc.noaa.gov/aquarium), 166 Water Street. When it opened in 1871, this was the first aquarium in the country. Today it's a fun place to learn about slippery fish, living shellfish (rather than the empty shells we're all accustomed to seeing), and other lesser-known creatures of the deep. Visitors delight in observing and interacting with lobsters, hermit crabs, and other crawling sea critters in a several tanks, including two touch tanks, a seal pool (feedings at 11 a.m. and 4 p.m. most days), and shallow pools of icy-cold bubbling seawater.

☙ **Woods Hole Oceanographic Institution (WHOI) and Ocean Science Exhibit Center** (508-289-2663; 508-289-2252 for tour reservations; whoi.edu), 15 School Street. Open mid-April through December. A Rockefeller grant of $2.5 million got WHOI off the ground in 1930, and since then its annual budget has grown to about $220 million. It is the largest independent oceanography lab in the country. About 1,000 students and researchers from all over the world are employed here year-round. During World War II, WHOI worked on underwater explosives and submarine detection. Today scientists study climate issues, undersea volcanoes, ocean and coastal pollution, deep-sea robotics and acoustics, and large and small marine life. Relatively unpolluted waters and a deep harbor make Woods Hole an ideal location for this work.

WHOI buildings cover 200 acres. One-hour guided walking tours are offered weekdays at 10:30 a.m. and 1:30 p.m. during July and August. The tour covers a lot of ground and is geared to adults and teenagers. The small exhibit center shows excellent videos and has an interactive display with marine-mammal sounds and a fascinating display of *Alvin*, the tiny submarine that allowed WHOI researchers to explore and photograph the *Titanic* in 1986. While you're at it, don't miss the exhibit on the *Titanic*. $; walking tour free, but reservations required.

❊ **Marine Biological Laboratory (MBL)** (508-548-3705; mbl.edu), 100 Water Street. Tours, weekdays from late June through August, are very popular and restricted in size, so reservations are required at least a week in advance. Visitor center open May through October. Founded in 1888 as "a nonprofit institution devoted to research and education

WOODS HOLE SCIENCE AQUARIUM KIM GRANT

in basic biology," the MBL, affiliated with the University of Chicago, studies more than fish. It studies life at its most basic level, with an eye toward answering the question, "What is life?" Marine creatures tend to be some of the most useful animals in that quest. MBL scientists (including 49 Nobel laureates over the years) study the problems of infertility,

WOODS HOLE OCEANOGRAPHIC INSTITUTE

hypertension, Alzheimer's, AIDS, and other diseases. It's not hyperbole to say there's no other institution or academy like it in the world. Guides lead excellent tours that include a video about what goes on at the MBL. History buffs will be interested to note that one of the MBL's granite buildings was a former factory that made candles with spermaceti (whale oil).

St. Joseph's Bell Tower, Millfield Street (north shore of Eel Pond). To encourage his colleagues not to become too caught up in the earthly details of their work and lose their faith in the divine, an MBL student designed this pink-granite Romanesque bell tower in 1929. He arranged for its two bells to ring twice a day to remind the scientists and townspeople of a higher power. (One bell is named for Gregor Mendel, the 19th-century botanist, the other for Louis Pasteur.) Nowadays the bells ring three times: at 7 a.m., noon, and 6 p.m. But really, do we need that much more reminding these days? The meticulously maintained **St. Mary's Garden** surrounds the tower with flowers, herbs, a bench, and a few chairs. Right on the harbor, this is one of the most restful places in the entire area.

WOODS HOLE HISTORICAL COLLECTION KIM GRANT

Church of the Messiah (508-548-2145; churchofthemessiahwoodshole.org), 22 Church Street. Nine Nobel Prize winners are buried in the churchyard. This 1888 stone Episcopal church is admired by visiting scientists, tourists, and townsfolk alike. The herb meditation garden is a treasure. Classical music lovers will enjoy the "Noontunes" concert series on Wednesdays in July.

🦞 🐚 **Woods Hole Historical Museum** (508-548-7270; woodsholemuseum.org), 579 Woods Hole Road. Museum open mid-June to September; archives open year-round by appointment. This is a little gem. Located at the end of Woods Hole Road, near the Woods Hole Library, this museum has two galleries with changing exhibits of local historical interest. It also maintains a good library on maritime subjects, more than 500 local oral histories, and a scale model of Woods Hole in the late 1800s. Dr. Yale's actual 1890s workshop is in a separate building. The adjacent Swift Barn exhibits small historic boats that plied these local waters long ago. Inquire about a free 60-minute

walking tour around Eel Pond once weekly in July and August. And if you're around on Saturday mornings, drop by to watch volunteers help restore boats in the collection.

The Dome (woodsholemuseum.org), Woods Hole Road. When Buckminster Fuller was teaching at MIT, he patented the geodesic dome design in 1954. One of his domes, which epitomizes doing more with less, is just north of town.

✳ To Do

BASEBALL ⚓ The **Falmouth Commodores** (falmouthcommodores.com), 790 Main Street, Falmouth at Fuller's Field. One of 10 teams in the Cape Cod Baseball League that plays in July and August.

BICYCLING & RENTALS The two most popular riding trails include the **Shining Sea Bike Path** (see "O' Beautiful" on page 74) and the 23-mile Sippewissett route. Rent bicycles and equipment at ✳ **Corner Cycle** (508-540-4195; cornercycle.com), 115 Palmer Avenue, Falmouth, located only a few hundred yards from the Shining Sea path.

BOAT EXCURSIONS & RENTALS The waters off Falmouth and Woods Hole are brimming with action. Whether you're interested in fishing charters, whale watching, cruising to Martha's Vineyard for the day, or just leisurely exploring the area, you can do it all here. For boating rules and regulations contact the **Harbormaster** (508-547-2550; falmouthmass.us), 180 Scranton Avenue, Falmouth Harbor.

✳ 🐾 **Patriot Party Boats** (508-548-2626; patriotpartyboats.com), 227 Clinton Avenue at Scranton Avenue, Falmouth. The Tietje (pronounced *teegee*) family has been chartering boats since the mid-1950s, and they know the local waters like the backs of their hands. Take advantage of their year-round water taxi service or freights to Martha's Vineyard. They also offer fishing charters. $$$. (See also *Fishing* and *Sailing* under **To Do**.)

FISHING The Chamber of Commerce (see *Guidance*) publishes a very good visitor fishing guide. Seasoned fishermen often brag about their luck at the Knob. Procure freshwater and saltwater fishing licenses and regulations online (mass.gov/eea/agencies/dfg/licensing).

Big game: **Islander Sportfishing** (508-847-6025; falmouthcharters.com). Open late May through October. Their specialty is catching big bass, but you can also battle a hungry bluefish, too. $$$$+.

Bluefin Charters (508-292-3244; Bluefin-charters.com), 180 Scranton Avenue, Falmouth Harbor. Open July through October. Book the popular combo trip with Captain Brian Courville and experience 2 hours of trolling for bass and blues, followed by 2 hours of bottom fishing for fluke, black sea bass, and scup. $$$$+.

Susan Jean (508-548-6901), Eel Pond, off Water Street, Woods Hole. Trips late May to mid-October. Capt. John Christian's 22-foot Aquasport searches for trophy-sized striped bass. This trip is for the serious angler—John usually departs in the middle of the night because of the tides. $$$$+.

⚓ **Patriot Party Boats** (508-548-2626; patriotpartyboats.com), departs from Falmouth Charterboat Marina, 110 Scranton Avenue, Falmouth Harbor. Trips mid-June to early September. $$$$+.

On shore: **Old Silver Beach** offers great fishing grounds, but it's also a popular swimming beach, making it nearly impossible to cast a line safely during the summer. In the fall, however, you will find plenty of open space. The south end of the beach gives

WATERFRONT BEAUTIES

Nobska Light, Church Street, off Woods Hole Road. Although there are no regular tours, visits can be arranged for groups of 15 or more by calling 508-457-3210. Built in 1828, rebuilt in 1876, and automated in 1985, the beacon commands a high vantage point on a bluff. The light is visible from 17 miles out at sea. It's a particularly good place to see the "hole" (for which Woods Hole was named), the Elizabeth Islands, and the north shore of Martha's Vineyard, and to watch the sunset. Some 30,000 vessels—ferries, fully rigged sailing ships, and pleasure boats—pass by annually, as does the internationally regarded Falmouth Road Race.

SPOHR GARDENS, WOODS HOLE   KIM GRANT

❄ **Spohr Gardens** (508-548-0623; spohr-gardens.org), 45 Fells Road off Oyster Pond Road from Woods Hole Road or Surf Drive; park on Fells Road. Thanks to Charles and Margaret Spohr, this spectacular 6-acre private garden is yours for the touring. More than 100,000 daffodils bloom in spring, followed by lilies, azaleas, magnolias, and hydrangeas. (You'll share the wide path with geese and ducks.) Don't miss the iris garden by the water; remarkably, it's maintained by only two people! Free.

Consider bicycling here via the **Shining Sea Bike Path** (see To Do), which also has great water views.

A VIEW FROM THE SHINING SEA BIKE PATH TO NOBSKA LIGHT   KIM GRANT

SCENIC DRIVE

Take Route 28A to Old Dock Road to reach placid West Falmouth Harbor. Then double back and take Route 28A to Palmer Avenue, to Sippewissett Road, to hilly and winding Quissett Avenue, and to equally tranquil **Quissett Harbor**. At the far edge of the harbor you'll see a path that goes up over the hill of the **Knob**, an outcrop that's half wooded bird sanctuary and half rocky beach. Walk out to the Knob along the water and back through the woods. It's great for picnicking and sunset watching. Sippewissett Road takes you past **Eel Pond** and **Woods Hole** via the back way. Surf Drive from Falmouth to **Nobska Light** is also picturesque.

KAYLA ROBERTSON/DO ART PHOTOGRAPHY

up larger bass in the late evening and after dark. The rest of the sandy beach will hold roaming schools of stripers feeding on sand eels and silversides, often late into the fall.

By bridge or jetty: To the right of the town dock, the harbor narrows into a channel that drains the upper reaches known as **Squeteague Harbor**. Stay below the high tide line and target the deeper water in the narrow channel, particularly during a falling tide. The rocky point in front of **Nobska Lighthouse** is the most productive and difficult fishing on the Upper Cape, but it's also where you will land your trophy catch. Recommended for pro-anglers only.

Freshwater: Fish for trout, smallmouth bass, chain pickerel, and white perch at the town landing on **Santuit Pond** and on the **Quashnet River**. The sea-run river herring provide a good forage base for game fish at **Connamessett Pond**, too.

Supplies: ❋ **Eastman's Sport & Tackle** (508-548-6900; eastmanstackle.com), 783 Main Street, Falmouth. Head to this knowledgeable shop for regulations, local fishing information, and rod and reel rental, too.

FOR FAMILIES See **Tony Andrew's Farm** under **Selective Shopping**.

GOLF ❋ **Cape Cod Country Club** (508-563-9842; capecodcountryclub.com), 48 Theater Drive, off Route 151, North Falmouth. A scenic course with great variety.

O' BEAUTIFUL

Shining Sea Bike Path. The easygoing 10.7-mile (one-way) trail is one of Falmouth's most popular attractions. Following the old Penn Central Railroad line between Falmouth and Woods Hole, the path parallels unspoiled beaches, marshes, and bird sanctuaries. It was named in honor of Katherine Lee Bates, composer of "America the Beautiful." The last line of her song—"from sea to shining sea"—is a fitting description of the trail, which offers lovely views of Vineyard Sound, Martha's Vineyard, and Naushon Island.

The trail connects with several other routes: from Falmouth to Menauhant Beach in East Falmouth, and from Woods Hole to Quissett and Sippewissett. You will find a trailhead and parking lot on Locust Street (at Mill Road) and another at Depot Avenue in Falmouth, as well as access points at Elm Road and Oyster Pond Road. Park here; it's very difficult to park in Woods Hole. Pick up a bike map at the chamber of commerce.

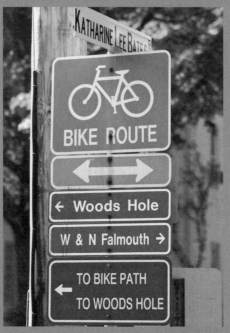

SHINING SEA BIKE PATH KIM GRANT

❊ **Paul Harney Golf Club** (508-563-3454; paulharneygolfcourse.com), 74 Club Valley Drive, off Route 151, East Falmouth. This par-60 course offers somewhat narrow fairways but is generally within the ability of weekend golfers.

❊ **Falmouth Country Club** (508-548-3211; falmouthcountryclub.com), 630 Carriage Shop Road off Route 151, East Falmouth. An 18-holer, par 72, with a good mix of moderate and difficult pars, and a nine-holer, par 37.

HORSEBACK RIDING ❊ ✍ **Haland Stable** (508-540-2552; halandstable.com), 878 Route 28A, West Falmouth. Reservations absolutely necessary. Haland offers excellent English instruction, individual and group lessons, and guided trail rides through pine wood groves, fields, a bird sanctuary, cranberry bogs, and salt-marsh land. Pony rides by appointment.

ICE-SKATING ✍ **Falmouth Ice Arena** (508-548-0275; falmouthicearena.com), 9 Technology Park Drive, off Palmer Avenue, Falmouth. Call for public skating times; $.

KAYAKS & PADDLEBOARDS ❊ 🐚 **Cape Cod Kayak** (508-563-9377; capecodkayak .com), 802 MacArthur Boulevard, Pocasset. Rent a one- or two-seater kayak and explore salt marshes, tidal inlets, freshwater ponds, and the ocean shoreline. If you want to go kayaking but don't know where to go, they will recommend spots or locations suited to your interests and level of ability. They also organize small tours. $$$$+. (See also **Waquoit Bay National Estuarine Research Reserve** under **Green Space**.)

Cape Cod Windsurfing & Paddleboards (508-801-3329; capecodwindsurfing.com). Open seasonally. Rent paddleboards by the day or by the week and have them delivered to wherever you're staying, or inquire about their two-hour windsurfing lessons. Old Silver Beach gets good, predominantly southwestern wind, so there's solid sailboarding here. $$$$+.

SAILING *The Liberté* (508-524-9121; theliberte.com), 227 Clinton Avenue, Falmouth Harbor. Sails from late June to early September. Docked in the mouth of Falmouth Harbor, this 74-foot, three-mast schooner carries up to 49 passengers on scenic sails across the bay. The location is important because when the sails go up, they go up quickly. Depending on wind

CAPE COD KAYAK   KIM GRANT

and tide, sails might head west to Woods Hole near Nobska Lighthouse and the Elizabeth Islands. If you are beckoned south, you will see Oak Bluffs and Vineyard Haven on Martha's Vineyard. To the east are Falmouth Heights Bluffs and the nature sanctuary of Waquoit Bay. Choose from morning, noon, and sunset sails. $$$$.

TENNIS ❋ The following courts are public: the **elementary school**, Davisville Road, East Falmouth; **Lawrence School**, Lakeview Avenue, Falmouth; the **high school**, Gifford Street Extension, Falmouth (call for reservations); **Nye Park**, North Falmouth;

AN AERIAL VIEW OF NOBSKA LIGHTHOUSE   MARCIA DUGGAN/CAPECODSOUL

Blacksmith Shop Road, behind the fire station, West Falmouth; and **Taft's Playground**, Bell Tower Lane, Woods Hole.

Falmouth Sports Center (508-548-7433), 33 Highfield Drive, Falmouth. Indoor and outdoor courts.

✳ Green Space

Ashumet Holly Wildlife Sanctuary (508-362-7475; massaudubon.org), 286 Ashumet Road (off Route 151), East Falmouth. Crisscrossed with self-guided nature trails, this 45-acre Massachusetts Audubon Society sanctuary overflows with holly: there are more than 8 species, 65 varieties, and 1,000 trees (from America, Europe, and Asia). More than 130 bird species also have been sighted here; since 1935, nesting barn swallows have made their home in the rafters of the barn from mid-May to late August. Other flora and fauna thrive, as well. Rhododendrons and dogwoods bloom in spring. Large white franklinia flowers (named for Benjamin Franklin) make a show in autumn, and in the summer Grassy Pond might overflow (depending on water levels) with rare wildflower blossoms. Pick up the informative trail map before setting out. By the way, local philanthropist Josiah K. Lilly III (of Heritage Museums & Gardens fame; see *To See* in "Sandwich") purchased and donated the land in 1961 after the death of Wilfred Wheeler, who cultivated most of these plants and had been very concerned about holiday overharvesting of holly. $.

ASHUMET HOLLY WILDLIFE SANCTUARY   KIM GRANT

Waquoit Bay National Estuarine Research Reserve (508-457-0495; waquoit bayreserve.org), 131 Waquoit Highway, East Falmouth. Part of a national system dedicated to research and education regarding coastal areas and estuaries, Waquoit Bay has four components: **South Cape Beach State Park** (see also **Green Space** in Mashpee), **Washburn Island**, **Quashnet River Property**, and the **headquarters**, which houses watershed exhibits. More than 3,000 acres of delicate barrier beaches, pine barrier beaches, and marshlands surround lovely Waquoit Bay. Stop in at the headquarters for a trail map and schedule of guided walks in July and August. In summer look for "Evenings on the Bluff" talks as well as other activities like the Watershed Block Party in August, with hands-on activities and demonstrations about the bay that are perfect for kids and families. Within South Cape Beach State Park is the little-used, mile-long **Great Flat Pond Trail** (accessible year-round). It winds past salt marshes, bogs, and wetlands and along

FALMOUTH BEACHES KIM GRANT

coastal pine forests. Pine-filled, 330-acre, Washburn Island is accessible year-round if you have a boat. The 11 primitive island campsites require reservations.

Falmouth Moraine Trail. These 10 miles of trails are part of Cape Cod Pathways (capecodcommission.org), "a growing network of walking paths linking open space in all 15 Cape Cod towns." Just a warning that directions and details can be confusing.

BEACHES Along Buzzards Bay and Vineyard Sound, 12 miles of Falmouth's 68-mile shoreline are accessible to the public via four beaches. (There are eight additional town beaches.) Generally, waters are a bit warmer off Falmouth than off northside beaches because of the Gulf Stream. Weeklong cottage renters qualify to purchase a beach sticker, obtainable at the Surf Drive Beach Bathhouse daily in summer. The permit costs $$$$+ for one week. Some innkeepers provide beach stickers. Otherwise, you may pay a daily fee to park at the following beaches. (The **Falmouth Beach Department** [508-548-8623] has further details.)

Menauhant Beach, on Vineyard Sound, off Route 28 and Central Avenue, East Falmouth. The best Sound beach, by far. Waters are less choppy on Vineyard Sound than they are on the Atlantic. Facilities include restrooms, a lifeguard, and a snack bar. Parking $.

⚓ **Old Silver Beach**, on Buzzards Bay, off Route 28A and Quaker Road, North Falmouth. One of the sandiest beaches in town, this is a good one for children, as an offshore sandbar creates shallow tidal pools. Facilities include a lifeguard and a snack bar. Parking $$.

Surf Drive Beach, on Vineyard Sound, on Surf Drive, off Main and Shore Streets, Falmouth. This beach attracts sea kayakers, walkers, and swimmers who want to escape "downtown" beach crowds. It's accessible via the Shining Sea Bike Path (see **To Do**); by foot it's 15 minutes from the center of Falmouth. Facilities include a bathhouse, a snack bar, and a lifeguard. Parking $$.

Falmouth Heights Beach, on Vineyard Sound, Grand Avenue, Falmouth Heights. Although there is no public parking, the beach is public and popular. Facilities include restrooms, a lifeguard, and lots of snack bars.

A WALK IN THE WOODS

Beebe Woods, access from Ter Heun Drive off Route 28A or Highfield Drive off Depot Avenue, behind the College Light Opera Company (see Entertainment), Falmouth. The Beebes, a wealthy family originally from Boston, lived in Falmouth from the late 1870s to the early 1930s. Generous town benefactors, they were among the first to purchase land in Falmouth. The 1878 Highfield Hall (508-495-1878; highfieldhallandgardens.org) was the centerpiece of the property and has been magnificently restored with the vision of Friends of Highfield. (They hold concerts, exhibits, and workshops here, all with marvelous acoustics. If you have an opportunity to get inside, seize it!) The 383 acres around it contain miles of public trails for walking, mountain biking, dog walking, and bird-watching. In autumn especially it seems like the whole town takes the trail to the Punch Bowl (a kettle pond). It's particularly pretty in May when the lady's slippers bloom. 🐾

HIGHFIELD HALL, FALMOUTH KIM GRANT

PONDS ✎ **Grews Pond**, off Route 28 at Goodwill Park, Route 28, West Falmouth. Lifeguard in-season, as well as picnic and barbecue facilities and a playground. There are also hiking trails all around the pond.

WALKS **Waterfront Park**, Water Street near the MBL in Woods Hole, with shaded benches and a sundial from which you can tell time to within 30 seconds.

Eel Pond, off Water Street in Woods Hole. The harborlike pond has a drawbridge that grants access to Great Harbor for fishing boats, yachts, and research vessels moored here. (The walk around the shore is lovely.) The little bridge goes up and down on demand; in summer boats line up to pass through.

🐌 🏠 **Bourne Farm** (508-548-8484; saltpondsanctuaries.org), Route 28A, North Falmouth. Bucolic grounds open year-round; house open by appointment. Owned by the nonprofit Salt Pond Areas Bird Sanctuaries, Inc., this 1775 historic landmark includes a

EEL POND, WOODS HOLE KIM GRANT

restored and furnished farmhouse, a bunkhouse (now a private residence), a barn, and 49 acres of orchards, fields, and wooded trails. It's a perfectly tranquil spot overlooking **Crocker Pond**, complete with a picnic area under a grape arbor. It's about as relaxing as it gets anywhere on the Cape! The property and barn are available for wedding rentals.

See also **Spohr Gardens** under "Waterfront Beauties" on page 72 and **Ashumet Holly and Wildlife Sanctuary, Grews Pond**, and **Waquoit Bay National Estuarine Research Reserve** under **Green Space**.

✳ Lodging

Falmouth has a variety of places to call home-away-from-home, but unfortunately, many of its family motels have been converted into timeshare units. Additionally, many bed-and-breakfasts and inns have switched ownership (for better or worse) since the last guidebook debuted.

ON/NEAR FALMOUTH HEIGHTS

BED-AND-BREAKFASTS 🦞 ✳ **Inn on the Sound** (508-457-9666; innonthe sound.com), 313 Grand Avenue. If you've stayed here before when Howard Grosser was commandeering this waterfront gem

of a bed-and-breakfast, you might be a little disappointed. Howard had a lovely ability to foresee people's want and needs, usually before they even knew it! With big shoes to fill, new owner Jon Saunders has taken the helm. Newbies to the area and first-timers give five-star reviews, while former guests are torn (change is hard, after all). Warren's first-class breakfast—categorized as artwork—has now been compared to carb-heavy La Quinta chain hotels. With that said, the location is clearly amazing (on the beach!) and the inn is clean and comfortable. Choose from 12 spacious rooms with private baths, contemporary-beach inspired décor, and fireplaces in some cases for the cooler months. Five guest-rooms have private balconies, and one is

INN ON THE SOUND   KIM GRANT

equipped with a kitchenette. Despite efforts to visit the inn, Jon was unable to accommodate prior to deadline. $–$$$$.

RESORTS & HOTELS ✧ **Mariner's Point Resort** (508-457-0300; marinerspoint resort.com), 425 Grand Avenue. Open mid-April to late October. This bilevel timeshare offers 37 efficiency studios and apartments within a short stroll of Falmouth Heights Beach (see **Green Space**). Most of the four-person units overlook the pool area; a few have unobstructed views of Vineyard Sound and a town-owned park popular with kite fliers. $–$$.

❅ ✧ 🐾 ⍦ **Seaside Inn** (508-540-4120; seasideinnfalmouth.com), 263 Grand Avenue. Across from Falmouth Heights Beach (see **Green Space**) and playing fields, this way-above-average, family-oriented motel has 23 rooms. Rates vary widely and are based on the degree of water view and amenities; whether the room has access to a deck, full kitchen, or kitchenette; and if the deck is shared or private. Rooms in the back building

are the nicest, but the reservation folks won't guarantee a particular room. Too bad, because the third-floor rooms are the best. By the way, the Falmouth branch of the **British Beer Company** (508-540-9600; britishbeer.com) is on the premises. It's a fine place for an authentic stout or ale on tap. (Note that I didn't mention the food.) Live music on weekends and most summer nights. $–$$.

ON/NEAR THE FAMOUTH GREEN

BED-AND-BREAKFASTS ❅ **Captain's Manor Inn** (508-388-7336; captains manorinn.com), 27 Main Street. Owners Randy and Pattie Laubhan have taken over the legacy of former hosts Trish and Kevin Robinson, and the reviews do not disappoint! The seven large and lush guestrooms include private baths, a café with refreshments, an elegant living room with an ornate original 1849 black marble fireplace and tall shuttered windows, and countless areas to relax on the 2,000-square-foot wrap-around veranda. Full breakfast at individual tables included. (As a footnote: Thinking of eloping? They have a package for that.) $$–$$$.

❄ 🐾 **The Palmer House Inn** (508-548-1230; palmerhouseinn.com), 81 Palmer Avenue. Innkeepers Tom von Zabern and Billy Brown bought the Palmer House in 2018 from longtime owners Pat and Bill O'Connell. This upscale Victorian bed-and-breakfast remains chock-full of period appointments and fanciful décor. The main house is a Queen Anne beauty with stained-glass windows, shiny hardwood floors, and front porch rockers. In all, there are 16 "bedchambers" and one cottage suite, all with robes, lots of lace, flowers, triple sheeting, and turndown service. Breakfast is elaborate and full, served at individual tables. Also, it's dog-friendly, and you will surely be greeted by Brody, "the ever-amusing and funny Leonberger, who has charmed his way into the hearts" of guests. $$–$$$.

CAPTAIN'S MANOR INN KIM GRANT

❄ 🐾 **Captain Tom Lawrence House Inn** (508-548-9178; captaintomlawrence .com), 75 Locust Street. Open February through December. This popular bed-and-breakfast also changed hands and is now owned by Iben, a delightful woman originally from Denmark but raised on the Cape. Innkeepers Bob and Barbara, along with Lynne Bishop, oversee the grounds and keep guests comfortable. This 1861 former sea captain's home is set back from the road, and offers five comfortable rooms and one cozy apartment cottage, all equipped with plush bedding and tasteful décor. The breakfast is spectacular, too. $–$$.

RENTAL HOUSES & COTTAGES **Real Estate Associates** (capecodhouses.com) in North Falmouth (508-563-7173), West Falmouth (508-540-3005), Falmouth (508-548-0200), or Pocasset (508-563-5266).

CAMPGROUNDS 🐾 **Sippewissett Campground & Cabins** (508-548-2542; sippewissett.com), 836 Palmer Avenue. Open mid-May to mid-October. This well-run, private campground has cabins, tepees, and 100 large campsites for tents, trailers, and RVs; clean, large bathrooms and showers; and free shuttles in July and August to Chapoquoit Beach, year-round to the Martha's Vineyard ferry. $.

See also **Waquoit Bay National Estuarine Research Reserve** under **Green Space**.

IN WOODS HOLE

BED-AND-BREAKFASTS ❄ 🐾 **Woods Hole Passage B&B Inn** (508-548-9575; woodsholepassage.com), 186 Woods Hole Road. On the road connecting Woods Hole and Falmouth, this quiet inn has a delightful feel. The 2 acres of gardens are best enjoyed from the hammock or from the plentiful lounge chairs. The attached barn has five renovated guest rooms; second-floor rooms are more

WOODS HOLE PASSAGE KIM GRANT

spacious, with vaulted ceilings and exposed beams. Décor is crisp country-modern, and each room has a bold splash of color. A full breakfast is included, as are loaner bikes, beach chairs, beach towels, and use of the outdoor shower. Bonus: The bed-and-breakfast is within walking distance of a beach. $$.

MOTELS **Sands of Time** (508-548-6300; sandsoftime.com), 549 Woods Hole Road. Open April to mid-November. This motel has been in Susie Veeder's family since the mid-1960s, and you'd be hard pressed to find as much family pride elsewhere. Who stays? Some guests missed the last ferry; others know it's a convenient place for exploring Woods Hole (a 5-minute walk away). And the rooms? There are 20 air-conditioned motel units (most with a delightful view of Little Harbor and two with kitchenettes), an apartment (eh), and 15 nice and large inn-like rooms in an adjacent 1870s house, many with a harbor view and working fireplace. Fresh flowers, morning coffee and doughnuts, a small heated

pool, and morning newspapers set this place apart. It's also a short walk to the beach and is adjacent to the Shining Sea Bikeway. $–$$.

RESORTS & HOTELS **Treehouse Lodge** (508-548-1986; mytreehouselodge.com), 527 Woods Hole Road. Though I was unable to stay here prior to deadline, a dear friend highly recommends this place for its stylish rooms, prime location, and budget-friendly prices. Despite the name, it's not really a tree house. Recently renovated rooms—canopy, canopy deluxe, pavilion, and hammock rooms—include barn board floors, cozy modern furniture, nautical décor, ambient lighting, and super-charged Wi-Fi (and Netflix)! Step outside and enjoy the courtyard equipped with a fire pit, yard games, and cozy furniture (like hammocks) perfect for unwinding after a busy day exploring. The Treehouse is within walking distance of the Martha's Vineyard ferry and the village of Woods Hole. Check online for special packages. My friend received free whale-watching tickets with her reservation. $–$$$.

✳ Where to Eat

Falmouth and Woods Hole restaurants satisfy all palates and budgets through upscale bistro dining, waterfront fish houses, taverns, and diners.

DINING OUT

IN FALMOUTH

✳ **The Glass Onion** (508-540-3730; the glassoniondining.com), 37 North Main Street. Open D. Dining in Falmouth (and the Upper Cape for that matter) hasn't been the same since The Onion burst onto the scene in 2010. Using market-fresh ingredients from start to finish, the chef/owners sure know how to please. I've been known to dine here three nights over a 10-day period, but I moderate in other ways by selecting lobster strudel only once per trip. No reservations. $$$$.

✳ 🐟 **La Cucina Sul Mare** (508-548-5600; lacucinasulmare.com), 237 Main Street. Open L, D. This Northern Italian and Mediterranean eatery with outdoor seating offers portions so large that you should think about sharing dishes. To make matters even better, the husband-and-wife team of Cynthia and Mark Cilfone do a super job of making it feel like one giant dinner party here (reservations only for parties of five or more). Intimate, charming, and villa-like, La Cucina has been offering fresh, Old World pasta and seafood specials since 2002. Live music on Sundays. L $–$$, D $$–$$$.

Anejo Mexican Bistro & Tequila Bar (508-388-7631; anejomexicanbistro.com), 188 Main Street. Open L, D. This place

THE GLASS ONION KIM GRANT

excels in adventurous Mexican dishes, tequila cocktails, and outside dining. It's almost impossible to go wrong with any of their house specials (like chile rellenos, carne asada, or pork carnitas), but don't overlook their excellent cod. I always judge places like this on their house margaritas and guacamole: the latter as a side dish would feed a small army, while the house version of the classic drink rules.

Osteria La Civetta (508-540-1616; osterialacivetta.com), 133 Main Street. Open L, D. When you want to linger, this Old World and family-style trattoria has few equals—partly because service is so "relaxed" and partly because that's the way things are done in the home country. (That didn't change when the Osteria doubled in size and a little something was lost in translation.) All of the six or seven main dishes (including the gluten-free pasta) are made completely from scratch. Come hungry and do it up with all four courses: antipasti, primi, secondi, and contorni. Or eat lighter at the little bar. L $$ (weekends only), D secondi $$$.

🍴 ❄ ❔ **Chapoquoit Grill** (508-540-7794; chapoquoitgrillwestfalmouth.com), 410 West Falmouth Highway. Open D. From the moment this eclectic New American bistro opened in the early 1990s, it was a success. Still run by the original owners, with their loyal chef overseeing the kitchen, "Chappy's" has a Grateful Dead kind of cult following (i.e., regulars who would follow them anywhere no matter what). You can spot the neighborhood folks who appreciate the low-key atmosphere: They order from the nightly specials menu. Pasta dishes are always superb. The popular wood-fired, super-thin-crust pizzas are also excellent. No reservations are taken, so get there when it opens at 5 p.m. or be prepared for a wait in the convivial bar. $$.

IN WOODS HOLE

❄ **Water Street Kitchen** (508-540-5656; waterstreetkitchen.com), 56 Water Street. Open D. Housed within the former Fishmonger, the casually romantic Kitchen offers upscale waterfront dining, plenty of seafood dishes, and fresh-from-the-farm seasonal fare. The ever-changing expressive menu might include pan-fried shishito peppers with lime ponsu; sea scallops with truffled beets and cauliflower puree; or a flat iron steak with lobster-bacon hash. The mint-lemonade soda is rather refreshing for a change, but as you can imagine, they have an ample selection of wines, sake, and a creative cocktail list. D $$$.

EATING OUT

IN FALMOUTH

🍴 **Jim's Clam Shack** (508-540-7758), 227 Clinton Avenue. Open L, D, late May to early September. There is rarely enough room inside this old-time and favored shack, but it's just as well—head to the back deck to munch on fried clams, scallops, and fish while watching pleasure boats and fishing boats come and go. No credit cards. $–$$.

🍴 **Simply Divine Pizza** (508-548-1222; divinepizza.com), 271 Main Street. This might be the Cape's best pizza: stone-fired Neapolitan with a thin and crispy crust. The whole package comes together here: creative offerings (like fig and bacon), relaxing atmosphere, and good service. There are pasta dishes, too. I bet you'll be tempted to eat here more than once.

❄ **Golden Swan** (508-540-6580), 323 Main Street. Open L, D. When you tire of New American cuisine or seafood, you won't be disappointed with the Indian cuisine here—unless you hail from Bangalore. Too bad the interior is so dark. $$.

❄ **Peking Palace** (508-540-8204; pekingpalacefalmouth.com), 452 Main Street. Open L, D. If you're hankering for takeout from your favorite suburban-style Chinese restaurant at home, the Peking Palace is your place. Along with a sushi bar, there must be 200 Mandarin, Szechuan, and Cantonese dishes on the menu. L $, D $–$$.

The Flying Bridge (508-548-2700; flyingbridgerestaurant.com), 220 Scranton Avenue. Open D. The only reason I'm including this is because of its prominent harborfront location. If that persuades you, the only thing I recommend is lobster. $$.

See also **Liam Maguire's** and **Boathouse** under **Entertainment**.

IN WOODS HOLE

❋ ⊘ **Quicks Hole Tavern** (508-495-0048; quicksholewickedfresh.com), 29 Railroad Avenue. Open L, D. Part taqueria, part tavern, part farm-to-table fine dining, the bustling Quicks Hole has an enviable perch right across from the ferry terminal for the Vineyard. Nothing like watching your ship come in—but please get in line way before that! L $-$$, D $$-$$$.

❋ ⊘ ⅋ **Captain Kidd** (508-548-8563; thecaptainkidd.com), 77 Water Street. Both the tavern and fancier waterfront section overlooking Eel Pond are open L, D. This local watering hole is named for the pirate who supposedly spent a short time in the environs of Woods Hole on the way to his execution in England. As such, a playful pirate mural hangs above barrel-style tables across from the long, hand-carved mahogany bar. The Kidd offers specialty pizzas, burgers, sandwiches, fish-and-chips, scrod, steaks, and blackboard fish specials. The glassed-in patio with a woodstove is a cozy place to be in winter. The only drawback here is that the staff is at times more attentive to the TV at the bar than they are to patrons. Still, it's an institution, with bouncers. Tavern $$, waterfront dining $$-$$$. No credit cards.

SWEET TREATS & COFFEE

IN FALMOUTH

❋ ⊘ **Betsy's Diner** (508-540-0060), 457 Main Street. Open B, L, D. The old-fashioned 1957 Mountain View Diner was transported in 1992 from Pennsylvania to Main Street, where it was placed on the site of another diner. The boxy addition isn't historic, just functional. Folks come for inexpensive fare: club sandwiches, breakfast specials, and the famous roast turkey dinner. Specials are generally very good, the portions large. Breakfast is served all day to tunes from the '60s. $.

❋ ⊘ **Mary Ellen's Portuguese Bakery** (508-540-9696), 829 Main Street. Open B, L. In addition to traditional Portuguese offerings like kale soup and malasadas, these super-friendly (and family-friendly) folks offer breakfast omelets throughout the day and cheeseburgers, too. It's small, but it's a find. No credit cards. $.

❋ **Dana's Kitchen** (508-540-7900; danas-kitchen.com), 881 Palmer Avenue. Open B, L. Arthur and Dana Tillman have been pleasing palates since they opened the kitchen doors in 2005. Full of fresh and local ingredients, the menu often changes, but you can always expect yummy sandwiches, homemade soups, beautiful pastries, and piled-high salads, all within a tranquil country-style setting. $.

Pickle Jar Kitchen (508-540-6760; picklejarkitchen.com), 170 Main Street. Open B, L. Pickle lovers rejoice! In addition to a full and delicious breakfast and lunch menu (breakfast salads, vanilla spiced oatmeal, pastrami spice cured salmon), you can buy pickles by the pound! Combos include the garlic-dill cukes, the Mexi-Cali (carrot and jalapeño), house garden, and spiced red onion.

❋ ◉ **Pies a la Mode** (508-540-8777; piesalamode.com), 352 Main Street #4. Open B, L. I love this hidden gem, which makes everything from scratch and on the premises. Take their amazing chicken pot pies (!!) and Cornish pasties to the beach, to the green, or home, and count yourself lucky to have found them! The excellence continues with dessert pies and gelato. $$-$$$.

Smitty's Ice Cream (508-457-1060; smittysic.com), 326 East Falmouth

PIE IN THE SKY   KIM GRANT

Highway, Route 28. My dear friend Jan loved this place and so do I—by extension and on its own merits. (Also seasonally in Barnstable on Route 6A, in Mashpee at the rotary of Routes 28 and 151, and in North Falmouth on Route 28A.) $.

❊ **Ben & Bill's Chocolate Emporium** (508-548-7878; benandbills.com), 209 Main Street. This old-fashioned sweets shop is lined with walls of confections, some made on the premises. The best offering is their excellent store-made ice cream, served in abundant quantities. $.

IN WOODS HOLE

❊ **Pie in the Sky** (508-540-5475; woods hole.com/pie), 10 Water Street. Open 364 days a year ("at least 5 a.m.–10 p.m."). This funky—in a good way—institution has strong coffee (they roast it them-selves), strong Wi-Fi, good handmade pastries, hearty sandwiches, and home-made soups. There are a few tables inside and garden/street side. In summer, fre-quent patio entertainment packs a crowd

that extends up the hillside. It's inevita-bly my first and last stop in Woods Hole. $–$$.

❊ **Coffee Obsession** (508-540-2233; coffeeobsession.com), 110 Palmer Ave-nue in Falmouth and 38 Water Street in Woods Hole. Caffeine addicts flock to "Coffee O" for bracing espressos, a slice of coffee cake, and a smidgen of counter-culture à la Falmouth and Woods Hole. Eggnog, apple cider, and other sea-sonal beverages, too. A retail shop serves all your chai-and coffee-related needs. $.

MARKETS

IN FALMOUTH

❊ **West Falmouth Market** (508-548-1139), 623 Route 28A. A great neighborhood place to stop for light groceries, deli sandwiches, and wine.

❊ **Windfall Market** (508-548-0099; windfallmarket.com), 77 Scranton Ave-nue. Prepared foods, a deli section, lob-sters, and homemade breads are baked fresh daily.

IN WOODS HOLE

Woods Hole Market & Provisions (508-540-4792; woodsholemarket.com), 87 Water Street. Located just over the Eel Pond drawbridge you will find this little homey-grocery store. Stop here for essentials, but also grab a snack and enjoy it on their outside seating

COFFEE OBSESSION   KIM GRANT

overlooking the water. (See also *Farms* under **Selective Shopping**.)

✳ Entertainment

Highfield Hall and Gardens (508-495-1878; highfieldhallandgardens.org), 56 Highfield Drive, Falmouth. Open April to November. After a $6.5 million labor of love, this magnificently restored 1878 manse opened as a community cultural center. It holds concerts, exhibits, and workshops, all with marvelous acoustics.

LIVE MUSIC 🎵 The **Falmouth Town Band** performs at Marina Park, on the

LIAM MAGUIRE'S IRISH PUB & RESTAURANT KIM GRANT

west side of the harbor on Thursday evenings in July and August. Bring a chair or a blanket and watch the kids dance to simple marches and big-band numbers. Or wander around and look at the moored boats. There are also free Friday concerts at 6 p.m. at Peg Noonan Park on Main Street in July and August.

Woods Hole Folk Music Society (508-540-0320; arts-cape.com/whfolkmusic), Community Hall, 68 Water Street, Woods Hole. Well-known folkies generally play on the first and third Monday of each month, except December. $$.

✳ **Liam Maguire's Irish Pub & Restaurant** (508-548-0285; liammaguire.com), 273 Main Street, Falmouth. It doesn't get any more fun than this unless you go to South Boston or Dublin. This place bumps with live tunes throughout the summer—take a peek at the packed schedule online to see who's playing.

MOVIES 🎵 **Movies Under the Stars** (falmouthvillageassociation.com), Peg Noonan Park on Main Street, Falmouth. Late June through August. Family-friendly movie starts at dusk every Wednesday. It's a charming way to spend the evening—rather like a drive-in of yore, except without the car!

✳ **Falmouth Cinemas** (508-495-0505 for movie hotline; falmouthcinemas .com), 137 Teaticket Highway, Falmouth. It's your average movie theater with all the new feature films you've been curious to see.

NIGHTLIFE **Shuckers** (508-540-3850; shuckerscapecod.com), 91A Water Street, Woods Hole. When you're in the mood for beer in plastic cups, this place has a seat with your name on it.

Pier 37 Boathouse (508-388-7573; falmouthpier37.com), 88 Scranton Avenue, Falmouth. Open late April to mid-October. The Boathouse jumps with live music and lively crowds.

OPERA **College Light Opera Company** (508-548-0668 for summer box office;

SHOPPING ON MAIN STREET, FALMOUTH   KIM GRANT

easily pass a couple of very pleasant
hours on Falmouth's Main Street.

ARTISANS **Woods Hole Handworks**
(508-540-5291; handworkswoodshole
.com), 68 Water Street, Woods Hole.
Open mid-May to mid-October. This tiny
artisans' cooperative, perched over the
water near the drawbridge to Eel Pond,
has a selection of fine handmade jewelry,
scarves, weaving, and beadwork.

Under the Sun (508-540-3603;
underthesunwoodshole.com), 22 Water
Street, Woods Hole. Joyce Stratton offers
an eclectic selection of handcrafted jewelry, pottery, glass, and wood. Although
the quality is somewhat uneven, the very
good far outweighs the all right.

BOOKSTORES 🐾 ✐ **Eight Cousins Children's Books** (508-548-5548; eightcous
ins.com), 189 Main Street, Falmouth.
Long before it won the equivalent of the
Pulitzer Prize for children's bookstores
in 2002, this excellent shop enjoyed
broad and deep roots in the community.
Named for one of Louisa May Alcott's
lesser-known works, Eight Cousins
stocks more than 17,000 titles and is a
great resource, whether you're a teacher,
a gift buyer, or entertaining a child on a
rainy afternoon. It continues to excel
with kids' programs, regular story times,
and great service. Don't miss artist
Sarah Peters's Alphabet Chair metal
sculpture in front of the store. It's a
favorite with kids *and* adults, who love to
sit on it and feel the different textures of
the individual letters that make up the
throne.

CLOTHING **Soul to Sole**, 422 Main
Street, Falmouth. I almost cried (okay, I
cried a little) when Theresa Cancelliere
closed her shop, Moda Fina, in Provincetown. Luckily, she joined forces with
Kristen Samok, owner of Mad as a Hatter
(also in Provincetown), and opened this
new boutique in Falmouth. (I'm still sad
because it's a hike for me and I no longer
can peruse her outside sale rack on

508-548-2211 off-season; collegelight
operacompany.com), 58 Highfield Drive,
Depot Avenue, Falmouth. Performances
late June to late August. Founded in
1969, this talented and energetic company includes music majors and theater
arts students from across the country.
Reserve early, as these performances sell
out quickly. $$$$.

THEATER **The Cape Cod Theatre Project** (508-457-4242; capecodtheatre
project.org), Falmouth Academy, 7 Highfield Drive, Falmouth. Established by two
New York actors who were vacationing in
Woods Hole in 1994, the project stages
readings of new American plays in July.
$$$.

✳ Selective Shopping

✳ Between the quality of its shops and
the strollability of the street, you can

FAIRS AND POWWOWS

KIM GRANT

arly July: Powwow (508-477-0208, Wampanoag Tribe; mashpeewampanoagtribe.com), 483 Great Neck Road South, Mashpee. The People of the First Light's Mashpee Wampanoag Powwow has been open to the public since before 1924, and the Mashpee Wampanoag Tribal Council has sponsored it since 1974. The powwow attracts American Indians in full regalia from nearly every state as well as Canada, Mexico, and some Central and South American countries. These traditional gatherings provide an opportunity for tribes to exchange stories and discuss common problems and goals. Dancing, crafts demonstrations, storytelling, pony rides, a "fire ball," a clambake, and vendor booths. Kids are encouraged to join in the dancing and nearly constant percussive music. $$. 🖉

Late July: Barnstable County Fair (508-563-3200; barnstablecountyfair.org), 1220 Nathan Ellis Highway, East Falmouth. A popular weeklong family tradition. Local and national musical acts, a midway, livestock shows, and horticulture, cooking, and crafts exhibits and contests. $. 🖉

Commercial Street.) Theresa has an unbeatable style. I've never met anyone with such prevailing taste. Everything is high quality, fun, flirty and fashionable, unique, chic, sexy—I can go on and on. You know that one item in your closet that makes you excited and happy every time you wear it? Theresa has provided that for me (and many others) time and time again. And she's the coolest, kindest person. If you have a few minutes, or an hour, be sure to swing by her store. I'm jealous of you already. Prices vary from average to designer.

Liberty House (508-548-7568 for Woods Hole; 508-548-3900 for Falmouth; libertyhousecapecod.com), 89 Water Street in Woods Hole and 119 Palmer Avenue in Falmouth. Falmouth store open mid-April to January; Woods Hole store open mid-April to December. Tasteful women's clothing at reasonable prices.

FARMS **Falmouth Farmers' Market,** (falmouthfarmersmarket.com), Marine Park at Falmouth Harbor, every Thursday from mid-May to mid-October.

🖉 **Tony Andrew's Farm** (508-548-4717), 394 Old Meeting House Road, East Falmouth. Open mid-June through October. Pick your own strawberries and other produce, all reasonably priced (especially if you pick your own). Turns out, strawberries have a big of a legacy in Falmouth. In 1927, Tony and his uncle Peter Andrews bought the acreage for what is now Tony Andrew's Farm. During this time, East Falmouth was at the height of strawberry production and local farms produced close to half the strawberry crop for the state. Strawberry season runs from early June to early July, more or less. You can also pick your own peas in June, tomatoes in August, sunflowers from July to October, and pumpkins in late September and October. There are lots of other family activities, too.

Nobska Farms, a.k.a. **Home of the Big Red Rooster** (617-480-0876; nobskafarms .com), 9 Nobska Road, Woods Hole.

Open mid-June to November. This micro-farm specializes in exotic, rare, super-hot, and hard-to-find chili peppers. Stop here for authentic hot sauces, jellies, ghost pepper chocolates, and other spicy concoctions.

GALLERIES **Falmouth Artists Guild** (508-540-3304; falmouthart.org), 137 Gifford Street at the corner of Dillingham Avenue, Falmouth. This nonprofit guild (active since the 1950s) holds eight to 13 exhibitions annually, a few of which are juried; classes; and various fundraising auctions.

MALL **Falmouth Mall** (508-790-2844; Falmouth-mall.com), 137 Teaticket Highway, East Falmouth.

SPECIALTY **Twigs** (508-540-0767), 178 Main Street, Falmouth. Practical, decorative, and functional accessories for the home and garden.

✳ Special Events

Early–mid-July: **Arts and Crafts Street Fair**. Main Street fills with crafts, artisans, and food stalls.

Late July–early August: **Woods Hole Film Festival** (508-495-3456; woodsholefilmfestival.com). This is the oldest independent film festival in Cape Cod. About 50 films by established and new filmmakers have been screened at various locations since the early 1990s.

Mid-August: **Annual Antiques Show**, Falmouth Historical Society; since 1970.

Falmouth Road Race (508-540-7000; falmouthroadrace.com). The event of the year in Falmouth: an internationally renowned 7-mile seaside footrace, limited to about 12,800 participants. Get your registration in before early May or you won't have a chance of running. Reserve your lodging ASAP—like when you send in your registration!

Mid- to late September: **Cape Cod Scallop Fest**, Cape Cod Fairgrounds, East Falmouth (capecodscallopfest.com). A weekend celebration with games, concerts, and restaurants and vendors offering dishes that celebrate—what else?—the scallop. Rain or shine, as the eating takes place under a big tent; since 1969. $.

Early October: **JazzFest** (artsfalmouth.org), Arts Foundation of Cape Cod, Marina Park.

Late October: **Cape Cod Marathon** (508-540-6959; capecodmarathon.com). A high-spirited event, beginning and ending on Falmouth's village green and attracting more than 2,000 long-distance runners and relay teams. Commit by September or you'll be disappointed.

Early December: **Christmas by the Sea**. Tree lighting, caroling at the lighthouse and town green, and a significant Christmas parade. Popular house tours are operated by the West Falmouth Library (508-548-4709).

MASHPEE

J ust east of Falmouth, fast-growing Mashpee (which means "land near the great cove") is one of two Massachusetts towns administered by American Indians (the other is Aquinnah on Martha's Vineyard).

The largest developed area of Mashpee is **New Seabury**, a 2.5-square-mile enclave of homes, condos, restaurants, golf courses, shops, and beaches. When developers won their lengthy legal battle with the Wampanoag, the tribe—and the town—lost much of its prettiest oceanfront property. The only noteworthy beach is **South Cape Beach**, a relatively pristine barrier beach with several miles of marked nature trails and steady winds that attract sailboarders. Compared with its neighbors, Mashpee is a quiet place, with a year-round population of 14,000, plenty of commuters into Boston, and an upscale outdoor mall, **Mashpee Commons**.

When the *Mayflower* arrived at Plymouth, the Wampanoag population was an estimated 30,000; there are about 1,600 Wampanoag in Mashpee today.

For 1,000 years prior to the colonists' arrival, the Wampanoag had established summer camps in the area, but with the settlement of Plymouth Colony, they saw larger and larger pieces of their homeland taken away from them and their numbers decimated by imported disease.

MASHPEE PUBLIC LIBRARY KIM GRANT

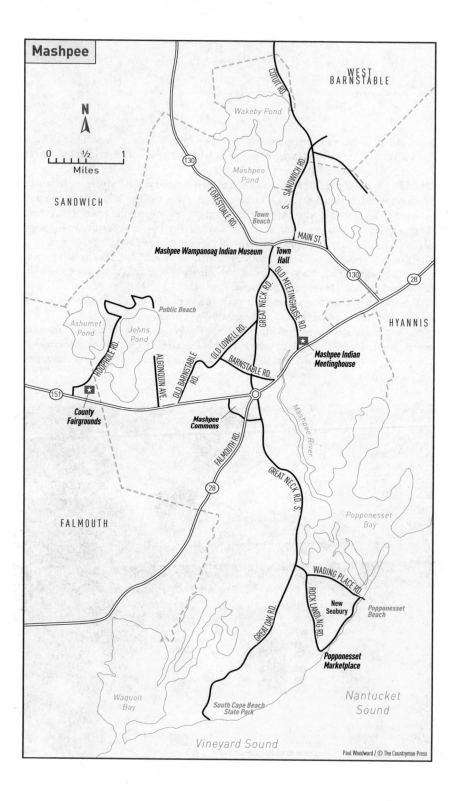

WHERE TO START IN MASHPEE

Morning: Fuel up with a carb-heavy breakfast from Bagel Haven before taking a guided kayak tour of Popponesset Bay with Rideaway Adventures. Or opt for a leisure walk in Lowell Holly Reservation and soak in the tranquility of this 135-acre preserve.

Afternoon: Slurp down some local oysters at the Raw Bar at Popponesset, or head to Estia for Modern Greek fare. Head to South Cape Beach for some fun in the sun, or test your abilities and wit at the Riddle Escape Room with family and friends.

Evening: Enjoy a fine French dinner at Blue or sophisticated cuisine at Trevi Café and Wine Bar. Afterward, stroll through Mashpee Commons for impromptu entertainment and window-shopping.

In 1617, three years after Capt. John Smith explored the area, six American Indians were kidnapped and forced into slavery. By 1665, the missionary Rev. Richard Bourne appealed to the Massachusetts legislature to reserve about 25 square miles for the American Indians. The area was called Mashpee Plantation (or Massapee or Massipee, depending on who's doing the translating), in essence the first American Indian reservation in the United States. In 1870 the plantation was incorporated as the town of Mashpee.

Mashpee wasn't popular with wealthy 19th-century settlers, so there are few stately old homes here. The Wampanoag maintain a museum and church, both staffed by knowledgeable tribespeople. In the 1930s classic *Cape Cod Ahoy!* Arthur Wilson Tarbell observed something about Mashpee that could still be said today: it's "retiring, elusive, scattered, a thing hidden among the trees."

GUIDANCE ❋ **Mashpee Chamber of Commerce** (508-477-0792; mashpeechamber .com), 5 Market Street within Mashpee Commons.

GETTING THERE *By car:* From the Sagamore Bridge, take Route 6 east to Route 130 south to North Great Neck Road to the Routes 151/28 Mashpee rotary. The Mashpee Commons shopping area at the rotary acts as Mashpee's hub.

GETTING AROUND *By shuttle:* The **Sealine** (800-352-7155; capecodtransit.org), travels from downtown Hyannis along Route 28 to Mashpee Commons.

PUBLIC RESTROOMS Mashpee Commons (see **Selective Shopping**).

PUBLIC LIBRARY ❋ ✐ ⬀ **Mashpee Public Library** (508-539-1435; mashpeepublic library.org), 64 Steeple Street, off Route 151 and adjacent to Mashpee Commons. One of the best on Cape Cod. Period.

EMERGENCIES **Mashpee Police Department** (508-539-1480; mashpeema.gov), 19 Frank E. Hicks Drive, or call **911**.

Medical: **Mashpee Family Medicine** (508-477-4282), Mashpee Health Center, 5 Industrial Drive at Route 28.

It's not an "emergency" (the kind you'd expect under this category, anyway), but many area water wells have been contaminated by years of training with grenades and other live munitions at the Massachusetts Military Reservation. I drink bottled water on the Upper Cape.

✳ To See & Do

HISTORIC HOUSES **Mashpee Indian Meetinghouse** (508-477-0208, Wampanoag Tribal Council; mashpeewampanoagtribe.com), 410 Meetinghouse Road off Route 28. Completely restored and located on the edge of what was once a Wampanoag-only cemetery ("They even took our burial ground away from us and made it theirs," laments a volunteer guide), this is the Cape's oldest surviving meetinghouse. It was built in 1684 by the descendants of Massasoit and moved to its current spot in 1717.

Mashpee Wampanoag Indian Museum (508-477-9339; mashpeewampanoag tribe.com), 414 Main Street, on Route 130 across from Lake Avenue. This small, early-19th-century house was built by Richard Bourne, minister and missionary to the Mashpee Wampanoag. (Check out the herring run at the end of the parking lot.)

BICYCLING & RENTALS If you're looking for a well-maintained paved path that follows main roads, this is the route for you. The **Great Neck South/Route 151 Path** travels from Mashpee Commons to South Cape via Great Neck Road. Park in the lot near Talbots in the Commons and follow the trail out the right corner, cross Route 28, and follow to South Cape Beach State Park. It ends around the Children's Museum, which is a fun place to take a breather and explore with the kiddos. (See also "O' Beautiful" on page 74). Rent bicycles and equipment from **Rideaway Adventures** (508-247-0827; rideawaykayak.com), 259 Shore Drive; or **Mocean Cape Cod** (508-477-1774; moceancapecod.com), 34 Steeple Street, Mashpee Commons. (See also *Kayaks & Paddleboards* below.)

MASHPEE INDIAN MEETINGHOUSE KIM GRANT

BOAT EXCURSIONS & RENTALS For boating rules and regulations, contact the **Harbormaster** (508-539-1450; mashpee ma.gov), 19 Frank E. Hicks Drive.

Plan Sea (508-687-2003; plan-sea .com), offers private daytime charters, sunset cruises, and ferry trips to Martha's Vineyard and Nantucket. Create an itinerary tailored to your wants and needs, and be sure to include a visit to the rarely visited Elizabeth Islands with a stop at Cuttyhunk for lunch. $$$$+.

FISHING There are plenty of fishing hotspots in Mashpee, you just need to know where to look. Do your research, ask around, or book a charter for the best results. Procure freshwater and saltwater fishing licenses and regulations online (mass.gov/eea/agencies/dfg/licensing).

WAMPANOAG INDIAN MUSEUM KIM GRANT

Big game: **Bucktail Fishing Charters** (774-313-0218; capecodbucktailcharters.com), 10 Charles Street. Join Captain Ron on his boat, the *Northernbelle* (named after his wife Debbie, "a Louisiana girl, living in a Massachusetts world"), for a rewarding day on the water. Land blues and stripers by trolling, casting, or jigging with live bait. Or drift and jig for bottom fish like seabass, fluke, and scup. Whether you're a seasoned angler or a first-timer, Captain Ron will surely teach you a thing or two (after all, he does have over 50 years of fishing experience). $$$$+.

On Shore: **South Cape Beach** is an excellent place for surfcasting and bottom fishing. Walk about 1 mile east along the shoreline for prime action (fishing along the featureless beach in front of the parking lot isn't worth the time). Strong rips and deep drop-offs attract decent-sized bass and blues.

By bridge or jetty: The **Waquoit Jetty** can only be described as a fish resting area. Here, Waquoit Bay and Nantucket Sound serve up a smorgasbord of baitfish, which as a result attract a variety of predators throughout the seasons. To fish the jetty, the best access point is by walking the soft sands of South Cape Beach (a little bit of a hike), or by boat or kayak. A public launch can be found at the Mashpee Boat Ramp in Waquoit Bay.

Freshwater: Fish for trout, large and smallmouth bass, chain pickerel, and yellow perch at the **Mashpee-Wakeby Ponds.** A large paved boat ramp with an attached parking lot is located on Fisherman's Landing Road to the north of Route 130. Parking sticker required in season. $.

Supplies: There are bait and tackle shops nearby, including **Canal Bait and Tackle** (508-833-2996; canalbaitandtackle.com), 101 Cranberry Highway, Sagamore; and **Eastman's Sport & Tackle** (508-548-6900; eastmanstackle.com), 783 Main Street, Falmouth.

FOR FAMILIES ✇ **Riddle Escape Room** (508-648-7664; riddlecapecod.com), 61 Market Street. Spend 60 minutes with family and/or friends testing your wit, creativity, inquisitiveness, and problem-solving skills in this live-action adventure. Players work together by solving a series of puzzles, riddles, and connecting clues to complete the mission. Expect themes like "The Secret of Dragon's Spire," "Game of Pirates," or "Like, Totally the '80s to the Max!" Games are public, so you might end up playing with other groups unless you purchase all the tickets for your room. Book your escape adventure online, credit cards only. $$$$.

✳ ✒ ⚓ **Cape Cod Children's Museum** (508-539-8788; capecodchildrensmuseum
.org), 577 Great Neck Road South. Toddlers love the castle, puppet theater, and 30-foot
pirate ship; younger kids enjoy arts and crafts. Older kids I know . . . not so much. Check
out the Starlab Planetarium and high-tech submarine with a working periscope, too. $.

GOLF ✳ **Quashnet Valley Country Club** (508-477-4412; quashnetvalley.com), 309 Old
Barnstable Road, off Great Neck Road. This semiprivate course winds around woods
and cranberry bogs; ponds and marshes surround 12 of 18 holes. Par 72, 18 holes. $$$$+.

KAYAKS & PADDLEBOARDS **Mocean Cape Cod** (508-477-1774; moceancapecod
.com), 34 Steeple Street, Mashpee Commons. Arrange your own group paddleboarding lesson, join a scheduled kayak tour, or rent a beach cruiser bike for the day. You can
also buy top-quality sports gear and equipment here. $$$–$$$$+.
     Rideaway Adventures (508-247-0827; rideawaykayak.com), 259 Shore Drive, Mash-
pee. Rent kayaks, paddleboards, and bikes from Rideaway and have them delivered to
your vacation rental. They also offer guided kayak tours of Popponesset Bay or "build
your own" tours, where you create your own adventure. $$$–$$$$+.

TENNIS **Mashpee High School**, 500 Old Barnstable Road (off Route 151), has public
courts.

✳ Green Space

Parking stickers for town beaches and ponds can be purchased at the **Mashpee Town
Hall** (508-539-1418; mashpeema.gov), 16 Great Neck Road. Stickers are required mid-
May to early September. $–$$.

BEACH **South Cape Beach State Park** (508-457-0495 ext. 101; waquoitbayreserve
.com), on Vineyard Sound, Great Neck Road. The 432-acre state park boasts a lovely
mile-long, dune-backed barrier beach, boardwalks, and nature trails. In-season facilities include restrooms and a handicap ramp onto the beach. $–$$.

PONDS **Mashpee** and **Wakeby Ponds**, off Route 130. Combined, these ponds create the
Cape's largest freshwater body (729 acres), wonderful for swimming, fishing, and boat-
ing. This area was a favorite fishing spot of both patriot Daniel Webster and President
Grover Cleveland.

✳ WALKS **Lowell Holly Reservation** (508-636-4693; thetrustees.org), off South Sandwich Road from Route 130. Open year-round. Donated by Harvard University President Abbott Lawrence Lowell to the Trustees of Reservations in 1942, this tranquil
135-acre preserve contains an untouched forest of native American beeches and more
than 100 varieties of wild hollies, as well as white pines, rhododendrons, and wildflowers. There is a small bathing beach (no lifeguard) and 4 miles of walking trails and
former carriage paths. $ parking fee late May to early September.
     Mashpee River Woodlands/South Mashpee Pine Barrens. Parking on Quinnaquis-
set Avenue (off Route 28 just east of the rotary) and at the end of River Road off Great
Neck Road South. The 8-mile hiking trail winds along the Mashpee River, through a
quiet forest, and along marshes and cranberry bogs. Put in your canoe at the public
landing on Great Neck Road.

SOUTH CAPE BEACH KIM GRANT

Jehu Pond Conservation Area. Established in the late 1990s, there are almost 5 miles of trails here on almost 80 acres encompassing woodlands, marshes, an abandoned cranberry bog, two islands, and Atlantic white cedar swamplands. Take Great Neck Road South toward South Cape Beach and follow the CONSERVATION AREA signs.

Great Flat Pond Trail, at South Cape Beach State Park. This easy-grade trail, a little less than a mile long, winds through woodland and wetland.

The Mashpee Environmental Coalition (mashpeemec.us) is a good source for trails.

✳ Lodging

Family-style accommodations rule in Mashpee.

RESORTS ✳ ♂ **The Club at New Seabury** (508-539-8322; newseabury.com), 95 Shore Drive West, Mashpee. This self-contained resort fronting Nantucket Sound consists of 13 "villages" of small, gray-shingled buildings that offer a variety of rental accommodations. Your best bet is to check VRBO and similar platforms. Facilities are de rigueur: restaurants, tennis courts, private golf courses, health club, outdoor pools, miles of private beach on Nantucket Sound, a small shopping mall, and mini-golf. You

needn't leave the grounds, although that would be a shame. $$$–$$$$.

✳ ♂ **Cape Cod Holiday Estates** (508-477-3377 or 800-228-2968 for reservations; capecodholidayestates .com), 97 Four Seasons Drive. These 34 upscale time-share houses consist of airy one-, two-, and three-bedroom units with a full modern kitchen, Jacuzzi (except one-bedroom units), central air-conditioning, separate living and family room, and private patio. On-premise activities and facilities include an indoor heated pool, shuffleboard, a game room, tennis, basketball, and a putting green. $–$$$$.

Sea Mist Resort (508-477-0549; sea mistcapecod.com), 141 Great Neck Road South, Mashpee. This family-friendly resort is nestled on 20 acres of quiet wooded land just 5 miles from Nantucket Sound beaches. Make yourself at home in their condos, which range in size but all come equipped with a full-size kitchen. On-site amenities include a clubhouse, indoor and outdoor pools, hot tubs and saunas, mini golf, tennis, shuffleboard, and volleyball courts. $–$$$$.

✳ Where to Eat

There aren't many choices in Mashpee, but the ones here are good. If you're not satisfied with these, stop at Mashpee Commons shopping area to see if any new restaurants opened recently.

DINING OUT **Trevi Café and Wine Bar** (508-477-0055; trevicafe.com), 25 Market Street. This classy, yet low-key eatery features an impressive rotating wine list with premium offerings by the glass. The stately and sophisticated Mediterranean menu boasts quality fare with satisfying portions. Start with a decadent charcuterie—my favorites includes the Barrel Aged Feta, made from tangy sheep's milk, or the Piave, a hard Parmesan-style cheese made from raw cow's milk. Accompany with hot Soppressata or salame toscano and *bon appétit*. Dinner options are just as lush: from lamb lollipops in chimichurri, handmade pasta Bolognese, or lighter fare like grilled artichoke hearts and Greek Mezze. The roman fountain replica ads a dash of European romance to the rather contemporary ambiance. $$–$$$$.

✳ ✿ **Bleu** (508-539-7907; bleurestaurant.com), 10 Market Street at the Mashpee Commons. Open L, D; B on wintertime Sundays. I really love Bleu—from the very cool blue interior to the cushy seats where you could sit all afternoon to the side-alley alfresco dining. It's upscale but casual and definitely stylin', with a smart waitstaff decked out in all black. French chef/owner Frederic Feufeu excels in both inspired

bistro and contemporary cuisine, from regional French classics like *cassoulet* with duck confit to seafood specialties. You'd almost be certifiably nuts not to save room for their caramel arborio rice pudding. In fact, let's just start and end with that. There's a nice wine selection, too. L $–$$, D $$$–$$$$.

✳ ✿ **Siena Italian Bar & Grill** (508-477-5929; siena.us), 17 Steeple Street at the Mashpee Commons. Open L, D. Graham Silliman's spacious Italian ristorante features a contemporary, sophisticated menu that has been dishing from an open kitchen since 2006. In general, I always expect the quality of the cuisine to be a tad higher for the prices. That said, the skewered seared scallops are absolute perfection! If you cannot live by scallops alone, consider their addictive Caesar salad, thin-crust pizzas, or the Cotuit oysters and clams that hail from waters less than 3 miles away. As an added bonus, Siena offers discounted movie tickets to patrons heading to a

BLEU KIM GRANT

MASHPEE COMMONS KIM GRANT

flick at Mashpee Commons. Although I like the buzz and the booths in the dining room, there is also popular patio dining in the summer (when service can hit some rough patches). Either way, the bartender is known for margaritas and pomegranate martinis; wines are poured liberally. L $–$$, D $$–$$$.

EATING OUT **Estia** (508-539-4700; estiacapecod.com), 26 Steeple Street. Open L, D. If you like Greek cuisine, you will surely be happy here. The menu features all the classics, but with modern and elevated twists. The coal-fired wings and pizza are both divine, as well as the dolmades (stuffed and rolled grape leaves), spanakopita, gyros (my mouth is watering just thinking about it), kabobs, and lamb chops. It's a lively place often filled with chatter, so don't come here expecting romance, unless you include falling in love with your food. $–$$$$.

The Raw Bar at Popponesset (774-228-2327; poppyrawbar.com), 259 Shore Drive. Open L, D mid-May to mid-October. You know this tiny place has something going for it because locals outnumber tourists. Part Cape Cod, part Caribbean, the raw bar boasts loyal staff, fresh seafood, and other casual goodies from hot dogs to lobster. Grab a picnic table outside and chow down. $–$$$$.

Wicked Restaurant and Wine Bar (508-477-7422; wickedrestaurant.com), 35 South Street. Open L, D. Wicked takes the traditional slice one step further. The dozen adventurous "fire-kissed pizza" offerings include organics, gluten-free, fig and prosciutto, scallop BLT, and barbecue chicken and pineapple. Choose from over 20 wines by the glass and 13 domestic beers on draft. You gotta love TVs and loud music to enjoy the experience here. $–$$$.

MARKETS **Rory's Market** (774-361-6075), 32 Market Street. This hidden gem of a natural market has been in business for over 35 years. Shop here for locally grown organic produce, supplements, beauty and wellness products, grocery staples, and more. The real steal here, though, is the small café inside. I always grab a smoothie while perusing the aisles.

SWEET TREATS & COFFEE **Bagel Haven** (508-477-4499), 681 Falmouth Road. Open B, L. This quick no-fuss bagel and breakfast bar offers the type of morning fuel needed for a day exploring. Order off the chalkboard and grab a seat or take it to go. The breakfast sandwiches are super-filling; I usually eat only half and save the rest for lunch. But what really gets me going here is the long list of homemade cream cheese flavors—chive, veggie, olive, jalapeño, lox, bacon-chive, sun-dried tomato, cinnamon, cranberry-walnut, blueberry-almond—to name a few. $–$$.

Washashore Bakery (508-419-6835; washashorebakery.com), 14 Central Street. Open B, L. As the name suggests, owner and baker Sandy McPherson is not a Cape native, but rather, a wash-ashore from the West Coast. And we don't care one bit because her baking is just that good! Stop here for sweet treats and be sure to try her famous cinnamon buns, sandbars, and lemon squares. Her tea breads are also uniquely yummy. $–$$.

✳ Entertainment

The **Mashpee Commons** (508-477-5400; mashpeecommons.com), Routes 151 and 28, and **Popponesset Marketplace** (508-477-8300; popponessetmarketplace .com), 259 Shore Drive, offer a variety of entertainment throughout the year. Check online for a schedule of listings.

LIVE MUSIC ⓨ **Naukabout Beer Co.** (naukabout.com), 13 Lake Avenue. I'm a big fan of this local brewery. "Our story started over 30 years ago with our cofounders' father. He would come home from work, change out of his work-a-bouts, and tell his sons to 'change into their nauk-a-bouts' in order to 'get outside for some fun!'" Stop here for a tasting—there are 15 brews on tap. Or grab a bite to eat from one of their local food truck partners and roam the grounds. Live music, workshops, games,

and festivals are often scheduled, so check online for further details.

MOVIES 🐾 ✳ ⓨ **Regal Mashpee Commons** (844-462-7342), Mashpee Commons, 15 Steeple Street.

✳ Selective Shopping

✳ **Mashpee Commons** (508-477-5400; mashpeecommons.com), Routes 151 and 28. Open daily. If you're familiar with Seaside, the planned community of architectural note in Florida, you might recognize elements of this 30-acre outdoor shopping mall–cum–new town center. It's located at what the Wampanoag used to call "pine tree corner," back when Mashpee was quieter than it is today. Developers have won numerous awards for transforming a strip mall into a veritable downtown commercial district. It's one of the most concentrated shopping venues on the Cape, boasting several good clothing stores, specialty boutiques, a movie theater, restaurants, cafés, and free outdoor entertainment in summer. Shops range from the likes of Talbots, Lane Bryant, and L.L. Bean to more one-of-a-kind, mom-and-pop shops, like the great independent **Market Street Bookshop** (508-539-6985, 31 Market Street); **Fox & Kit** (774-602-0447, 4 Central Square) for trending children's gear; or **Hot Diggity** (508-477-2663; hotdiggityonline.com, 1 Central Square), for cute accessories for your pooch.

Popponesset Marketplace (508-477-8300; popponessetmarketplace.com), 259 Shore Drive. If you're staying in the neighborhood, this little collection of shacks and seashell-lined pathways has interesting offerings, as well as coffee shops and a few casual eateries.

✳ Special Events

See "Fairs and Powwows" on page 89.

MID-CAPE

■

BARNSTABLE

HYANNIS

YARMOUTH

DENNIS

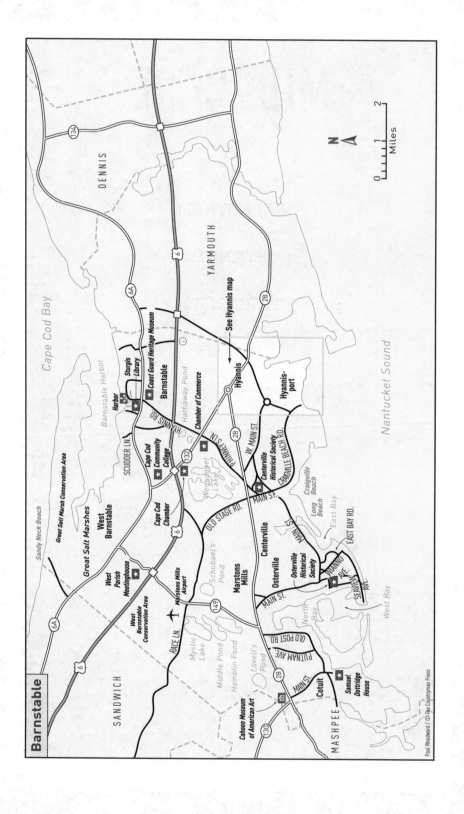

Barnstable

SANDWICH

DENNIS

YARMOUTH

MASHPEE

Cape Cod Bay

Nantucket Sound

Sandy Neck Beach

Great Salt Marsh Conservation Area

Great Salt Marshes

West Barnstable

West Parish Meetinghouse

West Barnstable Conservation Area

Marstons Mills Airport

RACE LN.

Mystic Lake

Middle Pond

Hamblin Pond

Lovell's Pond

Schubael's Pond

Marstons Mills

Centerville

Osterville

Osterville Historical Society

MAIN ST.

WIANNO AVE.

SEAVIEW AVE.

North Bay

West Bay

East Bay

East Bay

Long Beach

Craigville Beach

EAST BAY RD.

PUTNAM AVE.

OLD POST RD.

Cotuit

Samuel Dottridge House

Cahoon Museum of American Art

MAIN ST.

OLD STAGE RD.

MAIN ST.

Wequaquet Lake

Cape Cod Community College

Cape Cod Chamber

PHINNEY'S LN.

HYANNIS RD.

SCUDDER LN.

Barnstable

Harbor

Sturgis Library

Coast Guard Heritage Museum

Chamber of Commerce

Barnstable Harbor

Hathaway Pond

Hyannis

Hyannis-port

See Hyannis map

W. MAIN ST.

Centerville Historical Society

CRAIGVILLE BEACH RD.

West Barnstable

N

Miles

0 1 2

Paul Woodward / © The Countryman Press

BARNSTABLE

The Cape's largest town covers 60 square miles and is home to 48,000 year-round souls. It's also the Cape's second-oldest town, incorporated 2 years after Sandwich, in 1639. Barnstable actually comprises seven distinct villages—Cotuit, Marstons Mills, Osterville, Centerville, and Hyannis along Route 28, and West Barnstable and Barnstable along Route 6A. (Barnstable is sometimes referred to as Barnstable Village to distinguish it from Barnstable County, which embraces the whole of the Cape.)

On the bayside, Route 6A (also called Old King's Highway and Main Street) winds through **West Barnstable** and **Barnstable Village**. Development—or lack thereof—is rigidly controlled by the Old King's Highway Historical Commission, which regulates signage and does not allow gas stations, chain stores, or unconventional restorations within sight of the road. **Sandy Neck**, a haven for naturalists and beachgoers, is located off Route 6A, as are stately homes now converted into bed-and-breakfasts.

On the southside, off Route 28 you'll find **Centerville, Osterville,** and **Cotuit**—parts of which front Nantucket Sound. Centerville's Main Street is full of handsome old homes built during the 19th century by affluent sea captains and businessmen. Osterville boasts some of the Cape's largest summer mansions, all with **Nantucket Sound** as their front yard. Osterville's Main Street is lined with upscale shops. At the turn of the 20th century, Cotuit was dubbed "Little Harvard," because it was home to many academicians. Cotuit's Main Street is lined with impressive Federal, Greek Revival, and Queen Anne houses, with American flags and Adirondack chairs dotting the lawns. The popular **Craigville Beach** dominates this side of Barnstable.

Landlocked and wedged between Routes 28 and 6, **Marstons Mills** is tiny, quiet, and residentially developed. It was founded by the Marston family, who built and ran the mills driven by the Goodspeed River.

Barnstable was founded by English Congregationalist minister John Lothrop and a small band of religious renegades who found Plymouth Colony a bit too settled for them. The neighborhood of Oysterville, as it was called, was purchased from the American Indians in 1648 for "two copper kettles and some fencing." The area then was called Mattakeese, which translates as "plowed fields"—indeed, the land had already been cleared—but the settlers eventually named it for a similar harbor in Barnstaple, England.

GUIDANCE ✳ **Hyannis Area Chamber of Commerce** (508-775-2201; hyannis.com), 397 Main Street, Hyannis. The visitor center is located at the JFK Hyannis Museum, and the Hyannis chamber has information about all Barnstable villages.

GETTING THERE *By car:* Barnstable is 15 miles from the Cape Cod Canal. Take Route 6 to Exit 5 for West Barnstable (Route 149 North) and Marstons Mills, Cotuit, and Osterville (Route 149 South). Take Exit 6 for Barnstable Village (Route 132 West) and Centerville (Route 132 East).

By bus: The **Plymouth & Brockton** bus line (508-778-9767; p-b.com) connects Barnstable with other Cape towns, as well as with Boston's Logan Airport. The bus stops at the big commuter parking lot behind Burger King, Exit 6 off Route 6 at Route 132.

WHERE TO START IN BARNSTABLE

Morning: Accompany your morning coffee with sweet and savory breakfast delights from Amie Bakery. Take it to go and dine to sound of gently breaking waves at Sandy Neck Beach.

Afternoon: Pore over centuries-old primary sources of Cape Cod history at the Nickerson Memorial Room at Cape Cod Community College, or duck into the Anglicized and Japanese-style St. Mary's Church garden. Grab lunch at Barnstable Market or Kettle-Ho Tavern.

Evening: Take a road trip down Route 6A and pop into various antiques showrooms and gallery studios. Dine on seafood with the locals at Five Bays Bistro. Top the day off with ice cream from Four Seas.

GETTING AROUND *By shuttle and trolley:* The **Barnstable Villager** (800-352-7155; capecodtransit.org) connects Barnstable's Route 6A (at the courthouse) with the malls in Hyannis on Route 132, the Hyannis Transportation Center, and Barnstable Harbor. The **Sealine** starts at the **Hyannis Transportation Center** (800-352-7155; capecodtransit .org), 215 Iyannough Road and stops in Barnstable, Mashpee, Falmouth, and Woods Hole. Take the seasonal **Hyannis Area Trolley** (508-385-1430; capecodtransit.org) for popular stops within Hyannis or the **H2O** line, which travels Route 28 to Orleans daily in summer ($).

MEDIA The weekly *Barnstable Patriot* (508-771-1427; barnstablepatriot.com) has local news and gossip.

PUBLIC LIBRARIES **Osterville Village Library** (508-428-5757; ostervillefreelibrary .com.org), 43 Wianno Avenue, Osterville. (See also **Sturgis Library** under **To See.**)

EMERGENCIES **Barnstable Police Department** (508-775-0387; barnstablepolice.com), 1200 Phinney's Lane, or call **911**.

Medical: **Cape Cod Hospital** (508-771-1800; capecodhealth.org), 27 Park Street. Open 24/7.

❋ To See

ALONG OR NEAR ROUTE 6A

West Parish Meetinghouse (508-362-4445; westparish.org), 2049 Meetinghouse Road, off Route 149, West Barnstable. Open late May to early September. This fine example of early Colonial architecture is the second oldest surviving meetinghouse on Cape Cod. Don't miss it. (The oldest, the 1684 Old Indian Meetinghouse, is in Mashpee.) Its members belong to the oldest Congregationalist church fellowship in America, established in 1639 and descended from London's First Congregational Church. Founding pastor John Lothrop and his small band of followers erected their first meetinghouse in 1646. By 1715 the Congregational church had become so popular that Barnstable split into two parishes; the building you see today was constructed in 1717. Its bell tower, topped by a gilded rooster, holds a bell cast in Paul Revere's foundry in 1806; it still rings. Until 1834 the meetinghouse doubled as a town hall—so much for separation of church and state! In the 1950s, the meetinghouse was fully restored to its original modest, neoclassical beauty. Donations.

West Barnstable Cemetery, Routes 6A and 149. Near the stone wall along Route 6A, look for a large granite memorial bearing the following inscription: IN THIS CEMETERY LIE THE MORTAL REMAINS OF CAPT. JOHN PERCIVAL KNOWN AS "MAD JACK." BORN APRIL 3, 1779. DIED SEPTEMBER 17, 1862 IN COMMAND OF *Old Ironsides* AROUND THE WORLD 1844–1846.

✳ ⛵ **William Brewster Nickerson Memorial Room at Cape Cod Community College** (508-362-2131, ext. 4445; capecod .edu), 2240 Route 132, West Barnstable. Rainy day or not, visitors with more than a passing interest in the social history, literature, institutions, and people of the Cape and islands owe it to themselves to stop at the "4 C's." Students voted in 1966 to set up this collection to honor the college's second president's son, a Vietnam War hero and *Mayflower* descendant. The significant collection contains more than 5,000 documents: religious treatises, biographies, autobiographies, oral histories, letters by dune poet Harry Kemp, a scrimshaw, ship registers and logs, early diaries, US Lifesaving Service reports, telephone directories from 1886 on, and

WEST PARISH MEETINGHOUSE KIM GRANT

aerial photographs. The place is a treasure trove for researchers; several excellent books have been written solely using these materials.

✳ ✎ ⛵ **Sturgis Library** (508-362-6636; sturgislibrary.org), 3090 Main Street, Route 6A, Barnstable Village. Researchers from all over the United States (including entrepreneurs looking for information about shipwrecks) visit the country's oldest public library. It boasts one of the finest collections of genealogical records, dating to the area's first European settlers; more than 200 oral histories; an original 1605 Lothrop Bible; more than 1,500 maps and charts; and archives filled with other maritime material. William Sturgis, by the way, was born in the original part of the building, went off to sea at age 15 when his father died, and returned 4 years later as a ship's captain. Although he received no formal education, this self-made man obtained reading lists from a Harvard-educated friend and deeded the building to the town as a library. Use of the collections is free, although donations are welcome. The library also has a very good children's area.

Barnstable County Courthouse (508-375-6778), 3195 Main Street, Route 6A, Barnstable Village. Built in 1831–32, this imposing granite Greek Revival building is one of few reminders that tranquil Barnstable is the county seat for the Cape (and has been since 1685). Look for original murals and a pewter codfish in the main courtroom. On the front lawn, a bronze sculpture commemorates James Otis Jr., a West Barnstable "patriot" who wrote the famous 1761 Writs of Assistance speech. President John

Adams said Otis was the "spark by which the child of Independence was born." And on the side lawn, a memorial stands to Mercy Otis Warren, who self-published her Revolutionary War memoirs.

Lothrop Hill Cemetery, Route 6A, just east of Barnstable Village. Slate headstones are scattered across this little hillock, where John Lothrop and other Barnstable founders rest.

✂ ⚲ **Coast Guard Heritage Museum (Old Customs House)** (508-362-8521; coastguardheritagemuseum.org), 3353 Main Street, Route 6A, Barnstable Village. Open early May to early November. Before Barnstable Harbor filled with silt around 1900, it was the Cape's busiest port. The Old Customs House was built in 1856 to oversee the enormous stream of goods passing through the harbor. When harbor activity diminished, the brick Italian Renaissance Revival building served as a post office until the Barnstable Historical Commission made it its headquarters in 1959. The commission restored the beautiful building, painted it deep red, and opened this museum complex. On the grounds you'll find the Coast Guard Heritage Museum (showcasing the history of the Coast Guard and the lighthouse service), a blacksmith shop, and a circa-1690 jail cell (the oldest in the United States but closed because of a fire), complete with colonial "graffiti." $.

OFF ROUTE 28

⚲ ❋ ⚲ **Cahoon Museum of American Art** (508-428-7581; cahoonmuseum.org), 4676 Falmouth Road, Route 28, Cotuit. This magnificent 1775 Georgian Colonial farmhouse was once a stagecoach stop on the Hyannis-to-Sandwich route. Today it houses a permanent collection of 19th- and early-20th-century American art, and features the whimsical and often humorous paintings of the late neoprimitive artists Martha and Ralph Cahoon. The building's low ceilings, wide floorboards, fireplaces, and wall stenciling provide an intimate backdrop for the artwork. Don't miss it. The museum also offers summer workshops and classes. $.

OLD CUSTOMS HOUSE KIM GRANT

♪ ☂ **Centerville Historical Museum** (508-775-0331; centervillehistoricalmuseum .org), 513 Main Street, Centerville. Open May to mid-December. The 1850s Mary Lincoln House (no relation to Abraham) was built by Mary's father, Clark, a local tinsmith. Then along came Charles Ayling, a wealthy Cape businessman and philanthropist, who endowed a wing and assembled an entire Cape Cod colonial kitchen, complete with large open fireplace and dozens of iron utensils. The 14 rooms are filled with rare Sandwich glass, Civil War artifacts, maritime artifacts, historic quilts, costumes from 1750 to 1950, children's toys and games, perfume bottles, and A. E. Crowell's miniature duck carvings. Exhibits change throughout the season. $.

✳ **The 1856 Country Store** (508-775-1856; 1856countrystore.com), 555 Main Street, Centerville. With the exception of the original wooden floors, the store is more picturesque outside than inside. Crowds do flock here for the selection of cutesy country and perfumed things.

Osterville Historical Museum (508-428-5861; ostervillemuseum.org), 155 West Bay Road, Osterville. Open late May to mid-September. The museum comprises three properties, well worth a visit for local history buffs. The **Captain Jonathan Parker House**, built circa 1824, contains period art, antiques, furniture, and dolls, as well as paintings and porcelain from the China trade. The one-room-deep **Cammett House**, a simple Cape Cod farmhouse built circa 1790, is furnished with period pieces. And the **Boat Shop Museum** showcases the famous Crosby-designed catboat *Cayuga*, built in 1928, and the *Wianno Senior* and *Junior*. Half models, tools, and historic Osterville waterfront photographs are also displayed. Don't miss the period colonial gardens maintained by the Osterville Garden Club.

Samuel B. Dottridge House (508-428-0461; cotuithistoricalsociety.org), 1148 Main Street, Cotuit. Open late May to early September. Owned by the Historical Society of Sansuit and Cotuit, this 1790 house contains historical but otherwise fairly unremarkable objects pertaining to daily 19th-century life. $.

SPECIAL PROGRAMS ✦ **Tales of Cape Cod (at the Olde Colonial Courthouse)** (talesofcapecod.org), 3046 Main Street, Route 6A, and Rendezvous Lane, Barnstable Village. This simple, white-clapboard building served as the Barnstable County Courthouse from 1772 to 1832, when the "new" granite structure down the road was built. The secular Olde Colonial Courthouse then became a Baptist church until it was purchased in 1949 by Tales of Cape Cod, a nonprofit organization that preserves Cape folklore and oral histories. The organization sponsors an excellent summertime lecture series delivered by knowledgeable townspeople. (Refreshments alone are worth the price of admission.) $.

✳ To Do

AIRPLANE RIDES ✳ **Cape Cod Airfield** (508-428-8732; capecodairfield.com), Marstons Mills Airport, Route 149, Marstons Mills. These scenic tours, from the Cape's only grass-strip airport, can go virtually anywhere on the Cape. Reservations recommended. $$$$+.

BASEBALL ♪ The **Cotuit Kettleers** (508-420-9080; kettleers.org) play at Lowell Park (10 Lowell Avenue) in Cotuit from mid-June to mid-August.

BICYCLING & RENTALS If you don't have a friend with a summer place in the exclusive Wianno section of town, the best way to enjoy the village of Osterville is to cycle or

From the center of Centerville, take South Main Street toward Osterville. Turn left on East Bay, which will wind around and become Seaview; follow that to the end. Double back and turn left on Eel River, then turn left onto Bridge. You will not be able to go very far on this road (it empties into a gated community), but it does cross a sparkling waterway. After turning around, follow West Bay back to Main Street.

You can also take Main Street off Route 28 in Santuit (as you head toward Falmouth on Route 28, turn left onto Main Street just before the Mashpee town line). Follow Main Street through Cotuit center, jog left onto Ocean View overlooking Nantucket Sound, then jump back onto Main Street and follow it to the end for more pond and Sound views.

drive along Wianno Avenue to Seaview Avenue, then turn right onto Eel River Road to West Bay Road and head back into town. You can rent bicycles and equipment at **Corner Cycle in the Village** (774-228-2170; cornercycle.com), 876 Main Street, Osterville.

BOAT EXCURSIONS & RENTALS **Barnstable Harbor,** Millway Road, off Route 6A. This natural harbor is located about halfway along the "bicep" of Cape Cod's "arm." Sandy Neck shelters the harbor to the north and the city of Barnstable to the south. Fishing charters and whale-watching trips depart from this small harbor. Contact the **Harbormaster** (508-790-6273; 1189 Phinneys Lane, Centerville) for boating regulations.

Lou Lou's Leasing (508-362-4904 ext. 4; loulouleasing.com), 253 Millway Road. This family-owned and -operated rental business offers boats ranging from 18 to 22 feet. (See also **All Cape Boat Rentals** under *Boat Excursions & Rentals* in Hyannis.)

FISHING Procure freshwater and saltwater fishing licenses and regulations online (mass.gov/eea/agencies/dfg/licensing).

Big game: **Lady J. Sportfishing** (508-317-0016; ladyjsportfish.com), 186 Millway Road. Meet Captain Caliri and find out why he is called "the ocean operator." $$$$+.

On shore: **Craigville Beach** has plenty of parking and is a relatively short walk to the water.

Barnstable Harbor via **Scudder Lane** leads to a small creek that fills with fish at the top of the tide. It's not the greatest spot in the harbor, but at certain times it can be excellent, especially when schoolie stripers come in with the tide in search of small bait.

Sandy Neck Beach, off Route 6A on the border of East Sandwich and Barnstable, is perhaps the easiest area to fish. This is a very popular swimming beach, but with a short walk in either direction, you can always find water that's fishable (it's about 7 miles from the parking lot to the end of Sandy Neck beach). In the fall when there is a northeast breeze, bass and bluefish will be caught very close to the beach even in full daylight.

By bridge or jetty: Walk the large, easily manageable stone jetty at the south end of **Dowses Beach**, Osterville. There's also a pier, which is great for children and people with comprised mobility. Just off the end of the pier is a channel connecting East Bay (which feeds the Centerville River) to the Nantucket Sound.

Freshwater: **Wequaquet Lake** in Centerville has plenty of largemouth bass, sunfish, and northern pike to go around, but parking (along Shootflying Hill Road) can be tricky as it's quite limited. **Marstons Mills** has three ponds stocked with smallmouth bass, trout, and perch: **Middle Pond**, off Race Lane; **Hamblin Pond**, west of Route 149; and **Schubael's Pond**, off Race Lane.

Supplies: See Sports Port under *Fishing* in Hyannis.

FOR FAMILIES ❄ ♪ **Cape Cod YMCA** (508-362-6500; ymcacapecod.org), 2245 Iyannough Road, West Barnstable. Includes a fitness center, cardiovascular center, swimming pool, arts and crafts, and programs for adults. The Y also has a summer camp with weekly sessions.

Luke's Love Boundless Playground (508-375-0777; lukeslove.org), 2377 Meetinghouse Way, off Route 149, West Barnstable. This beautiful new playground is dedicated to Luke Vincent, a young boy who died in 2000 from a tragic medical error. Born from love, the gate to this supreme playground was unlocked in April 2019. New and modernized equipment will please the kiddos, while parents will enjoy the shaded benches. You might even see Luke's mom pulling weeds on a sunny day. The Luke Vincent Foundation helps fund opportunities for children in need.

WEQUAQUET LAKE, CENTERVILLE KAYLA ROBERTSON/DO ART PHOTOGRAPHY

GOLF ❄ **Cotuit Highground Country Club** (508-428-9863; cotuithighground .com), 31 Crocker Neck Road, Cotuit. Nine holes. $$–$$$.

Olde Barnstable Fairgrounds Golf Course (508-420-1141; barnstablegolf.com), 1460 Route 149, Marstons Mills. So close to the airport that you can see the underbellies of approaching planes from the driving range. $$$$+.

TENNIS Public courts are located at the **Centerville Elementary School** on Bay Lane; at the **Cotuit Elementary School** on Old Oyster Road; at the **Marstons Mills East Elementary School** on Osterville–West Barnstable Road; and at the **Barnstable–West Barnstable Elementary School** on Route 6A.

WHALE-WATCHING ♪ **Hyannis Whale Watcher Cruises** (508-362-6088; whales .net), Mill Way off Route 6A, Barnstable Harbor. Daily departures from April to mid-October. A convenient mid-Cape location and a fast boat make this a good choice for whale-watching. An on-board naturalist provides commentary. Summertime sunset clambake cruises, too. $$$$+.

❄ Green Space

Parking stickers are required at most spots and can be purchased at the **Hyannis Youth & Community Center** (508-790-6345; townofbarnstable.us/hycc), 141 Bassett Lane, Hyannis.

BARRIER BEACH BEAUTY

Sandy Neck Beach, on Cape Cod Bay, off Route 6A in West Barnstable, is one of the Cape's most stunning beaches. The entrance to this 6-mile-long barrier beach is in Sandwich. Encompassing almost 4,500 acres, the area is rich with marshes, shellfish, and bird life. Sandy Neck dunes protect Barnstable Harbor from the winds and currents of Cape Cod Bay. Sandy Neck was the site of an American Indian summer encampment before the colonists purchased it in 1644 for three axes and four coats. Then they proceeded to harvest salt-marsh hay and boil whale oil in tryworks on the beach. Today, a private summertime cottage community occupies the far eastern end of the beach. Known locally as the Neck, the former hunting and fishing camps, built in the late 19th century and early 20th, still rely on water pumps and propane lights.

Beach facilities include restrooms, changing rooms, and a snack bar. You can purchase four-wheel-drive permits at the gatehouse (508-362-8300). But six items must be in your car when the permit is issued: a spare tire, a jack, a ¾-inch board, a shovel, a low-pressure tire gauge, and something to tow the car. Parking $$.

SANDY NECK BEACH KAYLA ROBERTSON/DO ART PHOTOGRAPHY

BEACHES **Millway Beach**, just beyond Barnstable Harbor. Although a resident parking sticker is needed in summer, you can park here and look across to **Sandy Neck Beach** (see "Barrier Beach Beauty" above) in the off-season.

Craigville Beach, on Nantucket Sound, Centerville. This crescent-shaped beach—long and wide—is popular with teens and college crowds. Facilities include restrooms, changing rooms, and outdoor showers. Parking $$.

Long Beach, on Nantucket Sound, Centerville. Centerville residents favor Long Beach, at the western end of Craigville Beach; walk along the water until you reach a finger of land between the Sound and the Centerville River. Long Beach is uncrowded, edged by large summer shore homes and a bird sanctuary on the western end. Although

WHALE-WATCHING MARCIA DUGGAN/CAPECODSOUL

a resident sticker is required, I include it for my nonresident readers because it's the nicest beach, and Explorers can check it out off-season.

PONDS **Hathaway Pond**, Phinney's Lane, Barnstable Village, is a popular freshwater spot with a bathhouse and lifeguard. The following freshwater locations require a resident sticker: **Lovell's Pond**, off Newtown Road from Route 28, Marstons Mills; **Hamblin Pond**, off Route 149 from Route 28, Marstons Mills; and **Wequaquet Lake**, off Shootflying Hill Road from Route 132, Centerville.

WALKS **Sandy Neck Great Salt Marsh Conservation Area** (508-362-8300), West Barnstable; trailhead at the parking lot near the gatehouse off Sandy Neck Road. First things first: Hike off-season when it's not so hot. It takes about six hours to do the whole circuit. The 12-mile (round-trip) trail to Beach Point winds past pine groves, wide marshes, low blueberry bushes, and 50- to 100-foot dunes. It'll be obvious that this 3,295-acre marsh is the East Coast's second largest. Beginning in June, be on the lookout for endangered

SANDY NECK GREAT SALT MARSH CONSERVATION AREA KIM GRANT

ST MARY'S CHURCH GARDENS

piping plovers nesting in the sand. Eggs are very difficult to see and, therefore, easily crushed. If you're into camping they have a **primitive campground** open May to mid-October with four sites (first-come, first-served). Hike in the 3.3 miles with your gear; they provide wood, water (free), and bathroom facilities. Parking $$.

🛶 **Long Pasture Wildlife Sanctuary** (508-362-1426; massaudubon.org), 345 Bone Hill Road. These 100 acres include wooded trails, tidal flats, and incredible views of Sandy Neck dunes. Dip into their guided hikes, children's programs, or kayaking and paddleboarding. $.

St. Mary's Church Gardens (508-362-3977; stmarys-church.org), Route 6A (across from the library), Barnstable Village. Locals come to these peaceful, old-fashioned gardens to escape summer traffic swells on Route 6A. In spring, the gardens are full of crocuses, tulips, and daffodils. A small stream, crisscrossed with tiny wooden bridges, flows through the property; the effect is rather like an Anglicized Japanese garden.

Tidal flats, Scudder Lane, off Route 6A, West Barnstable. At low tide you can walk onto the flats, almost across to the neck of Sandy Neck.

West Barnstable Conservation Area, Popple Bottom Road, off Route 149 (near Route 6), West Barnstable. Park at the corner for wooded trails.

Armstrong-Kelley Park, Route 28 near East Bay Road, Osterville. This lovely 8½-acre park has shaded picnic tables, flowers blooming throughout the summer, wooded walking trails with specimens identified, and wetland and woodland walkways. Look for rare trees like the umbrella magnolia and the Camperdown elm. This park claims to be the oldest and largest private park on the Cape.

✳ Lodging

While a number of historic bed-and-breakfasts line Route 6A, I've included only a select few because each offers exceptional hospitality and are all quite different.

BED-AND-BREAKFASTS ✳ **Honeysuckle Hill** (508-362-8418; honeysucklehill.com), 591 Route 6A, West Barnstable. Among the most welcoming innkeepers on the Cape (since day one, when they opened in 2013), Nancy and Rick have applied their considerable talents to making this 1810 farmhouse a favorite. Their four rooms and two-bedroom suite (an extremely good value) have feather bedding, robes, fine English toiletries, flat-screen TVs, and marble baths. Friendly, elegant, and modestly furnished with a mix of white wicker and antiques, they're a breath of fresh air. I particularly like Wisteria, the largest, with a king bed, blue toile décor, and its own entrance. What's not to love, from the garden that boasts woodland walks and sitting areas to the spa tub with outdoor shower and a large screened-in porch? Nancy and Rick indulge guests with concierge services (they are fonts of local information) and bountiful breakfasts. $–$$.

✳ 👹 🐾 **Lamb and Lion Inn** (508-362-6823; lambandlion.com), 2504 Route 6A, Barnstable. Although it's the kind of place where guests are left alone if they want, proprietors Alice Pitcher and Tom Dott know a little something about service and hospitality: they operated a Relais & Châteaux restaurant in the Hudson Valley before coming here. This transformed inn consists of 10 guest rooms (including the Lamb's Retreat cottage and the most excellent Barn-Stable that can accommodate families) surrounding an open-air heated swimming pool and hot tub. Long hallways are brightened with sky murals, and the diverse rooms are pleasant, with wicker and antiques. I particularly like Room 9, which gets great afternoon sun, and the suite with a private deck, hot tub,

HONEYSUCKLE HILL KIM GRANT

and kitchenette. Although rooms are quite different, most have a fireplace, half have a kitchenette, and most have a spiffy motel-style bathroom. Before leaving, ask to see the rare, triple-sided fireplace in the original 1740 house. A fine expanded continental breakfast is included, and for $5 extra you can order a hot breakfast. $$–$$$.

✻ Where to Eat

Barnstable isn't overflowing with dining options, but it does have a few fine spots. (For more dining options, see **Where to Eat** in Hyannis.)

DINING OUT ✻ **Five Bays Bistro** (508-420-5559; fivebaysbistro.com), 825 Main Street, Osterville. Open D. Named for the five bodies of water that surround Osterville, this buzzy little place (or noisy, depending on your sensibilities) is urban and stylish—befitting a neighborhood awash with patrons sizing each other up and keeping up with the Joneses. As for the sophisticated fusion cuisine, it gets very good reviews across the board. Local seafood (perhaps done with an Asian twist) and lobster mac and cheese are always a good bet. $–$$$.

✻ ✤ ♈ **Dolphin Restaurant** (508-362-6610; thedolphincapecod.com), 3250 Main Street, Route 6A, Barnstable. Open L, D. This landmark restaurant in Barnstable Village has been serving reliable seafood dishes for over 70 years. Chef/owner Nancy Jean Smith's family recipes are heavy on fresh and locally caught seafood, but she rounds out the menu with various pasta dishes, veal and steak preparations, sandwiches and burgers. Dinner tends to be a bit more elaborate, with white tablecloths and flowers lining the fireplace. The Dolphin's long bar (separated from the main dining room) is often heavily patronized by locals who've been coming for years $–$$$.

Chart Room (774-602-8156; chartroomcrosbys.com), 330 West Bay Road,

Osterville. Open L (Friday through Sunday only) and D, April to November. This place can get a bit loud with music, families, and large parties of patrons, and you might find yourself shouting conservations across the table, but, in the end, the waterfront view is pretty great, and the food isn't bad either. Large portions and pleasant service, too. $–$$$.

EATING OUT **Earthly Delights** (508-420-2206; earthlydelightscapecod.com), 15 West Bay Road, Osterville. Open B, L. This bohemian eco-minded health food eatery offers a wide selection of vegetarian and vegan options at extremely good prices. Favorites include the veggie scramble, tempeh Reuben, and the organic sunshine burger (special thanks to my vegan friend for the recommendations). Meat eaters will enjoy the curry chicken salad, grilled chicken pesto wrap, or the raison walnut tuna sandwich. $.

♈ **Kettle-Ho Restaurant & Tavern** (508-428-1862), 12 School Street, Cotuit. Open L (weekends only) and D. When you want to hang out with locals for a beer or mixed drink (and a great burger!), this friendly joint is the place. Blink and you'll miss it, because Cotuit only consists of four or five buildings. Even though it's been refurbished, it still feels divey—in a good way. $–$$.

SWEET TREATS & COFFEE **Amie Bakery** (508-428-1005; amiebakery.com), 1254 Main Street, Osterville. Open B, L. There's no denying that owner/baker Amie Smith knows her way around a kitchen. This small specialty bakery pumps out delicious pastries, breads, muffins, scones, pies and tarts, and cakes. She also makes hearty soups, sandwiches, and salads (with a yummy house cider vinaigrette). Accompany your morning coffee with her daily quiche or the savory McAmie (sausage, egg, and cheese on a cheddar biscuit). The Osterville Bomb (a cinnamon roll smothered in a generous portion of

SINFUL SCOOPS

Four Seas Ice Cream (508-775-1394; fourseasicecream.com), 360 South Main Street, at Centerville Four Corners. Founded in 1934, Four Seas is owned by Dick Warren, who took over from his father—who had owned it since 1960, when he bought it from the folks who had given him a summer job as a college student. Got that? The walls of this funky place, a former blacksmith's shop, are lined with photos of preppy summer crews, newspaper articles about Four Seas (it wins national ice cream awards every year), and poems penned in honor of past anniversaries. You can see that this place really inspires folks! It's named for the four "seas" that surround the Cape: Buzzards Bay, Cape Cod Bay, the Atlantic Ocean, and Nantucket Sound. Oh yes, about that ice cream: the Cape's best is made almost daily, using the freshest ingredients. The only downside: Every time I stopped by this past summer, it was way too melty and I had to gobble it down too quickly. Try the coconut or black raspberry. Lobster salad sandwiches are great, too. Really great. 🏅 ❄ 🚀

glaze) is to-die-for. Amie also offers baking lessons with classes like how to make bagels from scratch or piping skills using a mum tip, for example. My only minor complaint is the limited seating. $–$$.

Nirvana Coffee Company (508-744-6983), 3206 Route 6A, Barnstable Village. What more can you ask for: strong coffee or green tea, a comfy vibe with pleasant service, breakfast sandwiches or gluten-free bagels, and some Adirondack chairs on the main drag when the weather is warm. $.

MARKETS **Barnstable Market** (508-362-4457; barnstableamarket.com), 3220 Main Street, across from the County Courthouse. This one-stop-shop opened in 2012, and folks couldn't be happier about it. Inside you will find everything from beer and wine to homemade soups, handmade pizzas, burgers, subs and more.

❄ **Cotuit Fresh Market** (508-428-6936; cotuitfreshmarket.com), 737 Main Street, Cotuit. This old multiuse building would go unnoticed in Vermont, but on the Cape, it's an anomaly. It's a convenience store–wine shop–grill–fruit and veggie market.

Fancy's Market (508-428-6954; fancysmarket.com), 699 Main Street, Osterville. This cozy, gourmet market is not only full of delicious foods, pantry staples, and such, but it is also full of rich history. Not only is the 176-year-old building nationally registered as "historic," but the store itself has been in existence since the early 19th century, when it was founded by Captain Harvey Scudder and his brother Erastus. (See also *Farms* under **Selective Shopping**.)

❋ Entertainment

Barnstable Comedy Club (508-362-6333; barnstablecomedyclub.org), 3171 Route 6A, across from the Barnstable Restaurant and Tavern, Barnstable Village. Performances November through May. Let's get something straight right off the bat—this is not an actual comedy club! Founded in 1922, the state's oldest amateur theater group performs more than comedies in this 200-seat theater—look for musicals and straight (though not heavy or provocative) theater. Since 1922 its motto has been "To produce good plays and remain amateurs." (Kurt Vonnegut got his feet wet here and was the club's first president.) $$$. No credit cards.

❋ Selective Shopping

❋ All shops are open year-round unless otherwise noted. Osterville center, with a number of upscale shops, is good for a short stroll.

ANTIQUES **Harden Studios** (508-362-7711; hardenstudios.com), 3264 Route 6A, Barnstable Village. This late-17th-century house was beautifully restored by Charles M. Harden in the mid-1990s and now functions as an antiques shop and gallery. It's a true family affair: Harden's son, Charles, operates an etching press and art gallery in the adjacent shed, and son Justin researches the fine antiques collection. The collection includes American antiques from the early 1700s to the 1840s; Empire and Federal pieces; and Oriental rugs, lamps, and chandeliers.

Sow's Ear Antiques (508-428-4931; sowsearantiqueco.com), 4698 Falmouth Road, Route 28 at Route 130, Cotuit. Americana and primitive folk art and furniture sold from an 18th-century house; some garden antiques, too.

Cotuit Antiques (508-420-1234), 70 Industry Road, behind Cotuit Landing off Route 28, Cotuit. Henry Frongillo enjoys people and keeping his shop folksy. Since he buys whole estates, you never know what you'll find. Primarily, though, he offers fine furniture, collectibles, some art, pottery, and lots of great old signage and advertising memorabilia.

BOOKSTORES ❄ **Books by the Sea** (508-771-9400; booksbythesea.net), 1600 Falmouth Road, Bell Tower Mall, Centerville. Head here to indulge in the strong local book selection; it's small but great. Look for special events by Cape Cod authors, too.

FARMS **Osterville Farmers' Market** (ostervillefarmersmarket.org), 155 West Bay Road, at Osterville Historical Museum, every Friday from mid-June to mid-September.

GALLERIES **Harden Studios** (508-362-7711; hardenstudios.com), 3264 Route 6A, Barnstable Village. This late-17th-century house was beautifully restored by Charles M. Harden in the mid-1990s and now functions as an antiques shop and gallery. It's a true family affair: Harden's son, Charles, operates an etching press and art gallery in the adjacent shed, and son Justin researches the fine antiques collection. The collection includes American antiques from the early 1700s to the 1840s; Empire and Federal pieces; Oriental rugs, lamps, and chandeliers.

Cape Cod Art Association (508-362-2909; capecodartcenter.org), 3480 Route 6A, Barnstable Village. This nonprofit was founded in 1948 and displays a fine range of juried art and artists in a beautiful and airy gallery. Shows change monthly. Indoor and outdoor classes and workshops are offered.

Tao Water Art Gallery (508-375-0428; taowatergallery.com), 1989 Route 6A, West Barnstable. The offerings of this contemporary Asian gallery, representing more than 35 artists from post-Cultural Revolution China and the States, run the gamut from exceptional abstract painting to landscapes, sculpture, and Chinese contemporary art. At more than 5,600 square feet, one of the largest galleries on the Cape.

SPECIALTY **West Barnstable Tables** (508-362-2676; westbarnstabletables.com), 2454 Meetinghouse Way, Route 149, West Barnstable. This showroom features the work of a dozen or so master craftsmen and artists, including that of Dick Kiusalas. Because it's difficult (not to mention prohibitively expensive) to find antique tables anymore, Dick makes tables using salvaged 18th- and 19th-century wood. His creations are exquisite and worth admiring, even if you don't have a couple thousand dollars to spare. Less expensive pieces include primitive cupboards made with old painted wood and found objects, as well as Windsor and thumb-back chairs.

Margo's (508-428-5664; margoshome.com), 27 Wianno Avenue, Osterville.

WEST BARNSTABLE TABLES KIM GRANT

Unusual picture frames, serving pieces, furniture, home accessories, bed linens, gifts, and interior design services.

✱ Special Events

Mid-July: **Osterville Village Day** (talk to Gail at 508-420-4590). Third Saturday; includes a crafts and antiques fair, a road race, children's events, and a parade.

July 4: **Hyannis Village Parade**, Main Street, Hyannis.

Early July: **Fireworks** over Lewis Bay at dusk (usually the Saturday of Fourth of July weekend); view from Veterans Beach. The Cape Symphony Orchestra plays at Aselton Park before the display.

⚲ Late July: **Barnstable County Fair** (508-563-3200; barnstablecountyfair .org), Route 151, East Falmouth. Local and national music acts, a midway, livestock shows (including horse, ox, and pony pulls), and horticulture, cooking,

and craft exhibits and contests. A week-long tradition, especially for teens and families. $$.

Early-August: **Centerville Old Home Week** (centervilleoldhomeweek.com). Main Street open houses, art auctions, live music, and bonfire gatherings; until it was resurrected in the mid-1990s, this event hadn't been held for 90 years.

Mid-October: **Osterville Village Fall Festival Day** (508-420-4590). Wine tasting, entertainment, an antiques show, a dog show, and food. Typically held the Saturday after Columbus Day.

Mid-December: **Osterville Christmas Open House and Stroll** (508-420-4590). Since 1972, the village has gussied itself up with traditional decorations for New England's second-oldest stroll. Upward of 2,000 to 3,000 participate in Friday-evening festivities, which include music, hayrides, trolley rides, wine tastings, and more.

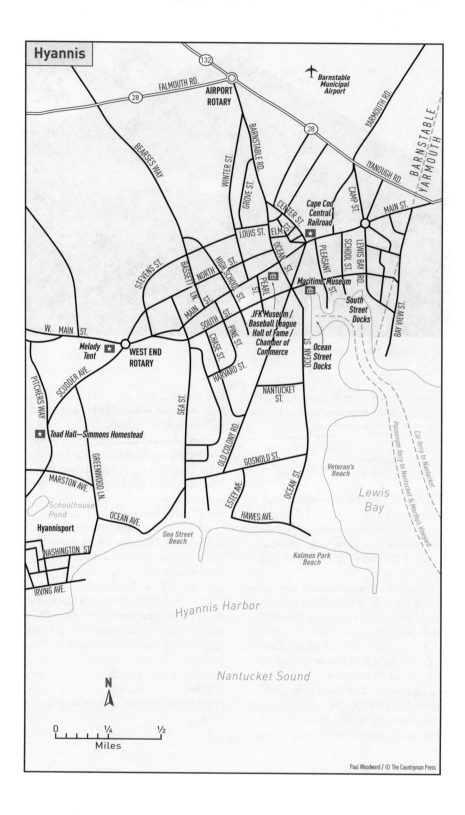

Hyannis

132

FALMOUTH RD.

28

AIRPORT ROTARY

Barnstable Municipal Airport

28

BARNSTABLE YARMOUTH

YARMOUTH RD.

Iyanough RD.

MAIN ST.

BEARSES WAY

WINTER ST.

BARNSTABLE RD.

GROVE ST.

CENTER ST.

CAMP ST.

Cape Cod Central Railroad

LEWIS BAY RD.

SCHOOL ST.

LOUIS ST.

ELM ST.

STEVENS ST.

BASSETT LN.

NORTH ST.

HIGH SCHOOL ST.

MAIN ST.

OCEAN ST.

PEARL ST.

PLEASANT

Maritime Museum

South Street Docks

BAY VIEW ST.

SOUTH ST.

PINE ST.

CHASE ST.

JFK Museum / Baseball League Hall of Fame / Chamber of Commerce

OCEAN ST.

Ocean Street Docks

W. MAIN ST.

Melody Tent

WEST END ROTARY

HARVARD ST.

NANTUCKET ST.

SCUDDER AVE.

PITCHERS WAY

SEA ST.

OLD COLONY RD.

GOSNOLD ST.

Veteran's Beach

Lewis Bay

Passenger ferry to Nantucket & Martha's Vineyard

Car ferry to Nantucket

Toad Hall—Simmons Homestead

GREENWOOD LN.

MARSTON AVE.

OCEAN AVE.

ESTEY AVE.

HAWES AVE.

OCEAN ST.

Schoolhouse Pond

Hyannisport

WASHINGTON ST.

Sea Street Beach

Kalmus Park Beach

IRVING AVE.

Hyannis Harbor

Nantucket Sound

N

0   ¼   ½

Miles

Paul Woodward / © The Countryman Press

HYANNIS

yannis is the Cape's commercial and transportation hub: Just under 1 million people take the ferry from Hyannis to Nantucket every year. Most Cape visitors end up in Hyannis at some point, whether by choice or by necessity.

Among Cape visitors, Hyannis seems to be everyone's favorite whipping post: a sigh of sympathy is heard when someone mentions he "has" to go into Hyannis in July or August. Yes, traffic is gnarly and Route 28 is overbuilt, but those same Cape residents and off-Cape visitors who moan about congestion in Hyannis couldn't live as easily without its services, including many fine restaurants. They come to buy new cars, embark to the islands, visit doctors, and shop at malls. Thus, because it is so distinct from the rest of Barnstable, I have given it its own chapter, even though Hyannis is technically one of Barnstable's seven villages.

Hyannis's **harborfront and Main Street** began to be revitalized in the 1990s, thanks in part to the encouragement of the late Ben Thompson, architect of Boston's Quincy Market shopping complex and other successful urban waterfront development projects. And it's received additional, phased face-lifts ever since. It's a downright pleasant place these days. Boating activity on Lewis Bay is active. Main Street is a study in contrasts: lined with benches and hanging flower baskets in an attempt to attract strollers, it also has lots of T-shirt shops, some vacant storefronts, and a growing crop of congregating youth and shops geared to them. (Hyannis is, after all, the closest thing to a "city" that the Cape has.) Look for the **Walkway to the Sea**—a nice, spiffy link between Main Street and the waterfront—and harborfront "shacks" from which artists sell their goods.

Hyannis has a bit of everything: discount outlets, upward of 50 eating establishments *in the waterfront district alone*, some quiet cottages and guest houses, plenty of motels geared toward overnight visitors waiting for the morning ferry, harbor tours, and lots of lively bars and nightlife.

Then there's the Kennedy mystique. **Hyannisport**—a neighborhood within

HYANNIS ABOUNDS WITH MYSTERY AND CHARM
KATY WARD

WHERE TO START IN HYANNIS

Morning: Enjoy breakfast at the Daily Paper, or grab coffee and pastries from Pain D'Avignon and indulge beneath a rare 200-year-old weeping beech tree.

Afternoon: Discover Camelot at the JFK Hyannis Museum, or stroll through the Artist Shanties at Bismore Park. Enjoy lunch at Spanky's Clam Shack on the harbor or opt for an afternoon football game, wings, and cold beer at DJ's.

Evening: Enjoy a quality meal at the Naked Oyster then head to the Cape Cod Melody Tent for a live performance.

HYANNIS HARBOR KATY WARD

Hyannis but quite distinct from Hyannis—will forever be remembered as the place where, in the early 1960s, President John F. Kennedy and his wife, Jacqueline, sailed offshore and played with Caroline and John. Visitors who come in search of the "Kennedy compound," or in hopes of somehow experiencing the Kennedy aura, will find only an inaccessible, residential, Yankee-style community of posh estates.

Lastly, let's talk historical perspective for a paragraph or two. Hyannis's harbor area was inhabited about 1,000 years ago by ancestors of the Eastern Algonquian peoples, who set up summer campsites south of what is now Ocean Street. The first European to reach Cape Cod, Bartholomew Gosnold, anchored in the harbor in 1602. Shortly thereafter, settlers persuaded American Indian sachem Yanno to sell them what is now known as Hyannis and Centerville for £20 and two pairs of pants.

Main Street was laid out in 1750, and by the early 1800s Hyannis was already known as the Cape's transportation hub. The harbor bustled with two- and three-masted schooners. When the steam-train line was extended from Barnstable in 1854, land-based trade and commerce supplanted the marine-based economy. Tourists began arriving in much greater numbers by the end of the 19th century. Yachts filled the harbor by the 1930s and continued to do so until John Kennedy (who tied up at the Hyannisport Yacht Club) renewed popular interest in traditional local sailboats, known as catboats, in the 1950s.

GUIDANCE ❄ **Greater Hyannis Chamber of Commerce** (508-775-2201; hyannis.com), 367 Main Street.

GETTING THERE *By car:* To reach Hyannis, about 30 minutes from the Cape Cod Canal, take Exit 6 off Route 6; follow Route 132 south to the airport rotary (at the junction of Routes 28 and 132). Take the second right off the rotary onto Barnstable Road, which intersects with Main, Ocean, and South Streets (for the harbor).

By bus: The **Plymouth & Brockton** bus line (508-746-0378; p-b.com) connects Hyannis with other Cape towns, as well as with Boston's Logan Airport. **Bonanza/Peter Pan** (888-751-8800; peterpanbus.com) connects Hyannis to Providence, T. F. Green Airport, and New York City. Both buses operate out of the Hyannis Transportation Center at Center and Main Streets.

❄ *By air:* **Barnstable Municipal Airport** (508-775-2020), at the rotary junction of Route 28 and Route 132, Hyannis. Small carriers serving Hyannis include **Cape Air** (508-771-6944; capeair.com) and **Nantucket Air** (800-227-3247; nantucketairlines.org)

GETTING AROUND *By car:* Hyannis suffers from serious summer traffic problems. Parking on Main Street is free if you can get a space. If not, try North Street, one block north of Main Street and parallel to it. Main Street (one-way) is geared toward strolling, but it's a long walk from end to end.

By rental: Call the big agencies based at the airport: **Hertz** (508-775-5825; hertz .com), **Avis** (508-775-2888; avis.com), and **Budget** (508-771-4734; budget.com). **Thrifty** (508-771-0450; thrifty.com) is across from the airport. **Trek** (508-771-2459; trekrentacar .com) is near the bus terminal, but they'll pick you up from the airport.

By shuttle and trolley: The **Hyannis Area Trolley** (508-385-1430; capecodtransit.org) operates from mid-May to early September. It starts at the **Hyannis Transportation Center** (800-352-7155; capecodtransit.org), 215 Iyannough Road, and makes a big loop, passing by all the popular destinations. Take the **Sealine** for connections in Barnstable, Mashpee, Falmouth, and Woods Hole, or the **H2O** line that travels on Route 28 to Orleans daily in summer ($).

GETTING TO THE ISLANDS From Hyannis, there is year-round auto and passenger service to Nantucket and seasonal passenger service to Martha's Vineyard. For complete information, see *Getting There* in "Martha's Vineyard" and "Nantucket." You can also fly to the islands.

MEDIA The daily *Cape Cod Times* (508-775-1200; capecodonline.com) is published in Hyannis (319 Main Street).

PUBLIC RESTROOMS At beaches (see **Green Space**), behind the JFK Hyannis Museum on Main Street, and at the Ocean Street Docks (Bismore Park).

PUBLIC LIBRARY ❄ ✎ ☂ **Hyannis Public Library** (508-775-2280; hyannislibrary.org), 401 Main Street. This charming little house has a much larger facility tacked onto the rear.

EMERGENCIES **Barnstable Police Department** (508-775-0387; barnstablepolice .com), 1200 Phinney's Lane, or call **911.**

Medical: **Cape Cod Hospital** (508-771-1800; capecodhealth.org), 27 Park Street. Open 24/7.

✳ To See

John F. Kennedy Hyannis Museum (508-790-3077; jfkhyannismuseum.org), 397 Main Street. Open mid-February through December. This museum opened in the early 1990s to meet the demands of visitors making the pilgrimage to Hyannis in search of JFK. People wanted to see "something," so the chamber gave them a museum that focuses on JFK's time in Hyannisport and on Cape Cod. The museum features more than 100 photographs of Kennedy from 1931 to 1963, arranged in themes: JFK's friends, JFK's family, JFK the man. He said, "I always go to Hyannisport to be revived, to know the power of the sea and the master who rules over it and all of us." (If you want to *really* learn something about the president and his administration, head to the JFK Museum in Boston.) A statue of JFK, sculpted by native-Cape-Codder David Lewis, graces the front of the museum.

JFK Memorial, Ocean Street. The fountain, behind a large presidential seal mounted on a high stone wall, is inscribed: I BELIEVE IT IS IMPORTANT THAT THIS COUNTRY SAIL AND NOT SIT STILL IN THE HARBOR. There is a nice view of Lewis Bay from here.

Kennedy Compound. Joe and Rose Kennedy rented the Malcolm Cottage in Hyannisport from 1926 to 1929 before purchasing and remodeling it to include 14 rooms, nine baths, and a private movie theater in the basement. (It was the first private theater in New England.) By 1932 there were nine children scampering around the house and grounds, which included a private beach, dock, tennis court, and pool. In 1956, then Senator John Kennedy purchased an adjacent house at the corner of Scudder and Irving Avenues, which came to be known as the "Summer White House." Bobby bought the house next door, which now belongs to his widow, Ethel. Senator Edward Kennedy's former house (it now belongs to his ex-wife Joan) is on private Squaw Island. Eunice (Kennedy) and Sargent Shriver purchased a nearby home on Atlantic Avenue.

JFK MEMORIAL KIM GRANT

RIDING THE RAILS

Cape Cod Central Railroad (508-771-3800; capetrain.com), 252 Main Street. Trips late May to late October. The 48-mile trip takes 2 hours and passes cranberry bogs, the Sandy Neck Great Salt Marsh, and the Cape Cod Canal. Because there are typically two trains daily, you take the first one, hop off in Sandwich, walk into the picturesque village (it's about a 10-minute walk), and then catch the next train back to Hyannis. The best part of this trip is the local narration—unless you've never been on a train before, in which case, the simple act of taking a train will tickle you more. Personally, I would fork out the extra cash for their dinner train, which includes a five-course meal served on white table linen in traditional rail style. Sip wine by soft candlelight as you transport yourself back in time on this 3-hour ride. The Sunday brunch train is also popular for families with children. $$$.

KATY WARD

It was at Malcolm Cottage that JFK learned he'd been elected president; at Malcolm Cottage that Jacqueline and the president mourned the loss of their infant son; at Malcolm Cottage that the family mourned the deaths of the president and Bobby Kennedy; at Malcolm Cottage that Sen. Edward Kennedy would annually present his mother with a rose for each of her years; at Malcolm Cottage that matriarch Rose Kennedy died in 1995 at the age of 104; and at Malcolm Cottage in 2009 where the clan gathered to transport Senator Kennedy's body from his beloved Cape Cod to services at the JFK Library in Boston (before he was interred in Arlington Cemetery in Washington, D.C., next to his brothers). In 2012 the Marchant house was donated to the Edward M. Kennedy Institute for the US Senate, with plans to open it to the public.

Although Kennedy sightings are rare, the Kennedys are still Hyannis's No. 1 "attraction."

If you drive or walk around this stately area, you'll see nothing but high hedges and fences. Those who can't resist a look-see will be far better off taking a boat tour (see **To Do**); some boats come quite close to the shoreline and the white frame houses.

RARE SPECIMENS

KIM GRANT

Weeping beech trees. In the courtyard behind 605 Main Street (Hyannis) and in the front yard of an inn on Route 6A (Barnstable; pictured here). To the town of Hyannis' knowledge, these specimens represent two of the seven remaining weeping beech trees in the entire country. They are awesome, magnificent, 200-plus-year-old beauties.

St. Francis Xavier Church, 347 South Street. Members of Rose Kennedy's clan worshiped here when they were in town. The pew used by JFK is marked with a plaque, while the altar is a memorial to JFK's brother, Lt. Joe Kennedy Jr., killed during World War II.

❋ **Cape Cod Maritime Museum** (508-775-1723; capecodmaritimemuseum.org), 135 South Street. Open mid-March to mid-December. This harborfront museum offers interactive exhibits, lectures, and classes in ship model making, maritime archaeology, and boatbuilding. It also displays boats that illuminate the region's past, present, and forthcoming connections with the sea. After the traditional catboat *Sarah* was built on the premises (quite a production), she was launched in Lewis Bay in 2007 and set out on excursions from ports between Chatham and Woods Hole. Don't miss a chance to go on 90-minute cruises with her (Thursday through Saturday, $$$). Museum $.

❋ ✐ ⵟ **Cape Cod Potato Chip Factory** (508-775-3358; capecodchips.com), 100 Breed's Hill Road, Independence Park, off Route 132. After Chatham resident Steve Bernard began the company in 1980 and parlayed it into a multimillion-dollar business, he sold it to corporate giant Anheuser-Busch and moved on to the business of purveying Chatham Village Croutons. But in the mid-1990s, when Anheuser-Busch wanted to sell or close it, Bernard bought the company back, saving about 100 year-round jobs. (Now it's owned by Lance, Inc., another snack manufacturer.) Take the 15-minute self-guided tour of the potato-chip-making process, then sample the rich flavor and high crunchability resulting from all-natural ingredients cooked in small kettles. Free.

Cape Cod Beer (508-790-4200; capecodbeer.com), 1336 Phinneys Lane. This microbrewery bills itself as a community space; think Friday farmers' market meets local happy hour. It has super informative tours and tastings, live music at times, fun games all the time, and a beer garden (i.e., a roped-off section of a parking lot when it's not indoors during inclement weather). All in all, people enjoy themselves here.

Town green, adjacent to the JFK Hyannis Museum. Note the life-sized bronze of the sachem Iyanough, chief of the Mattakeese tribe of Cummaquid and friend to the Pilgrims, created by Osterville sculptor David Lewis.

❋ **Toad Hall—Classic Sports Car Collection at the Simmons Homestead Inn** (508-778-4934; toadhallcars.com), 288 Scudder Avenue. Bill Putman relishes his quirkiness, and it's on full display here with an impressive collection of classic red sports cars—45 at last count. They're packed into a low-slung, garage-style barn, complete with fake Oriental carpets lining the gravel pathways between the cars. $.

✳ To Do

BASEBALL ⚓ The **Hyannis Harbor Hawks of the Cape Cod Baseball League** (cape codbaseball.org) plays from mid-June to early August under the lights at McKeon Park. (Take South Street to High School Road and turn right.)

BICYCLING & RENTALS The Hyannis Port bicycle trail is a short (10-mile) scenic ride from Hyannis Port to Craigville Beach. For easy access park at the Veterans Park Beach lot on Ocean Street. Check bike trails in nearby towns, too. You can rent bicycles and equipment at the **Bike Zone** (508-775-3299; bikezonecapecod.com), 323 Barnstable Road; or **Sea Sports** (508-790-1217; capecodseasports.com), 1441 Iyannough Road.

BOAT EXCURSIONS & RENTALS Lewis Bay and Hyannis Harbor are beautiful, and the best way to appreciate them is by water. Pine Island Cove is a great place to anchor up and swim, as well as off Egg Island, a sandbar that appears for 3 hours during low tide.

 All Cape Boat Rentals (508-827-2001; allcapeboatrentals.com), 177 Pleasant Street, at Baxter's Boathouse (see also under **Where to Eat**). Be your own personal tour guide and rent one these luxury boats. Choose your ideal watercraft: a Pontoon boat with capacity for up to 12 people; a bow rider built for relaxation available in various sizes, the largest being 21 feet in length, with capacity for up to 10 people; or a center console boat, perfect for watersports and fishing with its powerful motor and sturdy shape. Regardless of the boat, you will surely enjoy steaming around the harbor, relaxing in the sun and cooling off with a dip, or enjoying a picnic on the water. You can also rent tubes and waterskies. All boats are equipped with fishing rod holders, but you will need to bring your own equipment. $$$$+.

 ⚓ **Hyannis Harbor Cruises** (508-790-0696; hylinecruises.com), 220 Ocean Street. Trips Mid-April to mid-October. If you're like 85,000 other visitors each season and want the best possible view of the Kennedy compound, take this hour-long Hy-Line excursion. The boat comes within 500 feet of the compound's shoreline, which is closer than you can get by foot or car. $$.

 ⚓ **Pirate Adventures** (508-394-9100; capecodpirateadventures.com), 180 Ocean Street. Trips mid-June to early September. Particularly fun for children, this swash-buckling trip begins with face painting on the dock. Then kids sign on as the pirate ship's crew, take a pirate oath, search for sunken treasure, and fire water cannons against renegade pirates. On the return voyage, the booty is shared and pirates cele-brate with song and dance. $$$.

FISHING There are plenty of options in Hyannis when it comes to fishing. Troll the Atlantic for huge "cow" stripers along the coastline, or head offshore for bigger game. If you're just after some tasty food, you're in for a treat. It's called Cape *Cod* after all. Procure freshwater and saltwater fishing licenses and regulations online at (mass.gov/eea/agencies/dfg/licensing).

 Big game: ✳ *Helen H* **Deep Sea Fishing** (508-790-0660; helen-h.com), 137 Pleasant Street. This 100-foot, all-aluminum super-cruiser has a spacious cabin with cushioned

SLIP INTO HYANNIS HARBOR

Hyannis Marina (508-790-4000; hyannismarina.com), 1 Willow Street. Hyannis Harbor is beautiful, well protected, and one of the few natural deep harbors on Cape Cod. With over 180 slips, this resort marina can accommodate everything from small motorboats to deep draft sailboats to megayachts up to 200 feet long. Boat owners will be pleased with the marina's long list of amenities, while others will simply enjoy strolling down the finger piers and admiring the deluxe watercraft. This busy homeport is where you board for sightseeing tours, ferry boats, sportfishing charters, sailing, and more. The harbor also provides shelter for a bustling commercial fishing fleet. Not interested in water activities? The marina has two popular restaurants nearby, **Trader Ed's** and **Tugboats** (see under **Where to Eat**). Those renting dockage space get access to their large heated outdoor pool.

KATY WARD

seating and a full galley bar; a large upper sundeck for catching some rays; and resting bunks for multiday anglers. $$$$+.

Hy-Line Fishing Trips (508-790-0696; hylinecruises.com), Ocean Street Docks. Choose from bottom fishing charters or the "Captain's Choice" for sea bass, blues and flounder. $$$$+.

Predatuna Sportfishing (508-648-8411; predatunasportfishing), 110 School Street. Whether you want to catch jumbo porgies in the spring, bass and blues in the summer, or codfish in the early and late winter, Predatuna has you covered. As the name implies, bluefin tuna charters are also available. $$$$+.

By jetty: In early spring you might find black sea bass in the waters off the

Hyannisport Jetty, or some schoolie stripers in summer. Watch your step—it's a challenge hike along the rocks.

Supplies: ❋ **Sports Port Bait & Tackle** (508-775-3096; sportsport.us), 149 West Main Street. Surely you've seen the statue of a yellow guy in a red rowboat? That means the store is open. References for charters and tours; supplies for freshwater, saltwater, and fly-fishing; shellfish permits; and ice fishing details, too.

FOR FAMILIES **Hyannis Youth & Community Center** (508-790-6345; townofbarn stable.us/hycc), 141 Bassett Lane. A premier sports complex with twin ice-skating rinks, a gymnasium, and an indoor walking track, as well as a pro-shop, a game room, a computer lab, and more.

Island Carousel (508-771-0489; simon.com/cape-cod-mall), 796 Iyannough Road, near the food court in the Cape Cod Mall. Take a spin on this old-fashioned carousel. $.

GOLF ❋ **Hyannis Golf Course** (508-362-2606; barnstablegolf.com), Route 132, and ❋ **Twin Brooks Golf Course** (508-862-6980; twinbrooksgolf.net), 35 Scudder Avenue, offer challenging green.

SHANTIES **Artist Shanties** (508-862-4678; hyartsdistrict.com), 180 Ocean Street in Bismore Park and 51 Ocean Street at the harbor overlook. Open late May through September. Taking a page out of the playbook of Nantucket's waterfront area, these little shacks are occupied by juried artists. Mediums vary from watercolors and pastels to tapestries and jewelry to calligraphy and photography. It really livens up the area, whether or not you're waiting for a ferry.

TENNIS Public courts are located at **Barnstable High School** off West Main Street.

❋ Green Space

BEACHES Hyannis is not especially known for its beaches, but there are a couple that you might find enjoyable. Parking stickers are required and can be purchased in-person at the Hyannis Youth & Community Center (see *For Families* under *To Do*). $$.

Kalmus Park Beach, at the end of Ocean Street on Nantucket Sound. This beach is good for sailboarding. (Fun fact: The land was donated by Technicolor inventor, Herbert Kalmus, who also owned the Fernbrook estate in Centerville.) Facilities include a restroom, a picnic area, lifeguards, a snack bar, and a bathhouse.

🐾 **Veterans Beach**, on Hyannis Harbor (Lewis Bay), off Ocean Street. Fairly shallow calm water makes this beach ideal for children. It's also a great spot to watch sailboats because the Hyannis Yacht Club is next door. Facilities include a restroom, bathhouse, lifeguards, a snack bar, swings, grills, and a big wooded area with picnic tables.

PONDS & WALKS 🌳 **Hathaway Pond**, 1431 Phinneys Lane. A small pond with warm clear water and a decently sized sandy beach. The casual 1-mile loop around the pond takes about 30 to 45 minutes, with easily identifiable trail markers. There's also a newly renovated dog park that tends to be crowded.

Veterans Memorial Park, Hyannis Port. Along with the sentiment of the Veterans Memorial, this oceanfront park delivers panoramic views of the harbor, as well as manicured lawns, gardens, benches, and a small water fountain.

MAKING MEMORIES: THE MACRINOS

As a Connecticut resident, my family and I have fallen in love with Cape Cod. While my husband, two small children, and myself enjoy the tranquil shores of Truro, we also love the bustle of Hyannis. During one of our annual trips we discovered a true gem: The Cape Codder—a 30,000 square-foot hotel with an indoor/outdoor water park, situated in the heart of Hyannis. As a family we have a strict 2- to 30-hour drive rule, and this definitely fit the criteria. The Codder (as my kids call it) quickly became a place for our family to make memories. During our first stay, we bought a package for the "Pirates and Princesses Weekend," which included a themed dance and live shows for all the kiddos. The waterpark itself is something to be seen, and the whole experience is a fraction of the costs of similar waterpark resorts we had looked into. My husband enjoys the lazy river just as much as my nine-year-old son!

Another rule we have for our small family getaways is that we have options for food! After our 10-plus vacations at the Codder, we have come to find some favorite spots. We never leave Hyannis without eating at DJ's (see under **Where to Eat**). It is the ultimate sports bar, with a little something for everyone. The fact that you are literally eating inside an old train car is pretty fun! The food is fantastic and still voted the best wings our family has ever had! The Tiki Port has also become a family tradition. Besides the delicious authentic food (and leftovers for days), the atmosphere is just as special to us. My husband and son are avid tiki mug collectors, which you'd better believe they sell at the counter. And, in a world of dying malls, it wouldn't be a trip to Hyannis without a ride on the carousel at the Cape Cod Mall.

✱ Lodging

Hyannis has hordes of nondescript motels and many good family-oriented cottages. If you want a good bed-and-breakfast, stay in one of Barnstable's other villages.

RESORTS & HOTELS **Anchor In** (508-775-0357; anchorin.com), 1 South Street, on Hyannis Harbor. This charming hotel gets rave reviews for its bed-and-breakfast-like atmosphere and waterfront location. Perched on a hill at the water's edge of Hyannis Harbor, guests will enjoy watching ferries, fishing boats, and pleasure yachts cruise around the harbor from the comfort of their private balcony. Each of the 42 guest rooms comes equipped with plush bedding and the works. Enjoy the daily and delicious continental breakfast in the sunroom or poolside. The fire pit is also a nice choice for cooler summer nights. Hats off to owners Skip and Lisa, who truly run a flawless operation. $$–$$$$.

Cape Codder Resort & Spa (508-771-3000; capecodderresort.com), 1225 Route 132 Iyannough Road. Just a few miles from the center of town, this two-story destination property is owned by the Catania family (who have long owned the Dan'l Webster Inn in Sandwich and the family-style Hearth & Kettle restaurants), and they have poured millions into the Cape Codder. This ultra-family-friendly resort has 257 rooms, two indoor/outdoor waterparks complete with a 10,000 square-foot wave pool, four waterslides (two 160-foot high-speed slides and two 50- to 80-foot slides that wind through a pirate ship replica), and a continuous lazy river with waterfalls, rapids, and spouting whales. The resort also has a spa, two restaurants, a wine bar, a large fitness center, a game room, and tennis. (See also "Making Memories: The Macrinos" above.) $–$$$.

COTTAGES 🐾 🞗 **Harbor Village** (508-775-7581; harborvillage.com), 160 Marston Avenue. Open May to mid-October. Delightfully off the beaten path but still

HYANNIS PORT KIM GRANT

centrally located, these 20 private cottages are set on a private, wooded, 17-acre compound with a mere 2-minute walk to Quahog Beach. Cottages include a living room, dining area, fully equipped kitchen, dishwasher, fireplace, a deck or patio with a grill, and in some cases laundry service. Bring your own towels and beach chairs. $$–$$$.

❋ ✿ **Capt. Gosnold Village** (508-775-9111; captaingosnold.com), 230 Gosnold Street. This small village of boutique cottages sits on 4 acres of quiet residential property and is just a few minutes' walk from three beaches. The home-away-from-home accommodations include: one-, two-, and three-bedroom cottages as well as studio units. Kids will enjoy the wooded and grassy grounds with a fenced-in saltwater pool (heated, too), lifeguard, lawn games, and a play area. And parents will be at ease watching their kids play from the cottage's private deck. All have fully equipped kitchens and are comfortably furnished. $$–$$$$.

❋ Where to Eat

With more than 150 eateries around town, Hyannis offers everything from mod seafood to romantic Italian. Unless otherwise noted, all restaurants are open year-round.

DINING OUT ❋ ✿ **Alberto's Ristorante** (508-778-1770; albertos.net), 360 Main Street. Open L, D. Thanks to chef/owner Felis Barreiro, Alberto's has been catering to a loyal following since 1984. Elegant and romantic, done up with faux marble and off-white colors, it may look formal but without the stuffiness. The service is delightfully professional. The extensive and consistently fabulous Northern Italian menu features large portions of homemade pasta and regional specialties. Despite not having room, I still top off my meal with a rich cappuccino and a decadent dessert. Sidewalk tables are pleasant in the summer, and a jazz pianist draws diners on Friday and Saturday nights year-round. $$–$$$$.

❋ ▼ **Black Cat Tavern** (508-778-1233; blackcattavern.com), 165 Ocean Street. Open L, D. Local restaurateur Dave Colombo runs the Black Cat, an upscale-casual tavern located on the dock of Hyannis Harbor. Enjoy fresh seafood dishes and specialty cocktails as you watch sailboats cruise by. Casual gets kicked up a notch with the likes of pan-seared diver scallops with a Parmesan risotto, and the sesame seared tuna. The lobster bake, burgers, and grilled steak tips are also nice options. Stick around for a drink in the piano lounge and sway to the rhythm of live music. $–$$$.

❈ **Brazilian Grill** (508-771-0109; braziliangrillrestaurants.com), 680 Main Street. Open L, D. Using recipes passed down from generations, this family-owned restaurant delivers a truly authentic Brazilian culinary experience. The main attraction is the *churrascaria rodizio*, a traditional barbecue served tableside by gauchos who carefully carve up skewers of seasoned beef, chicken, pork, and lamb. Accompany your protein with a selection of Brazilian sides from the full-course salad bar. Did I mention it's all you can eat? Come hungry or don't bother. $$$–$$$$.

❈ ♈ **Naked Oyster** (508-778-6500; nakedoyster.com), 410 Main Street. Open L, D, year-round. This contemporary French-style bistro offers supreme culinary creations by executive chef Florence Lowell, a French native who grew up on the shoreline near Bordeaux. Start with primo appetizers like octopus and grilled watermelon, Cape Cod blonde mussels, or the house French country pâté. For the main event, choose puffed duck soup, fig mascarpone ravioli in a light lemon cream sauce, lobster risotto, or the 18-ounce cast-iron sirloin dressed in a Mezcal tomato sauce. Oyster aficionados will surely relish the farm-to-table (literally) Barnstable Harbor oysters, which are grown in the Northwest portion of the harbor near Sandy Neck. Leave room for dessert because Chef Lowell's *chocolat liegeios* (chocolate mousse layered with espresso) and crème brûlée are first-class. $–$$$$.

❈ **Pain D'Avignon** (508-778-8588; paindavignon.com), 15 Hinckley Road. Open B, L, D. Hidden off the beaten path, this exquisite French bakery, café, and gourmet restaurant is absolutely worth seeking out. From rustic breads, bagels, and home-baked crackers to café sandwiches like the open-faced Croque Monsieur layered with black forest ham and Gruyere. The French dinner fare—coquilles St. Jacques, steak frites, and crème brûlée—is excellent too. I often stop here for coffee and my family's favorite raspberry streusel, but it rarely survives the ride home. $–$$$$.

EATING OUT **Bangkok Kitchen** (508-771-2333), 339 Barnstable Road. Open L, D. This true hole-in-the-wall eatery has some of the best authentic Thai cuisine on the Cape (and believe me, I've searched high and low). While the food is grand in flavor, the family-owned operation has maybe eight tables total. Dine inside the tiny hideaway among delicate Asian dinnerware or take it to go. I've never disliked anything I've ordered, and my favorites include the chicken satay served with two dipping sauces: peanut and sweet cucumber, Tom Yum Goong (a soup with coconut milk, lemon grass, lime juice, mushrooms and shrimp), Pad Thai or Pad Kee Mao (a wide flat noodle in a decently spicy sauce), any of the curries, and the signature Bangkok Duck. Top it off with their decadent fried banana and homemade ice cream. It's also BYOB. $–$$.

DJ'S FAMILY SPORTS PUB KATY WARD

DJ's Family Sports Pub (508-775-9464; djsfamouswings.com), 165 Yarmouth Road. Open L, D. A sports bar inside a renovated train car. $$.

Y **Embargo** (508-771-9700; embargo restaurant.com), 453 Main Street. This modern lounge/bar is a popular spot for the 20-something crowd. The menu specializes in hand-tossed pizzas, tapas, sushi, and martinis. Enjoy live music and DJs on most nights. $$.

Tugboats (508-775-6433; tugboats capecod.com), 11 Arlington Street. Open L, D. Technically this restaurant is in West Yarmouth, but it overlooks Hyannis Harbor and most locals think it is in Hyannis, so I'm sticking with it. This is a bit of a tourist trap, but it does have water views and so-so food. $$–$$$.

Y **Trader Ed's** (508-790-8686; trader edsrestaurant.com), 21 Arlington Street. Open L, D, Mid-April to Mid-October. A popular Hyannis beach bar with frozen drinks and DJ-spun dance parties directly on the Hyannis Harbor. The food's pretty good too, especially after a few drinks. $$$.

Tiki Port (508-771-5220; tikiport .com), 714 Iyannough Road. Open L, D, and late night. This long-time purveyor of Chinese and Polynesian cuisine gets mixed reviews but, in the end, if you're craving lo-mein or boneless pork ribs, this is where to go in Hyannis. $$.

❊ **Common Ground Café** (508-778-8390; hyanniscommonground.com), 420 Main Street. Open L, D. When you step inside, let your eyes adjust to the darkness for a minute, and you'll find hand-hewn booths resembling hobbit houses and an old-fashioned community (a religious collective, actually) of folks serving honest food. The menu includes a few wholesome sandwiches and wraps, soups, salads, and daily specials. Everything is made from scratch. There is also a juice bar upstairs. $.

❊ ✐ **Sam Diego's** (508-771-8816; samdiegos.com), 950 Route 132. Open L, D. Decorated with lights, colorful serapes, toucans, and sombreros, this huge cantina-style restaurant is great for families. Enjoy extremely large portions of Mexican-inspired dishes from fajitas, burritos, enchiladas, and tacos. Not great food, but not terrible either. $–$$.

Spanky's Clam Shack (508-771-2770; spankysclamshack.com), 138 Ocean Street, on Hyannis Harbor. Open L, D, mid-April to mid-October. Directly on the harbor, this casual seafood place is the best of the fry bunch. Portions are huge, the prices are right, and you have a choice of inside or outside dining. Service can be the toughest thing to digest here. $$–$$$.

Baxter's (508-775-7040; baxters capecod.com), 177 Pleasant Street. Open L, D, mid-April to mid-October. Built on an old fish-packing dock near the Steamship Authority terminal, Baxter's has attracted a crowd since 1956, from beautiful people tying up at the dock to singles meeting at the bar and families who don't mind eating on paper plates on a harbor front picnic table. $$–$$$.

SWEET TREATS & COFFEE

The West End (508-775-7677; westend hyannis.com), 20 Scudder Avenue. Open for brunch on Sundays. This glam-meets-speakeasy restaurant is known for its dinner service, but it's their Sunday Jazz Brunch that I prefer. It's not cheap, but you get your money's worth at the make-your-own omelets and prime rib carving stations. The eggs Benedict and homemade Bloody Marys are pretty good, too. Wake up slow as you dine to the serenades of a rotating jazz lineup. $$$.

The Daily Paper (508-790-8800; dailypapercapecod.com), 644 West Main Street. Open B, L. This is by far my favorite place to have breakfast in Hyannis. The extremely casual diner-style atmosphere and comforting American classics menu make for an easy breakfast whether you're alone, with a spouse, or as a family. $–$$.

✤ ✦ **Spoon and Seed** (774-470-4634; spoonandseed.com), 12 Thornton Drive. Open B, L. From the hash and grits to cheesy biscuits and eggs Benny, you really can't go wrong. $–$$.

ICE CREAM **Katie's Ice Cream** (508-771-6889; katiesicecreamcapecod.com), 570 Main Street. Open mid-April to early September. Everyone seems to end up at this little shop sometime during the day or night for homemade scoops.

DINNER TRAIN See "Riding the Rails" on page 123.

✤ Entertainment

CONCERTS ✦ **Cape Symphony Orchestra** (508-362-1111; capesymphony.org), 744 West Main Street. The orchestra performs about 15 concerts for children and adults at the 1,400-seat Barnstable High School.

Enjoy **free concerts** (hyannismain street.com) on Thursday and Friday summer evenings on Main Street.

MOVIES ✤ 📽 **Regal Cape Cod Mall** (844-462-7342; regmovies.com), 793 Route 132 at intersection with Route 28.

NIGHTLIFE 🍸 The **Quarterdeck Lounge** (508-771-8850), 247 Iyannough Road, and **Duck Inn Pub** (508-827-7343), 447 Main Street, are both lively watering holes. True down-and-dirty local dives, if you dare. (See also **Cape Cod Beer** under **To Do**.)

✤ Selective Shopping

There are plenty of shopping outlets in Hyannis, most of which are open year-round.

BOOKSTORES **Barnes & Noble** (508-862-6310), Cape Cod Mall, Route 132, north of the airport rotary.

CLOTHING **Plush & Plunder** (508-775-4467; plushandplunder.com), 605 Main Street. Vintage and eccentric used clothing adorns those marching to an offbeat drummer, including fabled customers

HYANNIS KIM GRANT

STARSTRUCK

Cape Cod Melody Tent (508-775-5630; melodytent.org), 21 West Main Street. Shows June through early September. When this big white tent with a revolving stage was erected in 1950, entertainment was limited to Broadway musicals. Today, despite the occasionally less-than-perfect sound and acoustics (but still pretty good), it's the Cape's biggest and best venue for top-name musicians. Look for the likes of Chicago, Bonnie Raitt, ZZ Top, Shawn Colvin, Melissa Etheridge, Tony Bennett, Julio Iglesias, and Lyle Lovett. It's only "big" by Cape standards; you'll be surprised how close you are to your favorite stars here—about 20 rows max. That translates to about 50 feet.

CAPE COD MELODY TENT KATY WARD

like Cyndi Lauper, Joan Baez, and Demi Moore. You don't have to be an entertainer to shop here, although you'll end up entertained and entertaining (if you purchase something) while searching for gold lamé, a boa, or other retro accessories. Don't miss this place.

FARMS **Cape Cod Beer Farmers' Market** (capecodbeer.com/event/farmers market), 1336 Phinneys Lane, Hyannis, every Friday mid-May to mid-September.

GALLERIES **Black Whale Gallery** (508-771-8600; blackwhalegallery.com), 50 Pearl Street. Most selections found here, including jewelry, glasswork, pottery, and more, are by local artists. Rotating displays year-round, such as Nancy Lyon's beautiful scrimshaw art.

Red Fish Blue Fish (508-775-8700; redfishbluefish.com), 374 Main Street. The most fun and whimsical "gallery" in town carries unusual gifts and crafts. When it's not too busy, you can watch owner Jane Walsh making hand-blown glass jewelry in the store.

Guyer Art Barn (508-790-6370; artsbarnstable.com), 250 South Street. Part of the Harbor Your Arts scheme (see *Artist Shanties* under **To Do**). The Barnstable Arts and Humanities Council established this art gallery in 1986, which now showcases emerging and established local artists in a wide variety of genres.

MALL ♫ The **Cape Cod Mall** (508-771-0201; simon.com/mall/cape-cod-mall), 769 Iyannough Road, has a variety of ever-changing stores. Need a book? There's a Barnes and Noble. Husband needs a tie? There's an Eddie Bauer. Wife hates her outfit? There's a J.Jill. You get the idea.

SPECIALTY **Instant Karma** (508-827-4212; instantkarmahyannis.com), 547 Main Street. A new-age store and hippie boutique filled with tarot cards, sage, rare crystals, and the like.

Cellar Leather (508-771-5458; cellarleather.com), 578 Main Street. Shop here for quality leather goods: coats, vests, shoes, clogs, sandals, briefcases, hats, and wallets.

Kandy Korner (508-771-5313; kandykorner.com), 474 Main Street. Watch chocolates and fudge being made in the front windows before heading in to indulge your sweet tooth.

✳ Special Events

May: **Annual Figawi Sailboat Race Weekend** (figawi.com). The largest sailboat race in New England goes from Hyannis to Nantucket.

Late July: **Regatta** (hyannisyachtclub .org). At the Hyannis Yacht Club since the early 1940s.

Early August: **Pops by the Sea** (arts foundationcapecod.org). Cape Cod's single largest cultural event features the Boston Pops Esplanade Orchestra on the town green playing to an audience of 15,000. In the past, guest conductors have included Mike Wallace, Julia Child, Olympia Dukakis, and Walter Cronkite. Reserved-seating and general-admission tickets.

Early December: **Harbor Lighting and Boat Parade** (capecodchamber.org), Bismore Park, Ocean Street. The parade of boats includes the arrival of Santa; entertainment with a holiday theme.

YARMOUTH

Yarmouth, like neighboring Dennis, stretches from Cape Cod Bay to Nantucket Sound; it unfolds along quiet Route 6A *and* congested Route 28. It's a family-oriented town, with golf courses, tennis courts, and town-sponsored sailing lessons, as well as quite a few southside oceanfront resorts.

Although Yarmouth's 5.3-mile section of **Route 28** was planted with more than 350 trees in 1989 (on its 350th birthday), the road is still a wall-to-wall sea of mini-golf courses, shops, fast-food places, and family-style attractions like a billiards emporium and boating on the Bass River. A larger-than-life plastic polar bear, a lunging shark, and an elephant epitomize the Cape's kitschier side. They're alternately viewed as icons and eyesores.

It's difficult to imagine that Route 28 was once open land dotted with small farms and that Yarmouth's ports bustled in the 19th century: Packets sailed to New York City and Newark from South Yarmouth at the Bass River. Today the scenic Bass River and South Yarmouth Historic District provide a delightful detour south of Route 28.

On the northside, **Route 6A** (a.k.a. Main Street) was settled in the 1600s, traveled by stagecoaches in the 1700s, and reached its height of prosperity in the 1800s, when it was lined with houses built for and by rope makers, sea captains, bankers, and ship-builders. At one time, a mile-long section of Yarmouth Port was referred to as Captain's Row, as it was home to almost 50 sea captains. Many former sea captains' houses are now attractive bed-and-breakfasts.

Stephen Hopkins, a *Mayflower* passenger, built the first house in Yarmouth in 1638 (off Mill Lane), and the town was incorporated just one year later. Today Yarmouth is

ACCESS TO THE NANTUCKET SOUND MAKES YARMOUTH A POPULAR BOATING DESTINATION LEESA BURKE

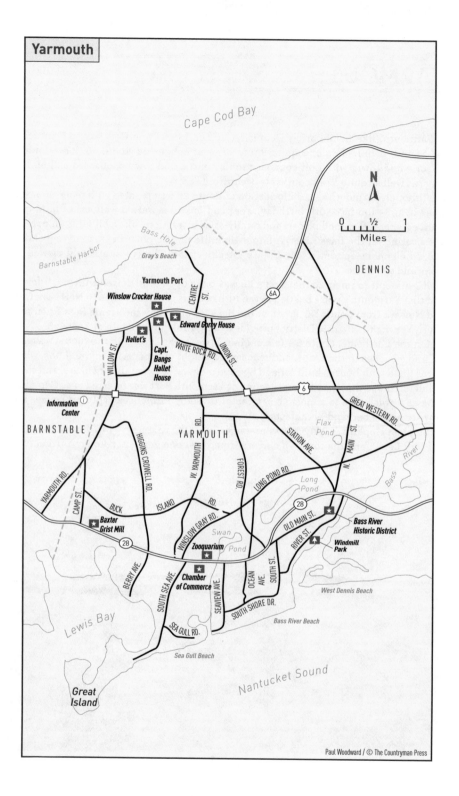

Morning: Order a filling breakfast from Anne and Fran's Kitchen.

Afternoon: Take the kids to the Cape Cod Inflatable Park and cool off with on their steep and very fast water slides, or take a Great Marsh Tidal Tour. Get in touch with your quirky side at the Edward Gorey House.

Evening: Enjoy a relaxing yet unusual dinner at the creative Inaho.

the third most populous town on the Cape, with 24,000 year-round residents. Meander along tranquil Route 6A and you'll find crafts and antiques shops, a quiet village green, a couple of fine historic houses open to the public, walking trails, and an antiquarian bookstore. Take any lane off Route 6A to the north, and you'll find picturesque residential areas and the bay, eventually.

GUIDANCE ❋ **Yarmouth Area Chamber of Commerce** (508-778-1008; yarmouth capecod.com), 424 Route 28, West Yarmouth. Along with a helpful chamber staff, the office has two self-guided historical tours of Yarmouth and Old South Yarmouth.

GETTING THERE *By car:* Yarmouth is 26 miles from the Cape Cod Canal; take Route 6 to Exit 7 for the northside (Yarmouth Port and Route 6A). For points along Route 28 on the southside, take Exit 7 south to Higgins Crowell Road for West Yarmouth. Take Exit 8 south for South Yarmouth and the Bass River.

GETTING AROUND *By shuttle:* The **H2O** line (800-352-7155; capecodtransit.org) travels Route 28 to Orleans daily in summer with several stops in Yarmouth (see schedule online). The **Sealine** starts at the **Hyannis Transportation Center**, 215 Iyannough Road, and stops in Barnstable, Mashpee, Falmouth, and Woods Hole. Take the seasonal **Hyannis Area Trolley** (508-385-1430; capecodtransit.org) for popular stops within Hyannis.

MEDIA The weekly *Register* (508-375-4945; wickedlocalcapecod.com) lists local happenings.

PUBLIC RESTROOMS On Route 6 between Exits 6 and 7; at the town hall, 1146 Route 28, South Yarmouth; and at Gray's Beach (open seasonally, off Centre Street from Route 6A).

PUBLIC LIBRARIES There are three public libraries: **Yarmouth Port Library** (508-362-3717; yarmouthportlibrary.org), 297 Route 6A; **South Yarmouth Library** (508-760-4820), 312 Old Main Street; and **West Yarmouth Library** (508-775-5206), 391 Route 28; or visit yarmouthlibraries.org.

EMERGENCIES **Yarmouth Police Department** (508-775-0445), 340 Higgins Crowell Road, West Yarmouth, or call **911.**

Medical: **Bass River Chiropractic** (508-394-1353; bassriverhealthcare.com), 833 Route 28, South Yarmouth. Call Dr. Reida if you are in need of healing during a holiday. She is an extraordinary chiropractor.

✳ To See

✳ ♂ **Edward Gorey House** (508-362-3909; edwardgoreyhouse.org), 8 Strawberry Lane, Yarmouth Port. Open mid-April to late December. *Curious, surreal, bizarre, whimsical,* and *quirky*: These have all been used to describe Gorey. His masterful pen-and-ink illustrations, as well as his offbeat sense of humor, endeared him to a wide audience. And the reputation he earned by doing the introductory credits for PBS's *Mystery* propelled him even further. So did the Tony Award he won for costume design for the Broadway production of *Dracula*. Closer to home, when Gorey moved to the Capefull time in the early 1980s, he contributed greatly to local theater productions. The restored house contains exhibits celebrating this marvelous artist, who lived here until his death in 2000. $.

🐾 ☂ **Hallet's** (508-362-3362), 139 Main Street, Route 6A, Yarmouth Port. Open April through December. Hallet's has been a community fixture since it was built as an apothecary in 1889 by Thacher Taylor Hallet. It's the oldest family-owned, old-fashioned soda fountain in the United States. Today, great-grandson Charles owns and operates the store, which boasts an old-fashioned oak counter and a marble-topped soda fountain. As time stands still, sit on a swivel stool or in one of the wrought-iron, heart-shaped chairs beneath the tin ceiling and relax over an ice cream soda (the food's not much to write home about). The second floor has been turned into something of a museum, documenting Yarmouth's history as seen through one family's annals and attic treasures. In addition to being a pharmacist (old medicine bottles are on display), T. T. Hallet was a postmaster (during his tenure, only 15 families had mail slots), selectman (the second

EDWARD GOREY HOUSE KIM GRANT

floor was used as a meeting room from 1889 to the early 1900s), and justice of the peace. The charming displays include store posters from the past 100 years and historical photographs. Tours $.

Village pump, Route 6A near Summer Street, Yarmouth Port. This wrought-iron pump has served the community since 1886. It's located just west of the Old Yarmouth Inn, the oldest inn (and stagecoach stop) on the Cape, dating from 1696. The pump's iron frame, decorated with birds, animals, and a lantern, is supported by a stone trough from which horses drank. Horse-drawn carriages traveling from Boston to Provincetown stopped here.

🌳 **Captain Bangs Hallet House** (508-362-3021; hsoy.org), 11 Strawberry Lane (park behind the post office on Route 6A), Yarmouth Port. Tours June to mid-October. The original section of this Greek Revival house was built in 1740 by town founder Thomas Thacher, but it was substantially enlarged by Capt. Henry Thacher in 1840. Captain Hallet and his wife, Anna, lived here from 1863 until 1893. The house, maintained by the Historical Society of Old Yarmouth, is deco-

VILLAGE PUMP KIM GRANT

rated in a manner befitting a prosperous sea captain who traded with China and India. Note the original 1740 kitchen, and don't miss the lovely weeping beech behind the house or the 1850 **Gorham Cobbler Shop**, which serves an archival research center. $.

🌳🌳 **Winslow Crocker House** (617-994-6661; historicnewengland.org), 250 Main Street, Route 6A, Yarmouth Port. Tours June to mid-October. Set back from Route 6A, this two-story Georgian home was built in 1780 with 12-over-12 small-paned windows and rich interior paneling. The house was constructed for a wealthy 18th-century trader and land speculator and moved to its present location in 1936 by Mary Thacher, a descendant of Yarmouth's original land grantee and an avid collector of 17th-, 18th-, and 19th-century furniture. She used the house as a backdrop for her magnificent collection. $.

Whydah Pirate Museum (508-534-9571, discoverpirates.com), 674 Route 28, West Yarmouth. This is more of an interactive science museum than the main Whydah museum in Provincetown (see **To Do**).

🐚 **Baxter Grist Mill**, 151 Route 28, West Yarmouth. Call Town Hall (508-398-2231, ext. 1292; hsoy.org) for opening hours. The original mill was built in 1710 with an exterior waterwheel. But in 1860, when water levels in Mill Pond became so low that the wheel froze, an indoor water turbine was added. (This is the Cape's only mill with an indoor water turbine.) Kids can help grind corn with "the Mill Man." Free.

Windmill Park, off River Street from Old Main Street, South Yarmouth. This eight-sided windmill on the Bass River was built in 1791 and moved here in 1866. This scenic spot also has a small swimming beach.

✳ To Do

BASEBALL ✐ The Cape League (ydredsox.pointstreaksites.com) sponsors the **Yarmouth–Dennis Red Sox**. Games are held from mid-May to early August, typically at 5 PM at the Dennis-Yarmouth Regional High School, Station Avenue, South Yarmouth.

BICYCLING & RENTALS Yarmouth has a surprisingly long list of bike trails. Pick up a map at the Chamber of Commerce (see *Guidance*), or at bike rental shops.

The **Cape Cod Rail Trail** offers 25 miles of paved road for your biking pleasure. The trail route starts in Yarmouth and passes through the towns of Dennis, Harwich, Brewster, Orleans, Eastham, and Wellfleet.

The **Yarmouth Bike Trail** begins on Old Townhouse Road, just off Route 6A in South Yarmouth. There are large parking areas at Homer Park, or at the new Station Avenue overpass bridge. Head west for views of the Cranberry Hills Golf area. Head east to connect with the Rail Trail. You can rent bicycles and equipment at the **Bike Zone Yarmouth** (508-694-5575; bikezonecapecod.com), 484 Station Avenue; and for those who would like some pep in their pedal, **Pedego Electric Bikes** (508-694-5977; pedegoelectricbikes.com), 20 Forsythe Avenue.

BOAT EXCURSIONS & RENTALS With its easy access to Nantucket Sound and beyond, Bass River is a mecca for boats both big and small. For boating regulations contact the **Harbormaster** (508-760-4800; yarmouth.ma.us/harbormaster), 424 Route 28, West Yarmouth.

Ship Shops Inc. (508-398-2256; shipshops.com), 130 Pleasant Street, South Yarmouth. Choose your preferred watercraft ranging from 16 to 24 feet in size. They also offer a full-service marina. $$$$+.

FISHING Procure freshwater and saltwater fishing licenses and regulations online at mass.gov/eea/agencies/dfg/licensing.

Big game: **Bass River Charters** (508-737-3162; bassriverfishingcharters.com), 10 Pleasant Street, South Yarmouth. $$$$+.

Shark Shark Tuna (774-212-0016; sharksharktuna.com), 17 Neptune Lane, South Yarmouth. Trips May through October. Book a charter with Captain Shane and his crew for a wicked experience targeting the big boys lurking down deep. $$$$+.

Emma Jack **Charters** (508-737-0363; emmajackcharters.com), 10 Pleasant Street. The *Emma Jack* is docked in Bass River and fishes the rips at Monomoy, up to Chatham, and down to Nantucket. Be sure to ask about their family recipes such as Rob B's mock lobster, which is really boiled hunks of striper, dipped in melted butter or cocktail sauce. Clever idea, Rob! $$$$+.

On shore: Test your luck casting from the shore at **Bass River Beach**, a.k.a. **Smuggler's**.

By bridge or jetty: On the Yarmouth side of **Bass River Bridge** there's a fishing pier just off Route 28. Large stripers, blues, and winter flounder are known to hang out in the shadows. See also **Smuggler's Beach Fishing Pier** and rock jetty.

Freshwater: Yarmouth has 28 freshwater ponds that are stocked with fish. **Long Pond** and **Dennis Pond** are the only freshwater ponds that offer public access and where it is possible to launch a boat on a trailer.

Supplies: ✳ **Riverview Bait & Tackle** (508-394-1036), 1273 Route 28, South Yarmouth. Among other services, the staff will direct you to local fishing spots.

FOR FAMILIES 🎣 **Cape Cod Inflatable Park** (508-771-6060; capecodinflatable park.com), 518 Route 28, West Yarmouth. Open mid-April to mid-October. My little friends Ella and Lilly could not stop talking about how much fun they had at this place over their school break. Cool down at the newly renovated H_2O park, with a lazy river, tipping buckets, lily pad pools, two slides, and three very large inflatable thrill slides. There's also a private pool for guests renting cabanas for the day. If you're in need of a break from the water, check out the "dry" rides: three-way bungee, batting cages, a sticky wall, the "fire rescue" (an inflatable fire truck for kiddos to explore), bull riding, and much more. Grab lunch at their on-site Shark Bites Café and be sure to play a few games at the arcade before you leave. $$$-$$$$+.

❄ 🎣 🎳 **Ryan Family Amusements** (508-394-5644; ryanfamily.com), 1067 Route 28, South Yarmouth. When rain strikes, head indoors to bowl away the blues. Choose from 10-pin and candlepin. $$$.

🎣 **Skull Island Adventure Golf & Sports World** (508-398-6070; skullisland capecod.com), 934 Route 2, South Yarmouth. Open April to early October. This

CAPE COD INFLATABLE PARK KATY WARD

Bass River sports complex has a little bit of everything, making it fun for kids and adults. In addition to the island-themed mini golf course with waterfalls, treasure caves, and a *Swiss Family Robinson* tree house, there's a golf driving range, an arcade, go-karts, batting cages, and kick ball/wiffle ball cages. (See also *Mini Golf* under **To Do**).

🎣 The **Fred Thatcher Playground** in Yarmouth Port and **Old Town House Road Park** in South Yarmouth both have decent playgrounds.

GOLF **King's Way Golf Club** (508-362-8870; kingswaycapecod.net), 81 Kings Circuit, Yarmouth Port. Open March to mid-November. A challenging Cornish and Silva course.

❄ **Bayberry Hills Golf Course** (508-394-5597; golfyarmouthcapecod.com), 635 West Yarmouth Road and ❄ **Bass River Golf Course** (508-398-9079), 62 Highbank Road. See the website for additional information on these two premium courses.

❄ **Blue Rock Golf Course** (508-398-9295; bluerockgolfcourse), 48 Todd Road, South Yarmouth.

KAYAKS & PADDLEBOARDS 🎣 **Great Marsh Kayak Tours** (508-470-4971; great marshkayaktours.com), West Yarmouth. Open June to September. Unsure of where to kayak or unfamiliar with local tides? Check out these wonderful 3-hour tours of Parker River, and tidal marshes, including Nauset Marsh in Orleans. (See also under **To Do** in Dennis.)

SCENIC DRIVES

South Yarmouth and the Bass River Historic District, on and around Old Main Street (off Route 28), South Yarmouth. The Pawkannawkut (a branch of the Wampanoag tribe) lived, fished, and hunted on a tract of land Yarmouth set aside for them along Long Pond and the Bass River in 1713. But by the 1770s, a smallpox epidemic wiped out most of the indigenous population. In 1790 David Kelley, a Quaker, acquired the last remaining Pawkannawkut land from the last surviving Pawkannawkut, Thomas Greenough. Quakers then settled the side streets off Old Main Street near Route 28 and built handsome homes. The Historical Society of Old Yarmouth publishes a walking-tour brochure to Old South Yarmouth, which you can get at the chamber of commerce (see *Guidance*). Note the simple traffic rotary at River and Pleasant Streets; it's thought to be the oldest in the country.

Yarmouth Port. From Route 6A, turn onto Church Street across from the village green. Follow it around to Thacher Shore Drive and Water Street. When Water Street turns left, head right down a dirt road for a wide-open view of marshland. Continue on Water Street across Keveney Bridge, which crosses Mill Creek; Keveney Lane takes you back to Route 6A. Turn left to head east, back into Yarmouth Port. This scenic loop is nice for a quiet walk, a bicycle ride, or an early-morning jog.

MINI GOLF ✐ **Pirate's Cove Adventure Golf** (508-394-6200 or 508-394-5252; piratescove.net), 728 Route 28, South Yarmouth. Open early April through October. At the granddaddy of all Cape mini-golf courses, kids have their choice of two 18-hole courses complete with lavish pirate-themed landscaping, extravagant waterfalls, and dark caves. Kids receive eye patches, flags, tattoos, and jaunty pirate hats (and multiple golf balls if you lose one in the water).

✐ **Wild Animal Lagoon** (508-790-1662; wildanimallagoon.com), 62 Route 28, West Yarmouth. Open mid-April through October. Kiddos will enjoy the wild animal-themed 18-hole course and its whimsical display. (See also **Cape Cod Inflatable Park** and **Skull Island** under *For Families*.)

PARASAIL & JET SKI **Cape Cod Parasail and Jet Ski** (508-398-7245; capecodparasail jetski.com), 17 Neptune Lane, South Yarmouth.

TENNIS The public can play at **Flax Pond** (off North Main Street from Route 28 in South Yarmouth); at **Sandy Pond** (from Route 28 in West Yarmouth, take Higgins Crowell Road to Buck Island Road); and at **Dennis-Yarmouth Regional High School** (from Route 28, take Station Avenue to Regional Avenue in South Yarmouth). All are free.

✳ Green Space

BEACHES Parking stickers are required at most beaches and can be purchased at the Yarmouth Town Hall (508-398-2231; yarmouth.ma.us), 1146 Route 28, South Yarmouth. Some lodging places offer discounted rates for daily beach stickers, so don't forget to ask!

Sea Gull Beach, off South Sea Avenue from Route 28, West Yarmouth. This long, wide beach is very popular with teens and college crowds. If volleyball and Frisbee are your thing, you will enjoy this beach. It's also very clean and tends to have less seaweed then other more narrow south side beaches. Facilities include a bathhouse, restrooms, and food service. Fun fact: The blue boxes you see are flytraps filled with

BOARDWALK, NOT PARK PLACE

Bass Hole (or Gray's) Beach, off Centre Street from Route 6A, Yarmouth Port. The small, protected beach is good for children, but the real appeal lies in the **Bass Hole Board-walk**, which extends across a marsh and a creek. From the benches at the end of the boardwalk you can see across to Chapin Memorial Beach in Dennis. It's a great place to be at sunset, although you won't be alone. The 2.5-mile **Callery-Darling Trail** starts from the parking lot and crosses conservation lands to the salt marsh. As you walk out into the bay, a mile or so at low tide, recall that this former harbor used to be deep enough to accommodate a schooner shipyard in the 18th century. Free parking; handicap ramp.

THE BASS HOLE BOARDWALK   LEFT: LEESA BURKE; RIGHT: KAYLA ROBERTSON/DO ART PHOTOGRAPHY

Octenol, a synthetic version of ox breath, that attracts the dreaded biting greenhead flies that terrorize sunbathers in July.

Bass River Beach (Smuggler's), off South Shore Drive, South Yarmouth. A spacious beach that is very popular for families with young children. Gentle breaking waves and delicate sand create perfect sandcastle conditions—so perfect, in fact, that Smuggler's is a destination on the **Yarmouth Sand Sculpture Trail** (508-771-1008; yarmouthcapecod .com), a "trail" featuring 33 family-friendly, extraordinarily intricate, and down-right amazing sand sculptures in various areas throughout Yarmouth. The popular attraction is open for viewing mid-May to mid-October and is sponsored by the Chamber of Commerce. You can download a trail map online.

WALKS **Botanical Trails of the Historical Society of Old Yarmouth**, behind the post office and Captain Bangs Hallet House, off Route 6A, Yarmouth Port. This 1.5-mile trail, dotted with benches and skirting 60 acres of pines, oaks, and a pond, leads past rhododendrons, holly, lady's slippers, and other delights. The trail begins at the gate-house, which has a lovely herb garden. A spur trail leads to the profoundly simple **Kelley Chapel**, built in 1873 as a seaman's bethel (a sacred space for sailors) by a father for his daughter, who was mourning the untimely death of her son. The interior contains a few pews, an old woodstove, and a small organ. It may be rented (508-360-9796) for small weddings and special events.

Taylor-Bray Farm, Bray Farm Road South, off Route 6A near the Dennis town line, Yarmouth Port. Open dawn to dusk. The Bray brothers purchased this land in the late 1800s and created a successful shipyard and farm. Now town-owned conservation land, this working farm offers a short walking trail and tidal-marsh views. It's a nice place for a picnic. You can't help but take a deep breath of fresh air here.

Captain's Mile. The Historical Society of Old Yarmouth has printed a booklet (look for it at the chamber of commerce or Captain Bangs Hallet House) that covers three walking tours of local sea captains' houses along Route 6A. It's an informative brochure and gives some perspective about the area.

Meadowbrook Road Conservation Area, off Route 28, West Yarmouth. This recommendation originally came from Joseph Molinari, a longtime explorer from New Jersey. A peaceful place to relax, this area has a 310-foot boardwalk with an observation deck that overlooks a swamp and salt marsh. Take Winslow Gray Road north from Route 28 in West Yarmouth. After a few miles, take Meadowbrook Lane to the right and park at the end.

See also **Bass Hole (or Gray's) Beach** in "Boardwalk, Not Park Place" on page 143. And, don't forget about the **walking-tour** brochure published by the Historical Society of Old Yarmouth (see *Guidance*).

✴ Lodging

Route 6A is lined with lovely bed-and-breakfasts, while the southside generally appeals to families (with a couple of notable exceptions).

RESORTS & HOTELS ✐ **Red Jacket Beach Resort** (508-760-9220; redjacketresorts.com), 1 South Shore Drive, South Yarmouth. Open early April to mid-October. Occupying 7 acres wedged between Nantucket Sound and the Parker's River, this extensive complex courts families. For beachgoers, the Blue Water Resort (highly recommend), or the more hotel-like Riviera and Red Jacket Resorts, all include water views, two large swimming pools, manicured grounds, and access to a private beach. Golf lovers will enjoy the Blue Rock Resort's par-3 course, outdoor pool, and on-site restaurant, and nature lovers will feel relaxed while watching wildlife on Lewis Bay at the Green Harbor Resort. $$$–$$$$.

Ocean Mist Beach Hotel & Suites (508-398-2633; oceanmistcapecod.com), 97 South Shore Drive, South Yarmouth. Open mid-May to mid-October. This shingled three-story complex fronting a 300-foot private beach offers 32 rooms and 32 loft suites. Each of the contemporary rooms has a wet bar or full efficiency kitchen, two double beds, and air-conditioning. Loft suites feature an open, second-floor sitting area—many of the rooms have ocean views, all have a sofa bed, and many have skylights and two private balconies. Mixed reviews are warranted but it's hard to beat the location for families. There's also an indoor pool on the premises. $$–$$$.

BED-AND-BREAKFASTS ❀ ✴ **Liberty Hill Inn** (508-362-3976; libertyhillinn .com), 77 Main Street, Route 6A, Yarmouth Port. Innkeepers John Hunt and Kris Srihadi offer the best bang for the buck in Cape Cod lodging. (Even more so now that they also rent a gloriously renovated house nearby! It's perfect for a romantic weeklong stay or family reunions.) The former 1825 whaling tycoon's home is nicely set back from Route 6A on a knoll. It features five comfortable rooms in the elegant main house and four in the adjacent post-and-beam-style carriage house. Light and airy rooms in the main inn benefit from lofty ceilings, floor-to-ceiling windows, a dramatic spiral staircase, and restored bathrooms. Crisp linens, triple sheeting, and arrival snack baskets are the norm. Next door, rooms might have a whirlpool, fireplace, or canopy bed. A sumptuous breakfast (served at individual tables) is included. $$.

※ **The Inn at Cape Cod** (508-375-0590; innatcapecod.com), 4 Summer Street, Yarmouth Port. Helen and Mike Cassels, innkeepers since the mid-2000s, have brought this 1820s gem back to life through keen decorating skills and quintessential British hospitality. I love being surprised, and their attention to this Southern Plantation-style inn is a delight. The seven guest rooms and two suites (the latter with a separate sitting room and private balcony) are lovely and elegant. Each is equipped with a flat-screen TV and gas fireplace, and each features spacious, high ceilings and an expertly renovated bathroom. A four-course breakfast is served at individual tables in the sunny breakfast room or terrace. As you might expect, afternoon tea served fireside with homemade treats is worth returning for. There's plenty of additional guest space, including elegant gardens, porches, and a sitting room with fireplace. $$–$$$.

※ ✿ **Village Inn** (508-362-3182; thevil lageinncapecod.com), 92 Main Street, Route 6A, Yarmouth Port. Open May to mid-October. If you want to understand genuine hospitality, stay with Robin and Claire, an Irish brother-and-sister team who took over this historic, colonial landmark in 2015. They provide a modest but spick-and-span, 10-room place where travelers can relax and interact, then toss in a few modern conveniences. When you're looking for value, look no further. And when you're here, walk 5 minutes down the adjacent lane to the old wharf on the water. $–$$.

Captain Farris House (508-760-2818; captainfarris.com), 308 Old Main Street, South Yarmouth. Open mid-February to early January. Located within a small pocket of historic homes off Route 28, the 1845 Captain Farris House offers understated elegance and luxurious modern amenities. Lovely window treatments, antiques, fine linens, and Jacuzzi tubs fill the guest rooms. Of the 10 rooms, four are suites, five have a fireplace, a

THE INN AT CAPE COD KIM GRANT

few have a private deck, and most have a private entrance. A fancy three-course breakfast is served at individual tables in the courtyard or at one formal dining-room table. $$.

COTTAGES ♫ **Seaside** (508-398-2533; seasidecapecod.com), 135 South Shore Drive, South Yarmouth. Open May to late October. These 41 one- and two-room cottages, built in the 1930s but nicely upgraded and well maintained, are very popular for their oceanfront location. Reserve by mid-March if possible; otherwise, cross your fingers. Sheltered among pine trees, the shingled and weathered units are clustered around a sandy barbecue area and sit above a 500-foot stretch of private beach. (A playground is next door.) Kitchens are fully equipped and linens are provided, as is daily maid service. Many of the tidy units have a working fireplace. The least-expensive units (without views) are decorated in 1950s style. Don't bother with the motel efficiencies. $$–$$$.

♫ ♫ **Beach House at Bass River** (508-394-6501; beachhousecapecod.com), 73 South Shore Drive, Bass River. Open early April to late October. This tasteful bilevel motor inn, built in the 1970s by Cliff Hagberg (who still operates it), sits on a 110-foot stretch of private Nantucket Sound beach. Each of the 26 rooms in the tidy complex is decorated differently with country antiques and wicker; generally the oceanfront rooms are a bit spiffier, with country-pine furnishings. All rooms have a private balcony or patio and a refrigerator. An expansive buffet breakfast is included. $$.

RENTAL HOUSES ♫ **Great Island Ocean Club** (508-775-0985; greatisland oceanclub.com), 618 Route 28, West Yarmouth. Open April through November. This gated residential community has about 30 rental homes, fully equipped houses with one to six bedrooms. Best of all, they're located on or within a quarter-mile of a private Nantucket Sound beach.

Shared facilities include tennis courts and a pool. $$$.

✳ Where to Eat

Route 6A has a couple of excellent restaurants, and while Route 28 is lined with dozens, most are not discernible from one another. I have reviewed only the few that are.

DINING OUT ♫ ✳ **Inaho** (508-362-5522; inahocapecod.com), 157 Main Street, Route 6A, Yarmouth Port. Open D, year-round. Year in and year out, Inaho remains on my list of top 10 restaurants on Cape Cod. Offering some of the most sophisticated and authentic Japanese cuisine this side of Tokyo, fearless diners are handsomely presented with the best-of-the-best from tuna nuta, tako wasabi, unagi don, or the chef's choice of five-piece nigiri sushi. Be sure to absorb the nightly specials, too. For those a bit less adventurous, try the bento box combination, or traditional teriyaki. Do not leave without trying desert, including the green tea mochi. $$–$$$.

SWEET TREATS & COFFEE ♫ **Ann and Fran's Kitchen** (508-775-7771; annand frans.com), 471 Route 28, West Yarmouth. Open B, L, March to December. If you go to one breakfast spot while you're on vacation, go here. Everything on the menu is delicious and the family service is wonderful. From savory options like the slow roasted hash and eggs or the popular "kitchen sink": a mix of potatoes, peppers, onions, and cheese, with homemade biscuits and sausage gravy; or sweeter treats like the blueberry ricotta pancakes or the fluffy thick-cut cinnamon French toast. Expect a country-fusion interior that is bustling with morning conversations and the smell of freshly brewed coffee and bacon. I also adore the Duarte family, especially the two children: chef Tyler Duarte, and his sister (and my dear Cape/college friend)

INAHO KIM GRANT

Kayla Duarte, who now goes by Robertson. Be sure to keep an eye out in this book for her featured Do Art Photography. $–$$.

❄ ✍ **Jack's Outback** (508-362-6690), 161 Main Street, Route 6A, Yarmouth Port. Open B, L. Classic American downhome cooking is served from an exposed, diner-like kitchen. Get there early for fluffy omelets, pancakes, and popovers, or be prepared to wait. $–$$.

❄ ✍ **Keltic Kitchen** (508-771-4835; keltickitchen.com), 415 Route 28, West Yarmouth. Open B, until 2 p.m. Chefowner and Irishman Dave Dempsey and his staff still sport thick brogues from the old country when they take your orders. How about an Irish farmhouse breakfast with rashers and black and white pudding or Keltic Benny's with poached eggs on an English muffin and corned beef hash? And despite having no ties to Ireland, the cranberry French toast, made with Portuguese bread, is a favorite. Lemon ricotta blueberry pancakes get raves as well. Come once to this friendly and cozy place and I bet you'll come back again. Try the beef and barley soup for lunch. And dine outside in fine weather. $.

❄ ✍ **Old Yarmouth Inn** (508-362-9962; oldyarmouthinn.com), 223 Main Street, Route 6A, Yarmouth Port. Open L, D. You have a choice to make at this 1696 inn, the oldest on the Cape: casual

ANN AND FRAN'S KITCHEN KAYLA ROBERTSON/DO ART PHOTOGRAPHY

pub dining or fine dining in one of three dining rooms. The fireplaces and white linens in the main dining rooms create a cozy elegance, but I often end up at the low-key tavern, a former stagecoach stop. It's just the perfect place for a grilled chicken Caesar, a cup of clam chowder, or a great burger. Lobster (baked, stuffed, in a roll, or whatever) is always a terrific choice. And the extensive Sunday buffet brunch is popular. $–$$$.

❋ **Gerardi's Café** (508-394-3111; gerardiscafe.com), 902 Route 28, South Yarmouth. Open L, D. This cute and casual place, with wooden booths, wooden chairs, a gas fireplace, and Oriental carpets, packs a big punch relative to its size. Thanks to chef Diego Gerardi, raised by restaurateurs in Boston's North End and trained at the Costigliole d'Asti at the Italian Culinary Institute for Foreigners, you can look with assurance for authentic Italian dishes like chicken Marsala and fettuccine Alfredo. You gotta love a place that knows what it is, doesn't overreach, and executes with aplomb. D $$–$$$.

EATING OUT **Skipper Chowder House** (508-394-7406; skipperrestaurant.com), 152 South Shore Drive, South Yarmouth. Open L, D, mid-April to mid-October.

OLD YARMOUTH INN   KIM GRANT

With a name like this, the "chowdah's" gotta rock—and it does! For a nice twist on two perennial faves, try the fried clam chowdah, which is fabu. Appetizers run the gamut from raw bar delicacies and Portuguese mussels to potato skins and buffalo wings; main dishes revolve around wicked awesome lobster variations, fish-n-chips and classic seafood rolls. Dine on the enclosed upper deck or on the patio, all the better to drink in the ocean. Save room for a little somethin' somethin' at their ice cream shack. $$.

❋ ♪ **Oliver's & Planck's Tavern** (508-362-6062; oliverscapecod.com), 960 Main Street, Route 6A, Yarmouth Port. Open L, D. Oliver's offers generous portions in cozy, tavernlike surroundings (or on the outdoor deck in summer). Oliver's attracts an older crowd at lunchtime; longtime Cape residents who like to keep things simple; and families who need to satisfy everyone. Specialties include seafood flatbread and broiled seafood, but hearty sandwiches, steak tips, and fettuccini are also quite popular. Live entertainment on weekends. L $–$$, D $$–$$$.

❋ ♪ **Royal II Restaurant and Grill** (508-362-2288; royalpizzagrill.com) 715 Route 6A, Yarmouth Port. Open L,D. Don't let the non-descript exterior fool you. This simple but pleasant family-friendly place offers fancy and traditional pizzas, classic Italian pasta dishes, some Mediterranean specialties like gyros and moussaka, and lots of requisite cheap eats like grinders, burgers, and fried seafood. (They also have a location on Lower Country Road in Dennis Port.) $$.

❋ Entertainment

♪ **Band concerts** (508-778-1008), Mattachesse Middle School band shell, Higgins Crowell Road, West Yarmouth. Monday night at 7 p.m. in July and August since 1970.

✳ Selective Shopping

✳ Unless otherwise noted, all shops are open year-round.

BOOKSTORE See "A Breed Apart" on page 150.

CLOTHING Wicked Thrift (508-648-5902 call or text; poprockvintageshop .com), 533 Route 28, West Yarmouth. Tammy Venneri has a unique business model when it comes to her colorfully modern yet vintage thrift store. "The secret sauce to Wicked Thrift is offering cash—everyone wants cash. The girl with that old prom dress, she wants cash; or the girl with Lululemon, she wants cash; even the guy that drives a Harley, he wants cash. So we end up with a really diverse mix, because we're handing out cash. You can't create a criteria that's so strict because then you lose all the fun stuff." Tammy likes to compare her store to ice cream: "I like vanilla ice cream, but it's gotta have lots of toppings. Like my store, we got vanilla and we got the top-pings." I won't deny that I was excited to come here for "guidebook research," and of course, I left with a brand new pair of Bernie Mevs at an unbeatable price. But it was the genuine vintage Italian leather cognac knee-high boots that I purchased over five years ago that secured me as a forever customer. I still have them and I refuse to ever give them up. You never know what treasures you will find at Wicked: from trendy mainstream brands and designer items to fabulous (yes, fab-ulous) vintage items, furs, costume pieces, shoes, and more. Shoppers will have a great time exploring her ever-changing racks. Prom season is also huge for Wicked. In 2019, Tammy had over 600 dresses on display from girls across New England. "Girls were travel-ing here from Connecticut and Rhode Island." Check online for specific buying times (genuine fur coats are accepted August through December for example,

and designer bags, boots, and shoes year-round). If you're savvy with social media, be sure to follow Wicked for updates, sales, and events.

FARMS Bass River Farmers' Market (bassriverfarmersmarket.org), 311 Old Main Street, South Yarmouth. Open Thursdays and Saturdays, mid-June to early September.

(See also **Taylor-Bray Farm** under **To Do.**)

SPECIALTY Design Works (508-362-9698; designworkscapecod.com), 159 Route 6A, Yarmouth Port. Scandinavian country antiques, home furnishings, and accessories like throws, pillows, and linens.

Botanique of Cape Cod (774-251-0066; botaniquecapecod.com), 23 Whites Path, South Yarmouth. This floral design studio offers custom arrangements and a flower bar where you create your own

WICKED THRIFT KATY WARD

A BREED APART

Parnassus Book Service (508-362-6420; parnassusbooks.com), 220 Main Street, Route 6A, Yarmouth Port. Deliberately avoiding signs and categories, the Muse family (proprietors since forever) wants people to browse and dig around, perhaps finding a first edition James or Melville in the stacks. Specializing in maritime, Cape Cod, and ornithology, the Muses have been selling new, used, and rare books since the mid-1950s. Shelves line the wall outside, where the books are available for browsing or purchase on a 24/7 honor system. In its former incarnations, this 1840 building served as a general store and a church. This really is one unique shop.

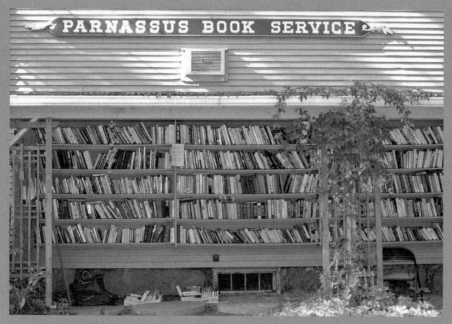

PARNASSUS BOOK SERVICE KIM GRANT

bouquets. There's also a grand collection of curated gifts and artwork.

✳ Special Events

Late May–late September: **Art shows** (yarmouthartguild.org). The Yarmouth Art Guild sponsors outdoor shows at the Cape Cod Cooperative Bank (Route 6A in Yarmouth Port) on many Sundays (10 a.m.–5 p.m.).

Mid-October: **Seaside Festival** (yarmouthseasidefestival.com). Begun in 1979, this festival features jugglers, clowns, fireworks, field games, a parade, sand castle competitions, arts and crafts, and bicycle, kayak, and road races.

Mid-November: **Trolley Tour Taste of Yarmouth**. Join the local culinary tour trend with this (new) annual event. More than a dozen restaurants participate, offering a variety of appetizer-sized dishes at each stop. Festivities are hosted at different venues each year.

✿ *Early December:* **Yarmouth Port Christmas Stroll** (hsoy.org). Tree lighting on the village common, caroling, and special children's activities; wreaths for sale.

DENNIS

L ocated at the Cape's geographic center, Dennis is a convenient base for day trips. Some visitors are drawn to Dennis for fine summer theater; others come for family-style attractions along Route 28. Indeed, to outsiders (including the 40,000 or so summer visitors), Dennis suffers from a split personality. Luckily, the 14,000 year-round residents have long since reconciled the village's conflicting natures.

On the **northern side of town**, Route 6A (a.k.a. Main Street) continues along its scenic way, governed by a historical commission. Skirting Dennis and **East Dennis**, Route 6A is lined with a smattering of antiques shops, crafters, and sea captains' gracious homes. (During the 19th century, more than 400 sea captains called Dennis home.) Colonial side roads off Route 6A lead to beach communities, such as **Quivett Neck** (settled in 1639) and Sesuit Marsh and **Sesuit Harbor**, where the fishing industry once flourished and fishing charters now depart. Note the streets in this area, named for methods of preserving fish: Cold Storage Road and Salt Works Road.

The Cape's oldest cranberry bog is also off Route 6A; Dennis resident Henry Hall cultivated the first cranberries in 1807. He discovered that the berries grow much better when covered with a light layer of sand. His brother, Isaiah, a cooper, patented the

AERIAL VIEW OF SESUIT HARBOR MARCIA DUGGAN/CAPECODSOUL

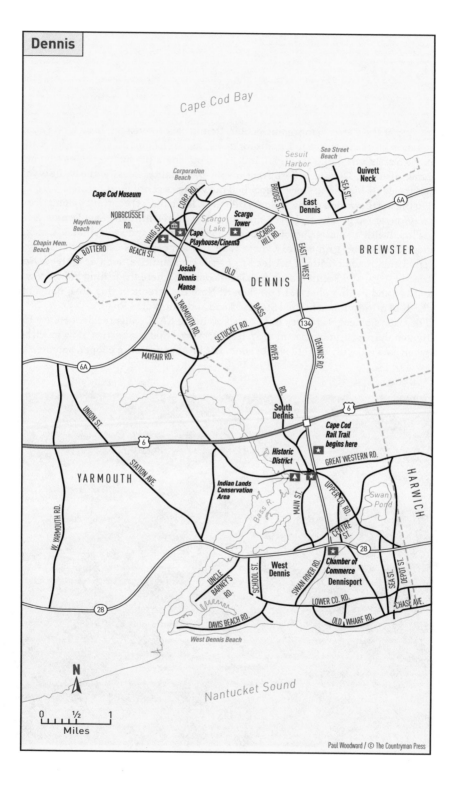

Dennis

Cape Cod Bay

Corporation
Beach

Sesuit
Harbor

Sea Street
Beach

Quivett
Neck

6A

Cape Cod Museum

NOBSCUSSET
RD.

Mayflower
Beach

Scargo
Lake

Scargo
Tower

East
Dennis

BRIDGE ST.

Chapin Mem.
Beach

WHIG ST.

CORP. RD.

Cape
Playhouse/Cinema

SCARGO
HILL RD.

EAST — WEST

BREWSTER

DR. BOTTERO

BEACH ST.

Josiah
Dennis
Manse

OLD

DENNIS

S. YARMOUTH RD.

SETUCKET RD.

BASS

134

DENNIS RD.

6A

MAYFAIR RD.

RIVER

RD.

South
Dennis

6

Cape Cod
Rail Trail
begins here

UNION ST.

STATION AVE.

YARMOUTH

Historic
District

GREAT WESTERN RD.

HARWICH

Indian Lands
Conservation
Area

Bass R.

MAIN ST.

UPPER CO. RD.

Swan
Pond

W. YARMOUTH RD.

CENTRE ST.

28

SCHOOL ST.

West
Dennis

SWAN RIVER RD.

Chamber of
Commerce

SEA ST.

DEPOT ST.

28

UNCLE
BARNEY'S
RD.

Dennisport

LOWER CO. RD.

CHASE AVE.

DAVIS BEACH RD.

OLD WHARF RD.

West Dennis Beach

Nantucket Sound

N

0   ½   1
Miles

Paul Woodward / © The Countryman Press

Morning: Get up early and head over to the Red Cottage for a diner-style breakfast that will knock your socks off, or grab a liquid breakfast at Three Fins Coffee Roasters.

Afternoon: Climb Scargo Tower early in the day for a clear view of Provincetown. Skip stones in Scargo Lake afterward. Rent an electric paddleboat or kayak from Cape Cod Waterways and explore Swan River. Then, fuel up with a traditional and delicious lobster roll at Sesuit Harbor Café.

Evening: Savor top-notch cuisine at the Pheasant, followed by a show at Cape Playhouse. Or relish in upscale bar food, live music, and local art at Harvest Gallery and Wine Bar.

barrels used to transport the harvest. It wasn't until the 1840s, when sugar became more readily available, that anyone could do much with these tart berries, though.

The center of Dennis has a quintessential white steeple church, town green, and bandstand.

On the **southern side of town**, the 6-mile-long **Bass River** is the largest tidal river on the eastern seaboard. It serves as a natural boundary between Yarmouth and Dennis, offering numerous possibilities for exploration, fishing, and birding. Although it has never been proved, it's widely believed that Viking explorer Leif Eriksson sailed up the Bass River about 1,000 years ago, built a camp, and stayed awhile. Follow Cove Road off Route 28 and Main Street for nice views of the Bass River and sheltered Grand Cove. (The villages of **South Dennis** and **West Dennis** were once connected by a bridge here.) In **Dennis Port**, kids will enjoy the smaller **Swan River** in a paddleboat.

Each side of Dennis has its own nice, long beach: **Chapin Memorial Beach** on Cape Cod Bay and **West Dennis Beach** on Nantucket Sound. Head to **Scargo Tower** for an expansive view.

GUIDANCE ❊ **Dennis Chamber of Commerce** (508-398-3568; dennischamber.com), 242 Swan River Road, West Dennis.

GETTING THERE *By car:* From the Cape Cod Canal, take Exit 9 off the Mid-Cape Highway (Route 6). Head north on Route 134 to Route 6A for Dennis and East Dennis. Head south on Route 134 to Route 28 for West Dennis and Dennis Port. The tiny historic district of South Dennis is just west of Route 134 as you head south. Depending on traffic, it takes 20 to 30 minutes to get to various points in Dennis from the canal.

GETTING AROUND As the crow flies, Dennis is only about 7 miles wide from Cape Cod Bay to Nantucket Sound. When navigating, keep a couple of things in mind: South Dennis is actually the geographic center of Dennis, and Dennis Port (the southeastern portion of town) doesn't have a harbor on the ocean, as you might have expected (given its name!). In general, there isn't much to interest travelers between Routes 6A and 28. Year-rounders make their homes here, visit doctors' and lawyers' offices, and buy food and gardening supplies. Concentrate your meandering north of Route 6A and around the tiny historic district on Main Street in South Dennis.

PUBLIC RESTROOMS Sesuit Harbor in East Dennis; Town Hall, Main Street, South Dennis; Dennis Port Public Library, 5 Hall Street, Dennis Port.

PUBLIC LIBRARIES ❄ ⚓ ⚕ There are five small village libraries, but the biggest is **Dennis Public Library** (508-760-6219; dennispubliclibrary.org), 5 Hall Street.

EMERGENCIES **Dennis Police Department** (508-394-1315), 90 Bob Crowell Road, South Dennis, or call **911**.

❄ To See

⚓ **Scargo Tower**, Bass Hill Road, Dennis. (Bass Hill Road is just off Scargo Hill Road from Route 6A.) The 30-foot stone tower sits 160 feet above sea level atop the area's tallest hill, and on a clear day the panoramic view extends all the way to Provincetown. Even on a hazy day you can view the width of the Cape from Nantucket Sound to Cape Cod Bay. **Scargo Lake** (see **Green Space**), a glacial kettle pond, is directly below the tower.

⚓ **Josiah Dennis Manse Museum** and **Old West Schoolhouse** (508-385-3528; dennishistoricalsociety.org), 61 Whig Street, Dennis. Open late June through August. This 1736 saltbox was home to

SCARGO TOWER   KAYLA ROBERTSON/DO ART PHOTOGRAPHY

the Reverend Mr. Dennis, for whom the town is named. Today it's set up much as it would have been during the reverend's time, with a keeping room, children's room,

JOSIAH DENNIS MANSE   KIM GRANT

A WORTHY CULTURAL STOP

Cape Cod Museum of Art (508-385-4477; ccmoa.org), 60 Hope Lane, off Route 6A, Dennis. Open May to mid-October. The museum is a winner, with eight exhibition spaces, a glassed-in sculpture court, and the Weny Education Center. At the CCMA, Cape Cod's important, historical, and contemporary artists—both living and dead—are represented by almost 2,000 works on paper and canvas as well as sculpture. It should definitely be at the top of your list of things to do. The museum also sponsors lectures and art classes for adults and children, and features first-run independent and foreign films in their Screening Room. Stop in to the Artful Hand Gallery museum shop before leaving. $. ❋ ✐ ☂

CAPE COD MUSEUM OF ART   KIM GRANT

maritime wing, and spinning exhibit in the attic. Costumed interpreters are on hand to answer questions. The 1745 one-room schoolhouse, filled with wooden and wrought-iron desks, was moved to its present location in the mid-1970s.

Congregational Church of South Dennis (508-394-5992, congregationalchurchof southdennis.org), 216A Main Street, South Dennis. The staff will let you into this 1835 church on weekday mornings. What's there? The chapel features a chandelier made with Sandwich glass and a 1762 Snetzler pipe organ, the country's oldest, which is still in use during services. The church is also called the Sea Captains Church because more than 100 of its founding members were sea captains.

❋ ✐ **Jericho House and Barn Museum**, (508-398-6736; dennishistoricalsociety.org), 90 Old Main Street, West Dennis. Open by appointment (when there are enough volunteers). The 1801 full Cape-style house contains period furnishings, and the 1810 barn is filled with antique tools, carriages, and a fanciful collection of folk art animals (a veritable "driftwood zoo") crafted in the 1950s by Sherman Woodward.

❋ To Do

BICYCLING & RENTALS The **Cape Cod Rail Trail** offers 25 miles of paved road for your biking pleasure. The trail route starts in Wellfleet and passes through the towns of Eastham, Orleans, Brewster, Harwich, Dennis, and Yarmouth. Hop on the trail across from Hall Oil, off Route 134 and South Dennis. You can rent bicycles and equipment at **Barb's Bike Shop** (508-760-4723; barbsbikeshop.com), 430 Route 134,

SCENIC DRIVES

The **South Dennis Historic District**, on and around Main Street from Route 134, gets wonderful afternoon light and relatively little traffic. Escape the crowds and head for this little gem; it's worth a short drive or quiet walk. Note the South Dennis Free Public Library (circa 1858)on Main Street, a cottage-style building covered with wooden gingerbread trim. Liberty Hall is also noteworthy; it was used for concerts, fairs, lectures, and balls when the second story was added in 1865. Edmond Nickerson, founder of the Old South Dennis Village Association, deserves much of the credit for initiating fundraising drives and overseeing restoration projects.

For a pleasant alternative to Route 134, which also connects the north- and southsides, take Old Bass River Road, which turns into Main Street in the South Dennis Historic District.

KAYLA ROBERTSON/DO ART PHOTOGRAPHY

South Dennis; and **Dennis Cycle Center** (508-398-0011; denniscyclecenter.com), 249 Great Western Road, South Dennis. Both shops provide parking and easy access to the rail trail.

BOAT EXCURSIONS & RENTALS If you're looking to rent watercraft during your stay, check out boat excursions and rentals in Yarmouth or Harwich. For boating regulations contact the **Harbormaster** (508-385-5555; town.dennis.ma.us/harbormaster), 351 Sesuit Neck Road.

FISHING Several competitive fishing charters depart from Sesuit Harbor and only a few are listed below. Otherwise, test your luck in freshwater for smallmouth bass and trout. Procure freshwater and saltwater fishing licenses and regulations online at mass .gov/eea/agencies/dfg/licensing.

Big game: **Sea Dog Fishing Team & Charters** (508-269-3003; seadogfishingteam charters.com), Cold Storage Road, East Dennis. Trips mid-May through September. Join Captain Paul Spear and first mate Kevin Spear on their 24-foot Boston Whaler for a fishing trip you surely won't forget. Time flies when you're having fun. $$$$+.

SCENIC BIKE RIDES ARE A CLASSIC CAPE COD TRADITION MARCIA DUGGAN/CAPECODSOUL

Janine B. Sportfishing (508-790-7820; or cell 774-212-0538; capecodsportfishing .com), 352 Sesuit Neck Road, West Dennis. With over 30 years of charter experience, Captain Wayne Bergeron has a keen eye for prime fishing areas. His son and first mate, Michael, joined the business at 14 years old and has almost paid off his college tuition thanks to the family business. $$$$+.

On shore: **Corporation Beach** is a nice place to spend the day with rod, reel, and a bucket of sand eels.

By bridge or jetty: On the West Dennis side of **Bass River Bridge** off Route 28, park along the shoulder. Large stripers, blues, and winter flounder tend to hang in the shadows. Although fishing is not officially allowed here, the rule is not enforced (they'll get you more for parking on the bridge than they will for the fishing).

Freshwater: **Scargo Lake** is one of the best places for freshwater fishing on Cape Cod (shh!). It's deeper than you'd expect and stocked with fish every spring (including smallmouth bass and three types of trout: rainbow, brook, and brown).

Supplies: The **Goose Hummock Seasonal Shop** (508-258-0929; goose.com), 1369 Route 134, South Dennis. Open May to October. (Check out the year-round store under *Fishing* in Orleans.)

FOR FAMILIES 🚲 **Cartwheels** (508-394-6755; capecodcartwheels.com), 11 South Gages Way, across from Tony Kent Arena, South Dennis. Open in the summer. "Indy-style" go-carts, batting cages, an arcade, moon walk, Italian ice, and ice cream.

GOLF **Dennis Highlands** and **Dennis Pines** (508-385-8347; dennisgolf.com), 825 Old Bass River Road and 50 Golf Course Road, South Dennis.

KAYAKS & PADDLEBOARDS **Cape Cod Waterways** (508-398-0080; capecodwater ways.com), 16 Main Street, Dennis Port. Open daily mid-April to mid-October. The small and winding Swan River heads about 0.75 mile north to the 200-acre Swan Pond and 2 miles south to Nantucket Sound. Cape Cod Waterways rents electric and manual paddleboats, canoes, and kayaks that can accommodate a family with two small children.

ICE-SKATING ✳ **Tony Kent Arena** (508-760-2400; tonykentarena.com), 8 South Gages Way, South Dennis. Located off Route 134, this rink served as Olympic silver medalist Nancy Kerrigan's training ground back in the early 1990s.

MINI GOLF **Holiday Hill** (508-398-8857; holidayhillinnandsuites.com), 350 Main Street, Dennis Port. Open late April to mid-October. Route 28 is lined with mini-golf courses similar in quality, but can others claim that they plant more than 10,000 flowers annually, as Holiday Hill can?

PARASAILS & JETSKIS **Dennis Parasail** (508-385-8359; capecodparasail.com), 1372 Route 134, South Dennis.

✳ Green Space

BEACHES Cottage renters may purchase a weekly parking pass at Town Hall (508-394-8300), 485 Main Street, South Dennis. Day-trippers pay ($$$) to park at the following beaches:

🏄 **West Dennis Beach** (off Lighthouse Road) on Nantucket Sound is the town's finest and longest beach (it's more than a mile long). Like many Nantucket Sound beaches, though, it's also rather narrow. While there's parking for more than 1,300 cars, the lot rarely fills. If you drive to the western end, you can usually find a few yards of beach for

BEACH JETTY KAYLA ROBERTSON/DO ART PHOTOGRAPHY

MAYFLOWER AND CHAPIN BEACH STRETCH KAYLA ROBERTSON/DO ART PHOTOGRAPHY

yourself. The eastern end is for residents only. Facilities include 10 lifeguard stations, a snack bar at the eastern end, showers, and restrooms. It's difficult to imagine that fishing shanties, fish weirs, and dories once lined the shores of West Dennis Beach. But they did.

Chapin Memorial Beach, off Chapin Beach Road on Cape Cod Bay, is open to four-wheel-drive vehicles. It's a nice, long, dune-backed beach. As you drive up to Chapin, you'll probably notice an incongruous-looking building plunked down in the marshes and dunes. In fact, it's the headquarters for the Aquaculture Research Corporation (known as the Cultured Clam Corp.), the only state-certified seller of shellfish seed. Begun in 1960, the company is a pioneer in the field of aquaculture. There's no better place to study shellfish. Facilities at the beach include portable restrooms.

Corporation Beach, off Corporation Road on Cape Cod Bay, is backed by low dunes and was once used as a packet-ship landing by a group of town residents who formed the Nobscusset Pier Corporation (hence its name). The crescent-shaped beach has concession stands, a playground and picnic area, lifeguards, and restrooms.

Ⓜ **Mayflower Beach**, off Beach Street on Cape Cod Bay, has a boardwalk, restrooms, and a concession stand. **Sea Street Beach**, off Sea Street, and **Howes Street Beach**, off Howes Street, are backed

PRINCESS BEACH KAYLA ROBERTSON/DO ART PHOTOGRAPHY

by low dunes; both have boardwalks. The Sea Street parking lot fills up by noon. These three beaches are relatively small and good for families with young children because the water is shallow. As at Corporation and Chapin Memorial beaches, at low tide you can walk a mile out into the bay.

There are seven other public beaches on Nantucket Sound, but all are quite small. Of those, the **Crowes Pasture Conservation** area is a favorite.

PONDS & LAKES **Scargo Lake**, a deep, freshwater kettle hole left behind by retreating glaciers, has two beaches: **Scargo Beach** (off Route 6A) and **Princess Beach** (off Scargo Hill Road). Princess Beach has a picnic area; bathers at Scargo Beach tend to put their beach chairs in the shallow water or on the narrow, tree-lined shore. There are two legends concerning the lake's creation—you decide which you prefer: Did an American Indian have the lake dug for fish that she received as a present? Or did a giant named Maushop dig the hole as a remembrance of himself to the local American Indian tribe?

Swan Pond Overlook, off Centre Street from Searsville Road and Route 134. A small overlook best for bird-watching.

WALKS **Indian Lands Conservation Area**, behind Town Office on Main Street, South Dennis. This easy, 2-mile round-trip walk skirts the banks of the upper Bass River. In winter you'll see blue herons and kingfishers; lady's slippers bloom in May. From the northern end of the Town Hall parking lot on Main Street, follow the power line right-of-way path for half a mile to the trailhead. The adjacent cemetery near the parking lot offers gravestones of Dennis' ancestors from the 1690s.

✳ Lodging

🐾 Dennis lodging establishments represent very good values. One place off Route 6A *really* stands out on the northside, while the southside is loaded with family places (with one noteworthy exception). Most southside places are on or quite close to the beach.

RESORT 🐚 **Lighthouse Inn** (508-398-2244; lighthouseinn.com), Lighthouse Inn Road, West Dennis. Open mid-May to mid-October. They don't make them like this anymore. This classic Cape Cod, family-friendly resort on Nantucket Sound has 68 rooms and tidy cottages on 9 grassy, waterfront acres. The resort, expertly operated by the Stones since 1938, has lots of amenities: supervised children's activities, special children's dinners, a heated pool, tennis, shuffle-board, mini-golf, volleyball, and the Sand Bar Club and Lounge. On rainy days guests gather in the common rooms of the lodge-style main building, stocked with games, books, and a TV. Oriental carpets lend it a delightful, old-shoe, Adirondack-camp feel. And a staff of more than 100 hustle around, keeping guests happy. A full breakfast is included. Its Bass River Lighthouse is the only privately owned working lighthouse in the country. $$–$$$.

BED-AND-BREAKFASTS ✳ 🐚 **Isaiah Hall Bed and Breakfast Inn** (508-385-9928; isaiahhallinn.com), 152 Whig Street, Dennis. On a quiet street off Route 6A, this rambling 1857 farmhouse is one of the most comfortable and welcoming places on Cape Cod. It feels like one big nonstop social event here, with guests lingering in the pass-through kitchen and hanging around in the "great room." Main inn guest rooms are furnished with country-style antiques, while rooms in the attached carriage house are newer, each decorated with stenciling, white wicker, and knotty-pine paneling. Check out the newer Isaiah Hall Suite, a jewel of a two-bedroom suite with a fireplace. All 12 rooms are air-conditioned and

ISAIAH HALL B&B INN   KIM GRANT

equipped with flat-screen TVs, DVDs, and 600–thread count sheets. There is plenty of indoor and outdoor common space, including that cathedral-ceilinged great room (with a guest computer), a delightfully relaxing garden, and a deep lawn that leads to the Cape's oldest cranberry bog. A full breakfast is served at one long, extraordinarily convivial table. $–$$.

❄ **Shady Hollow Inn** (508-694-7343; shadyhollowinn.com), 370 Main Street, South Dennis. This off-the-beaten-path bed-and-breakfast, with a tranquil side garden, is a graciously renovated sea captain's house that dates to 1839. Beth and Gary Albert's three guest rooms, with Mission-style furnishings and quilts, are outfitted with a hefty dose of attention, soothing color palettes, and tasteful bathroom renovations. $.

✐ **An English Garden B&B** (508-398-2915; anenglishgardenbb.com), 32 Inman Road, Dennis Port. Open late April through October; guest house and suites open year-round. This is a very good, comfortable, contemporary choice. Within a 2-minute walk of the beach,

this bed-and-breakfast has nine tasteful rooms, two suites, and a three-bedroom guest house. Each boasts hardwood floors, quilts, and a deck or small balcony; some have a whirlpool or ocean view. Both airy living rooms are perfect for reading on a rainy afternoon. A full breakfast is served at individual tables in a spacious and bright breakfast room. $$.

✐ **By the Sea Guests B&B** (508-398-8685; bytheseaguests.com), 57 Chase Avenue at Inman Road, Dennis Port. Guest house open late April through September, while suites are available year-round. You can't get closer to Inman Beach than this. Each of the 12 large rooms, with refrigerator and cable TV, is basically but pleasantly outfitted. Look for well-maintained 1950s-style cottage furniture, white cotton bedspreads, and white curtains. It's all very summery, charming, and breezy. On rainy days, guests can head to the enclosed porch overlooking the private beach (just steps away) or to the large living room with books, games, and a ready supply of snacks. There are also five contemporary, fully equipped one- and two-bedroom suites for weekly stays. Full breakfast included with bed-and-breakfast rooms: $$–$$$.

COTTAGES ✐ **Dennis Seashores** (508-778-8108; dennisseashores.com), 20 Chase Avenue, Dennis Port. Open May through October. These 35 housekeeping cottages are some of the best on Nantucket Sound; make reservations a year in advance. The two-, three-, and four-bedroom shingled cottages, with knotty-pine paneling and fireplaces, are decorated and furnished in a "Cape Cod Colonial" style. Cottages, with fully equipped kitchens, towels, and linens, are either beachfront or nestled among pine trees; each has a grill and picnic table. The resort's private stretch of beach is well tended. $$$–$$$$+.

❋ Where to Eat

Dennis has embarrassing riches of good and great restaurants to satisfy every budget and whim. Surrounding towns should be so lucky.

DINING OUT **The Pheasant** (508-385-2133; pheasantcapecod.com), 905 Main Street, Route 6A, Dennis. Open D. After 30 years of perfect service, Bill Atwood and his wife Denise, passed over the key to their iconic restaurant. Meet new owners Adam and Erica Dunn, a married team dedicated to continuing the Pheasant's legacy, while adding a little flavor of their own. Low ceilings, wood floors, a large brick fireplace laced with small lights, and a brightly hand-painted floral mural sets a truly rustic and romantic tone. Located in a 200-year-old renovated barn (actually, a former ship chandlery on Corporation Beach), the elegant restaurant enjoys a fine reputation for attentive service and first-rate cuisine. Cranking up the heat in the kitchen is Executive Chef Toby Hill with dishes like crispy skin "brick" chicken (literally cooked under a brick); or the tomato and olive braised monkfish, gnocchi, and crispy quinoa. Adventurous foodies will be curious to try the bone marrow burger, or the curried goat. Be sure to start with appetizers like the pan-roasted scallops topped with fresh peaches and a refreshing watermelon relish. The housemade soft cheese is also impressive. Chef Toby works with several local farms on the Cape and the menu changes seasonally depending on available produce, seafood, and game. I recommend penciling the Pheasant into your book of vacation dining musts. $$$–$$$$.

Fin (508-385-2096; fincapecod.com), 800 Main Street, Route 6A, Dennis. Open D, mid-February through December. This upscale contemporary seafood bistro (intimately housed in a two-story antique Cape building) has been all the rage since it opened. Don't miss the day boat sea scallops or flounder (a house specialty)—most is locally sourced. And the chef/owner, Martha Kane, hails from the acclaimed Brewster Fish House. Oh, and hubby Jonathan Smith is an oyster grower, so don't miss the oyster chowder or Nobscussett oysters. $$$.

🦞 Ÿ **Ocean House** (508-394-0700; oceanhouserestaurant.com), 425 Old Wharf Road, at the end of Depot Street, Dennis Port. Open B, D, mid-March to early January. Everyone loves the Ocean House, but don't let appearances deceive you: The boxy brick building belies the ocean views that await. Go before sunset to drink in the views; it's half the fun. The other half is artful chef Anthony Silvistri, who prepares seasonal, contemporary, New American dishes with a local influence. Look for fusion dishes like cedar-roasted teriyaki salmon, grilled Hawaiian tuna steak, or a 12-ounce Wolfneck's Farm rib eye. If you don't have reservations, dine at the bar on gourmet pizzas and appetizers. Definitely save room for distinctive desserts, and consider starting with a signature martini. $$–$$$$.

❋ ✐ Ÿ **The Oyster Company Raw Bar & Grille** (508-398-4600; theoyster

GINA'S BY THE SEA KIM GRANT

company.com), 202 Depot Street, Dennis Port. Open L, D. This is one hip and happening place to nosh with pals. And to think you don't have to drive to Wellfleet to enjoy magnificently fresh oysters anymore! Although the Oyster Company offers other fishy temptations besides briny delicacies, the $1.25 oysters (available from 5 to 6:30) really pack 'em in. Oysters are harvested daily from Quivet Neck in Dennis. Try summertime oysters barely broiled in cilantro and butter. The regular menu is fairly limited because the chef relies on the daily catch for inspiration. $$–$$$.

♆ **Gina's by the Sea** (508-385-3213), 134 Taunton Avenue, Dennis. Open D, April through November. Gina's is a very friendly and fun place, with a low-key bar, knotty-pine walls, a fireplace, and exposed beams. A fixture in this beachside enclave since 1938, Gina's really is as consistently good as everyone says. Its Northern Italian menu features signature dishes like garlicky shrimp scampi, mussels marinara, and chicken "gizmonda." Because the restaurant is small, very popular, and doesn't take reservations, arrive early or wait until after 9 p.m. Otherwise, put your name on the waiting list and take a walk on nearby Chapin Memorial Beach, or have a drink and watch the sunset.

Gina's epitomizes the essence of summer. $$–$$$.

🍴 ❄ ❧ **Scargo Café** (508-385-8200; scargocafe.com), 799 Main Street, Dennis. Open L, D. The friendly staff here are particularly adept at getting patrons (most of whom are older) to Cape Playhouse shows (see **Entertainment**) on time without hurrying them. If you're really late, light bites and finger foods such as shrimp martini and calamari are served in the pleasant bar. Otherwise, dependable specials include seafood strudel, a vegetable-and-Brie sandwich, rack of lamb, and lobster risotto. As for the atmosphere, the bustling, renovated former sea captain's house is awash in wood: paneling, wainscoting, and floors. Brothers Peter and David Troutman have presided over the extensive and well-executed menu since 1987. It's hard to beat the prices and quality here. L $–$$, D $$–$$$$.

Clean Slate Eatery (508-292-8817; cleanslateeatery.com). 702 Route 28, West Dennis. Open D. The entrepreneurs behind Clean Slate (in the "pop-up" dining business prior to opening this brick-and-mortar place in 2016) are putting a fresh and adventurous spin on the local dining scene with two prix-fixe seatings at two different price points. Choose from traditional and vegetarian tasting menus, which might include roasted blue hubbard squash with apple cider–braised kale dumplings in a sweet onion tarragon veloute; halibut romesco with pickled dragon beans, cherry tomatoes, and roasted eggplant; or olive oil cake with ginger ice cream and vanilla compressed peaches. Proclaiming this "dinner as an event" is about right. $$$$+.

EATING OUT **Chapin's Bayside** (508-385-7000; chapinsbayside.com), 85 Taunton Avenue, Dennis. Open L, D, June through October. Now under new ownership, this casual eatery boasts a lively outdoor scene with a small marble counter bar, modern steel tables and chairs, towering heaters, and overhead string lights. There's inside seating, too. The menu offers something for everyone, which generally means the food isn't gourmet quality, but it also means that most folks will walk away fairly happy. There's a lot to be said for that. Chapin's is near to two bayside beaches—Mayflower and Corporation—and offers a slew of nightly entertainment (check schedule online). $–$$$.

Harvest Gallery Wine Bar (508-760-1633; harvestgallerywinebar.com), 776 Main Street, Route 6A, Dennis. Open D. A great place to sip fine wine, chat with friends, munch on apps and soak in tunes. Be careful—after a few glasses of wine, the contemporary artwork might whispering in your ear, "Buy me." The diverse gallery features more than 30 artists of different genres—paintings, collages, sculptures, textiles, photography, and more. The gourmet bar-style menu offers upscale classics for the "locavore-minded." The full-service wine bar (inspired by West Coast and European nightlife) highlights wines from around the world, as well as craft cocktails and beer. And a nightly rotating lineup of local musicians only enhances the lively atmosphere. There's quite the variety—I've seen jazz, folk and reggae performers at this place. Owner/artist Michael Pearson hit the nail on the head when he decided to combine his passions into one endeavor. To top it off—the service is friendly (and open late hours). $$.

Waterfront Restaurant (508-398-2244; lighthouseinn.com), 1 Lighthouse Road, off Lower County Road at the Lighthouse Inn. Open B, L, D, mid-May to mid-October. The décor and cuisine here are decidedly old-fashioned; it's the kind of place you might expect in the Catskills, à la 1950, except it's perched seaside of West Dennis Beach. Along with peaked ceilings and knotty-pine paneling, the large and open dining room features a full wall of windows overlooking the ocean. $–$$$.

Sesuit Harbor Café (508-385-6134; sesuit-harbor-cafe.com), 357 Sesuit Neck Road, Dennis. Open B, L, D, April through October. Wildly, wildly popular

SESUIT HARBOR CAFÉ MARCIA DUGGAN/CAPECODSOUL

with good reason, this café offers excellent lobster rolls and trips aboard a retrofitted lobster boat (508-385-1686; lobsterrollcruises.com). If you prefer to keep your feet on terra firma, make a beeline through the marina and boatyard for their simple harbor front shack. It's nothing to look at, but the raised herb beds augur well for quality ingredients. Order off the scallop shell blackboard menu and eat at picnic tables, inside or outside, with mismatched umbrellas. BYOB and cash only. $–$$$.

Captain Frosty's (508-385-8548; captainfrosty.com), 219 Main Street, Route 6A, Dennis. Open L, D, mid-April through September. This no-frills roadside clam shack uses premium ingredients like hooked (not gillnetted) Chatham cod, Gulf shrimp, native clams, lobster, and small sea scallops, so you'll want to look for daily specials. Save room for the Cape's best soft-serve ice cream. $–$$.

Kream n' Kone (508-394-0808; kreamnkone.com), 961 Main Street, West Dennis. Open L, D, mid-February to mid-October. This place dishes honest-to-goodness kitsch, not kitsch imported from any consultant who says kitsch is cool. Come for self-serve fried seafood (fresh, never frozen), ice cream, and clams. Although it's campy, it's not necessarily cheap; a family can easily spend a fortune here. $–$$.

Lost Dog Pub (508-385-6177; lost dogpubs.com), 1374 Route 134, East Dennis. Open L, D. I wouldn't waste good daylight hours at this tavern at lunchtime, but it makes a cozy spot after dark—when you just want something homey and decent, with good service. Their burgers and pizza are good; seafood, fishcakes, and clam chowder are specialties. $–$$. (See also under **Where to Eat** in Orleans.)

The Dog House (508-398-7774; doghousedennis.com), 189 Lower County Road, Dennis Port. Open L, D, mid-May to mid-October. Calling all hot dog lovers (like me)! This old-fashioned hot dog stand dispenses dogs with sauerkraut or bacon, cheese or chili, and lots of other odd combos like flamin' hot Cheetos, macaroni and cheese, pastrami meat or salsa. Lemonade aficionados take note, too: they serve it fresh squeezed here. After you've ordered from the take-out window, have a seat at one of a few covered picnic tables. $–$$.

SWEET TREATS & COFFEE **The Red Cottage** (508-394-2923; redcottage restaurant.com), 36 Old Bass River Road, South Dennis. Open B, L. This homey joint run by the Rosenbach family offers some of the best diner-style breakfasts this side of the bridge. First timers take note: eggs are cracked to order (no cartons of pre-scrambled here); their bacon is thick (nine slices per pound and cured exclusively for them); there's always a lengthy wait (but well worth it); and don't show up with large parties. Be sure to ask your server about signature dishes like the crowd-favorite Red Cottage home fries: hand cut potatoes, onions, ham, green peppers, mushrooms, and herbs topped with an airy lemon hollandaise; or the cinnamon bun French toast and 1776 sausage (a savory, juicy, mild pork sausage). This cheery morning dive

THE CAPE'S SIGNATURE LOBSTER ROLL MARCIA DUGGAN/ CAPECODSOUL

HEAVENLY SCREENINGS

Cape Cinema (508-385-2503; capecinema.com), 35 Hope Lane, off Route 6A, Dennis. Built in 1930 as a movie theater, Cape Cinema continues to bring fine art films, foreign films, and independent productions to Cape audiences. The exterior was designed after the Congregational church in Centerville, while the interior ceiling was designed by Rockwell Kent to represent his view of heaven, filled with comets and constellations. When Kent refused to set foot in Massachusetts because he was protesting the 1921 verdict in the Sacco and Vanzetti trial, Jo Mielziner supervised the painting and installation of the 6,400-square-foot art deco mural, which was done by the Art Students League in a New York theater and shipped by train to the Cape. There are about 300 seats in this theater, which was chosen to premiere *The Wizard of Oz* in 1940. Don't miss catching a flick here. ❄

nestled on the 1828 Captain Wilbur Harden Homestead, originally started out as a 2½-room cottage, built in 1936 by Walter Weeman. Later the house was expanded and a restaurant opened in the garage. At one point in time, there was also a boat-building shop where the restaurant is today. In 2009 the restaurant received a top-to-bottom "period" restoration, returning to its 1950s splendor. Take a gander at the vintage art collection of South Dennis lining the walls. For more information about the Red Cottage history, pick up a copy of "A History of the Red Cottage" by Edmond Rhodes Nickerson. Cash only. $–$$.

The Breakfast Room (508-398-0581; thebreakfastroomcapecod.com), 675 Route 28, West Dennis. Open B, L, April through December. Another local and lively breakfast den serving up hearty morning fare at reasonable prices. In addition to griddlecakes, choose from traditional egg dishes, or go whole hog and chow down on steak, eggs, and potatoes. They have other classics like French toast and pancakes, too. $.

Wee Packet (508-394-6595; weepacketrestaurant.com), 79 Depot Street, Dennis Port. Open B, L, D, early May to late October. Since 1949, this small and sweet place has been serving full Irish breakfasts, tons of egg dishes, hot and hearty lobster rolls at lunch, and clambakes with all the fixing for dinner. The outdoor patio and summer cocktails are a nice addition. As for the name, many years ago, "Packet Ships", as they were known, were used to transport goods and services from Boston to Cape Cod and the Islands. The words "Wee Packet" in layman's terms mean "small ship." The height of the Cape Cod packet ships spanned most of the 19th century. $–$$.

Three Fins Coffee Roasters (508-619-3372; threefinscoffee.com), 581 Route 28, West Dennis. "We love coffee and we love talking about coffee—it is a magical bean in our view." This specialty coffee bar focuses on small farm and small lot brews, which is apparent in each sip. It's all part science, part art. Come here for lattes, Americanos, and the likes.

Sundae School Ice Cream Parlor (508-394-9122; sundaeschool.com), 381 Lower County Road, Dennis Port. Open mid-April to mid-October. This old-fashioned parlor is replete with a marble soda fountain, marble tables, tin signage, and a nickelodeon. Some confections are delightfully modern, though: frozen yogurt and ice cream are made with two-thirds less fat. I refuse to take a stand, by the way, in the Sundae School versus Smuggler debate of which is better. You can't make me walk the plank on that one.

Ice Cream Smuggler (508-385-5307; icecreamsmuggler.com), 716 Main Street, Dennis. Open April to mid-October. Stop here for delicious homemade ice cream and frozen yogurt.

MARKETS **Dennis Public Market** (508-385-3215; dennispublicmarket.com), 653 Main Street, Route 6A. Locally known as DPM, this neighborhood market opened its doors to the public in 1907 as a five & dime shop. Today, although the prices may have changed, that's about it. Stop here for all the essentials: produce, deli meats, condiments, sandwiches, and liquor, beer, and wine.

Swan River Fish Market (508-398-2340; swanriverrestaurant.com), 5 Lower County Road, Dennis Port. Open mid-May to mid-October. Family owned and operated, this casual market's appeal is fresh hook-caught fish, local lobsters, steamers, oysters, littlenecks, and cherrystone clams. The fresh catch selection—halibut, swordfish, cod, and haddock—changes daily. Adjoining the market is the Swan River Restaurant. Arrive early to secure a table overlooking a river, a marsh, Nantucket Sound, and a windmill. $$–$$$$.

See also *Farms* under **Selective Shopping**.

Entertainment

LIVE-MUSIC **O'Shea's Olde Inne** (508-398-8887; osheasoldeinne.com), 348 Main Street, West Dennis. A very lively Irish pub with a range of nightly entertainment. From traditional Irish jigs, to Sunday blues jams, Round Ups quartet, open mike nights, and Celtic rock bands—O'Shea keeps the boat rockin' all night long. I've never eaten here before, but I've heard decent reviews from local folks. Probably not a great spot for people who are easily annoyed by rowdy children. $–$$

See also **Harvest Gallery Wine Bar** and **Chapin's** under **Where to Eat**.

MOVIES **Entertainment Cinemas** (508-394-4700; entertainmentcinemas.com), 2–6 Enterprise Road, South Dennis. Feel like hiding from the sun in the dark corners of an air-conditioned movie theater? Or maybe it's raining and you've been dying to see a newly released flick. Stop here. $–$$.

See also **Cape Cinema** in "Heavenly Screenings" on page 166.

THEATERS **Cape Playhouse** (508-385-3911; capeplayhouse.com), 820 Main Street, Dennis. Shows mid-June to early September. The Cape Playhouse was established in 1927 by Californian Raymond Moore, who initially went to Provincetown to start a theater company, but found it too remote. Moore's attitude when he purchased this former 1830s Unitarian meetinghouse for $200 was, "If we fix it up, they will come." Sure enough, the playhouse proudly claims the title of the country's oldest continuously operating professional summer theater and the Cape's only full Equity theater. Basil Rathbone starred in the company's first production, *The Guardsman*. Over the years, the playhouse has featured the likes of Helen Hayes, Julie Harris, Olivia de Havilland, and Jessica Tandy, when they were already "stars." Henry Fonda, Bette Davis, Humphrey

CAPE PLAYHOUSE KIM GRANT

WHIMSY IN THE WOODS

Scargo Pottery (508-385-3894; scargopottery.com), 30 Dr. Lord's Road South, off Route 6A, Dennis. Down a path through the woods, Harry Holl's four daughters (Tina, Kim, Mary, and Sarah) make whimsical and decidedly untraditional birdhouses, fountains, and architectural sculptures, among other things. The "gallery" is a magical world that you won't want to miss: Pieces hang from tree branches and sit on tree stumps. The work isn't cheap, but it isn't run-of-the-mill, either. There's no question that this is pottery as art. ✽

SCARGO POTTERY KAYLA ROBERTSON/DO ART PHOTOGRAPHY

Bogart, and Gregory Peck acted here before they were "discovered." Check the summertime schedule for worthwhile children's theater. If you make it to only one summer production, let it be here. $$$–$$$$+.

✽ Selective Shopping

✽ Unless otherwise noted, all shops are open year-round.

ANTIQUES Dennis Port center is a quiet place for year-round antique browsers. Chief among the half-dozen shops "downtown" is the **Main Street Antique Center** (508-760-5700), 691 Main Street.

With more than 30 dealers, it's just one of many retailers trying to revitalize the little district.

Antiques Center of Cape Cod (508-385-6400; antiquecenterofcapecod.com), 243 Main Street, Route 6A, Dennis. With more than 250 dealers, this two-story (former) building supply store is the Cape's largest cooperative, offering curios large and small. Don't miss it or the giant warehouse next door. Most objects sell for under $200 and are classified as "old," "vintage," or "collectible" rather than "antique."

Eldred's Auctions (508-385-3116; eldreds.com), 1483 Main Street, Route 6A, East Dennis. This high-end auction house—the Cape's largest—moves magnificent collections. In July the weekly auctions concentrate on books, collectibles, marine items, and paintings. During August there is an Americana auction the first week; a contemporary Cape Cod art auction the second week; and a weeklong Asian art auction late in the month. In spring and fall, call about the monthly specialty auctions.

ARTISANS **Eden Hand Arts** (508-385-9708; edenhandarts.info), corner of Dr. Lord's Road and Route 6A, Dennis. When I was in high school, your level of "cool" was determined by how many Cape Cod bracelets you had stacked on your wrist (you know, the classic silver cuff bracelet with a gold ball—then two balls, three balls, etc.). And if Eden made it, you were that much cooler because everything is custom made and limited edition. So limited, in fact, that the only way to visit this tiny artisanal shop is by booking (free) tickets online. It's on a first-come-first-served basis and only a handful of tickets are available. Though I never fell into this trap (and still managed to be cool somehow, I think), my friends are pleased with their triumph.

Fritz Glass (508-394-0441; fritzglass .com), 36 Upper County Road, Dennis Port. Fritz Lauenstein creates and sells his colorful, striking, extraordinarily decorative, and functional glass pieces here. Watch him work and check out the inventory of fun and intricate marbles (sold in museums around the country) and sand dollars, honey pots and bud vases. Chances are that Fritz's wife, June, and his daughter Coco will be in the shop, too.

A Touch of Glass (508-398-3850; atouchofglasscapecod.com), 711 Route 28, West Dennis. For over 30 years, Bob Micznik has been crafting beautiful lamps, ornaments, windows, cabinet doors, and plates using the sturdy "Tiffany" method for assembling stained glass. He also creates jewelry from beach glass and local seashells found along Cape Cod's shore.

BOOKSTORES **I Cannot Live Without Books** (508-760-4959), 314 Main Street, West Dennis. Hence the name of the store, this great little bookstore is stocked with a well-rounded selection of reading material. The owners are wonderful, too. Book enthusiasts will surely find something here to keep them busy.

CLOTHING **Mermaids on Cape Cod** (508-369-1401; mermaidsoncapecod .com), 855 Route 28, West Dennis. This beachy boutique started like most hip clothing stores on the Cape—from the back of a big, bright, mobile bus! The bus became a brick-and-mortar-reality three short months later and Mermaids on Cape Cod took off in waves. Official mermaid gear includes everything from beach blankets, beach must-haves, Nauti clothes, hats and visors, jewelry, and more. The boutique also partners with local charities whose mission to protect the ocean environment.

FARMS **P&D Fruit** (508-394-9099), 349 Lower County Road, Dennis Port. Open mid-May to mid-September. A seasonal stand with tons of local fruits and veggies (especially the corn—do not leave without a few cobs!) and select grocery items like cookies, salad dressing, and their amazing, gooey, and sweet and sticky cinnamon roll bread.

GALLERIES **Ross Coppelman and Kate Nelson** (508-385-7900; rosscoppelman .com and katenelson.com), 1439 Main Street, East Dennis. Ross has been fashioning stunning jewelry for more than 20 years. His shop is a special-occasion kind of place, and his creations have lots of zeros on the price tags. Kate's work is some of the most sophisticated abstraction I've seen on the Cape. Her nonrepresentational paintings and prints are extraordinary and, as she says, "ever-changing, like the path to the outgoing tide on the Brewster flats." She continues to fuse the experience of exterior landscape with the "inscape," the inner landscape of psyche and spirit.

See also **Harvest Gallery Wine Bar** under **Where to Eat**.

SPECIALTY **Elburne** (508-694-5536; elburne.com), 744 Main Street. Style your home with Cape Cod-esque décor from this locally owned and eco-friendly shop. From rugs to lamps, picture frames, pillows, dressers, mirrors, art, and other odds-and-ends, Elburne offers an upscale chic collection. Sisters and creative partners Laura and Simone Pereira named the shop after their childhood street, "Elburne" in their hometown of Brazil. Don't waste precious cargo space—order online and have it delivered.

On the Fringe (508-394-9000; love livelocal.com), 672 Main Street. This family-affair artisanal boutique is driven by Wendy Howard, her son Conor Howard-Rose and his girlfriend Janna Powell. Shop here for handcrafted coasters and tiles made with vintage materials such as old maps, brochures and advertisements. They make custom tiles, too.

Salt Yarn Studio (508-694-6189; saltyarnstudio.com), 620 Main Street. Not your grandmother's yarn store, that's for sure. This studio is a "fiber resource and craft school" tucked within a 200-year-old Cape cottage. Here you will find an array of hand woven treasures from woolfolk, bluesky fibers, malabrige, dirty water dyeworks, berroco, schoppel wolle, cascade, koigu, and more. If you know yarn, you will be in thread-heaven here, and most definitely leave with an armful of inspiration. They also offer drop-in classes and private lessons, check online for details.

Stage Stop Candy (508-394-1791; stagestopcandy.com), 411 Main Street, Dennis Port. Ray and Donna Hebert originated the ultimate chocolate-covered cranberry. You must try it. They'll make chocolates in any shape, including computer boards and TV remote controls.

✳ Special Events

✎ *Mid-August:* **Sandcastle Contest** (508-398-3568), on Mayflower Beach in the morning. Free.

THE LOWER CAPE

■

BREWSTER

HARWICH

CHATHAM

ORLEANS

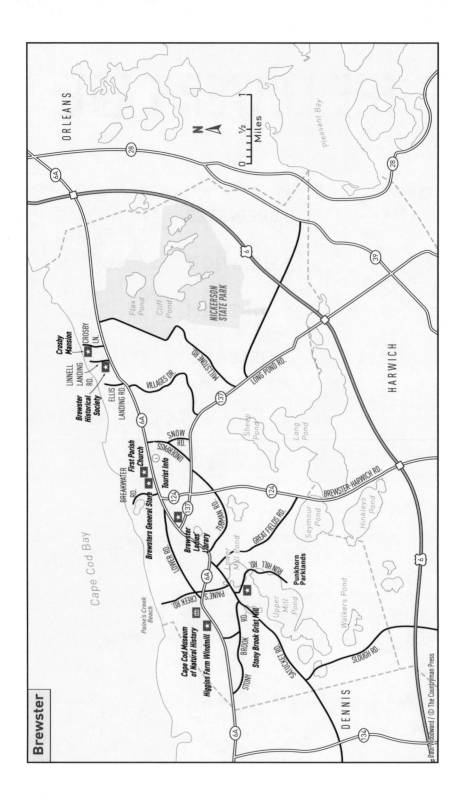

Brewster

ORLEANS

HARWICH

DENNIS

Pleasant Bay

Cape Cod Bay

NICKERSON STATE PARK

Flax Pond

Cliff Pond

Sheep Pond

Long Pond

Seymour Pond

Hinkleys Pond

Walkers Pond

Upper Mill Pond

Lower Mill Pond

Mill Pond

N

0   ½   Miles

Crosby Mansion

Brewster Historical Society

First Parish Church

Tourist Info

Brewsters General Store

Brewster Ladies Library

Punkhorn Parklands

Stony Brook Grist Mill

Cape Cod Museum of Natural History

Higgins Farm Windmill

Paine's Creek Beach

CROSBY LN.

LINNELL LANDING RD.

ELLIS LANDING RD.

VILLAGES DR.

MILLSTONE RD.

LONG POND RD.

SNOW RD.

UNDERPASS

BREAKWATER RD.

TUBMAN RD.

GREAT FIELDS RD.

BREWSTER-HARWICH RD.

LOWER RD.

PAINE'S CREEK RD.

LOWER MILL RD.

RUN HILL RD.

STONY BROOK RD.

SATUCKET RD.

SLOUGH RD.

6A

28

6

39

137

124

124

137

34

6A

6

Paul Woodward / © The Countryman Press

BREWSTER

You could spend a charmed week in Brewster with plenty to occupy you. While the 2,000-acre Nickerson State Park boasts facilities for a dozen outdoor activities, there is also Punkhorn Parklands, an undeveloped, 800-acre parcel of conservation land in town. Although Brewster has only 10,000 year-round residents, it has more than its share of attractions, including two good golf courses, horseback-riding trails, an outstanding museum of natural history, and exceptional dining choices.

Brewster's section of Route 6A is a vital link in the 80-square-mile Old King's Highway Historic District. Known for its selection of fine antiques shops, Brewster also attracts contemporary artists who are drawn to a landscape more evocative of the countryside than the seaside—the land south of Route 6A is dotted with ponds, hills, and dales.

Brewster, settled in 1659 and named for *Mayflower* passenger Elder William Brewster, wasn't incorporated until 1803, when it split from Harwich. By then the prosperous sea captains who'd built their homes on the bay side wanted to distance themselves from their less-well-off neighbors to the south. Between 1780 and 1870, 99 sea captains called Brewster home (although they sailed their clipper ships out of Boston and New York), a fact that even Henry David Thoreau commented on during his 1849 trip. Many of these beautiful houses on Route 6A have been converted to bed-and-breakfasts and inns.

In the early 1800s, Breakwater Beach was a popular landing for packet ships, which transported salt and vegetables to Boston and New York markets and brought tourists to the area. Salt making was big business in 1837, when more than 60 saltworks dotted Brewster beaches. Windmills pumped seawater into 36-by-18-foot vats, where it was left to evaporate (this process was developed in Dennis). During the late 18th and early 19th centuries, Brewster's Factory Village sold cloth, boots, and food to people all over the Cape.

GUIDANCE ❋ **Brewster Chamber of Commerce** (508-896-3500; brewster-capecod .com), 2198 Route 6A, about half a mile east of Route 124, in Town Hall.

GETTING THERE *By car:* Brewster is 30 minutes from the Cape Cod Canal (take Route 6 east to Exit 9, to Route 134, to Route 6A); it is 45 minutes from Provincetown, at the tip of the peninsula.

GETTING AROUND It's very easy to get around Brewster. There's no real "center" to the town; places of interest are strung along Route 6A.

By shuttle: **The Flex** (508-385-1430; capecodtransit.org) offers north and south-bound trips from Provincetown to Harwich with reserved stops. The Flex stops at the Brewster Council on Aging and Underpass Road.

PUBLIC RESTROOMS Nickerson State Park and the Visitor Information Center, both on Route 6A.

WHERE TO START IN BREWSTER

Morning: Read the morning paper on the front porch of The Brewster Store or indulge in sweet breakfast delights at the Eat Cake 4 Breakfast Bakery. Explore Nickerson State Park's woodlands and ponds before the temperature heats up.

Afternoon: Discover shallow pools on the Brewster Flats, or poke around the Stony Brook Grist Mill. Stop by Lemon Tree Village for a shopping spree and gallery gaze.

Evening: Enjoy a classic fried seafood dinner from Kate's before heading to Paine's Creek Beach for sunset. For a casual-fine dining experience head over to Spinnakers, or make reservations in advance for authentic French cuisine at historic Chillingsworth.

Late-Night: Look for shooting stars while relaxing in Drummer Boy Park (you might even catch a show) or check out the Woodshed's list of local rowdy performers.

PUBLIC LIBRARY **Brewster Ladies' Library** (508-896-3913; brewsterladieslibrary .org), 1822 Main Street. In 1852, two teenage Brewster girls established this "library," which began as a shelf of books lent from the girls' houses. After local sea captains donated funds in 1868, the ever-expanding library moved to a handsome red Victorian building. The two original front-parlor rooms—each with a fireplace, stained-glass windows, and armchairs—are still filled with portraits of sea captains and ships. Not just for ladies, the modern library has a large child's area, DVDs, CDs, periodicals, newspapers, and computers. Call for details about lectures and art exhibits.

EMERGENCIES **Brewster Police Department** (508-896-7011; brewsterpolice.org), 631 Harwich Road, or call **911**.

✳ To See

✳ ◈ **Cape Cod Museum of Natural History** (508-896-3867; ccmnh.org), 869 Route 6A. Founded by naturalist John Hay (along with seven local educators) in 1954, this is a terrific resource for learning about the Cape's natural world. The museum takes its mission seriously: to "inspire and foster an understanding and appreciation of our environment through education, and a means to sustain it." Check out marine tanks (containing rotating displays with native crabs, lobsters, mollusks, turtles, eels, frogs, and mesmerizing moon jellies), a live "osprey cam" which shows a bird family nesting nearby, whale displays, a natural history library, as well as many interactive, hands-on exhibits for children. The gift shop is packed with fun and educational toys, books, and games. The Wing's Island Trail—just one trail traversing the museum's 80 acres of marshes, beaches, and woodland—begins from here. $.

Stony Brook Grist Mill and Museum and Herring Run (508-896-1734; brewster-ma .gov), 830 Stony Brook Road. Open June through September; inquire about corn grinding on Saturdays. This mill side pond is one of the Cape's most picturesque places, especially during the spring migration (mid-April to early May), when the herring are "running" and the natural "ladders" are packed with the silver-backed fish. In 1663 America's first water-powered mill stood on this location. The present gristmill,

BREWSTER LADIES' LIBRARY KIM GRANT

constructed on 1873 woolen mill foundations (part of the 19th-century Factory Village), contains old milling equipment and an antique loom. The museum includes early American artifacts and American Indian stone tools.

The Brewster General Store (508-896-3744; brewsterstore.com), 1935 Main Street. Purveying groceries and general merchandise since 1866, this quintessentially Cape Cod store was built in 1852 as a Universalist Church. As always, locals and visitors sit outside on old church pews, sip coffee, read the morning newspaper, eat penny candy and ice cream, and watch the world go by. Upstairs has been re-created with memorabilia from the mid-1800s to the mid-1900s; downstairs has a working antique nickelodeon and often-used peanut roaster.

Brewster Historical Society Museum (508-896-9521; brewsterhistoricalsociety .org), 739 Lower Road at the Captain Elijah Cobb house. Open late June through August. Highlighting Brewster's rich heritage this small museum has an 1884 barbershop, a 1830s sea captain's room, toys, and gowns. Special summertime exhibits feature little known aspects of Brewster history. The society also maintains the **Higgins Farm Windmill, Harris-Black House, and Hopkins Blacksmith Shop**, located at Drummer Boy

STONY BROOK GRIST MILL KIM GRANT

Park, 773 Route 6A, West Brewster. Volunteer members of the BHS are on hand to regale you with historic anecdotes, like how a family raised 10 children in the one-room house (possibly the "last remaining primitive one-room house on the Cape"). The 1795 windmill is known for its octagonal design, while its top resembles a boat's hull. A walking trail originates from the house (see **Spruce Hill Conservation Area** under **Green Space**).

Crosby Mansion (508-896-1744; crosbymansion.com), 163 Crosby Lane, off Route 6A. Call for opening months. Once the elegant home of Albert and Matilda Crosby, this Colonial Revival structure sits on 19 acres of bayside property. The state acquired the land (and the house by default) by eminent domain in 1985 so that the public could access Cape Cod Bay from Nickerson State Park. Because the state couldn't afford to maintain it (the 28-room mansion requires millions in repairs), a volunteer group, the Friends of Crosby Mansion, stepped in. They've done an impressive job repairing the worst structural damage and much of the interior. Once upon a time, Albert Crosby owned the Chicago Opera House and fell in love with one of the showgirls, Matilda. When she came to live in Albert's modest turn-of-the-20th-century house, she was so unhappy that Albert had a mansion built for her around his original four-room house! (Kids compare stepping into the smaller house to what Alice must have felt like in Wonderland). Matilda is said to have entertained in the larger mansion while Albert stayed in his interior boyhood home.

First Parish Church (508-896-5577; firstparishbrewster.org), 1969 Route 6A, on the town green (a.k.a. The Egg, because of its shape and natural depression). Gothic windows and a bell tower mark the church's 1834 clapboard exterior, while interior pews are marked with names of prominent Brewster sea captains. Wander around the graveyard behind the church, too.

✳ To Do

BASEBALL ✐ The **Brewster Whitecaps** (508-896-7442; brewsterwhitecaps.com), who joined the Cape Cod Baseball League in 1988 as an expansion team, play behind the school, 384 Underpass Road, from mid-June to early August. The Whitecaps also sponsor weeklong clinics and a baseball camp in June and July.

BICYCLING & RENTALS The **Cape Cod Rail Trail** offers 25 miles of paved road for your biking pleasure. The trail route starts in Wellfleet and passes through the towns of Eastham, Orleans, Brewster, (and **Nickerson State Park**), Harwich, Dennis and Yarmouth. You can rent bicycles and equipment at **Cape Cod Rail Trail Bike & Kayak** (508-896-8200; railtrailbikeshop.com), 302 Underpass Road, which rents and sells bikes. As the name implies, they also rent kayaks for use on the kettle ponds, sandy lake beaches, and salt marshes along the trail; and **Brewster Bike** (508-896-8149; brewsterbike.com), 442 Underpass Road.

If you brought your own bikes, there is rail trail parking on Route 137, on Underpass Road off Route 137, and at Nickerson State Park on Route 6A. Trailers and alley cats (rented above) are great for hauling kids on this stretch because it's shady and fairly flat. (See also "A Supreme State Park" on page 179).

FISHING Brewster has almost 70 freshwater ponds. Procure freshwater and saltwater fishing licenses and regulations online (mass.gov/eea/agencies/dfg/licensing).

Big game: **Liberty** *Fishing Charters* (508-240-1613; libertyfishingcharters.com), 1 Bay View Drive. Open May to October. Book the *Liberty* for a half-day, full day, or extended day (with overnight charters) in pursuit of striped bass, bluefish, and the ultimate game fish, bluefin tuna. The *Liberty* is appointed with all the comforts of home: brew a fresh cup of coffee in the galley or grab a cold drink from the fridge. On your way to and from the fishing grounds, relax in the air conditioned/heated salon or step up to the roomy bridge for a Captain's view of the bay. The family owned and operated business is based in Brewster, but departs from Rock Harbor in Orleans.

Freshwater: The following ponds are stocked: **Sheep Pond**, off Route 124; **Upper Mill,** Run Hill Road; and **Flax, Little Cliff**, and **Higgins Ponds** within Nickerson State Park. For shellfishing permits (and specifics about where and when to find the creatures), head to Town Hall (508-896-3500), 2198 Route 6A.

Supplies: **Brewster Ace Hardware**, (508-896-6610; hardwarestorebrewster.com/bait-and-tackle), 2632 Route 6A. In addition to paint and screwdrivers, this Ace Hardware offers a full-service bait and tackle shop.

NICKERSON STATE PARK KIM GRANT

FOR FAMILIES **Eddy Elementary School**, 2298 Route 6A. A smaller playground with a jungle gym, tires to climb through, bars to swing on, four slides, eight swings, and more.

Playground by the Bay, Drummer Boy Park, Route 6A. Shaped like a packet ship to honor Brewster's seafaring history, this play structure has separate areas for toddlers and older children. Picnic tables, too.

Summer Camp (508-896-3867; ccmnh.org), 869 Route 6A at the Cape Cod Museum of Natural History. If you have a child ages 3 to 12 and a few extra hours (or days for that matter), check this place out. Classes explore "Mudflat Mania," "Extreme Science," tidal flats, archaeology, and Monomoy's barrier beach. The emphasis is on fun, outdoor adventure, and education.

(See also **Cape Repertory Theatre** under **Entertainment** and **First Parish Church** under **To See.**)

GOLF **The Captain's Golf Course** (508-896-1716; captainsgolfcourse.com), 1000 Freemans Way and **Ocean Edge Golf Club** (508-896-9000; oceanedge.com), 2907 Main Street, are highly rated courses. The Ocean Edge course was designed by the Nicklaus Design Group and is for members and resort guests exclusively.

HORSEBACK RIDING **Woodsong Farm** (508-896-5800; woodsongfarm.com), 121 Lund Farm Way. Open by appointment. Established in 1967, Woodsong offers riding instruction, boarding, training, coaching for competitive riders, children's day programs, horse shows, and an on-premises tack shop. Despite the ideal location, they do not rent horses for trail rides.

KAYAKS & PADDLEBOARDS **SUPfari Adventures** (508-205-9087; supfariadventures .com), multiple locations in Orleans and Brewster. Stand-up paddleboarding brought from Maui to Cape Cod by Brewster's former harbormaster. $$$$.

Lea's Boat Rentals, Flax Pond in Nickerson State Park. Open June to early September. Stop here for a range of watersport rentals at extremely fair prices. $.

SAILING **Cape Sail** (508-896-2730; capesail.com), out of Brewster's Upper Mill Pond and Harwich Port's Saquatucket Harbor. Late May to mid-October. A Coast Guard–licensed captain since 1983, Bob Rice offers customized sailing lessons and an overnight sailing school, as well as sunset and moonlight cruises and custom charters. Call him to discuss your interests.

See also **Pleasant Bay Community Sailing** under **To Do** in Harwich.

TENNIS Check the free public courts located behind the Fire Department near the town offices, Route 6A. There is a small court fee at the Brewster Community Tennis Courts (508-896-9430; brewsterrecreation.com), 384 Underpass Road.

✳ Green Space

Though Brewster is not famous for its salty waterfront, there are over 8 miles of coast and a few beaches that are definitely worth visiting.

BEACHES **Paine's Creek Beach**, Paine's Creek Road. Friend and local Brewster-native Brianna's favorite beach: a little quieter, but still perfect for families and children, this beach offers a superior sunset experience. It's also close to **Kate's Seafood** (see **Where to Eat**).

Other beaches ideal for children, swimming and sunsets include: **Breakwater Beach**, Breakwater Road; **Crosby Landing Beach**, Crosby Lane; and **Linnell Landing**, Linnell Landing Road.

PONDS **Long Pond** and **Sheep Pond**, both off Route 124, have freshwater swimming and small sandy beaches. Sheep Pond is a favorite among locals who praise the clean warm water.

Flax Pond and **(Big & Little) Cliff Pond**, both off Flax Pond Road in Nickerson State Park. Both have small beaches with limited sandy spots for lounging, some parking, a boat ramp, and a roped off swimming area. Perfect for watersports like kayaking and paddleboarding (see under **To Do**). Parking permits are required for residents and visitors and some with restrooms and seasonal lifeguards. Daily nonresident parking permits can be purchased at the lower level of Town Hall (508-896-4511; brewster-ma .gov), 2198 Main Street (see also "A Supreme State Park" on page 179).

WALKS Famed nature writer John Hay lived in Brewster and certainly had plenty of places nearby to enjoy Mother Nature. You can follow in his footsteps.

Wing's Island Trail, **South Trail**, and **North Trail**, at the Cape Cod Museum of Natural History (see **To See**), 869 Route 6A. Named for Brewster's first settler, a Quaker forced to leave Sandwich due to religious persecution, the Wing's Island Trail (about 1.5 miles round-trip) meanders past sassafras groves and salt marshes, which provide habitat for diverse plants and animals. Traversing a tidal island, it ends on the dunes with a panoramic bay view. South Trail is on the opposite side of Route 6A and extends for about a mile past Stony Brook, a beech grove, and the remnants of a cranberry bog.

A SUPREME STATE PARK

Nickerson State Park (508-896-3491; mass.gov/dcr), 3488 Route 6A. Open 8 AM–8 PM daily during camping season, dawn to dusk off-season. This former estate of Roland Nickerson, a Chatham native and multimillionaire who founded the First National Bank of Chicago, contains just under 2,000 acres of pine, hemlock, and spruce and 11 to 14 kettle ponds, depending on water levels. Nickerson and his wife Addie, who entertained such notables as President Grover Cleveland, had a fairly self-sufficient estate, with their own electric generator, ponds teeming with fish, vegetable gardens, and game that roamed the land. When the mansion that Roland's father, Samuel, built for him burned down in 1906, a disconsolate Roland died two weeks later. (The "replacement" is now the Ocean Edge Conference Center.) Addie ultimately donated the land in 1934 to honor their son, who died in the 1918 influenza epidemic.

Nickerson State Park has been developed with walking trails, bicycling trails, jogging paths, more than 400 campsites (including yurt camping) picnic sites, boat launches, an amphitheater, and sandy beaches. Winter conditions often provide for ice skating and ice fishing and occasionally for cross-country skiing. (Snow rarely stays on the ground for more than a few days, though.) If you're at all interested in the out-of-doors, don't bypass Nickerson, one of the Cape's real treasures. Almost 500,000 people visit annually. In summertime, look for park programs like bayside strolls, night walks, campfires, and "kiddiescope" bird-watching. Parking $.

Camping (877-422-6762 reservations; 508-896-3491 information; reserveamerica .com), mid-April to late October. Because Nickerson is very popular, summer reservations are absolutely essential. They're accepted 6 months in advance for all of the 400+ sites. There is a 14-day limit in summer. 🖐 🐾 🚲

See also *Bicycling & Rentals*; *Fishing*; and *Kayaks & Paddleboards* under **To Do**.

NICKERSON STATE PARK LEFT: KATY WARD; RIGHT: KIM GRANT

FAMOUS FLATS

The Brewster Flats are one of the largest flats in North America, measuring about 12,000 acres from North Eastham through Brewster during low tide. This natural phenomenon is created by the ebb and flow of the daily tides, when the waters recede out of Cape Cod Bay, revealing over 2 miles of sandbars, clam beds, and tidal pools. During Prohibition, townspeople walking on the flats would often stumble into cases of liquor thrown overboard by rumrunners. But encounters are tamer these days. Check the tides and grab your baseball cap or floppy hat and walk out to the middle of the bay. Here you can see where the original landing was built to allow packet ships to come into Breakwater Landing (where they ferried cargo and travelers to and from Boston). The flats are also perfect for small children who can explore the warm tidal pools teeming with sea life, play in the channels left by receding tides, and marvel at the streaked "garnet" sand. The flats are also home to oyster grants or "farms." Be respectful of commercial shellfishermen and steer clear of their gear. If you're curious what Brewster oysters taste like, you can usually find them on the menu at the Brewster Fish House or Mahoney's in Orleans (see under Where to Eat in Orleans). The distinct flavor of an oyster is largely a result of the water in which it grows. In this case, Brewster's clean and clear water provides a definite bite. To experience this natural daily beauty, visit any of Brewster's bayside beaches.

THE BREWSTER FLATS MARCIA DUGGAN/CAPECODSOUL

The short North Trail wends around the museum's immediate grounds, crossing a salt marsh. Naturalist-led walks depart from the museum (508-896-3867) twice daily on weekdays in summer; free with museum admission.

Punkhorn Parklands, at the end of Run Hill Road, off Stony Brook Road. Miles of scenic trails on 880 acres—some overlooking kettle ponds—traverse oak and pine forests, meadows, and marshes. Trails are used by birders and mountain bikers, even coyotes and foxes. Pick up a detailed trail and off-road map from the Visitor Information Center (see *Guidance*).

Spruce Hill Conservation Area, behind the Brewster Historical Society Museum, 3171 Route 6A. This trail, and the uncrowded little beach at the end of it, is a secret treasure. The 20-minute, round-trip trail (¼ mile each way) follows an overgrown, old, clay dirt carriage road—probably used for off-loading fish and lumber and rumored to have been used by bootleggers during Prohibition—which runs from the museum to the bay and a private stretch of sandy beach. The Conservation Commission manages the 25-acre area.

See also "A Supreme State Park" on page 179.

❋ Lodging

Brewster has it all, from first-class inns and homey bed-and-breakfasts to resort condos and family cottages.

BED-AND-BREAKFASTS **Captain Freeman Inn** (508-896-7481; captainfreeman inn.com), 15 Breakwater Road. This former gem has been resurrected by veteran innkeepers, Donna and Byron Cain (formerly of Brewster by the Sea fame). Sitting proudly on the town's oval-shaped green and next door to the iconic general store, the inn does its namesake proud. Each of the 11 guest rooms is tasteful and tranquil: some are distinguished by luxurious baths, others by private porches. Even the most humble "boutique rooms" might make other innkeepers envious. I particularly like the private third-floor rooms. Pack a bathing suit for the pool but leave your scale at home, because of the indulgent breakfasts. $$–$$$.

Brewster by the Sea Inn & Spa (508-896-3910; brewsterbythesea.com), 716 Route 6A. Amy Chesnut and her brother Chris (and Sweet Pea, the third musketeer and on-site therapy dog for those who miss their pups at home) offer true old-fashioned hospitality. Breakfast is by far one of the main highlights for guests with their coveted blueberry pancakes and apricot scones. In the summer expect homemade raspberry jam and in winter warm spiced chai tea. Stay in the newer adjacent carriage house (a.k.a. the Old Orchard House) or the main Greek revival farmhouse built in 1846. Either way, you'll find English country décor in seven luxurious and spacious suites and stylish guest rooms. All feature flat screen TVs and luxurious amenities like thick towels, fine bedding, and nightly turndown with a truffle. One has a private deck; most have a fireplace; three have a whirlpool tub. Spa services (poolside in summer and fireside in winter) include a full range of massages, facials,

CAPTAIN FREEMAN INN MARCIA DUGGAN/CAPECODSOUL

BREWSTER BY THE SEA INN & SPA KIM GRANT

reflexology, and body scrubs. Inquire about lots of packages and special weekends, and enjoy the surprise contents of the departure goodie bag. $$–$$$.

The Ruddy Turnstone Inn (508-246-4907 and they respond to texts if you prefer; theruddyturnstone.com), 463 Route 6A. Open April through October. This is one of only two bed-and-breakfasts on Route 6A with a view of Cape Cod Bay and the salt marsh—and what a view it is! If the weather is good, you'll enjoy it from the garden, deck, under the fruit trees, or from a hammock. Bring bug spray. All three Cape-style guestrooms boast private entrances and plenty of privacy and hospitality. Inquire about weekly rates, otherwise, nightly. $$–$$$.

COTTAGES **Michael's Cottages** (508-209-4726; michaelscapecodcottages.com) 618 Route 6A. Weekly rentals May through October. I can't say enough complimentary things about Michael's (now owned and run by Matthew). These authentic old Cape Cod accommodations include four crisp and tidy cottages with comfortable bedding, fully equipped galley kitchens, a screened in porch, and some with a fireplace. The larger 1800s farmhouse is perfect for those traveling with a big crowd. With three bedrooms and bathrooms, a full eat in kitchen and an extensive outdoors area with oversized granite picnic tables with enough seating for up to 12 people. Set back from the road this place is timelessly charming. $–$$.

CAMPGROUNDS In addition to Brewster's popular **Nickerson State Park** (see "A Supreme State Park" on page 179), alternatives include:

Shady Knoll Campground (508-896-3002; shadyknoll.com), 1709 Route 6A at Route 137. Sites available from mid-May to mid-October. Combining the conveniences of modern campgrounds with all the age-old traditions that make camping fun, Shady Knoll's offers both hookup and non-hookup campsites for tents, pop-ups, and RVs up to 38 feet. Amenities include Wi-Fi, hot showers, clean restrooms, a laundry facility, and a playground. Campfires are permitted until 11 p.m. so bring on the s'mores. $.

Sweetwater Forest Cape Cod Family Campground (508-896-3773; sweetwaterforest.com), 676 Harwich Road. Sites available April through October. This family-owned campground has 250 nicely shaded wooded sites spaciously spread throughout 75-plus acres and abutting a freshwater pond. In addition to the traditional amenities, Sweetwater offers a slew of recreational activities for children including a large playground, horseshoe pits, a newly renovated mini-golf course, kayak and canoe rentals, and more. $.

INNS **Old Sea Pines Inn** (508-896-6114; oldseapinesinn.com), 2553 Route 6A. I'm always impressed when I visit this delightful, period-perfect hostelry. In 1907 the building housed the Sea Pines School of Charm and Personality for Young Women. When Michele and Steve Rowan renovated it in 1981, they combined 1920s and '30s nostalgia with modern but unfussy comforts to create palpable authenticity. Few innkeepers work harder. All 24 rooms and three suites are pleasant, furnished with old brass or iron beds and antiques. The less expensive "classrooms" are small and share baths—it will be easy to imagine yourself as a young girl at boarding school. The rear annex has less charm but still features the Rowans' attention to detail; family suites are quite economical. The inn is set on 3.5 acres, and there's plenty of space to relax inside, too, including a large, comfy living room with fireplace that leads onto the wraparound porch set with rockers. On Sunday evenings in summer, the Cape Repertory Theatre holds a well-received Broadway musical dinner revue here (see **Entertainment**). And no matter the day, a buffet-style breakfast is always included in the rates. $.

Chillingsworth (508-896-3640; chillingsworth.com), 2449 Route 6A. Open late May to late November. This 1689 house, believed to be Brewster's second oldest, rents three European-style guest rooms above the restaurant (see *Dining Out*). The antique-filled Stevenson Room boasts a private entrance and four-poster double bed—it's the largest and nicest of the rooms. The Foster Room has views of the back gardens and gazebo. Though the Ten Eyck Room is small and without a view, it's charming nonetheless. All have a private bath, TV, and air-conditioning. Rates include afternoon wine and cheese, a continental breakfast, access to a private beach at the end of the street, and privileges at a private club with an indoor/outdoor pool, tennis courts, and golf. $.

RESORTS & TOWNHOUSES **Ocean Edge Resort** (508-896-9000; oceanedge.com), 2660 Main Street, Route 6A. Town houses available seasonally. Once part of the vast Roland Nickerson estate (see "A Supreme State Park" on page 179), this 380-acre complex includes a Gothic and Renaissance Revival stucco mansion (now mainly a conference and event center) and 11 private, contemporary condominium "villages". Rental units are configured as apartments, two-story town houses (with one, two, and three bedrooms), and Cape cottages. Some units are bayside; the majority overlooks the golf course. Most have backyards and are within walking distance of resort facilities, which include indoor and outdoor pools, a private 1,000-foot bayside beach (for bayside rentals only), restaurants, a playground, and organized programs for children (for a fee). Golf packages, without instruction, are available through the resort on a "pay-as-you-play" basis. $$$–$$$$+.

✳ Where to Eat

Brewster has a wide variety of great restaurants.

DINING OUT 🦞 🍷 **Brewster Fish House** (508-896-7867; brewsterfish.com), 2208 Route 6A. Open L, D, late March through

December. This long-beloved, small roadside bistro doesn't look like much from the outside, but inside it's an intimate and pleasant place with fresh flowers, high ceilings, and a small bar. It's consistently excellent. Alongside creative and eclectic specials you'll find grilled and broiled seafood and fish served on mod plates; go for the catch of the day. Try the superb chowder or lobster bisque, which has a nice, spicy kick to it. In season, arrive before 6 p.m. or expect to wait at least an hour (no reservations taken here). Put your name on the list and walk across the street to the beach; they'll honor your position on the list when you return. $$–$$$.

Chillingsworth (508-896-3640; chill ingsworth.com), 2449 Route 6A. Open D, May to late November. The art of fine dining is not yet lost, thanks to Chef "Nitzi" Rabin and his wife, Pat, who continue to proudly preside after 40 years. While the focus remains steadfast on quality food, one can't help but soak in the unique dining atmosphere: small bedrooms turned into candlelit dining areas adorned with white tablecloths, mismatched China, and century antiques. It's truly beautiful. There's also a dedicated corner of the house with correspondence from friend and fan Julia Child. The sophisticated service is well paced and discreet. Indulge in a six-course, prix-fixe menu featuring superlative French/California-style haute cuisine, or choose items a la carte. For lighter fare, the Bistro and bar offer contemporary appetizers, soups, and salads. Choose from barstool seating, a table in the airy greenhouse, or dine alfresco on the peaceful terrace, which overlooks 6 acres of landscaped lawns, willow trees, and budding gardens (see also under **Lodging**). $$–$$$$

Spinnaker (508-896-7644; spincape .com), 2019 Route 6A. Open D. When husband-and-wife team Rob and Andrea DiSimone bought the former Bramble Inn in 2017, they knew they had big shoes to fill. The iconic restaurant and

CHILLINGSWORTH KATY WARD

bed-and-breakfast had been a Brewster crowd favorite for over 30 years. Today, the newly named restaurant, Spinnaker, continues to be a fan favorite. The atmosphere is breezily elegant with an emphasis on comfort (grab one of the pretty throw blankets available to guests who are chilly). The contemporary Italian–inspired menu includes appetizers like: Pillows & Blankets, a crispy tempura fried Parmigiano cheese, thinly sliced prosciutto di parma, and finished with a drizzle of aged balsamic. Or the roasted beets with sunchoke puree, blue cheese, orange segments, and walnuts also makes a lovely light starter. Entrées range from vegetarian options like the Roasted Eggplant Boat with a bright San Marzano tomato sauce, to perfectly grilled lamb Chops Scottadito, or grilled East Coast swordfish served with a red pepper and onion agrodolce sauce. The Porcini-dusted filet mignon is also exquisite. $$–$$$$.

EATING OUT Kate's Seafood (508-896-9517; liamsandkates.com), 284 Paine's Creek Road. Open mid-May to mid-September. Just minutes down the street from Paine's Creek Beach, Kate's has been pumping out delicious seafood and ice cream since they opened their doors in 1986. The menu offers classic American favorites like dogs and burgers, as well as fresh seafood (fried, grilled or stuffed in a bun), tempura veggies, salads and other munchies. The ice cream and frozen yogurt top the chart with dozens of flavors to choose from. Brewster-native Brianna highly recommends stopping here before heading to the beach for a stellar sunset. $–$$.

Side note: Curious about Liam's? Once a popular seafood shack at Nauset Beach in Orleans, Liam's (formerly Philbrick's since the 1940s) was torn down in March 2018 after severe storm damage and loss of beach. The favorite seafood joint withstood 28 years of sandy abuse before buckling to Mother Nature. Kate's continues the Liam legacy.

Guapo's Tortilla Shack (508-896-3338; guaposcapecod.com), 239 Underpass Road. Open L, D, March through November. Brewster-native Kyle Parker and his wife Danna have taken the Cape by storm with their Mexican-inspired tortilla shack, so much so that they opened a second year-round location in Orleans (see under **Where to Eat** in Orleans). Stop here for their popular fish tacos, grilled street corn (hand-shaved off the cob, thank you), zesty guacamole with warmed house made chips, and other traditional Mexican favorites. $–$$.

Café Alfresco (508-896-1741), 103 Lemon Tree Village Square, off Route 6A. Open B, L, year-round. This modest café offers breakfast (eggs any style and great muffins), sandwiches, soups, homemade bread, and specials like fish-and-chips, scallop rolls, and chicken salad. Snag a seat outside near the trickling fountain or settle inside with the rest of the local folks. $–$$.

Cobie's (508-896-7021; cobies.com), 3260 Route 6A. Open L, D, May to mid-October. Owner Rob Slavin has operated this old-fashioned summertime seafood and ice cream shack since 1984, and his staff is quite loyal, which says a lot. Favorites include the lobster roll, onion rings, fried scallops, charbroiled burgers, and sweet potato fries (a healthier fast food indulgence). Dine under covered picnic tables near pine trees with plastic utensils and a cold soda. Some people prefer JT's (a very similar menu and atmosphere) across from Ocean's Edge, but I'm a Cobie's fan. $$.

Stone L'oven Pizza (508-896-9400; stoneloven.com), 280 Underpass Road. Open D. If you're craving pizza, stop here. Napolitano-style pizzas cooked directly on a stone-fired hearth set to 625°F to lock in the flavor. Choose from traditional combinations: Margherita, Greek; or specialty pies such as Fig & Prosciutto or Sweet Potato (or Scallop) and Bacon for example. $$–$$$.

MARKETS **Ferretti's Market** (508-896-8919; ferrettismarket.com), 501 Underpass Road. Open daily, year-round. Owned by the Ferretti family since 2001, this market has everything you need to check off your shopping list. Plus they do deli sandwiches to go.

Brewster Farms Market (508-896-2727), 2771 Route 6A. This tiny market has a variety of convenience options, including gas.

See also *Farms* under **Selective Shopping**.

SWEET TREATS & COFFEE **Eat Cake 4 Breakfast Bakery** (508-896-4444; eatcake 4breakfastbakery.com), 302 Underpass Road. Open B, L, year-round. This killer place dispenses buttery croissants, mouth-watering brownies, quiches, and so much more. Grab a cup of coffee to balance out your sugar high. $.

Brewster Coffee Shop (508-896-8224), 2149 Route 6A. Open B, L, April through November. The place is always packed to the gills and for good reason. Order up a short stack of pancakes, share some eggs Benedict, and then go for a walk and burn off those calories. $–$$.

Snowy Owl Coffee Roasters (774-323-0605;), 2624 Route 6A. Open B, L, year-round. If you're one of those people (like me) who needs coffee before anything else, the Snowy Owl has you covered, from fancy espresso drinks to hot black brews. $.

Brewster Scoop (508-896-7824), 1935 Route 6A. *Open late May to mid-September.* Behind The Brewster Store, this small shop is a purveyor of Bliss Dairy's sugar-free ice cream and nonfat frozen yogurt. Don't worry they have sugary delights, too. $.

(See also **Kate's Seafood** and **Cobie's** for frozen sweet treats.)

BREWSTER SCOOP KIM GRANT

✳ Entertainment

⚑ **The Woodshed** (508-896-7771; the brewsterwoodshed.com), 1993 Route 6A near The Brewster Store. Open late April to late November. Live acoustic rock nightly in summer, weekends in fall and spring. This answers the question, "Where do all the summer workers go on their night off?" With wooden rafters and well-worn wooden floors (reeking of stale beer), this dark joint jumps with locals.

⚐ **Band concerts**, Drummer Boy Park, 773 Route 6A, 2.5 miles west of Route 124. Summertime concerts at 6 p.m. Sunday during July and August at the gazebo. Bring a blanket and lawn chairs.

⚐ **Cape Repertory Theatre** (508-896-1888; caperep.org), 3299 Route 6A. On the grounds of the former Camp Monomoy in Nickerson State Park, this company presents performances in a 200-seat open-air theater in the woods and at a 129-seat indoor theater. There is also a popular summertime Broadway musical dinner revue at the Old Sea Pines Inn (see **Lodging**). Shows May through November; $$$. Children's productions in July and August; $.

✳ Selective Shopping

ANTIQUES **Mews at Brewster Antiques** (508-896-4887; the-mews-at-brewster-antiques.com), 2926 Route 6A. A high-end store with slightly overpriced finds and definitely no junk. Stop here for bigger items like country furniture, artwork, and glassware.

Wayne's Antiques (508-896-0299), 1589 Route 6A. Let's be real: the thrill of the hunt is the find, and here you will surely catch sight of something that revs your engine. Peruse the glass cases, walls, and shelves chock full of collectibles (at great prices).

Wisteria Antiques (508-896-8650; wisteria-antiques.com), 1199 Route 6A. The lavender exterior, plus the scent of wisteria, plus three rooms exploding with amethyst glassware and porcelain, all equal one beautifully unusual establishment. Clearly the owners have an eye for Limoges porcelain, mirrors, chandeliers, and Venetian glass, even if the presentation is over the top. Decide for yourself: if the stuff is good enough for Barbra Streisand (which it is), it might be right up your alley.

ARTISANS **Heart Pottery** (508-896-6189; dianeheartpottery.com), 1145 Route

ROUTE 6A'S ANTIQUES AND GALLERIES KIM GRANT

homespun pottery. I adore her mugs, her minnow shaped dishes, and her rustic earthy vases. Ruby also continues to create some of her father's signature pieces such as his popular fish platters and wall hangings. She also does super cute custom designs (with proper advance notice) for items like wedding plates, dinnerware sets and baby feet tiles.

BOOKSTORES **Brewster Book Store** (508-896-6543; brewsterbookstore.com), 2648 Route 6A. Looking for a book to read at the beach? Perhaps an imaginative bedtime story for your little one, or a classic Cape novel filled with local history? This bookstore has it all, and some. If you visit the shop at the right time, you might find yourself at a book signing.

CLOTHING **Pelo Mar** (774-323-3397; pelomarcapecod.com), 2007 Route 6A. Interior designer Stephanie Meads and her daughter Mackenzie Meads are the dream team when it comes to all things fashion and lifestyle. Shop their carefully chosen selection of handmade and vintage treasures from across the globe. In case you were curious, the name, Pelo Mar translates to "by the sea" in Portuguese.

6A. Specializing in functional and decorative porcelain and raku, Diane Heart spends most days at her wheel here in the shop. Her raku (made by using an ancient Japanese firing technique) is stunning.

Sydenstricker Galleries (508-385-3272; sydenstricker.com), 490 Route 6A. Stop in for glass-fusing demonstrations using a technique developed by Brewster-native Bill Sydenstricker (who died in 1994). Sydenstricker glass is used in two American embassies and displayed in museum collections around the country.

Wildflower Pottery (774-722-1680), 3820 Route 6A. I am thrilled to feature Ruby Calderwood's gallery in this edition of the guidebook! Daughter of Brewster's famed ceramic artist, Clay Calderwood (the retired owner of Clay Works Studio), Ruby is now keeping the family craft alive through her own

WILDFLOWER POTTERY KATY WARD

BREWSTER BOOK STORE KIM GRANT

FARMS **Brewster Farmers Market** (508-896-9521; brewsterfarmersmarket.com), 51 Drummer Boy Road at Windmill Village, every Sunday from late June to early September.

Allard Farm (508-896-8306), 68 Eldridge Road. Allard Farms is a seasonal farm and garden center with an honor-system farm stand open May through September. The staffed garden center is open May through June.

GALLERIES Brewster has a surprisingly long list of galleries. Only a few favorites are listed below.

Aries East Gallery (508-896-7681; arieseastgallery.com), 2805 Route 6A. Owner and artist Geoffrey Smith is known for his fine art collections worldwide.

Underground Art Gallery (508-896-3757; undergroundartgallery.com), 673 Satucket Road. Amazingly, this working studio sits beneath 100 tons of soil and

is supported by 10 tree trunks. The gallery features the work of watercolorist Karen North Wells, who also uses oil and acrylic for her seascapes and landscape florals. (Check the website for her classes and other events.) Karen's late husband, Malcolm Wells, designed earth-covered solar buildings like this one and wrote books on sustainable architecture (malcolmwells.com).

Teichman Gallery (508-896-2395; teichmangallery.com), 6 Sachem Drive. Milton Teichman showcases a little bit of everything in his contemporary-styled gallery. From abstract paintings to non-objective collages to sculptures made in bronze, wood, clay, brass, aluminum, and other found objects—Milton has a unique style.

SPECIALTY **Great Cape Herbs** (508-896-5900; greatcape.com), 2624 Route 6A. Your senses will surely be heightened after visiting this herbal apothecary. Proprietor Stephan Brown, who opened the shop in the early 1900s, showcases over 170 varieties of Western and Chinese herbs as well as New Age literature on health and well-being. Walk through the modest herb and community agricultural gardens and revive yourself with a cup of strong matcha tea before leaving.

HandCraft House (508-240-1412; handcrafthousegallery.com), 3966 Route 6A. This cozy artsy shop is celebrating over 30 years in business. Shop here for locally made decorative and functional crafts including candles, clocks, garden art, jewelry, home décor, wind chimes, and more.

Lemon Tree Village Shops (lemontreevillageshops.com), 1069 Route 6A. A collection of eateries and shops worth poking around for gifts and souvenirs. Favorite stores include: **Lemon Tree Pottery** (508-896-3065; lemontreepottery.com), for handcrafted wares; **Brewster Birdhouse** at **Woodworks Gallery** (508-896-3133; woodworksgallery.com); the **Village Toy Store** (508-896-8185; thevillagetoystorebrewster.com) for

ALLARD FARM   MARCIA DUGGAN/CAPECODSOUL

obvious and not-so-obvious toys; and the **Cook Shop** (508-896-7698; cookshopcapecod.com), for whimsical kitchen gadgets, gourmet treats, and high-quality cookware.

LEMON TREE   KIM GRANT

✳ Special Events

Mid-April–early May: **Herring Run**. Hundreds of thousands of alewives (herring) return from the salt water to lay their eggs in the same freshwater ponds where they were born (see **Stony Brook Grist Mill** and **Herring Run** under **To See**).

Early May: **Brewster in Bloom** (brewsterblooms.com). A three-day scholarship fundraiser for local teens pursuing higher education, this festival features a golf contest, self-guided antiques and arts tour, 5K run, children's festival, juried fine arts and crafts show, and tour of historic inns.

Late June: **Open Air Antiques Fair** sponsored by the Brewster Historical Society (508-896-9521) at Drummer Boy Park. $.

HARWICH

Harwich isn't nearly as developed as its westerly neighbors, although its stretch of Route 28 does have its share of bumper boats, mini-golf courses, and go-carts. In fact, the town exudes a somewhat nonchalant air. It's as if the 12,200 year-rounders are collectively saying, "This is what we have and you're welcome to come and enjoy it with us if you wish"—which is not to say that Harwich doesn't attract visitors. It boasts a wide range of places to stay and eat, from humble bed-and-breakfasts to family-friendly cottages, from exceptional New American fare to roasted chicken-on-a-spit. At the same time, while Harwich has more saltwater and freshwater beaches than any other town on the Cape, only a few have parking for day-use visitors.

Harwich, mostly blue collar and middle class, comprises seven distinct villages and is blessed with one of the most picturesque harbors on the Cape, **Wychmere Harbor**. Nearby, lovely **Saquatucket Harbor** is reserved for fishing charters and ferry service to Nantucket. It's worth poking around the quiet center of **Harwich**, with its historic homes standing in marked contrast to the heavily developed areas just a mile or so away. Harwich, which bills its annual **Cranberry Harvest Festival** as "the biggest small-town celebration in the country," lays claim to cultivating the first commercial cranberry bog.

GUIDANCE **Harwich Chamber of Commerce** (508-430-1165; harwichcc.com), 1 Schoolhouse Road, and **Harwich Information Center** (508-432-1600), Route 28, are both very helpful. Stop here to use biking and walking trail maps as well as their handy (free) street map.

GETTING THERE *By car:* From the Cape Cod Canal, take Route 6 to Exit 10 (Route 124 South and Route 39 South) to Route 28, or take Exit 11 to Route 137 for East Harwich. It takes 35 to 40 minutes to reach Harwich from the canal.

WYCHMERE HARBOR

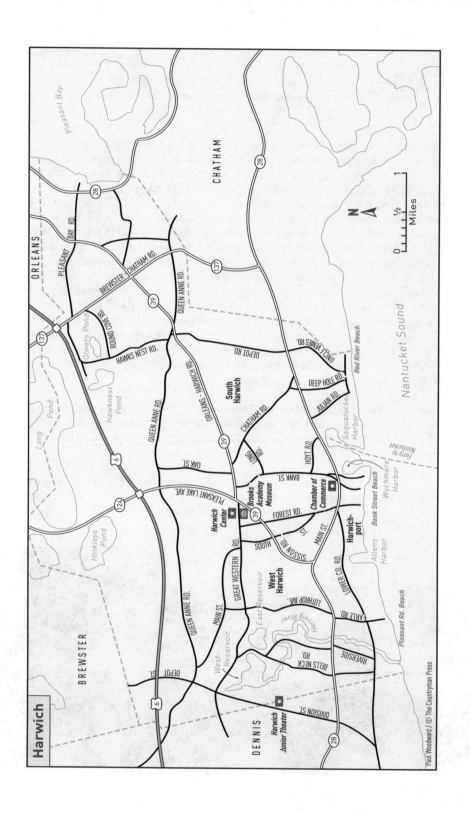

By bus: The **Plymouth & Brockton** bus (508-746-0378; p-b.com) connects Harwich with Hyannis and other Cape towns, as well as with Boston's Logan Airport. The bus stops at the Park & Ride commuter lot near the intersection of Routes 6 and 124.

GETTING AROUND *By car:* Route 28 is also called Main Street. (This is not to be confused with Main Street, a.k.a. Route 39, in the center of Harwich, which is inland.) Although most points of interest are located along Route 28, head inland to explore Harwich's ponds and conservation areas.

By shuttle: **The Flex** (508-385-1430; capecodtransit.org) offers north and south-bound trips from Harwich to Provincetown with reserved stops. The shuttle stops at the Harwich Community Center; Star Market; the Lighthouse Charter School; Route 28 bus stop; and Stop and Shop. (Both Stop and Shop and Route 28 connect with the **H2O** ($) line, which travels to and from the Hyannis Transportation Center and Orleans daily in summer.

GETTING TO NANTUCKET According to my dear friend Julia (a local native and Harwich lover) jumping on the ferry to Nantucket is a must do.

Freedom Cruise Line (508-432-8999; freedomferry.com), 731 Route 28. Open late May to mid-October. Why does she recommend this? Well, not only is Nantucket gorgeous (see the Nantucket chapter), but parking is conveniently located and free for day-trippers. Another bonus: You avoid Hyannis summertime traffic. Freedom Cruise also offers overnight parking in their private lot. A ferry ride takes less than 80 minutes. Purchase tickets online or at the ferry dock. $$$$.

PUBLIC RESTROOMS At the chamber (see *Guidance*).

PUBLIC LIBRARY ❋ ⌀ ⌂ **Brooks Free Library** (508-430-7562; brooksfreelibrary.org), 739 Main Street, Harwich.

EMERGENCIES **Harwich Police Department** (508-430-7541; harwich-ma.gov), 183 Sisson Road, or call **911.**

Medical: **Fontaine Medical Center** (508-432-4100; capecodhealth.org), 525 Long Pond Drive, off Route 137, Harwich.

❋ To See

⌂ **Brooks Academy Museum** (508-432-8089; harwichhistoricalsociety.org), 80 Parallel Street, Harwich Center. Open late June to early October. This imposing 1844 Greek Revival schoolhouse was home to one of the country's early vocational schools of navigation, established by Sidney Brooks. Now operated by the Harwich Historical Society, the museum features a history of cranberry farming, historical photographs, and changing exhibits on Harwich's past. There is also a permanent display of art by C. D. Cahoon, a gunpowder house used from 1770 to 1864, and a restored 1872 outhouse. Genealogical resources and a significant manuscript collection round out the research facility. $.

First Congregational Church (508-432-1053; firstchurchofharwich.org), 697 Route 6A. Built in the mid-1700s, this historic church anchors Harwich's tiny town center. You can't miss the sky-high cathedral: a common style of gothic architecture that is believed to evoke ethereality and reach toward the heavens.

Morning:	Start your day with a classic breakfast from Ruggie's or grab coffee and bagels to-go from Perks. Take an informative Cranberry Bog Tour or lose yourself in a fiction novel from Reed's Books while you lounge in a shady spot at Long Pond.
Afternoon:	Head over to Brax Landing for a casual seafood lunch overlooking the harbor. Rent a canoe and explore the Herring River and Sand Pond Conservation lands or bring the little ones to Bud's Go-Karts for some bumper fun.
Evening:	Enjoy a romantic dinner at Cape Sea Grille or indulge in authentic Italian cuisine at Buca's. Follow up with live jazz music at Wequassett, or cure your sweet tooth at Sundae School.

Saquatucket Harbor and **Wychmere Harbor** are twin harbors located within a half-mile of each other. Wychmere was originally a coastal pond until 1887 when fifty-or-so men dug a channel (by hand no less) from the harbor to Nantucket Sound. In the late 1920s the town was gifted land on Harbor Road (between Wychmere and Saquatucket) by the Gray family for the purpose of building a town pier. In order to do so, an inlet was dredged in 1968 to accommodate the new marina. The unique and often mispronounced name, Saquatucket Harbor, was chosen for the American Indian tribe who once inhabited the shore from Harwich Port to Brewster. Today, Saquatucket Harbor is one of the largest municipal marinas on the Cape with over 200 berths and a handful of slips reserved for transient visitors. Contact the **Harbormaster** (508-430-7532; harwich -ma.gov), Route 28.

You can also launch at **Allen Harbor**, the third largest humanmade harbor in Harwich. Only private seasonal ramp passes are available here. You can contact **Allen Harbor Marine Service** (508-430-6008; allenharbor.com), 335 Lower County Road.

✷ To Do

BASEBALL ✐ **The Harwich Mariners** (harwichmariners.org) play baseball from mid-June to mid-August at Whitehouse Field behind the high school in Harwich Center, off Oak Street from Route 39. They also host weekly clinics from late June to early August; $$$$+.

BICYCLING & RENTALS The **Cape Cod Rail Trail** offers 25 miles of paved road for your biking pleasure. The trail route starts in Wellfleet and passes through the towns of Eastham, Orleans, Brewster, Harwich (about 5 miles total), Dennis and Yarmouth. Hop on the trail near the Pleasant Lake General Store (see *Markets* under **Where to Eat**) and pick up a trail map at the Chamber of Commerce (see under *Guidance*). You can rent bicycles and equipment at **Old Colony Bikes** (508-545-3283; oldcolonybikes.com), 1 Old Colony Road; or **Cape Cycle** (774-327-0027; capecyclecc.com), 199 Route 28.

BOAT EXCURSIONS & RENTALS **Down Cape Charters and Boat Rentals** (508-430-6893; downcapeboating.com), at the Wequassett Resort, Route 28. Open mid-June through September. Rent kayaks, catamarans, powerboats, and Sunfish, as well as guided tours and lessons. Enjoy cocktail and hors d'oeuvre cruises through Pleasant Bay and Chatham Harbor on the weekends. $$$$+.

FISHING There are plenty of fish in the waters off Harwich, especially on Nantucket Sound. For big game (like bass, cod, tuna, and shark) I recommend splurging on a charter. It's one of the most rewarding and thrilling experiences. The sound of the reel buzzing as you hook a tuna and the hour-plus battle that ensues, or watching a thresher shark jump out of the water as it attacks your bait—it's a combat you will never forget.

Big game: ***Magellan*** **Deep Sea Fishing Charters** (508-237-9823; capecodsportsmen .com), 715 Route 28. Open June through September. Some people say Captain Len Greiner is a fish whisperer—and maybe he is. With over 20 years of experience running fishing charters on the Cape (and also time served as a Gulf War veteran, former merchant marine, and commercial fisherman), Captain Len knows his stuff. Step aboard the 35-foot Duffy boat *Magellan* and head offshore to test the waters for striped bass, bluefish, fluke, cod and haddock, bluefin tuna, or mako and thresher sharks. $$$$+.

Jail Break Fishing Charters (508-237-3962; fishjailbreak.com), 715 Route 28. Open May through September. Book a charter with Captain Seamus Muldoon if you want to experience the thrill of fighting a monster, or if you just want an "escape from everyday life" (which is the definition of "jail break"). Spend the day, or half day, fishing off the 42-foot Duffy for striped bass and bluefish, or head a bit further offshore to battle bluefin tuna and shark. Be sure to say hi to the first mate: a chocolate Labrador named Fiona. $$$$+.

Yankee II **Deep Sea Fishing** (508-432-2520; yankee2deepseafishingcapecod.com), 704 Route 28. Open mid-May through September. Bring the entire family on this comfortable and spacious 65-foot vessel for a memorable fishing adventure. Trips are suited for all levels of experience, and rod, reel, and bait are included (and free parking at Saquatucket Harbor). Enjoy a nice boat ride across Nantucket Sound to fish for black sea bass, fluke, and scup, as well as Tautog starting early September.

A FISHER'S PARADISE MARCIA DUGGAN/CAPECODSOUL

CRANBERRIES (NOT THE ROCK BAND)

Cranberry Bog Tours (508-432-0790; cranberrybogtours.com), 1601 Factory Road. You might be picturing a scene from an Oceanspray commercial, but I can assure you that is not the case. Reserve a tour of Leo and Andrea Cakounes' year-round organic cranberry operation. The 90-minute tour includes an overview of the tart and tangy berry's history of growing on the Cape, as well as views of the bog and the equipment used. I guarantee you will be surprised at how much time and labor goes into harvesting cranberries. Keep an eye open for grazing farm animals and be sure to stop at the farm stand on your way out for cranberry related goodies. Tours are offered seasonally and fill up quickly, so be sure to reserve in advance. Cash only. $$.

LEESA BURKE

By bridge or jetty: Try your luck casting from a jetty at Red River Beach (see *Beaches* under **Green Space**) or from Herring River Bridge in West Harwich. Procure freshwater and saltwater fishing licenses and regulations online at mass.gov/eea/agencies/dfg/licensing.

Supplies: **Sunrise Bait & Tackle** (508-430-4117), 431 Route 28. Stop here for the essentials and chat up the very knowledgeable and friendly staff for local fishing tips.

FOR FAMILIES **Grand Slam Entertainment** (508-430-1155; capecodbumperboats .com), 322 Route 28. Open mid-May to early September. This fun zone offers a little bit of everything for most ages. From batting cages (baseball, softball, and wiffleball), to bumper boats, a rock wall, and a zip line over the pool. $-$$$.

Trampoline Center (508-432-8717), 296 Route 28. Open May to mid-September. There are no age or height restrictions; the only limit at this outdoor center is that kids can't do flips. One recent reviewer referred to this place as the "GOAT: Greatest of All Trampolines." $–$$.

Bud's Go-Karts (508-432-4964), 9 Sisson Road, off Route 28. Open May through September. Everyone is really a kid at heart. Stop here for some good old-fashioned bumper fun. Kids have to be more than 54 inches tall and at least 8 years old to drive without parents at this busy track. $–$$.

Harwich Elementary School, 263 South Street. This giant wooden playground known as, Castle in the Clouds lends plenty of space for children to run, climb, and play hide-and-seek. There are also monkey bars, swinging rings, and a basketball court.

GOLF **Cranberry Valley Golf Course** (508-430-5234; cranberryvalley.golf) 183 Oak Street, off Route 28. *Open March through December.* An 18-hole, par-72 course with a driving range and practice putting green space. Golf carts available and on-site pro shop.

Harwich Port Golf Club (508-432-0250), 51 South Street. Enjoy this modest nine-hole, par-34 course.

SAILING **Pleasant Bay Community Sailing** (508-945-7245; pbcb.cc/wp), 2287 Route 28. Open late June to October with educational programs year-round. Located on the Pleasant Bay waterfront where the towns of Brewster, Orleans, and Harwich connect, this community center offers sailing excursions for children and teens (as well as "Mothers and Others" after the school season begins), educational classes on marine life, kayak tours, catboat lessons, seminars, and more. Open to residents and visitors. $$$$–$$$$+.

TENNIS Free public courts are located at **Brooks Park** (508-430-7553), Route 39 and Oak Street. In summer there are morning programs for children.

✳ Green Space

BEACHES There are a number of beaches lining the town's shoreline on Nantucket Sound. However, unlike most beaches, Harwich has some of the softest and finest sand I've encountered on Cape Cod. (I'm more accustomed to the rock tumbled sand that tends to hurt your feet if they are not weathered, or if you're a big baby.)

Most beaches (and ponds, see below) require a parking sticker and can be purchased at the **Town Hall** (508-430-7501; harwich-ma.gov), 732 Main Street. You can also buy one at the **Chamber of Commerce** (508-432-1600; harwichcc.com), 1 Schoolhouse Road, for a small added convenience fee.

Red River Beach, at the end of Uncle Venie's Road (there are other streets that will get you there, but I recommend this route). This is a popular beach for locals and visitors alike for its wide-stretching shoreline, soft sand, gentle waters (perfect for splashing and swimming), and accessible parking. In-season amenities include lifeguards, restrooms, handicap access and a mobile food vendor with American classics. Local native, Harwich lover, and dear friend, Julia, favors this spot. Though it can get crowded in summer, this beach is large enough to accommodate many.

Bank Beach, off Bank Street. Though this beach is a tad-bit smaller, it's very similar (including amenities) to Red River Beach. Stop here for beautiful panoramic views of Nantucket Sound.

Pleasant Road Beach, off Pleasant Road, is another relatively large beach, as far as Harwich beaches go. It's salt water, but calm, like a pond.

Earle Road Beach, off Earle Road. This medium-sized beach is a little quieter than other Harwich beaches—perhaps a little too quiet for families with children who are looking for lots of activity. Rock jetties and gentle breaking waves create supreme serenity.

PONDS There are over 20 freshwater swimming holes in Harwich. Some have easy access, while others take a little bit of a hike to get too. Most ponds in Harwich are kettle ponds that were formed by melting ice blocks as glaciers retreated over 18,000 years ago. Be sure to check with the town hall about swimming and fishing closures. Some ponds, such as **Hinckley's Pond**, have recently tested positive for excessive phosphorus, which has led to numerous algae blooms and fish kills. It is also dangerously toxic for humans and pets.

Long Pond, off Long Pond Drive's south side, or off Cahoon Road's east side. This is the largest and deepest pond in Harwich (measuring 66 feet deep) with two sandy beaches. Rent a kayak or paddleboard and explore the hidden banks. Parking stickers required (see *Beaches* for purchase info).

Bucks Pond, off Clearwater Drive, has a large beach, picnic tables and great fishing conditions. There are no restrooms or lifeguards; parking stickers required.

Sand Pond, off Great Western Road. This clean little pond has a small beach (half sun and half shade), a roped-off swimming area, and a dock used primarily for swimming lessons and playful jumping. Park in the large pine-needle lot and take the wooden stairs down. A great place for families and often crowded with excited kids.

Seymour Pond, west of Long Pond. The best way to access this hidden freshwater gem is via Cape Cod Rail Trail. There are some benches, a sandy beach and refreshingly cool water that feels oh-so-good after peddling in the midday sun.

SAQUATUCKET HARBOR KIM GRANT

WALKS Contact the **Harwich Conservation Trust** (508-432-3997; harwichconservation trust.org) or the **Chamber of Commerce** (see under *Guidance*) for information and walking trail maps of the area.

Herring River/Sand Pond Conservation Area/Bells Neck, park off Bells Neck Road from Great Western Road. The story has it that, in 1668, settler John Bell acquired much of the land from the Saquatucket (see also **Saquatucket Harbor** in Chatham). For the next 300 years, the land passed through the hands of multiple owners until the town purchased it in order to protect the Herring River, West Reservoir (freshwater), East Reservoir (brackish), and buffering woodlands. With 250-plus acres of marshland, tidal creeks, and reservoir, there's plenty to explore. Watch for ospreys and the secretive black-crowned night heron in spring and summer. Each April, herring swim upstream along a herring ladder at the west trailhead. Canoeists and kayakers can launch near each trailhead.

Thompson's Field, park off Chatham Road from Route 39 (south trailhead) or at the intersection of Route 39 and Route 124 (north trailhead). This 57-acre preserve with dirt trails will give you an idea of what the Cape probably looked like 100 years ago. Purchased by the town in 1984, the mosaic of woods and fields were preserved primarily to protect groundwater flowing toward the adjacent public well field. Some land south of the rail trail has remained open field habitat, but is gradually being succeeded by pitch pine, eastern red cedar and other non-native invasive plants. (Every April, AmeriCorps, the conservation trust, and the town partner with volunteers to maintain the open fields and enhance the wildlife habitat.) Pitch pine dominates the land north of the bike path. Thompson's is also a popular spot for dog-walkers.

✳ Lodging

Check out rentals on Airbnb, HomeAway, and VRBO.

BED-AND-BREAKFASTS ✳ **The Platinum Pebble Boutique Inn** (508-432-7766; platinumpebble.com), 186 Belmont Road, West Harwich. Decidedly different (in a good way) from most every other bed-and-breakfast or inn on Cape Cod, the Platinum Pebble will knock your socks off with its service, tickle your fancy with its mod décor, and pamper you silly with its luxe amenities. The centrally located boutique property features some rooms with private patios with direct access to the pool and others with soaking. All have fine linens and bedding. Schedule a time and dine in your room or the lounge, poolside or in the garden, on a sumptuously sweet or savory full breakfasts. $$-$$$.

Tern Inn (508-432-3714; theterninn .com), 91 Chase Avenue. Hands-on owners Sue and Dan run a spotless operation and it pays off. This combination bed-and-breakfast and cottage colony is located on over 2-acres of quiet woodland. A 10-minute walk from the beach, these five nicely maintained cottages and 12 Cape house guestrooms include a delicious and bountiful buffet breakfast, manicured lawns with lounging chairs, and an outdoor swimming pool. $$-$$$.

RESORTS & INNS **Commodore Inn** (508-432-1180; thecommodoreinn.com), 30 Earle Road. Dan and Kelley McNamara have traveled the country, nothing quiet compares to their time spent on Cape Cod. So it was only fitting when they took the plunge and purchased the inn. Though the couple resides in Texas you'll likely see them in the summertime. Meanwhile (when Dan and Kelley are off duty), innkeepers John and Barbara-Anne Foley, year-round residents of Harwich since 1987, take the helm. Each of the 27 newly renovated rooms come equipped with comfortable bedding, daily housekeeping, and a freshwater (temperature-controlled) swimming pool accessible to all guests. Choose from a queen room with two queen beds and a full bathroom and shower tub; or a king room with one king bed, a deluxe soaking tub, and gas fireplace. Each room opens onto the pool and recreation area, where guests will find a variety of lawn games as well as a fire pit and comfortable seating. Stop by their on-site beach bar (open to guests and non-guests) for light bites, specialty cocktails, and ice-cold beer. $–$$$.

Winstead Inn & Beach Resort (508-432-4444; winsteadinn.com), 116 Parallel

WINSTEAD INN & BEACH RESORT KIM GRANT

Street. You might pay handsomely for a stay at these privileged properties—but you won't regret it. The Winstead offers the best of both worlds: leisure lovers will enjoy the 14 waterfront rooms at the beach resort, while families will enjoy the ease of the inn and its 15 guestrooms and suites. Both are near the Cape Cod Rail Trail and steps from the center of town. Guests have access to most amenities including a continental breakfast, free parking, beach towels, umbrellas and lounge chairs. A shuttle brings guests to and from the private secluded beach. Only inn guests have access to the outdoor (and heated) saltwater pool open mid-May to September. Enjoy lemonade and cookies in the afternoon. $$–$$$$.

Wequassett Resort and Golf Club (508-784-7966; wequassett.com), 2173 Route 28. Open April through November. Just 10 minutes north of Chatham on picturesque Pleasant Bay, this resort is known for an attentive staff, exceptional service, and understated elegance. Consisting of 23 buildings set on 22 beautifully landscaped acres, it boasts an excellent restaurant, Twenty-eight Atlantic (see under *Dining Out*), four tennis courts, sailing, and an oh-so-suave pool renovated with cabanas, a Jacuzzi, and a waterfront bar. Other resort amenities include a fitness center, boat rentals, and launch service to a secluded section of National Seashore beach. For families, childcare and summer programs for kids are available. The resort also offers guests playing privileges on the otherwise private Cape Cod National Golf Course, a challenging Silva course (golf packages available). As for the 116 rooms, some have cathedral ceilings and private decks, though not all have views of the boat-studded Round Cove. Triple sheeting, morning delivery of the newspaper, and turndown service are standard. Light lunches are served at the pool; nightcaps are soothing at the charming Thoreau's. $$$$–$$$$$+.

WONDROUS WEQUASSETT

Wequassett Resort and Golf Club (508-784-7966; or 508-432-3000 for reservations; wequassett.com), 2173 Route 28, has several premier dining options to choose from.

Twenty-Eight Atlantic, open B, D, April through November. I can't decide whether it's the water views or the food that reigns supreme, it's truly hard to say, since they both rise above lofty expectations. Chef James Hackney oversees the regional and contemporary American menu, full of artfully presented dishes packed with great flourishes and flavors. The seasonal menu is served on Limoges china in a genteel, understated, open, elegant dining room, which has a nice buzz to it as the evening wears on. Service is seamless. While jackets and ties are not required, torn jeans, flip-flops, and T-shirts are not permitted. $$$–$$$$$.

If you'd rather dine alfresco, check out The Verandahs at Twenty-Eight Atlantic, a two-tiered dining venue surrounded by beautiful stonework and overlooking the grand lawn and bay.

Thoreau's, open daily April through November. This club-like bar oozes sophistication with its warm rich undertones, overstuffed leather chairs, stone and granite fireplace, and large open windows overlooking Pleasant Bay. Stop here for a light lunch (think gourmet soups, salads, and sharing plates) or dinner and a nightcap. Thoreau's offers an excellent and extensive wine list, as well as unique specialty cocktails.

Outer Bar & Grille, open L, D, mid-June to mid-September. This waterside eatery is a great spot to enjoy a lunchtime lobster roll, salad, grilled pizza, or panini. Soak in the scenic vistas from the open-air dining room and seaside deck. The food might not be 100 percent worth it, but the views surely are. $$–$$$.

You can also dine at LiBAYtion, a beachside bar housed under a very posh pergola. While the menu is the same as at Outer Bar & Grille, this intimate spot hosts live entertainment in season.

✳ Where to Eat

One comment: You won't go hungry in Harwich.

DINING OUT **Buca's Tuscan Roadhouse** (508-432-6900; bucasroadhouse.com), 4 Depot Road. Open D, year-round. From the hills in Tuscany to the hills in Harwich, this intimate and cozy trattoria serves sophisticated Italian-inspired cuisine like the excellent *cacciucco* (Tuscan fish stew served over linguini), *merluzzo di prada* (pistachio crusted local cod), and *vitello rosa* (veal scallopine with a red wine balsamic butter sauce). Buca's old world eggplant parmigiana also gets rave reviews. The atmosphere is relaxing and romantic with its high-backed booths, red-and-white-checked tablecloths and warm ambient lighting.

Furthermore, portions are generous, desserts are homemade, and there's a decent selection of wines by the glass. $$–$$$.

BUCA'S TUSCAN ROADHOUSE   KIM GRANT

CAPE SEA GRILLE KIM GRANT

Check out their fast food cart, **Depot Dogs** (depotdogs.net), parked in their lot. You can't miss the fire-engine red gourmet hotdog stand.

Cape Sea Grille (508-432-4745; capeseagrille.com), 31 Sea Street. Open D, April to mid-December. This contemporary bistro offers well-prepared, creative New American cuisine with a French Mediterranean influence. Because it's also served by twinkling candlelight in a lovely old sea captain's home, it's more like a grand slam. Outstanding signature dishes include pan-seared lobster with pancetta and asparagus and duck confit. Dishes change seasonally, but preparations always play with the classics. You'd better save room for strawberry shortcake or silky ginger crème brûlée. The three-course sunset menu is a steal. Chef/owner Doug Ramler has presided over this upscale eatery since the early 2000s. $–$$$$.

L'Alouette Bistro (508-430-0405; frenchbistrocapecod.com), 787 Route 28. Open D, year-round. Enjoy fine French creations by Chef Christian Shultz in this newly renovated bistro. Dishes are rich yet simple and full of country-inspired flavor. The prix-fixe dinner is lovely, especially with a glass of their estate-grown wine. $$$–$$$$.

EATING OUT **Ten Yen** (774-209-3160; 10yenharwichport.com), 554 Route 28. Open D, year-round. I'm very pleased to include chef/owner Michael Jacek's urban-style sushi bar in this edition of the guidebook. (Side note: Michael and I worked together several years ago, so I know he's the real deal.) Using the freshest ingredients, Chef Michael heightens traditional sushi dishes with bold sophisticated flavors and perfect preparations. His plates are truly a work of art. The intimate setting is livened up by his hands-on presence both inside and outside the kitchen. You will often see him conversing with tables or serving up robatayaki-style sashimi by tableside flame. This is by far the best sushi on Cape Cod.

Brax Landing Restaurant (508-432-5515; braxlanding.com), 705 Route 28. Open L, D, April through December. Bar open year-round. Overlooking Saquatucket Harbor, this casual tavern-like restaurant offers a varied menu full of local favorites. Their steamers are particularly renowned. A few indoor seats have choice views, but the real draw is the outdoor seating by the tranquil harbor. A bountiful brunch buffet on Sunday brings in a crowd. Regardless of the time of day, there is often a 45-minute wait. $–$$$.

Ember (508-430-0407; emberpizza .com), 600 Route 28. Open L (weekends only) and D, year-round. Baked inside a 1,000-degree coal fired oven, Ember puts out delicious wings and bubbly, cheesy, saucy pizzas. They also serve burgers, sandwiches, and pasta dishes. Stop in for live music on select evenings. $$–$$$.

Hot Stove Saloon (508-432-9911; hotstovesaloon.com), 551 Route 28. Open L, D, year-round. Offering good-value pub grub since the mid-2000s, this place sports the requisite low lighting and boisterous quality you want in a (primarily) sports bar. The cheeseburgers are great, but you could also go for thin-crust pizza, fish-and-chips, or any number of sandwiches (BLT, cheesesteak, or hot pastrami, for instance). A couple picnic tables out front provide good watching on Main Street. $–$$.

The Port Restaurant (508-430-5410; portcapecod.com), 541 Route 28. Open L, July and August only, and D, April to November. Slurp back $1 Chatham oysters during the Port's raw bar happy hour before diving into one of their signature entrées like the butter-poached lobster, scallop risotto, and chimichurri chicken. This is a great place to take a break from shopping Harwich Port's main strip. $$$.

SWEET TREATS & COFFEE **Perks Coffee Shop and Beer Garden** (774-209-3460; perkscapecod.com), 545 Route 28. It might be an odd combo—coffee and beer—but it works. Established in 2010 by Taylor and Sarah Powell, this lively joint has a bit of everything: espresso, smoothies, and bagels to burgers, brats, and beer.

Ruggie's Breakfast & Lunch (508-432-0625; ruggiescapecod.com), 707 Route 28. Open B, L, year-round. This popular morning spot offers traditional diner-style meals at diner-style prices. Feeling extra hungry? Test your luck with "The Duke": two waffles, six eggs "their way," ¼ pound of cheddar cheese, ¼ pound of American cheese, hash browns, homemade sausage gravy, two buttermilk pancakes, six strips of bacon, three sausage patties, and two pieces of boneless country style fried chicken. *Yikes*. The rules: You have 30 minutes to finish everything on your plate and are allowed one 8-ounce glass of juice. If you succeed, your meal is on the house and you get a T-shirt and photo on their wall of fame. $–$$.

Lighthouse Café (508-432-5399), 216 Route 28. Open B, year-round. This quaint family-owned eatery specializes in home-style breakfast classics. A local favorite. Cash only. $.

Sundae School Ice Cream (508-430-2444; sundaeschool.com), 606 Route 28. Open mid-May to late September. This olde-fashioned shoppe is the place to go for homemade ice cream concoctions. They also have locations in Orleans and Dennis Port. $.

MARKETS **Pleasant Lake General Store** (508-430-0200; localflavorcapecod.com), 403 Pleasant Lake Avenue. Stop here for sandwiches, wraps, burritos, baked goods, desserts, penny candy, and craft beer and wine. Located next to the Cape Cod Rail Trail, this is a great place to take a break and refuel. They also offer prepared dinner pies to-go.

See also *Farms* under **Selective Shopping**.

✳ Entertainment

Band concerts are held on select evenings at Brooks Park, 1 Oak Street.

Harwich Jr. Theatre (508-432-2002; capecodtheatrecompany.org), 105 Division Street. This semiprofessional theater—the country's oldest children's theater, established in 1951—produces up to 12 shows a year for both children and adults. In summer, children star in kids' roles, manage the sound and lighting, and sell refreshments. Whether your child is considering acting or you want to introduce him or her to theater, this is an imaginative alternative to another round of mini-golf. Classes or workshops are offered year-round. In the off-season, the theater offers shows geared toward an older crowd. $$.

Annual Jazz Festival, at Wequassett Resort and Golf Club (see **Lodging** and "Wondrous Wequassett" on page 201). Performances take place on the Garden Terrace overlooking Pleasant Bay every Tuesday and Wednesday evening from late June through August. Cocktails and a light menu are available, but performances are free and open to the public.

❊ Selective Shopping

❄ All establishments are open year-round unless otherwise noted.

BOOKSTORES **Reed Books** (508-432-5293), 537 Route 28, has a decent selection of new and gently used books for your reading pleasure.

CLOTHING **Whimsy** (508-430-4100; capewhimsy.com), 121 Route 28. This unique consignment boutique gets a glowing and well-deserved recommendation in my book. Owner Beth Pedicini is not only super cool but sophisticatedly fashionable. Her eye for quality clothing, shoes, and accessories is apparent as you peruse the carefully curated displays. Take your time wandering around the six handsomely decorated rooms within the old sea captains home. If you rush your shopping, you might miss the silky scarf tucked delicately inside a display dresser, the strand of pearls hanging from a bookcase, or the vintage dress draped from a window shutter. You will surely find the perfect item to compliment your style and personality. It's not often that I leave here empty-handed, and the same goes for my mother. Despite the age difference, Beth covers all bases. If you're interested in selling clothes, contact Beth directly.

WHIMSY KATY WARD

FARMS **Harwich Farmers Market** (508-432-8089), 80 Parallel Street, every Thursday from June to October.

Cape Cod Lavender Farm (508-432-8397; capecodlavenderfarm.com), Weston Woods Road. Open March through December with peak bloom in late June to mid-July. Smell the lavender at this family-owned operation. I recommend only coming during peak season; otherwise there's not much to look at.

SPECIALTY **Dr. Gravity's Kite Shop**, (508-430-0437; drgravitys.com), 560 Route 28. Yes, it's a bit touristy, but Dr. Gravity has some pretty cool kites, and more. They don't call it "the emporium of fun" for nothing.

Sativa (508-430-4410; shopsolis.com), 517 Route 28, offers an eclectic mix of gifts and goods from nautical-inspired home décor, organic body care products, locally made jewelry and accessories, adorable children's clothes, and more. You will surely find something unique and affordable here.

CAPE COD LAVENDER FARM KATY WARD

Solis (774-408-7088; shopsolis.com), 521 Route 28 (Sativa's sister store). Shop here for Cape Cod Scout products like beach bags, totes, coolers, and clothing.

Yankee Doodle Shop (508-432-0579; yankeedoodleshop.com), 181 Route 28. Bemis Boies (the "Yankee" of Yankee doodle) founded this Americana gift shop in 1952 and it remains family operated today. Shop here for unfinished, stained, or painted woodenware, glassware, and metalware. You will surely find something of interest and at the right price.

❋ Special Events

Mid-May: **Fooding Around Harwich. Formerly the Toast of Harwich,** this trolley tasting tour of the town's chefs includes (for VIPs) a reception with wine and bourbon tastings at the Wequassett Resort on the Harwich-Chatham town line. $$$$$.

July through September: **Guild of Harwich Artists** (guildofharwichartists .com) sponsors Monday "Art in the Park" programs at Doane Park, off Lower County Road. (Rain date is Wednesday.)

Mid-September: **Fall for Harwich** (harwichcranberryfestival.org) at the Harwich High School off Oak Street. Community spirit prevails at this popular celebration, which boasts an attendance of almost 40,000 people. Events include fireworks, a parade, a carnival, and hundreds of top-notch crafts displays.

Early December: **Christmas Weekend in the Harwiches** (harwichcc.com) includes hayrides, strolling minstrels, a choral group, and merchant open houses.

HARWICH CRANBERRY FESTIVAL KAYLA ROBERTSON/DO ART PHOTOGRAPHY

CHATHAM

Although Chatham is less accessible from Route 6 than are its neighbors, even the most hurried Cape visitors stop here. Occupying the tip of Cape Cod's elbow, the town offers a good mix of archetypal Cape Cod architecture, a classic Main Street, a refined sensibility, plenty of excellent beaches and shops, and a rich seafaring history.

Chatham is known for its calm, genteel, independent spirit. The town's vigilant zoning commission has kept tourist-trap activity to a minimum. Bordered on three sides by water, the town is populated by descendants of its oceangoing founders, many of whom continue in their ancestors' footsteps. Despite the difficulty in navigating the surrounding waters, Chatham sustains an active fleet of fishermen and leisure-time sailors. Fishermen, sailors, shop owners, and an increasing number of retirees live quietly in this delightfully traditional village.

Chatham, along with the spectacularly desolate **Monomoy National Wildlife Refuge**, boasts 65 miles of shoreline. As such, Chatham's **beaches** are varied: some are hit by pounding surf, sandbars shelter others; some are good for shell collecting, others are wide and sandy. A walk along the shore reveals gentle inlets and beautiful seafront homes. An inland drive or bicycle ride takes you past elegant shingled cottages and stately white houses surrounded by picket fences and boasting primroses and tidy lawns.

In the center of Chatham, **Main Street** is chock-full of upscale shops, offering everything from tony antiques and nautically inspired gifts to jewelry, clothing, and

AERIAL VIEW OF CHATHAM'S MONOMOY MARCIA DUGGAN/CAPECODSOUL

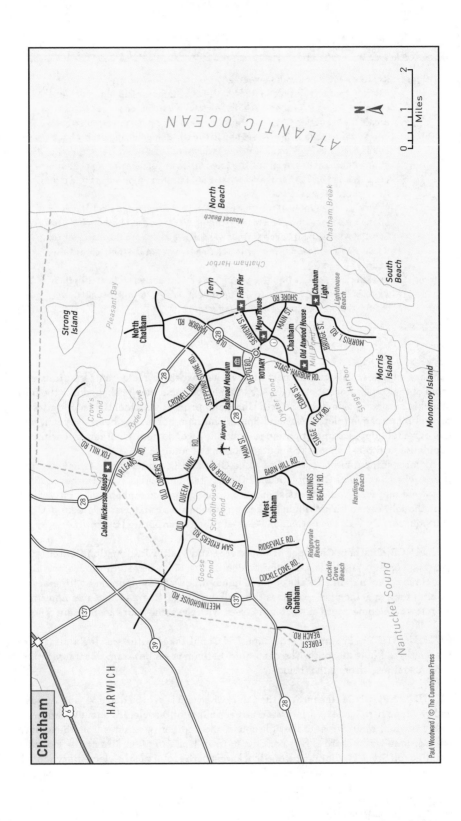

Chatham

ATLANTIC OCEAN

North Beach

Nauset Beach

Chatham Break

South Beach

Chatham Harbor

Tern I.

Fish Pier ★

Mayo House ★

SHORE RD.

MAIN ST.

SEAVIEW ST.

Chatham ①

Old Atwood House ★

Chatham Light ★

Lighthouse Beach

BRIDGE ST.

MORRIS I. RD.

Morris Island

OLD HARBOR RD.

28

ROTARY

DEPOT RD.

Railroad Museum 🏛

STAGE HARBOR RD.

Mill Pond

CEDAR ST.

STAGE NECK RD.

Stage Harbor

Monomoy Island

North Chatham

Strong Island

Pleasant Bay

Crow's Pond

Ryder's Cove

STEPPING STONE RD.

CROWELL RD.

28

FOX HILL RD.

28

Caleb Nickerson House ★

ORLEANS RD.

OLD COMERS RD.

QUEEN ANNE RD.

Airport ✈

GEO. RYDER RD.

MAIN ST.

28

Schoolhouse Pond

Oyster Pond

BARN HILL RD.

HARDINGS BEACH RD.

Hardings Beach

West Chatham

SAM RYDERS RD.

Goose Pond

OLD

RIDGEVALE RD.

Ridgevale Beach

COCKLE COVE RD.

Cockle Cove Beach

Nantucket Sound

South Chatham

MEETINGHOUSE RD.

137

FOREST BEACH RD.

39

28

6

HARWICH

137

N

0 1 2
Miles

Paul Woodward / © The Countryman Press

WHERE TO START IN CHATHAM

Morning: Act like a local and wake up early to snag a seat at the Hangar B Eatery, a sunny spot on the second floor of the Chatham Municipal Airport that opens at 7 a.m. Prefer something quick with a little less fuss? Grab a picnic table outside Chatham Perk and enjoy their freshly brewed coffee and homemade muffins. Then, hop in the car and drive the scenic back roads overlooking Pleasant Bay, Oyster Pond, and Stage Harbor. Walk sandy Chatham Break or use the telescopes to get a better long-distance view. While you're there, explore the old Chatham Lighthouse and climb the rickety staircase to the top.

Afternoon: Grab a barstool table at the Chatham Squire for lunch and a cold beer, or spend a bit more time (and money) dining waterside at Chatham Bars Inn. Stroll down Main Street and window-shop. Head over to the Fish Pier for a seal tour on the *Rip Ryder*, or watch fishermen unload their plentiful bounty.

Evening: Practice chopstick etiquette as you dive into creative rolls at Bluefin's Sushi & Sake Bar, or head to the Impudent Oyster for an upscale Cape/Mediterranean-inspired dining experience.

culinary supplies. This central part of town has excellent restaurants and inns and some of the Cape's finest bow houses (so named because they're shaped like the bow of a ship turned upside down). North Chatham, primarily residential, is dotted with several picturesque inlets. West and South Chatham border the beaches; you'll find lots of rental houses, summer cottages, and piney woods here. Chatham's year-round population of 6,600 balloons to about 35,000 in the summer.

As for a snippet of history and to place Chatham in context with its neighboring towns: when Samuel de Champlain and his party tried to land at Stage Harbor in 1606, they were met with stalwart resistance from the indigenous inhabitants. Fifty years later, though, Yarmouth's William Nickerson purchased a great deal of land from Chief Mattaquason. By 1712, the permanent "settlers" had incorporated the town.

GUIDANCE **Chatham Chamber of Commerce and Visitor Information Center** (508-430-7455; or 800-715-5567; chathaminfo.com), 2377 Main Street, in the historic Bassett House. The map-lined walls come in handy when you're planning an itinerary or looking for a specific place—as does the walking guide. There is also a summertime downtown welcome booth at 533 Main Street, with the same hours as the main office.

GETTING THERE *By car:* From the Cape Cod Canal, take Route 6 east to Exit 11 (Route 137 South) to Route 28 South. The center of Chatham is 3 miles from this intersection, about 45 minutes from either bridge.

GETTING AROUND Like most of the Cape, Chatham is crowded in July and August, and you'll be happiest exploring Main Street on foot or bicycle. It's about a 15-minute walk from mid-Main Street to the lighthouse, and another 15 minutes from the light to the pier (one-way). There is free parking at Town Hall (off Main Street), the Colonial Building (off Stage Harbor Road), one block west of the rotary at the elementary school, and on Chatham Bars Avenue, behind the Impudent Oyster restaurant off Main Street.

If you decide to ride your bike, there are numerous free racks to lock up at while you explore.

PUBLIC RESTROOMS Year-round facilities are located at the town offices on Main Street, at the Fish Pier on Shore Road, and the parking lot behind St. Christopher's Church on Main Street. Summertime restrooms are located behind Kate Gould Park (off Main Street).

PUBLIC LIBRARY **Eldredge Public Library** (508-945-5170; eldredgelibrary.org), 564 Main Street. One of the Cape's most beautiful libraries. The Renaissance/Romanesque revival–style building boasts traditional West Barnstable red brick walls and pink mortar, terra cotta cresting and slate roof, and gorgeous eyebrow dormers. And the interior is just as lush: quartered oak wainscoting, a carved oak fireplace mantle, Italian marble mosaic in the vestibule, and two stained glass windows with solid medallion facsimiles of the marks of L. Giunta and Aldus, both early Italian book crafters.

EMERGENCIES **Chatham Police Department** (508-945-1213; chatham-ma.gov), 249 George Ryder Road or call **911.**

✳ To See

Chatham Light (newenglandlighthouses.net), Main Street and Bridge Street. Built in 1808 and rebuilt in 1877, the lighthouse has a beacon visible 23 miles out to sea. The US Coast Guard–operated lighthouse is open in the afternoon on most/many Wednesdays from May to mid-October. Climbing the lighthouse requires some exertion, because there are 44 steps followed by eight steps up a ladder. Parking limit of 30 minutes during the summer.

    Chatham Break Coin-operated telescopes across from the lighthouse allow visitors to take a closer peek at Chatham Break. The main break was the result of a ferocious nor'easter on January 2, 1987. During the historic storm, the barrier beach (the lower portion of Nauset Beach) that had previously protected Chatham Harbor from the open ocean was breached. As a result, low dunes were flattened, tidal waters rose, and waves and high winds forced a channel through Nauset Beach. Over the next few years, expensive waterfront homes were destroyed by the ensuing unrestrained pounding of the fierce Atlantic Ocean. Although fishermen now have a more direct passage through the (formerly) long barrier beach, boating around the harbor's strong currents remains difficult. In a matter of hours in 1987 (rather than over the natural course of 50 years), the break altered Chatham's way of life—as do new breaks. The effects are still felt and debated today. But ocean currents have a mind of their own; in 1846 a previous break in South Beach repaired itself. That hasn't happened to this breach yet. But some beachfront is returning, and some of it belongs to folks who saw their lots washed away in the late 1980s. Sand, like birds, migrates south; Wellfleet and Eastham's beach losses are Chatham's gain. Lighthouse Beach is directly below the lookout area; South and North Beaches are visible across the harbor (see **Green Space**).

    Built in 1800, the original **Stage Harbor** Lighthouse helped mark and define the anchorage area for vessels waiting to round Monomoy Point and Pollock Rip Channel during times of low visibility. It also lined up perfectly with the Chatham Twin Lights making an effective range for Chatham Roads—the deep water channel crossing Nantucket Sound (a.k.a. the Vineyard Sound before 1920) from south of Bishop & Clerks Reef off Point Gammon in Hyannis—to the staging area (hence the name Stage

Harbor). The Lighthouse (now privately owned) was discontinued in 1933, when it was replaced by a skeleton tower 200 feet west, which continues to be an active aid to navigation. Today, **Stage Harbor Marine** (508-945-1860; 80 Bridge Street) remains busy with some Chatham-based fishing fleets, charters, private craft owners, and sailboats and yachts from Stage Harbor Yacht Club. The lighthouse does not offer public tours.

Chatham Railroad Museum (508-945-5100; chathamrailroadmuseum.com), 153 Depot Road. Open mid-June to mid-September. This carefully restored 1887 depot on the National Register of Historic Places features decorative "railroad gothic" architecture (unique to the

CHATHAM LIGHT KATY WARD

United States) from its turret to its gingerbread trim. In fact, this is such a good example of this architecture that students come to Chatham to study it. On the track in front of the station, you will find a 1910 New York Central train caboose (visitors are free to climb on the caboose and explore its interior); inside the museum are such treasures as photos, models, and equipment pertaining to the Cape's railroad history.

Josiah Mayo House (508-945-4084; chathamconservationfoundation.org/Josiah -mayo-house), 540 Main Street. Open limited weekdays and hours, late June to early September. Built in 1818 by Josiah Mayo (who served for 40 years as Chatham's first postmaster) and filled with period antiques, the Mayo House is owned

CHATHAM BREAK KATY WARD

RAILROAD MUSEUM KIM GRANT

and maintained by the Chatham Conservation Foundation. The tiny, gray-with-red-shutters, three-quarter Cape isn't the "best this" or the "oldest that"—it's just a nice little old house.

Caleb Nickerson House (508-945-6086; nickersonassoc.org), 1107 Orleans Road (Route 28). Open mid-June to late September. This near pristine full-Cape home, which dates to 1772, is a "jewel box of authentic Colonial architecture." Don't miss it. Although the house was moved from its original location overlooking Oyster River, it ended up on homestead land that originally belonged to the great-great-great-great-grandfather of the founder of Chatham, William Nickerson.

Atwood House Museum (508-945-2493; chathamhistoricalsociety.org), 347 Stage Harbor Road. Open June through October. Sea captain Joseph Atwood built this gambrel-roofed home in 1752, but the Chatham Historical Society has maintained the property since 1926. Except for the addition of electricity, the old house is unchanged from when it was built and furnished centuries ago. The museum includes a gallery devoted to the history of fishing on Cape Cod and seven additional galleries that display antique dolls, tools, toys, portraits of sea captains, Sandwich glass, and other Chatham seafaring artifacts. The adjoining Mural Barn features a permanent exhibit by Alice Stallknecht. On the Atwood grounds, you will find the Chatham School Bells display

ATWOOD HOUSE MUSEUM, CHATHAM SCHOOL BELLS KATY WARD

FISH-N'-SHIPS

Chatham Fish Pier (508-945-5185 for harbormaster; chatham-ma.gov/chatham-fish-pier), 613 Stage Harbor Road. Watch as the fleet of fishing boats return (from as far away as 100 miles) to the pier each afternoon. From the pier you can watch fishermen unload their catch of haddock, lobster, cod, halibut, flounder, and dogfish. While you're there, look for the Fisherman's Monument. A 1992 call for designs attracted nearly 100 applicants from around the world, but the local government chose Sig Purwin, a Woods Hole sculptor, to memorialize the town's fishermen. In recent years, as stocks have begun to dwindle, fishermen have increasingly turned to shellfish harvesting. (Local bay scallops harvested in late fall are like nothing you've ever tasted.) In fact, more commercial licenses are purchased yearly in Chatham than anywhere else on the Cape. (See also **Chatham Fish Market** under **Where to Eat**.)

A FISHERMAN UNLOADS DOGFISH AT THE CHATHAM FISH PIER KATY WARD

and the Chatham Light Display, featuring the lantern house from Chatham's twin light with its original Fresnel lens, which flashes its beam whenever the museum is open.

Monomoy National Wildlife Refuge North and South Monomoy Islands (fws.gov/refuge/monomoy), acquired by the federal government as part of a wildlife refuge in 1944, comprise a 7,600-acre habitat for more than 285 species of birds. Birds and seaside animals rule the roost; there are no human residents, no paved roads, no vehicles, and no electricity. (Long ago the island did support a fishing community, though.) It's a quiet, solitary place. Monomoy, one of four remaining "wilderness" areas between Maine and New Jersey, is an important stop for shorebirds on the Atlantic Flyway—between breeding grounds in the Arctic and wintering grounds in South America. Conditions here may well determine whether the birds will survive the journey. Some beaches are closed from April to mid-August to protect threatened nesting areas for piping plovers and terns. The lovely old lighthouse, built in 1823 and not used since 1923, was restored in 1988. In the mid-1990s, the US Fish and Wildlife Service embarked on a long-term management project to restore avian nesting diversity to Monomoy by creating habitat for terns, which historically numbered in the thousands. Restoring the nesting space was controversial because the government considered it necessary to "remove" (with bread chunks laced with poison) about 10 percent of the aggressive seagulls that also nested here. As a result, by the late 1990s, the number of nesting terns, including 18 pairs of roseate terns, increased dramatically. Some protesters still maintain that the Fish and Wildlife Service took this action under pressure from off-road-vehicle drivers, who are often banned from driving on mainland beaches because of nesting endangered birds. But by the late 1990s, Monomoy had become the

SCENIC DRIVES

Chatham is one of the most scenic Cape towns. Route 28 toward Orleans offers some of the loveliest scenery, with views of Pleasant Bay to the east. Shore Road passes handsome cedar-shingled houses. The causeway to Morris Island affords harbor views as well as views of the open ocean beyond tall grasses and sandy shores. And the road to Cockle Cove Beach from Route 28 in South Chatham runs along a picturesque salt marsh and tidal river.

second largest tern-nesting site on the East Coast, and the biggest between here and the Canadian Maritimes. In 1998 the refuge was dogged by another controversy: dens of coyotes (and their pups) were feasting on newborn chicks. Management "removed" them as well. These days, commercial clammers and crabbers are sparring with the refuge over the issuance (or lack thereof) of permits. Monomoy was attached to the mainland until a 1958 storm severed the connection; a storm in 1978 divided the island in two. The islands are accessible only by boat and only under favorable weather conditions (see under *Boat Excursions & Rentals*). Today, South Monomoy Island contains the largest gray seal haul-out site on the US Atlantic Coast.

✳ To Do

AIRPLANE RIDES ✳ 🐾 **Stick'n Rudder Aero Tours** (508-945-2563; chathamairport .com), Chatham Municipal Airport, 240 George Ryder Road. To really appreciate Chatham's shoreline and the fragility of the Outer Cape landscape, head 900 feet above it in a four-seater Cessna. These wonderful sight-seeing rides are pricey but special. Prices are per ride, whether it's for one person or three (maximum). Walk-ups are welcome, but reservations are wiser ($$$$+).

ART CLASSES ✳ **Creative Arts Center** (508-945-3583; capecodcreativearts.org), 154 Crowell Road. The center offers classes during July and August in pottery, drawing, photography, painting, jewelry making, and other fine arts. Work is shown at the center's on-site **Edward A. Bigelow Gallery**, alternating student/teacher work with regional shows by other artists. Since 1971, the center has held an annual art festival in August (see **Special Events**), where you may meet the artists and purchase their work.

BASEBALL ✐ **The Chatham Anglers** (508-945-5511; chathamanglers.com), one of 10 teams in the Cape Cod Baseball League, usually play ball at 7 p.m. from mid-June to early August at Veterans Park, Route 28, just west of the rotary. The information booth (see *Guidance*) has schedules. The As sponsor weekly clinics for youngsters from mid-June to July. Inquire about particulars and bring your own glove.

BICYCLING & RENTALS **The Cape Cod Rail Trail** offers 25 miles of paved road for your biking pleasure. The trail route starts in Wellfleet and passes through the lower and mid-Cape towns, ending in Yarmouth. Personally, I prefer bicycling as a means of getting around town. It's a great way to explore and visit the many beaches and shops while avoiding summer traffic, and you're always guaranteed parking at one of the many bicycle racks on Main Street. After cycling through town, head over to Monomoy Island on Chatham's southern end, or the "causeway" as locals call it. The long stretch of sanding uniting Chatham and Monomoy lends scenic views of the Atlantic on one side with Ryder's Cove Boatyard opposite.

OUTERMOST ADVENTURES, CHATHAM KIM GRANT

You can rent bicycles and equipment at **Chatham Hood Bikes** (508-469-0210; chathamhoodbikes.com), 400 Main Street; or at **Wheelhouse Bike Co.** (774-840-4156; wheelhousebike.com), 48 Crowell Road.

BOAT EXCURSIONS & RENTALS The **Wellfleet Bay Wildlife Sanctuary** (508-349-2615; massaudubon.org) sponsors numerous activities, including kayak trips around Tern Island and guided tours of Monomoy Island. Call to register for a trip. $$$$+.

Outermost Adventures (508-945-2030; outermostharbor.com), 83 Seagull Road. Open June to mid-September. Take advantage of their shuttles to and from Chatham's South Beach; bird watching and seal spotting tours off North Monomoy Island; and fishing charters on the 33-foot *Grady White*. Outermost offers a little bit of everything. $$$.

Beachcomber (508-945-5265; sealwatch.com), 174 Crowell Road. Open June through September, but call for tours because there's no set schedule until July. Chatham has no shortage of seals. Don't believe me? Take a tour. Take away the seals and it's still a beautiful experience. $$$.

Monomoy Island Ferry (508-237-0420; monomoyislandferry.com), Stage Harbor Marine, 80 Bridge Street. Open April through November; make reservations the night before. Join Captain Keith Lincoln aboard the *Rip Ryder* for a memorable ocean adventure. Marvel at the beauty of Monomoy Island as you watch seals frolic and bask in the sun with protected native birds flying above. Captain Keith also offers shuttle trips to South Monomoy. When he drops you off, tell him what time you want to be picked up. $$$.

FISHING Chatham's abundant coastline offers excellent fishing conditions for pro-anglers and blooming sportsmen alike. Procure freshwater and saltwater fishing licenses and regulations online at mass.gov/eea/agencies/dfg/licensing.

Big game: **Capeshores Charters** (508-237-0399; sportfishingcapecod.com), Barcliff Avenue Extended, Chatham Fish Pier. Trips typically begin May/June through October/November. Book a charter on the 34-foot *Marilyn S* for some of the best big game action in New England. Test your patience, luck, and stamina with a full-day trip hunting for bluefin tuna or feisty striped bass. Captain Bruce Peters is a 16th-generation skipper and Cape Cod native from a long genetic line of lifesavers, whalers, and watermen. When he's at the helm, you are guaranteed a rewarding trip. $$$$+.

On shore: **Morris Island** is a premier area for shore fishing. Multiple channels between sandbars, with deep drop offs, and plentiful bait like sand eels. Begin fishing just below the Monomoy Wildlife Refuge Visitor Center and work your way along the beach casting into any "dark" water you see. Keep going until you reach **Oyster River**, which tends to hold larger bass. Cast and wading is necessary in some spots and it requires a fair amount of walking to fish the entire area thoroughly.

By bridge: Follow Stage Harbor Road to Bridge Street, where **Mill Pond** empties into **Stage Harbor**. You'll haul in crabs, small flounder, eels, and perhaps even a bluefish. Locals will certainly be there harvesting shellfish with long rakes. Stop even if you don't fish; it's picturesque.

Freshwater: **Schoolhouse Pond** (reached via Sam Ryder's Road) and **Goose Pond** (off Fisherman's Landing) offer freshwater fishing for rainbow trout. Freshwater permits can be obtained from **Goose Hummock** (508-255-0455; goose.com; 15 Route 6A, Orleans).

COMMERCIAL FISHING IN CHATHAM MARCIA DUGGAN/CAPECODSOUL

Supplies: Stop at **Cape Fishermen's Supply Inc.** (508-945-3501; capefishermens supply.com), 67 Depot Road, for everything marine-related or **North Chatham Outfitters** (508-348-1638; northchathamoutfitters.com), 300 Orleans Road. Here you will find rods and reels, lures and bait for salt and freshwater fishing, as well as apparel, coolers, and kayak and paddleboard rentals.

FOR FAMILIES **Veteran's Field Playground** on Depot Street across from the Chatham Railroad Museum.

GENEALOGY **Nickerson Family Association** (508-945-6086; nickersonassoc.org), 1107 Orleans Road. Chatham's founder, William Nickerson, has more than 350,000 descendants. Think you're one of them? This genealogical research center will help you find out. In addition to mapping the Nickerson family tree, the volunteer association casts a wide net, compiling information on folks associated with the Nickersons and original settlers of Cape Cod and Nova Scotia.

GOLF **Chatham Seaside Links** (508-945-4774; chathamseasidelinks.com), 209 Seaview Street, next to the Chatham Bars Inn. Open March through November. Founded in 1895, this nine-hole course will delight any avid golfer. They also offer lessons. $$$–$$$$+.

Wequassett Resort and Golf Club (508-432-5400; or 508-690-6692 to book tee time; wequassett.com/golf), 2173 Route 28 in Harwich. Open late May to mid-October. With 18 challenging holes, a 72-par, and 6,954 championship quality yards, it's not your average run-of-the-mill course. $$$$+.

KAYAKS & PADDLEBOARDS **The Chatham Kayak Company** (508-241-2389; chatham kayakcompany.com), 391 Barn Hill Road. Choose from a wide variety of quality kayaks and stand-up paddleboards, powerboat rentals, guided tours, lessons, and more. Each rental comes fully equipped with gear for all ages and depths of experience. $$$–$$$$+.

SAILING **Chatham Sailboat Rentals** (508-432-4339; chathamsail.com), 434 Ridgevale Road. This family owned and operated business offers top-notch Hobie Catamaran and Sunfish rentals. Sailing guests receive complimentary beachside parking, life jackets, launching and rigging services to ensure a hassle-free day on the sea. You can rent kayaks and stand-up paddleboards here, too.

SEAL TOURS See *Boat Excursions & Rentals.*

TENNIS Free public courts are located on **Depot Road** by the Railroad Museum and at **Chatham High School** on Crowell Road.

Chatham Bars Inn (508-945-6759; chathambarsinn.com), 297 Shore Road. Courts open mid-April to mid-November. CBI has waterfront courts made of synthetic "classic-clay" (they play like clay but are much easier to maintain) which they rent to nonguests ($$$/hour). Summertime lessons, too.

✳ Green Space

BEACHES There are six major beaches in Chatham. Each requires a parking sticker from late June to early September. Daily and weekly passes (cash only) are available at town beach kiosks at Harding, Ridgevale, and Cockle Cove Beach only and the

YOU HAD ME AT HYDRANGEA

Heading north on Shore Road from Main Street you will find a road lined with stately private homes overlooking the ocean. But one landscape is sure to stand out, the Hydrangea Walk, especially during mid-June to September when the front walkway is awash with more than 50 blooming hydrangea plants. The public facade is an icon that has been the subject of tourists' photos and postcards since the house was originally built in 1938.

HYDRANGEA WALK MARCIA DUGGAN/CAPECODSOUL

Harbormaster's office (508-945-5185; 613 Stage Harbor Road). Residential passes can be purchased at the **Chatham Permit Department** (508-945-5180; chatham-ma.gov), 261 George Ryder Road across from Chatham Municipal Airport.

Harding Beach, off Harding Beach Road on Nantucket Sound. Small waves, soft sand, and lifeguards make this beach ideal for families and large groups. I recommend a game of beach bocce while you're here. Military personnel—active or retired—are allowed free access with military photo ID.

Ridgevale Beach, off Ridgevale Drive on Nantucket Sound. This popular large beach is very similar to Harding Beach (with the same amenities like lifeguards), but with creeks for children to splash around in.

Cockle Cove Beach, off Cockle Cove Road. Parents will appreciate the calm waves and long stretches of soft sand, while children enjoy building sandcastles and watching adventurous windsurfers shred water.

Pleasant Bay Beach, a.k.a. **Jackknife**, off Route 28, North Chatham. The 7,000-acre inlet with its warm water and sheltered cove is great for children, but there are no lifeguards or restrooms, so be mindful.

EASTWARD HO MARCIA DUGGAN/CAPECODSOUL

North Beach, CCNS, Chatham's section of Nauset Beach. If you want solitude, this is the closest you will get. North Beach is actually the southern end of Nauset Beach (see *Beaches* under **Green Space** in Orleans) and is only accessible by boat or permitted ORV. No restrooms or lifeguards. (Fun fact: North Beach was the topic of Henry Beston's *Outermost House* and Tim Wood's *Breakthrough: the Story of Chatham's North Beach*.)

Lighthouse Beach and **South Beach**, across from Chatham Lighthouse. This beautiful expanse of sandy terrain offers some of the best ocean views on Cape Cod. But don't let your guard down—strong currents and tides can be extremely dangerous. Keep an eye on the flagpole at the top of the stairs, which signals dangerous conditions. If you see a red flag, it means swimming is prohibited. Lighthouse Beach is not guarded by lifeguards and is swim-at-your-own-risk. Parking is limited to 30 minutes, but you can bicycle or walk from Morris Island Road just beyond the lighthouse (a sign points the way to South Beach). It's a bit of a walk and you will need a parking pass, but you can also try parking on Bridge Street.

See also "Shark Awareness" on page 282.

PARKS **Chase Park** and **Gristmill** on Cross Street are ideal places for a picnic reprieve from the summertime madness on Main Street.

PONDS **Schoolhouse Pond,** off Indian Hill Road. Take a breather from the beach and head over to this freshwater paradise. Parents in need of a reprieve will enjoy watching their little ones frolic in the cool water, play in the soft sand, or search for tadpoles in the low grass marsh. Parking sticker required.

Oyster Pond, off Stage Harbor Road. One of the few places that does not require a parking pass. Contrary to most ponds, this one is very open, sunny, and bright. Warm sparkling water and grills meshed with nearby neighborhood traffic makes this pond ideal for families but not so peaceful.

WALKS Chatham Conservation Foundation (508-945-4084; chathamconservation foundation.org). With more than 645 acres, the foundation has created three distinct walking areas traversing marshes, wetlands, and meadows. Contact the town information booth on Main Street (see *Guidance*) for directions to Frost Fish Creek, Barclay Pond, and Honeysuckle Lane.

The Dog Runs, as it's known locally. Walk 10 minutes along Bridge Street away from the lighthouse to find this forested coastal trail along Stage Harbor. Enjoy a picnic in the cattail marshes. (See also **Monomoy National Wildlife Refuge** under **To Do**.)

✳ Lodging

Generally, Chatham is one of the more expensive places to stay on Cape Cod. Its motels, though, are some of the best on Cape Cod. Two-night minimum stays in July and August are normal, and many of Chatham's most notable places are booked for July and August well in advance. (See also **Lodging** in Harwich, which has several worthy places that are just across Chatham's town line.)

BED-AND-BREAKFASTS **The Captain's House Inn** (508-945-0127; captainshouse inn.com), 369–377 Old Harbor Road. Jill and James Meyer have been successfully wooing guests since the mid-2000s with their 12 handsomely decorated rooms, four sumptuous suites, and 2 acres of perfectly tended gardens. It's easily among the top 10 places to stay in New England. The Captain's Cottage contains one particularly historic room with wood-burning fireplace, walnut-paneled walls, and pumpkin-pine flooring; a hideaway attic suite; and a honeymoon-style room with a double whirlpool. Full breakfasts are served on linen, china, and silver in a wonderfully airy room abutting the inn's beautiful gardens. Smoked salmon graces the sideboard every morning, an authentic English tea is

CAPTAIN'S HOUSE INN OF CHATHAM KIM GRANT

offered every afternoon, cookies always seem to be baking throughout the day, and the DVD library always has port in the evening. The inn also has an oh-so-exclusive-feeling swimming pool and a small but expert fitness room. Check for minimum stays, even outside of high season. $$–$$$$.

Carriage House Inn (508-945-4688; thecarriagehouseinn.com), 407 Old Harbor Road. Formerly the homestead of sea Captain Isaac Loveland, this beautiful 1850s building has undergone extension renovations. Under the new management of Chef Peter Varns and Brian O'Connor, this adults-only bed-and-breakfast is perfect for romantic couples and serious foodies. Amenities include a spacious rooftop deck with a peek of the ocean, a large sunny breakfast room and outside patio adorned with white tablecloths and private seating, and lush well-manicured gardens. Guestrooms include quality bedding with 600-thread count sheets, spa robes and slippers, artisanal bath

amenities, and a rustic multicourse breakfast and afternoon tea by Chef Peter. $$–$$$$.

COTTAGES **Metters Cottages** (508-432-3535; chathambeach.com), 94 Chatham Harbor Lane. Open late May through October. These three rustic and simply stated cottages are located within short walking distance to Cockle Cove Beach (see also *Beaches* under **Green Space**). Think linoleum floors, natural wood furniture, a large brick fireplace, and a quiet spacious deck overlooking the harbor. Call for availability and reservations. $$–$$$.

RESORTS & HOTELS **Chatham Inn** (508-945-9232; chathaminn.com), 359 Main Street. This two-story, 18-room boutique hotel (a 10-minute walk from Chatham Light and a 5-minute walk from the heart of downtown) was recently renovated with aplomb. Upscale guestrooms might have a fireplace, private balcony

CHATHAM BARS INN KATY WARD

(overlooking the parking lot), wet bar, and signature spa bathtubs. Behind the inn sits a little nature trail and unharvested cranberry bog, but most guests enjoy the rocking chairs on the long veranda. Come late afternoon (and for Sunday brunch) to their on-site **Chatham Wine Bar and Restaurant** (508-945-1468; chathamwinebar.com), which is also open to the public. $$–$$$.

Chatham Bars Inn (508-945-0096; chathambarsinn.com), 297 Shore Road. This grande dame's gracious elegance is rivaled by only a handful of places in New England. Built in 1914 as a hunting lodge, it's now the quintessential seaside resort. And after extensive million-dollar renovations, it's better than ever. Scattered over 25 acres, the main inn and cottages have 217 rooms and suites comfortably decorated in traditional Cape Cod style, some with private balconies or decks. The complex includes a private beach, a heated outdoor pool, a spa, gift shop, three tennis courts, croquet, a health and wellness center, a nine-hole golf course, launch service to Nauset Beach, sailing lessons, and a full and complimentary children's program. They also offer morning harbor seal cruises aboard their custom-designed *Bar Tender* vessel (it can hold up to 18 people), as well as sportfishing and lessons for kids. Although prices don't normally include meals, bed-and-breakfast packages offer a lavish buffet every morning (which is otherwise $$$). Enjoy picture-perfect views of the ocean from the veranda or dine oceanside at the **Beach Bar Grille** (see **Where to Eat**), or at the resort's elegant **The Sacred Cod** for upscale tavern cuisine from the resort's local farm.

Chatham Tides (508-432-0379; chathamtides.com), 394 Pleasant Street. Open mid-May to mid-October. This beachfront gem does not fit the description of a hotel in any way shape or form. Delightfully off the well-trodden path and about 4 miles from the center of town, this quiet beachfront complex of 24 rooms and suites is a real find. Each room—whether it's a standard bedroom, efficiency, town house or studio, or beach house (yes, an entire house)—they all offer water views of Nantucket Sound. After all, it is located directly *on* a private beach. Each room has its own secluded deck with tables and chairs and prepped kitchens/kitchenettes. Guest reviews praise owners John and Mary Ellen for their hospitality. After staying here once, you'll probably return again and again. Try booking in February after the repeat guests have their pick of the litter in January. $$–$$$.

Chatham Wayside Inn (508-945-5550; waysideinn.com), 512 Main Street. Open year-round. Located just steps away from bustling Main Street, the Wayside Inn offers 46 comfortable guestrooms and five suites that are both bright and airy, furnished with flair and reminiscent of the historic 1860 hostelry. Triple sheeting, thick towels, and top-notch bathroom amenities are standard. Some rooms have canopy or four-poster beds and reproduction period furniture, a fireplace, a whirlpool tub, or a private patio or balcony. Amenities include an outdoor heated pool, exercise room, lounge

CHATHAM TIDES KIM GRANT

with light fare and drinks, a continental breakfast, and access to the on-site **Wild Goose Tavern** (see *Dining Out* under **Where to Eat**). The Wayside Inn also rents nearby private homes equipped with full kitchens, outside dining areas, and the works: a two-bedroom home at 391 Main Street; a three-bedroom home at 393 Main Street; and a quaint two-bedroom cottage at 58 Cross Street. $$–$$$$$.

Pleasant Bay Village Resort (508-945-133; pleasantbayvillage.com), 1191 Orleans Road. Open May through October. Chose from efficiency units, three types of suites, and six different styles of hotel rooms. All accommodations feature luxurious bedding, high-end bath products, contemporary coastal décor, and 6 acres of stunning garden views and Japanese style landscaping—it's a horticulturist's delight. There's also a heated pool and Jacuzzi. The spacious lobby is filled with Oriental carpets and is a great place to hang out on a rainy day, as is the airy breakfast room. Walk across the street and down Route 28 to Pleasant Bay Beach (see **Green Space**). Don't make the mistake of guests who book for 2 or 3 days and end up wanting to stay for 5 or 6 days, but can't because of limited availability. $–$$.

MOTELS **Hawthorne Motel** (508-945-0372; thehawthorne.com), 196 Shore Road. Open mid-May to mid-October. This place is all about location, location, location. Every time I stop in, it feels like coming home. A 10-minute walk from Main Street, this motel is popular because there's nothing standing between it and the ocean except a grassy green lawn and a path to the private beach. *Nothing.* The simple complex consists of 16 motel rooms and 10 efficiencies and cottages (with kitchens). They all provide delightfully easy access to sunning, swimming, and lazing on the beach. I particularly like the corner rooms, as they're much larger. $$–$$$.

Chatham Highlander Motel (508-945-9038; chathamhighlander.com), 946 Route 28. All rooms open April to mid-November with few available year-round. An excellent choice for budget-minded travelers; this favored motel is

HAWTHORNE MOTEL KIM GRANT

just a stone's throw from the center of town. The two adjacent buildings sit on a little knoll above a well-traveled road. Each of the 29 rooms has a TV, a small refrigerator, a newly tiled bathroom, and air-conditioning; the one-bedroom apartment has a bona-fide kitchen. The cheery rooms are sparkling white; other aspects are charmingly retro. There are also two heated pools. $–$$.

RENTAL HOUSES & COTTAGES **Sylvan Vacation Rentals** (508-945-7222; sylvanrentals.com), 1715 Route 28, West Chatham.

Chatham Home Rentals (508-945-9444; chathamhomerentals.com), 1370 Route 28.

BLUEFIN'S SUSHI & SAKE BAR KATY WARD

✳ Where to Eat

Dining options in Chatham run the gamut, from elegant to child-friendly places. Reserve ahead in summer (especially at *Dining Out* eateries) or be prepared for a lengthy wait.

DINING OUT **Bluefin's Sushi & Sake Bar** (508-348-1573; bluefinschatham.com), 513 Main Street. Open D, year-round. Make reservations whether you are a sushi fan or not! Specialty rolls such as the Red Sox, Dynamite, Toro Jalapeño, and Chatham's Sunset are divine. You can't go wrong with the Tornado, Shaggy Dog, and Tiger-Eye cooked rolls, either. For starters: the Korean Ribs, asparagus fries, and deconstructed lobster rangoons are fight-worthy, as well as the obvious edamame and blistered shishito peppers. Not into seafood? Try their Wagyu beef burger or Chatham pad thai. You will leave happy regardless of what you order. Plus the service is top-notch. $$$–$$$$.

Pisces (508-432-4600; piscesof chatham.com), 2653 Main Street. Open D, late April to mid-May. A foodie's delight tucked inside an inconspicuous yellow cottage. This charming and contemporary bistro offers 40 seats in the dining room and a cozy five-seat bar. The menu includes Mediterranean and coastal cuisine dishes like local cod sautéed in a spiced cornmeal crust with lemon caper aioli, toasted orzo pasta, and summer vegetables. The simple décor features local art on the walls, but the plates are anything but simple. It's always crowded here and, if they had twice the space, twice as many people would be salivating. $$$–$$$$.

Del Mar Bar & Bistro (508-945-9988; delmarbistro.com), 907 Main Street. This place fills up quickly in summer, so I suggest making reservations well in advance (2 days preferably). Start with Chef Maria Pollio's Japanese pumpkin ravioli, the warm tomato and burrata bruschetta, or wood fired oysters. For the main course: the maple glazed roasted duckling with sweet potato puree, broccolini, and bourbon-soaked black cherries is spectacular; as is the grilled filet mignon paired with bacon mashed potatoes; and the Portuguese steamed littlenecks over linguini. Be sure to also check the blackboard menu for nightly specials. My recent indulgence was the Berbere boneless short ribs with Ethiopian spice, tomato and coconut milk, coriander basmati rice, and a crisp curry slaw with charred pineapple relish and

IMPUDENT OYSTER KATY WARD

plantain chips—YUM. One reviewer said, "My wife and I were fortunate enough to dine here during our Chatham vacation, and I can say without question that not only was it the best meal of our stay, it was one of the best meals of my life. We should have eaten here every night; it's that much better than the rest of the area's high-end options." $–$$$$.

Impudent Oyster (508-945-3545), 15 Chatham Bars Avenue. Open L, D, year-round. Ask around in Chatham and this place is still top of the list, even though it's been around since the mid-1970s. The atmosphere is certainly pleasant and almost rustic: peaked ceiling with exposed beams, skylights, and hanging plants. And the extensive menu highlights internationally inspired fish and shellfish dishes. Try the deservedly popular Impudent Bouillabaisse; their Cape Cod twist on Devils on Horseback; Coop's meatballs; or Cod Lisbon for dinner. For lunch order a simple lobster roll, fish tacos, or the Cape Fish-Wich. The Thai fisherman's stew, Nantucket scallop

sandwich, and Bang Bang Roll Up are also delicious options. $$–$$$$.

Chatham Bars Inn (508-945-0096; chathambarsinn.com), Shore Road. Open B, D, year-round. The grand hotel's veranda, overlooking the ocean, makes a picture-perfect setting for a late afternoon drink and/or light meal. As for the other draws, panoramic ocean views and grand Sunday-night buffets in the main dining room are legendary. (Long pants and collared shirt are requested at dinner.) If you normally avoid buffets, break that rule here. $$$–$$$$.

EATING OUT **Wild Goose Tavern** (508-945-5590; wildgoosetavern.com), 512 Main Street. Open L, D, year-round. If you overhear a local say, "Meet me at the Goose," this is where they are talking about. Because of its prominent location on Main Street and a constant parade of strollers-by, this pleasant room really packs in visitors. The street side patio is pleasant offering a mid-day menu of sandwiches, salads, pizzas, and panini. The indoor bar has a flat-screen TV when you need to catch a game or some breaking news. $–$$$.

Bistro on Main and Chatham Raw Bar (508-945-5033; bistroonmainchatham .com), 595 Main Street. Open L, summer, and D, year-round. You would think Chatham is chock-full of raw bars, but it turns out this is the one and only! Whether you dine inside at the long mahogany bar or outside on a patio table, this place has a relaxed vibe with dynamite food and lovely service. Plus the inside captain's wheel is pretty cool. $$–$$$$.

Chatham Squire (508-945-0945 restaurant; 508-945-0942 tavern; thesquire.com), 487 Main Street. Open L, D, year-round. A local favorite watering hole where the beer runs cold and the food is deliciously inexpensive. A friendly place, Chatham's best family restaurant offers something for everyone—from burgers and daily seafood specials to multiethnic dishes and excellent chowder. Paisley carpeting, low booths, captain's chairs at wooden tables, exposed beams, and pool tables (off-season only) add to the family-den feel of the place. License plates and local signs adorn the walls and ceiling. $$–$$$.

Beach House Grill (508-945-0096; chathambarsinn.com), 297 Shore Road at Chatham Bars Inn. Open L, D, mid-June to mid-September. One of the Cape's few alfresco oceanside eateries, the grill's deck is anchored in the sand, overlooking a wide, golden beach. Settings rarely get better than this. The overpriced menu features upscale seaside standards: burgers, summer salads, lobster rolls, peel-and-eat shrimp, and fried seafood platters. Popular dinners revolve around family-friendly themes like clam and lobster bakes or Caribbean night (where folks dress up in pirate garb). There's live music nightly. $$–$$$$.

Red Nun Bar & Grill (508-348-0469; rednun.com), 746 Main Street. Open L, D. A casual place with a creative tavern-style menu. Think burgers (the Nun burger with the works and the High Thai'd burger with spicy Thai peanut sauce), nachos, beer-battered onion rings, and fried local seafood—all wrapped in red-and-white-checkered paper and placed in an old-school red basket. Kids get to play artist with an open paper table "cloth" and crayons. See their second location under **Where to Eat** in Dennis. $–$$$.

The Talkative Pig (508-430-5211; thetalkativepig.com), 2642 Main Street. Open B, July to September only; L and D, year-round. Everything on the Mediterranean-inspired menu is delicious, but it's Chef Jeff Mitchell's pizza that's the talk of the town. Choose from signature hand-pulled pizzas like the Melanzane with grilled eggplant and caramelized onion, or the tender grilled shrimp scampi with tomatoes, garlic, and a ricotta cream thyme sauce. You can also build your own pizza: start with your choice of sauce (tomato, pesto, ricotta cream, barbecue, or olive oil) and top it off with a variety of oven-roasted veggies, meats (the homemade sausage is sumptuous), and fresh Parmesan and mozzarella. They also offer gluten-free pizza, salads, and market sides. $$–$$$.

Carmine's (508-945-5300), 595 Main Street. Open L, D. When you're tired of pricy lobster rolls and other seafood bites, Carmine's is a great alternative. Pizza (slice and pies), calzones, subs, and salads rounds out the menu. $–$$.

Corner Store (508-432-1077; chatham cornerstore.com), 1403 Old Queen Anne Road. I've never met anyone who disliked a Corner Store burrito. Choose from white or wheat wrap (with or without cheese) and go down the line of fillings: steak, chicken, veggies, rice, beans, guac, and corn salsa, to name a few. These burritos are stuffed to the brim and tailored to your taste buds. They also serve panini, sandwiches, and soups at this location (see also under *Eating Out* in Orleans). $–$$.

SWEET TREATS & COFFEE **Chatham Perk** (508-945-5005; chathamperk.com), 307 Orleans Road. Open B, L. Tired? This place will surely perk you up. Start your day off on the right foot with delicious coffee, espresso drinks, and freshly baked pastries: muffins, bagels, cinnamon rolls, and more. They also serve lunch: café sandwiches, salads, soups, and grilled panini; and hand-pressed juices, smoothies, and smoothie bowls. $–$$.

Chatham Cookware (508-945-1250; chathamcookware.com), 524 Main Street. Open B, L, year-round. No, this is not a place to buy pots and pans, but rather coffee, baked goods, sandwiches, and the like. $–$$.

Chatham Village Café and Bakery (508-945-3229; 508-945-2525; chatham villagecafeandbakery.com), 69 Crowell Road. Open B, L. Relocated from its former home on Main Street, this upscale bakery offers creative sandwiches, excellent baked goods, and quality coffee and espresso drinks. $–$$.

MARION'S PIE SHOP LEESA BURKE

Hangar B Eatery (508-593-3655), 240 George Ryder Road in the Chatham Municipal Airport. You may not expect a gourmet breakfast in an airport, but Hangar B will surprise you. Favorites include the Red Flannel Hash made with beets, sweet and gold potatoes, and served with big slices of sourdough toast, bacon, and poached eggs with horseradish crème fraîche. Craving something sweet? Try their indulgent lemon ricotta pancakes topped with whipped butter, Vermont maple syrup, and fresh berries. You can't go wrong here. Expect a (worthwhile) wait if you don't get there early. $–$$.

Marion's Pie Shop (508-432-9439; marionspieshopofchatham.com), 2022 Main Street. Open B, L, takeout only. Using the same pastry crust recipe that has been passed down for over 70 years, Cindy and Blake continue Marion's tradition of filling bellies and souls with good old-fashioned comfort cooking. While all the pastries are heavenly: muffins, croissants, fruit breads, and coffee cake— it's really about the pies. With over a dozen fillings, it's hard to choose: apple, blackberry, wild blueberry, strawberry rhubarb, lemon meringue, and chocolate cream, to name just a few. They also have savory pies: chicken and gravy, beef steak, clam, seafood, and hamburger. If you're not in the mood for pie, grab something from their prepared specialty comfort food menu with options such as lasagna, meatballs, or stuffed Italian peppers. Careful with the children— misbehaving ones "will be made into pies." $–$$$.

Chatham Candy Manor (508-945-0825; candymanor.com), 484 Main Street. This sweet spot has been making hand-dipped chocolate, fudge, and liqueur-flavored truffles since 1955.

MARKETS **Chatham Village Market** (508-945-9783; chathamvillagemarket .com), 20 Queen Anne Road. Open daily, year-round. Swing by this truly full-service market and stock up on essential groceries for your vacation stay. You can also take advantage of their local home delivery option: just place your order over the phone and let them do the shopping and deliver the bags to your door.

Delivery extends to all of Chatham, with a $5 fee on purchases over $25.

Chatham Pier Fish Market (508-945-3474; chathamfishpiermarket.com), 45 Barcliff Avenue Extension. Open daily, year-round. Located at the base of Chatham's busy pier, you will find fresh, locally caught day-boat seafood like lobsters, shellfish, bluefin tuna, cod, sole, haddock, flounder, scallops, and so much more. The market's to-go menu, though comprised of simple Cape classics like fish and chips, fried clams, and lobster bisque, is also fantastic. $–$$.

Chatham Fish & Lobster Company (508-945-1178; or 508-945-1173; chathamfishandlobster.com), 1291 Main Street, in the Cornfield Market Place. Open daily, year-round. Prices change daily just like the tides. Common seafood stock includes fresh fish, shellfish, lobsters, and other specialties like octopus, Pete's stuffed clams, and their offshore seafood spread. $$–$$$.

See also *Farms* under **Selective Shopping**.

SPECIALTY **High Tea at The Captain's House Inn** (508-945-0127; captainshouse

HIGH TEA AT THE CAPTAIN'S HOUSE KIM GRANT

inn.com), 369 Old Harbor Road. This inn serves an exceptional afternoon tea to nonguests by reservation. With a vast assortment of savories and sweets, all beautifully presented, it's well worth it. $$.

CHATHAM PIER FISH MARKET KATY WARD

NOSTALGIA REIGNS

Band concerts at Kate Gould Park (chathamband.com), off Main Street. Every Friday night at 8 p.m., late June to early September, this brass-band concert is the place to be. Upward of 6,000 lighthearted visitors enjoy music and people watching as they have for the past 60 years. Dance and swing to Sousa marches, big band selections, and other standards. Between the bandstand, the balloons tied to strollers, the bags of popcorn, the blankets on the grass (set yours out at 10 a.m. for the best position), and the "Star-Spangled Banner" finale, the concert hasn't changed a "whit" since it began. (Except that beloved Whit Tileston, who led the band for almost 50 years, passed away in 1995. The bandstand was renamed in his honor.)

KATE GOULD PARK KIM GRANT

✳ Entertainment

THEATERS **Chatham Orpheum Theater** (508-945-0874; chathamorpheum.org), 637 Main Street. A historic theater, turned CVS, turned back into a theater. The original Orpheum opened in 1961 as Chatham's first and only movie house. From the early days of silent films to the blockbuster era of *Jaws*, the theater remained vibrant for 72 years. Then it started to go downhill. First it was purchased by the Interstate Theater's Corporation, which eventually became known as Chatham Theater, but ceased in 1987 like many other cinemas across the country. The historic building remained dark and deserted for several years until it was bought by CVS. "The entire town mourned the loss of this iconic Main Street treasure, but the tradition was never forgotten." The Orpheum returned in November 2013, thanks to a grass roots team led by founding president Naomi Turner. The first $1.3 million raised helped purchase the building, followed by another $4 million to restore and rehabilitate the 100-year old structure. Today the nonprofit community theater offers a variety of films: sports documentaries, dramas, comedies, mysteries and thrillers, as well as book talks and the popular fall art film series. And who doesn't like to snack while watching a movie? Order from the Orpheum Café and enjoy upscale bar food like truffle fries, tempura chicken bites, lamb sliders, or even lobster rolls. You can order wine, beer and specialty cocktails, too.

Monomoy Theatre (508-945-1589; monomoytheatre.org), 776 Main Street. Performances held mid-June through August. Since 1958, this small summer theater company has been entertaining folks through a variety of mediums. Over the 12-week period you can expect shows like Rodgers and Hammerstein musicals, William Shakespeare comedies, and other contemporary classics. Monomoy Theatre is known for encouraging young artists by working alongside professional directors and guest artists. Enjoy the stage from any of the 263 seats—there isn't a bad view in the house. $$$.

CONCERTS & BANDS **Chatham Methodist Church** (508-945-0474; chatham methodist.org), 569 Main Street. The church sponsors free Chatham Chorale concerts on select weekends (see the event calendar online), as well as lobster roll suppers on Fridays starting late June through August from 5 to 7 p.m., market price.

Live music and DJ dance nights are offered at several Chatham establishments, including the Chatham Squire, the Red Nun, Del Mar Bistro, and Chatham Bars Inn (see under **Where to Eat**).

✳ Selective Shopping

Main Street in Chatham is a great place to window-shop and pop in and out of stores. There are lots of tasteful options, but a forewarning: expect your wallet to feel lighter afterward. Just like Chatham's real estate—it's expensive.

CHATHAM POTTERY   KIM GRANT

ARTISANS **Chatham Pottery** (508-430-2191; chathampottery.com), 2058 Main Street. Open May through October. Gill Wilson and Margaret Wilson-Grey's large studio offers a wide array of functional, decorative stoneware, hand-thrown pots, pitchers, sinks, plates, bowls, tiles, and tables. Take a piece of the Cape home with you.

Chatham Glass Company (508-945-5547; chathamglass.com), 758 Main Street. James Holmes designs and creates unique, colorful glass items—candlesticks, platters, bud vases, and marbles—which are sold at Barneys, Neiman Marcus, and Gump's. The working studio is just behind the brilliantly lit displays, so you can watch the creative process of glassblowing.

Main Street Pottery (508-945-0128; mainstreetpotterychatham.com), 645C Main Street. Stop here for Barbara Parent's function and stylish pottery.

BOOKSTORES **Yellow Umbrella Books** (508-945-0144; yellowumbrellabooks

WHERE THE SIDEWALK ENDS KIM GRANT

Fisherman's Daughter (508-292-5463; fishermansdaughtermarket.com), 521 Main Street. Open May through January; open online year-round. Just as the name implies, this nautical bohemian–inspired boutique is owned and operated by a fisherman's daughter! Owner Taylor Brown features her own collection as well as over 50 other local artists and designers. All handmade and eco-friendly with quality organic cottons—expect to pay a bit more, but it's worth it. I can't thank her enough for having the coziest and cutest sweatshirt to warm me up after a bipolar bout of Cape weather—rookie move on my part. Take note: When the wind switches to the north, get ready for a cooler ocean breeze and have a sweatshirt on hand.

The Trading Company (508-945-9191), 614 Main Street. This boutique has come a long way since owner Christine and her late husband purchased it in the '70s. This high-end women's clothing shop is filled with high-quality Italian designers. Send your husband to the "waiting room" in the back while you shop. Decked out with a TV, books, magazines, and comfortable chairs, you might have a hard time getting him to leave when you're done.

FARMS **Chatham Farmers' Market** (508-945-0240; localcolorchatham.com /farmersmarket), 1652 Main Street, every Tuesday afternoon from mid-May to late October.

GALLERIES **Munson Gallery** (508-945-2888; munsongallery.net), 1455 Main Street. Open April through December. Sally Munson, a fourth-generation art dealer with a keen eye for fine art, showcases contemporary talent on the walls of her wonderfully restored barn studio. The collection offers something for everyone in both price and taste. Stop by her satellite gallery space at Pisces Restaurant and Bistro on Main, too.

Odell Studios and Gallery (508-945-3239; odellarts.com), 423 Main Street.

.net), 501 Main Street. Owner Eric Linder has gathered a fine selection of Cape Cod titles and some used books, too, for all ages and interests. Long live the independents!

Where the Sidewalk Ends (508-945-0499; booksonthecape.com), 432 Main Street. Open daily, year-round. This mother-and-daughter run bookstore is one of the best independents I've encountered in years. From outdoor and fireside seating and children's story hours to coffee-with-the-author book signings and a great staff, this airy place has it all.

CLOTHING **Beach Bum Surf Co.** (beachbumsurfcompany.com), 4 Seaview Street, off Main Street. Candice, a salty young entrepreneur, decided to combine her love of surfing and the ocean with her passion for fashion. Her tiny shop offers a specialty clothing line for men and women. All made with love on the Cape.

Tom (a metalsmith) and Carol (a painter) have lived and worked together in their lovely Greek revival historic home since 1975. Carol excels in colorful nonobjective, multimedia paintings and prints, monotypes, oils, and encaustic. Her work complements Tom's jewelry and sculptures, which he fashions from precious metals and alloys.

Steve Lyons Gallery (617-529-1378; stevelyonsgallery.com), 463 Main Street. Open April through December. An internationally celebrated artist, Steve Lyons is best known for his ability to reinvent traditional painting techniques and test the waters with new ones. Personally I gravitate toward his impasto artwork, an old Italian technique of sculpting and molding acrylic to create heightened dimensions. The gallery also features artists such as Eric Davis, Nick Heaney, Eric Layne, Boston Logan, Scott Panuczsk, and Emmet Towey.

SPECIALTY **Artful Hand Gallery** (508-945-5681; artfulhandgallery.com), 459 Main Street. Joe Porcari's curatorial eye for innovative and impeccable crafts-

THE ARTFUL HAND GALLERY KATY WARD

manship shines bright in this not-so-average gallery. Here you will find jewelry, home décor, and a variety of gifts and gadgets from a child's tooth fairy box to picture frames, cutting boards, and copper nail fish clippers.

Chatham Jam & Jelly Shop (508-945-3052; chathamjamandjelly.com), 16 Seaquanset Road. This colorful family run shop sells over 100 variations of homemade jams and jellies. Obviously, their

FISHERMAN'S DAUGHTER KATY WARD

best seller is Beach Plum Jelly, but feel free to taste as many as you'd like before committing. They also have chutney and a delicious zucchini relish.

Gustare Oils & Vinegars (508-945-4505; gustareoliveoil.com), 461 Main Street. As the name implies, here you will find exotic quality oils and vinegars including their Sicilian Gold Nocellara EVOO, Herbs di Napoli (an 18 year traditional style balsamic vinegar base), or Lemon-Thyme Vinaigrette and crispy kale chips for munching. Join owners Dave and Catherine Ferraresi on Sunday evenings for a tasting, but call ahead.

Maps of Antiquity (508-945-1660; mapsofantiquity.com), 1409 Main Street. These folks carry rare antique and reproduction maps of the 19th century and earlier from around the world. If you want to know what the Cape or a specific town looked like 100 years ago, this shop will have a map that will show you. It's a treasure trove.

Mark August (508-945-4545; markaugust.com), 490 Main Street. Open daily, year-round. Stop here for fun and contemporary jewelry and home décor made by local artists.

Mermaids on Main (508-945-3179), 410 Main Street. Open late May through December. If a mermaid lived in a shack (above water), this is what it would look like. The exterior boasts classic weather-washed shingles, aqua-blue Adirondack chairs, lobster traps, and nautical lighting framing the sea blue door. Step inside to a bright oceanesque interior full of seashells, jewelry, wind chimes, bags of sea glass, and nautical artwork. It's basically a mermaid's paradise.

Yankee Ingenuity (508-945-1288; yankee-ingenuity.com), 525 Main Street. This eclectic assortment of unique finds extends from glass and jewelry to clocks and lamps. You never know what you will find, isn't that exciting?

The Mayflower (508-945-0065; themayflowershop.com), 475 Main Street. Established in 1885, this venerable, old-time variety store has joined the modern era of swanky Main Street.

✳ Special Events

Check Chatham's **Chamber of Commerce** website (chathaminfo.com) for a full list of calendar events.

July 4: **Independence Day Parade** (chathamparade.com), from Main Street to Veterans Field. After the parade is the annual **Strawberry Festival**, with shortcake at the First United Methodist Church (16 Cross Street).

Late July: The **Annual Chatham Antiques Show & Sale**, held at the Chatham Elementary School, 147 Depot Road. It's basically a collector's dream weekend and has been happening since the mid-1950s.

Mid-August: The **Festival of Arts** (508-945-3583; capecodcreativearts.org), located at Chase Park on Cross Street. Sponsored by the Creative Arts Center, this weekend festival has over 120 exhibitors—from painters and quilters to sculptors and more.

Mid-December: **Christmas by the Sea** and **Christmas Stroll** (chatham merchants.com/christmasbythesea). This annual event includes a tree lighting ceremony, candy-cane-making demonstrations, caroling, mulled cider served at the Mayo House (see **To See**), hayrides, open houses, and much more.

New Year's Eve: **First Night Celebration** (508-945-1122 in November and December only; firstnightchatham .com). This family-friendly town-wide celebration rings in the New Year with fireworks over Oyster Pond at the stroke of midnight.

ORLEANS

Many could argue, with some success, that Orleans's biggest draw is **Nauset Beach (in East Orleans)**, an Atlantic Ocean barrier beach more than 9 miles long. It can accommodate hundreds of sun seekers and sand-castle builders in summer. But in the off-season, you'll be practically alone, walking in quiet reflection, observing shorebirds and natural rhythms. It's a beautifully haunting place during a storm—so long as it's not a huge storm. Nauset Beach also has historical significance. Gosnold explored it in 1602 and Champlain in 1605. It was the location of the first recorded shipwreck on the eastern seaboard, in 1626, when the *Sparrow Hawk* ran aground near Pochet. It is the only place in the continental United States to be fired upon in the War of 1812 (by the British) and in World War I (in 1918 it was shelled by a German submarine). More recently, two Englishmen set off from nearby Nauset Harbor to row successfully across the Atlantic Ocean.

The real charm of Orleans, which has few historical sights, lies not in the sand but in the waters that surround the town. A large number of fingerlike inlets creep into the eastern shoreline from aptly named **Pleasant Bay**, dotted with tiny islands. And most of these quiet inlets are accessible via back roads and town landings. Excursion boats explore the rich habitat of **Nauset Marsh** to the north, while bayside, **Rock Harbor** is home to the Cape's most active charter fishing fleet.

Because Routes 6, 6A, and 28 converge in Orleans, traffic is heavy in summer; getting anywhere takes time. But Orleans straddles the two distinct worlds of the Outer Cape and the Lower Cape. On the one hand, Orleans serves as a year-round commercial and retail center for the area. It offers plenty of activities and a variety of dining and lodging options. On the other hand, Orleans has its share of exclusive residential areas and plenty of quiet waterside spots. In the summer, Orleans balloons to a population of about 22,000 from its year-round count of 6,700.

Orleans is the only Cape town without an American Indian or English name. Incorporated in 1797 after separating from Eastham, Orleans was named for Louis-Philippe de Bourbon, Duke of Orléans (and later king of France), who sojourned here in 1797 during his exile.

GUIDANCE **Orleans Chamber of Commerce** (508-255-7203; orleanscapecod.org), 44 Main Street, and **Information Booth** (508-255-1386; orleanscapecod.org), exit 12 off Route 6A. Questions about your stay? They will surely have answers here, as well as free booklets, maps, itineraries, etc.

GETTING THERE *By car:* Take Route 6 east from the Cape Cod Canal for about 48 miles to Exit 12. Route 6A East takes you directly into town.

By bus: The **Plymouth & Brockton Bus** (508-746-0378; p-b.com) connects Orleans with Hyannis and other Cape towns, as well as with Boston's Logan Airport. It only stops at the CVS on Main Street.

GETTING AROUND *By shuttle:* The **Flex** (508-385-1430; capecodtransit.org) offers north and southbound trips from Provincetown to Harwich with reserved stops. The shuttle stops at Stop & Shop, the Land Ho, and Skaket Corners. The flex also connects

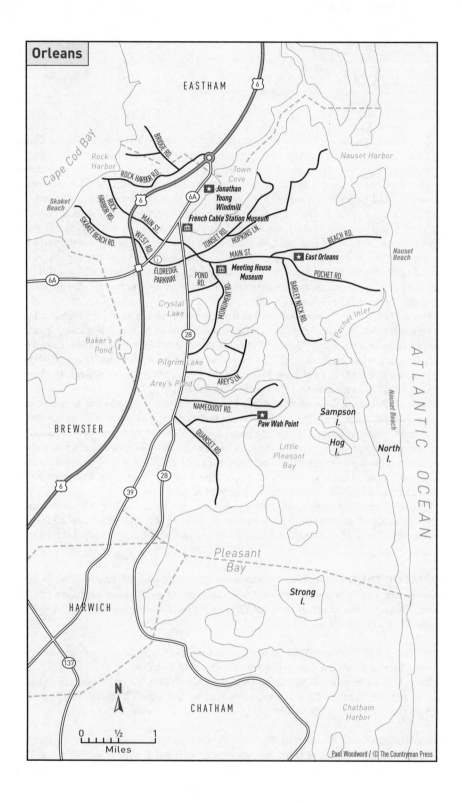

Orleans

EASTHAM

Cape Cod Bay

Rock Harbor

Skaket Beach

Nauset Harbor

Town Cove

★ Jonathan Young Windmill

🏛 French Cable Station Museum

Nauset Beach

BRIDGE RD.

ROCK HARBOR RD.

ROCK HARBOR RD.

SKAKET BEACH RD.

MAIN ST.

WEST RD.

TONSET RD.

HOPKINS LN.

MAIN ST.

BEACH RD.

★ East Orleans

POCHET RD.

Nauset Beach

6A

ELDREDGE PARKWAY

POND RD.

🏛 Meeting House Museum

Crystal Lake

MONUMENT RD.

BARLEY NECK RD.

Pochet Inlet

Baker's Pond

28

Pilgrim Lake

Arey's Pond

AREY'S LN.

NAMEQUOIT RD.

★ Paw Wah Point

Sampson I.

Hog I.

North I.

QUANSET RD.

Little Pleasant Bay

BREWSTER

28

39

6

Pleasant Bay

Strong I.

HARWICH

137

N

CHATHAM

Chatham Harbor

ATLANTIC OCEAN

0   ½   1
Miles

Paul Woodward / © The Countryman Press

Morning: Start your day off with buttery breakfast delights from Cottage Street Bakery or head over to Viv's Kitchen for fuel-packed smoothies and savory breakfast sandwiches.

Afternoon: Grab your beach essentials and head out to Nauset Beach for sunbathing and a refreshingly cold and salty dip in the Atlantic. Looking for solitude? Kayak in the refreshing Pleasant Bay or Nauset Marsh. Stop for a fish feast lunch at Cap't Cass Rock Harbor Seafood or grab a quick burrito from the Corner Store. Stroll and shop the main strip in Orleans.

Evening: Enjoy a sophisticated and creative dinner at ABBA or try the Jailhouse Tavern and Hog Island Beer Co. for a laidback atmosphere. Listen to twilight at Rock Harbor while watching the fishing fleet return for the day.

with the **H2O** line at these locations and travels Route 28 between the Hyannis Transportation Center and Orleans daily in summer ($).

PUBLIC RESTROOMS At the information booth and 44 Main Street.

PUBLIC LIBRARY **Snow Library** (508-240-3760; town.orleans.ma.us/snow-library), 67 Main Street at Route 28.

EMERGENCIES **Orleans Police Department** (508-255-0117; town.orleans.ma.us /orleans-police-department), 99 Eldredge Park Way, or call **911.**

Medical: Orleans Medical Center (508-255-9577; 508-255-8825; orleansmedical center.org), 204 Main Street, or Exit 12 off Route 6.

✳ To See

⌖ **Meeting House Museum** (508-240-1329; orleanshistoricalsociety.org), 3 River Road at Main and School Streets. Open July and August. Built in 1833 as a Universalist meetinghouse, and now operated by the Orleans Historical Society, the museum contains artifacts documenting Orleans's early history. Among the items are an assessor's map of Orleans homes in 1858, photographs, American Indian artifacts, and a bicentennial quilt. The building itself is a fine example of Greek Revival Doric architecture. Down at Rock Harbor, the museum also has a Coast Guard rescue boat that was used during a 1952 shipwreck off the Chatham coast. That 32 people piled into this tiny boat is beyond belief. You can board the boat; in fact, following restoration, it now once again travels the waters on Cape Cod and beyond. A tour schedule is posted on-site. Free.

⌖ **French Cable Station Museum** (508-240-1735; frenchcablestationmuseum.org), Route 28 at Cove Road. Open June through September. Before the advent of the information superhighway and wireless communications, there was the French Cable Station. Direct transmissions from Brest, France (via a 3,000-mile underwater cable), were made from this station between 1890 and 1941, at which time transmissions were automated. Among the relayed news items: Charles Lindbergh's successful crossing of the Atlantic and his 1927 Paris landing, as well as Germany's invasion of France. Much of the original equipment and instruments are still set up and in working order. (Alas, the cable is no longer operational.) The displays, put together with the help of

FRENCH CABLE STATION KIM GRANT

the Smithsonian Institution, are a bit intimidating, but someone is on hand to unravel the mysteries. Free.

Jonathan Young Windmill (508-240-1329), 27–33 Route 6A at Windmill Park Conservation Area. Open July and August. This circa-1720 gristmill was built in South Orleans, transported to the center of town in 1839, moved to Hyannisport in 1897, and returned to Orleans in 1987. Although it's no longer operational, the windmill is significant because of its intact milling machinery. Inside you'll find interpretive exhibits, including a display of a 19th-century miller's handiwork, as well as a guide who might explain the origins of "keep your nose to the grindstone." (Because grain is highly combustible when it's ground, a miller who wasn't paying close attention to his grain might not live to see the end of the day.) The setting, overlooking Town Cove, provides a nice backdrop for a picnic. Free.

Rock Harbor, on Cape Cod Bay, at the end of Rock Harbor Road from Main Street. This protected harbor, the town's first commercial and maritime center, served as a packet landing for ships

JONATHAN YOUNG WINDMILL KIM GRANT

transporting goods to Plymouth, Boston, and Maine. When the harbor filled with silt, several old houses in the area were built from the lumber of dismantled saltworks. During the War of 1812, Orleans militiamen turned back Britain's HMS *Newcastle* from Rock Harbor. And what about those dead trees in the water? They mark the harbor channel that is dredged annually for the charter fishing fleet. This is a popular sunset spot for watching the boats come in, if you can tolerate the bugs.

✳ To Do

BASEBALL ✄ **The Orleans Firebirds** (508-255-0793; orleansfirebirds.com) play ball at Eldredge Park Field, off Route 28 at Eldredge Park Way, from mid-June to early August. Their clinics for boys and girls begin in late June. As many as 60 or 70 young sluggers might show up, but there is always a good ratio of instructors to children. $$$$$+ for the first week, or $$$ per day.

BICYCLING & RENTALS The **Cape Cod Rail Trail** offers 25 miles of paved road for your biking pleasure. The trail route starts in Wellfleet and passes through the towns

ROCK HARBOR AT SUNSET MARCIA DUGGAN/CAPECODSOUL

THE REAL "FISH" STORY BEHIND ROCK HARBOR CLAM TREES: MARCIA DUGGAN

So how did these pine trees get nicknamed "clam trees"? As the lore goes, quahog seeds were planted at the base of the trees out in the channel of Rock Harbor in the 1970s. The seed would dig their way into the sand, spread, and grow into legal size quahogs ready to be raked by recreational shellfish permit holders. Supposedly, you could have a basketful of clams for dinner by digging right by the trees. Like a game of telephone, the locals started referring to the channel markers as "clam trees," when asked by visitors why the trees were in the water.

This is a popular spot for a day at the beach, booking a charter boat for sportfishing, and enjoying incredible sunsets at dusk. The combination of the setting sun over the water and the line of trees attracts thousands of visitors in the summer and off-season. The beat of a local steel drum band serenading a gazing crowd as the charter fleet steams in from a day on the water only heightens the spectacularly unique view.

One can only wonder about the origin of this fun "fish" story about the clam trees. Either way, these trees contribute to the most beautiful sunsets in the world (I am a little partial as this is my hometown and my backyard, sort of). I spend as much time as I can here photographing sunsets, taking long walks during low tide, visiting the local oyster grants, and fishing for striped bass, blues, and tuna.

Rock Harbor is tidal. During low tide, you can walk all the way out to the farthest clam tree in the bay. The trees serve as channel markers for the fleet of the Rock Harbor Charter Fishing boats and other recreational boats.

THE ANNUAL "PLANTING" OF ROCK HARBOR'S ICONIC CLAM TREES   MARCIA DUGGAN/CAPECODSOUL

of Eastham, Orleans, Brewster, Harwich, Dennis, and Yarmouth. You can rent bicycles and equipment at **Orleans Cycle** (508-255-9115; orleanscycle.com), 26 Main Street; **Idle Times Bike Shop** (508-240-1122; idletimesbikes.com), 29 Main Street; or **Mike's Bike Trail Rentals** (508-240-1791; capeescapeadventures.com), 15 Canal Road.

BOAT EXCURSIONS & RENTALS **Blue Claw Boat Tours** (508-240-5783; blueclawboat tours.com), 235 Main Street at Nauset Marina. Trips daily mid-May to early October. Enjoy an up-close and personal view of the ocean's "puppies" (as some locals call them) on a narrated seal tour. The guides are comical and will surely keep you entertained with stories about pirates, seals, sharks, shipwrecks, and more. The sea-blue certified Coast Guard boat carries an entire family in comfort to the seal colonies (you might even see a shark if you're lucky) or for an afternoon beachcombing an island. They also offer private and custom tours. The family company has been operating for over a decade under Captain Robert Wissman, licensed by the Coast Guard since 1982 with a 100 Ton Master's license—basically, he's top-grade. $$$$+.

BOWLING **Orleans Bowling Center** (508-255-0636 for lanes; 774-801-2116 for restaurant; alleybowlingbbq.com), 191 Route 6A. OK, so you didn't come to the Cape to go bowling, but if it's raining and you've got kids in the car, it's a great idea. Dave Currier and partner Brooke Carlson renovated the 1970s bowling alley in 2014. The OBC now offers an authentic barbecue restaurant with high-top tables and a seasonal enclosed garden patio heated with an outdoor fireplace. The OBC offers 12 candlepin lanes and some arcade games like table hockey and Buck Hunt. Enjoy pitchers of beer, salt and vinegar wings, and beef brisket tips while you sport your best bowling pose.

FISHING **Rock Harbor Charter Fleet** (508-255-9757; rockharborcharters.com), Rock Harbor. Trips daily mid-May to early October. This family-run charter service offers 10 fully equipped sportfishing boats designed for catching striped bass, bluefish, shark, and bluefin tuna depending on the season. The crews are all knowledgeable, courteous, and will do their best to accommodate the needs of both experienced and novice anglers alike. If you have a lucky day on the water, your mate will clean your catch.

    Goose Hummock (508-255-0455; goose.com), Town Cove, 15 Route 6A at the rotary. This outfitter fulfills all fishing-related needs, including rod rentals, fishing trips, instruction, and wintertime fly-tying seminars. They also offer shellfishing and hunting equipment. The great staff offers lots of free advice and information.

    Procure freshwater and saltwater fishing licenses and regulations online (www .mass.gov/eea/agencies/dfg/licensing), then head to **Crystal Lake**, off Monument Road (see **Green Space**), which has perch, trout, and bass. There are also a dozen fresh- and saltwater town landings in Orleans.

ICE-SKATING **Charles Moore Arena** (508-255-5902; charlesmoorearena.org), 23 O'Connor Road. Although this big arena is reserved most of the year, public skating times are set aside, including Friday nights, when it's strobe-lit for kids. The popular "snowball"—holding hands and skating in a circle to the rhyme of music—is popular among 13-year-olds (including myself, way back when).

KAYAKS & PADDLEBOARDS The **Wellfleet Bay Wildlife Sanctuary** (508-349-2615; massaudubon.org) sponsors numerous activities including kayak trips around Pleasant Bay. Call to register for a trip. $$$$+.

GOOSE HUMMOCK KIM GRANT

SUPfari Adventures (508-205-9087; supfariadventures.com), multiple locations in Orleans and Brewster. Stand-up paddleboarding brought from Maui to Cape Cod by Brewster's former harbormaster. The full moon sunset glow tours are quite fun. $$$$.

See also **Pump House Surf & Paddle** under *Surfing*.

MINI-GOLF ⚓ **Cape Escape** (508-240-1791; capeescapeadventures.com), 14 Canal Road, off Route 6A near the Orleans rotary. Open April to mid-October.

MODEL RAILROADING ⚓ **Nauset Model Railroad Club** (nausetmodelrailroadclub .com), Hilltop Plaza (around the back), 180 Route 6A. And now for something completely different: head to this open house (Wednesdays and Fridays) as an alternative to more common Cape Cod activities for kiddos and aficionados of any age. Free.

SAILING **Arey's Pond Boat Yard** (508-255-0994; areyspondboatyard.com), 43 Arey's Lane off Route 28. Open June through September. Just off of Little Pleasant Bay and the Namequoit River, Arey's Pond offers services for sailboats and powerboats alike, as well as quick access to Cape Cod's largest estuary and some of the best sailing and scenic views in the area.

See also **Pleasant Bay Community Sailing** under **To Do** in Harwich.

SKATEBOARDING ⚓ **Jean Finch Skateboard Park**, located at the middle school fields, 70 Route 28. Helmets required. $.

SURFING **Nauset Surf** (508-255-4742; nausetsports.com), 2 Route 6A, in Jeremiah Square near the rotary. Open April through January, but rentals are only provided in-season. Stop here to rent surfboards, paddleboards, skim boards, boogie boards, and wet suits.

Pump House Surf & Paddle (508-240-2226; pumphousesurf.com), 9 Route 6A, off near the rotary. Open June through September. Fully stocked one-day rentals:

CANOEING AND KAYAKING

The protected, calm waters of northern Pleasant Bay offer delightful paddling opportunities. And the folks at Goose Hummock (508-255-2620; goose.com), off Route 6A on Town Cove, are the experts in this neck of the bay. Talk to them about Southern Pleasant Bay, for instance; it can be tricky for the uninitiated. Pick up the Nauset Harbor tide chart and rent a canoe or recreational kayak ($$$ for 3 hours). Parking is limited at the town landings, but it's free. If you're new to kayaking, take their 3-hour introductory course ($$$$$+) to learn basic paddle strokes and skills. Otherwise, they have a huge array of other courses and specialty tours: intro to kayaking, tidal currents and navigation, open-water kayaking, sunrise tours, kids in kayaks, and more.

surfboard, SUP, body board, kayaks, wetsuits, and roof racks. They also sell trendy top-brand beachwear. $–$$$$+.

For lessons, Pump House has partnered with **Sugar Surf Cape Cod** (508-240-4166; sugarsurfcapecod.com).

TENNIS You'll find three public courts at **Eldredge Park** (off Route 28 at Eldredge Park Way) and three at the **elementary school** (off Eldredge Park Way), both with seasonal fees.

✳ Green Space

BEACHES 🏊 ♿ **Nauset Beach** (508-240-3780), on the Atlantic Ocean, off Beach Road, beyond the center of East Orleans. It doesn't get much better than this: good bodysurfing waves and 7 miles of sandy Atlantic shoreline backed by a low dune. (Only about a half-mile stretch is covered by lifeguards; much of the rest is deserted.) A gently sloping grade makes this a good beach for children. Facilities include an in-season lifeguard on weekends, restrooms, a snack bar, a boardwalk over dunes, outside showers, chairs and umbrellas for rent, and plenty of parking. $–$$, depending on the day/month.

Four-wheel-drive vehicles with permit are allowed onto Nauset Beach. Certain areas, though, may be restricted during bird breeding and nesting periods. Obtain permits at the Nauset administrative offices, Parks and Beaches Department (508-240-3775), 18 Bay Ridge Lane.

🏊 ♿ **Skaket Beach** on Cape Cod Bay, off West Road. Popular with families, as you

SUPFARI ADVENTURES KIM GRANT

SCENIC DRIVES

Pleasant Bay, Little Pleasant Bay, Nauset Harbor, and Town Cove creep deep into the Orleans coastline at about a dozen named inlets, ponds, and coves. With the detailed centerfold map from the Orleans Chamber of Commerce guide in hand (see *Guidance*), head down the side roads off Tonset Road, Hopkins Lane, Nauset Heights Road, and Barley Neck Road to the town landings. After passing beautifully landscaped residences, you'll be rewarded with serene, pastoral scenes of beach grass and sailboats. Directly off Route 28 heading toward Chatham, there are two particularly lovely ponds with saltwater outlets: **Arey's Pond** (off Arey's Lane from Route 28) and **Kescayogansett Pond** (off Monument Road from Route 28). There's a little picnic area with limited parking at **Kent's Point** near here, off Frost Fish Lane from Monument Road.

can walk a mile out into the bay at low tide; at high tide, the beach grass is covered. The parking lot often fills up early, creating a 30-minute wait for a space. Parking $$ in season. (The parking fee is transferable to Nauset Beach on the same day.) Facilities include an in-season lifeguard, a bike rack, restrooms, a boardwalk, outside showers, and a snack bar.

Pleasant Bay Beach, Route 28, South Orleans. A saltwater bayside inlet beach with limited roadside parking.

See also "Shark Awareness" on page 282.

PONDS **Crystal Lake** (off Monument Road and Route 28) and **Pilgrim Lake** (off Herring Brook Road from Route 28) are both good for swimming. Pilgrim Lake has an in-season lifeguard, restrooms, changing rooms, picnic tables, a dock, and a small beach; parking stickers only. At Crystal Lake, parking is free but limited; no facilities.

WALKS & PICNICS **Paw Wah Point Conservation Area**, off Namequoit Road from Eldredge Park Way, has a loop trail leading to a nice little beach with picnic tables.

Rhododendron Display Garden, Route 28 and Main Street. A nice place for a picnic.

Sea Call Farm, Tonset Road, just north of the intersection with Main Street. Overlooking Town Cove, this is another fine picnic spot.

NAUSET BEACH MARCIA DUGGAN/CAPECODSOUL

✳ Lodging

📍 Lodging in Orleans is a very good value. You'll find everything from super-stellar and friendly bed-and-breakfasts to almost-beachfront motels and family motor inns.

BED-AND-BREAKFASTS **A Little Inn on Pleasant Bay** (508-255-0780; alittle innonpleasantbay.com), 654 South Orleans Road. Open May to late October. I affectionately dub my favorite place to stay, marvelously and tastefully renovated, "a little slice of heaven on high." The European innkeepers (Sandra, Pamela, and Bernd) have transformed this 1798 house into a priceless diamond with commanding views of Pleasant Bay and a thoroughly contemporary aesthetic. Formerly a stop on the Underground Railroad, the main house has plenty of common space, including a big living room filled with windows. It's all quite conducive to luxuriating. Guestrooms feature whitewashed barn board and lovely bathroom tilework; some have private decks or patios. Blue stone patios grace the front and backyard, which are beautifully landscaped. The Bay Rooms (carved from a former paddock) and the carriage house have also been renovated with similar doses of grace and style. Late-afternoon sherry and access to a private beach and dock are all included. $$$.

Nauset House Inn (508-255-2195; 800-771-5508; nausethouseinn.com), Beach Road. Open May through mid-October. Nestled in East Orleans, this charming 1810 farmhouse has 14 guestrooms (eight with private bath and six with shared baths) that are tastefully appointed with hand-painted furniture, floral stencils, trompe l'oeil walls, and lace curtains. Inn rooms tend to be smaller than those in the carriage house. One reviewer was extremely pleased with his impromptu stay in the one-bedroom Johnny Walker room, tucked beneath the stairwell. Just past the 100-year-old apple tree sits the Outermost Cottage, my personal favorite, with its cathedral ceiling, a sunken bathroom and arched doorway, and a natural barn board loft, all brightened by stained glass windows. It's the epitome of rustic Cape living. Cindy and John

A LITTLE INN ON PLEASANT BAY KIM GRANT

are lovely hosts and will surely make you feel right at home (as will their resident dog, Louie). They've taken the reins from Cindy's mother, Diane Johnson, who opened the inn in the 1980s. Start the day with a full complimentary breakfast in the brick-floored dining room with its open hearth and beamed ceilings, or step outside into the greenhouse

NAUSET HOUSE INN KATY WARD

conservatory, which reminded me of the classic book, *Secret Garden*. This place does not skimp on quiet places to relax. Oh, and it is only a half-mile from Nauset Beach. $–$$.

The Parsonage Inn (508-255-8217; 888-422-8217; parsonageinn.com), 202 Main Street, East Orleans. This pleasant, rambling, late 18th-century house has eight guest rooms comfortably furnished with a blend of contemporary furnishings and country antiques (only two rooms have adjoining walls, so there is plenty of privacy). Wide pumpkin-pine floors, canopy beds, and redone bathrooms are common. Willow, the studio apartment, has a kitchenette and private entrance, while the roomy Barn, with exposed beams and eaves, has a sitting area and sofa bed. $$.

MOTELS & HOTELS **The Cove** (508-255-1203; thecoveorleans.com), 13 South Orleans Road. This modest complex of 47 rooms and suites is situated on the waterfront along Town Cove and close to bike paths. Pluses include a free boat tour of Town Cove and Nauset Beach, an outdoor heated pool, a dock for sunning and fishing, and picnic tables and grills that are well situated to exploit the view. Deluxe rooms have a sitting area and sofa bed. Most waterfront rooms have a shared deck overlooking the water, two-room suites have a kitchen (some with a fireplace and private deck), and inn rooms have a bit more décor (some also have a fireplace and private deck). $–$$.

RENTAL HOUSES & COTTAGES **The Rental Company at William Raveis** (508-240-2222; capecodvacation.com), 213 Main Street, East Orleans.

✻ Where to Eat

DINING OUT ✻ **The Beacon Room** (508-255-2211; beaconroom.com), 23 West Road. Open L, D, year-round. For casual fine dining on the way to Skaket Beach, this intimate bistro offers sizable portions of well-presented dishes at reasonable prices. Dinnertime entrées range from pasta and lamb (quite popular) to seafood and chicken saltimbocca. Sandwiches and burgers are offered at lunch. No reservations, but you can call ahead for dinner. $$–$$$.

EATING OUT **Rock Harbor Grill** (508-255-3350; rockharborgrill.net), 18 Old Colony Way. Open D, year-round. This upscale yet casual restaurant is one of my favorites in town. Take a stool at the long rustic bar or at one of the closely situated tables or cushioned booth seats in the rear of the restaurant, which tend to be quieter. The menu offers creative "snacks" like Devils on Horseback (medjool dates stuffed with feta, wrapped in a pecan wood smoked bacon, and drizzled with a balsamic glaze) or the Octopus of the Day (soaked in marinade for 24 hours and served on a bed of baby arugula with marinated olives and a lemon vinaigrette). Starters that are ideal for sharing include options like the Lobster Mac & Cheese, Three Cheese Vegetable Dip,

Pork Belly Slides, or mussels. "Hand Held" menu items include the RHG burger and my personal favorite, the Portabella Burger (topped with roasted red peppers, caramelized onion, chevre, and sun-dried tomato pesto, and served with fries). Other entrée options include the pan-seared cod served over their nightly risotto, or NY strip of pork. They also serve amazing wood-fired pizza that can be seen baking to perfection in their oven near the bar. Expect some wait time in season. $$–$$$.

✻ ⅄ ♘ **Mahoney's Atlantic Bar & Grill** (508-255-5505; mahoneysatlantic.com), 28 Main Street. Open D, year-round. Consistent and appealing across the board, this cozy storefront bistro serves contemporary New American dishes like pan-roasted lobster, tuna sashimi, and roasted chicken. Salads and a few veggie dishes round out the choices. It's hard to go wrong here. Their lively and upscale martini bar sports a few satellite TVs, all the better to catch a Sox game. $$–$$$$.

Cap't Cass Rock Harbor Seafood, 117 Rock Harbor Road. Open L, D, mid-April to mid-October. This classic lobster shack is adorned with colorful buoys on the outside and checkered tablecloths on the inside. As for the food, it's a cut above: the lobster roll is enormous and arguably one of the best on the Cape; the she-crab stew is outrageously delectable; and the fish-and-chips are pretty darn good, too. The menu is posted on cardboard, as it has been since 1958. There really was an 80-something-year-old Captain Cass, by the way, but today the "shack" is run by the fish market next door. BYOB and cash only. $$–$$$.

Land Ho! (508-255-5165; land-ho.com), 38 Main Street. Open L, D, year-round. A favorite local hangout since 1969, John Murphy's place is very colorful (literally), from red-and-white-checked tablecloths to old business signs and license plates mounted on the walls and hanging from the ceiling. Newspapers hang on a wire to separate the long bar from the dining area. Beyond club sandwiches,

BOOK 'EM DANNO

Jailhouse Tavern (508-255-JAIL or 508-255-5245; jailhousetavern.com), 28 West Road. Open D, year-round. During the 1920s and '30s, there were many tales of Prohibition-era rum running on the Lower Cape. Bootleggers smuggled liquor into the small coves and inlets dotted along the bay by way of boats. Accomplices had fast trucks and would drive the goods off-Cape during the night. Some tell stories about how these lawbreakers got caught in the early hours of the morning. Given that Orleans has always been a town to extend a helping hand, it comes as no surprise that the town constable Henry Perry offered the front bedroom of his house on West Road as a Saturday night lockup. This property is now the Jailhouse Tavern, where you can sit today. Constable Perry was the only senior law enforcement officer in town at the time, and because there was no place on Saturday nights to transport those who would flout the law, he opened the doors of his home. Perry, a friendly and trusting soul, simply locked his prisoners in a spare bedroom, secured with bars and locks, and retired to his room for a good night's sleep. In the morning, the prisoners were taken up Cape to more secure surroundings.

In 1984 the old jailhouse was transformed into a restaurant. Think polished jail cell bars, three unique dining areas, an outdoor patio, and a handsome oak bar. Combine all this with an eclectic menu of fresh seafood, traditional New England fare, and a great selection of libations, and you won't leave disappointed.

Though a separate operation, be sure to also check out Hog Island Beer Company (508-255-2337; hogislandbeerco.com), 28 West Road, located in the back of the restaurant. The brewery is "built by locals, brewed by locals, drank by locals." Choose from the White Shark Wheat (one of my favorites), the Far Out Stout, the Pig Pen Pharmhouse, Moon Snail Pale Ale (also another favorite), Outermost IPA, and Day Sail Session IPA. Stop here for a pint of cold beer or pick up a 64-ounce growler or 32-ounce Big Hog can to go. They also offer lawn games like corn hole, as well as indoor games such as shuffleboard and foosball. $–$$$.

THE HOG ISLAND BEER COMPANY KATY WARD

CAP'T CASS ROCK HARBOR SEAFOOD MARCIA DUGGAN/
CAPECODSOUL

fried seafood dishes, and great burgers, look for specialties like fish-and-chips, barbecue ribs, stuffed clams, and the Cod Reuben. You'll find lots of families, college students, and old-time locals here. $$.

The Knack (774-316-4595; theknack
capecod.com), 5 Route 6A off highway rotary. Stop here for delicious burgers (single or doubles) topped with all the fixings and Knack's famous burger sauce; griddled and split-down-the-middle hot dogs (the mustard dog with onion rings, house made pickles, and whole grain beer mustard is my go-to); and hand-cut fries. They also serve lobster rolls and fish sandwiches, but I've had better elsewhere. Place your order at the window and wait until your number is called, then find a seat on the outside patio and enjoy. $–$$.

The Corner Store (508-255-5454; freshfastfun.com), 54 Main Street. Open B, L, year-round. I've never met anyone who disliked a Corner Store burrito. Choose from white or wheat wrap (with or without cheese) and go down the line of fillings: steak, chicken, veggies, rice, beans, guac, and corn salsa, to name a few. These burritos are stuffed to the brim and tailored to your taste buds (see also under *Eating Out* in Chatham). $–$$.

Guapo's Tortilla Shack (508-255-3338; guaposcapecod.com), Staples Plaza, off Route 6A. Open L, D, year-round. A casual, Baja-style tortilla shack in the heart of Orleans. Start off with warm crisp chips and homemade salsa before diving into their fish tacos, California-style burger, or Mexican street corn. They also have a feisty margarita selection (spicy habanero, please!). Check out their second location under *Eating Out* in Brewster. $–$$.

Nauset Farms (508-255-2800; nausetfarms.com), 199 Main Street. Stop here for lunch before heading out Nauset Beach. Their lobster roll is one of my favorites: big pieces of claw and knuckle meat mixed with mayonnaise, a touch of celery, chive, and lemon scooped onto a buttery, toasted brioche roll. Afterward, stop here again and order fresh cuts of specialty meats from Butcher Rick Backus. His kabobs and grill-ready chicken are delicious. Don't forget to grab a bottle of tastefully chosen wine by certified sommelier Susi Keyes. $–$$.

SWEET TREATS & COFFEE **Sunbird Kitchen** (508-237-0354; birdinthesun .com), 85 Route 6A. Open B,L, year-round; D Friday nights in off-season. This neighborhood café doubles down on seasonally inspired comfort food. Expect

THE CORNER STORE KATY WARD

VIV'S KITCHEN & JUICE BAR

Viv's Kitchen & Juice Bar (508-255-3354; vivskitchencc.com), Staples Plaza, off Route 6A. Open B, L, year-round. I've known Viv and Mike for several years, and I'm thrilled to include them in this edition of the guidebook. Since opening their doors in 2017, the powerhouse couple has etched their name into the hearts (and bellies) of locals and visitors alike. The small Brazilian-meets-Cape Cod eatery offers a menu unlike most on the Lower Cape. For breakfast, try their Mornin' Bowl: fried egg with fresh avocado and Viv's pico served over rice and black beans; or the Lokal Yokal and Portuguese Sunset on griddled and pressed Brioche. For lunch, the Primo Steak & Cheese, The Bella, and What the Cluck? are all delicious hot options, while the Rooster and Charlie's Lunch (named after their first son) are great for bringing to the beach. Viv's Kitchen also serves Marmita Plates, a traditional Brazilian dish consisting of rice, beans, pico, and a simmered and slow-roasted protein jam-packed with flavor. The recipes are from her mother, who also helps prep in the

KATY WARD

items such as the Bird Breakfast Sandwich (farm eggs, smoky bacon, citrus mayo, and organic greens on grilled ciabatta), quinoa porridge, eggs Benedict, fresh leafy green salad, and grain and seed bowls. Add proteins like the fish fillet (griddled and local), smoked mozzarella, and pork shoulder; and veggie add-ons like kimchi and pickled red onions. In the off-season, Sunbird opens for Noodle Night on Fridays only. Choose between a pho noodle bowl or miso/pork ramen and order small sharing bites for the table—favorites include the Brussels sprouts in a bacon, soy, pickled cherry sauce or the roasted carrots served with a spicy pepper relish and Meyer lemon kosho.

KATY WARD

kitchen. And, as if that weren't enough, they also offer freshly pressed juices and a smoothie bar. $-$$.

"The idea for Viv's Kitchen & Juice Bar came from a feeling of pure necessity for my husband and me," said Viviane Dufresne, "We were thirsty and we were in search of flavorful food in the dead of winter on Cape. Although I was born in Brazil, I grew up on Martha's Vineyard, where the Brazilian community was thriving; we never lacked Brazilian food and products growing up. Upon meeting my husband and moving to his hometown of Eastham, I quickly realized that was not the case here! With more than a decade of restaurant experience, I saw an opportunity to share the delicious and fresh foods Brazil has to offer with the year-round crowd. Familiar with the seasonality of the Cape, we knew we wanted to devote as much time and effort necessary to providing something good for everyone who sticks it out all winter long. My mom joined the venture as the force behind our daily crowd favorite: Marmita Plates. And with the addition of the healthy and fresh juice and smoothie bar (100-percent gluten-free and vegan), our family tries to provide something for everyone."

Cottage Street Bakery (508-255-2821; cottagestreetbakery.com), 5 Cottage Street. Open B, L, year-round. This European-style bakery, buttering up the community since 1984, has a number of oddly named specialties including Dirt Bombs, an old-fashioned French doughnut recipe that requires baking, not frying. Their breads are also great.

Knead I say more? Okay, I will: you can get homemade soups, lasagna, chicken pies, and sandwiches here, too. There are a few indoor and outdoor tables. $-$$.

The Hole in One (508-255-3740; theholecapecod.com), 98 Route off 6A. Open B, L, year-round. A real local hangout, The Hole is usually packed at

COTTAGE STREET BAKERY KIM GRANT

read a newspaper, chat with friends, or grab a beverage to go. $.

Sundae School Ice Cream (508-255-5473; sundaeschool.com), 210 Main Street. Open late May through early September. This sweet little rustic landmark has been churning small delicious batches of ice cream since 1976. Using a fresh mixture of milk, cream, and sugar with high butterfat content, you can expect silky smooth deliciousness. With over 40 flavors, it might be hard to choose: pistachio (with real pistachios), black raspberry (again, real black raspberries), butter pecan (you get the theme here), coffee, creamsicle, grapenut—the list goes on. Can't decide? Ask one of the seasoned employees. "It has become a tradition that employees hired as high school students continue to work with us throughout their college years," said the Endres family: "We also have a large number of siblings who work together, and once again the Sundae School takes on a family atmosphere. We watch with pride as 'our' kids get accepted to great colleges, go on to successful careers, and start their own families of little scoopers." They also have a location in Harwich Port (508-430-2444; 606 Main Street) and Dennis Port (508-394-9122; 381 Lower County Road). $.

MARKETS **Friends Marketplace** (508-255-0963; friendsmarketplace.net), 57 Main Street. Open daily, year-round. Need to stock up on supplies? Friends Marketplace offers everything from fresh produce, deli items (and butcher shop with organic quality meats), prepared foods, beer and wine, baked goods, and other grocery staples. The garden center is popular among locals around Christmas time, when they sell trees and wreaths.

Orleans Whole Food Store (508-255-6540; orleanswholefoodstore.com), 46 Main Street. Open daily, year-round. This small market offers a variety of carefully chosen organic produce, supplements,

breakfast time, when eggs-your-way and a short stack of pancakes rule. $–$$.

Homeport Restaurant (508-255-4069; homeportrestaurant.com), 55 Main Street. Open B, L. This tiny hole-in-the-wall eatery serves average food at affordable diner prices. Think basic breakfast staples: the breakfast standard (two eggs your style, meat, home fries, and toast), corned beef hash, buttermilk pancakes, and Texas-style French toast. Be patient with the service and expect some wait time for a table. $–$$.

The Hot Chocolate Sparrow (508-240-2230; hotchocolatesparrow.com), 5 Old Colony Way, behind CVS on Route 6A. Open daily (with late hours) year-round. The Sparrow is a prime spot to get delicious coffee and espresso drinks, tea, baked goods, and candy. Of course, their hot chocolate is wonderfully popular. Catch up on emails (yes, free Wi-Fi),

ORLEANS WHOLE FOOD STORE KATY WARD

and body care products, as well as sandwiches, salads, and soups to go.

Young's Fish Market (508-255-3366; nausetfishandlobster.com), Rock Harbor Road. After walking the Rock Harbor flats and checking out the charter boats, stroll over to Young's for the catch of the day. Located right by the docks at Rock Harbor, it literally cannot get any fresher than this. Take it back to your "home away from home" and chef it up however you like.

See also *Farms* under **Selective Shopping**.

✳ Entertainment

ENTERTAINMENT **Academy Playhouse** (508-255-1963 for tickets; apacape .org), 120 Main Street. This 162-seat playhouse, established in 1975, hosts a handful of drama, comedy, and musical productions each year. Think popular productions like *Romeo & Juliet, The Legend of Sleepy Hollow,* and an adaptation of the popular Disney movie, *Frozen* (as part of the Summer Youth Theater program). $$$.

See also "Book 'Em Danno" on page 246.

YOUNG'S FISH MARKET KIM GRANT

✳ Selective Shopping

ARTISANS **Nauset Lantern Shop** (508-255-1009; nausetlanternshop.com), 52 Route 6A. In keeping with the rich history of the 60-year old shop, Chris and Kelly Berardi use the same hand-operated equipment and crafting process used by their forefathers. Flat sheets of copper, brass, or pewter are cut using century-old templates as guides. Those sheets are folded, beaded, and ridged by hand. Even the hinges, latches, and handles are handcrafted. Popular lanterns include reproductions of Early American, Colonial, Onion, and Nautical Marine lighting fixtures.

Kemp Pottery (508-255-5853; kemppottery.com), 9 Cranberry Highway, near the rotary. This studio/gallery has been in existence since 1978 under the clay-caked hands of Steve Kemp. In 2002, Steve's son Matt jumped on board and became part owner. The store boasts handcrafted, wheel-thrown artwork, such as functional porcelain and stoneware pieces like lamps, platters, mirrors, dinner sets, bathroom sinks; and less common decorative objects for the home and garden, such as pagodas, torsos, fountains, and tile.

BOOKSTORES **Main Street Books** (508-255-3343; mainstreetbooksonline.com), 46 Main Street. The husband-and-wife team, Janis and Don, have presided over a small but worthy selection of titles since 1975.

KEMP POTTERY KIM GRANT

MAIN STREET BOOKS KATY WARD

CLOTHING **The Salty Crown Boutique** (508-221-5753; saltycrownboutique.com), 39 Main Street. This little shop reflects everything that is wonderful about its owner, Kelly Lungo, and her keen eye for all things fashionable, stylish, sexy, sophisticated, and witty. A Cape Cod native and mother of three, Kelly provides fun and modern options for women of various ages. Her bohemian chic collection mirrors carefully curated clothing at affordable prices, trending fashion accessories, home goods (think cute beachy signs with sassy sayings), romantic bralettes, locally made jewelry, and this season's best footwear.

Homegrown Boutique (603-325-5328; homegrownboutique.com), 34 Main Street. Emily's vision for her dream boutique started in 2003 in the back of a VW bus; driving around the country, stopping at music festivals, and setting up shop with her own line of bags designed by hand. Fast forward to today: Emily now owns Homegrown, a modern bohemian lifestyle boutique. Shop here for clothing, accessories, beach must-haves, beauty and wellness products, and home

A MUST-SEE FOR ART LOVERS

Addison Art Gallery (508-255-6200; addisonart.com), 43 South Orleans Road. If you only stop at one gallery, make it this one. Helen Addison represents internationally sought-after artists working in representational and traditional realms. Find fresh oils, watercolors, pastels, encaustics, and sculpture. New to the art scene or serious collector, you'll be comfortable browsing and collecting in this charming Cape building. Intriguing shows and receptions year-round.

goods. In addition to a superb women's line, she also sells items for men, kids, and babies.

Ragg Time Ltd. (508-240-0925; ragtimeltd.com), 43 Main Street. Shop here for casual and comfortable women's clothing. They also have a seasonal location in Wellfleet that sells Wellfleet Oyster clothing and Billingsgate Bass T-shirts for men, women, and children (508-349-1266; 25 Bank Street).

FARMS **Orleans Farmers' Market** (orleansfarmersmarket.com), 21 Old Colony Way, every Saturday from May through November; and 70 Route 28, Orleans at Nauset Middle School every Saturday from December through April.

GALLERIES **Gallery 31 Fine Art** (508-208-6703; gallery31capecod.com), 34 Main Street. Voted best fine art gallery on the Lower Cape in 2019 by *Cape Cod Life*, expect high-caliber artwork by Tony Allain, Jeanne Rosier Smith, Paula David, Richard McKinley, William Gotha, and Kelly Milukas, to name a few. The gallery interior boasts small intimate areas in an office home-like setting. Gallery 31 specializes in pastel and oil paintings, as well as watercolor, alcohol ink, collage, and sterling silver items. There's plenty to look at.

Tree's Place Gallery (508-255-1330; treesplace.com), 60 Route 6A at Route 28. Tree's offers a vast collection of unusual gifts (like kaleidoscopes and antique jewelry) as well as an excellent collection of representational New England painters. Wander through each of the nine

display rooms or call for meet-the-artist champagne receptions.

Left Bank Gallery (508-247-9172; leftbankgallery.com), 8 Cove Road. Ceramic, glass, jewelry, furniture, pottery, and estate items are just a few things you might find here.

SPECIALTY **Bird Watcher's General Store** (508-255-6974; birdwatchers generalstore.com), 36 Route 6A off the rotary. If you're a bird lover, you'll be in heaven here. From feeders, houses,

SALTY CROWN BOUTIQUE KATY WARD

fountains, birdseed, children's books, jewelry, and more this place has everything bird-related. It is also an invaluable resource for birdie-news: where the purple martin colony was last seen, when the bank swallows are nesting, or a lesson on fishing in the midst of hungry ospreys.

Earth House (508-240-0257; earthhouse.com), 121 Route 6A. Bring out your inner hippie! Come here for banners and flags, bumper stickers, candles, crystals, clothing, Haitian art, incense, jewelry, and body products.

Honey Candle Co. (508-255-7031; honeycandle.com), 37 Main Street. The light is bright; the scent is natural and sweet. That's because Honey Candle offers candles made entirely from beeswax.

Hidden Gem (774-801-2667; hidden gemcapecod.com), 47 Main Street. Expect the unexpected in this tiny consignment shop tucked off the main strip in Orleans. Anne Kiefer offers an eclectic mix of vintage Americana and quirky collectibles. From nautical chart jewelry to goat's milk soap and pottery, this shop has a bit of everything. Additional consignment profits go to NAOMI, the National Alliance on Mental Illness.

Cape Cod Photo, Art & Framing (508-255-0476; capecodphotoandart.com), 60 Route 6A, inside Tree's Place. Print and frame your vacation photos here! They also sell painting supplies, 1-hour photo process, everything digital, and custom frames.

✳ Special Events

Because print guidebooks circulate for years—and because events are changeable—I normally only include big annual events around which you'd want to plan. In this case, I suggest checking orleanscapecod.org.

THE OUTER CAPE

■

EASTHAM

WELLFLEET

TRURO

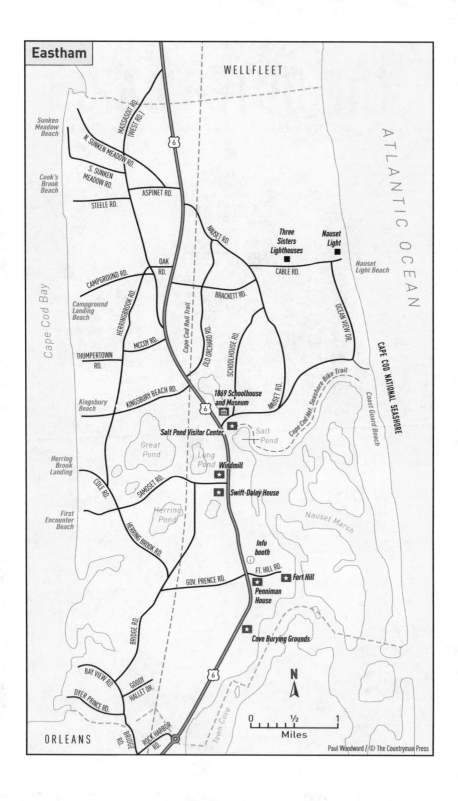

Eastham

WELLFLEET

ATLANTIC OCEAN

Sunken Meadow Beach

Cook's Brook Beach

MASSASOIT RD. (WEST RD.)

N. SUNKEN MEADOW RD.

S. SUNKEN MEADOW RD.

ASPINET RD.

STEELE RD.

NAUSET RD.

Three Sisters Lighthouses

Nauset Light

Nauset Light Beach

CABLE RD.

OAK RD.

CAMPGROUND RD.

HERRINGBROOK RD.

Campground Landing Beach

Cape Cod Bay

MCCOY RD.

THUMPERTOWN RD.

Kingsbury Beach

KINGSBURY BEACH RD.

Cape Cod Rail Trail

OLD ORCHARD RD.

SCHOOLHOUSE RD.

BRACKETT RD.

NAUSET RD.

OCEAN VIEW DR.

CAPE COD NATIONAL SEASHORE

Cape Cod Nat. Seashore Bike Trail

Coast Guard Beach

1869 Schoolhouse and Museum

Salt Pond Visitor Center

Salt Pond

Great Pond

Long Pond

Windmill

Swift-Daley House

Herring Brook Landing

COLE RD.

SAMOSET RD.

Herring Pond

Nauset Marsh

First Encounter Beach

HERRING BROOK RD.

Info booth

FT. HILL RD.

Fort Hill

GOV. PRENCE RD.

Penniman House

Cove Burying Grounds

BRIDGE RD.

BAY VIEW RD.

GOODY HALLET DR.

DYER PRINCE RD.

6

ORLEANS

BRIDGE RD.

ROCK HARBOR RD.

Town Cove

N

0   ½   1
Miles

Paul Woodward / © The Countryman Press

EASTHAM

Eastham is content to remain relatively undiscovered by 21st-century tourists. In fact, although almost 29,000 folks summer here, year-rounders (fewer than 5,500) seem perfectly happy that any semblance of major tourism development has passed them by. There isn't even a Main Street or town center per se.

What Eastham does boast, as the gateway to the Cape Cod National Seashore (CCNS), is plenty of natural diversions. There are four things you should do, by all means. Stop in at **Salt Pond Visitor Center**, one of two CCNS headquarters, which dispenses a wealth of information and offers ranger-guided activities and outstanding nature programs. Consider taking a boat trip onto **Nauset Marsh**, a fragile ecosystem that typifies much of the Cape. Hop on a bike or walking trail; a marvelous network of paths traverses this part of the seashore, including the **Fort Hill** area. And of course, head to the beach.

The Cape's renowned, uninterrupted stretches of sandy beach, backed by high dunes, begin in earnest in Eastham and extend all the way up to Provincetown. One of them, Coast Guard Beach, is also where exalted naturalist Henry Beston spent about 2 years during the mid-1920s, observing nature's minute changes from a little cottage and recording his experiences in *The Outermost House*, which was published in 1928.

Eastham is best known as the site where the *Mayflower*'s Myles Standish and a Pilgrim scouting party met the Nauset American Indians in 1620 at First Encounter Beach. The "encounter," in which a few arrows were slung (without injury), served as sufficient warning to the Pilgrims: They left and didn't return for 24 years. When the Pilgrim settlers, then firmly entrenched at Plymouth, went looking for room to expand, they returned to Eastham. Led by Thomas Prence, they purchased most of the land from American Indians for an unknown quantity of hatchets.

Although the history books cite these encounters as the beginning of Eastham's recorded history, the 1990 discovery of a 4,000-year-old settlement (see "Coast Guard Beach" on page 264) is keeping archaeologists and anthropologists on their toes.

GUIDANCE **Eastham Information Booth** (508-240-7211 chamber; 508-255-3444 info booth; easthamchamber.com), 1700 Route 6, near Fort Hill. Open June to mid-October.

EASTHAM'S FAMOUS BUOY TREE MARCIA DUGGAN/ CAPECODSOUL

Morning:	Start the day off with a full belly at Laura & Tony's buffet breakfast. If you'd rather keep it simple, stop at the Hole in One for fresh donuts, bagels, and coffee. Take it to go and enjoy it with panoramic views atop Fort Hill.
Afternoon:	Bike the Cape Cod Rail Trail up to Wellfleet and down to Dennis or sink your toes in the sand at the bayside First Encounter Beach. For lunch, stop for tacos and delicious street corn at Joey's Joint or grab a fresh and buttery lobster roll from the Friendly Fisherman.
Evening:	For dinner head over the Brine and enjoy one of Chef Zia's special entrées or try the Local Break for upscale bar food. Build a bonfire at the National Seashore (after having picked up a permit), or check what's scheduled at the First Encounter Coffee House.

🦞 ❄ ⚓ **Salt Pond Visitor Center** (508-255-3421; 508-771-2144; nps.gov/caco), 50 Nauset Road, off Route 6. In 1961 newly elected president John F. Kennedy, Sen. Leverett Saltonstall, and Rep. Hastings Keith championed a bill to turn more than 43,000 acres into the **Cape Cod National Seashore** (CCNS), protected forever from further development. (About 600 private homes remain within the park.) Today, more than 5 million people visit the CCNS annually. The excellent center shows short films on Thoreau's Cape Cod, Marconi, the ever-changing natural landscape, and the history of whaling and lifesaving. And the fine museum includes displays on the salt and whaling industries and the diaries of Captain Penniman's wife, Augusta, who accompanied him on several voyages. Rangers lead lots of activities during the summer, from sunset campfires on the beach to talks on tidal flats and bird walks. Two short loop trails depart from here around Salt Pond and are worth your time. Programs are also offered during spring and fall. Free.

GETTING THERE *By car:* Eastham is 40 miles from the Cape Cod Canal via Route 6.

By bus: The **Plymouth & Brockton** bus line (508-746-0378; P-B.com) connects Eastham with Hyannis and other Cape towns, as well as with Boston's Logan Airport. The bus stops across from Town Hall on Route 6 and at the Village Green Plaza at Bracket Road on Route 6.

GETTING AROUND *By shuttle:* **The Flex** (508-385-1430; capecodtransit.org) offers north and southbound trips from Provincetown to Harwich with reserved stops. The shuttle stops at the Eastham Town Hall, Salt Pond Visitor Center, Four Points by Sheraton Hotel, and Bracket Road on Route 6.

PUBLIC RESTROOMS Salt Pond Visitor Center, 50 Nauset Road off Route 6.

PUBLIC LIBRARY **Eastham Public Library** (508-240-5950; easthamlibrary.org), 190 Samoset Road. The recently renovated building (which was purchased by the town in 1878 for $175) offers a variety of public resources. From computers and printing, classes for children and teens/tweens, endless reading options and audio books, as well as a range of events: Ayurveda and holistic wellness meetings, knitting groups, performances by the Toe Jam Puppet Band, DIY crafts, device advice, and more. Check the website's calendar of events for a complete list.

✳ To See

Edward Penniman House (508-349-3785), off Route 6 in the Fort Hill area, CCNS. Open early May to late October; inquire about tour times/days. At age 11 Penniman left Eastham for the open sea. When he returned as a captain 26 years later, he had this 1868 house built for him. Boasting indoor plumbing (the first in Eastham to make that claim) and a kerosene chandelier, this French Second Empire–style house has Corinthian columns, a mansard roof, and a cupola that once afforded views of the bay and ocean. Ever-helpful National Park Service guides dispense lots of historical information. Even if it's closed, peek in the windows. Free.

   Swift-Daley House and **Tool Museum** (508-240-1247; easthamhistoricalsociety .org), next to the post office at 2375 Route 6. Open July and August. In the late 1990s one of the seashore dune shacks (see "Dune Shacks" on page 332) was moved to this site. Although it's difficult to imagine what dune-shack life might have been like, this helps. As for the Swift-Daley House, it's a completely furnished full Cape Colonial built by ship's carpenters in 1741. It has wide floorboards, pumpkin-pine woodwork, narrow stairways, and a fireplace in every room on the first floor. The Tool Museum behind the house displays hundreds of old tools for use in the home and in the field. And the Olde Shop sells antiques and local arts and crafts. Donations.

   1869 Schoolhouse and Museum (508-255-0788; easthamhistoricalsociety.org), 25 Schoolhouse Road, off Route 6 across from the Salt Pond Visitor Center. Open July and August. During the time when this former one-room schoolhouse served the town (1869 until 1936), there were separate entrances for boys and girls. Inside you'll learn about Henry Beston's year of solitude, spent observing natural rhythms on nearby Coast Guard Beach. Thanks to the Eastham Historical Society, you can also learn about

EDWARD PENNIMAN HOUSE KIM GRANT

PLEIN-AIR PAINTING AT THE EDWARD PENNIMAN HOUSE KIM GRANT

the town's farming history, daily domestic life, local American Indian tribes, offshore shipwrecks, and the impressive Lifesaving Service. Donations.

Oldest windmill (easthamhistorical society.org), on Route 6 at Samoset Road. Open July and August. Across from Town Hall, the Cape's oldest working windmill was built in Plymouth in the 1680s and moved to Eastham in the early 1800s.

First Encounter Beach, off Samoset Road and Route 6. A bronze marker commemorates where the Pilgrims, led by Captain Myles Standish, first met the indigenous people. The exchange was not friendly. Although arrows flew, no one was injured. The site goes down in history as the place where the American Indians first began their fateful interaction with European settlers. On a more modern note of warfare history, for 25 years the US Navy used an offshore ship for target practice. Until recently, it was still visible on a sandbar about a mile offshore. The beach, with its westward vista, is a great place to catch a sunset. Seasonal parking $$.

Doane Homestead Site, between the Salt Pond Visitor Center and Coast Guard Beach, a mile down Nauset Road on the southside, CCNS. Only a marker remains to identify the spot where Doane, one of Eastham's first English settlers, made his home.

Cove Burying Grounds, Route 6 near Corliss Way. Many of these graves date back to the 1700s, but look for the memorial to the three *Mayflower* Pilgrims who were buried here in the 1600s.

SWIFT DALEY HOUSE AND TOOL MUSEUM KIM GRANT

OLDEST WINDMILL KIM GRANT

Nauset Light (508-240-2612; nausetlight.org), at the corner of Cable Road and Ocean View Drive, CCNS. Inquire about tour times May through October. This light was originally built in Chatham in 1877, one of a twin, but was moved here shortly thereafter. In the mid-1990s, when Nauset Light was just 37 feet from cliff's edge, the large red-and-white steel lighthouse was moved—via flatbed truck over the course of three days—from the eroding shoreline. And a few years later, the keeper's house (which dates to 1875) was also moved back. For now, the cast-iron behemoth sits a respectable distance from the shoreline, its beacon still stretching 17 miles to sea. Free, but you might have to pay to park at Nauset Light Beach (see **Green Space**).

Three Sisters Lighthouses (508-255-3421), inland from Nauset Light, CCNS. Inquire about tour times May through October. In 1838 this coastal cliff was home to three brick lighthouses that provided beacons for sailors. They collapsed from erosion in 1892 and were replaced with three wooden ones. When erosion threatened those in 1918, two were moved away; the third was moved in 1923. Eventually the National Park Service acquired all three and moved them to their current location, nestled in the woods far back from today's coastline. (It's a rather incongruous sight: lighthouses, surrounded by trees, their light unable to reach the water.) Head inland from the beach parking lot along the paved walkway. Free, but you'll have to pay to park at Nauset Light Beach (see **Green Space**).

✴ To Do

BICYCLING & RENTALS **The Cape Cod Rail Trail** offers 25.5 miles of paved road for your biking pleasure. The trail route starts in Wellfleet and passes through the towns of Eastham, Orleans, Brewster, Harwich, Dennis, and Yarmouth.

Nauset Bike Trail, CCNS. This 1.6-mile (one-way) trail connects with the Cape Cod Rail Trail and runs from the Salt Pond Visitor Center, across Nauset

THREE SISTERS LIGHTHOUSE KIM GRANT

Marsh via a boardwalk, to Coast Guard Beach. The trail passes large stands of thin, tall black locust trees not native to the area—they were introduced to return nitrogen to the soil after over farming.

You can rent bicycles and equipment at the family-owned **Little Capistrano Bike Shop** (508-255-6515; littlecapistrano bikeshop.com), 30 Salt Pond Road. This superb little bike shack is located right on the rail trail and across the street from the Nauset Bike Trail. Owners Melissa and Josh are wonderful.

LITTLE CAPISTRANO BIKE SHOP KIM GRANT

BOAT EXCURSIONS & RENTALS The **Wellfleet Bay Wildlife Sanctuary** (508-349-2615; massaudubon.org) sponsors numerous activities including kayak trips on the Town Cove (Hemenway Landing) and Great Pond. Call to register for a trip. $$$$+.

FISHING Procure freshwater and saltwater fishing licenses and regulations online at www.mass.gov/eea/agencies/dfg/licensing. Then head to **Goose Hummock** (508-255-0455; goose.com), 15 Route 6A at the Orleans rotary.

FITNESS CLUB **Willy's Gym** (508-255-6370; willysgym.com), 4730 Route 6. A large fitness center with all the essentials: cardiovascular machines, free weights, sauna and steam rooms, classes, a juice bar, and supervised childcare. Lap swimmers will appreciate the indoor unheated pool. $$.

FAMILIES & KIDS **Recreational programs** (508-240-5974) are held mid-June to mid-August. Visitors and summer residents are encouraged to bring their younger children to the playground at **Nauset Regional High School** (508-255-1505; nausetschools.org; 100 Cable Road) for various programs. In the past they've included archery, arts and crafts, and soccer. Supervised swimming and instruction are also offered at Wiley Park (see **Green Space**) and classes and story-time at the Eastham Public Library (see *Public Libraries*). Fees vary.

TENNIS **Nauset Regional High School** (508-255-1505; nausetschools.org), 100 Cable Road. The public can use these eight courts for free after school gets out. (See also **Willy's Gym** under *Fitness Club*).

✳ Green Space

BEACHES The CCNS manages Eastham's ocean beaches while the town maintains the bayside beaches. Both require different stickers 8 a.m. to 4 p.m., starting late June through early September. Parking is first-come, first-serve. Town beach stickers are available from the Town of Eastham's Sticker Office (508-240-5976), 555 Old Orchard Road (off Route 6 or Brackett Road). Parking $.

Nauset Light Beach, CCNS (nps.gov/caco), on the Atlantic Ocean. An idyllic, long,

NATIONAL SEASHORE BONFIRES

A beach bonfire, with or without a clambake, defines the essence of summertime on the Outer Cape. That said, officials prefer the term campfire—nothing too big, just cozy and toasty compared to anything rip-roaring. Here's the process you need to follow to secure a permit: In July and August head to the **Salt Pond Visitor Center** (508-255-3421; nps .gov/caco) three days before you want a permit and request one. For instance, if you want it for Wednesday, go on Sunday. Be there when the center opens (9 AM). On the day of your big event, be at the visitor center by 3:30 PM or you'll lose your permit to someone waiting in line. In the off-season, you can call three days ahead of your desired date without a problem. There are limits on the number of permits given out: four at Coast Guard Beach, four at Nauset Light Beach, and four at Marconi Beach; there are also limitations on the sizes of the groups allowed to congregate. Beach rangers will check permits. BYOF—bring your own firewood—and don't forget to extinguish the flames. Fires are permitted year-round from 5:30 to 11:30 p.m.

SALT POND VISITOR CENTER KIM GRANT

broad, dune-backed beach. Facilities include changing rooms, restrooms, and a lifeguard in-season. Get there early because the lot fills by 10 a.m. in summer.

(See also "Shark Awareness" on page 282.)

First Encounter Beach, Campground Beach, and **Cook's Brook Beach.** These bayside beaches are a paradise for children (and their parents) because of the shallow water and gradual slopes. Small pools of water offer the perfect opportunity to build sandcastles, splash in the sun-warmed water, and explore. First Encounter Beach has a bathhouse; the others are equipped with portable toilets.

PONDS **Herring Pond** and **Great Pond**, both west of Eastham center off Samoset, has sufficient parking, beaches, lifeguards, and swimming areas (including **Wiley Park**, with a beach, playground, and bathhouse).

COAST GUARD BEACH

This long National Seashore beach, backed by grasses and heathland, is perfect for walking and sunning. Facilities include changing rooms, restrooms, and in-season lifeguards. In summer a shuttle bus ferries visitors from a parking lot that fills by 10 a.m.; it's a mile from the beach, and it's no use trying to drop off passengers at the beach *before* parking; the seashore banned it to control traffic and protect resources. Parking entrance fee per car $$ (good all day on any CCNS beach; no charge after 4 PM) from late June to early September and on shoulder season holidays.

At times during the winter, you might be lucky enough to spot gray seals and small brown harbor seals congregating at the southern tip of Coast Guard Beach. They feed on the ever-present sand eels. Take the walk at low tide and allow an hour to cover the 2 miles.

Henry Beston published his 1928 classic, *The Outermost House*, about the year he lived in a two-room bungalow on Coast Guard Beach. The book chronicles Beston's interaction with the natural environment and records seasonal changes. The cottage was designated a national literary landmark in 1964, but the blizzard of 1978 washed it into the ocean. Bundled up (tightly!) against the off-season winds, you'll get a glimpse of the haunting isolation Beston experienced.

After a brutal 1990 storm washed away a large chunk of beach, an amateur archaeologist discovered evidence of a prehistoric dwelling on Coast Guard Beach. It is one of the oldest undisturbed archaeological sites in New England, dating back 1,100 to 2,100 years to the Early and Middle Woodland cultures. Because Coast Guard Beach was then 5 miles inland, the site provided a safe encampment for hunters and gatherers. In response to the thousands of ships that were wrecked off this treacherous coast, the Life-Saving Service established in 1872 morphed into the US Coast Guard. After the Cape Cod Canal was built in 1914 and ships could pass through instead of going around the Cape, fatalities off this coastline decreased dramatically. And so, by 1958, the Coast Guard Station at the top of the cliff could be decommissioned. It now serves as a CCNS educational center.

COAST GUARD BEACH LEFT AND RIGHT: KIM GRANT

WALKS **Nauset Marsh Trail**, CCNS; trailhead behind the Salt Pond Visitor Center (see *Guidance*). About 1 mile round-trip; some log steps. This trail runs along Salt Pond and yields expansive vistas of Nauset Marsh, which was actually Nauset Bay when French explorer Samuel de Champlain charted it in 1605. As the barrier beach developed, so did the marsh. Along those same lines, Salt Pond was a freshwater pond until the ocean broke through from Nauset Marsh. This complex ecosystem sustains all manner of ocean creatures and shorebirds.

Buttonbush Trail, CCNS, trailhead at the Salt Pond Visitor Center. The trail is half a mile (round-trip), with some boardwalk, some log steps. It was specially designed with Braille markers for the blind and visually impaired.

❋ **Eastham Hiking Club.** The club meets on Wednesdays from September to late May for a vigorous two-hour walk somewhere between Yarmouth and Provincetown. The contact person and phone number changes from year to year, so it's best to Google or ask around. Generally about 45 to 50 people gather for the 4- to 6-mile hike along wooded trails and ponds. Call for the meeting place. Free.

❋ Lodging

Route 6 is lined with cottage colonies, but there are a few quite notable alternatives.

BED-AND-BREAKFASTS **Whalewalk Inn & Spa** (508-255-0617; whalewalkinn .com), 220 Bridge Road. Open April to December. This upscale 19th-century whaling captain's home has been run like a tight ship by Elaine and Kevin Conlin since the mid-2000s. Expect a range of accommodations including a romantic cottage, four suites, a luxuriously renovated carriage house, and the most romantic room: the spa penthouse. (Book it now!) Carriage house rooms are outfitted with four-poster beds and gas fireplaces; all have a small private deck or balcony and some have a large whirlpool. Inn rooms are decorated with country sophistication: a smattering of fine

WHALEWALK INN & SPA KIM GRANT

antiques, and breezy floral fabrics. I particularly like the brick patio, where a full breakfast (mesclun salad with pecans, Gorgonzola, and pear slices, followed by a killer Grand Marnier oatmeal pie with vanilla yogurt) and afternoon hors d'oeuvres are served. The inn also boasts a first-rate spa with an exercise facility, sauna, hot tub, and indoor pool—massages can be arranged. The inn is around the corner from the rail trail and within walking distance of bay beaches. $$–$$$$.

Fort Hill Bed and Breakfast (508-240-2870; forthillbedandbreakfast.com), 75 Fort Hill Road. Open January through November. This bed-and-breakfast has car-stopping street appeal, and I could live out the rest of my days here. Perched on a little knoll overlooking Nauset Marsh, Jean and Gordon Avery's two suites and cottage enjoy one of the Cape's best locations. The casual yet refined 19th century Greek revival farmhouse is a charmer with wonderful hosts (who have separate guest quarters). As for the rooms, the second-floor Lucille is sweet with slanted eaves, wide-pine

FORT HILL BED & BREAKFAST KATY WARD

floors, and a detached bathroom. The first-floor two-room Emma Suite features a little library, a piano, and an oversized tub. The *pièce de résistance*, however, is the ever-so-private Nantucket Cottage that boasts a secluded garden, distant marsh views, cathedral ceilings, and a sitting room with a gas fireplace. Folks who stay tend to become serious repeat visitors. A delectable full breakfast might include zucchini quiche or piping-hot baked apples with "jammy" muffins. (The cottage has a self-catering option). $$$.

700 Samoset (508-255-8748), 700 Samoset Road. Open May through October. The ever-resourceful Sarah Blackwell moved this abandoned 1870 Greek revival farmhouse to its current location on the bayside of Route 6, on a quiet road near the bike trail. She also did a wonderful job restoring it, sanding floors and woodwork, and blending period pieces with contemporary accents like a painted checkerboard floor and tin lamps. It's all quite tasteful. Too bad for us, there are only two guest rooms. From the open country kitchen, guests enjoy an expanded Continental breakfast while you plan your day from the front porch rocking chairs. No credit cards and rented by the week (call for rates).

Inn at the Oaks (508-255-1886; inattheoaks.com), 3085 Route 6. Open mid-March to late December. This big yellow Victorian house is hidden from Route 6 and across from the Salt Pond Visitor Center. Guests enjoy relaxing on the wide wraparound veranda, the billiards room, or parlor with velveteen curtains. All 10-guestrooms have lacy curtains and a smattering of antiques; some have a cathedral ceiling and skylight. The Garden Room (my favorite) has a private porch and fireplace. Afternoon tea, cider, and cookies are included, as well as an expanded Continental breakfast. As a historical footnote, Henry Beston stayed on the property during bad weather while he was writing *The Outermost House*. $$–$$$.

AN ABSOLUTE FAVORITE VIEW & WALK

Fort Hill area, CCNS; trailhead and parking off Route 6. The trail—one of my all-Cape favorites—is about 1.5 miles round-trip with a partial boardwalk, some log steps, and some hills. It offers lovely views of Nauset Marsh, especially from Skiff Hill, but also winds through the dense Red Maple Swamp and past the Edward Penniman House (see **To See**). Birders enjoy this walk year-round, but it is particularly beautiful in autumn when the maples turn color. Pastoral Fort Hill was farmed until the 1940s, and rock walls still mark boundaries.

FORT HILL TRAIL KIM GRANT

The Rugosa (508-255-1248; therugosa .com), 4885 Route 6. Open year-round, call for availability. This historic home was built in 1751 on Billingsgate Island, Wellfleet, and floated across the bay to its present location in Eastham. Its original owner, Captain Isaiah Horton, was a direct descendent of Constance Hopkins, who traveled to the New World on the *Mayflower*. Her father was one of the 41 passengers to sign the Mayflower Compact of 1620. The building remained a family residence until the Penney Family turned it into a hotel in the 1980s. In 2019, Joey Rugo claimed ownership (see **Joey's Joint** under **Where to Eat**). Hidden behind a row of trees on the highway, the Rugosa offers eight completely and tastefully renovated guestrooms—Joey's upgrades are careful to keep

the footprint of the original home. Step inside the main foyer to large open windows, lush green plants, a decorative fireplace, leather furniture, fur skin rugs, and bright artwork. Wander among the skinny and brightly painted hallways until you reach the communal kitchen equipped with cooking essentials and a small library, or the paved patio abutting a remote lawn that's equipped with a small ceramic fountain and relaxing hammock. Stroll along the brick walkway (admiring Joey's abilities to grow pineapple on Cape Cod) until you reach the heated outdoor saltwater swimming pool. Each of the eight rooms comes fitted with comfortable bedding, large pine wood floors, air conditioning, and Wi-Fi. Some have fireplaces and a private balcony. $–$$.

THE RUGOSA KATY WARD

COTTAGES **Cottage Grove** (508-255-0500; grovecape.com), 1975 Route 6. Open May through October. You can tell this is not your average cottage colony just by the unusually aesthetic fence that fronts the highway. Although these are individually owned condos, they're expertly managed during the summer like rental units. No matter how you categorize them, I call them some of the most charming places to stay on the Outer Cape. The nine cozy cottages have been nicely renovated and are set back off the road on 3 acres of remote land. Cottages are rustic, with knotty-pine walls, but have upgraded bathrooms and kitchens, firm new mattresses, and cotton sheets. $$-$$$.

Gibson Cottages (508-240-7229; gibsoncottages.com), 80 Depot Road. Open April through October. Some of the Cape's best lakeside cottages are down a little dirt road marked only with GIBSON. Each of these seven well-spaced one-, two-, and three-bedroom cottages has a screened porch or deck and a fully equipped kitchen. A swimming dock, a sailboat, rowboats, a kayak, a canoe, and a barbecue area are shared by all. There

are also two bike trails on the other side of the pristine lake, which boasts a private sandy beach. This is a gem; call early. No credit cards. $$-$$$.

Midway Motel & Cottages (508-255-3117; midwaymotel.com), Route 6. Open March to mid-October. Pine and oak trees shield this reasonably priced complex from the road. The tidy grounds, over which the Knisely family has presided since 1983, feature a nice children's play area, shuffleboard, badminton, horseshoes, picnic tables, grills, and direct access to the rail trail. All rooms have refrigerators, microwaves, and coffee makers. Rooms rented nightly and weekly. $-$$.

HOSTEL **HI Eastham Hostel** (508-255-2758; hisusa.org), 75 Goody Hallet Drive. Open mid-June to early September. Relieve your fondest memories of summer camp. Located in a quiet residential neighborhood, this hostel has about 46 beds in seven coed, same-sex, and family cabins. The hostel boasts no lockout times and has an array of summertime events. Take advantage of the fully equipped kitchen, bike shelter, outdoor shower, volleyball net, and barbecue area. $.

✳ Where to Eat

Brine (774-561-2967; brinedining.com), 4100 Route 6. Open D, year-round, and for brunch on weekends only. It's no surprise that Brine is becoming a blooming success, and I hope it continues. Though the menu changes seasonally, chef/owner Zia Auch's homemade gnocchi and ragu Bolognese are delicious dinner entrées. Or come for breakfast—my personal favorite—for the eggs Benedict (five different variations), her homemade slow-roasted corn beef hash, or the almond-scented strawberry crêpes. Be sure to opt for dressed mixed greens (I could drink Zia's homemade white balsamic dressing, it's that good). Brine also caters to vegetarians and vegans. The only downfall is the unassuming location (hidden off the highway), but the inside's

rustic and nautical inspired décor makes up for it. Customers are greeted with a collection of strung-together sea weathered bottles dragged off the ocean floor during her father's fishing days. Choose from booth and table seating or grab a stool at the bar. $–$$$$.

Karoo Restaurant (508-255-8288; karoorestaurants.com), 3 Main Street, Route 6. Open D, year-round; closed Tuesdays. Looking to spice things up? Be sure to stop at Karoo and try Chef Sanette Groenewald's South African hometown cooking, like Bobotie (a mild curry meat loaf), the Cape Malay stew, peri-peri wings, or beef or vegetable samosas. It's even better than some meals I had while in Cape Town! $$–$$$.

Local Break (508-255-6100; local-break.com), 4550 Route 6. Open daily, year-round. A favorite local spot. Take a seat at one of the booths, or grab a stool seat at the bar. Local Break offers a long list of locally crafted beers and delicious sangria and wines. Start with an app

BRINE KATY WARD

A PIPE DREAM TURNED INTO REALITY

Joey's Joint (508-237-8493; joeysfoodtruck.com), 4100 Route 6. Open L, mid-June through September. A taco shop with a whole lot of personality! I first met Joey Rugo (the mastermind behind the taco operation) during an English class in college, but that's a different story for another time. In 2014, Joey made a bold move. He quit his job, took all of his savings, and bought a used hot dog trailer. He painted it green, added some kangaroo logos, and decided he was going to cook tacos out of it. (Wondering why the kangaroo branding? A "joey" is a young kangaroo or "beginner"). With a bunch of recipes in mind and zero experience working in a commercial kitchen, Joey recruited the help of his friend, Zia Auch (see Brine under Where to Eat). Oh, and she was nine months pregnant at the time. The two made it work, and soon enough Joey's tacos came to life. In 2018, Joey opened his first landlocked joint, adjoined to Zia's restaurant. Stop by for a taco or two, *or three*—it's hard to choose just one from the colorful handwritten menu. They also offers quesadillas and burritos, vegan and vegetarian options (such as the Pot Head with sweet potato), as well as my favorite: Mexican street corn rolled in ancho chili butter and smothered with feta cheese and chipotle aioli. $$.

KATY WARD

such as the Cod Tacos, lightly fried and served with a mango salsa and spicy avocado dressing. Move on to the Southern Fried Chicken with braised green beans and mac and cheese, or the seared Faroe Islands Salmon. Feeling basic? Try their house burger topped with house relish and bacon-mayo; or go for something not-so-basic, like the tuna burger topped with a risotto spread and avocado-wasabi sauce. $$–$$$.

The Friendly Fisherman (508-255-6770; friendlyfishermaneastham .com), 4580 Route 6. Open mid-May to mid-October. This popular and rustic shack offers the requisite fish-and-chips, but I always gravitate to their excellent lobster rolls. Come hungry as they serve large portions. See also under *Markets*. $$–$$$.

Arnold's Lobster & Clam Bar (508-255-2575; arnoldsrestaurant.com), 3580 Route 6. Open L, D, mid-May through September. Operating under the same stewardship for years, Arnold's offers excellent fried seafood baskets (with award-winning fried clams), a raw bar, lobster clambake dinners, and home-made ice cream. Abutting the rail trail, Arnold's has a nice fenced-off area with tables under pine trees and an open-air patio. There's always a line, so expect to wait. See also under *Mini-Golf*. $$–$$$.

Red Barn Pizza (508-255-4500; theredbarnpizza.com), 4180 Route 6. Open L, D, mid-May through September. Just as the name implies, this big red barn eatery, off the highway, pumps out some seriously delicious pizza. $$–$$$.

Sam's Deli (508-255-9340), 100 Brackett Road. Open L, D, mid-March through December. These folks make great hot and cold sandwiches, prepared salads like black bean, orzo, and curried chicken. Or take home one of their delicious potpies. Just pop it in the oven and let it bake. A perfect dinner for a night when you don't feel like going out, or spending hours in the kitchen, and it's large enough to feed the entire family, but make sure to ask for extra homemade gravy. $$–$$$.

SWEET TREATS & COFFEE **Laura & Tony's Kitchen** (508-240-6096; lauraand tonyskitchen.com), 5960 Route 6 (across from the Wellfleet Drive-In & Flea Market). Open B, mid-May through late September. This is one of the best breakfast joints in Eastham. Laura and Tony (the nicest husband and wife team I have ever met), offer a buffet-style breakfast with all the fixings. Fresh fruit, granola and yogurt, eggs, home fries, bacon, Tony's famous sausage gravy and biscuits, a bagel bar, assorted frittatas, and much *much* more. Sip on fresh squeezed orange juice, Beanstock coffee, or $3 mimosas and Bloody Mary's. Make sure you save room for one of Laura's decadent cinnamon rolls—they are to die for—or you can order premade rolls to bake at home. $$–$$$.

The Hole in One (508-255-3893; the holecapecod), 4295 Route 6. Open daily, year-round. This hole-in-the-wall bakery (pun intended) offers freshly made doughnuts, muffins, pastries, bagels, and more. If you're looking for a morning bite to go, I recommend this place. They also offer a sit-down full breakfast menu next door at their sister restaurant, The Fairway, but I'd stick to the baked goods. $–$$.

Brine (774-561-2967; brinedining .com), 4100 Route 6. Offers a delicious brunch on weekends—see under **Where to Eat.** $$–$$$.

MARKETS **Eastham Superette** (508-255-0530; easthamsuperette), 2475 Route 6. Open daily, year-round. If you're in need of supplies, this is a convenient one-stop shop. In addition to all the basics, they have a deli counter with made to order sandwiches and are attached to a liquor store.

LAURA & TONY'S KITCHEN KATY WARD

Mac's Seafood Market & Kitchen (508-255-6900; macseafood.com), 4680 Route 6. Open daily, year-round. Here you'll find fresh fish and shellfish, house-smoked seafood and pâtés, along with a great selection of deli salads, cooked lobsters, meat, cheese, and produce. Don't feel like cooking? Order at the counter and dine on the shaded porch or picnic tables.

Friendly Fisherman (508-255-3009; friendlyfishermaneastham.com/market), 4580 Route 6. Open daily from mid-May to mid-October. Another great seafood market with fresh and affordable items.

See also *Farms* under **Selective Shopping**.

✳ Entertainment

First Encounter Coffee House (508-255-5438; firstencounter.org), 220 Samoset Road. Open year-round, except December and May. Performances (usually) take place on the second and fourth Saturday of each month. Acoustic, folk, blues, and bluegrass reign here, attracting musicians with national reputations—including Wellfleet's Patty Larkin and Vineyarder Livingston Taylor. Home to the 1899 Unitarian Universalist church (a.k.a. Chapel in the Pines) since 1974, the intimate venue has only 100 seats beneath its stained-glass windows. Off-season, it's a very local affair, where everybody knows your name and knows to arrive early to get a good seat. $$.

✳ Selective Shopping

SPECIALTY **Pure Vita** (774-561-2395; purevitacapecod.com), 4205 Route 6. Open daily, year-round. This modern apothecary boutique offers verified CBD products, an essential oils tap-bar, home-made soaps (and refill station), and botanical body/home care goods. Husband and wife team, Katie and Steve Scott, opened this tiny natural shop in January 2019. Stop by and smell the roses.

Buddha & Beads (774-207-0105), 2390 Route 6. Open mid-May through

PURE VITA KATY WARD

ARTICHOKE   KATY WARD

October. Also known as Buddha Bobs, this little shack is filled with unique finds. Look for dozens of Buddha statues scattered across the lawn and you'll know you've found the right place.

Three Sisters Gifts (781-424-2022), 4380 Route 6. Open late June to early September, and weekend fall hours. Stop here for unique gifts and other curiosities. Expect Cape inspired T-shirts, pillows, jewelry, wall décor, and more.

CLOTHING **ARTichoke** (774-316-4550; artichokecapecod.com), 4550 Route 6. Powerhouse sisters Katy and Lizzy Escher found their niche after turning their DIY apparel hobby into a brand. Their beachy-boho vibe is apparent right off the bat by the store's turquoise and lime green boutique trimming. Step inside to a small cozy space filled with everything from women and men's clothing to jewelry, art, home and beauty products, and children's apparel. They also have a printing studio in the back where they make their own designs. Their witty prints are very popular among locals and tourists: "Oysters are for lovers," "Oysters & Beer Kind of Girl," "Salty AF," "Shuck Norris," and their

classic "Mutha Shucka," are a few examples.

ANTIQUES **Collector's World** (508-255-3616; collectorsworldcapecod.com), 4100 Route 6. Since 1974, Chris Alex has been selling an eclectic lineup of antiques, gifts, and collectibles like Russian lacquer boxes, scrimshaw, pewter, Civil War artifacts, and toy soldiers. It's one of the wackiest collections on the Cape.

✳ Special Events

July–August: **Eastham Painters' Guild** (easthampaintersguild.com), at the Old Schoolhouse Museum, Route 6 at the Salt Pond Visitor Center. Outdoor art shows are held here most Thursdays and Fridays, as well as over the Memorial Day and Labor Day weekends.

Early to mid-September: **Windmill Weekend** (easthamwindmillweekend .org). This three-day community festival is staged for locals and features a road race, a band concert, an arts-and-crafts show, square dancing, and a parade.

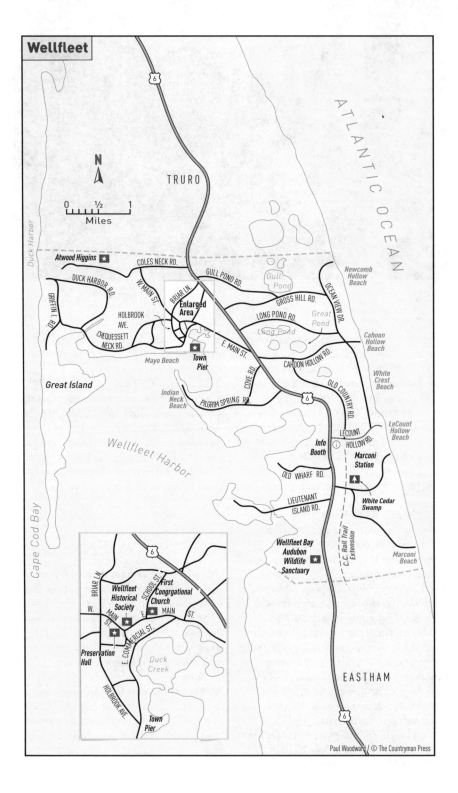

Wellfleet

TRURO

ATLANTIC OCEAN

N

0   ½   1
Miles

Duck Harbor

Atwood Higgins ★

COLES NECK RD.

GULL POND RD.

Gull Pond

Newcomb Hollow Beach

DUCK HARBOR RD.

W. MAIN ST.

BRIAR LN.

Enlarged Area

GROSS HILL RD.

OCEAN VIEW DR.

GRIFFIN I. RD.

HOLBROOK AVE.

LONG POND RD.

Great Pond

CHEQUESSETT NECK RD.

Long Pond

Cahoon Hollow Beach

Mayo Beach

Town Pier ★

E. MAIN ST.

White Crest Beach

Great Island

Indian Neck Beach

COVE RD.

CAHOON HOLLOW RD.

OLD COUNTRY RD.

PILGRIM SPRING RD.

Wellfleet Harbor

LeCount Hollow Beach

LECOUNT HOLLOW RD.

Info Booth ⓘ

Marconi Station ★

Cape Cod Bay

OLD WHARF RD.

White Cedar Swamp

LIEUTENANT ISLAND RD.

C.C. Rail Trail Extension

Marconi Beach

Wellfleet Bay Audubon Wildlife Sanctuary ★

EASTHAM

BRIAR LN.

SCHOOL ST.

Wellfleet Historical Society ★

First Congragational Church ★

W. MAIN ST.

E. MAIN ST.

E. COMMERCIAL ST.

Preservation Hall ★

Duck Creek

HOLBROOK AVE.

Town Pier

WELLFLEET

lthough a whopping 70 percent of Wellfleet is conservation land, the town is perhaps best known as an art stronghold. Wellfleet's two principal thoroughfares, **Main Street** and **Commercial Street**, are dotted with 25 or so **galleries** representing a wide range of art: from souvenir works to images that transcend their media. Many artists and artisans who exhibit here call Wellfleet home, at least for a short time each year, gaining inspiration from pristine landscapes and an unrelenting ocean.

After art, Wellfleet's other main draw is nature. The outstanding **Wellfleet Bay Wildlife Sanctuary** offers practically unparalleled opportunities for observing marine and bird life through guided activities and self-guided walks. A mostly sandy, 8-mile-long **National Seashore trail on Great Island** yields solitude and commanding views of **Wellfleet Bay**. On the **Atlantic side**, dunes and cliffs back broad and uninterrupted beaches. Any of Wellfleet's meandering roads are perfect for cycling, leading you past ponds, salt marshes, heathlands, and scrub pines.

Wellfleet appeals to a distinct crowd, many of whom have returned year after year for decades. In fact, many non-native families—wash-ashores—rent houses here for the entire summer. When shopkeepers and restaurateurs begin dusting off the shelves in early to mid-June, it feels like a real homecoming—old friends catching up over coffee in a café, neighbors renewing relationships as they tend their gardens.

And although Wellfleet is very popular with vacationing Freudian analysts, there's also a notable seasonal contingent of lawyers, professors, and writers. They've all come for the same purpose: to commune with their thoughts, recharge their batteries, and lead a simpler life (albeit only temporarily). Summer folks also venture out of their

SHELLS AND SEAWEED LEESA BURKE

WHERE TO START IN WELLFLEET

Morning:	Dip into Gull Pond or walk the Atlantic shoreline at Newcomb Hollow before parking stickers are needed. Savor an omelet at the Wicked Oyster or a short (or tall) stack of pancakes topped with Vermont maple syrup at the Flying Fish.
Afternoon:	Trek trails, identify birds, and beach yourself on the sand at the Wellfleet Bay Wildlife Sanctuary. Looking for shade? Hike the primordial Atlantic White Cedar Swamp Trail. Then, dine alfresco at Winslow's Tavern or enjoy a cold drink on the Pearl's patio while listening to live music.
Evening:	Enjoy sushi from Mac's or a fishwich from PJ's. Follow up with a movie under the stars at the Wellfleet Drive-In Theatre or a provocative show at Wellfleet Harbor Actors Theater.

cocoons to dine on wonderful food in laid-back settings, to square dance outdoors, and to engage in lively conversation after a particularly spirited performance by the **Wellfleet Harbor Actors Theater**.

Wellfleetians are an independent bunch. Almost 30 percent of the 3,000 year-rounders are self-employed (proverbial Jacks and Jills of all trades), more than in any other Cape town, and almost 20 percent are unemployed in winter. (If you do visit midwinter, you'll find a few warm beds and the frozen bay—a romantic sight on an overcast day.) While most of the town rolls up its shutters from mid-October to mid-May, Wellfleet may also feel like a ghost town on a weekday in mid-June. But on any given summer day, about 17,000 folks will be overnighting in Wellfleet.

Wellfleet was most likely named for a town in England, which, like "our" Wellfleet, was also renowned for its oyster beds. As early as the 17th century, when Wellfleet was still a part of Eastham known as Billingsgate, the primary industries revolved around oyster and cranberry harvesting. Whaling, fishing, and other related industries also flourished until the mid-1800s. And by the 1870s, commercial markets had really opened up for littlenecks, cherrystones, and clams for chowder. Today, with the depletion of natural fish and shellfish stocks, year-round fishermen have turned to aquaculture. Currently more than 100 aquaculturists lease 120 acres of Wellfleet Harbor; you'll see them off **Mayo Beach** at low tide. Shellfish like **quahogs and oysters** are raised from "seed," put out in "protected racks," and tended for 2 to 3 years while they mature. Because as many as 2 million seeds can be put on an acre of land, this is big business. For those looking for fishing charters, though, the harbor and pier are still centers of activity.

GUIDANCE **Wellfleet Chamber of Commerce** (508-349-2510; wellfleetchamber.com), 1410 Route 6. Open spring through fall. The information booth is well marked right off Route 6 in South Wellfleet.

GETTING THERE *By car:* Wellfleet is 50 miles beyond the Cape Cod Canal via Route 6.

By bus: The **Plymouth & Brockton Bus** (508-746-0378; p-b.com) connects Wellfleet with Hyannis and other Cape towns, as well as with Boston's Logan Airport. The bus stops at Bank Street and the Cape Cod National Seashore Marconi Site in South Wellfleet.

OFF THE BEATEN PATH SECRET

Atwood Higgins House (508-255-3421), 269 Bound Brook Island Road, off Pamet Point Road from Route 6. Open for tours late June to late October (by reservation only). The pastoral 5-acre homestead, under the auspices of the CCNS, has a tour that focuses on the architecture and versatility of the 18th-century full Cape that was restored by its early-20th-century owners. Don't miss it. This is one of my favorite places on the entire Cape. Free.

ATWOOD HIGGINS HOUSE KIM GRANT

GETTING AROUND *By shuttle:* **The Flex** (508-385-1430; capecodtransit.org). The Flex offers trips from Provincetown to Harwich with reserved stops. The Flex stops at the Wellfleet Dunkin Donuts off Route 6.

PUBLIC RESTROOMS Seasonally at **Bakers Field** across from **Mayo Beach** (on Kendrick Avenue), as well as at the **Town Pier** and the marina (both at the end of Commercial Street). Year-round at the **Town Hall** on Main Street.

PUBLIC LIBRARY **Wellfleet Public Library** (508-349-0310; wellfleetlibrary.org), 55 West Main Street. Housed within the former Candle Factory, this outstanding library offers more than just books—from children's story hour to readings, screenings, and speakers.

EMERGENCIES **Wellfleet Police Department** (508-349-2100; wellfleetpd.org), 36 Gross Hill Road, or call **911.**

 Medical: **Outer Cape Health Services** (508-349-3131; outercape.org), 3130 Route 6, not an urgent-care facility.

✳ To See

Marconi Wireless Station, CCNS, off Route 6 at the Marconi Area. In 1901 Guglielmo Marconi began construction of the first wireless station on the US mainland, in little

SCENIC DRIVES

Ocean View Drive. Take LeCount Hollow Road to Ocean View (despite its name, it has only limited views) and head back to Route 6 via Gull Pond Road or Long Pond Road. You'll pass heathlands, cliffs, and scrub pines.

Chequessett Neck Road. Cross the dike at Herring River and head to the end of the road for magnificent sunset views. Although there is room for only a few cars at the very end of the road, you can park near the Great Island Trailhead and walk down to the beach (about 15 minutes).

Pilgrim Spring Road. Not to be confused with the Pilgrim Spring Trail in Truro, where the Pilgrims got their first taste of fresh water, this quiet road offers lovely inlet and cove views; at the end of the road, look back toward Wellfleet Harbor.

old Wellfleet. Two years later the first US wireless transatlantic message was transmitted between this station and England: President Roosevelt sent King Edward VII "most cordial greetings and good wishes." (Canada beat the United States in sending a wireless transatlantic message by one month.) A mere 14 years later, the station was closed for wartime security reasons; it was dismantled and abandoned in 1920 because of erosion and the development of alternative technologies. There are few remains today, save the concrete foundation of the transmitter house (which required 25,000 volts to send a message) and sand anchors that held guy wires to the 210-foot towers.

The Cape Cod peninsula is at its narrowest here, and from a well-positioned **observation platform** you can scan the width of it—from Cape Cod Bay, along Blackfish Creek, to the Atlantic Ocean. (See the **Atlantic White Cedar Swamp Trail** under **Green Space.**)

Wellfleet Historical Society Museum (508-349-9157; wellfleethistoricalsociety .com), 266 Main Street. Open June to mid-October. The society has collected photographs, toys, shipwreck detritus, marine artifacts, displays on Marconi and oystering, and household items to illustrate and preserve Wellfleet's past. Join one of their historical walks around town in the summer; meet at museum; $. (Self-guided audio walking tours are also available.)

First Congregational Church of the United Church of Christ (508-349-6877; well fleetchurch.org), 200 Main Street. Although the church was organized in 1721, this Greek Revival meetinghouse dates to 1850. The interior is graced with a brass chandelier, eggshell-yellow walls, curved pews, and a Tiffany-style stained-glass window depicting a 17th-century ship similar to the *Mayflower*. The bell-shaped cupola, by the way, was added in 1879 after a storm destroyed the traditional one. (It was thought that a bell-shaped tower would be sturdier—perhaps it has been.) Select concerts feature a restored Hook and Hastings pipe organ. Check the church's website for myriad special events, including a summer concert series in July and August.

Town clock, First Congregational Church, 200 Main Street. According to the arbiter of strange superlatives, *Ripley's Believe It or Not*, this is the "only town clock in the world that strikes ship's time." Listen for the following chimes and try to figure out what time it is for yourself: Two bells distinguish 1, 5, and 9 o'clock; six bells signify 3, 7, and 11 o'clock; eight bells toll for 4, 8, and 12 o'clock. To make matters even more interesting, adding one chime to the corresponding even hours signifies the half hours. (After all these years of hanging out in Wellfleet, I still double-check my cell phone!)

Preservation Hall (508-349-1800; wellfleetpreservationhall.org), 335 Main Street. On the occasion of the country's 1976 bicentennial, two troubadours expressed their thanks to the town after a long celebration by donating the handsome painted carvings attached to the doors. More recently, the town purchased the former church and rechristened it as a nonprofit cultural center in the late 2000s. After years of renovations, the hall now houses live concerts, film screenings, art exhibitions, poetry readings, Vegas nights, oyster and strawberry festivals, and garden tours. A life-sized blue heron, created by local sculptor Del Filardi and symbolizing good luck, now proudly tops the reinstalled cupola.

✷ To Do

BICYCLING & RENTALS The **Cape Cod Rail Trail** offers 25 miles of paved road for your biking pleasure. The trail route starts in Wellfleet and passes through the towns of Eastham, Orleans, Brewster, Harwich, Dennis, and Yarmouth.

Nauset Bike Trail, a 1.6-mile (one-way) trail connects with the Cape Cod Rail Trail and runs from the Salt Pond Visitor Center across Nauset Marsh via a boardwalk to Coast Guard Beach. The trail passes large stands of thin, tall black locust trees not native to the area—they were introduced to return nitrogen to the soil after over farming.

You can rent bicycles and equipment at **Wellfleet Bike Rentals** (508-349-1316; wellfleetbikerentals.com), 464 Route 6; **Idle Times Bike Shop** (508-349-9161; idletimesbikes.com), 2616 Route 6; or the **Little Capistrano Bike Shop** (508-255-6515; littlecapistranobikeshop.com), 1446 Route 6. These shops also provide a free and very detailed trail map.

BOAT EXCURSIONS & RENTALS **Wellfleet Marine Corp.** (508-349-6417; wellfleet marine.com), 25 Holbrook Ave. This family-run business has Stur-Dee Cat sailboats and Boston Whalers for hourly or daily rental at the town pier and marina. They also offer a full-service boatyard with bait and tackle, a retail shop, and a fish market.

WELLFLEET PIER KATY WARD

WICKED WELLFLEET

Wellfleet Harbor & Marina (508-349-0320; wellfleet-ma.gov), 255 Commercial Street, Town Pier. Even before the first settlers arrived, Wellfleet Harbor was known for its abundance of fish and oysters, and, by the early 1700s, whaling had become a thriving industry, with a fleet of ships that cruised as far as the coast of Africa. This brought great wealth to the town, but all of this prosperity was brought to a sudden halt during the American Revolution when the British blockade condemned ships of the fleet to rot at their moorings. After the war, a lack of capital to replace the great whaling fleet ended Wellfleet's glory as a whaling port.

By the turn of the 19th century, fishing began to flourish, and Wellfleet became one of the leading fishing ports in the state. At the same time the local shell fishermen were shipping in oysters from Buzzards Bay, Connecticut, and the Chesapeake, planting them in the harbor to pick up the famous Wellfleet flavor and reharvesting them for the Boston market. By the 1900s, the mackerel fishery began to decline, but the shellfish industry remained active. It was no longer profitable to transplant oysters in large quantities, as the production of native oysters had gradually increased. The harvests of oyster, quahogs, soft-shelled clams, bay scallops, and sea clams have fluctuated widely from year to year but on the average have remained an important part of the town's economy. Today, Wellfleet's shellfish industry brings in a whopping $6.3 million annually.

WELLFLEET HARBOR AT SUNSET KATY WARD

FISHING Procure freshwater and saltwater fishing licenses and regulations online at mass.gov/eea/agencies/dfg/licensing.

Big game: See *Fishing* under Truro and Provincetown for sportfishing charters.

On Shore: Try your luck surf casting early in the morning or at night at the following Atlantic beaches: Newcomb Hollow, White Crest, and LeCount Hollow, or at Duck Harbor on the bayside.

Freshwater: Freshwater fishing holes include Great Pond, Gull Pond, and Long Pond (see also under **Green Space**).

Shellfish: Permits are required for the taking of oysters, clams, and quahogs. To purchase a recreational license, contact the Wellfleet Shellfish Department in Town Hall (508-349-0325; wellfleet-ma.gov), 300 Main Street.

FOR FAMILIES **Summer recreation programs** (508-349-0314; wellfleetma.org), Baker's Field and Gull Pond, are held early July to mid-August. Sports, arts and crafts, swimming lessons, yoga on the beach, tennis courts, and a skateboard park.

GOLF **Chequessett Yacht & Country Club** (508-349-3704; cycc.net), 680 Chequessett Neck Road. Open April through October. This nine-hole, par-35 course offers beautiful views of Wellfleet Harbor.

KAYAKS & PADDLEBOARDS **Fun Seekers** (774-722-0764; funseekers.org), 2480 Old Kings Highway. Open mid-May to September. Private and group surfing lessons for people of all ages and experience levels are offered here. They also give guided lessons in kiteboarding, windsurfing, and stand-up paddleboard.

Jack's Boat Rentals (508-349-9808; jacksboatrental.com), 2616 Route 6 near Cahoon Hollow Road. Open late June to early September. This friendly outfit rents

CAPE COD CATAMARAN KATY WARD

SHARK AWARENESS

Did you know there is a foolproof way to find out if sharks are in the water? *Follow carefully now:*

Step 1: Acquire a silver spoon, or any spoon from the kitchen drawer will do.

Step 2: Bring the silver spoon with you to the beach. Walk down to the shoreline with spoon in hand and gather just the tiniest bit of ocean water.

Step 3: Gently take a sip from the spoon.

Step 4: If it tastes salty, there are sharks in the water.

All jokes aside, Cape Cod has sharks. Great white sharks, blue sharks, thresher sharks, dogfish (also a shark), and even Orcas—a pod was spotted in Chatham just recently.

There's no skirting around the fact that Cape Cod has recently become a hotspot for great white shark activity. If you're wondering why the sudden influx, most people will agree it's thanks to our extremely dense seal population. What to do about it is another topic of debate. Some people call for culling (or killing) of seals and/or sharks; some believe nature will run its course (mostly the surfers, surprisingly); others are hopeful that technology will keep our beaches safe. But as of this edition, no compromise or solution has been found.

In the meantime, towns have made conscious efforts to stock the beaches and their lifeguards with Stop the Bleed Kits and other lifesaving materials (most beaches also have a civilian bleed kit in the event there is no lifeguard on duty), and remote service-less beaches now have call boxes. The need for better emergency access became apparent after a series of encounters in 2018, which included one fatality.

My advice is: Don't let it ruin your vacation.

KATY WARD

canoes, pedal boats, sea cycles, surf bikes, kayaks, and Sunfish. If you want to paddle somewhere besides Gull Pond, pick up a boat at the shop (508-349-9808) on Route 6.

The Wellfleet Bay Wildlife Sanctuary (508-349-2615; massaudubon.org) sponsors numerous activities, including kayak trips around Great Island, Pochet Island, Lieutenants Island, Little Sipson Island, and Gull Pond. Call to register for a trip. $$$$+.

SAILING **Chequessett Yacht & Country Club** (508-349-3704; cycc.net), 680 Chequessett Neck Road, offers junior and adult sailing late June to late August. Group instruction by the week for youths; individual instruction by the hour. Call ahead for availability.

Cape Cod Catamaran (508-349-3816; capecodcatamaran.com), 255 Commercial Street. Open June through early October. Book a charter sail around Wellfleet Harbor with Captain Keith on the *Discovery*. On deck there is comfortable seating for up to six passengers around the helm with a Bimini top providing shade. The *Discovery* has a

The beaches are still beautiful and the water is still refreshing—just play it a little safer than you might have in the past. Don't go in deep, don't play or swim near seals, stay within the presence of others, and don't go surfing alone. Listen to the lifeguards and look for the waving purple flag signaling "shark." I also recommend downloading the Atlantic White Shark Conservancy's mobile app, Sharktivity, which will send you notifications on temporary and permanent beach closures due to shark sightings. While the Atlantic is a common place for great white sightings (specifically Truro and Wellfleet, but also Province-town, Eastham, Orleans, and Chatham), the bayside isn't shark-free either. Also remember, sharks do not care for humans! Most bites are accidental.

And if none of my suggestions ease your worries about coming in contact with one of these massive ocean predators, luckily you have this guidebook that is chock-full of alternative activities!

A SINGLE ROSE RESTS ON THE SHORELINE FOLLOWING A MEMORIAL FOR 26-YEAR-OLD ARTHUR MEDICI, WHO DIED AFTER BEING BITTEN BY A GREAT WHITE SHARK AT NEWCOMB HOLLOW BEACH, WELLFLEET IN 2018 KATY WARD

full galley and head (bathroom) with showers for rinsing off after a salty swim. Glide through the waters effortlessly, thanks to the two-hull design and the captain's expertise (over 30 years working the waters on Cape Cod). Choose from a 4-hour morning or afternoon cruise, a 2-hour sunset cruise, or a private charter. $$$$+.

Postcard Harbor Tours (508-214-0176; postcardharbortours.com), 65 Cannon Hill Road, but trips depart from the Wellfleet Pier. Open June to October. Join Captain John Wolf on his traditional catboat, *Gala VI*, for a picturesque sail across the harbor.

TENNIS Practice your front- and backstroke at the town courts near **Mayo Beach**.

Oliver's Red Clay Tennis Courts (508-349-3330; oliversredclaytennis.com), 2183 Route 6. Open June through September. Rent these seven courts by the hour. Lessons available, too. $$$.

Chequessett Yacht & Country Club (508-349-3704; cycc.net), 680 Chequessett Neck Road. Open March through November. Five hard courts are available to the public. $$.

Wellfleet Bay Wildlife Sanctuary (508-349-2615; massaudubon.org), 291 Route 6. This is one of my Top 10 places on Cape Cod. With almost 1,100 acres of pine, moors, freshwater ponds, tidal creeks, salt marsh, and beach, the Audubon sanctuary is one of New England's most active. Despite that, you'll appreciate the relative lack of human presence after a day of gallery hopping and sunbathing. ✶

Three trails total more than 5 miles: Silver Spring Trail, a lovely, wooded walking trail alongside a long pond; Goose Pond Trail (an all-person accessible trail), past ponds, woodlands, a marsh, and heathland (a boardwalk leads to the bay from here); and Bay View Trail.

The sanctuary also offers a steady stream of activities throughout the summer (plenty year-round, for that matter): canoe trips, family seashore hikes, evening natural history talks, birding expeditions, and trips to Monomoy Island.

Call about their 90-minute seal cruises off the waters of Chatham, and don't miss one if your schedule jives with theirs. They also have a 2-hour Sea Bird and Seal Cruise in late fall, which goes out on an open commercial fishing vessel. On-board naturalists will educate you about the habits and habitats of harbor and gray seals. Reservations required.

Wellfleet Bay Wildlife Sanctuary Natural History Day Camps are offered June through August. Geared toward children,

WELLFLEET BAY WILDLIFE SANCTUARY   KIM GRANT

these excellent weeklong programs are designed to "expand curiosity about and respect for the environment through hands-on outdoor experiences . . . and to develop skill in discovering the natural world using the principles of scientific inquiry." Indeed.

The sanctuary's summertime Adult Field School incorporates multiday, hands-on courses. Topics include Cape Cod natural history, ornithology, marine life, nature photography, local endangered habitats, and sketching in the field. Instruction is expert.

Before departing, don't miss the eco-friendly Esther Underwood Johnson Nature Center, and especially don't miss the environmentally friendly composting toilets, which save 100,000 gallons of water per season. It's a beautiful example of green architecture, with solar heating and graywater planter beds. Exhibits feature Cape Cod natural history as well as two 700-gallon aquariums displaying life beneath the water of salt marshes and tidal pools. Trails are free to members, $ nonmembers. Members may tent in the wooded natural setting (call for fees and reservations).

✶ Green Space

BEACHES Parking permits for town beaches can be purchased online or at the Beach Sticker Booth (508-349-9818) on the Town Pier from July to early September. CCNS permits are available upon beach entrance and are valid at all six federally protected beaches (508-255-3421; www.nps.gov/caco/planyourvisit/fees).

The four popular Atlantic beaches include **Newcomb Hollow, Cahoon Hollow, White Crest,** and **Lecount Hollow.** Backed by steep dunes, these sandy coastal beaches offer refreshing cold water, wide sandy banks, and idyllic surfing conditions. Take the steep dune path down to the shoreline and claim your spot. As intriguing as the steep dunes might be to children (and some adults), stay on the marked paths and do not climb the dunes—that amplifies erosion. Newcomb and White Crest have ample parking, but get there early because it fills up fast. (White Crest is also a favorite spot for hang gliders.) Cahoon Hollow's parking lot is usually full by 9 a.m., thanks to the popular Beachcomber restaurant (see **The Beachcomber** under *Eating Out*). All beaches are equipped with lifeguards, restrooms, and an emergency call box—there's very little cell service. Parking permits are required from mid-May to September (Beachcomber patrons get a parking pass with entrance to the restaurant.)

MARCONI BEACH

Fun Fact: In late January 2008, after a fierce midwinter storm, a visitor washed ashore at Newcomb Hollow Beach: a mid- to late-19th-century schooner that had shipwrecked who knows when and had taken down who knows how many sailors with it (if

NEWCOMB HOLLOW BEACH KATY WARD

SWAMP THING

tlantic White Cedar Swamp Trail, CCNS, Marconi Area. One of my favorite year-round trails on the Outer Cape. The swamp is navigable by boardwalk, and then it traverses into quiet woodlands and sandy shoals. The 1.2-mile loop has some stairs, making the 1-hour hike moderately difficult—be careful not to stray off the boardwalk (the swamp is 24 feet deep with peat in some areas). A stunted forest offers hikers coverage from the blazing sun or harsh winter winds. The trail is home to some of the last remaining strands of white cedar on the Cape, hence its name. Prized by settlers for its light weight and ease of handling, cedar wood became a popular and sought-out material. Today, cedar struggles to repair itself from overuse and continues to be choked out by other trees such as pine and red maple. But another rare plant is making a comeback: the Lady's Slipper, also known as the Moccasin Flower (named after its resemblance to a delicate pair of feminine slippers) continues to bloom in this area. If you are lucky enough to spot one, admire it from a distance, because a picked lady's slipper will not rejuvenate itself. The orchid has a less than 5 percent transplant success rate, making it "off limits" to pickers and diggers. While some species of the lady's slipper are listed as endangered in New England, others, such as the pink lady's slipper are listed as a "special concern" under the Native Plant Protection Act. Once established, lady's slipper will propagate on its own and live for many years if left undisturbed.

KATY WARD

KATY WARD

any). The beached keel and ribs, upright in the sand, looked like the ribs of a 50-foot whale, and it captured the attention of locals and visitors from hundreds of miles away. The National Park Service suggested the ship was the largest to wash ashore in 15 years; another marine specialist suggested it could have been the *Logan*, a coal barge wrecked in 1920. What is known for sure is that 18 ships failed to navigate the treacherous shifting sand bars and shoals near the Cahoon Hollow Lifesaving Station between 1800 and 1927.

Marconi Beach, CCNS, on the Atlantic. A boardwalk and steep staircase (repeatedly replaced after winter storms) lead to this long and narrow beach. Lifeguards, outdoor showers, and changing facilities are available from mid-May to September. Parking permit valid all day at any CCNS beach with no charge after 4 p.m.

Mayo Beach, Kendrick Avenue. The water is calm and warm here, but it's certainly not my top pick when it comes to beaches. Settled next to the Wellfleet Harbor Pier, it only offers pleasant swimming around high tide, and even then it can get a bit mucky. On the upside: free parking and great sunset views. At low tide, you will see shellfishermen tending to their grants (farms), which are defined by yellow buoys.

Other beaches include: **Maquire Landing** off Ocean View Drive on the Atlantic Ocean; **Burton Baker Beach** (the only place in town where sailboarding is permitted) and **Indian Neck Beach,** both off Pilgrim Spring Road on the bayside; and **Powers Landing** and **Duck Harbor**, both off Chequessett Neck Road, also bayside.

PONDS **Great Pond, Long Pond**, and **Gull Pond** offer freshwater swimming. If you're staying at an inn or cottage, you'll be eligible for the requisite parking sticker (available on the Town Pier; 508-349-9818). Swimming may be closed periodically in the summer due to bacteria (especially after hot days). Lifeguards available at all ponds.

WALKS **Great Island Trail**, CCNS, off Chequessett Neck Road. About 8 miles roundtrip, this trail is relatively flat, but soft sand makes for a challenging four-hour roundtrip trek. Walk at low tide, when the sand is firmer. (Besides, Jeremy Point, the tip of

UNCLE TIM'S BRIDGE MARCIA DUGGAN/CAPECODSOUL

land farthest out to sea, is covered at high tide.) You'll be rewarded with scant human presence and stunning scenery. Great for birders; best on a sunny spring day or a crisp autumn one. Bring plenty of water and sunscreen.

This area was once an island, hence its name. Over time, Cape Cod Bay currents deposited sandbars that eventually connected it to the mainland. Long ago, Great Island was home to various commercial enterprises—oystering, cranberry harvesting, and shore whaling—and the land was dotted with lookout towers used to spot whales. There was even a local watering hole and overnight hostelry, the Great Island Tavern, built in 1690 and used until about 1740. But as shore whaling died, so did the Great Island community. By 1800 the island was deserted and deforested. (Pines have been planted in an effort to keep erosion under control.)

Uncle Tim's Bridge, East Commercial Street. The often-photographed wooden footbridge connects Commercial Street to a small wooded island, crossing a tidal creek (Duck Creek) and marshland. Short, sandy trails circle the island.

Wellfleet Conservation Trust (508-349-2162; wellfleetconservationtrust.org) is constantly purchasing and opening up new trails and tracts of land—including Bayberry Hill, Fox Island Marsh and Pilgrim Spring Woodlands, and Box Turtle Woods. The easiest thing to do is go online and print trail maps.

See "Trails, Birds, Seals & Classes" on page 284.

✳ Lodging

BED-AND-BREAKFASTS The Wagner at Duck Creek (508-349-9333; thewagner atduckcreek.com), 70 Main Street. This 27-room boutique hotel sits on a historic property overlooking the marsh. The legacy of long ownership began with The Holiday House (1930s to 1980), and subsequently became The Inn at Duck Creeke (1980 to 2015) until today's new ownership. Prior to offering guest accommodations, the property operated as a true Captain's house and was the Price family residence. Buildings were added to the property at different points in time, with the most historic dating back to the 1700s. $$–$$$$.

COTTAGES Surf Side Cottages (508-349-3959; surfsidecottages.com), 45 Ocean View Drive. Open early April through November. These 1950s-style housekeeping cottages are within a minute's walk of the dunes and ocean. Larger cottages have a roof deck; each has a screened-in porch (with the classic wooden-door slamming sound), a woodburning fireplace, and a private outdoor shower. Modern kitchens, knotty-pine paneling, and tasteful rattan furnishings are the norm. Bring sheets and towels, and leave the cottage clean and ready for the next tenants. Reserve early. $$–$$$.

🏄 **The Even'tide** (508-349-3410; eventidemotel.com), 650 Route 6. Open late April to early September. These nine cottages, which rent weekly, are a cut above. Wooded and set back from Route 6, the complex has a nice children's play area, a big heated indoor pool, an exercise room, a billiard table, mini-golf, shuffleboard, table tennis, badminton, horseshoes, basketball, direct access to the rail trail, and a walking trail to Marconi Beach. Phew! Is that enough for you? All cottages have fully tiled bathrooms and full kitchens (except Tern). They also have some above-average motel rooms and suites that rent nightly, early May to mid-October. Inquire about the Kingfisher House, a five-bedroom place that rents weekly.

See also **Maurice's Campground** under *Campgrounds*.

MOTELS & HOTELS Wellfleet Motel (508-349-3535; wellfleetmotel.com), 170 US Route 6. Open mid-April through October. It may not look like much from the highway, but this motel is a score.

SURF SIDE COTTAGES KIM GRANT

This family-owned motel offers comfortable rooms (clean and spacious with soft cozy bedding) at reasonable prices. Amenities include both indoor and outdoor saltwater pools, a Jacuzzi and barbecue area, free parking and Wi-Fi, and an on-site cafe with a cocktail lounge and smoothie bar. It's within rock-throwing distance of the Cape Cod Rail Trail and Wellfleet Drive-In Theatre and less than a half-mile from the Wellfleet Bay Wildlife Sanctuary. Great for families with kids. $$–$$$.

CAMPGROUNDS **Wellfleet Hollow State Campground** (508-349-3007; or 877-422-6762 for reservations; reserve america.com), 180 Old County Road. Open late May to September. Forever remembered as Paine's Campground, the family-owned business was sold to the state Department of Conservation & Recreation in 2017. The 28-acre campground, with 155 campsites reopened under new management in May 2019. It will be run similarly to other state-owned campgrounds, such as Nickerson State Park in Brewster. $–$$.

Maurice's Campground (508-349-2029; mauricescampground.com) 80 Route 6. Open late May to mid-October. This campground first established its roots in 1949 with only seven cabins and four cottages. Today, Maurice's has about 220 wooded sites for tents and trailers, as well as cottages, cabins, and a duplex

WELLFLEET PIER KATY WARD

cabin that can sleep up to six people. Direct access to the Cape Cod Rail Trail is a real plus for folks. $–$$.

✻ Where to Eat

Wellfleet oysters are renowned: legend has it that England's Queen Victoria served them at her state dinners (no others would do). According to aficionados, Wellfleet oysters taste better when harvested from the cooler waters in the off-season, but you'll have little choice if you vacation in July or August: order them anyway. Wellfleet is also known for its hard-shell quahog and steamer clams. In fact, these waters yield millions of dollars' worth of shellfish annually.

DINING OUT **Ceraldi** (508-237-9811; ceraldicapecod.com), 15 Kendrick Avenue. Open D, May to mid-October. My biggest regret for this edition was not being able to indulge in Ceraldi's seven-course menu. Dining at the chef's table with an open kitchen allows Chef Michael to interact with his guests and servers and to share stories about local food purveyors and wine subtleties.

"Amazing" is the most whispered adjective when folks try to describe Ceraldi. $$$$+.

Winslow's Tavern (508-349-6450; winslowstavern.com) 316 Main Street. Open L, D, mid-May through October. This upscale bistro and tavern (resurrected in the mid-2000s) features New England classics, fresh fish, and imaginative specials. It's easy on the palate and the wallet. Start with one of three various oyster preparations: on the half shell (raw) with a Pernod-cucumber mignonette, broiled with basil pesto (my favorite), or roasted with a rosemary lemon butter, chive butter, or Tabasco lime butter. Move on to local mussels bathed in a curry, Riesling, and crème fraîche broth; or the grilled chicken paillard with local baby arugula and mixed cherry tomatoes. This is just lunch; don't get me started on the dinner menu. Come early for a drink upstairs in the cozy bar or dessert and wine. $$–$$$$.

EATING OUT **Wicked Oyster** (508-349-3455; thewickedo.com), 50 Main Street. Open B, D, mid-January to late November, and L in summer only. This upscale casual bistro lives up to its name. For

WINSLOW'S TAVERN KIM GRANT

BEACHCOMBIN'

Built in 1897, the 'Comber was one of nine federally constructed and staffed lifesaving stations on Cape Cod. In 1953, Russell Gallagher, who summered as a child at Cahoon Hollow Beach, bought the station and converted it into an inn. He dubbed it The Beachcomber after finding driftwood and nautical bric-and-brac that was "combed" off the beach. In 1978 he sold the business to its current owners, Todd LeBart and Hugh Dunbar. Luckily for them, the property fell under a grandfather clause when President John F. Kennedy created the Cape Cod National Seashore in 1960 and purchased over 43,500 acres of land along the Atlantic-Eastern Oceanside, spreading through the towns of Provincetown, Truro, Wellfleet, Eastham, Orleans, and Chatham. Thanks to the clause, the Beachcomber was (and still is) allowed to remain within the Seashore as a privately held commercial property. In the daytime, the 'Comber overlooks a steep dune that leads to the popular Cahoon Hollow Beach. Though this spot was a favorite in my 20s, I now find it a bit crowded during high summer season. Take a reprieve from the sun and trek up the dune (yes, be sure to pace yourself and take a big breath, it's a hike) and head to the outside cabana-style bar for a raw bar snack and a cold drink. At night, the 'Comber turns into a special concert venue with popular returning artists such as G. Love, Dub Apocalypse, the Spampinato Brothers, Donovan Frankenrieter, and DJ Bud E Green (21+ only after 9 p.m.). Depending on the type of music, the age of the crowd will vary, but generally there is a very mixed crowd. A must-see on your vacation itinerary!

One other note: There is very little to NO cellphone service! And if you're curious what the beach crowd or waves look like (for all you surfers out there), check the beach camera link on thebeachcomber.com.

breakfast, try the "wicked" three-egg omelet and trust the chef's daily preparation. For dinner, order the pan-roasted cod served over a light paprika-cream broth with littlenecks, sunchokes, leeks, and bacon. Not in the mood for seafood? Try the seared duck breast with mushroom and duck bacon gratin. Either way you will be pleased. $$–$$$$.

Moby Dick's (508-349-9795; mobys .com), 3225 Route 6. Open L, D, mid-May through mid-October. This place is always packed, and for good reason. Order off the blackboard menu and take a seat downstairs, surrounded by weathered nautical paraphernalia, or at a picnic table on the open upper level. Some say they have the best lobster roll on the Cape: big hunks of tail and claw meat mixed with a hint of mayo on a soft buttered bun. Another popular feature is that you can BYOB (or wine). $$–$$$$.

The Pearl (508-349-2999; wellfleet pearl.com), 250 Commercial Street. Open L, D, mid-May to mid-October. Hats off to the Pearl for having one of the most spirited happy hours I can remember. Sip on a handcrafted drink to the sound of local musicians, or request a table with your choice of indoor-outdoor seating on multilevel decks. Did I mention the stunning panoramic view of the harbor, town pier, Mayo Beach, and Great Island? $$–$$$$.

The Well Tavern + Kitchen (508-214-0038; thewelltavernandkitchen.com), 70 Main Street. Open D, year-round. One of the few places open year-round in Wellfleet, and we locals are happy about it! The Well, as it's nicknamed, offers upscale tavern food. Try the tavern's mac and cheese—a creamy cheese blend with bacon, spinach, and cracker crumbs. Or snack on one of their signature flatbreads or blackened cod fish tacos. In the summer months (and on some winter weekends), the Well has live music. Check the website for a list of performers and times. $–$$$$.

Mac's Shack (508-349-6333; macs seafood.com), 91 Commercial Street.

Open D, May to mid-October. If you want to know the definition of summer, visit Mac's Shack. As some people have said to me, "it's the kind of food that makes you happy." Beyond the seashell-crushed parking lot sit a lively outdoor bar and raw bar with limited stool seating. Or you can put your name down for a seat at the inside sushi bar and watch them work their magic. See also **Mac's on the Pier.**

The Flying Fish (508-349-7292; flyingfishwellfleet.com) 29 Briar Lane. Open B, L, D, mid-May to mid-October. Owners Sarah Robin and Anthony "Jelly" Hill have created a funky favorite in Wellfleet. The cherry wood bar (built by Sarah's woodworking father) and the outdoor patio make it a favorite for locals and tourists alike. Jelly offers everything from pizza (he really knows what he's doing) to seafood dishes (be sure to try one of his Caribbean inspired plates) to burgers and steaks. If visiting in July or August, stop by for local entertainment on the deck. Check the website for a list of performing artists. $–$$$$.

Van Rensselaer's (508-349-2127; vanrensselaers.com), 1019 Route 6. Open B, weekends only; D, early April to late October. A popular family style restaurant, I recommend this place for people with children, seniors, and anyone with a large appetite. In addition to the early bird dinner specials and all-you-can-eat breakfast buffet, VR's offers a diverse menu that will surely satisfy everyone's needs, including those customers with pickier palates. $$–$$$$.

Bookstore & Restaurant (508-349-3154; wellfleetoyster.com), 50 Kendrick Avenue. Open B, weekends only; L, D, mid-February to late December. Try to steal a patio table on the outside deck for drinks and apps with friends, but consider having dinner elsewhere. $$–$$$.

PJ's Family Restaurant (508-349-2126; pjscapecod.com), 2616 Route 6. Open L, D, mid-May to mid-October. My all-time favorite fast-food seafood joint in Wellfleet. Start with a cup of the homemade lobster chowder, filled to the brim with big hunks of lobster meat. Follow up with a fried cod or haddock sandwich (the cod is the best) or share a seafood platter: whole belly clams, scallops, shrimp, and fish with fries—it's more than enough to stop the hungries. Top it all off with a root beer float, milkshake, or soft-serve cone. Both indoor and outdoor seating available; expect some wait time. $–$$.

Mac's on the Pier (508-349-9611; macsseafood.com), 265 Commercial Street on Town Pier. Open L, D, mid-May through September. Order at the window and scout for an empty picnic table or sandy spot on the beach. This fast-food joint offers everything from hot dogs and burgers to sushi, burritos, sandwiches, and more. $–$$$.

The Beachcomber (508-349-6055; thebeachcomber.com), 1120 Cahoon Hollow Road. Open L, D, mid-May through early September. If you've never heard of the Beachcomber, then you must be living under a rock. This historic Oceanside restaurant, bar, and prime jam spot has received numerous awards. The 'Comber serves surprisingly large and fresh platters of fried oysters, clams, fish, and scallops. The tuna sashimi and seaweed salad at the raw bar are also dynamite, and the rolls and wraps are perfect for taking down to the beach. Be sure to try the famous Goombay Smash, but don't be deceived, this bad boy contains hefty amounts of Cruzan rums (yes, plural) and juices, topped with a Myers float (see also "Beachcombin'" on page 291). $–$$$.

SWEET TREATS & COFFEE **PB Boulangerie Bistro** (508-349-1600; pbboulangeriebistro.com), 15 Lecount Hollow Road. Open Tuesday through Sunday; with D on Wednesday through Sunday. A busy bakery so come prepared to wait in line. PB offers an array of French pastries (the mille-feuille and cream puff are my two guilty pleasures), as well as freshly baked breads and coffee. If you're lucky enough to snag a croquette monsieur before they sell out,

OPEN-AIR SCREEN WITH STARS

WELLFLEET DRIVE-IN   KIM GRANT

Wellfleet Drive-In (508-349-7176; 508-349-2450 to speak to a human being; wellfleetdrivein.com), Route 6. Shows early May to early September. One of the last holdouts of a vanishing American pastime, this drive-in has lured patrons since 1957, when the number of US drive-ins peaked at 4,000. Today there are fewer than 800 left—only a handful in New England, and no others on the Cape. Hence, it is a treasured local institution. Late owner John Jentz, a former engineering professor at MIT, designed the 100-by-44-foot screen with his MIT pals; perhaps that's why it's withstood hurricanes with winds up to 135 mph. Double features are shown nightly at dusk. Movies change once a week, and there's a play area behind the reasonably priced Dairy Bar & Grill. Films are generally family-oriented.

then it's your lucky day; they are unbelievably yummy (and fattening, but you're on vacation after all, right?). PB also serves a bistro dinner, which I've heard is great, but wasn't impressed the few times I went. $$–$$$$.

The Chocolate Sparrow (508-349-1333; hotchocolatesparrow.com), 326 Main Street. Open mid-June to early September. The closest you will get to an old-school penny candy store. The Chocolate Sparrow opened in 1990 and continues its tradition of hand-dipped delicious chocolates. $.

The Flying Fish offers Beanstock coffee, scones, muffins, and a full breakfast menu. See under Where to Eat.

MARKETS Catch of the Day (508-349-9090; wellfleetcatch.com), 975 Route 6. Open L, D, mid-April to late October. This seafood market and no-frills eatery features fresh catch (grilled or blackened); buckets of local shellfish; and daily specials like fish tacos, fisherman's stew, or baked Chatham scrod. Bring it to the beach, cook it at home, or dine on their patio.

Hatch's Fish Market (508-349-2810; hatchsfishmarket.com), 310 Main Street. Open daily mid-May to late September. Family-owned and -operated for over 50 years, this tiny shack of a market is one of the best. The selection of fish, lobsters,

BOULANGERIE BISTRO   KIM GRANT

HATCH'S FISH MARKET KATY WARD

and shellfish is always outstanding, but it's the smoked fish and pâté that gets my mouth drooling every time. Hatch's also offers an abundance of local fruits, vegetables, breads, and herbs.

Wellfleet Market Place (508-349-3156), 295 Main Street. Open daily year-round. This quaint and centrally located downtown market offers premade items like macaroni and chicken salad, meats, vegetables, wine, and beer, as well as having a full-service deli.

See also *Farms* under **Selective Shopping.**

✳ Entertainment

Wellfleet Harbor Actors Theater (508-349-9428; what.org), 2357 Old Route 6 Route. Open from mid-March to November. Offers matinees and kids' shows as well as a half-price "student rush" just prior to curtain time. $$–$$$$.

Harbor Stage Company (508-514-1763; harborstage.org), 1 Kendrick Avenue. This intimate (90-seat) local landmark produces original and classic theater on the edge of the harbor. It's

decidedly Wellfleet and I highly recommend treating yourself to a performance here. $$–$$$.

Square dancing at the Town Pier. On Wednesday evening in July and August, the waterfront takes on a different tone. Dancing begins at 7 p.m. and the steps get progressively more difficult until 9 p.m. or so. Though I've never tried my footing here, I've been told it's a blast.

Wellfleet Cinemas & Drive-In Theatre (508-349-7176; wellfleetdrivein.com), 51 Route 6. Cinemas open year-round, drive-in open mid-May to October. Check online to see what shows are playing. See "Open-Air Screen with Stars" on page 293. $–$$.

✳ Selective Shopping

ARTISANS Narrow Land Pottery (508-349-6308; narrowlandpottery.com), 2603 Route 6, adjacent to the service station. Joe McCaffery, who studied at the School of the Museum of Fine Arts in Boston, is a master at throwing pots, vases, mugs, lamp bases, and plates. His glazes, porcelain, and stoneware come in a variety of colors.

BOOKSTORES Herridge Books (508-349-1323), 140 Main Street. Used books covering a wide range of subjects.

CLOTHING Sickday (508-214-4158; sickday.cc), 3 West Main Street. Do you have a teenager? This shop offers an array of swim and beach apparel, clothing, hats, sunglasses, and more. You will get an A+ for being cool but a D in frugal shopping. Be prepared to spend money. $$$–$$$$+.

FARMS Wellfleet Farmers' Market (wellfleetfarmersmarket.com), 200 Main Street, every Wednesday from mid-May to mid-October.

GALLERIES Cherry Stone Gallery (508-246-5486; cherrystonegallery.com), 70

SHUCKIN' AWESOME

Wellfleet OysterFest (508-349-3499; wellfleetspat.org; Shellfish Promotion and Tasting—SPAT—are the event promoters), Main Street. This two-day annual festival in mid-October celebrates the deep-rooted shellfishing traditions in Wellfleet. Since its inception, OysterFest has outrageously grown in size. The festival kicks off the weekend after Columbus Day, rain or shine, bringing in over 50,000 people to the center of downtown Wellfleet. You know you're in the right spot when you see T-shirts sporting, "Shuck You," "Shuck Norris," or "Mutha Shucka" (yes, I am guilty of owning this one—shout out to the Artichoke girls for these clever cottons; see Selective Shopping in Eastham). Tickets for OysterFest are $10 per day. Food, retail, and classes are priced individually. Taste-test your favorite oysters by sampling from numerous vendors, or stand in line for local beer and wine. Street corn, fried lobster on a stick, chowder, and stuffed clams are a few vendor options available. If I had to pick a favorite part of OysterFest (in addition to the food, beer, friends, and fun), it would be the highly anticipated Oyster Shuck-Off. Whoever shucks 24 oysters as quickly and cleanly as possible takes the title of Shuck-Off champion. Controversial rulings have been known to fire up a crowd of thousands, including devastating time penalties for broken shells, massacred oysters, and blood shed from slashed fingers. The Shuck-Off takes place on the Main Stage behind Town Hall with preliminaries held on Saturday and the finals on Sunday. The winning Shucker earns $1,000 cash and qualifies to compete in the National US Oyster Shucking Championship Contest in St. Mary's County, Maryland. The Shuck-Off is only open to professional shuckers—shellfishermen, raw bar shuckers, restaurant chefs, or others who regularly open oysters. Like most small-town events, parking can be an issue. Try the town beach lot ($10 per car) with frequent shuttle service to town center from 9:30 a.m. until 5:30 p.m. Free parking with walking access to OysterFest is also located at the Wellfleet Elementary School on Lawrence Road, at the Cove Corner on Route 6 and the Mayo Beach Parking Area. If you park illegally, be prepared for a ticket.

OYSTERFEST MICHELA CAREW-MURPHY

WELLFLEET FLEA MARKET KIM GRANT

East Commercial Street. Open daily (except Sundays) from June to September. Celebrating over 48 years, this long-established gallery carries works by Abbott and Atget, Motherwell and Tworkov, and other local Cape artists. Unpretentious and friendly, it's for serious collectors.

Off Main Gallery (offmaingallery.com), 326 Main Street (rear). Open limited hours and by appointment from May through October. Housed in an 1875 barn in downtown Wellfleet, this gallery "thinks locally" with exhibits in paintings, collages, prints, and photography of the Outer Cape. Considered a "community gallery," it also offers poetry readings, musical events, and art demonstrations.

Blue Heron Gallery (508-349-6724; blueheronfineart.com), 20 Bank Street. Open Mother's Day weekend through mid-October. Founded in 1978, this gallery continues to maintain an impressive roster of award-winning artists from around the country. The Blue Heron displays an extensive collection of contemporary art (including oil, egg tempera, watercolor, pastels, acrylic, and more).

Berta Walker Gallery Wellfleet (774-383-3161; bertawalkergallery.com), 40 Main Street. "The History of American Art" as seen through the eyes of Provincetown, and now Wellfleet. Berta opened her second shop in 2015.

Marrinan Gallery (508-776-2804; marrinangallery.com), 14 Commercial Street. As a friend of mine would label it "a vanity gallery, but with interesting stuff."

Other worthy galleries include **Cove Gallery** (508-349-2530; covegallery.com), 15 Main Street; **Gaa Gallery** (gaa-gallery.com), 230B Main Street; **The Frying Pan Gallery** (508-514-7090; fryingpangallery.com), 250 Commercial Street; **Harmon Gallery** (harmongallery.com), 95 Commercial Street; **Left Bank Gallery** (508-349-9451; leftbankgallery.com), 25 Commercial Street.

SPECIALTY **Wellfleet Flea Market** (508-349-7176; wellfleetcinemas.com), Wellfleet Drive-In, 51 Route 6. There's more junk than treasure, but you never know what you'll find: name-brand clothing, a hat to ward off the summer sun, used and antique furniture, trinkets, tea sets, colored glasses, and much, *much*, more. Open early May to mid-October ($ per car) but booths get pricey. $–$$$.

✻ Special Events

July 4: **Independence Day parade.**
Mid-October: **Oysterfest**—see "Shuckin' Awesome" on page 295.

TRURO

onsidered to be the last vestige of "old Cape Cod," Truro has no stoplights, no fast-food outlets, no supermarket. It does have, though, the last working farm on the Outer Cape. And it has a lot of new construction—second homes that lie dormant during the off-season and lots of new year-round houses. Yes, Dorothy, the landscape is changing in Truro. Still, though, both Truro Center and North Truro consist of only a few shops. Nothing more, nothing less. And local folks, summer people (vacationing writers and urban professionals who have built large houses in the rolling hills and dunes), and even the newcomers are determined to keep it that way.

North Truro is also tiny but has blue-collar ties to Provincetown. As you head toward Provincetown, the only real development—in a nod to the tourist industry—consists of hundreds of tiny cottages, motels, and houses lining a narrow strip of shore wedged between Cape Cod Bay and the dramatic parabolic dunes on Pilgrim Lake. It's an odd juxtaposition, but one I always look forward to.

There aren't many human-made sites to explore, except for **Highland Light** and the **Truro Historical Museum**, but there are plenty of natural ones. Almost 70 percent of Truro's 42 square miles (one of the largest towns on the Cape, in acreage) falls within the boundaries of the **Cape Cod National Seashore (CCNS)**. There are hiking and biking trails as well as expanses of beach.

Rolling moors and hidden valleys characterize the tranquil back roads east and west of Route 6. Windswept dunes, lighthouses, beach grass, and austere shorelines will inspire you, as they did Edward Hopper. The painter built a summer home in Truro in the 1930s and worked there until 1967. In the late 2000s a land dispute erupted with the Klines, developer-owners who wanted to build a trophy house on 9 acres of what many view as sacred Hopper land and views. Neighbors wanted to preserve the landscape made famous by the artist. The Cape Cod Commission, arbiters of all things potentially contentious and historic, ruled that the Klines could go ahead and build their 6,500-square-foot house. Such is progress.

Truro, established in 1697, has endured many name changes. Originally it was called Payomet or Pamet, after the American Indian tribe that inhabited the area before the Pilgrims. In 1705 it was known as Dangerfield because of the

PILGRIM LAKE KATY WARD

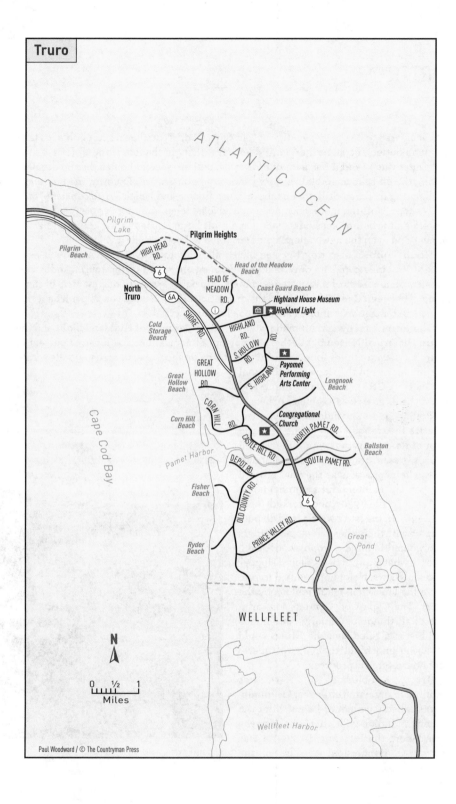

Truro

ATLANTIC OCEAN

Pilgrim Lake

Pilgrim Heights

Pilgrim Beach

HIGH HEAD RD.

6

Head of the Meadow Beach

North Truro

6A

HEAD OF MEADOW RD.

Coast Guard Beach

Highland House Museum

★ Highland Light

Cold Storage Beach

SHORE RD.

HIGHLAND RD.

S. HOLLOW RD.

GREAT HOLLOW RD.

Great Hollow Beach

S. HIGHLAND

★ Payomet Performing Arts Center

Longnook Beach

CORN HILL RD.

Corn Hill Beach

★ Congregational Church

NORTH PAMET RD.

Ballston Beach

Pamet Harbor

CASTLE HILL RD.

DEPOT RD.

SOUTH PAMET RD.

Cape Cod Bay

Fisher Beach

OLD COUNTY RD.

6

Ryder Beach

PRINCE VALLEY RD.

Great Pond

WELLFLEET

N

0   ½   1
Miles

Wellfleet Harbor

Paul Woodward / © The Countryman Press

WHERE TO START IN TRURO

Morning:	Grab coffee and/or easy breakfast at Savory & the Sweet Escape. Afterward, play the Scottish-style Highland Golf Links or tour the Cape Cod Light and historic Highland House Museum. Test the waters by taking a cold dip in the Atlantic at Head of the Meadow Beach.
Afternoon:	Eat under a shaded picnic table at Salty Market or Captain's Choice. Truro Vineyards also offers tastings of their local wines and spirits.
Evening:	Indulge in top-notch cuisine at the ever-popular Blackfish. Head over to Fisher Beach with a blanket and catch the last remnants of sunset on the bayside.

large number of offshore sailing disasters. Eventually it was named Truro, for a Cornish coastal town in England.

Although today Truro is sleepy and rural, it has been, at times during the past few centuries, a hotbed of activity. The *Mayflower*'s Myles Standish spent his second night ashore in Truro. His band of 16 fellow Pilgrims found their first fresh water in Truro, as well as a stash of corn (which belonged to the American Indians) from which they harvested their first crop. And although you wouldn't know it today, because **Pamet Harbor** choked up with sand in the mid-1850s, Truro's harbor once rivaled neighboring Provincetown as a whaling and cod-fishing center. By the late 1700s, shipbuilding was thriving and the harbor bustling. Vessels bound for the Grand Banks were built here, and a packet boat sailed from Truro to Boston. The whaling industry also owes a debt to early Truro residents, one of whom (Ichabod Paddock) taught Nantucketers how to catch whales from shore.

In 1851 the population soared to a rousing 2,000 souls. But in 1860 the Union Company of Truro went bankrupt due to declining harbor conditions, and townspeople's fortunes and livelihoods sank with it. Commercially, Truro never rebounded. Today, the year-round population is also about 2,100 (despite a recent housing boom); the summer influx raises that number tenfold.

GUIDANCE **Truro Chamber of Commerce** (508-487-1288; trurochamberofcommerce .com), Route 6. Open late May to mid-October.

GETTING THERE *By car:* The center of Truro is about 60 miles from the Cape Cod Canal via Route 6. Route 6A and Shore Road are synonymous.

By bus: The **Plymouth & Brockton Bus** (508-746-0378; p-b.com) connects Truro with Hyannis and other Cape towns, as well as with Boston's Logan Airport. The bus stops at Salty Market in North Truro, as well as at the post office & Jams' convenience store near the Pamet.

GETTING AROUND *By car:* Beaches, sites, and roads are well marked off Route 6. Generally, the CCNS is east of Route 6. The Shore Road exit in North Truro takes you into North Truro and eventually to Beach Point, choked with motels as it approaches Provincetown. At its most narrow, Truro is only a mile wide, while it stretches for 10 miles north to south.

By shuttle: The **Provincetown Shuttle** (508-385-1430; capecodtransit.org) operates on weekends starting in late May through June then switches to a daily route with stops every 30 minutes until early September. The shuttle provides service from

Provincetown to Truro's Route 6A, Beach Point, Salty Market, and Horton's Campground. Flag the bus down anywhere along the route. $.

PUBLIC RESTROOMS Stop at the Pilgrim Heights rest area in summer.

PUBLIC LIBRARY **Truro Public Library** (508-487-1125; trurolibrary.org), 7 Standish Way, North Truro. This contemporary library has programs for adults and kids.

EMERGENCIES **Truro Police Department** (508-487-8730; truropolice.org), 322 Route 6, or call **911**.

✳ To See

Cape Cod Light, or **Highland Light**, CCNS, 27 Highland Road, off South Highland Road, North Truro. The original lighthouse that guarded these treacherous shores was erected in 1797. It was the first on Cape Cod and had to be rebuilt in 1853, the year that a whopping 1,200 ships passed by within a 10-day period. Almost as important to landlubbers as mariners, the lighthouse provided shelter to Henry David Thoreau during one of his famous Outer Cape walks. The spot where he once stood and proclaimed that here a man could "put all America behind him" is thought to be 150 feet offshore now, thanks to erosion. One of only five working lighthouses on the Outer Cape, it was the last to become automated, in 1986. The original light shone with whale oil from 24 lamps, while later lamps were fueled with lard and kerosene. The modern light has a 110-kilowatt halogen bulb. Visible 21 miles out to sea, it's the brightest lighthouse on the New England coast. And at 120 feet above sea level, it's aptly named Highland.

In the mid-1990s the National Park Service, Coast Guard, Truro Historical Society, and the state joined forces to avert a looming disaster. Engineers cautioned that the lighthouse would crumble into the ocean. Erosion, at the rate of 3 to 4 feet per year, had chewed away the cliff upon which the lighthouse was built. (Thanks to ferocious storms in 1990, some 40 feet were lost in one year alone!) And when cliffs erode to within 100 feet of a lighthouse, it is too dangerous to bring in the heavy equipment needed to move it. So at a cost of $1.5 million, and over a period of 18 days, the 430-ton historic lighthouse and keeper's house was jacked up onto steel beams and pushed along steel tracks by hydraulic rams. At a rate of 25 feet per day, it was moved 450 feet west and 12 feet south (that is, inland), to a spot on the golf course. It should be safe for another 150 years, unless we get a lot of nor'easters.

Lighthouse tours (508-487-1121; trurohistorical.org and capecodlight.org), which include a short video and exhibit in the keeper's house, are offered mid-May through October; $. No children under 48 inches allowed. An observation deck, where the lighthouse recently stood, overlooks the ocean. Mark your calendar to ascend the lighthouse under the light of a full moon from April through December. It's quite something, watching the sunset and moonrise from here. Reservations are required and space is limited; donations.

🏛 **Highland House Museum** (508-487-3397; trurohistorical.org), 6 Highland Light Road, North Truro. Open June through September. Operated expertly by the Truro Historical Society and housed in the circa-1907 Highland Hotel, this museum is wholly dedicated to preserving Truro's maritime and agricultural past. Permanent items on display include a pirate's chest, fishing and whaling gear, 17th-century firearms, photos of Truro residents and places, toys, and ship models. In essence, all 12 of the former

HEARD IT THROUGH THE GRAPEVINE

Truro Vineyards of Cape Cod (508-487-6200; trurovineyardsofcapecod.com), 11 Route 6A. Open daily from May to late September. This hands-on family business has been gaining momentum since the Roberts took it over in 2007. The Vineyard first sprouted roots in 1992, but the gorgeous carriage-style building and its accompanying estate date back nearly two centuries. The main house (the Vineyards' Federal House) was built in 1813 and first owned by John and Hannah Hughes. Their granddaughter, Amelia, and her husband, Michael Rich, eventually took the property over and cultivated the estate into a prosperous farm selling grain, milk, and coal. During the 1940s, cantaloupes were grown on the warm, well drained, sandy soil, which later proved to be the perfect spot for growing grapes. Enjoy a tasting under the pavilion and take a free guided tour of the Vineyard, including their state of the art barrel room. Be sure to also check out their on-site distillery, **South Hollow Spirits**, where they make Twenty Boat Rums and Dry Line Gin in a 250-gallon copper pot still. Sip samples or try a cocktail while hanging with friends on their beautiful green lawn. Come hungry because the Blackfish Restaurant's **Crush Pad Food Truck** (see also **Where to Eat**) serves lunch and snacks that are

LEESA BURKE

mouth-wateringly delicious. Stop at the gift shop on your way out and buy a bottle of their wine (the lighthouse-shaped bottle makes for a great gift). Starting at the end of June, the Vineyard hosts free Summer Sundays on the lawn with live music and a raw bar (free parking too). It's the perfect way to kick off—or end—a Cape Cod weekend. Check the website for a list of full events including the Truro Treasures Grape Stomp & Music Fest, and the annual Vinegrass Music Festival. See also under **Special Events**. $$–$$$.

hotel rooms are set up as mini museums furnished with period pieces. One room is dedicated to Courtney Allen, the Truro Historical Society founder, artist, model maker, and wood carver. Upstairs is reserved for rotating exhibits. The building is a fine example of the kind of fashionable, once prominent, turn-of-the-20th-century summer hotels that were common in Cape Cod. $.

HIGHLAND HOUSE MUSEUM KATY WARD

✣ **Truro Center for the Arts at Castle Hill** (508-349-7511; castlehill.org), 10 Meetinghouse Road at Castle Hill Road, Truro. Classes and workshops year-round, although the majority are held in summer. A nonprofit educational institute, Castle Hill was founded in 1972 and has evolved into an important cultural voice on the Outer Cape art scene. Classes and workshops are offered in a converted 1880s barn to people of all ages in painting, drawing, writing, printmaking, book arts, photography, clay, and sculpture. Castle Hill also sponsors lectures, concerts, and artist receptions. Nationally renowned artists and writers lead week-long (and longer) classes.

Jenny Lind Tower, CCNS, off Highland Light Road, North Truro. Between the Highland Golf Links and the former **North Truro Air Force Base**, this 55-foot tower of granite seems out of place. And in fact, it is. The short story goes like this: In 1850 P. T. Barnum brought Swedish singing legend Jenny Lind to America. When Barnum oversold tickets to her Boston concert, and when Lind heard the crowds were going to riot, she performed a free concert from the roof tower for the people in the street. When the building was to be destroyed in 1927, a Boston attorney purchased the tower and brought it here (he owned the land at that time). The CCNS owns the property now and the entrance is blocked, but the granite tower still stands 150 feet above sea level, visible to passing ships and those of us on the ground.

Congregational church and **cemetery**, off Bridge Road, Truro. A marble memorial commemorates the terrible tragedy of the 1841 October Gale, when seven ships were destroyed and 57 crewmembers died. Renowned glassmakers from Sandwich made the church windows, and Paul Revere cast the steeple bell. Take Route 6 to Snow's Field to Meetinghouse Road to Bridge Road.

Susan Baker Memorial Museum (508-487-2557), 46 Route 6A, Truro. Not really a museum, but more of a gallery. One of the most irreverent painters on the Cape, Baker

THE SHORE ROAD

Roll the windows down and breathe in the salty air as you drive Shore Road (also known as Route 6A and runs parallel to the highway). This slow speed single lane takes you along the bayside with intermittent views of the water and quaint Cape cottages tucked neatly together. Also be sure to enjoy the highway stretch across East Harbor (also known as Pilgrim Lake) that abuts the beautiful vast oceanside dunes.

KATY WARD

is a humorist at heart. She has a great body of work exploring the history of Provincetown and a recent book of European chapels and churches. She's perhaps best known for her sculptural, three-dimensional frames that take their cue from the architecture of whatever European building is in the painting. It's hard to keep a good woman in one medium.

Old Cobb Library (508-349-0200; trurohistoricalsociety.org/cobb-library), 13 Truro Center Road. Built in 1912, this building originally served as the town's first true public library. Located in the town's center, it is now used and maintained by the Truro Historic Society as a

OLD COBB LIBRARY KATY WARD

HIGHLAND LIGHT LEESA BURKE

safe holding place for troves of maps, charts, books, photographs, family memorabilia, and other historical documents. Open for public viewing and research on select days, year-round. Free but welcomes donations.

✳ To Do

BICYCLING & RENTALS **Head of the Meadow Bike Trail,** CCNS, off Route 6, North Truro. Just south of Pilgrim Lake, this 2-mile trail connects at the dirt path parking lot at High Head Road (2 hour parking limit) and Head of the Meadow Beach (seasonal beach parking fees apply). Personally, I find this trail rather easy with some bumpy surfaces, slight hills, and a winding single lane path. In the summer months, keep your eyes open for rosehips, beachplums, wild blueberries, and bayberries. I also recommend bug spray—the mosquitos love the abutting wetlands. In the off-season you might spot a deer, a coyote, or a feisty fisher cat. Four-wheel-drive vehicles with proper stickers can enter the dunes at High Head too, depending on piping plover activity. See *Bicycling & Rentals* under **To Do** in Provincetown & Wellfleet.

BOAT EXCURSIONS & RENTALS **Pamet Harbor,** 75 Depot Road, at the end. Contact the harbormaster for launching information (508-349-2555; truro-ma.gov/harbor -master). See also "Truro's Salty Landmark" on page 306.

FISHING Like most of the Cape, Truro offers fully stocked waters, both salty and fresh. Procure fishing licenses and regulations online at mass.gov/eea/agencies/dfg/ licensing.

Big game: **Reel Deal Fishing Charters** (508-487-3767; fishreeldeal.com), 5 Great Hollow Road. With over 20 years of commercial fishing and 15 years in the charter

SCOTLAND COMES TO CAPE COD

Highland Golf Links (508-487-9201; highlandlinks.com), 10 Highland Light Road, off South Highland Road, North Truro. Open late April through November. Perched on a high windswept bluff, the Cape's oldest course (founded in 1892) is one of the country's oldest, too. At the turn of the 20th century, the course was part of the Highland House resort (now a museum; see *To See*), which drew Boston visitors by train. Today the museum sits between the eighth and ninth holes. The course exemplifies the Scottish tradition, with deep natural roughs, Scotch broom, heath, unirrigated open fairways, occasional fog, and spectacular ocean views. That's why golfers come to this nine-hole course. That, and for the dime-sized greens, whale sightings from the sixth tee in summer, and the view of Highland Light adjacent to the seventh hole. Avoid the crowds by playing on Sunday. It's the only public course between Orleans and Provincetown. $$$$; clubs $$.

KATY WARD

business, Captain Bobby Rice knows what works. Experience a true fishing experience as you land stripers, blues, and tuna on one of their fully loaded boats. $$$$+.

Jigged-Up Sportfishing (774-200-1180; jiggedupsportfishing.com), 75 Depot Road. Captain Mike Wisniewski and his crew are waiting to take you on a certainly unforgettable fishing adventure. Expect common catch like striped bass, bluefish and bluefin tuna, cod, and sharks. $$$$+.

On shore: Surfcasting is good all along the Atlantic coastline, but not as plentiful as it once was. You're better off booking a charter if you want to catch anything worthwhile.

Freshwater: Kids love fishing from the grassy shores off **Pond Road** (which leads to Cold Storage Beach); it's a tranquil place for picnicking and watching the sunset, too. **Great Pond**, off Savage Road from Route 6 can also be hit or miss.

FOR FAMILIES **Puma Park Playground** at the Truro Public Library, 7 Standish Way is quite elaborate and ADA accessible. See also **Truro Agricultural Fair** under **Special Events**.

KAYAKS & PADDLEBOARDS **Pamet Harbor Yacht and Tennis Club** (508-349-3772; pametclub.com; 7 Yacht Club Road) offers easy kayak and paddleboard access to protected waters of the harbor with a membership. The club provides plenty of parking, lockers to store equipment, and hoses to clean off sandy feet and gear after an adventurous trip. The clubhouse sports a stone fireplace, a full kitchen, and glassed-in porch

TRURO'S SALTY LANDMARK

A safe and scenic haven for boaters who ply the waters of Cape Cod bay, **Pamet Harbor** comes equipped with the bare essentials: a small harbormaster's office, a dual launch ramp, and a small protruding dock with floating moorings—and that's about it. There's no marina, stores, restaurants, or ice cream stands cluttering the large parking lot, and that's just the way Truro likes it. Found at the **Pamet River** (hence its name), the harbor's history dates back centuries. In the late 1700s, Pamet Harbor was the site of vibrant shipbuilding and fishing enterprises, as well as salt works, despite its notoriously shallow inlet. Rail service came to the Lower Cape in the 1870s, when a trestle and a depot were constructed (where the parking lot is now), along with a high berm that divided the marsh. (Fun fact: The west end of **Depot Road** was once a bustling train station. By the fall of 1960, the tracks leading from Eastham to Provincetown were dismantled by the New York, New Haven & Hartford Railroad Co., leaving behind only remnants.) Following the Civil War, the shipbuilding industry declined and the fishing stock dwindled. The neglected harbor sat vacant and mostly deserted for almost a century. In 1918, the present inlet was carved through the dunes in an attempt to straighten the course of the river and increase the current flow to prevent silting. But within five years the inlet silted, again, and became unnavigable to most vessels except boats with a shallow-draft. In the 1950s a pair of stone jetties were constructed, which helped mitigate the silting problem for some time. (Tip: Park at Corn Hill Beach and walk left until you reach the jetty. It's a wonderful spot to cast a line and/or watch recreational boats pass through.)

Today, Pamet Harbor can comfortably launch boats up to 26 feet on most tides, although the channel can get pretty dicey in some spots due to continual shoaling. The area is also a wonderful place to explore marsh habitat and bird life; in fact the area is home to one of the state's largest nesting colonies of least terns. Kayakers often depart from the harbor and traverse into the Pamet River—be sure to pay attention to the tide. "It is really beautiful, but you can get stuck somewhere in the Pamet estuary at low tide, with a very long walk in black mud as you pull your kayak behind you," said one fellow Truro lover.

PAMET HARBOR KATY WARD

with a large deck boasting expansive views of the Pamet. Club members also have access to tennis courts, water sport rentals, storage racks, and club events like Pickleball, needlework classes, football game night, and book clubs. Choose from an annual pass or seasonal (summer/winter). I recommend this for people staying longer lengths of time in Truro or nearby. $$$$+.

TENNIS See the **Pamet Harbor Yacht and Tennis Club** above.

✻ Green Space

BEACHES Truro offers 11 town beaches to visit during your stay, but parking stickers are required 8 a.m. to 4 p.m., starting late June through Labor Day. Parking is first-come, first-serve. Ample beach parking (160+ spots) can be found at **Head of the Meadow Beach** and **Corn Hill,** which are the only two beaches that allow daily passes and are handicapped accessible. Stickers can be purchased weekly or seasonally at the **Recreation and Beach Department** (508-487-6983; truro-ma.gov/beach-office; 36 Shore Road).

　　Head of the Meadow Beach, on the Atlantic Ocean. Half the beach is maintained by the town and half by the CCNS. Both sides have lifeguards, but the only difference is the latter half has restrooms; otherwise it's the same wide, dune-backed beach.

　　Corn Hill Beach, on the bayside, off Corn Hill Road. The name "Corn Hill Beach" originated in 1620, when the Pilgrims sailed to this area and found a cache of corn buried by the local American Indians. The bayside water is always warmer and less intimidating. Walk the shoreline to the "jetty" and watch recreational boats steam in and out of the Pamet Harbor. No lifeguards or restrooms.

HEAD OF THE MEADOW BEACH KATY WARD

CORNHILL BEACH LEESA BURKE

Longnook Beach, on the Atlantic Ocean, off Long Nook Road. A true local favorite. Drive down a winding road until you see the ocean. This beautifully secluded beach fills up fast in the summertime with only a handful of parking spots. Trek down the overly steep dune and enjoy the remoteness. Also, there's *no* cellphone service, lifeguards, or restrooms.

Coast Guard Beach, off Highland Road, and **Ballston Beach**, off South Pamet Road; both on the Atlantic Ocean. Each is owned by the town and requires a sticker, but anyone can bicycle in for free. (This Coast Guard Beach is not to be confused with Henry Beston's Coast Guard Beach in Eastham, under the auspices of CCNS.) And yes, there are lifeguards and restrooms.

Other bayside beaches include **Beach Point Beach**, off Route 6A near the Top Mast Resort; **Cold Storage Beach**, off Pond Road in North Truro; **Fisher Beach**, at the end of Fisher Road; **Great Hollow Beach**, at the end of Great Hollow Road; **Noon's Landing**, off Route 6A, and **Ryder Beach,** off Ryder Beach Road. There are no lifeguards at any bayside beach.

See also "Shark Awareness" on page 282.

WALKS **Pilgrim Heights Area**, CCNS, off Route 6, North Truro. Two short walks yield open vistas of distant dunes, ocean, and salt marsh. As the name implies, the easy 0.75-mile round-trip **Pilgrim Spring Trail** leads to the spot where the Pilgrims reportedly tasted their first New England water. Or so historians say; it's debatable. One subsequently penned: "We . . . sat us downe and drunke our first New England water with as much delight as ever we drunke in all our lives." A small plaque marks the spot.

Small Swamp Trail (about the same distance as the Pilgrim Spring Trail, above) was named not for the size of the swamp or trail, but rather for the farmer (Mr. Small) who grew asparagus and corn on this former 200-acre farm. By August,

A MINI LENDING LIBRARY AT COAST GUARD BEACH KATY WARD

blueberries are ripe for the picking. In spring look for migrating hawks. There's a wooded picnic area.

Pamet Area/Bearberry Hill, North Pamet Road, Truro. You won't want to pick this tangy and sour fruit come late September, but take the lovely walk to the top of Bearberry Hill for views of the Atlantic and the bog landscape. The trailhead is located at the parking lot below the youth hostel/education center.

✳ Lodging

RESORTS & HOTELS **Top Mast** (508-487-1189; topmastresort.com), 209 Shore Road, North Truro. Open early May through late October. Owned and operated by the Silva family since 1971, this nicely maintained motel flanks Route 6A well before the congestion begins. Beachfront units are built into the bayside, with sliding glass doors that open onto individual balconies. Choose among motel rooms, one- and two-room efficiencies, and two-bedroom cottages with full kitchens. For larger parties, consider renting one of three private shore houses that sleep up to 14 people (seven queen beds) plus all the amenities: kitchen, washer and dryer, central AC, and sun decks with water views. The indoor pool complex features a 50-foot heated saltwater pool, kiddie pool and slide, hot tub, sauna, aromatherapy steam room, and fitness room. They also sport big screen TVs, Wi-Fi, and lawn games such as Corn Hole and Ping Pong. The on-site Topmast Café is open for breakfast and lunch, with a special fish fry on Fridays from 4–9 p.m. $$–$$$$$+.

Dune Crest Hotel (508-487-9090; dunecresthotel.com), 535 Route 6. Open year-round. One word describes this place: location! Nestled high on the dune cliffs, this hotel offers panoramic views of the bay, the Provincetown Monument, and the cascading dunes and Pilgrim Lake. It is also very dog-friendly (with non-pet rooms available, too). Walking trails (see **Green Space**), relief areas throughout the property, and a private on-site dog park are just a few amenities geared toward your furry friend. $$–$$$.

TOP MAST RESORT KATY WARD

DAYS GET LONGER

Days Cottages (508-487-1062; dayscottages.com), 271 Shore Road. After decades of ownership, the Day's family sold their iconic cottages in 2017. Today each cottage is privately owned and operated. But what hasn't changed is the look—and it never will. Deed restrictions placed on the property prevent owners from altering the exteriors (interiors are game on). This means all 23 cottages will forever remain white clapboard (now vinyl) with a sea-foam green window trim and a floral nickname. The popular flower names, "Peony," "Violet," and "Daisy" (to name a few), were chosen by Joseph A. Days' wife, Amelia, who decided to label each cottage as a way for visitors to easily locate the right one. She and her husband moved to North Truro from Provincetown by taking their house apart and hauling it to the little strip of sand between Pilgrim Lake and Cape Cod Bay, where he promptly scrapped the rebuilding idea and had a bonfire. When the Depression hit, Joe enlisted help and started constructing what is now known as Days Cottages. Only a few man-made objects in the history of Cape Cod have been immortalized in art as often and lovingly as Days Cottages, as in the work of painter John Dowd, photographer Joel Meyerowitz, and countless others. The location made lasting impressions on the hearts and minds of thousands of summer vacationers as well, some of whom stayed a night, some a week or two, many year after year. One set of those vacationers happened to be my grandparents, Katie and Ed, who rented the Daisy cottage for a week every summer. Somewhere on the antique nonfunctioning fireplace (if it's still there) is the signature of a 5-year-old girl. A chalk scribbled "Katy Ward," along with several drawings of a kitty and my cousins' names. I will cherish the memories of walking the shore with my grandma combing for wampum, American Indian pottery, and the perfect skipping rock. (See also under *Markets*).

LEESA BURKE

COTTAGES **Oceana by the Sea Cottages** (508-487-3014; oceanacottages .com). Open early June through September. A bit rustic with its wooden paneled walls and seashell curtains, but true old-school Cape Cod style. The amenities are basic: an equipped kitchen, towels and linens, etc. So what makes this place so special? Waking up to the sound of the waves gently rolling onto the shore, seagulls squawking, and drinking your morning coffee in the sand. That's what. $$–$$$.

Kalmar Village (508-487-0585, 617-277-0091 in winter; kalmarvillage .com), 674 Shore Road. Open early June through September. Owned by the Prelacks since 1968, the quaint Kalmar Village still stands out. It's particularly good for families because Kalmar sits on 400 feet of private bay beach. All 45 cottages are roomy inside, with modern kitchens. Other perks include daily housekeeping and a coin-operated laundry; each unit has its own picnic table and grill. There are also large and small efficiencies, as well as motel rooms. Rented weekly in-season. $$$–$$$$.

CAMPGROUNDS 🦐 🐾 **North of Highland Camping Area** (508-487-1191; cape codcamping.com), 52 Head of the Meadow Road, North Truro. Open late May to mid-September. On 60 acres of scrub pine forest within the CCNS, these 225-plus sites are suitable for tents and tent trailers only (no hook-ups, though) and are a 10-minute walk from Head of the Meadow Beach (see **Green Space**). There are strict quiet hours. From mid-July to mid-August, reservations must begin and end on a Saturday or Sunday. $.

🦐 🐫 **Adventure Bound Camping Resorts** (508-487-1847; abcapecod .com), 46 Highland Road, North Truro. Open April through October. Within the CCNS, these 22 acres of wooded sites accommodate about 325 tents and RVs. It's less than a mile to Coast Guard Beach (see **Green Space**), and only 6 miles to Provincetown.

KALMAR VILLAGE KIM GRANT

HOSTEL 🦐 **Hostelling International, Truro** (508-349-3889; 888-901-2085 in-season reservations; hiusa.org), 111 North Pamet Road, Truro. Open mid-June to early September. Originally a US Coast Guard station, the 42-bed hostel commands a dramatic location—amid dunes, marshes, and a cranberry bog. The hostel is within the CCNS and just a 7-minute walk from Ballston Beach (see **Green Space**). National Park Service interpreters host special programs each week; they're free to all and not to be missed.

✱ Where to Eat

DINING OUT **Blackfish** (508-349-3399), 17 Truro Center Road. Open D, mid-May to late October. Resurrected from its longtime incarnation as the Blacksmith Shop, this upscale tavern has been under the direction of chef/owner Eric Jansen since the late 2000s. The menu is heavy on meat (pork, rabbit, duck) and locally caught fish dishes. The dining room can feel crowded, but the clientele thinks of it more like a buzz. All in all, it reaches for (and hits) a high note. See also "Heard It Through the Grapevine" on page 301. $$–$$$$.

TERRA LUNA KATY WARD

Terra Luna (508-487-1019; terraluna restaurant.com), 104 Shore Road. Open D, mid-May to mid-October. Peaked ceilings, shellacked wooden tables, and candlelight transforms this unassuming roadside eatery into a very desirable place to spend a couple of hours (except when it's really hot, since there's no air-conditioning). Chef/owner Tony Pasquale's dishes are rustic with a focus on fresh ingredients. The menu might feature dishes like roasted Chatham cod or pan-fried goat cheese with grilled figs, local honey, and balsamic. The cocktail menu is always creative. $$–$$$$.

EATING OUT **Montanos** (508-487-2026; montanos.com), 481 Route 6. Open D, year-round. This family restaurant serves dependable and authentic Italian favorites such as handcrafted pastas and homemade sauces and pizza. Their crab cakes get rave reviews. $$–$$$$.

Savory and the Sweet Escape (508-487-2225), 316 Route 6. Open B, L, D, year-round. You can't miss this big red building and I bet you'll come back more than once. From breakfast sandwiches to stone-fired pizzas, grilled burgers, and roast beef sandwiches, this place has all

the bases covered. Dine outside or inside at one of the long window stools. See also under *Sweet Treats & Coffee*. $–$$$.

Captain's Choice (508-487-5800; captainschoicetruro.com), 4 Highland Road. Open L, D, mid-May through October. A casual place with family-friendly prices and the freshest seafood around. See "It's a Shore Thing" on page 314. $$–$$$$.

SWEET TREATS & COFFEE **Chequessett Chocolate** (774-538-6249; cheques settchocolate.com), 8 Highland Road. Open daily, year-round. When owners Katie Reed and Josiah Mayo are not traveling Central America in search of the finest cacao bean, you can find them here packaging homemade chocolate bars, stocking the glass case with truffles and bonbons, or slinging Asian street food from their High Tide food truck out front. Make sure you try their best seller: the Wellfleet Sea Salt Chocolate Bar. In addition to the endless array of sweet treats, they also serve coffee and other special beverages such as Mexican hot chocolate, the Cold Storage Mocha, or their Watermelon Lemonade. $$–$$$.

Savory and the Sweet Escape (508-487-2225), 316 Route 6. Choose from an endless list of flavors, all of which are

CAPE TIP SEAFOOD MARKET KATY WARD

MARKET-FRESH AND MADE-TO-ORDER

Salty Market (508-487-0711; thesaltymarket.com) 2 Highland Road. Open daily, year-round. A true mom-and-pop business, Salty Market, formerly known as Dutra's Market, offers a range of items including made-to-order sandwiches, bagels, prepared foods, grocery items, and top-notch wines and local brews. Andrea Freeman, the general manager, told me, "The owners, Claire and Ellery, took over what had been a corner store for over 50 years. In spite of their lack of experience in the field, they kept the store's legacy going with a fresh take on a classic business, making it an ever-surprising, ever-changing, ever-bettering work in progress. With a diverse crew of homegrown locals, washashores, and a sprinkle of college students making the most of their summer, Salty Market wears many hats. In true neighborly fashion, we're a breakfast and lunch café, an information booth, a weather channel, a bus station, a wine tasting room, a catering service, and whatever else might suit your needs of the day. Through the ups and downs of the bipolar nature of Cape Cod seasons, we keep the OPEN flag waving. We cater to all—from the year-round neighbors who support us in the cold winter months, to the summer dwellers who return every season, to the weekend visitors who need a one-stop-shop to stock up for a backyard barbecue or a day at the beach. So next time you find yourself in North Truro, stop in and see how we can make your day better!" $–$$.

crafted in-house. Grab a scoop or two of the Lavender Fig, the Wicked Mud Flats, or the Ryder Beach Rubble. Cash only, open seasonally. $–$$.

MARKETS **Jams** (508-349-1616), 14 Truro Center Road, off Route 6 in Truro

DAY'S MARKET KATY WARD

Center. Open late May to early September. A great place to grab sandwiches, rotisserie chickens, cold beverages, and other grocery staples. For those of you who don't live nearby, carry your picnic fixings across the street to the park. A perfect reprieve for bicyclists and the car-weary. $$–$$$.

Cape Tip Seafood (508-487-0259 for sales; 508-487-2164 for retail; cape tipseafood.com), 300 Route 6. Fishing boats from Provincetown, Truro, and Wellfleet supply this string of fish markets. Take your pick of fresh seafood or grab a lobster roll and cup of clam chowder while your order is neatly folded into paper wrapping. See also "It's a Shore Thing" on page 314. $$–$$$.

Day's Market (508-487-2855), 271 Route 6A. Thank you, Mylan and Camilla, for turning this market into something truly worthy! Gone are the days of penny candy, but that's quite all right. After gutting and renovating the market in 2019, the couple transformed the outdated shop into a beachy yet modern roadside dive. Stop in for a fresh lobster roll on a buttered bun and choose from one of several preparations: original (mayo), the Connecticut (butter),

IT'S A SHORE THING

The story behind Cape Tip Seafood and Captain's Choice begins with Chris King, a fourth-generation Provincetown native. My fondest childhood memories include celebrating the Blessing of the Fleet on his 65-foot fishing vessel, the *Second Effort*, which he purchased in 1991. Friendly faces, barbecues, cold drinks, jumping off the pilothouse into the ocean, or reeling into the water via rope swing . . . it was the best.

After 18 good years, the boat was retired and replaced with the *Donna Marie*, a 60-foot steel hulled vessel that continues to fish out of Provincetown Harbor today. But Chris is not only a fisherman; he's a businessman. In 1999, Chris opened Cape Tip Seafood, selling not only his catch but that of other local fishermen, as well of the former Cabral Pier (now Provincetown Marina). After finding success, Chris (and his business partner, John White, another notable local) opened a trio of seafood markets, including one in Provincetown (near Stop & Shop), Truro (near Box Lunch), and Orleans (Old Colony Way). But that wasn't enough. In 2015, Chris and John opened Captain's Choice, a casual seafood joint in North Truro. You cannot get any fresher than this.

KATY WARD

the Californian (BLAT), the Mexican (salsa), or the Moroccan (curry mayo and pineapple). They also offer cold and hot sandwiches, salads, and a fully stocked market with all the necessities. If passing by early, or any time of day for that matter, pick from their "Brekky" menu, which offers savories, sweets, and healthier options. $–$$$.

❋ Entertainment

LIVE MUSIC **Summer Concerts on the Green**, sponsored by the Truro Public Library (508-487-1125; trurolibrary.org), 7 Standish Way. Enjoy a free concert on Thursday evenings in July and August at Snow's Park in the town center.

Payomet Performing Arts Center (508-487-5400; payomet.org), 29 Old Dewline Road. Open mid-April to mid-September, with off-season events at various locations on the Outer, Lower, and Mid-Cape. In the summer months, Payomet offers an array of talent underneath their large white tent in North Truro. Showcasing both national and local talent through music, circus, and theater performances as well as circus classes for children and "meet the artist" opportunities. $$–$$$$+.

Truro Vineyards of Cape Cod (508-487-6200; trurovineyardsofcapecod.com), 11 Route 6A. The Vineyard offers live music on Sundays, as well as other events throughout the summer. See their website for a calendar of events. See also "Heard It Through the Grapevine" on page 301. $–$$.

✳ Selective Shopping

FARMS Truro Farmers' Market (sustainablecape.org), 20 Truro Center Road, next to the Post Office, every Monday mid-June to late August. See also **Truro Agricultural Fair** under **Special Events**.

GALLERIES Jobi Pottery & Gallery (508-349-2303; jobipottery.com), 314 Route 6, Unit 3. Original owners Joe Colliano and Bill Hastings (Jo-bi) began their business in a little hot dog stand near the Cape Cod Highland Lighthouse in 1953. Today, owner/designer Susan Kurtzman uses the same methods and original mid-century casting molds to create Jobi Pottery by hand in her Truro studio. The retro and mid-century look of her pottery shapes and designs can be traced back to Cape Cod–inspired originals with added colors and motifs to compliment the Jobi line. Open weekends in April, or make an appointment to tour the production studio and see how the pottery is made, painted, and designed.

Post Office Gallery (508-487-3111; postofficegallery.com), 38 Shore Road. This gallery (see its sister, **Larkin Gallery**, in Provincetown) offers group and juried exhibits starting mid-July through the New Year.

Thomas A. D. Watson Studio (508-349-1631; thomasadwatson.com), 45 Depot Road. This studio gallery showcases the work of Thomas A. D. Watson, an award-winning third-generation artist known for his representational landscape paintings of Cape Cod and New York's Adirondack mountains. The studio has infrequent opening hours so I recommend calling in advance.

SPECIALTY Atlantic Spice Co. (508-487-6100; 800-316-7965; atlanticspice.com), 2 Shore Road, North Truro. Culinary herbs and spices, botanicals, make-your-own potpourri, teas, spice blends, nuts, and seeds. They're here, they're fresh, and they're in a cavernous bright blue warehouse. Although this is primarily a wholesaler, you can purchase small quantities (less than the usual 1-pound increments) of most products. You may also be tempted by an assortment of practical souvenirs, kitchen gadgets, spice jars, and much more. I often find myself holiday shopping here. $–$$.

Jules Besch Stationers (508-487-0395), 3 Great Hollow Road. Open April

ATLANTIC SPICE CO. KATY WARD

to late November. This gorgeous shop features product that will make you want to take pen (perhaps an antique 1880s pen or a quill) to paper (perhaps some handmade paper or a bound journal). It also sells unique wrapping paper, collectible postcards, artsy boxed note cards, specialty albums, and blank books. A part of the shop resembles a study, set up with writing tables, leather blotters, and stylish desk lamps. Buy a blank card and ask Michael Tuck (a.k.a. Jules) to personalize it (overnight); he's known for his calligraphy and verse.

❋ Special Events

Early September: **Truro Agricultural Fair** (sustainablecape.org), 20 Truro Center Road. This popular 1-day event put Truro on the map! Truro's Ag Fair brings thousands of people to the tiny town center. Walk around Snow's Park, going booth to booth, surveying the lush local harvest including fresh veggies, fruits, eggs, honey, flowers, crafts, and more. Grab a quick bite from one of the fair's featured food trucks and enjoy it on the lawn or in the shade of a pine tree. Be sure to have your camera ready for the kid's zucchini 500 race, the pie-eating contest, and burlap sack race, and don't forget to cast your vote in the Barnyard Beauty Contest by dropping a bean into the jar of your favorite chicken, rooster, rabbit, sheep, and the like. The event is sponsored by Sustainable Cape and is free to the public. Parking can be found on the roadside and can be difficult to find at times. If traveling through the area, expect traffic and delays.

Mid-September: **Truro Treasures** (trurotreasures.org). Since the early 1990s, this folksy 2-day weekend in mid-September features a crafts fair, an antique car show, a treasure hunt, a pancake breakfast, a silent art auction, and more.

PROVINCETOWN

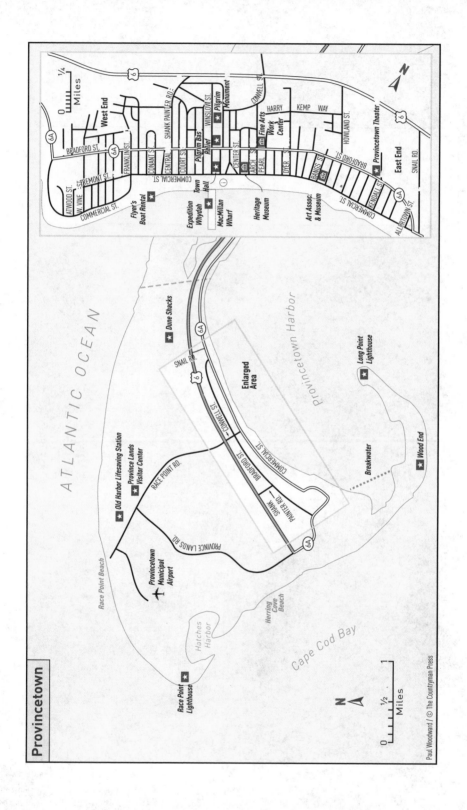

Provincetown

ATLANTIC OCEAN

Race Point Lighthouse

Race Point Beach

Old Harbor Lifesaving Station

Province Lands Visitor Center

Provincetown Municipal Airport

RACE POINT RD.

PROVINCE LANDS RD.

Dune Shacks

6A

SNAIL RD.

6

COMMERCIAL ST.

BRADFORD ST.

SHANK PAINTER RD.

Enlarged Area

6A

Provincetown Harbor

Long Point Lighthouse

Breakwater

Wood End

Hatches Harbor

Herring Cove Beach

Cape Cod Bay

N

0   ½   1
Miles

Paul Woodward / © The Countryman Press

West End

6A

6A

BRADFORD ST.

FRANKLIN ST.

ATWOOD ST.

W. VINE

TREMONT ST.

COMMERCIAL ST.

Flyer's Boat Rental

CONANT ST.

CENTRAL

COURT ST.

SHANK PAINTER RD.

WINSLOW ST.

Pilgrim Monument

Pilgrim Bas Relief

CARWELL ST.

Fine Arts Work Center

HARRY   KEMP   WAY

HOWLAND ST.

BRADFORD ST.

Provincetown Theater

East End

6

SNAIL RD.

COMMERCIAL ST.

Town Hall

Expedition Whydah

MacMillan Wharf

CENTER ST.

ARCH ST.

PEARL

DYER ST.

Heritage Museum

BANGS ST.

Art Assoc. & Museum

KENDALL ST.

COMMERCIAL ST.

ALLERTON ST.

6A

N

0   ¼
Miles

PROVINCETOWN

As you cross into Provincetown, where high dunes drift onto Route 6, you begin to sense that this is a different place. This outpost on the tip of the Cape, where glaciers deposited their last grains of sand, attracts a varied population. Whether seeking solitude or freedom of expression in the company of like-minded souls, visitors relish Provincetown's fringe status. (Although it's becoming less "fringey" every day, but more on that later.) P-town, as it's often referred to by nonlocals but not by locals, is perhaps best known as a community of tolerant individuals. The LGBTQ community, Portuguese fishermen and families, artists, writers—all call it home and welcome those who are equally tolerant.

Visitors parade up and down **Commercial Street**, the main drag, ducking in and out of hundreds of shops and galleries. The town has a carnival-like atmosphere, especially in July and August, testing the limits of acceptability. As you might imagine, people watching is a prime activity. On any given Saturday, the cast of characters might include cross-dressers, leather-clad motorcyclists, barely clad in-line skaters, children eating saltwater taffy, and tourists from "Anytown, USA," some of whom can't quite figure out what they've stumbled into and some of whom have come to scope out (gawking or relishing) the alternative scene.

LONG POINT KATY WARD

Morning:	**Stroll Commercial Street while everyone is still asleep. Walk the calm bayside flats during low tide. Flip a coin for breakfast at Yolqueria or Liz's Café.**
Afternoon:	**Hike to the top of the Pilgrim Monument for panoramic views of the town and beyond and explore the museum while you're there. Feeling beachy? Grab Flyer's Shuttle to Long Point and soak in the sun, salt, and beauty of the northernmost tip of Cape Cod. Grab a late lunch at Ross' Grill overlooking the bay, or dine alfresco at Bubalas and people-watch (you will not be bored). Afterward book a trip with Art's Dune Tours and cruise the soft sand on the Seashore's backside dunes.**
Evening:	**Watch the sunset at Herring Cove Beach. Head over to Farland on the Beach for live music, snacks, and beer and wine. Enjoy a late dinner at Front Street or the Mews.**
Late Night:	**Cruise the gallery district in the East End or opt for a live and maybe promiscuous show at the Crown & Anchor.**

Provincetown's history began long before the *Mayflower* arrived. It's said that Leif Eriksson's brother, Thorvald, stopped here in 1004 to repair the keel of his boat. The Wampanoag fished and summered here—the tiny strip of land was too vulnerable to sustain a year-round settlement. In 1620 the Pilgrims first set foot on American soil in Provincetown, anchoring in the harbor for 5 weeks, making forays down-Cape in search of an agreeable spot to settle. By the late 1600s and early 1700s, only 200 fishermen lived here.

But from the mid-18th to the mid-19th century, Provincetown was a bustling whaling community and seaport. After the industry peaked, Portuguese sailors from the Azores and Cape Verde Islands, who had signed on with whaling and fishing ships, settled here to fish the local waters. The Old Colony Railroad was extended to Provincetown in 1873, transporting iced fish to New York and Boston. Upward of four trains a day departed from the two-room station, located where the Duarte Motors parking lot is today, two blocks from MacMillan Wharf. But by the early 1900s, Provincetown's sea-driven economy had slowed. Trains stopped running in 1950. Today, although a small fishing industry still exists, tourism is the steam that drives the economy's train.

In 1899 painter Charles W. Hawthorne founded the Cape Cod School of Art. He encouraged his Greenwich Village peers to come north and take advantage of the Mediterranean-like light. By 1916 there were six art schools in town. By the 1920s, Provincetown had become as distinguished an art colony as Taos, East Hampton, or Carmel. Hawthorne encouraged his students to flee the studio and set up easels on the beach, incorporating the ever-changing light into their work. By the time Hawthorne died in 1930, the art scene had a life of its own, and it continues to thrive today.

Artistic expression in Provincetown wasn't limited to painting, though. In 1915 the Provincetown Players, a group of playwrights and actors, staged their works in a small waterfront fish house. In their second season they premiered Eugene O'Neill's *Bound East for Cardiff* before moving to 133 MacDougal Street in New York City, where they are still based.

Provincetown's natural beauty isn't overshadowed by its colorful population. **Province Lands**, the name given to the **Cape Cod National Seashore (CCNS)** within Provincetown's borders, offers bike trails and three remote beaches, where, if you walk far enough, you can find real isolation. Most summertime visitors venture onto the water—to whale-watch, sail, or sailboard in the protected harbor. A different perspective comes with a dune or aerial tour.

For all the history and natural beauty that doesn't change in Provincetown, the town itself is changing—like the rest of the United States, condos have sprung up on every empty strand of sand, turning Provincetown into a bedroom community for Bostonians. Nightlife isn't *quite* as vibrant as it once was; more visitors stay in, have dinner parties, and nest with their children. It's more expensive than ever for a new generation of gay youth, and the older generation is getting, well, older. Since gays moved into the mainstream and gay marriage was legalized across the country, it's no longer quite *the* gay destination it used to be. When *Queer Eye* brings its aesthetic into everyone's households, Ellen and Portia's wedding makes the cover of *People* magazine, and a different singer comes out as bisexual every week (it seems), it becomes a little easier for the LGBTQ community to vacation anywhere they want. Cisgendered folks are filling in around the edges and enjoying what gays and artists have long known: this is still one of the most special destinations in North America.

Provincetown is a delight in late spring and fall, when upward of 80,000 summer visitors return to their homes off-Cape. Commercial Street is navigable once again, and most shops and restaurants remain open. Tiny gardens bloom profusely well into October. From January to March, though, the town is given back to the almost 3,000 hardy year-rounders—almost half of whom are unemployed during this time. Although about 80 percent of the businesses close during January and February, there are still enough guest houses (and a handful of restaurants, especially on the weekends) open all winter, luring intrepid visitors with great prices and stark natural beauty. Steel yourself against the wind and take a walk on the beach, attend a reading at the **Fine Arts Work Center**, or curl up with a good book.

GUIDANCE **Provincetown Chamber of Commerce** (508-487-3424; ptownchamber .com), 307 Commercial Street near Lopes Square, and the **Provincetown Tourism Office** (508-487-3298; provincetowntourismoffice.org), 330 Commercial Street, are

PIPING PLOVER LEESA BURKE

both extremely informative and helpful resources. Here you can find guides and maps, ask questions about local history and town culture, or get help with scheduling travel accommodations. While you're there, pick up a free copy of the event calendar, which lists dozens of nightlife events and more.

Provincetown Business Guild (508-487-2313; ptown.org), 3 Freeman Street. Founded in 1978, the PBG is a non-profit organization that supports LGBTQ tourism. The PBG has over 300 members and is the working force behind popular events such as the highly anticipated Carnival in August, Holly Folly in the fall, and First Light on New Year's Eve.

Province Lands Visitor Center (508-487-1256; nps.gov/caco), Race Point Road, CCNS. Open early May to late October. Climb atop the observation deck for a 360-degree view of the outermost dunes and ocean. Also check out the Visitor Center, which offers informative exhibits on Cape history, local flora and fauna, dune ecology, as well as short films and other organized activities such as birding trips and dune tours.

GETTING THERE *By car:* Provincetown is the eastern terminus of Cape Cod, 63 miles via Route 6 from the Cape Cod Canal and 128 miles from Boston and Providence. It takes almost 2½ hours to drive to Provincetown from Boston.

By boat from Boston: **Bay State Cruise Company** (617-580-0147; baystatecruise company.com) offers daily 90-minute rides from Boston's Seaport District to Province-town's MacMillan Wharf starting mid-May through mid-October. Instead of staring at brake lights, stare at the ocean's horizon and watch the tip of Cape Cod magnify as you get close to docking. Personally this company is my favorite. The seats are comfortable, there's concierge service and plenty of outdoor space when you need fresh air. The staff is also beyond helpful and has gone to great lengths to accommodate me in the tightest of situations. Round trip and one-way options are available and there are no additional fees for luggage (including your bicycle). Reserve tickets online or buy at the booth. $$$$+.

Boston Harbor Cruises (617-227-4321; bostonharborcruises.com), another fast-ferry service that offers daily trips from Boston's Long Wharf to MacMillan Pier. Open mid-May through mid-October. $$$$+.

By boat from Plymouth: **Captain John Boats** (508-927-5587; captjohn.com) provides fast ferry service from Plymouth's State Pier to MacMillan Pier. The passenger ferry only offers two trips daily, both 90 minutes with round-trip and one-way

FERRY DEPARTS PROVINCETOWN FOR BOSTON

options available. Runs from mid-May to mid-September. $$$.

By bus: The **Plymouth & Brockton Bus** (508-746-0378; p-b.com) connects Provincetown with Hyannis and other Cape towns, as well as with Boston's Logan Airport. Travel time to Boston is about 3.5 hours and requires a bus change in Hyannis. The bus stop is behind the Provincetown Chamber of Commerce. Tickets must be purchased online or at a ticket agency terminal. $$$$.

By air from Boston: **Cape Air** (800-227-3247 for reservations; 508-487-0241 for the airport; capeair.com) provides year-round service from Logan Airport to Provincetown's Municipal Airport. This is my other favorite mode of transportation. Grab a window seat and look down at the Cape's sandy arm as you glide above

KATY WARD

the Atlantic. The flight takes about 25 minutes and the airport is 3 miles north of Provincetown near Race Point Beach and Hatches Harbor. Tickets can be reserved online with one-way and round-trips available. $$$$+.

GETTING AROUND Provincetown's most popular strip is **Commercial Street**, a 3-mile-long, narrow road, abutting the water with one-way vehicle traffic (bicycles can go both ways, so be careful). The street is often clogged with traffic—mostly people, bikers, drag queens, local workers, and delivery trucks (in the morning only)—making this drive *rather* difficult. Ask any local, it can be a bit of a nightmare trying to get to the post office or local bank in the summertime. As my grandmother used to say, "patience is a virtue." To quickly drive from one side of the town to the other I recommend using **Bradford Street** (parallel to Commercial). There are limited sidewalks with less foot traffic, but keep your eyes open for bicyclists. Take any of the side streets (unless it states one way) to get back onto Commercial.

Finding parking in Provincetown is *by far* the number one frustration among both tourists and locals. A single-parking space was recently listed for sale at a whopping $150,000. Finding free parking is very unlikely in the height of summer (after October, when the parking season ends, it's *much* easier). Try the **Municipal Parking Lot** near MacMillan Pier (it also offers limited electric vehicle charging station ports) or the **Grace Hall Lot** (at the intersection of Bradford and Prince Streets). Kiosks and other metered spaces are available on the East and West end of Commercial Street, at the Johnson Street lot; West End Lot; Alden Street Lot; as well as limited spaces on Ryder Street. There are also privately owned lots such as the one at Riley's on Bradford Street near the center of town, or the Provincetown Marina adjacent to MacMillan Pier. The Pilgrim Monument and Provincetown Museum offers daily parking, which includes one free ticket into the museum.

By car: The first exit off Route 6 (Snail Road) leads to the East End of town (street numbers in the East End are higher than in the West End). Take the second exit (Conwell Street) for MacMillan Pier and the Municipal Parking Lot. The third exit (Shank Painter Road) leads to the West End. Follow Route 6 to its end for Herring Cove Beach (on the right), or take a left and head toward the breakwater. A right off Route 6 (at

THE MAYFLOWER TROLLEY KATY WARD

the lights and opposite of Conwell Street) takes you to the Province Lands section of the CCNS and the municipal airport.

By shuttle: **The Provincetown Shuttle** (508-385-1430; capecodtransit.org) operates on weekends starting in late May through June then switches to daily routes with stops every 30 minutes until September. The shuttle provides service to Herring Cove Beach, the Provincetown Inn (near breakwater), Beech Forest, Race Point, Provincetown Airport and the Province Lands Visitor Center. It also travels Route 6A toward Truro, stopping at Beach Point Beach, Salty Market, and campgrounds. Pull the shuttle's rope to request a stop along the route. The **Flex** (508-385-1430; capecodtransit.org) offers trips from Provincetown to Harwich with reserved stops. The Flex stops at MacMillan Pier and Stop and Shop on Shank Painter Road. $.

By trolley: **The Mayflower Trolley** (508-487-8687; mayflowertrolley.com), Commercial Street at Town Hall. If you're visiting Provincetown there's no better introduction than a trip on the Trolley. The 45-minute narrated tour will give you a complete overview of the town, both past and present, before delving into it yourself. $$.

By taxicab: Call **Mercedes Cab** (508-487-3333; mercedescab.com) or **Cape Cab** (508-487-2222; capecabtaxi.com). This is usually my last alternative when in need of a ride. $$–$$$.

Atypical travel: **Ptown Pedicab** (508-487-0660; ptownpedicabs.com) Tired of walking? Curious what the West End looks like but stuck in the East End? Or maybe you and your partner just said, "I do," and you're looking for a modernized carriage to celebrate the big day. Whatever your needs are, let one of the friendly muscled hunks (and chiseled women) from Ptown Pedicab chauffer you and your friends around town. Flag one down anywhere on Commercial Street really, but surely in front of Town Hall or Lewis Brother's Ice Cream. You can also call and request a ride in advance. Sit back on the comfy padded cushion and experience the childlike thrill as your "driver" weaves through traffic, peddles up and down hills, and squeezes through narrow side streets. Rides are based on a pay-what-you-think-it's-worth system. I always end up tipping extra because it's just that much fun and the drivers are awesome. $–$$.

The Funk Bus (508-487-0111; thefunkbus.com) is not your average school bus. Choose from one of several party buses dressed in brightly colored graffiti animal print to transport you and your big

PTOWN PEDICAB KATY WARD

and rowdy group around Cape Cod. The Funk Bus offers buses for 14 people up to 30 people. Mini buses come equipped with a sound system. $$–$$$$.

MEDIA The *Provincetown Banner* (508-487-7400; wickedlocal.com/provincetown) and *The Provincetown Independent* (provincetownindependent.org) both deliver weekly newspapers focused on the Outer Cape towns. The *Provincetown Magazine* (508-487-1000; pmag.provincetown magazine.com) also has great information. Tune into **WOMR Outermost Community Radio** at 92.1 FM (508-487-2619; womr.org) or watch **Provincetown Community Television** on Comcast's community channel 99 or PTV's government channel 18 (508-487-0648; provincetowntv.org).

PUBLIC LIBRARY KIM GRANT

PUBLIC RESTROOMS Look behind the Chamber of Commerce (307 Commercial Street), Whaler's Wharf (237 Commercial Street), Town Hall (260 Commercial Street), Old Firehouse #2 (189 Commercial Street, across from Spiritus Pizza), and MacMillan Pier.

PUBLIC LIBRARY **Provincetown Public Library** (508-487-7094; provincetownlibrary .org), 356 Commercial Street (at Center Street). This magnificent facility is housed in the former Heritage Museum.

EMERGENCIES **Provincetown Police Department** (508-487-1212; provincetown-ma .gov), 26 Shank Painter Road, or call **911**.

  Outer Cape Health Services (508-487-9395; outercape.org), 49 Harry Kemp Way.

WEBSITES Check out the work of David Dunlap at buildingprovincetown2020 .org (and keep reading for a few snippets from his research); provincetownfor women.com for all things women, including Girl Splash and Single Women's Week; and provincetown.com.

✻ To See

Listings are organized from east to west.

Commercial Street. Until Commercial Street was laid out in 1835, the shoreline

A TRIBUTE TO PTOWN'S SINGING AMBASSADOR, ELLIE LEESA BURKE

MacMILLAN WHARF: DAVID W. DUNLAP

(While neither is wrong, "wharf" comes closer to describing what this structure is—in the sense of having multiple piers and docks.)

Stretching 1,450 feet (as long as the Empire State Building is high), MacMillan Wharf is in many ways the real heart of town, and its chief gateway. Like any great civic hub, it embraces a multitude of functions and users—each all but oblivious to the other. First and foremost—though they often complain that they are treated last and least—come the commercial fishermen, whose boats hug two finger piers on the east side of the wharf. Closer to shore, perpendicular floating docks accommodate smaller commercial vessels, including lobstermen. On the west side is the terminus for two fast ferry services to Boston, where passengers queue up or disembark by the dozens, sometimes hundreds. Even more crowds are drawn to the gleaming white, dolphin-nosed whale-watching vessels. Sailboats and party boats complete the lively mix. Before we wander any farther out on the 950-foot causeway, let's talk nomenclature. MacMillan Wharf honors Provincetown's most famous native son and its preeminent hometown hero: Rear Admiral Donald Baxter MacMillan of 473 Commercial Street, an intrepid and imaginative Arctic explorer, anthropologist, geographer, and naturalist. MacMillan Wharf is the successor to the Railroad Wharf of 1873, which was also known as Town Wharf, since it was given to the town by the New York, New Haven & Hartford Railroad after freight service to the water's edge was abandoned. You'll sometimes hear old-timers refer to MacMillan as Town Wharf. That's led to a bit of confusion in some historical accounts, which state that MacMillan Wharf is an updated and renamed Railroad Wharf. It isn't. It's a completely separate structure that was built to the east of Railroad Wharf, and closely parallel, from 1955 to 1957. The wharf was built on 14- to 18-inch-diameter pilings of creosote-treated Southern pine, warranted for a 50-year lifespan. The last slab of concrete in the roadbed was poured in June 1956, with 11 days to go before the Blessing of the Fleet, which was the first time the pier was put to public use. The formal dedication of the pier occurred more than a year later, in July 1957.

KATY WARD

served as the town's main thoroughfare. Because houses had been oriented toward the harbor, many had to be turned around or the "front" door had to be reconstructed to face the new street. Some houses, however, still remain oriented toward the shore.

Provincetown Art Association & Museum (PAAM) (508-487-1750; paam.org), 460 Commercial Street. Established in 1914 by a group of artists and townspeople (including Charles Hawthorne and E. Ambrose Webster), this nationally recognized cultural institution is an essential part of Provincetown's community and art colony. The donation of works by the organizing artists and two juried exhibitions mounted in the summer of 1915 began PAAM's traditions of collecting and exhibiting the work of the local community of artists. By then, the art community at the tip of Cape Cod had become a refuge of artists and expatriates returned from war-torn Europe. Today, PAAM includes five sparkling galleries with over 2,000 selections in its permanent collection. There are also rotating exhibits by both established and emerging artists and a series of events, such as Secret Garden Tours, Summer Jazz concerts and lectures, as well as educational workshops and youth programs. Open daily and year-round with free admission after 5 p.m. on Fridays. $–$$$$.

Expedition Whydah (508-487-8899; discoverpirates.com), 16 MacMillan Wharf. Open mid-May through October. This museum is devoted to chronicling the story of the *Whydah*, the only pirate ship ever salvaged. Story has it, the *Whydah* sank 1,500 feet offshore from Wellfleet's Marconi Beach on April 26, 1717, and Cape Codder Barry Clifford discovered it in 1984. They also have a Whydah Pirate Museum that has more interactive science activities, located at 674 Route 28 in West Yarmouth. $–$$.

Provincetown Marina (508-487-0571; ptownmarina.com), 9 Ryder Street Extension. After 46 years of ownership under Provincetown's prominent Cabral family, the former Fisherman's Wharf sold in 2016 to its current owner, Charles "Chuck" Lagasse. Much needed renovations have taken place over the years including the name change, but Chuck has proven to be a town player, keeping some key historic features in place, such as the ever-popular waterfront tribute, *They Also Faced the Sea* (see also "Provincetown's Sea-Women" on page 330), on the old fish house building at the end of the pier.

PROVINCETOWN ART ASSOCIATION & MUSEUM   KIM GRANT

HISTORY WAS MADE HERE

Old Harbor Lifesaving Station (508-487-1256; nps.gov/caco), Race Point Beach. Open July and August. This 1898 structure, one of nine original Lifesaving Service stations on the Outer Cape, was floated by barge from Chatham to its present location in 1977—just in the nick of time. One year later the great nor'easter of 1978 blew through and wiped out its original location. The Lifesaving Service, precursor to the Coast Guard, rescued crews from ships wrecked by shallow sandbars and brutal nor'easters. The boat room contains the original equipment, but on Thursday at 6 p.m. (confirm the time before going), hourlong demonstrations are given using the old-fashioned techniques. "Surfmen" launch a rescue line to the wrecked ship and haul in the distressed sailors one at a time. Plaques lining the boardwalk to the museum explain how the service worked. In June and July there are also "breeches buoy rescue reenactments" conducted on Thursday evenings. Donation suggested, and you'll have to pay to park at Race Point Beach.

Provincetown Marina has 100 private slips, 85 moorings with launch service, and the capacity to accommodate vessels up to 300 feet. If you're not staying on a slip, it's still fun to walk the pier and admire all the fancy boats.

Bas Relief Park, 106 Bradford Street, behind Town Hall. In anticipation of the 400th anniversary of the Pilgrims' landing in Provincetown, the town gave the historic park a much-needed facelift. Most importantly were repairs made to the 6-by-9 foot bronze plaque and surrounding 70-by-20 foot granite structure that was created in 1921 by Cyrus Edward Dallin, a renowned American sculptor. The plaque's design represents a scene in a cabin of the *Mayflower* during the signing of the Mayflower Compact. Two of the secondary on-site monuments were also restored, including a memorial on the western side of the park for the five Pilgrims who perished aboard the *Mayflower* while it was anchored in Provincetown Harbor, as well as a monument to the east of the park dedicated to the 41 men and women who signed the Mayflower Compact.

Provincetown Town Hall (508-487-7000; provincetown-ma.gov), 260 Commercial Street. Constructed in 1886, the building serves as the seat of local government and community agencies. The beautiful auditorium is also used for concerts and lectures. Look for an art collection throughout and for the Works Progress Administration–era murals of farmers and fishermen by Ross Moffett and a portrait by Charles Hawthorne.

Pilgrim Monument and Provincetown Museum (508-487-1310; pilgrim-monument .org), 1 High Pole Hill Road, off Winslow Street from Bradford Street. Open April through November. The 252-foot monument (the tallest all-granite US monument) commemorates the Pilgrims' first landing in Provincetown on November 11, 1620, and their 5-week stay in the harbor while searching for a good place to settle. President Theodore Roosevelt laid the cornerstone in 1907 and President Taft dedicated it in 1910. Climb the 116 stairs of the monument—modeled after the Torre del Mangia in Siena, Italy—for a panoramic view of the Outer Cape. On a clear day, you can see 42 miles to Boston. At the museum, one wing is devoted to early Pilgrim travails: the *May-flower*'s first landing, finding corn and fresh water, the unsuccessful search for a place to settle. Another wing is dedicated to the local Wampanoag tribe, including arrowheads, implements, tools, and images. The museum also showcases artifacts brought in by Donald MacMillan, who explored the Arctic with fellow explorer Robert Peary; the town's first fire engine, built in the 1830s by an apprentice of Paul Revere; exhibits dedicated to a whaling captain's life ashore; the birth of modern theater; shipwrecks; and much more. Parking ($$$) is good for the day, so feel free to go downtown after you've had enough of PMPM. It also gets you one free admission into the museum.

Center for Coastal Studies (508-487-3622; coastalstudies.org), 5 Holway Avenue. This independent, nonprofit institution is dedicated to research, public education, and conservation programs for the coastal and marine environments. Among other things, researchers study the endangered right whale (there are only about 350 to 400 in the world) and maintain the largest population database of humpback whales in the Gulf of Maine. They have raised important environmental questions about the overall health of our oceans and have implemented programs such as the Marine Debris and Plastics Program, which aims to reduce waste from recreational and commercial users. Stop by the center to see the life-size skeleton of Spinnaker, a humpback whale found dead in Maine off the shore

PROVINCETOWN TOWN HALL   KATY WARD

of Acadia National Park in 2015. She was well known to naturalists and scientists alike, spending her first summer with her mother off Massachusetts. Later she came to prefer more northerly areas of the Gulf of Maine (the body of water stretching between the Bay of Fundy in Canada and Cape Cod and Georges Bank to the south and east). During her life she was known to have been entangled at least four times. Her second-known entanglement was lethal, something the CCS now knows due to the preservation of her skeleton. The center is the only East Coast organization authorized to disentangle whales trapped in fishing gear.

✻ **Universalist Meetinghouse** (508-487-9344; uumh.org), 236 Commercial Street. This 1847 Greek Revival church contains trompe l'oeil murals (by Carl Wendte, who painted similar murals for Nantucket's Unitarian Universalist Church), a Sandwich glass chandelier, and pews made with Provincetown pine. The pews are decorated with medallions carved from whales' teeth.

Pilgrims' First Landing Park, West End of Commercial Street, near the breakwater. It's difficult to imagine that centuries ago the Pilgrims dropped anchor just a few feet offshore from this park. But indeed, it's true. There's a common misconception that Plymouth was the Pilgrims' first landing spot. Yes, they did land there, dubbing it "New Plymouth" because they departed from Plymouth, England (and they have Plymouth Rock to prove it). But what many people do not know is that 5 weeks before discovering Plymouth, the Pilgrims sailed into Provincetown Harbor, where they docked and produced the first written document alluding to government in the new colony, the Mayflower Compact. (Pick up a copy of Edward Winslow's *Mourt's Relation,* which describes the discovery and shows maps of where the first steps of land were supposedly taken). Although the park is an understated tribute (with only one placard, a few memorial stones, and unkempt greenery), plans to rehab the space are in place.

SCENIC DRIVES Drive Race Point Road from Route 6 and around Province Lands, passing by Herring Cove Beach, until you hit the West End rotary near the breakwater.

PROVINCETOWN'S SEA-WOMEN

An amazing tribute to the Portuguese matriarchs of Provincetown, the installation, *They Also Faced the Sea*, created by Ewa Nogeic and Norma Holt, was installed on the old fish house building on Fisherman's Wharf (now Provincetown Marina) in 2003. These five women—Bea Cabral, Mary Janson, Frances Raymond, Almeda Segura, and Eva Silva—were local women whose lives were predicated on the wharf and by the uncertainty of the sea. When their husbands left shore, they watched the ships disappear into the horizon as they waved goodbye. When the men returned, their wives anxiously waited on the wharf eager for their arrival. When a fishing vessel had been gone too long, the wives would stand together on the wharf sharing their dread and worry, later consoling each other when the boat returned at half-mast—if it returned at all. They were the mothers, sisters, daughters, lovers of the fishing fleet, often overlooked when men accounted for the heroism of the fishery. Over the years, harsh weather and salt water faded the installation's photographs. In 2015, several locals sought donations for repairs, raising over $12,000 for the reinstallation and printing of these soul-bearing images. I hope these women forever remain perched above our harbor, keeping watch over Provincetown.

PAUL SCHULENBURG

❋ To Do

Despite its scanty size, Provincetown offers a punch of excitement for anyone visiting. Within the 16-mile stretch of land, there are endless activities, restaurants, galleries, beaches, and more. But personally, I find the energy of the street's crowd is what makes this town so special. Whether it's a drag queen strutting her stuff down Commercial Street, pleading you to come to a show while posing for selfies, or the face-painting and balloon animal booths lined up in front of Town Hall, ready to glamour and excite your child. There's also the statuesque military man who perches on the corner of Standish and Ryder Streets looking eerily fake—until he winks at you. It's a bustling unique town full of curiosities.

AIRPLANE RIDES **P-Town Airs** (508-237-5563; p-townairtours.com), 176 Race Point Road. Soar high in the sky in the completely renovated 1940 Waco UPF7 biplane or the restored Cessna 172. Reservations recommended. $$$$+.

BICYCLING & RENTALS **Province Lands** offers 8 miles of scenic trails perfect for bike riding. Soak in the solitude as you wind through dunes, peddle around ponds, and pass the Cape tip's popular beaches, including Race Point and Herring Cove Beach. Trails are paved and marked with access points on Race Point Road near Route 6 and parking areas at Beech Forest, Province Lands Visitor Center, and both beaches. It's a beautiful and rewarding ride, but prepare yourself for some steep hills. At a steady pace it takes about 2 hours to complete the 8-mile loop, or you can pack lunch and take a more leisurely pace. All logistics aside, it's glorious and will be a highlight of your trip.

You can rent bicycles and equipment from several places including **Gale Force Bikes** (508-487-4849; galeforcebikes.com), 144 Bradford Street; **Provincetown Bike Rentals** (774-447-4539; provincetownbikerentals.com), 136 Bradford Street; and **Ptown Bikes** (508-487-8735; ptownbikes.com), 42 Bradford Street. Shops are open mid-April to mid-October and bikes can be rented by the hour or daily. $$$–$$$$.

Pedal Ptown Bike Tours (pedalptown.com), 6 Standish Street. Enjoy a guided tour with Rik Ahlberg, a year-round bicycling enthusiast and talented storyteller. Rik offers two-hour tours (3 miles total). Tours lend an opportunity to explore aspects of town that casual visitors often miss. Bring your own bike or rent one from Rik. Tours run from April to early December with private tours available year-round by request. $$$$+.

BOAT EXCURSIONS & RENTALS **Hindu Charters** (508-542-2996; sailschoonerhindu .com), MacMillan Wharf. Open mid-May through October. The story behind this historic wooden sailboat rivals the tall tales of any salty dog. Built for pleasure during the roaring 1920s, the schooner *Hindu* is weathered in history, from pleasure trips to sailing spices from India to the United States, or assisting the US Coast Guard Coastal

THE *HINDU* AND *BAY LADY II* DOCKED SIDE BY SIDE ON MacMILLAN WHARF KATY WARD

DUNE SHACKS

In the dunes between Race Point and High Head in North Truro, beyond the end of Snail Road, along 2 miles of ridges and valleys, stand a line of weather-beaten dune shacks. Constructed between 1935 and 1950 from driftwood and scavenged materials, the shacks are the subject of local legend. Over the years, notable writers and artists have called them home for weeks, months, even years: among the tenants have been Jack Kerouac, e. e. cummings, Norman Mailer, Jackson Pollock, poet Harry Kemp, and Eugene O'Neill.

When the CCNS was created in 1961, the federal government set up 25-year or lifelong leases with squatters who were living in the shacks. (Only one of the inhabitants held a clear title to the

KATY WARD

land.) Some shacks are still occupied. In 1985, Joyce Johnson, a dune dweller since the early 1970s, founded the Peaked Hill Trust to oversee some of the shacks. Members of the trust can win stays through a lottery system; write to P.O. Box 1705, Provincetown, MA 02657, for membership information (or try thecompact.org). Since Province Lands was added to

KATY WARD

KATY WARD

the National Register of Historic Places in 1989, the maintenance and fate of most of the historic shacks have fallen to the National Park Service. At this point, policies are decided from season to season. The park service still sets aside a few shacks, though, for an artist-in-residence program.

I've won weeklong stays in a shack owned by Hazel Hawthorne Werner. On my first visit, it took until the fifth day to shake the first thought that came to my mind after returning to the shack from a walk: I wonder who called while I was out? Remarkable. Remarkable that the shack felt so much like home and remarkable that it was such a deeply ingrained response to being away. I wrote many other impressions but didn't produce anything approaching Cynthia Huntington's *The Salt House*, which she wrote over many, many months of living in that shack. It's well worth reading.

There are a few off-road parking spots at the end of Snail Road. Take the short woodland trail and hike up the first steep dune, then over the next two crests; the shacks will appear in the distance. You can also reach the shacks by walking east from Race Point Beach. Remember, however, that most shacks are still occupied, and people live out there for privacy, to pursue the creative process uninhibited, to contemplate in isolation.

KATY WARD

Patrol along the Eastern Seaboard during World War II. Following the war, the *Hindu* settled in Provincetown in 1946 and remained there for decades, serving primarily as a charter vessel. Eventually she fell into disrepair, spending some time in Key West, Florida, until her revival, when father and son team Bill and Josh Rowan bought her in 2012. Since then she's undergone extensive restoration and is back in action, sailing across the harbor in all her glory. Hindu Charters offers day sails, as well as private and sunset sailing charters. $$$–$$$$+.

Bay Lady II (508-487-9308; sailcapecod.com), MacMillan Wharf. Trips offered mid-May to mid-October. All aboard this traditionally gaff-rigged schooner for a 2-hour harbor sail across Cape Cod Bay. It's a really relaxing way to see the area and spend time on the water. $$$.

Flyer's Boat Rental (508-487-0898; flyersboats.com), 131A Commercial Street. Open mid-May through September. Flyer's has been a working boatyard for more than 75 years. Here you can rent large pontoon boats (perfect for families), speedboats, skiffs, sailboats, kayaks, and paddleboards by the hour, half-day, or full day. Flyer's also offers moorings, sunset cruises, and the popular Long Point Shuttle, which transports people from MacMillan Wharf to Long Point every half hour in season. $$–$$$$+.

DUNE TOURS **Art's Dune Tours** (508-487-1950; artsdunetours.com), 4 Standish Street. Trips mid-April to mid-November. The Costa family has expertly led tourists on these narrated, hour-long, off-road 4x4 trips through the CCNS dunes since 1946. I highly recommend taking one. The GMC Suburbans stop at least once (on the beach or atop a high dune) for photos, so you can take in the panoramic views. Reservations necessary for sunset trips. One of Art's Dune Tours drivers, Paul Benson, told me, "When I drive a Dune Tour, I'm trying to put the entire Provincetown story into context, so people can see the whole town in a deeper way. I talk about the whaling ships that brought the Portuguese to town, and the art colony and writer's colony that helped turn Provincetown into a funky and special place. I talk about how the magic landscape of the dunes nurtured those artists and writers, and how they found a home away from home that fed

FLYER'S BOAT RENTAL KATY WARD

their creativity. I tell of the ice sheets that made the Cape, and the blinding storms that wrecked thousands of ships on this shore. I want to help people see this place more fully, experience it more deeply, feel the centuries of stories that built our present day. And regardless of what I do or don't say, the beauty of the landscape arrests everyone. There's a reason locals recommend the Dune Tours. They showcase what makes this place special." $$$.

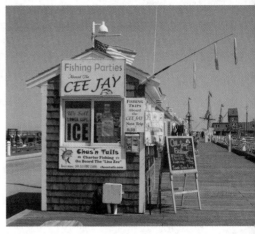

KATY WARD

FISHING *Big game:* **Beth Ann Charters** (860-716-0202; provincetowncharter fishing.com), MacMillan Wharf. Open daily from early May to late October. Fish and cruise the harbor aboard the 38-foot *Beth Ann* with Captain Rich Wood. Charters offer sportfishing for striped bass, bluefish, cod, haddock, or maybe bluefin tuna if you're lucky; whale watching trips off Stellwagen Bank Marine Sanctuary; and other specialty charters for those looking for more than just fish and whales. $$$$+.

Other fishing charters located on MacMillan Wharf include the **Cee-Jay** (508-487-4330; provincetowncjfishing.com); **Chas'n Tails Charter Fishing** on board the *Lisa Zee* (508-241-3469; chasntails.com); **Cape Tip'N Charter Fishing** (508-277-0840; capetipn fishing.com); and **Hook Charters** (508-681-9490; fishingcharterprovincetown.com) with Captain Steve.

On shore: **Herring Cove Beach** is a very popular place for shore casting, as well as the Race Point and Hatches Harbor stretch. Decades ago (before the seals) surfcasters would on occasion catch 50-pound bass, 10-pound blues, Pollock, and even tuna from shore.

FITNESS CLUBS **Mussel Beach Health Club** (508-487-0001; musselbeach.net), 35 Bradford Street, and **Provincetown Gym** (508-487-2776; ptowngym.com), 81 Shank Painter Road, are equipped with the workout essentials. Muscle Beach tends to be

ART'S DUNE TOURS   PAUL BENSON

S-4 CRASH SITE: DAVID W. DUNLAP

On 17 December 1927, 34 sailors, four officers, and two visitors were aboard the USS *S-4*, which was on a trial run when it surfaced unexpectedly in the path of the oncoming destroyer, USCG *Paulding*, on rum-running patrol. The sub quickly sank more than 100 feet, unable to surface on its own. Twenty-four hours later, a Navy diver managed to communicate with survivors in the forward torpedo compartment by pounding out Morse code on the hull. He asked how many survivors were there. "There are six; please hurry. Will you be long now?" The Navy rebuffed offers of assistance from an experienced commercial salvager in Boston and from the fishermen of Provincetown. But gale-force winter winds hindered the official rescue efforts. "Please send us oxygen, food, and water," said a coded message on December 19th. To Provincetown's growing distress and anger, the Navy was unable to do so. The rescue effort was called off on the 22nd.

The *S-4* was raised in March 1928 and returned to service as a test ship used to devise rescue and salvage methods. She was credited with having indirectly helped save 33 crewmembers of the USS *Squalus*, which sank in 1939 off New Hampshire. A memorial cross is placed in the yard of the Church of St. Mary of the Harbor, 517 Commercial Street. "Provincetown never forgets the *S-4*," Mary Heaton Vorse wrote in *Time and the Town*. "There is a special terror in the memory of those men waiting, tapping their patient messages, and dying. Everyone in Provincetown had a feeling that it was their individual task to save these men and no one could do anything."

geared more toward men, while Provincetown Gym might feel less intimidating for women. Day use and weekly passes available. $$–$$$.

FOR FAMILIES 🍴 **Playgrounds** are located at both ends of town: at Bradford and Howland Streets (East End) and at Bradford and Nickerson Streets (West End).

KAYAKS & PADDLEBOARDS **Provincetown Aquasports** (508-413-9563; ptownaquasports.com), 333 Commercial Street #1 (rear), offers a variety of rental options and guided tours. **Flyer's Boat Rental** (see under *Boat Excursions & Rentals*) offers reasonable rates on kayaks and paddleboards, too.

BOAT RENTALS KATY WARD

SAILING **Dog Gone Sailing Charters** (508-566-0410; doggonesailingcharters .com), MacMillan Wharf. Sail aboard the 30-foot cutter *Moondance II* with Captain Ro and Spinnaker (the saltiest dog you will ever meet, literally). Reserve a full or half day on the water whale watching, or enjoy a sunset sail near Long Point. They also cater to wedding parties, and even burials at sea.

SPECIAL PROGRAMS ❋ **Fine Arts Work Center** (508-487-9960; fawc.org), 24 Pearl Street. The center was founded in 1968 by a group of writers, artists, and patrons, including Robert Motherwell, Hudson Walker, Stanley Kunitz, and Myron Stout. And its intent was to provide a place for emerging artists to pursue independent work within a sympathetic community of their peers. In 1972 the center purchased Days Lumber Yard, where artists have worked in small studios since 1914. (Frank Days Jr., who had been concerned about the plight of artists, built 10 studios over his lumberyard. And Charles Hawthorne was one of the first tenants in 1914.) Writing and visual arts residencies, which include a monthly stipend and materials allowance, run October through April. Twenty candidates are chosen from a pool of about 1,000. Year-round readings, seminars, workshops, and exhibits are open to the public. There's also a great summer program for creative writing and visual arts, which offers weeklong and weekend workshops in printmaking, sculpture, fiction writing, and the like. Keep your eyes open for talks, presentations, and readings by visiting instructors like Kate Clinton. (File under fun trivia: Annie Dillard once completed a residency here.) Donations.

✳ ✿ **Provincetown Museum School** (508-487-1750; paam.org), 460 Commercial Street at Bangs Street. Programs run year-round; galleries open in summer. Printmaking, painting, monotypes, and watercolor are just some of the classes taught by notable artists at the Provincetown Art Association & Museum. Children's classes are also offered; some courses are accredited.

SWIMMING POOLS Both the **Provincetown Inn** (508-487-9500; provincetowninn .com), 1 Commercial Street, and the **Boatslip Resort & Beach Club** (508-487-1669; boatslipresort), 161 Commercial Street, have giant Olympic-size pools that tend to attract a lively crowd, usually gay men. The **Harbor Hotel Provincetown** (508-487-1711; harborhotelptown.com), 698 Commercial Street, is more geared toward families (and free). Regardless of where you go, be prepared to spend money on food and drinks at the outside cabana bars. $$.

TENNIS Town courts are located at Motta Field off Winslow Street.

   Provincetown Tennis Club (508-487-9574; provincetowntennis.com), 288 Bradford Street. Open May through October. Clay and hard courts.

WALKING TOURS **Historic Walking Tour of Provincetown** (508-487-1310; pilgrim -monument.org). Call for schedule and reservations, runs July through August. Led by staff members from the Pilgrim Monument and Provincetown Museum (PMPM) and the CCNS, this 90-minute tour is a great introduction to art and architecture, to whalers and writers. Please, don't be too cool to take a walking tour in Provincetown. $$.

WHALE WATCHING For many people, seeing whales breech and frolic is one of the most exhilarating and sacred things they've ever done. There's something so inspiring about watching these enormous and ancient creatures feed and play just a few feet from the boat. If you've never done it, put it on your to-do list. Located just 8 miles from Provincetown are the fertile feeding grounds of Stellwagen Bank, home to a variety of marine life including migrating finback

WHALE WATCHING ANNE GREENBAUM

LONG POINT, WOOD END, AND RACE POINT LIGHT

At the very tip of Cape Cod sits **Long Point Beach**, an unspoiled spit of sand that simultaneously delivers views of the Atlantic Ocean and the town's bayside beach. The "Point" (as locals call it) is often far less crowded than other beaches because it's only accessible by boat or by foot. **Long Point Lighthouse**, at the tip of the spit, was built in 1826, two years before a community of fishermen began to construct homes out there. By 1846 there were 61 families on Long Point, all of whom returned to town during the Civil War (two Civil War forts were built on Long Point). At the southwest end of Long Point sits **Wood End** and the remnants of **Wood End Light Lookout Station**, a historic lighthouse built in 1872. The station was originally used as a navigational aid for vessels coming into the harbor. Wood End looks like Long Point and, like Long Point, it's under the care of the American Lighthouse Foundation, but when Long Point flashes green, Wood End flashes red, every 10 seconds. Its foghorn was especially chatty. The keeper's house was torn down after the light was automated in 1961, but an oil house remains (see also "*S-4 Crash Site: David W. Dunlap*" on page 336). To get to Long Point or Wood End, jump on Flyer's Shuttle at MacMillan Pier (see **Flyer's Boat Rental** under *Boat Excursions & Rentals*) or trek the 2½-hour hike across the West End's breakwater and along the shoreline until you reach the tip's end (see **Breakwater** under *Walks*). There are no restrooms, facilities, or lifeguards, and both Wood End and Long Point Lighthouses are closed to the public.

Not to fret, the elder **Race Point Lighthouse** (855-722-3959; racepointlighthouse.org) offers guided tours. Race Point Light was first illuminated in 1816 after travel became treacherous for vessels trying to navigate the sand bars near the Cape's most northern tip. The tower's light was 25 feet above sea level and was one of the earliest revolving lights—in an attempt to differentiate it from other lighthouses on Cape Cod. By 1876 the old stone tower was falling apart, and replaced by a 45-foot lighthouse, lined with brick. It wasn't until 1957 that Race Point Light was electrified, and not until 1994 that the beacon and fog signal became solar-powered. In 1995, the lighthouse and the keeper's house were renovated including a new roof, new windows and doors, and other modernized upgrades to the interior and exterior. Three keepers and their families lived at the lighthouse in the two separate keeper's houses. The children walked almost 3 miles over sand to school every day. In the 1930s, a keeper named James Hinckley made the trip much quicker by customizing a Ford into a dune buggy; the trip now took just 30 minutes. We now use a newer form of dune buggy: a Suburban! Today, the lighthouse optic is still an active aid to navigation, maintained by the US Coast Guard. Tours are typically held on first and third Saturdays, June through October. You can get to the lighthouse by walking or by your own four-wheel vehicle and permit (see **Hatches Harbor** under *Beaches*). Overnight stays in the Keeper's House are wonderful for families and groups, with three differently sized bedrooms that share 1.5 baths as

and humpback whales. Whale sightings vary each season. Some summers sightings are a dime a dozen, although it never feels that blasé; and other times, not so much. Most whale-watch cruises last about 3½ hours and have an on-board naturalist. Bring a sweater (even in summer) and seasickness pills if you think you'll need them.

Dolphin Fleet Whale Watch (508-240-3636; whalewatch.com), 307 Commercial Street and MacMillan Wharf. Offers trips starting in mid-April through October. The Dolphin Fleet works in conjunction with the CCS. $$$$.

Before or after your trip, stop by the **Stellwagen Bank National Marine Sanctuary** (781-545-8026; stellwagen.noaa.gov), 205 Commercial Street at Carver Street. There's

well as a living room (maximum occupancy of 11). You can also rent the remodeled Whistle House, which opened in 2007 and can accommodate eight people in two bedrooms. Solar energy powers appliances in the kitchen; bring your own food, water, and linens. It's glorious out there. Be sure to check the website beforehand, as tours and overnight stays might be cancelled due to piping plover activity.

WOOD END LIGHTHOUSE MARCIA DUGGAN/CAPECODSOUL

a small exhibit with touch-screen computers offering images and information about local marine life, as well as two "video-scopes" that allow you to look into the underwater world of Massachusetts Bay. (See also the **Center for Coastal Studies** under to **To Do**). Free.

✳ Green Space

BEACHES "A man may stand there and put all America behind him." —Henry David Thoreau, describing the great Outer Cape beaches in the 1800s.

RACE POINT BEACH LEESA BURKE

Provincetown has over 30 miles of pristine beach, protected and maintained by the CCNS.

Race Point Beach, CCNS, off Route 6. This beach is great for sunbathing as it faces north and gets sunshine all day long. Find a spot amidst the wide swatch of sand that stretches far off into the distance (Thoreau could not have said it better). Race Point tends to have long, and sometimes rough, breaking waves. The strong undercurrent and steep slopes in the ocean floor can make it difficult for inexperienced swimmers. Small "kiddie" pools sometimes trickle in between low and high tide, making the perfect playpen for children. Keep your eyes open for seals playing in the waves (but stay away, as great white sharks have been spotted in this area). In spring, with binoculars, you might see a whale spouting offshore. Facilities include lifeguards, showers, and restrooms, in season. Parking late June to early September (and fall weekends) costs $$ daily (permit valid all day at any CCNS beach). The lot generally fills up by 11 a.m. in summer and frees up after 5:30 p.m.

Hatches Harbor, CCNS. One of the most difficult beaches to get to, but worth it. There are two ways to get there: by foot or with an off-road-vehicle permit. Hatches Harbor extends north of Race Point with an outer and inner driving path. I recommend this for people who are spending a fair amount of time on the Outer Cape and prefer the beach to everything else. Cruising the sandy trail is an experience in itself. Take the inner path and glide up and down dunes before passing lush rose hips and the historic Race Point Lighthouse, until you reach the shoreline (see also "Long Point, Wood End, and Race Point Light" on page 338). Take the outer path for views of the ocean and abutting dune. Scale the beach until you find the perfect spot to park. Another bonus? You don't have to lug anything with you. It's the epitome of "living your best life." However, there are some downfalls. ORV access is regularly affected by piping plovers, causing closures because Rangers will section off large areas and driving paths in an effort to protect hatchlings, which often nest in the tracks left by vehicles and footprints. Closures often cause overcrowding as vehicles try to squeeze into the one open area. You can visit the park service website for a map showing current ORV trail openings and closures. Permits are costly and available at the Ranger's Station (to the left at Race Point Beach). You must have a four-wheel drive vehicle with a valid inspection sticker and license, as well as other safety equipment such as a tire gauge, a shovel, a rope, and a wooden board. You will be required to view the Orientation Program by the CCNS prior to receiving a permit and agree to abide by the rules and regulations, such as the "low and slow" initiative. Permits are issued on a first-come, first-serve basis with up to 400 weekly permits and 3,000 annual permits available. $$$$+.

Herring Cove Beach, CCNS, at the end of Route 6. If you've visited Herring Cove in the past, you might be a little confused by its new look. No longer can you pull up to the beach, park, and watch the sunset from the comfort of your driver's seat. A series of nor'easters and winter storms decimated the famous parking lot, sending large chunks of asphalt into the ocean and scattered along the shoreline. Entire sections of the lot eroded, leaving only a few spaces open for parking. Under the direction of the CCNS, the parking lot was given a complete makeover and moved 50 feet back, allowing for ample space and a new life span. Though the convenience is gone, the beach still boasts spectacular sunsets. Facilities include lifeguards, showers, and restrooms, and accessibility by shuttle. See also **Farland by the Beach** under **Entertainment**.

Harbor Beach, a.k.a. the town's bayside beach, is about 3.5 miles long and parallel to Commercial Street. Although there is little beach at high tide, it's great to walk the flats at low tide. Access the beach to the right of Provincetown Marina, near the breakwater in the West End, or across the street from the Harbor Hotel in the East End. Keep your eyes open for town landings along Commercial Street, which serve as public beach access points.

(See also "Shark Awareness" on page 282.)

WALKS **Beech Forest Trail**, CCNS, off Race Point Road from Route 6. This 1-mile loop takes you into Cape Cod's sandy forest and around one large freshwater pond. At a leisurely pace the trail takes about 45 minutes. Expect varied terrain of soft and hard

HERRING COVE BEACH KATY WARD

WALKING ON WATER (SORTA)

The West End Breakwater/Long Point Dike easily qualifies as Provincetown's most imposing architecture. With roughly 1 mile of giant granite boulders stretching out like a highway to the sea, it's my most favorite walk in town.

Though technically not a "breakwater" but rather a "dike" (the only official breakwater in town can be seen at the end of MacMillan Wharf), it serves as a footpath across the harbor to the secluded Wood End and Long Point. A walk across the 6,150-foot dike can be challenging at times and I don't recommend it to those who are ill footed. The most important thing (besides sunblock, water, and sneakers) is to check the tide chart before heading out! At high tide, sections of the dike become impassable and the rocks extremely slippery. There have been numerous 911 calls from people stranded on the dike during a big tide or swept into the sea in a strong current, as well as broken arms, legs, and noses. It can be dangerous. With that said, just be mindful of the tide, because it waits for no man.

Built in 1910 (finished in 1915), the Long Point Dike was constructed to protect the harbor from offshore coastal hazards and prevent a permanent breach from separating Long Point. But the dike was no match for Mother Nature. Strong riptides and storms continuously battered the dike and continue today. There is also new evidence that the dike may have done more harm than good by restricting the ebb and flow of the salt marsh, a vital breeding ground for fish. Studies and restoration plans by the US Army Corp. of Engineers are being discussed with the town.

MARCIA DUGGAN/CAPECODSOUL

sand, as well as one steep wooden stairway through a forest of beech trees. In summer, be sure to wear insect repellent and long pants to avoid mosquito bites and poison ivy. Starting in mid-May, warblers migrating from South America pack the area. Do not feed the birds, because Rangers will charge you a fine. This trail is especially beautiful in autumn, when the forest fills with color, as well as in winter, when snowy drifts blanket the dunes. If it stays cold long enough, the ponds will freeze, creating a local ice-skating rink.

Nicky's Park, off Harry Kemp Way. This park is nearly 4 acres in size and half-wooded, half-wetland. Protected by the town's conservation trust, it includes a small pond (Jimmy's Pond) and is surrounded by high bush blueberry and red maple swamp. It is the town's most important habitat for the water-willow borer moth, the threatened few-flowered sedge, and the bog twayblade orchid (which can be spotted near the pond).

Clapps Pond, off Route 6. This 3- to 4-mile trail takes you around beautiful Clapps Pond and through a mixed terrain of sand, woodland, and marshy wetlands. It's a peaceful hike through the woods, and I recommend it highly. You can also bring your dog. Clapps Pond and the surrounding acreage are co-owned by the CCNS, the state Division of Marine Fisheries and Wildlife, and the town of Provincetown.

Hatches Harbor, CCNS, near Race Point. Expect varied terrain with marsh and ocean views, sandy shoals, and utter

BEECH FOREST TRAIL KIM GRANT

remoteness. Park in the small lot off Province Lands Road and follow the dike trail to the dunes. It's not the easiest walk in the park, but more of a serene adventure. See also under *Beaches*; "Dune Shacks" on page 332; and **Province Lands** under *Bicycles & Rentals*.

✳ Lodging

BED-AND-BREAKFASTS & GUEST HOUSES **Lands End Inn** (508-487-0706; landsendinn.com), 22 Commercial Street. Book now, and I promise you will not be disappointed. Nestled on the top of Gull Hill in the West End of town, this inn not only delivers stunning panoramic views of the harbor but also a visual feast inside, chock-full of Victoriana, woodcarvings, heirloom antiques, and gorgeous stained glass floor lamps. Built in 1904, the inn offers 16 rooms and two apartments; the tower rooms and loft suite are magnificently decorated and situated. Most rooms have access to private decks; some sleep four. If you're looking for peace and quiet coupled with

impressive views and eclectic décor, this is the place to stay. $$$–$$$$.

Queen Vic Guesthouse (508-487-8425; queenvicptown.com), 166 Commercial Street. A historic sea captain's home turned boutique bed-and-breakfast. Each of the nine rooms comes fitted with lush bedding, some with gothic stained four-poster beds, bright white bead board, and some with private balconies. Built in the 1870s, the inn boasts large windows and mirrors enhancing the antique narrow design. Start the day with a simple yet delicious breakfast of fresh fruit, baked goods, and Belgium waffles made by your hosts (Josh and Stan are the benchmarks of hospitality). The cozy and comfortable front-yard patio bordering Commercial Street is another guest favorite. Sip drinks around the fire pit on a cool

LANDS END INN KIM GRANT

evening or head across the street to the Boatslip and enjoy its famous Tea Dance (see under **Entertainment**). $$–$$$.

❄ **White Porch** (508-364-2549; whiteporchinn.com), 7 Johnson Street. This completely remodeled guest house and carriage house burst onto the scene in the late 2000s, and I couldn't be happier about it. The nine soothing and sophisticated rooms ooze a contemporary beach aesthetic and have been updated with

QUEEN VIC GUESTHOUSE STAN COTTNER

iPod docking stations, flat-screen TVs, and luxe bedding. It's all quite stylin'. Although you might be tempted to cocoon here (at least you girls out there), gather for drinks with the gang on the front porch. In- and off-season, it's a very mixed guest house, with all welcome, of course. Expanded continental breakfast. $–$$$.

❄ 🐾 **Benchmark Inn** (508-487-7440; benchmarkinn.com), 6 Dyer Street. Hospitality has been redefined by the Swiss innkeepers who purchased the inn in the early 2000s. Their seven rooms and penthouse are welcoming and upscale. Service is supreme (think nightly turndown), amenities are top-notch (think marble bathrooms), and the aesthetic is simple but elegant with clean lines. Fireplaces, wet bars, outdoor space, and fresh flowers are the norm. Extended continental breakfast included. $$–$$$$.

The Brass Key (508-487-9005; brasskey.com), 67 Bradford Street. Open April through December. More like a luxurious private enclave—fenced-in and gated—the Brass Key catapulted Provincetown accommodations to new heights when it opened. Purchased by the Crowne Pointe Inn in the late 2000s, all 43 rooms surrounding the enclosed pool and courtyard are completely different from one another. In addition to being elegant and

A FEW GENERALITIES ABOUT SLEEPING IN PROVINCETOWN

If you care about where you stay, don't go to Provincetown in summer without reservations. If you must wait until the last minute, there are often vacancies midweek in July. Most places have lengthy minimum-night stays during special events and holiday weekends—again, reserve early. (Rates for holiday weekends are always higher than I've reported.) Because the East End tends to be quieter than the West End, I've indicated where each lodging is located, unless it's in the middle of town. All guest houses included below welcome everyone, gay and straight, although there are always more gay visitors in the summer.

sophisticated, rooms have vaulted ceilings, working fireplaces, whirlpool baths, upscale amenities, nightly turndown, and antiques. Some have balconies; all have access to a widow's walk and three living rooms. An expansive continental breakfast buffet is served in the country inn–style Gatehouse. No children. $$–$$$$+.

Eben House (508-487-0386; ebenhouse.com), 90 Bradford Street. Paying homage to Captain Eben Snow and his Federal-style 1770s home, owners Kevin O'Shea and David Bowd hired local artist Michael Gredler to interpret and create large-scale, 18th-century, primitive-style portraits of the Snow family (with a touch of contempo flair, of course). Be sure to closely admire these paintings adorning each of the 14 guestrooms (as well as luxury bedding, restored hardwood floors, and some with claw foot tubs and fireplaces). Over the past two centuries, the house had various owners and uses, including David Fairbanks, who resided here in the early 1800s and founded what is now Seamen's Bank. In 1976, the house was restored and opened as David Fairbank's House, a museum that featured an extensive collection of early American folk art. In 1985, the museum was converted into a guesthouse and still operates as one today. The Eben House also has three additional houses located close to the main house. The Studio is a quaint one-bedroom cottage tucked into an ivy-covered hillside at the rear of the property; The Cottage, a historic artist studio located across the street from the main house, features two bedrooms, a large dining room with an overlooking loft, and an outdoor terrace; and The Residence, the largest of them all, is situated behind the Eben House property. This 2,700-square-foot building comes with four en-suite king bedrooms, a large eat-in kitchen, a living room, a dining room, and a brick courtyard furnished for outdoor entertaining. All guests have access to the main house amenities, which include an outdoor saltwater pool and a signature rustic breakfast. $$$–$$$$$.

The Inn at Cook Street (508-487-3894; innatcookstreet.com), 7 Cook Street (East End). Owners John Jay and Patrick operate a mixed house (gay, straight, men, women), which is just the way they like it. The gracious 1836 Greek revival sea captain's house offers four rooms, two suites, and two cottages. They are all very tasteful and highly recommended. Pick your room based on its sleigh bed (Garden Suite), how much sun it gets (the Retreat is very bright), or its deck access (some have a private deck). $$–$$$.

❄ 🐾 ✐ **Tucker Inn** (508-487-0381; thetuckerinn.com), 12 Center Street. This cozy eight-room inn, dating to 1872, is one of the most comfy, welcoming, and well-priced places to stay in town, thanks to owner Howard Burchman. He's constantly upgrading the offerings with things like flat-screen TVs and little gardens. The rooms are both soothing and simply decorated. One of the big pluses: The inn also offers arguably the best full breakfast in town, including eggs any style any morning, served on the brick patio in warm weather. Take time to hang out in the hot tub or relaxing garden, and I bet you'll return. Inquire about the nice little cottage, which rents weekly. The inn is a mixed house of gay, straight, men, women. (Still, like most other places, it's more gay than straight.) $–$$.

Inn at 7 Central (508-487-8855; innat7central.com), 7 Central Street. Open April to late October. This is a great spot. Centrally located, this renovated contemporary guesthouse offers something that most do not: each room has a private entrance and most have a private balcony. The shared courtyard deck is also relaxing and convivial. $$–$$$$.

APARTMENTS, COTTAGES & STUDIOS ✳ **Watermark Inn** (508-487-0165; watermark-inn.com), 603 Commercial Street at Wiley Street (East End). These 10 contemporary suites are right at the water's edge. They feature triangular gable windows, skylights, spacious living areas, and either a full kitchen or a kitchenette. (Two rooms have a fireplace.) Six

suites have sliding glass doors that open out onto private decks—perfect for when high tide laps at the deck. It's a 20-minute walk from town, and it features a rarity: on-site parking. Weekly and nightly rentals in summer; off-season $–$$$ nightly.

✳ ♪ **The Masthead** (508-487-0523; themasthead.com), 31–41 Commercial Street (West End). At the far end of the West End, about a 15-minute walk from the center of town, The Masthead offers a superb variety of distinctly "old Provincetown" apartments, cottages, and rooms. The neatly landscaped complex, operated by the Ciluzzi family since 1959, has a boardwalk with lounge chairs and access to the 450-foot private beach below. Each cottage has a large picture window facing the water. The units, in buildings more than 100 years old, have fully equipped kitchens, low ceilings, pine paneling, and Early American furnishings that are dated but nonetheless comfortable. Although most units can accommodate four people, one sleeps eight. It's a great place for families; children under 12 stay free. $$$–$$$$+.

Captain Jack's Wharf (508-487-1450; captainjackswharf.com), 73A Commercial Street at West Vine Street (West End). Open late May to late October. On a rustic old wharf, these 15 colorfully painted bohemian apartments (condos, actually) transport you back to Provincetown's early days as an emerging art colony. Many units have whitewashed interiors with skylights and lots of windows looking onto the harbor. Some first-floor units have narrow cracks between the planked floorboards—you can see the water beneath you! I particularly like Australis, a two-story unit with a spiral staircase and more than 1,000 square feet of space. The wharf is strewn with bistro tables, pots of flowers, and Adirondack chairs. Weekly rentals; $–$$$ off-season.

🐚 **White Horse Inn** (508-487-1790; whitehorseinnprovincetown.com), 500 Commercial Street at Daggett Lane (East

WATERMARK INN KIM GRANT

THE MASTHEAD KIM GRANT

End). Call to find out which months the inn is open. This low-key, artsy hostelry has been taking in guests since 1963, intent on providing clean, comfortable rooms at good prices. Mary Martin presides over six studio apartments that have been individually decorated with an eclectic, bohemian flair. Some are light and airy; some are dark and cozy. All defy description—although one bathroom is truly "postmodern nautical." Suffice it to say each is a work of art in progress. Although the 12 guest rooms are basic (most with a shared bath), they are filled with local art from the past 30 years. They're a real find and are very popular with Europeans. No credit cards. $ rooms, $$ studios.

MOTELS & HOTELS **Surfside Hotel & Suites** (508-487-1726; surfsideinn.cc), 543 Commercial Street at Kendall Lane. Open mid-April through October. A wonderful contemporary-styled hotel located in the East End of town. The resort has 83 guestrooms within two buildings—one sits on the harbor front beach and the other overlooks the heated saltwater pool. Inquire about the Jacuzzi Suites and one- and two-bedroom apartments. $$$–$$$$ rooms; $$$$+ suites.

AWOL (508-413-9820; awolhotel .com), 59 Provincelands Road (West End). Formerly the Inn at the Moors, this newly renovated boutique hotel, now owned by Lark Hotels, is nestled on the outskirts of town. Rooms and suites include top-notch amenities such as Sole beach cruisers (basically a bike that peddles in sand), Tivoli Bluetooth speakers, daily housekeeping, and Waffle kimono robes (ahh, so cozy after a day in the sun). Most rooms can accommodate two guests, while the Lark Suite (and its rooftop deck) and Double Queen Patio rooms can accommodate up to four. Pets are welcomed for an extra fee. Enjoy a fiery sunset (this area puts on quite the show) while warming up by the fire pit. Within walking distance of the West End breakwater and 15 minutes from town center. $$–$$$$$+.

CAMPGROUNDS **Coastal Acres Campground** (508-487-1700; coastalacres provincetown.com), 76R Bayberry. Open mid-April through October. A remote place to pitch a tent or park your Airstream, but only if you can find the place. After you turn onto West Vine Street you will pass a horse stable, followed by a wealthy neighborhood. Head straight but keep your eyes open for the Coastal Acres signs. Now under new management, this 22-acre campground along Shank Painter Pond has over 200 trailer and tent sites, on-site water and electric connections, and bathrooms. Pets are also welcome, and it's within walking distance of town, bike trails, and beaches. $.

Dunes' Edge Campground (508-487-9815; thetrustees.org/places-to-visit /cape-cod-islands/dunes-edge-camp ground), off Route 6. Open May through September. Within earshot of the highway, this campground is clean and well-kept with a family-friendly atmosphere. But the sites can feel small if you've got more than one tent, and bike access to downtown with kids can be scary because of cycling on Route 6. $.

✴ Where to Eat

DINING OUT **The Mews Restaurant and Café** (508-487-1500; mewsptown.com), 429 Commercial Street. Open D, year-round; Sunday brunch in summer. One of Provincetown's most sophisticated restaurants, the beachfront Mews is elegant and romantic, awash in peach tones and bleached woods. Long-time chef Laurence deFreitas offers a popular mixed seafood grill along with dishes like seared peppercorn-crusted tuna. Sauces are rich and delicious, and the servers are very knowledgeable. The more casual upstairs café, with the same water views and lower prices, also has great burgers, appetizers, salads, and pasta. It's a great place for a before-dinner drink or an after-dinner dessert and coffee. (The Mews stocks the largest selection of vodka in New England, by the way.) There's also entertainment in winter. Dine before sunset to better appreciate the water view. $$–$$$$.

THE RED INN KIM GRANT

A FEW GENERALITIES ABOUT EATING IN PROVINCETOWN

The quality of Provincetown restaurants continues to impress me. In fact, Provincetown has the greatest concentration of fine restaurants of any town on the Cape. You'll have plenty of choices to suit your budget and taste buds. Opening and closing months listed here are only a guideline. If you have your heart set on a particular place, call ahead off-season to see if they are open. And always make reservations whenever and wherever you can, especially in summer.

The Red Inn (508-487-7334; theredinn .com), 15 Commercial Street. Open brunch and D, April through December. This refined restaurant, perched on the water's edge, comes decked out in white linens and soothing colors. The beautifully restored old building has sanded floors and huge picture windows—perfectly blending a contemporary and classic aesthetic. That just about sums up the cuisine, too. The menu exudes finesse: pepper-crusted filet mignon with truffle mashed potatoes or pan-roasted local cod with lemon garlic confit and rosemary potatoes (this is my go-to, my mouth is already watering). Then there's the specialty rack of lamb, with a secret rub of spices and their savory vegetable bread pudding (oddly yummy). If you can't come for dinner, stop in for happy hour. Enjoy cocktails on the outside deck overlooking the bay and munch on a fusion of appetizers such as the panko-crusted shrimp or bacon wrapped oysters. The Red Inn also rents guestrooms, but I recommend just coming for the food and drinks. $$–$$$$.

Front Street (508-487-9715; frontstreetrestaurant.com), 230 Commercial Street (between Gosnold and Masonic Streets). Open D, May to early December. Located in the cozy brick cellar of a Victorian house, Front Street is one of the Outer Cape's most consistent and noteworthy restaurants. It's a convivial place, made more so by small tables placed very closely together, antique booths, local artwork, and stained glass. Dim lighting creates a cozy ambiance. Their top-notch service gets five stars in my book with a long-time, returning front-of-house staff. Expect tentative yet unobtrusive service (how they recite the long list of nightly specials without a notepad blows my mind every time). Donna Aliperti, chef/ owner since opening the restaurant in 1987, reigns over the kitchen creating much-lauded Mediterranean-American fusion. The repertoire of Italian, French, and Continental dishes changes weekly, but signature dishes include herb-crusted rack of lamb, tea-smoked duck, and Gorgonzola-stuffed filet mignon. The wine list is excellent as well as dessert. $$$–$$$$.

SAL'S PLACE MICHELA CAREW-MURPHY

Sal's Place (508-487-1279), 99 Commercial Street. Open D, early June to late September. The legacy of this deliciously historic beachside restaurant began in 1963 under the vision of local artist, Salvatore Del Deo (see also **Ciro & Sal's**). Sal, a painter himself, believed two things: first, that "good artists make good cooks," and second, that the secret to maintaining good health was through fine quality food, hence he adopted the motto, "Qui si sana," which means "Here you find health" or "Here you are healthy." In 1989, the business was taken over by Jack and Lora Papetsas, who continued the Sal's Place tradition for the next 20-plus years. Today, Siobhan Carew and her daughter, Michela Carew-Murphy, are at the helm and the reviews continue to remain favorable. Popular items include the scallop ceviche, burrata summer salad (out of this world), bluefish pate, the slow cooked octopus, veal Milanese, and seafood fra diavlo. Try one of their handcrafted batch cocktails or a selection from their sustainable wine menu. Ask for a seat on the outdoor deck and listen to waves kiss the shoreline as you sip and dine on quality food. Dessert is limited to complimentary fudge with lavender sea salt. Cash only. $$–$$$$.

Ciro & Sal's (508-487-6444; ciroandsals.com), 4 Kiley Court (off Commercial Street). Open brunch on weekends only; D, year-round. The primary reason to eat here is historical: Ciriaco Cozzi and Salvatore Del Deo founded it in 1951 as a coffee shop. The two young Italian-American men met in Provincetown in 1947 as students of Henry Hensche, the famed American painter and teacher. In order to make a living while learning to paint, Ciriaco and Salvatore decided to open an after-hours sandwich shop. It was an overnight success and became the gathering place for Provincetown's art colony and local fishing community. Their partnership dissolved in 1959 (see also **Sal's Place**). Today, Ciro & Sal's continues operating as an artists' restaurant and you may find yourself dining next to Anne Packard or Paul Resika. The ground floor still looks the same as it did back then: cozy with brick and plaster walls and Chianti bottles hanging from the low rafters. Chef Larry Luster reigns in the kitchen, but has passed the head chef title to his son, Caleb. The extensive Northern Italian menu features traditional dishes, such as veal Marsala, Bolognese, and seafood specials. My experiences here have always been okay, but the staff is very friendly and the ambiance is intimate. $$–$$$$.

EATING OUT **Ross' Grill** (508-487-8878; rossgrillptown.com), 237 Commercial Street (within Whaler's Wharf). Open L, D, year-round. Overlooking the harbor from a second-floor vantage point, this casual American grill has a bit of everything. With good music, a structural steel ceiling, an exposed kitchen, and a range of menu choices from burgers to duck à l'orange. There's also an impressive list of 75 wines by the glass and a dozen international beers. Because this place is tucked away, it feels like you need to be in the know to know, which is fun. $$–$$$$.

Strangers & Saints (508-487-1449; strangersandsaints.com), 404 Commercial Street. Open D, year-round. This modern interpretation of a portside tavern blends the history of a sea captain's "salt, swank, and swagger" with a deep sense of hospitality, food, and drink. The former 1850s captain's home may look unassuming from the outside, with its tall colonial style architecture, white plank boarding, and black shutters. but step inside (and back in time) and you will find gorgeous natural wooden beams lining the ceiling, glossy wide paneled floors, teal trim, modernized lanterns, antique furniture, and an array of nautical décor. The Mediterranean-inspired menu is composed of small and large plates perfect for sharing with small groups of friends. Presided over by chef Fred Latasa-Nicks from the Culinary

Institute of America and his husband, Steven, menu items might include charred shishito peppers and chorizo, duck fat popcorn and cracklins, curried octopus and chickpea smash, grilled halibut sliders with pickled watermelon, spicy stuffed mussels, and rustic brick oven pizzas, to name a few. $$–$$$$.

Napi's (508-487-1145; napisptown .com), 7 Freeman Street. Open L, D, year-round. Chef/owner Napi Van Dereck and his wife, Helen, opened this unusual restaurant in 1973. Behind the brightly frosted stained glass windows you will find an endless array of local art including sculptures by Al Davis, cartoons from the pen of Howie Schneider, and paintings by George Yater, Frank Milby, and Salvatore Del Deo. But my most favorite artwork is the spectacular brick mural crafted by the nonpareil Conrad Malicoat. It's extremely impressive. The international menu includes a bit of everything from Portuguese kale soup, Jamaican jerk chicken, cod Provençal, and several vegetarian choices. Free parking for customers. $$–$$$.

Fanizzi's by the Sea (508-487-1964; fanizzisrestaurant.com), 539 Commercial Street. Open for brunch on weekends, L, D, year-round. If you're lusting for a killer view of the water, Fanizzi's is the place. The East End restaurant boasts 180-degree views through three walls of windows overlooking the harbor. At high tide, it almost feels like you are in the dining room of a cruise ship. If you're lucky enough to come here during a nor'easter or some other crazy blast of Cape weather, you might experience the thrill of waves crashing under the building and spraying the dining room windows with force. The menu features comfort cuisine, seafood, and American dishes. The Buffalo wings and stuffed artichoke are two of my favorites. $$–$$$$.

Lobster Pot (508-487-0842; ptown lobsterpot.com), 321 Commercial Street. Open L, D, April through November. This venerable waterfront institution might feel touristy, but I can attest it's a favorite townie spot, too. Put your name down with the host for bar seats at the "Top of the Pot" or in one of the large waterfront dining rooms (there's *always* a wait). The service is usually hurried, but lively. When your table is ready, walk through the narrow hallway, passing the open kitchen and seasoned staff, working like a well-oiled cooking machine. Be sure to steer clear of servers carrying abnormally large trays of food up and down the steep second floor staircase (above their head no less). The lengthy menu offers variety, but is memorable for its seafood. Strap on a bib and get down and dirty cracking lobster shells and dipping fresh tail meat in warm drawn butter. I usually go for appetizers: the scallops au gratin, tuna sashimi, lobster ravioli, blackened shrimp, peanut chicken, and clams casino are all great choices. I also prefer the upstairs bar with my favorite bartenders, Cassie and Winston, watching them shake and stir martinis with a smile. First-timers must try the award winning clam chowder by Chef Timmy McNulty. Say yes to the breadbasket as it comes with a variety of delicious carbs including pumpkin bread prepared by Warren W. Costa. The plates are rich and large, so come hungry. $$–$$$$.

Nor'east Beer Garden (508-487-2337; thenoreastbeergarden.com), 206 Commercial Street. Open L, D, mid-May to mid-September; full bar serving cheese and snacks on weekends until Halloween. Hidden behind lattice and climbing ivy is this small outdoor garden eatery. The menu specializes in unique craft cocktails and of course, beer. When it comes to food, aficionado Michela (and the brains behind the menu at **Sal's Place**) could not have said it better: "Beer Garden is my favorite for lunch this year. They've made a gradual switch to a fully Middle Eastern menu. The shakshuka is the best I've ever had; the eggplant makes it less acidic, which makes it easy to eat every day. The dry-rubbed wings are also a favorite (I dip them in their house made aioli), and their cocktails and rotating beer menu are second to none. The décor is incredibly well thought out and the menus are made out of recycled shingles." You heard the lady, it's a must-try. $$–$$$$.

Local 186 (508-487-7555), 186 Commercial Street. Open L, D, mid-May through October. What I would consider the Cadillac of Provincetown's burger joints; with over a dozen signature burger options, you can't go wrong. Popular options include the El Guapo, with fried avocado and chipotle aioli; the Brit, with local lager and aged Cheddar pub cheese and fried onion strings; and the Frenchie, with frenched onions, smoked Gruyère, and au jus (to name *just* three). The lamb and turkey burgers are also delicious, and the popular Sophie Lou is a yummy option for vegetarians. $$–$$$$.

Bubalas By The Bay (508-487-0773; bubalas.com), 185 Commercial Street. Open L, D, mid-May through October. Grab a seat on the lively outdoors patio and watch the interesting foot traffic pass by. Say yes to the complimentary roasted garlic bulbs and EVOO that accompany the breadbasket. On cooler nights, steal a seat at the bar. The espresso martinis made with real coffee will give you that extra boost of energy you might be craving. For dinner, favorites include the duck quesadilla app, the braised boneless short ribs, and the lobster ravioli. My go-tos for lunch are the Caesar salad with pan-seared shrimp or the grilled tuna wasabi sandwich. $$–$$$$.

1620 Brewhouse (774-593-5180; 1620brewhouse.com), 214 Commercial Street. Open L, D, year-round. Though the name screams brewery, that's not the case (or at least not in time for this edition). But it doesn't mean they don't have a lengthy beer list! The pub-style menu includes high-quality bar food, burgers, salads, and subs. Personal favorites include the buffalo fried shrimp and chowder fries (a Cape-twist on classic poutine but with clam chowder and crumbled bacon—I know it sounds odd, but it works). The steak and cheese with shaved rib eye and Portobello mushrooms is messy but amazing, and the house-made veggie burger is unreal (and I'm not a vegetarian). If you're

NOR'EAST BEER GARDEN KATY WARD

LOCAL 186 KIM GRANT

feeling adventurous, try the peanut butter burger, with bacon and pepper jack. $$–$$$.

Squealing Pig (508-487-5804; squealingpigpubs.com/provincetown), 335 Commercial Street. Open B, L, D, year-round. Dear Squealing Pig, thank you, thank you, *thank you*, for staying open year-round and continuing to serve the most delicious and comforting curry this side of the bridge (in my opinion). This laid-back upscale Irish pub offers the typical bar food staples: wings, burgers and fries (the parmesan and truffle oil ones, please), and seasonal Irish specials such as shepherd's pie, beef stew, and corn beef and cabbage. Oh, and a long list of beers! Breakfast choices include bangers, rashers, and the traditional black and white puddings, but don't worry, there's an American breakfast too. In winter the Pig holds trivia nights and rowdy sports games on their indoor projection screen. $–$$.

Liz's Café, Anybody's Bar (508-413-9131; lizscafeptown.com), 31 Bradford Street. Open B, L, D, year-round. It's no surprise that Liz Lovati's newest restaurant would make the list. She's a genius in the kitchen (see also **Angel Food's** under *Markets*). Despite her take-no-$%!# attitude, anyone in town will agree that Liz has a heart of gold, always lending a helping hand for her community. Flippers, eggs Benedict, Queen Mary's, and Bellinis are a few morning choices. Liz also offers a section on her menu that pays tribute to the old Tip For Tops'n restaurant, which the Carreiro family operated in the same building from 1966 to 2013. The odd moniker stood for, "Tip of the Cape for Tops in Service" and was a townie favorite known for their breakfast specials. After lunch service— think soups, salads and sandwiches—the restaurant closes for a few hours and prepares for the dinner crowd. Entrée options might include Liz's homemade meat loaf, chicken Milanese, sole Florentine, or local mussels in a white wine, shallot, and butter sauce. The white exterior of the building, dressed with a bright yellow awning with white cast-iron chairs and pinstriped cushions will surely catch your eye. Step inside to a cozy restaurant with roughly 20 tables, filled with rich colors and historic maritime décor. The Dory Bar is definitely the restaurant's central focus, almost giving the appearance of being at sea especially with the large ship's wheel sitting prominently above the bar. The name, Liz's Café, Anybody's Bar, reaches back into Provincetown's history. Ernest L. Carreiro, an early immigrant from the Azores, Portugal, originally ran Anybody's Market, dating back to at least 1942.

The Canteen (508-487-3800; thecanteenptown.com), 225 Commercial Street. Open B, L, D, year-round. From the backyard-style "patio" overlooking the bayside to the wooden indoor tables meant for sharing with strangers, the Canteen has made its mark on Provincetown. Owners and partners Rob Anderson and Loic Rossignon opened the Canteen in 2014. "We built the Canteen to be a gathering place, a spot where everyone—local or visitor, artist or fisherman, culinary adventurous eight-year-old or fish-and-chips-loving 88-year-old—can find a seat and something great to eat." This casual upscale bohemianesque eatery has the best crispy Brussels sprouts I've ever had. The lobster roll, clam chowder, and house-made peanut butter crunch and jelly sandwich (with fresh strawberries) are select favorites. In the off-season, the Canteen showcases special events such as their popular Holiday Market in December (in France, they call it a *Marché de Noël*, in Germany the *Weihnachtsmarkt*, and in Spain *Mercadillos de Navidad*). Enjoy German brats, homemade pretzels, and spiked mulled cider while perusing local artisanal vendors and enjoying a faux ice-skating rink with the little ones. $–$$.

Mac's Fish House Provincetown (508-487-6227; macsseafood.com), 85 Shank Painter Road. Open L, D, year-round. The sushi is superb, as well as the entrées and apps. Happy hour from 3 to 5 p.m. with $1 oysters and clams on the half-shell makes for a fun and slightly cheaper way to spend the later part of an afternoon. Reserve a table in the cozy dimly lit dining room or opt for the livelier bar room area, with its long granite bar, stool top tables, and leather-cushioned booths. In winter months, I sometimes like to sit at the sushi bar and watch them prepare delicate orders, and in summer the outdoor patio area is a nice option. (See also under *Markets* and *Dining Out* in Wellfleet). $$–$$$.

GRAB & GO **Kung Fu Dumplings** (774-538-7106; kfdumplings.com), 293 Commercial Street. There are very few ethnic dining options in Provincetown, but tucked down the alley near Portuguese Bakery (see under *Sweet Treats & Coffee*), you will find this hole-in-the-wall dumpling delight. Owner Stephen Rome was born and raised in Provincetown, but moved to Shenyang in Liaoning Province (commonly referred to as Northeast China) when he was 17 years old. He spent eight years there, where he studied at the Provincial University and learned Mandarin. Stephen moved back to the Cape in 2010 to help out with the family business—his mother, Leslie Packard, is proprietor of the Packard Gallery and its reproduction store, Packard Gallery II (see under *Galleries*). Rome and his business partner, Chuang "Leon" Tony (also

THE CANTEEN KATY WARD

from Northeast China), opened the dumpling doors in 2014. In addition to dumplings (fried or steamed), they offer fried rice, lo mien, spring rolls, chicken teriyaki, and more. Heads up: It's not exactly grab and go—emphasis on the "go." Each order is made fresh and can sometimes take upwards of 30 minutes wait time. But it's so worth it. I often call my order in ahead of time and pick it up. They also deliver to the Outer Cape for a nominal charge. $.

John's Foot Long (508-487-7434), 309 Commercial Street in Lopes Square. Open L, D, mid-May to September. This old-school hotdog stand dates back to 1961 and hasn't changed a bit since. Stop at the counter and order off the whiteboard: their foot-long hotdog (griddled with a buttered bun), burgers, Portuguese kale soup, and fried seafood baskets are the best in town. Sit outside in Lopes Square or head upstairs (it's a bit of a hidden gem—climb the staircase to the left). $–$$.

Spiritus (508-487-2808; spirituspizza .com), 190 Commercial Street. Open daily with late-night hours, April to early December. If you didn't stop for a slice at Spiritus while you were in town, then I'm sorry to say that you missed out. This family-run pizzeria offers some of the best pizza on Cape. Slices include cheese, pepperoni, and their famous Greek, or order a whole pie (one size only). The Spiritus scene gets especially rowdy between midnight and 2 a.m. when the bars let out. They also offer Lewis Brother's homemade ice cream (see under *Sweet Treats & Coffee*), and their famous espresso shake is second to none. Spiritus also showcases local rotating art exhibits. Cash only. $–$$.

POP+DUTCH (774-538-6472; pop anddutch.com), 147 Commercial Street. Open B, L, mid-May through early September. This sandwich shop and pint-sized general store in the West End of town offers house-cured meats, cheeses, juices, and prepared foods. I'm a big fan of the Helltown sandwich: deviled-egg

STEPPING BACK IN TIME

Provincetown may be filled with second homes and condos purchased by baby boomers dining on $35 entrées and homemade vodkas, but there are still vestiges where you can step back three and more decades. Let's do the time-warp again: head to the **Mayflower Café** (300 Commercial Street) for a quick meal; the **Portuguese Bakery** (299 Commercial Street; see above); **Sal's Place** (99 Commercial Street) for an outdoor, waterside Italian dinner; and the **Porchside Bar at the Gifford House** (9 Carver Street).

salad topped with radishes and celery leaves on potato bread. $–$$.

Provincetown House of Pizza (508-487-6655; ptownpizza.com), 50 Bradford Street. Open L, D, mid-April to late November. This Greek-inspired pizza joint (locally called P-HOP), offers pizzas, calzones, subs, wraps, fried foods, and more. You could feed an army here for less than most places in town. Two pluses: free parking and delivery. $–$$.

George's Pizza & Bar (508-487-3744; georgespizzaandbar.com), 275 Commercial Street. Open L, D, year-round. If you were to come here in the dead of winter, you would surely find the barstools and booths filled with locals chatting and venting to one another about an issue aired during a board meeting across the street at Town Hall. The pizza and subs are okay (this is only place I know of that serves mushroom by the slice), but they win big in my book for staying open year-round and having a bar. $–$$.

Aquarium Mall, 207 Commercial Street. Open mid-May through September. This little mini-mall has a handful of diverse and inexpensive eateries. Come for quick and good burritos, Chinese food, breakfast sandwiches and bagels, gelato, and more. Take your food onto the Aquabar's beachside deck located at the rear of the building.

Café Maria (508-487-9116; cafemaria
ptown.com), 277 Commercial Street.
Open mid-May to September. This
teeny-tiny hole-in-the-wall cafe is one
of my favorites. Maria's veggie panini
is usually my go-to: fresh mozzarella,
tomatoes, onions, roasted red peppers,
and pesto on ciabatta that is pressed and
griddled for toasted golden perfection.
Her subs and wraps are also fantastic, as
well as her breakfast sandwiches, daily
baked goods, and coffees. The café also
serves ice cream and handcrafted watermelon lemonade that truly quenches
your thirst. There are only a few outdoor
umbrella-shaded patio tables. I usually
place my order to go and enjoy it on the
benches near the parking lot that overlooks MacMillan Wharf. $–$$.

MARKETS **East End Market** (508-487-
2339; eastendmarketplace.com), 212
Bradford Street. Open daily, year-round.
Offerings include specialty sandwiches,
breakfast items, pantry staples, and beer
and wine. Check the glass case for prepared meals, such as Chef Claudio's
amazing mushroom and goat cheese
lasagna. For those who rented a lavish
home for the week and would rather dine
in but don't feel like cooking, place an
order off the meal services menu, which
includes starters, main course entrées,
sauces, sides, and dessert. You can pick
up from the store, or they will deliver it
fresh and warm right to the doorstep (for
a small additional fee). $–$$$$.

Angel Foods (508-487-6666; angel
foods.com), 467 Commercial Street
(directly across from PAAM). Open
daily, year-round. This tiny grocery store
embodies old-school Provincetown, with
its crushed seashell parking lot, creaky
wooden porch entrance, rocking chairs,
and rustic interior. Expect gourmet com-
fort cooking and high-end pantry items
by the talented Liz Lovati (see also **Liz's
Café, Anybody's Bar**). $–$$$$.

Far Land Provisions (508-487-0045;
farlandprovisions.com), 150 Bradford
Street. This centrally located sandwich

shop and grocery market is always busy,
and for good reason. Stop here for the
market basics: sandwiches, soups, pas-
tries, and prepared items. They also offer
beer and wine. Dine inside or on a front
porch rocking chair. (See also **Far Land
on the Beach** under **Entertainment**).
$–$$$$.

Relish (508-487-8077; ptownrelish
.com), 93 Commercial Street. Open daily,
year-round. For all you West Enders, this
is the spot to stop for baked goods, sand-
wiches, wraps, cookies, and more. $–$$.

If you are looking for a seafood market, stop at **Mac's Seafood Market** (508-
487-6227; macsseafood.com/markets), 85
Shank Painter Road (see also **Mac's Fish
House Provincetown**). $$–$$$$.

See also *Farms* under **Selective
Shopping**.

SWEET TREATS & COFFEE **Yolqueria**
(508-487-0600; yolqueria.com), 401½
Commercial Street. Open for brunch
daily, late May to September. Chef and
owner Brandon Quesnell's menu infuses
traditional American brunch with Mexi-
can flair. Enjoy a hot cup of coffee from
Manzanita Roasting Co. (sourced from
Brandon's hometown of San Diego).
Breakfast options include house-cured
salmon gravlax, fried chicken and waf-
fles, chilaquiles, eggs Benedict with a
homemade smoky hollandaise, freshly
baked cinnamon rolls, and homemade
granola. Opt for the spicy kale salad over
home fries. $–$$.

Café Heaven (508-487-1991; cafe
heavenptown.com), 199 Commercial
Street. Open B, L, D, late May to September. With floor-to-ceiling windows, this
is a great place to brunch while watching
the bustle of Commercial Street. Come
for breakfast: think Brioche French toast,
banana cornmeal pancakes, eggs Benedict (swap a crab cake for an English
muffin), omelets, and more. They also
serve lunch and dinner, but breakfast has
always been my favorite. $–$$.

Chach (508-487-1530; chachprovince
town.com), 73 Shank Painter Road.

LOCAL MARKETS KIM GRANT

Open B, L, mid-May to September. This diner-style breakfast spot offers red cushioned stool seating at the bar and booths for larger parties. There's no air-conditioning, so dress lightly. The menu boasts classic American breakfast and lunch staples. Be sure to check the daily chalkboard specials. $–$$.

The Coffee Pot (508-487-2580; ptown coffeepot.com), 315 Commercial Street (Lopes Square). Open daily from mid-May to October. Stop here for cheap and decent coffee, quick breakfast foods (for those with big belly's try the Rescue Squad Special), subs, wraps, and salads. I recommend going elsewhere for quality food. $–$$.

Joe Coffee (508-487-6656; joecoffee ptown.com), 170 Commercial Street. Open daily, mid-May through early December. The trio of new owners—Mark Shaw, Peter McBrien, and Glenn Siegmund, collectively known as "MPG"—took over the coffee shop in the spring of 2019. Stop here for quality espresso, lattes, mochas, and pastry items. The outdoor patio is a prime spot for people watching or catching up on emails (free Wi-Fi). $.

Kohi (774-538-6467; kohicoffee.com), 199 Commercial Street. Open daily, year-round. A tiny coffee shop tucked off the main strip. Exceptional brews, but expensive. $–$$.

Connie's Bakery (508-487-2167; conniesbakery.com), 205 Commercial Street (in the Aquarium Mall). Open B, L, mid-May through October. Come here for the unbeatable challah and pastries as well as sandwiches and prepared foods. Their savory pies are dynamite (ask for them heated). $–$$.

The Portuguese Bakery (508-487-1803), 299 Commercial Street. Open daily, April through October. Short of hopping on a plane to Lisboa, you haven't tried Portuguese breads and pastries until you've dropped into this classic place. Think *pasteis de coco* (meat pies), *pasteis de nata* (a custard tart), and *tarte de amêndoa* (almond tart). In summer the ovens are cranking 24 hours a day, and the *mallassadas* (fried dough) flies out faster than they can make it. $–$$.

The Penney Patch (508-487-2766; penneypatch.com), 281 Commercial Street. Open daily April through September. This family-run candy shop offers a variety of childhood delights from gobstoppers, caramels, fizz pops, saltwater taffy, and more. You won't be able to resist the sweet smell of sugar wafting through the air when they make fudge. $.

Cabot's Candy (508-487-3550; cabots candy.com), 276 Commercial Street. You would think this candy shop would be in competition with its neighbor (see **The Penny Patch** above), but that's not the case. Fill a bag with all your favorite goodies: saltwater taffy (try the local

CAFÉ HEAVEN KIM GRANT

while adults enjoy the boozy ice cream options (yes, real booze: think Limoncello, Mint Julep, White Russian, and Mudslide, for example). They've got toppings, sundaes, waffle cones, and more. If you're an indecisive person, I recommend taking a peak at the large whiteboard menu inside before stepping in line. $.

✳ Entertainment

MOVIE **Water's Edge Cinema** (508-413-9369 for show times; 508-487-3456 for box office; provincetownfilm.org), 237 Commercial Street (third floor of Whaler's Wharf). This tiny theater hidden upstairs at Whaler's Wharf is cozy yet complex, but a warning: it's not your typical movie theater. Come for a trending blockbuster hit, an indie film, or documentary. (My last movie night was the thriller *Us*, which ended up being scarier and funnier than I ever could have imagined, but only thanks to the shrieking gay men in the back and the laughing lesbian couple to my right. I had a blast!) Whaler's Wharf is part of the nonprofit organization the Provincetown Film Society (PFS), also responsible for the Provincetown International Film Festival (see **Special Events**).

NIGHTLIFE Provincetown's after-dark scene can get rather spicy. There's something for everyone: gay, straight, and in-between. Heads up: When the bars and clubs close around 1 a.m., crowds flock to **Spiritus** (see **Where to Eat**). It's rather extraordinary when you think about it: there can be 300 people hanging out in front of Spiritus in the middle of the night eating pizza without any problems—for the most part.

Crown & Anchor (508-487-1430; onlyatthecrown.com), 247 Commercial Street. The diversity of entertainment is impressive here. The Crown features the town's largest nightclub (**Paramount**), video bar (**Wave**), cabaret venue,

beach plum taffy or sea salt caramel), beer brittle made with fresh peanuts, gummi bears, licorice, and jelly beans, oh my! $.

Provincetown Fudge Factory (508-487-2850; ptownfudge.com), 210 Commercial Street. Open daily May through October. Hands down, this tiny store makes the best fudge in town. Favorites include the penuche, peanut butter, Oreo cookie, rocky road, cappuccino, and cranberry walnut fudge. Be sure to ask for a sample before trying, just because you can. They also make delicious peanut butter cups, truffles, and caramel turtles. $–$$.

Lewis Brother's Homemade Ice Cream (508-487-0977; lewisbrothers icecream.com), 310 Commercial Street near Lopes Square. If you like options, this place has plenty. Kids will savor one of over 30 premium handmade flavors,

THE PENNEY PATCH   KATY WARD

poolside bar with heated pool, a piano bar, and an ever-popular leather bar (**The Vault**). There's also a new outdoor patio bar and bistro fronting Commercial Street. It's home to some of the best entertainers in town, including the incomparable comedian Kate Clinton. You can't miss it: drag queens will be strutting up and down Commercial in the late afternoon, handing out fliers for their shows.

Bingo at the Unitarian Universalist Meeting House (508-487-9344; uumh .org), 236 Commercial Street (across from Whaler's Wharf and Water's Edge Cinemas). When you need a dose of quirky Provincetown, nothing beats this mostly LGBTQ crowd at Wednesday night bingo.

Grotta Bar (508-487-7555; local186 .com/grotta), 186 Commercial Street. Open mid-May through October. This spot successfully manages something for everyone: live entertainment, jukebox tunes, DJs, and a killer lineup of signature drinks. It's an easy place to hang with friends.

Post Office Cabaret (508-487-0006; postofficecabaret.com), 303 Commercial Street. Open mid-May through September. Don't be shy. If you're open-minded and ready to blush with curiosity and squeal with laughter this is the place

to go. The Ptown Male Call and Mama Tits are shows that will surely raise your eyebrows.

The Club (508-487-1527; theclub ptown.com), 193A Commercial Street. Lea Delaria took ownership of the former Pied Piper Bar in 2019, turning it into Provincetown's version of New York City's Smoke and Jazz nightspot. The first time I checked it out, I had the pleasure of witnessing an impromptu stage performance by Dawn Derow. Her voice was silky and strong, and it echoed off the stage. My friends (who I promptly ditched at the sound of her voice) continued drinking on the waterfront porch lit up by string lights and decorated with comfortable white plush lounge furniture. Lea is a well-known comedian, actor, and jazz singer, more recently recognized for her role as Carrie "Big Boo" in the Netflix series, *Orange is the New Black*.

Old Colony (508-487-2361), 323 Commercial Street. Open April through November. You might feel drunk, but it's really just the slanted floors and uneven tables—or is it? Come here for an authentic old-school townie experience. Don't be scared. No one bites, but you're sure to meet some drunken characters.

Governor Bradford (508-487-2781), 312 Commercial Street. To get a different but equally "real" flavor of Provincetown, stop into this townie tavern. Live music, karaoke, and a rowdy crowd will keep you entertained.

The Underground (508-413-6948; the undergroundbarptown.business.site), 293 Commercial Street, downstairs. Open year-round. This downstairs cellar bar is a popular hang-out spot for locals, seasonal workers, tourists, and everyone else in between. With live DJs and a dance floor, pool tables, air hockey, and themed nights throughout the year. Plus, bartenders Michelle and Jenna are my favorites.

THEATER **Provincetown Theater** (508-487-7487; provincetowntheater.org), 238 Bradford Street. This year-round theater offers plays, touring shows, dance

WHALER'S WHARF FIRE: DAVID W. DUNLAP

The most spectacular fire in Provincetown's living memory—on the mild night of Tuesday, February 10, 1998—destroyed the 79-year-old Provincetown Theater (by then known as Whaler's Wharf), the abutting Handcrafter store, and much of the Crown & Anchor, incidentally damaging Marine Specialties and threatening the Julie Heller Gallery before it was brought under control by firefighters and emergency workers who had rushed to the Cape End from as far away as Plymouth (the fire could be seen in Dennis!). "There goes our history," one onlooker was quoted as saying in the *Provincetown Banner*. And, yes, a lot of history was lost that night—though, fortunately, no lives were.

With more than 600 seats, the Provincetown Theater was a coming-of-age statement for the town when it opened in 1919. It looked like a big-city cinema: a solid work of masonry in a town of lumber, unabashed in identifying itself in big chiseled letters under the exterior proscenium arch. In its early years, the theater was a franchisee of First National Pictures, one of the most powerful studios of its day. The house was used for other programs as well, including at least one appearance by Donald B. MacMillan, who showed his movies of the Arctic in 1925. During its heyday, the Provincetown Theater was owned and run by Victor Lewis, a powerful businessman. He was also the proprietor of Lewis's New York Store on what is now Lopes Square. In 1931, on the petition of more than 500 residents, the [town's board of selectmen] allowed Lewis to show movies on—gasp!—Sunday nights.

In 1973, Dale Elmer bought the old theater to create Whaler's Wharf, a kind of artisans' collective and craft market that was set up in what had been the orchestra level of the auditorium. Dennis Dermody, who once managed the theater, wrote of it in 1997 for *Provincetown Arts*: "I not only hired the handicapped, I made a point of *only* hiring alcoholics, drug addicts, the mentally unstable, and children who smoked. Our projectionist had a bit of a drug problem, so you never knew what was going to happen. There was the sweet thrill of coming to work on nights that we showed Bertolucci's *The Conformist,* Altman's *Thieves Like Us,* Malick's *Badlands,* or Cocteau's *Orpheus.* Just sitting at the top of those stairs, basking in those images—while the audience used their movie schedules as makeshift fans—was so wonderful on those humid, airless nights. So what if the ticket taker had passed out and was slumped over the counter, or the concession stand boy was sneaking his friends up the back exit or the projectionist was speaking in tongues and had his clothes on backward. There was magic in the air." That magic came to an end in the 1980s, when the theater closed and the balcony was converted into use as a storage space for the Whaler's Wharf shops. But the 20 or shops kept the old theater lively and cheap space at Whaler's Wharf helped the artists and artisans. Elmer would rent by the square foot.

On the evening of February 10, 1998, the night watchman, David Bragdon, a 65-year-old artist, saw the beginnings of a fire in a fuse box. He said he tried to extinguish it with blankets but could not, and so fled the building. Police officer Fernando deSousa was the first to respond, at about 6:30 p.m. Within 40 minutes, the fire had jumped the alleyway to the Crown & Anchor. Fire trucks were arriving from Yarmouth, Barnstable, Harwich, and

performances, and readings. They also provide education for youth and adults and foster the development of emerging playwrights. Home to the Provincetown Theatre Company (PTC), this place has been a fixture since it opened its doors in 2006. Founded in 1963 to further the goals of the early-20th-century Provincetown Players, PTC is a collaborative of professional, semiprofessional, and amateur actors, writers, directors, technicians, teachers, and theater lovers.

The Art House (508-487-9222; ptownarthouse.com), 214 Commercial Street. Open late May to mid-September.

Bourne. A fifth alarm was sounded a little more than an hour into the blaze. The battle lasted deep into the night. "In many ways, it was nothing less than a battle to save the very town itself," Sue Harrison recalled in the *Provincetown Banner* two years later. "For anyone who saw the fire at its peak, the idea that it could be stopped seemed impossible, and the horror of what would happen to the entire downtown area if it wasn't, unthinkable. Townspeople poured out of their homes and businesses to line the beach and nearby streets as fire engine after fire engine poured into town to lend support. . . . As the sky over Commercial Street blazed orange against the black of the February night, a fine rain fell, mixing water with flying sparks, some half-dollar-sized. Hoses snaked and coiled like a riot of pale anacondas, and the street was turned into a shallow river for hours as millions of gallons of water were thrown at the inferno." Two weeks after the fire, Bragdon—who was seemingly blameless in the event—killed himself by leaping into the harbor. Harrison reported in the *Provincetown Banner*, "He never seemed to completely shake his feeling of dishonor in not being able to contain the fire, and his friends say that sense of honor led him to take his own life." The broken-up chunks of the inscription from the monumental blind arch of the facade can be

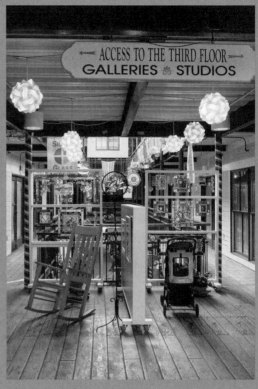

LEESA BURKE

found on the harbor side of Whaler's Wharf, out the back entrance and half buried in sand. Lest the memorial be taken too gravely, its fragments frame a zaftig mermaid (or merman?) with a broad smile on its face.

See also **Water's Edge Cinema** under Entertainment, "MacMillan Wharf: David W. Dunlap" on page 326, and **Cold Storage** under Truro's *Beaches*.

Under the leadership of artistic director Mark Cortale, this venue offers a full lineup of unique entertainment. Stop in for stellar cabaret, dance performances, stand-up comedy acts, or drag shows with Provincetown's famous: Varla Jean Merman, Miss Conception, the Kinsey Sicks, and Bob the Drag Queen, to name just a few. The singing string quartet, Well-Strung, is another favorite.

Peregrine Theatre Ensemble (774-539-9084; peregrinetheatre.com), 12 Winslow Street (in Fisherman's Hall at the former Provincetown High School). This professional performing arts company has upped the entertainment ante

FOR THE BOYZ

The Boatslip Beach Club (508-487-1669; boatslipresort.com), 161 Commercial Street (between Central and Atlantic Streets), is known around the LGBTQ world for its packed, oh-so-gay summertime Tea Dance from 4 to 7 p.m. daily (May to mid-October). Every member of the LGBTQ community should experience the euphoria at least once. Last dance on Labor Day is particularly heady. If you like to dance, be here. You can also rent pool chairs and a towel ($) if you're not staying here, as long as you depart by tea time.

Atlantic House (508-487-3821; ahouse.com), 6 Masonic Place, more commonly referred to as the A-House, has three diverse bars: the so-called Macho Bar (a nationally known men's leather bar); the nautically decorated disco Dance Bar; and the Little Bar (more intimate, with a roaring fireplace in the off-season). I'm confident that no other 18th-century house sees such action. Open 365 days a year until 1 a.m. Seems like there isn't a gay guy in town who doesn't stop into the A-House off-season. Some credit the A-House with establishing Provincetown's "off-season" versus "closed for the season."

in town. Peregrine co-founders Adam and Ben Berry first washed ashore in Provincetown during their college days—Adam coming from Boston to perform *Hair* and Ben from Minnesota to perform Shakespeare. They scrambled to make ends meet and sometimes worked two or three jobs during the day and performing at night. (Adam vowed to never return to Provincetown after working tirelessly and having no money to show at the end of the season.) Today, the Berrys live in town and use Peregrine as a way to give aspiring young adults a similar experience, but with half the stress. Peregrine casts college students from top training programs in their annual summer musical—past performances include *Cabaret, Hair,* and my all-time favorite, *Chicago*—and they don't have to pay rent. Despite the youth of the cast, Peregrine students are highly skilled. I recommend catching a show, plus the seats in Fisherman's Hall are comfortable. No matter where you sit, you will surely have a decent view of the stage.

✳ Selective Shopping

There are upward of 300 shops lining Commercial Street and the nearby area, making it nearly impossible to list each one. Generally, the East End of town is considered the Arts District. The center of town is livelier, with specialty retail shops, eateries, and entertainment venues. The West End tends to be quieter, with very few shops but rather refined dining and lodging. A few notes: Provincetown can be a difficult place to survive as a small business owner, due to the unpredictable seasonal economy, high rental prices, and available help (among other things). With that said, businesses often change hands from season to season or move to new locations. Most shops are open mid-April to mid-October, although some galleries keep a shorter season (mid-June to mid-September). Many shops stay open until 11 p.m. in July and August, and a number of them offer sales on weekends in the fall and early winter (there's not much going on in February and March). *Provincetown Arts* (provincetownarts.org), a 150-page annual published in July, is a great guide for everything related to visual arts, literature, and theater.

ARTISANS **Victor Powell's Workshop** (508-487-9075; victorpowellsworkshop .com), 323 Commercial Street above Old Colony Tap. My mother worked for Victor during my early and impressionable childhood, so I will be first to admit this review is semi-biased. But I'm not the only one who is rightfully impressed by his leatherwork—the *New York Times* reviewed Victor's workshop in late September 2019 as one of the top five places to visit in Provincetown. His specialty is custom-made hand-cobbled sandals, but also leading edge handbags and other one-of-a-kind accessories. Victor started his artisanal career in the mid-1970s, when more than 20 leather crafters "plied their trade in Provincetown." Today, Victor's is the last working studio. His apprentice **Florence Mauclere** recently launched her own line of custom-designed, hand-stitched leather bags. She also makes great wallets, sandals, and other goodies, which you can find at Victor's workshop or at local Provincetown venues like the Holiday Market. See her work at mauclereleather.com.

BOOKSTORES **Provincetown Bookshop** (508-487-0964), 246 Commercial Street. A good selection of children's books, Cape titles, and cookbooks; established in 1932.

Tim's Used Books, 242 Commercial Street. Hidden down an alley off the main strip, this used bookstore offers an exciting variety of classics chosen by Tim. The older books have a sweet, musky smell that wafts into any book-lover's nose.

CLOTHING Shopping for clothing other than witty, scandalous, hilarious, souvenir T-shirts is not really an option. Peruse **Wild Rice** (508-487-4220), 333 Commercial Street; **Board Stiff** (508-487-2406; boardstiffprovincetown.com), 273 Commercial Street; **David Oliver's Cape Tip Sportswear** (508-487-3736; capetip sports.com), 224 Commercial Street; and **Chameleon** (508-487-2720), 389 Commercial Street. Be sure to also check out **Marine Specialties** and if you're a tie-dye fan stop at **Shop Therapy** (see both under *Specialty*).

FARMS **Provincetown Farmers' Market** (ptownevents.com/provincetown -farmers-market), at the corner of

BOATSLIP BEACH CLUB KIM GRANT

NATIONAL SEASHORE BONFIRES

A beach bonfire, with or without a clambake, defines the essence of summertime on the Outer Cape. Here's the process you need to follow to secure a permit: In July and August head to the Province Lands Visitor Center (508-487-1256; nps.gov/caco) on Race Point Road 3 days before you want a permit and request one. For instance, if you want it for Wednesday, go on Sunday. Be there *before* the center opens (there will be a line). On the day of your big event, be at the visitor center by 3:30 p.m. or you'll lose your permit to someone waiting in line. In the off-season, you can call 3 days ahead of your desired date without a problem. Fires are permitted year-round. During the off-season, permits must be obtained at the Race Point Ranger Station (518-487-2100).

Commercial and Ryder Streets, every Saturday from mid-May to mid-October.

GALLERIES Provincetown is brimming with galleries—after all, it was founded as an artists' colony in the late 1890s. Most studios are spread throughout town, but the East End is mostly dedicated to artists. My suggestion is to start there and work your way down the main strip. Most galleries hold Friday openings staggered between 5 p.m. and 10 p.m. You can stroll the street, catching most of the reception and meet-the-artist opportunities. Most galleries change exhibits every two weeks.

See also **Provincetown Art Association & Museum** under **To See** and the **Fine Arts Work Center** and **Provincetown Museum School** under *Speacial Programs*.

Schoolhouse Gallery (508-487-4800; galleryschoolhouse.com), 494 Commercial Street. Located in a mid-19th-century Greek Revival schoolhouse, this venture features four galleries. Look for contemporary photography, paintings, and sculpture.

Julie Heller Gallery (508-837-9607; juliehellergallery.com), 2 Gosnold Street and **Julie Heller East,** 465 Commercial Street. Stop by these two galleries for a taste of Provincetown's rich heritage, showcased through varied exhibitions that "survey over a century of vibrant innovation and timeless tradition in the visual arts."

Berta Walker Gallery Provincetown (508-487-6411; bertawalkergallery.com), 208 Bradford Street. This excellent gallery represents Provincetown-affiliated artists of the past, present, and future. See her second gallery under Wellfleet's **Selective Shopping.**

Outermost Home (508-413-9370; outermosthome.com), 427 Commercial Street. The best gallery/shop to open in 2019 features aesthetically sublime paintings, wooden bowls, pottery, bespoke candles, and other hand-crafted objects (like their mahogany

COMMERCIAL STREET ART GALLERIES KIM GRANT

Adirondack chair). I want to live in this space, with its soothing palette inspired by Outer Cape colors and its local ethos reflecting modern and vintage sensibilities.

William-Scott Gallery (508-487-4040; williamscottgallery.com), 439 Commercial Street. This venue showcases contemporary art and preeminent regional artists like John Dowd, Will Klemm, and other major painters.

Simie Maryles Gallery (508-487-7878; simiemaryles.com), 435 Commercial Street. Simie's vibrant landscapes were so popular in local galleries that the artist decided to open her own shop. She also features contemporary artists.

Rice Polak Gallery (508-487-1052; ricepolakgallery.com), 430 Commercial Street. A favorite gallery for many art enthusiasts and critics. Marla Rice represents more than 40 contemporary artists working in painting, photography, assemblages, graphics, and sculpture.

Albert Merola Gallery (508-487-4424; albertmerolagallery.com), 424 Commercial Street. You'll find very fine contemporary art here, as well as notables like Milton Avery, Michael Mazure, and other major artists including John Waters. It's always worth dropping in.

Packard Gallery (508-487-4690; packardgallery.com), 418 Commercial Street. Leslie Packard showcases paintings by her sister, Cynthia, and her mother, Anne.

Gaa Gallery (508-413-9621; gaa-gallery.com), 494 Commercial Street. This gallery's roster promotes the work of emerging and established international artists such as Peter Zimmermann, Judy Pfaff, Martin Mannig, Erika Wastrom, and Heidi Howard.

AMP Gallery (646-298-9258; art marketprovincetown.com), 432 Commercial Street. A lively and interactive studio specializing in contemporary work by multidisciplined artists such as filmmakers, performance artists, and writers.

KATY WARD

Exhibitions are primarily cutting-edge and often process-based.

Alden Gallery (508-487-4230; aldengallery.com), 423 Commercial Street. This open and intimate gallery exhibits paintings and sculptures by emerging and established artists with local, national, and international followings. Founders Stephen Syta and Howard Karren provide excellent guidance and attention to everyone from first-time art buyers to seasoned collectors. Side note: I adore Howard. Not only is his discerning eye for the arts applauded, but his witty word-play and polished editorial skills are second to none. I feel honored to have worked with

OUTERMOST HOME   KIM GRANT

him during our time at the *Provincetown Banner*.

Kiley Court Gallery (508-487-4496; kileycourtgallery.com), 445 Commercial Street. This fine collection of mostly representational oil paintings features artists such as Frank Milby, Joan Cobb Marsh, and father and son Robert Cardinal and Julian Cardinal (who have very different styles).

On Center Gallery (508-413-9483; oncentergallery.com), 352 Commercial Street. This contemporary and transitional art gallery offers a diverse and stable collection of talent from around the globe.

Kobalt Gallery (508-487-1132; kobalt gallery.com), 366 Commercial Street. Owner and director Francine D'Olimpio has assembled a diverse group of artists whose work upholds a collective level of intrigue, vision, and integrity. Exhibitions are consistently dynamic and engaging in this lively venue.

Oils by the Sea/Roccapriore Gallery (508-280-1278; oilsbytheseagallery.com), 437 Commercial Street. Owned and operated by long-time Provincetown resident, artist, and filmmaker Shirl Roccapriore, the gallery features her own abstract work with the nude figure as well as other select noted area artists.

Galeria Cubana (508-487-2822; lagaleriacubana.com), 357 Commercial Street. A contemporary Cuban art gallery featuring internationally renowned and emerging artists currently living in Cuba.

Gary Marotta Fine Art (617-834-5262; garymarottafineart.com), 162 Commercial Street. There's something satirically sexy about this gallery's rotating collection of eclectic artists. It's bright, it's fun, it's a bit naughty, and it's very impressive. Look for the names of Ria Brodell, Katy Bisby, Joe McCaffery, Manuel Pardo, and Segundo Planes, to name a few.

Bakker Gallery (508-413-9758; bakker project.com), 359 Commercial Street. Jim Bakker is a major figure within the local arts community. Peruse his collection from mostly estates of classic Provincetown art.

Evaul Studios & Gallery (508-237-3080; evaul.com), 359 Commercial Street. Since 1970, Bill Evaul has been creating vibrant oil paintings in figurative expression. He is also popularly known for his white-line woodblock prints.

Memories of Provincetown (508-487-9911), 169 Commercial Street, West End. I'm a big fan of Michael Brown's optical artwork, so much so that I have one of his prints hanging on my wall. Using a lenticular printmaking technique combined with original photography, Michael creates art that animates, morphs, or zooms in response to the viewer's movement. In addition to his diverse interactive collection (which he is more than happy to share and talk about), he also features surreal photomontages by internationally known artist Thomas Barbey, as well as Roy and Dennis Barloga, a father/son tandem based out of California that combines modern technology with traditional photography to create a variety of unusual and "unphotographic" techniques. The tiny gallery also sells inexpensive photographs and signed prints that make perfect gifts and mementos.

JEWELRY **Exuma** (508-487-2746; exumajewelry.com), 283 Commercial Street. Gunter Hanelt opened his shop in the early 1970s after emigrating from Germany. Specializing in quality one-of-a-kind pieces, his unique style and hands on craftsmanship keeps a diverse and faithful clientele. Display cases are chock-full of variety from sapphires to rubies, diamonds, and emeralds, some of which are crafted by Gunter; other modern items and classic antiques. In the fall of 2005, he opened C.C.'s Cape Cod Jewelry, a smaller seasonal store that features sterling silver items influenced by the Cape Cod lifestyle. Fun fact: The store is named after his two daughters, Chloe and Cecilia (my forever best friend). Today, his son Alex oversees the day-to-day operations, but Gunter can sometimes be spotted in the back of his shop amidst a cluttered desk with magnifying glasses perched on his head.

Sparks Jewelry (508-487-9377), 364 Commercial Street. Elizabeth Adler has a great eye for costume jewelry, stunning sterling silver, decorative hair accessories, and other odd items such as fairy nightlights, musical ornaments, and other intricate keepsakes. I often come here in search of gifts for others and leave with something for myself.

Another favorite jewelry store is **Christina's Jewelry** (508-487-2228; christinasprovincetown.com), 215 Commercial Street. Despite the tiny size of the store, it's jam-packed with quality jewels at reasonable prices.

SPECIALTY **Impulse** (508-487-1154; impulseartgallery.com), 188 Commercial Street. This contemporary American crafts shop and gallery offers a large selection of kaleidoscopes, wind chimes, wood objects d'art, fragile and colorful glass creations, jewelry, and signed celebrity photos and letters.

Lands End Marine Supply (508-487-0784; landsendmarinesupply.com), 337 Commercial Street. It's amazing that this old-fashioned two-story hardware store continues to thrive. But it does, by selling beach chairs, umbrellas, coolers, suntan lotion, and more.

Marine Specialties (508-487- 1730), 235 Commercial Street. Everyone has to stop here and poke around when visiting Provincetown. This eclectic shop set up in a warehouse-like space offers a jumble of Army-Navy items, brand name clothing (but you'll have to dig through because it's quite unorganized), shoes, trinkets, stuffed animals, hats, costumes, glassware—you name it. You'll undoubtedly walk out with something you hadn't even thought of buying but you just couldn't pass up for the price.

Provincetown Human Rights Campaign Store (508-487-7736; shop.hrc .org), 205 Commercial Street. For all your Human Rights Campaign equality T-shirt, jacket, jewelry, accessory, gift, and bumper sticker needs. And for those "Make America Gay Again" caps.

Roots (508-487-2500; roots.com), 193 Commercial Street. Beautiful accessories for the home, like rugs and ornate lamps, as well as jewelry, décor, and a feisty selection of hilarious socks, aprons, dishtowels, and pot holders. I always find unique gifts here.

Shop Therapy (508-487-9387; shop therapy.com), 286 Commercial Street. This landmark, psychedelic-swathed building proclaims: "Monsters attack P-town. Shop Therapy blamed." No doubt. Merchandise revolves around current alternative lifestyles and the retro look. It's a head shop without the dope, and it was opened in 1972. The sex toy selection upstairs is quite outrageous.

The Captain's Daughters (774-593-3010; captainsdaughters.com), 384 Commercial Street. Think a little bit tea bar, a little bit boutique, and a little bit gallery.

Utilities (508-487-6800; utilitieshome .com), 393 Commercial Street. They're

MARINE SPECIALTIES KIM GRANT

purveyors of whimsical, colorful, summery, frivolous, and functional items for the bath, home, and kitchen. Bed, Bath & Beyond they are not!

Whaler's Wharf, 237 Commercial Street. This three-story open structure brims with artisans, a cooperative, shops, and a few restaurants. You're bound to find something interesting (see also "Whaler's Wharf Fire: David W. Dunlap" on page 360).

✳ Special Events

Off-season, there are dozens of special event weekends geared toward every segment of the LGBTQ and cisgendered world. If you want to be assured of a quieter off-season retreat, call the chamber of commerce (see *Guidance*) for an up-to-the-minute listing of events.

Mid-April: Whale-watching begins and seasonal shops begin to reopen.

Mid-May: **Single Women's Weekend** (provincetownforwomen.com). Although the title is self-explanatory, the weekend is filled with more events than you can imagine.

Late May: **Memorial Day** weekend kicks off the summer season.

Early June: **A Night at the Chef's Table** (508-487-9445; asgcc.org). An annual benefit for Provincetown's AIDS Support Group. This festive, multicourse gala dinner includes champagne and wine at many of the town's finest restaurants. More than 50 restaurants from Falmouth to Provincetown participate. It's a very local thing, but that doesn't mean you aren't welcome.

Women of Color Weekend (womenofcolorweekend.com). Finally, a few days devoted to diversity.

Mid-June: **International Film Festival** (ptownfilmfest.com). Established in 1999, with special screenings, features, documentaries, international selections, and LGBTQ shorts.

Late June: **Portuguese Festival and Blessing of the Fleet** (508-246-9080;

provincetownportuguesefestival.com) This four-day celebration is one of my all-time favorites. Not only does it signal the summer kickoff, but it also supports the rich Portuguese heritage and fishing traditions that Provincetown was built upon—and it happens to be a lot of fun, too. Festival events are held all over town, but the majority of action is at the intersection of Commercial and Ryder Street. Festivities include live music, dancing, a parade, kids' fishing derbies, competition lobster-pot pulls, and the lively lobster bake. The celebration is capped off with the annual Blessing of the Fleet, a longstanding tradition where boats parade past MacMillan Wharf to receive a sprinkled blessing for a safe and prosperous season from the Bishop. Afterward, the party starts. Boats tie up and get the grills cranking, the music bumping, and cold ones flowing. If you're not a local and if you don't know any locals, you might have a hard time getting in on the fun.

July 4: **Independence Day.** A spirited parade organized for and by the entire town, and a spectacular fireworks display.

Mid-July: **Secret Garden Tour** (508-487-1750). A popular annual benefit for the Provincetown Art Association & Museum.

Late July: **Girl Splash** (girl-splash.com). A full week of women's events during fine summer weather! Think Dinah Shore East.

Late July to early August: **Family Week.** At this popular event, the definition of *family* is expanded to include Heather and her two mommies as well as daddy-and-poppy nuclear families.

Mid- to late August: **Fine Arts Work Center Annual Auction** (508-487-9960; fawc.org). A benefit for the nationally recognized fellowship program for artists and writers. Since 1969, this has been an Art-with-a-capital-A event.

Carnival (508-487-2313; ptown.org). This weeklong celebration of the LGBTQ life brings in nearly 100,000 visitors annually. Sponsored by the Province-town Business Guild (see under *Guidance*), festivities include parties, art fairs, a costume ball, and the extremely popular, eyebrow-raising Carnival Parade. Themes change from year to year—past ones include Mardi Gras, Candyland, Space Odyssey, Wild Wild West, and Peace, Love, and Go-Go Boots, to name a few. Themes are announced on the back of the last parade float. Expect outrageously flashy and promiscuous costumes, lots of skin, and role-playing groups parading up and down the street modeling for any photo op; lawn chairs lining the sidewalk (and a few turf fights); and lots of beads, glitter, and candy. It's kind of like Halloween, but in the hot August sun. Traffic and parking is a nightmare so give yourself plenty of extra travel time.

Early September: **AIDS Support Group's Annual Silent and Live Auction** (508-487-9445; asgcc.org), at Fisherman's Wharf. It seems as if every artist in Provincetown donates work to this auction. Don't miss it.

Early September: **Provincetown Harbor Swim for Life & Paddler Flotilla** (swim4life.org). During this harbor swim from Long Point to the Boatslip Beach Club—to raise money for AIDS research—a "paddler flotilla" carries close to 300 swimmers across the bay so they can swim the 1.4 miles back to town. After the swim, the Boatslip holds a free "Mermaid Brunch" open to the public. The event often raises more than $150,000; since its inception it's raised more than $2 million. **The Great Provincetown Schooner Regatta** (provincetownschoonerrace.com). Two classes of sailing vessels parade along the waterfront (west to east) and then race.

Late September: **Tennessee Williams Theater Festival** (866-811-4111 for tickets; twptown.org). Four days of theater, dance, music, film, and fun sharing "the writer's vision of the healing power of love."

Mid-October: **Women's Week** (womeninnkeepers.com). It all started back in 1984, with a small weekend clambake on the beach. These days it spreads over a 10-day period with hundreds of events, including "Meet other women who . . ." mixers and dance parties at the Pied Bar. Hosted by Women Innkeepers of Provincetown, the weeklong extravaganza features women artists and entertainers.

Mid- to late October: **Fantasia Fair** (fantasiafair.org). This seven-day event brings cross-dressers, transgendered persons, and others to town.

Late October: **Halloween.** This is a big event, as you might imagine, with lots of costumes and contests. The children's parade starts at the Pilgrim Monument and ends at the Provincetown Community Center.

Late November: **Lighting of the Monument** (pilgrim-monument.org). The Wednesday before Thanksgiving. Nearly

BLESSING OF THE FLEET KATY WARD

MY MOM AND I INDULGING AT THE ANNUAL PORTUGUESE FESTIVAL LOBSTER BAKE KATY WARD

CARNIVAL AFTERMATH 2019 KATY WARD

5,000 white lights (4 miles' worth) illuminate the Pilgrim Monument and remain lit until early January.

Lighting of the Lobster Pot Tree (provincetownview.com). At Lopes Square in the center of town.

Early December: **Holly Folly Festival** (ptown.org). An annual LGBTQ festival featuring a concert by the Boston Gay Men's Chorus, seasonally decorated house tours, street caroling, shopping galore, special holiday menus, and general gay merriment and revelry.

December 31: **First Light**, ringing in the New Year.

MARTHA'S VINEYARD

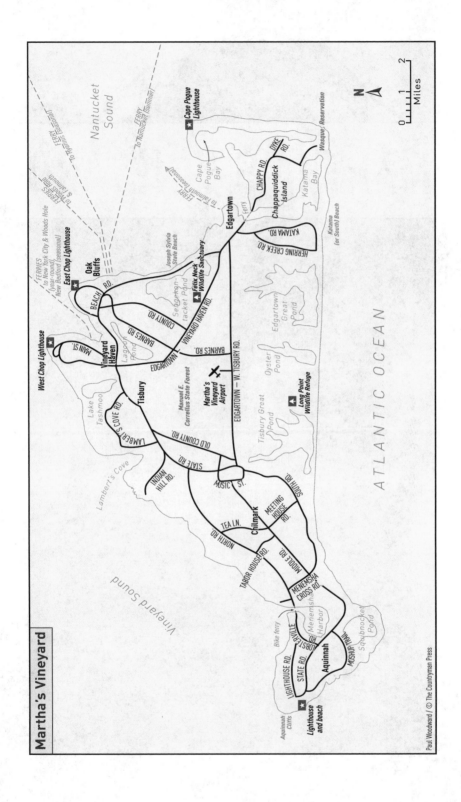

Martha's Vineyard

Nantucket Sound

FERRY
to Nantucket (Summer)

Cape Pogue
Lighthouse

DYKE
RD.

CHAPPY RD.

Cape
Pogue
Bay

Chappaquiddick
Island

Katama
Bay

Wasque Reservation

Katama
(or South) Beach

FERRY
to Falmouth (Seasonal)

Edgartown
Ferry

KATAMA RD.

HERRING CREEK RD.

Joseph Sylvia
State Beach

Felix Neck
Wildlife Sanctuary

Sengekontacket Pond

Edgartown
Great
Pond

VINEYARD HAVEN RD.

BARNES RD.

COUNTY RD.

BEACH RD.

East Chop Lighthouse

Oak
Bluffs

FERRIES
to New York City & Woods Hole
(year-round)
New Bedford (seasonal)

FERRIES
to Falmouth &
Hyannis (seasonal)

West Chop Lighthouse

MAIN ST.

Vineyard
Haven

Lagoon
Pond

Lake
Tashmoo

Tisbury

LAMBERT'S COVE RD.

Lambert's Cove

BARNES RD.

Martha's
Vineyard
Airport

EDGARTOWN — W. TISBURY RD.

Manuel E.
Correllus State Forest

EDGARTOWN — W. TISBURY RD.

Oyster
Pond

Long Point
Wildlife Refuge

Tisbury Great
Pond

OLD COUNTY RD.

STATE RD.

INDIAN HILL RD.

MUSIC ST.

Chilmark

TEA LN.

NORTH RD.

MEETING HOUSE RD.

SOUTH RD.

TABOR HOUSE RD.

MIDDLE RD.

MENEMSHA CROSS RD.

Menemsha
Harbor

Squibnocket
Pond

Bike ferry

LOBSTERVILLE RD.

LIGHTHOUSE RD.

STATE RD.

Aquinnah

MOSHUP TRAIL

Aquinnah
Cliffs

Lighthouse
and beach

Vineyard Sound

ATLANTIC OCEAN

N

0   1   2
Miles

Paul Woodward / © The Countryman Press

MARTHA'S VINEYARD

ntrepid explorer Bartholomew Gosnold was the first European known to have visited Martha's Vineyard (in 1602), although Leif Eriksson may have done so earlier. Gosnold named the island for its bounty of wild grapes, but Martha's identity remains a mystery; she may have been Gosnold's daughter. The island was formally colonized in 1640, when a shipload of English settlers bound for Virginia ran short of supplies. They docked in Edgartown, found the resident Wampanoag friendly, and decided to stay.

The settlers converted the Wampanoag to Christianity with startling success, perhaps aided by the imported diseases that were killing Wampanoag by the thousands. A century after Edgartown was founded, the island's American Indian population had dropped from 3,000 to about 350. During that time, Vineyarders learned (from the surviving Wampanoag) how to catch whales. They also farmed in Chilmark and fished from Edgartown and Vineyard Haven.

During the American Revolution, islanders suffered extreme deprivation after British soldiers sailed into Vineyard Haven Harbor and looted homes and ships. Among their plunder were some 10,000 head of sheep and cattle from island farms. The island didn't fully recover until the 1820s, when the whaling industry took off. The Vineyard enjoyed a heyday from 1820 until the Civil War, with hundreds of whaling vessels sailing in and out of Edgartown. Whaling captains took their enormous profits from whale oil and built large Federal and Greek Revival homes all over the island. Many still stand today as gracious inns, renowned restaurants, and private homes.

After the Civil War, with the whaling industry in decline, tourism became the Vineyard's principal source of income. By 1878 the Methodist Campground of Oak Bluffs had become a popular summer resort, with 12,000 people attending annual meetings. Over the next 30 years, other travelers discovered the island and returned summer after summer to enjoy its pleasant weather, relatively warm water, excellent fishing, and comfortable yet genteel lifestyle. By the turn of the 20th century, there were 2,000 hotel rooms in Oak Bluffs alone—there aren't that many bed-and-breakfasts or inns on the entire island today! Summertime traffic was so high that a rail line was built from the Oak Bluffs ferry terminal to Katama. Daily ferry service ran from the New York Yacht Club to Gay Head (present-day Aquinnah).

Although the whaling industry rapidly declined, other sea-related businesses continued to reap healthy profits. In 1900, Vineyard Sound was one of the busiest sea-lanes in the world, second only to the English Channel. Heavy sea traffic continued until the Cape Cod Canal was completed in 1914. Tourism picked up again in the early 1970s. And when the Clintons began spending summer vacations here in the mid-1990s, they created a tidal wave of national and international interest in the island. As of late, the Obamas have continued the tradition with visits in 2009, 2010, 2011, and 2013.

Today the year-round population of 15,000 mushrooms in July and August to about 150,000. Grumpy year-round Vineyarders are fond of saying that the island sinks 3 inches when ferries unload their passengers.

The terms *up-island* and *down-island* are holdovers from the days when the island was populated by seafarers—as you travel west, you move up the scale of longitude. *Up-island* refers to the less developed, hilly western end, including West Tisbury,

EDGARTOWN HARBOR KIM GRANT

Chilmark, the village of Menemsha (in Chilmark), and Aquinnah. Edgartown, Oak Bluffs, and Vineyard Haven, which are the most developed towns, are all *down-island*.

THE TOWNS

Elegant **Edgartown** is chock-full of grand, white Greek Revival ship captains' houses, with fanlights and widow's walks. Many of these private homes are clustered on North and South Water Streets, while elsewhere downtown you'll find chic shops, galleries, and restaurants.

Although it's less showy than Edgartown, **Vineyard Haven** maintains a year-round level of activity that Edgartown doesn't. It's the commercial center of the island, where

VINEYARD HAVEN HARBOR KIM GRANT

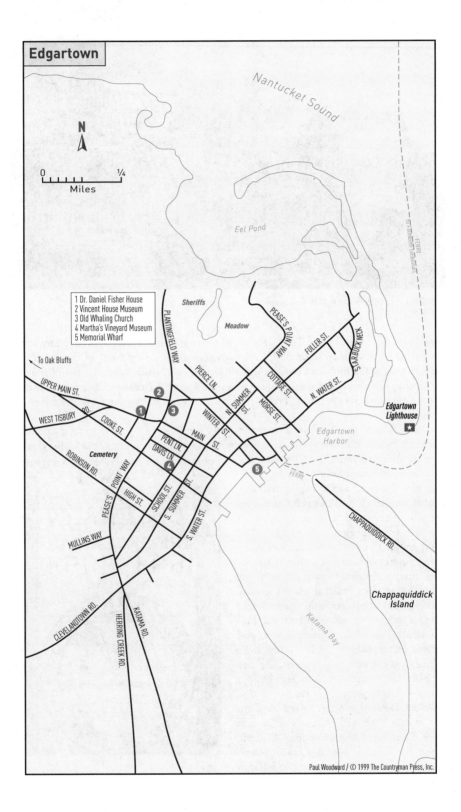

Edgartown

N

0 ———— 1/4
Miles

1 Dr. Daniel Fisher House
2 Vincent House Museum
3 Old Whaling Church
4 Martha's Vineyard Museum
5 Memorial Wharf

Nantucket Sound

Eel Pond

FERRY TO WOODS HOLE

Sheriffs

Meadow

To Oak Bluffs

UPPER MAIN ST.

WEST TISBURY RD.

COOKE ST.

ROBINSON RD.

Cemetery

PEASE'S POINT WAY

MULLINS WAY

CLEVELANDTOWN RD.

HERRING CREEK RD.

KATAMA RD.

HIGH ST.

SCHOOL ST.

S. SUMMER ST.

S. WATER ST.

DAVIS LN.

PENT LN.

MAIN ST.

WINTER ST.

N. SUMMER ST.

PLANTINGFIELD WAY

PIERCE LN.

COTTAGE ST.

MORSE ST.

PEASE'S POINT WAY

FULLER ST.

N. WATER ST.

STARBUCK NECK

Edgartown
Lighthouse

Edgartown
Harbor

FERRY

CHAPPAQUIDDICK RD.

Chappaquiddick
Island

Katama Bay

Paul Woodward / © 1999 The Countryman Press, Inc.

GINGERBREAD HOUSES IN OAK BLUFFS KIM GRANT

"real" people live and work. The harbor is home to more wooden boats than any other harbor of its size in New England. For an experience straight out of the 19th century, stop in at Gannon and Benjamin Boatbuilders on Beach Road; it's one of the few remaining wooden-boat rebuilding shops in the country. Dozens of big-name literary and journalistic personalities have all called Vineyard Haven their second home for decades.

Oak Bluffs today is at once charming and honky-tonk. A number of prominent African Americans have vacationed here over the years, including Spike Lee, Vernon Jordan, Dorothy West, and Charles Ogletree. In fact, Oak Bluffs has a long history of welcoming and attracting African Americans: in 1835, Wesleyan Grove was the site of the Methodist congregation's annual summer-camp meetings. The campers' small tents became family tents; then primitive, wooden, tentlike cottages; and finally, brightly painted cottages ornamented with fanciful trim. Cupolas, domes, spires, turrets, and gingerbread cutouts make for an architectural fantasyland. The whimsical, precious, and offbeat cottages are worlds away from Edgartown's traditional houses. So are Oak Bluffs' nightclubs and the baggy-pants-wearing, pierced youth.

CHILMARK KIM GRANT

West Tisbury is often called the Athens of the Vineyard because of its fine New England Congregational Church, Town Hall, and Grange Hall. Music Street, where descendants of the island's

19th-century ship captains still live in large houses, was so named because many of these families used whaling profits to purchase pianos. Over the years, West Tisbury summer residents have included *Washington Post* owner-publisher Katharine Graham, cartoonist Jules Feiffer, and historian David McCullough. Other A-list celebs clamoring for their place in the Vineyard sun (in Hollywood East) have included Ted Danson and Mary Steenburgen, Larry David, film mogul Harvey Weinstein, John Cusack, and Michael J. Fox.

Chilmark is a peaceful place of rolling hills and old stone fences that outline 200-year-old farms. You'll find dozens of working farms up-island, some still operated by descendants of the island's original European settlers.

Travel down North Road to **Menemsha**, a small, truly picturesque village and working harbor that you may recognize as the location of the movie *Jaws*. The surrounding area is crisscrossed by miles and miles of unmarked, interconnected dirt roads, great for exploring. (Alas, many are private.) Chilmark is sparsely populated, to the tune of 1,050 or so year-rounders, and they aim to keep it that way. In order to limit growth, they issue the island's only 3-acre-minimum building permits.

Chilmark, which is among the 50 wealthiest towns in America (the average price of a single family home in 2016 was $2.1 million), has hosted such disparate personalities as photographer Alfred Eisenstaedt and John Belushi. (Belushi is buried on-island; "Eise's" photos are found in galleries and at his beloved retreat, the Menemsha Inn and Cottages.) Harvard Law School professor Alan Dershowitz is a denizen of Lucy Vincent Beach, one of the island's many residents-only beaches—and a nude one at that.

Aquinnah, a must-see destination, occupies the island's western tip. (If you haven't visited the Vineyard for a while, you may know Aquinnah as Gay Head. It was renamed Aquinnah, "land under the hill," in mid-1997 by a narrow 79–76 town vote.) Of the 1,100 members listed on the Wampanoag tribal rolls, approximately 300 still reside on the Vineyard, half in Aquinnah. Tribal legend holds that the giant Moshup created the Vineyard, taught the Wampanoag how to fish and catch whales, and remains a protector. The Wampanoag own the brilliantly colored bluffs and the face of the Clay Cliffs of Aquinnah.

Martha's Vineyard has always attracted celebrity summer visitors. But in recent years, many who visited decided they wanted to own a piece of it. Beginning in the late 1980s and continuing to this day, a tremendous building boom has changed the face of the Vineyard. While the Vineyard had been a place where the well-heeled and well-off

MENEMSHA HARBOR KIM GRANT

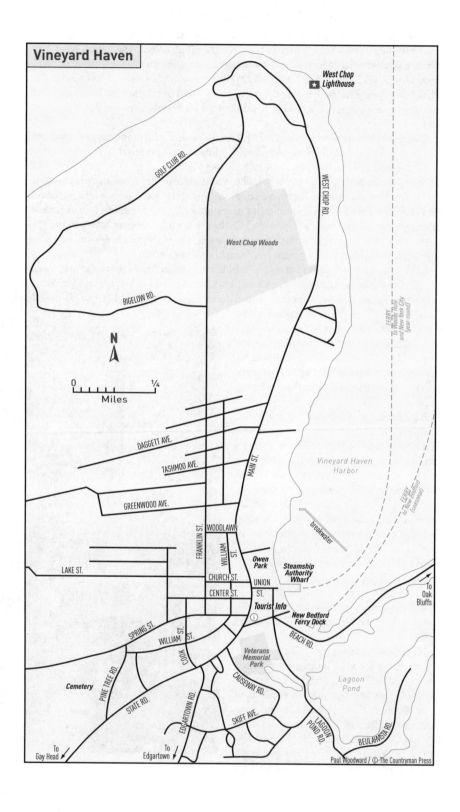

Vineyard Haven

West Chop
Lighthouse

GOLF CLUB RD.

WEST CHOP RD.

West Chop Woods

BIGELOW RD.

N

0   ¼
Miles

DAGGETT AVE.

TASHMOO AVE.

GREENWOOD AVE.

MAIN ST.

FRANKLIN ST.

WOODLAWN

WILLIAM ST.

LAKE ST.

CHURCH ST.

CENTER ST.

UNION ST.

Owen Park

Steamship Authority Wharf

Vineyard Haven Harbor

breakwater

FERRY
To Woods Hole
and New York City
(year-round)

FERRY
To New Bedford
(seasonal)

To Oak Bluffs

Tourist Info
ⓘ

New Bedford Ferry Dock

BEACH RD.

SPRING ST.

WILLIAM ST.

COOK ST.

PINE TREE RD.

Cemetery

STATE RD.

EDGARTOWN RD.

CAUSEWAY RD.

SKIFF AVE.

Veterans Memorial Park

LAGOON POND RD.

BEULAH'S TA RD.

Lagoon Pond

To
Gay Head

To
Edgartown

Paul Woodward / © The Countryman Press

came to escape notice, today the celebrities and power brokers come as much to see as to be seen. Although residents are generally unfazed by their celebrity neighbors—movie stars, authors, journalists, musicians, financial moguls—many locals and long-time visitors agree that the Vineyard is no longer the quaint, tranquil island it was prior to the mid-1980s.

Martha's Vineyard is unlike most of the rest of America; people tend to get along pretty well with one another. They work hard to maintain a sense of tolerance and community spirit. Most lengthy debates center on land use and preservation rather than on race or religion. (Of course, there are notable exceptions.) Everyone relies, to some extent, on the hectic summer season that brings in most of the island's annual income, though residents do breathe a sigh of relief when the crowds depart after mid-October.

To experience the Vineyard at its best and still have a dependable chance for good weather, plan your visit from May to mid-June or from mid-September to mid-October. From January to March, the Vineyard is truly a retreat from civilization.

GUIDANCE ❊ **Martha's Vineyard Chamber of Commerce** (508-693-0085; mvy.com), 24 Beach Road, Vineyard Haven. There are good, free street maps of Vineyard Haven, Oak Bluffs, and Edgartown available at all chambers.

There are two seasonal **information booths**: one at the Steamship Authority terminal, Vineyard Haven; and the other at Circuit Avenue, Oak Bluffs (adjacent to the Flying Horses Carousel).

Edgartown Information Center, Church Street, Edgartown. Around the corner from the Old Whaling Church, this small center has restrooms and a post office, also serving as a shuttle-bus stop (see also *Getting Around*).

GETTING THERE ❊ *By boat from Woods Hole:* **The Steamship Authority** (508-477-8600 for advance auto reservations; 508-548-3788 in Woods Hole for day-of-sailing information only; no reservations accepted—don't count on getting lucky; steamship authority.com), 1 Cowdry Road. The Steamship is the only company that provides

STEAMSHIP AUTHORITY FERRY KIM GRANT

ISLANDER FERRY DOCKING IN VINEYARD HAVEN KIM GRANT

daily, year-round transport—for people and autos—to Vineyard Haven and Oak Bluffs. The Vineyard is 7 miles from Woods Hole, and the trip takes 45 minutes. About nine boats ply the waters daily.

The Steamship annually carries upward of 2 million people to the Vineyard. *Here's the best advice in the entire book:* Make car reservations as soon as possible. Call as soon as you know your dates. Auto reservations are mandatory/essential year-round. Otherwise, the Steamship has a standby policy that's first come, first served.

Round-trip tickets: $$ adults; $ bicycles; more than $150 for autos. Off-season, auto prices drop to just less than $100. If you are not taking your car, the Steamship Authority provides free, frequent buses between the parking lots and the ferry dock. Each bus has a bike rack that holds two bikes. Parking is $$ per calendar day.

By boat from Falmouth: **Island Queen** (508-548-4800; islandqueen.com), 75 Falmouth Heights Road. This passengers-only service (smaller and more comfortable than the Steamship Authority's boat) operates late May to mid-October and takes about 35 minutes; departures are from Falmouth Inner Harbor to Oak Bluffs. There is plenty of parking near the *Island Queen*'s dock ($$ per calendar day). Round-trip fares: $$ adults; $ bicycles.

Falmouth–Edgartown Ferry (508-548-9400; falmouthedgartownferry.com), 278 Scranton Avenue. From late May to mid-October, this service plies the waters three to five times daily between Falmouth and Edgartown (Memorial Wharf). Round-trip fares: $$$$$ adults; $ bicycles. Parking is $$–$$$ per calendar day.

By boat from Hyannis: **Hy-Line Cruises** (508-778-2600; hylinecruises.com), 220 Ocean Street Dock. Two to five passenger boats (55 minutes) to and from Oak Bluffs from May to late October. If you haven't purchased advance tickets, it's wise to arrive an hour early in July and August. Round-trip, in-season fares: adults $$$$$+/high-speed ferry, traditional ferry less; bicycles $$. Parking $–$$.

By boat from New Bedford: **Seastreak Ferry** (866-683-3779; nefastferry.com) operates passenger boats from 49 State Pier to Vineyard Haven from late May to mid-October. The ferry crossing takes one hour. Round-trip fares: $$$$$+ adults, $$ bicycles. Parking is $$ per calendar day. For visitors coming from the south, New Bedford is a more convenient departure point than Woods Hole. Even those driving from points north may wish to consider taking the New Bedford ferry to avoid Cape Cod Canal bridge traffic.

By boat from Nantucket: **Hy-Line Cruises** (508-778-2600 Hyannis; 508-693-0112 Oak Bluffs; 508-228-3949 Nantucket; hylinecruises.com) offers interisland service between Oak Bluffs and Nantucket from mid-June to mid-September. The trip takes 1¼ hours; there is only one trip daily. One-way fares cost $$$$$ adults, $ bicycles.

By boat from New York City: **Seastreak Ferry** (866-683-3779; nefastferry.com) This 5-hour voyage runs during the summer months.

See also **Patriot Party Boats** under *To Do* in "Falmouth and Woods Hole."

By bus: **Bonanza/Peter Pan** (888-751-8800; peterpanbus.com) provides daily year-round service to Woods Hole from Boston, New York, Hartford, and Providence. Buses are scheduled to meet ferries, but ferries won't wait for a late bus.

By air: With a booming increase in jet-setting visitors, it's no wonder a new terminal was built in the late 1990s. **Cape Air** (866-227-3247; capeair.com) flies to the Vineyard from Boston, Providence, Nantucket, New Bedford, Hyannis, and White Plains.

GETTING AROUND *By car:* The infamous Five Corners is the trickiest and most dangerous intersection on the island. It's also the first thing you'll encounter as you disembark from the Vineyard Haven ferry terminal. If you're going to Oak Bluffs, Katama, Edgartown, and Chappaquiddick, take the left lane. For West Tisbury, North Tisbury, Lambert's Cove, Menemsha, Chilmark, and Aquinnah, enter the right lane and turn right.

When making plans, consider these sample distances: Vineyard Haven to Oak Bluffs, 3 miles; Vineyard Haven to Edgartown, 8 miles; Oak Bluffs to Edgartown, 6 miles; Vineyard Haven to Aquinnah, 18 miles.

Unfortunately, summertime traffic jams are commonplace in down-island towns. Try to park outside of town and take shuttles (see *By Shuttle*). Why would you want to stop and crawl in a picturesque village on a vacation day?

In-season, expect to pay more than $100 daily for the least-expensive rental car and upward of $200 daily for four-wheel drives and minivans. A word of note: Rates change according to weekday, weekend, and holiday rentals. Before heading out, invest a few bucks in the very detailed gold-and-orange Martha's Vineyard Road Map produced by Edward Thomas (508-693-2059). It's an excellent, accurate resource and even lists mileage between intersections. It's available at most bookstores, grocery stores, and liquor stores.

Car rental companies include **Budget Rent-a-Car** (508-693-1911; budgetmv .com), Edgartown, at the Triangle; 45 Beach Road, Vineyard Haven; 9 Oak Bluffs Avenue (at the ferry dock), Oak

OAK BLUFFS KIM GRANT

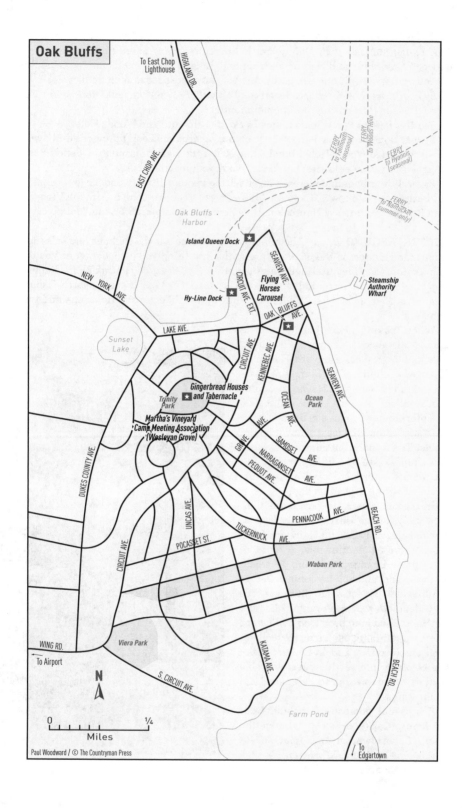

Oak Bluffs

To East Chop Lighthouse

HIGHLAND DR.

EAST CHOP AVE.

Oak Bluffs Harbor

NEW YORK AVE.

FERRY to Falmouth (seasonal)
FERRY to Woods Hole
FERRY to Hyannis (seasonal)
FERRY to Nantucket (summer only)

Island Queen Dock

Hy-Line Dock

CIRCUIT AVE. EXT.

SEAVIEW AVE.

Flying Horses Carousel

OAK BLUFFS AVE.

Steamship Authority Wharf

LAKE AVE.

Sunset Lake

CIRCUIT AVE.

KENNEBEC AVE.

OCEAN AVE.

SEAVIEW AVE.

Gingerbread Houses and Tabernacle

Trinity Park

Martha's Vineyard Camp Meeting Association (Wesleyan Grove)

GROVE AVE.

SAMOSET AVE.

Ocean Park

NARRAGANSETT AVE.

PEQUOT AVE.

DUKES COUNTY AVE.

UNCAS AVE.

PENNACOOK AVE.

BEACH RD.

POCASSET ST.

TUCKERNUCK AVE.

Waban Park

CIRCUIT AVE.

Viera Park

WING RD.

To Airport

S. CIRCUIT AVE.

KATAMA AVE.

Farm Pond

BEACH RD.

To Edgartown

N

0   1/4
Miles

Paul Woodward / © The Countryman Press

Bluffs; and 71 Airport Road at Martha's Vineyard Airport. I've always found these outfits helpful: **Adventure Rentals** (19 Beach Road, Five Corners, Vineyard Haven, 508-693-1959); and **Island Hoppers** (23 Lake Avenue, Oak Bluffs, 508-696-9147; islandhoppersmv.com). By the way, gas is usually cheapest at the airport, but **Mobil** (North Line Road, Edgartown) and **Up-Island Automotive** (1074 State Road, West Tisbury) have decent prices, too.

MOPEDS FOR RENT   KIM GRANT

By moped: If most Vineyarders and emergency-room doctors had their way, mopeds would be banned. Once you've seen the face, arms, and legs of a fellow Explorer skinned, you'll know why. Sand, mopeds, winding roads, and speed do not mix. Take a look at the mopeds you might be renting; many of their plastic hulls have been cracked from accidents. Having said that and not wanting to appear maternalistic, here goes: many rental agencies are located near the ferry terminals in Oak Bluffs and Vineyard Haven. **Adventure Rentals** has mopeds (often $100/day). Extra training, yellow diamond road signs (at notorious intersections), and maps (with danger spots and distances between points) should help reduce casualties.

❄ ♺ *By shuttle:* **Martha's Vineyard Transit Authority (VTA)** (508-693-9440; vineyardtransit.com) operates an excellent system of buses. Twelve buses travel among Vineyard Haven, Oak Bluffs, Edgartown, West Tisbury, Chilmark, Menemsha, and Aquinnah year-round. Buses seem to stop everywhere you want to go; you can also flag them down. They even have bike racks. Get a copy of the very helpful VTA map with stops and routes clearly listed. Carry it with you wherever you go. One-day passes cost $, three-day $$, seven-day $$$. Exact change is strongly suggested because change is given only in the form of credit vouchers for future trips. All routes run year-round except Edgartown Park & Ride and South Beach; the latter operates May to mid-October.

Of particular use are the following routes:

Edgartown Park & Ride. VTA has an alternative to wrangling for a parking place in Edgartown's car-choked streets. Leave your car at the Triangle (at the corner of Edgartown–Vineyard Haven Road and Oak Bluffs Road) and ride the shuttle. Parking and rides are free.

Tisbury Park & Ride, State Road (across from Cronig's Market). Avoid the parking nightmare in Vineyard Haven and let the VTA shuttle drop you off downtown. The free shuttle runs year-round. Parking is free for 7 consecutive days; after that you must purchase tickets in advance at Town Hall (508-696-4200, William and Spring Streets) in Vineyard Haven. Seasonal passes available.

South Beach. This route runs from Edgartown's information building (near Church and Main Streets) to three points at South Beach.

Bus tour: **Gay Head Sightseeing** (508-693-1555) and **Martha's Vineyard Sightseeing** (508-693-4681) offer tours from mid-April to late October. The clearly marked buses meet incoming ferries. The Gay Head tour covers all six towns but makes only one stop—at the Clay Cliffs of Aquinnah—where there are small food stands, souvenir shops, public restrooms, and a wonderful view of the cliffs and the ocean. The only potential drawback: You may tire of hearing the constant running commentary about which celebrities live down which dirt roads. They also offer charter tours for large groups. $$$.

Taxi tour: Most taxis conduct island sight-seeing trips for a price, but you don't want to go with just anyone. I highly recommend **Jon's Taxi** (508-627-4677). Trips with Jon or his drivers cost $$$$$+ per hour for one to six people. Schedule these private trips at your convenience.

❋ **Adam Cab** (508-627-4462; adamcabmv.com) is also very good and gives a general 2½-hour tour twice daily from Edgartown from late May to early September (less often off-season) for $$$$ per person.

By taxi: Uber and Lyft are on-island, but I'd personally rather support local taxis.

🚲 *By bicycle:* Bicycling is a great way to get around, but it requires stamina if you're heading up-island (see **To Do**).

MEDIA *Vineyard Gazette* (508-627-4311; vineyardgazette.com), 34 South Summer Street, Edgartown. The newspaper, which first rolled off the press on May 14, 1846, is a beloved island institution. Although its year-round circulation is only 10,000, the paper is mailed to island devotees in all 50 states and internationally. There's no single better way for an Explorer to get a handle on island life.

Martha's Vineyard Times (508-693-6100; mvtimes.com), 30 Beach Road, Vineyard Haven. For over 35 years, this weekly publication and its corresponding website has been delivering up-to-date news as well as feature material on island life, arts, and entertainment. Their *Vineyard Visitor* publication and website (vineyardvisitor.com) have lots of travel tips and info on things to do.

MORE WEBSITES For a complete guide visit **mvol.com** as well as **vineyardstyle.com** for articles and info about local artisans, gardening, home décor and interiors, shopping, and other island trends.

PUBLIC RESTROOMS In Vineyard Haven head to the top of the Stop & Shop parking lot (seasonal) and to the Steamship Authority terminal (year-round) off Water Street. In Oak Bluffs, restrooms can be found at the Steamship Authority terminal on Seaview Avenue (seasonal); on Kennebec Avenue, one block from Circuit Avenue (seasonal); and next to Our Market (seasonal) at Oak Bluffs Harbor. In Edgartown, they're at the visitor center (year-round) on Church Street. Seasonal facilities are also located near the parking lot for the Clay Cliffs of Aquinnah, at Dutcher's Dock in Menemsha Harbor, and in West Tisbury at the Grange Hall next to Town Hall.

LAUNDROMATS **Airport Laundromat** (508-693-5005; takemmycleaners.com/airportlaundramat, off the Edgartown–West Tisbury Road. Open daily 8 a.m.–7 p.m.

PUBLIC LIBRARIES ❋ 🖊 ☂ Most of these libraries have story times and Internet access; call ahead or look online for hours and schedule vagaries:

BIKES FOR RENT KIM GRANT

A DOWN-ISLAND DAY ON THE VINEYARD

Morning: Order everything on the menu at Art Cliff Diner. Then watch quiet morning harbor activity from Owen Park. Take a stroll in Oak Bluffs and admire the whimsy of the gingerbread houses. Sit for a minute in the solid Old Whaling Church in Edgartown.

Afternoon: Have a quick (sidewalk) lunch at Alchemy or grab an award-winning cup of clam chowder from M.V. Chowder Co.

Evening: Breathe in the salty air with a walk to the Edgartown Lighthouse or a leisure sunset cruises on Sail Ena. Enjoy fine cuisine at The Dunes (Edgartown) or a romantic table for two at Sweet Life Café. Resolve to visit the Vineyard longer next time.

Aquinnah (508-645-2314; aquinnahlibrary.org), 1 Church Street at State Road.
Chilmark (508-645-3360; chilmarklibrary.org), 522 South Road, Chilmark Center.
Edgartown (508-627-4221; edgartownlibrary.org), 26 West Tisbury Road.
Oak Bluffs (508-693-9433; oakbluffslibrary.org), 56R School Street.
Vineyard Haven (508-696-4211; vhlibrary.org), 200 Main Street.
West Tisbury (508-693-3366; westtisburylibrary.org), 1042 State Road.
See also **Martha's Vineyard Museum** under *To See.*

HERITAGE TRAILS **Aquinnah Cultural Trail** (508-645-9265; wampanoagtribe.net). For those interested in something other than beaches and shops, look for the excellent and informative map once you're on-island. You can always find it at the Aquinnah Cultural Center, 35 Aquinnah Circle, Aquinnah. It is full of interesting facts about the "first people of Noepe," place-name translations, Moshup legends, local government, and a schedule of events.

African American Heritage Trail (508-693-4361; mvheritagetrail.org). Tours on request late May to early September. The brainchild of a Martha's Vineyard Regional High School history teacher and NAACP archivist Elaine Weintraub, this developing trail currently has about 16 sites devoted to telling the story of the island's strong association with African Americans. Weintraub researched the story of the Island's own African American whaling captain, William A. Martin, and two generations of his family, establishing an African American presence on Martha's Vineyard before the American revolution. Every town has sites, including abandoned graveyards; the home of Dorothy West, a Harlem Renaissance writer who lived on the island and died in 1999; a site dedicated to Rebecca Amos, an African woman enslaved on the Vineyard; and a decrepit Gospel Tabernacle. The book *Lighting the Trail: The African American Heritage of Martha's Vineyard* is sold in all the island bookstores. Choose from three different tours of varying durations and scopes.

EMERGENCIES **Edgartown Police Department** (508-627-4343; edgartownpolice.org), 72 Peases Point Way; **Tisbury Police Department** (508-696-4240; tisburypolice.org), 32 Water Street; **Oak Bluffs Police Department** (508-693-0750; oakbluffspolice.com), 2 Oak Bluffs Avenue; or call **911.**

Medical: **Martha's Vineyard Hospital** (508-693-0410; mvhospital.com), 1 Hospital Road, off Beach Road, Oak Bluffs. Includes a 24-hour emergency room. In 2010, the hospital opened a new 90,000-square-foot building.

✳ To See

IN EDGARTOWN

✳ 🦆 **Martha's Vineyard Museum** (508-627-4441; mvmuseum.org), 59 School Street. This excellent collection is housed in several buildings. Perhaps the most interesting exhibit is the Oral History Center, which preserves the island's history through more than 1,400 interviews with some of the island's older citizens. (The project was begun in the mid-1990s.) Other facilities include a fine pre–Revolutionary War house which has undergone little renovation since the mid-19th century. Ten rooms at the Thomas Cooke House focus on various aspects of the island's history, including ethnic groups, architecture, natural history, and agriculture. The society also has a maritime gallery, a historical reference library, a tryworks replica, a carriage shed that houses boats and vehicles, and a historic herb garden. The enormous original Fresnel lens from the Aquinnah Lighthouse is here, too, and it's illuminated for a few hours after sunset every day. $.

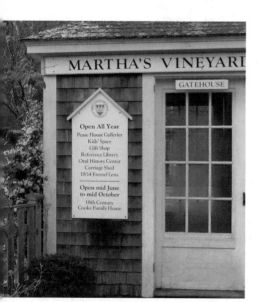

MARTHA'S VINEYARD MUSEUM KIM GRANT

Dr. Daniel Fisher House (508-627-4440; mvpreservation.org), 99 Main Street. The island's best example of Greek Revival architecture, this 1840 house has an enclosed cupola (perhaps more correctly called a "lantern"), roof and porch balustrades, a shallow hipped roof, large windowpanes, and a portico, all exquisitely preserved. Dr. Fisher was a Renaissance man: doctor, whaling magnate, banker (he founded the Martha's Vineyard National Bank), merchant, and miller. He insisted that his house be constructed with the finest materials—with Maine pine timbers soaked in lime for two years, and brass and copper nails, for instance. The house is headquarters for the Martha's Vineyard Preservation Trust, which is charged with saving, restoring, and making self-sufficient any important island buildings that might otherwise be sold for commercial purposes or radically remodeled. Combination tours (45 minutes; $) with the Vincent House and the Old Whaling Church (see below) are offered May to mid-October.

Vincent House Museum (508-627-4440; mvpreservation.org), behind the Old Whaling Church. Open May to early September. Dating to 1672, the Vineyard's oldest residence was in the same family until 1941, and was eventually given to the Preservation Trust in 1977. Reproduction and antique furniture in three rooms depicts how the residence looked in the 17th, 18th, and 19th centuries. $.

Old Whaling Church (508-627-4440; mvpreservation.org), 89 Main Street. Built in 1843, this thriving parish church also serves as a performing arts center, hosting plays, lectures, concerts, and films. Owned by the Martha's Vineyard Preservation Trust, the building originally housed the Edgartown Methodist Church and was constructed with the same techniques used to build whaling ships. Free.

FRESNEL LIGHT KIM GRANT

DR. DANIEL FISHER HOUSE KIM GRANT

OLD WHALING CHURCH   KIM GRANT

Memorial Wharf, adjacent to the Chappy Ferry on the water. This two-story landing is a terrific spot from which to watch harbor boat traffic in one direction and stately manses in the other.

North Water Street. Some of these fine Colonial, Federal, and Greek Revival houses may look familiar because many clothing companies, including Talbot's, have sent crews of models and photographers here to shoot their catalogs. Architectural detailing on these white houses trimmed in black is superb.

Edgartown Lighthouse (508-627-4441; mvmuseum.org), at the end of North Water Street. The first lighthouse to direct boats into and around Edgartown Harbor was built in 1828 on a small island. Shortly after a new lighthouse replaced it in 1938, the island became connected to the "mainland" of the Vineyard by a spit of sand. Today the lighthouse, renovated in 2007, is accessible by foot. Take note of the granite cobblestone foundation (dubbed the Children's Lighthouse Memorial), a tribute to Vineyard children who have died. Open to the public late May to mid-October. $.

IN VINEYARD HAVEN

Sovereign Bank (508-696-4400), 75 Main Street. This distinctive 1905 beachstone building has lovely stained glass and great acoustics. On this site, incidentally, stood the harness shop where the Great Fire of 1883 started. The conflagration destroyed 60 buildings.

William Street. The only street in town that survived the devastating 1883 fire boasts some fine examples of Greek Revival architecture. The **Richard G. Luce House**, near the corner of William Street and Spring Street, is prime among the carefully preserved sea captains' homes. Captain Luce never lost a whaling ship or a crew member during his 30-year career, and apparently his good fortune at sea extended to life on land.

Jirah Luce House, near the corner of South Main and Main Streets. Built in 1804, this is one of the few buildings to survive the Great Fire of 1883.

Old Schoolhouse, Main Street at Colonial Lane. Built in 1829, the schoolhouse now houses a youth sailing program, but the Liberty Pole in front of it recounts the story of three courageous girls who defied British troops.

West Chop Lighthouse, at the western end of Main Street. Built in 1817 with wood and replaced with brick in 1838, the lighthouse has been moved back from the shore twice, first in 1848 and again in 1891. Today the lighthouse is inhabited and not open for touring.

Katharine Cornell Theatre/Tisbury Town Hall (508-696-4200; tisburyma.gov), 51 Spring Street. This 1844 performance center features murals by Stan Murphy, depicting island scenes, whaling adventures, seagulls, and American Indians. The 130-seat theater boasts no box office per se; event listings are best found at mvtimes.com or mvgazette.com.

IN OAK BLUFFS

East Chop Lighthouse (508-627-4441; mvmuseum.org/eastchop), Telegraph Hill, off East Chop Drive, Oak Bluffs. Open Sunday 90 minutes prior to sunset and 30 minutes after, June through August. This circa-1850 lighthouse was built by Capt. Silas Daggett with the financial help of prosperous fellow seafarers who wanted a better system of relaying signals from the Vineyard to Nantucket and the mainland. Up to that point, they'd used a complex system of raising arms, legs, flags, and lanterns to signal that ships were coming in. In 1875 the government purchased the lighthouse from the consortium of sea captains for $6,000, then constructed the cast-iron structure that stands today. There are nice ocean views from here. $.

WEST CHOP LIGHTHOUSE KIM GRANT

✒ **Flying Horses Carousel** (508-693-9481), Circuit Avenue at Lake Avenue. Open mid-April to mid-October. The oldest operating carousel in the country, carved in New York City in 1876, is marvelously well preserved and lovingly maintained. It was brought by barge to the island in 1884, complete with four chariots and 20 horses with real horsehair manes. Adults visit this national historic landmark even without a child in tow to grab for the elusive brass ring, which entitles the catcher to a free ride. (Here's a public service announcement: A few folks every year are not returning the brass ring when they grab it, and the carousel is getting precariously close to running out of them.) $.

Trinity Park Tabernacle, (508-693-0525; mvcva.org/tabernacle), behind Lake, Circuit, and Dukes County Avenues. The enormous, tentlike tabernacle was built in 1879 to replace the original meeting tent used by the Methodists who met here. Today the tabernacle is one of the largest wrought-iron structures in the country. There are community sing-alongs at 8 p.m. on Wednesdays in summer.

EAST CHOP LIGHTHOUSE KIM GRANT

UNION CHAPEL KIM GRANT

Wesleyan Grove surrounds the tabernacle, which, in turn, is encircled by rows of colorful **"gingerbread" cottages**, built during the late 19th century to replace true tents. Owners painted the tiny houses with bright colors and pastels to accentuate the Carpenter Gothic architecture and woodwork. There are upward of 320 cottages today, still leased from the Camp Meeting Association. Visitors are welcome to wander around the mainly Protestant (but always ecumenical) community. No bicycles are allowed in Wesleyan Grove, and quiet time is strictly observed after 11 p.m.

Union Chapel, 55 Narragansett Avenue, at the corner of Kennebec and Samoset Avenues. This 1870 octagonal chapel holds interdenominational services and hosts seasonal performing arts events.

Cottage Museum (508-693-7784; mvcma.org), 1 Trinity Park. Open seasonally. The interior and exterior of this 1867 cottage are typical of the more than 300 tiny cottages in Wesleyan Grove. Memorabilia and photographs span the ages from 1835 to present day. $.

UP-ISLAND

Mayhew Chapel and **Indian Burial Ground**, Christiantown Road, off Indian Hill Road, West Tisbury. This tiny chapel, burial ground, and memorial to the Praying Indians (who were converted to Christianity by the Reverend Mayhew Jr. in the mid-1600s) is a quiet place, owned by the Wampanoag tribe of Aquinnah.

Grange Hall (508-627-4440; mvpreservation.org), State Road, West Tisbury. Open seasonally. The original Agricultural Society Barn now hosts functions and events.

Beetlebung Corner, at the intersection of Middle, South, State, and Menemsha Cross Roads; the center of Chilmark. The intersection was named for the grove of beetlebung trees (the New England name for tupelos), which are unusual in this region. Tupelo is a very hard wood, an excellent material for making mallets (also called beetles) and the plugs (or bungs) that filled the holes in wooden casks and barrels during whale oil days.

CHERISHED INSTITUTION

Alley's General Store (508-693-0088; mvpreservation.org), State Road, West Tisbury. Alley's is a beloved Vineyard landmark. "Dealers in almost everything" since 1858, the store has a wide front porch where locals have gathered over the decades to discuss current events and exchange friendly gossip. In the early 1990s, though, economic conditions almost forced Alley's to close. In true island spirit, the Martha's Vineyard Preservation Trust stepped in to renovate the building and ensure its survival. Alley's continues to feel like a country store, selling everything utilitarian: housewares, mismatched cups and saucers, and locally grown produce.

KIM GRANT

Abel's Hill Cemetery, South Road, about ½ mile beyond Meeting House Road, Chilmark. John Belushi, of *Saturday Night Live* and Blues Brothers fame, was buried here after a drug overdose in 1982 at the not-so-ripe age of 33. He'd been partying with Robert DeNiro and Robin Williams at the Chateau Marmot in West Hollywood on March 5 when a mainline cocktail of heroin and cocaine did him in. According to legend, the only place Belushi ever said that he got a good night's sleep was on the Vineyard, where he and his wife had some property. You'll easily find the marked grave near the entrance of the cemetery, but his body lies in an unmarked grave about 11 feet north of where his original headstone was placed.

Quitsa Overlook, off State Road. At Beetlebung Corner, bear left onto State Road, heading toward Aquinnah. After a mile or so, you'll pass over a bridge; Nashaquitsa Pond (also known as Quitsa) is on your right and Stonewall Pond is on your left. Just beyond, a spot overlooks Quitsa and Menemsha Ponds. About half a mile farther, locals fill water jugs from a fresh, sweet stream that's been siphoned off to run out of a pipe. Local lore attributes various cures to the water—from stress relief to a flu antidote to a hangover remedy.

Aquinnah Community Baptist Church (508-693-1539; wampanoagtribe.org), 1 Church Street at State Road, Aquinnah. Turn left at the small red schoolhouse (now the town library). The lovely church is the country's oldest American Indian Baptist church. It might have the prettiest location, too, overlooking windswept grassy dunes, stone walls, and the Atlantic Ocean.

Menemsha Harbor, at Menemsha Cross Road near Beetlebung Corner. This working fishing village is filled with small, sturdy docks and simple, weathered boathouses. Some islanders still earn a living from the boats of Menemsha's fishing fleet. For the rest of us, the harbor is a great location from which to watch the setting sun. It's one of several locations throughout the Cape and islands where the ritual of applauding the sun for its day's work is observed the moment it slips below the horizon. A few little shacks (shops and fast-food eateries) line the road to Dutcher's Dock.

Aquinnah Tribal Administrative Building (508-645-9265; wampanoagtribe.org), 20 Black Brook Road, Aquinnah. Housed inside this eco-friendly building (made almost completely of recycled materials and run by solar power) are a number of interesting small displays about the Wampanoag tribe. Look for an elders gallery with pictures of the tribal elders past and present, traditional native gardens, and a wetu, a traditional native home. When visiting, be aware that this is a working environment for the government of the tribe, not just a tourist destination.

Clay Cliffs of Aquinnah. The brilliantly colored clay cliffs, a designated national landmark, rise 150 feet above the shore and were formed 100 million years ago by glaciers. For a fine view of the full magnitude of this spectacular geological formation, and distant views of Noman's Land Island and the Elizabeth Islands, walk beyond the souvenir shops. A wooden boardwalk also leads to the beach, where you can appreciate the towering clay cliffs from sea level. It's important to note that the Wampanoag have lived here for more than 5,000 years and own most of this land, although most of the beach is public; only they may remove clay from the eroding cliffs.

Gay Head Lighthouse (508-627-4441; gayheadlight.org). This redbrick lighthouse was built in 1844 to replace a wooden lighthouse that had stood since 1799. In 1856 a powerful Fresnel lens was mounted atop the lighthouse, where it warned ships away

MENEMSHA HARBOR KIM GRANT

from the perilous Aquinnah coast; it was used for almost 100 years. The Gay Head light was named one of America's 11 Most Endangered Places by the National Trust for Historic Preservation in 2013, and in order to preserve it for generations to come, the "Keep On Shining" committee successfully raised funds to relocate the light away from the eroding cliffs; the committee continues its fundraising efforts to complete restoration. From late June to mid-September, you can ascend the lighthouse to enjoy the sunset. It opens 90 minutes prior to sunset and closes 30 minutes after sunset; $.

CLAY CLIFFS OF AQUINNAH KIM GRANT

Aquinnah Cultural Center (508-645-7900; wampanoagtribe.org), Aquinnah. Open late June to early September. This 1880s homestead, which serves as the Indigenous Museum of the Aquinnah Wampanoag and community cultural center, enjoys some of the most wonderful windswept vistas on the island. It's no wonder that their 6 acres are leased for weddings. Donations.

Moshup Beach Overlook, on the northern end of Moshup Trail and south of the parking lot for the lighthouse, off State Road. This scenic coastal road has nice views of wild, low heathlands.

SCENIC DRIVES Instead of making a beeline up-island, detour onto Lambert's Cove Road from State Road out of Vineyard Haven. Take North, South, or Middle Roads up-island. I particularly like cutting between the roads on Tea Lane and Meeting House Road. As you approach Aquinnah, take a left onto Moshup Trail to the lighthouse and circle back via Lighthouse Road and Lobsterville Road (but do follow Lobsterville to the very end, across the cut from Menemsha).

AQUINNAH CULTURAL CENTER KIM GRANT

✳ To Do

AIRPLANE RIDES **Classic Aviators** (508-627-7677; biplanemv.com), off Herring Creek Road at the Katama Airfield, Edgartown. Open seasonally. Open-cockpit rides in a 1941 Waco biplane, solo or with a friend, with Snoopy-like leather caps and goggles. Rates start at $229 for one or two people for a 15- to 20-minute flight.

BICYCLING & RENTALS Several excellent (albeit crowded) bicycle paths connect the main towns: Vineyard Haven to Oak Bluffs, Oak Bluffs to Edgartown, Edgartown to West Tisbury, and Edgartown to South Beach via Katama Road. Because the roads from West Tisbury to Aquinnah are rather hilly, you need to be in pretty good shape to tackle the ride. A less ambitious but rewarding journey would entail taking your bike to Aquinnah and then pedaling the hilly but scenic up-island circular trail that begins at the Aquinnah Lighthouse: take Lighthouse Road to Lobsterville Road and backtrack up Lobsterville Road to State Road to Moshup Trail. The Manuel E. Correllus State Forest (see **Green Space**), off Edgartown–West Tisbury Road, also has several bicycle paths.

Rubel Bike Maps (bikemaps.com) are the best, most detailed maps available. Rubel produces a combination map that covers both the Vineyard and Nantucket ($), as well as another that includes the islands, Cape Cod, and the North Shore ($).

The **Martha's Vineyard Commission** (508-693-3453; mvcommission.org) also produces a free map that tells you what to expect on major routes: for instance, narrow roadways (shared with cars), gently rolling terrain, steep rolling terrain, and so on. It does not give estimated times or exact mileage, though.

Menemsha Bike Ferry (508-645-5154) operates 9 a.m.–5 p.m. (on demand) late May to early September. Some people riding out to Menemsha and Aquinnah will be thrilled to know about Hugh Taylor's little ferry, which takes cyclists across Menemsha Creek, which separates the picturesque harbor from Lobsterville Beach and Aquinnah beyond. This 150-yard ferry ride saves cyclists a 7-mile bike ride. $.

Dozens of shops rent bikes, including **R. W. Cutler Bikes** (800-627-2763; marthas vineyardbike.com) on the harborfront at 1 Main Street in Edgartown; and **Wheel Happy** (508-627-5928), 8 South Water Street, and (508-627-5881), 204 Upper Main Street, both in Edgartown. Mountain bikes and hybrids are rented for 1-, 3- and 7-day periods. Most shops are open April through October; ask about delivery and pickup service. $$$ daily.

✳ **Cycle Works** (508-693-6966), at 351 State Road in Vineyard Haven, repairs bicycles. John Stevenson and his enthusiastic and helpful crew have the largest selection of cycling equipment (for sale and rent), accessories, and parts on the island. They've been here since 1975.

BOAT EXCURSIONS & RENTALS **Martha's Vineyard Boat Rentals** (508-693-4174; marthasvineyardboatrentals.com), on Lagoon Pond, Edgartown. Choose from a large selection of fully equipped center console powerboats ready for cruising around the Vineyard and Nantucket Sound. $$$$+.

Martha's Vineyard Ocean Sports (508-693-8476; mvoceansports.com), 12 Circuit Avenue, in Oak Bluffs Harbor's dockside marina. In addition to daily, weekly, and monthly powerboat and jet ski rentals, Ocean Sport offers parasailing, fly boarding, and banana boat rides, as well as private charters and sunset cruises. $$$$+.

Island Time Charters (508-499-9126; myislandcharter.com), Vineyard Haven Harbor, call for pick-up location. Sit back and relax while Captain JoJo Wild charters you and your crew around the coastline. No matter the crowd you're with, JoJo offers something for everyone—choose from three sunset cocktail cruise packages (the romantic, the pre-gamers, or the ritzy); a private secluded beach excursion rounded off with your choice of a classic New England clambake or beachside barbecue; or the True Islander package, which includes a full day of exploring the area with a true island native as your guide. Other offerings include watersport rentals, private boat transfers, and private yacht getaways. $$$$+.

FISHING STORES   KIM GRANT

Pirate Adventures (508-687-2739; mvpirates.com), 12 Circuit Avenue, Oak Bluffs. The *Sea Gypsy* is a 40-foot custom-built pirate ship (don't worry, it is safely staged at sea) equipped to spark your child's imagination. Kiddos will dress and talk like pirates, assemble a treasure map, battle rivals with water cannons, and hoist sunken treasure from the ocean floor.

FISHING If you're unsure how to speak "fisherman," you will surely be able to learn the language here. Procure freshwater and saltwater fishing licenses and regulations online at mass.gov/eea/agencies/dfg/licensing.

Big game: **North Shore Charters** (508-645-2993; bassnblue.com), out of Menemsha Harbor. May through October. Captain Scott McDowell takes anglers in search of bass and blues. All levels of experience welcomed. $$$$+.

The Skipper (508-693-1238; mvskipper.com), 2 Circuit Avenue Extension, Oak Bluffs. Year after year this charter-slash-party-boat business operated by Captain John Potter and his second-hand-man, Captain John Nelson, continues to get five-star reviews. For 29 years, The Skipper has been voted best fishing charter in Martha's Vineyard. Whether you embark on a daytime fishing trip, a sunset cruise, or a private charter, expect a lively atmosphere on board. $$$$+.

On shore: Surfcasting is best from south-facing beaches, including **Aquinnah Beach**. On **Chappaquiddick, East Beach at Cape Pogue Wildlife Refuge,** and **Wasque Point** are famed for fishing (see "Chappaquiddick" on page 396).

By jetty or bridge: The bridge between **Oak Bluffs and Edgartown** is perfect for anglers. There's also a wide area that hangs over the swiftly running channel between **Nantucket Sound** and **Sengekontacket Pond**. You're most likely to catch the island's prized striped bass and bluefish before sunrise.

Supplies: **Coop's Bait & Tackle** (508-627-3909; coopsbaitandtackle.com), 147 West Tisbury Road, Edgartown. This is your basic one-stop shopping for bait, tackle, boat charters, and information on "hot spots" for catching the big ones.

Dick's Bait & Tackle (508-693-7669), 108 New York Avenue in Oak Bluffs, also rents fishing rods, tackle, and other necessary equipment.

FITNESS CLUBS ❄ **Airport Fitness** (508-696-8000; airportfitnessmv.com), off Edgartown–West Tisbury Road, at the airport. A full-service center.

❄ **B-Strong** (508-693-5997; b-strong.com), 29 Kennebec Ave, Oak Bluffs. This small gym downtown has a good variety of equipment and the best hours on the island.

CHAPPAQUIDDICK

Accessible via the "Chappy ferry," *On-Time II* and *On-Time III* (508-627-9427; chappyferry.com), at the corner of Dock and Daggett streets. The crossing between Edgartown and Chappy is completed in the blink of an eye. The ferry runs 6:45 a.m.–midnight in-season, but doesn't really have a schedule; it just goes when it's needed, and thus it's always "on time." Because it's the only method of transportation between the two islands and a surprising number of people live on Chappy year-round, the ferry runs daily. Round-trip for car and driver $$, walk-on passengers $, bikes $.

Chappaquiddick contains several lovely beaches and wildlife refuges, including the 516-acre Cape Pogue Wildlife Refuge, the 14-acre Mytoi, and the 200-acre Wasque Reservation. Unfortunately, though, the beautiful island is perhaps best known because of Dike Bridge, the scene of the drowning incident involving Sen. Edward Kennedy in July 1969. To reach Dike Bridge, stay on Chappaquiddick Road after you get off the ferry until the road turns into Dike Road. When the road takes a sharp turn to the right (in about a mile), continue straight on the dirt road until you reach the bridge.

When the bridge was rebuilt in the mid-1990s, pedestrians once again had direct access to Cape Pogue, a thin ribbon of sand that stretches along the east side of Chappaquiddick and the remote Cape Pogue Lighthouse. Four-wheel-drive vehicles can use the bridge when endangered shorebirds like the

CAPE POGUE LIGHTHOUSE KIM GRANT

piping plover are not nesting. Cape Pogue is also accessible by foot or by four-wheel-drive vehicle, over the sand of Wasque Point, several miles south of the beach.

Cape Pogue Wildlife Refuge and Wasque Reservation (508-627-7689; thetrustees.org). These adjoining tracts of land on the southeastern corner of Chappaquiddick—called Pogue or Poge, depending on whom you are talking to—are relatively isolated, so that even on summer weekends you can escape the crowds. This seaside wilderness contains huge tracts of dunes, the long and beautiful **East Beach**, cedars, salt marshes, ponds, tidal flats,

KIM GRANT

and scrub brush. Overseen by the Massachusetts Trustees of Reservations, Cape Pogue (516 acres) and Wasque (200 acres) are the group's oldest island holdings. Half of the state's scallops are harvested each autumn off the coast near the **Capue Pogue Lighthouse** (on the northern tip of the cape). The lighthouse was built in 1893 and automated in 1943. Note: It is dangerous to swim at Wasque Rip because of the forceful tide. Limited East Beach parking $, reservation entrance $ (late May to mid-October). 🏖

The outstanding three-hour natural history tours (508-627-3599; thetrustees.org) of Cape Pogue are naturalist-led, in an open-air four-wheel-drive vehicle, and depart from Mytoi Garden (see below) daily, May through October. It'll be one of your best island adventures. $$$$. 🏖

Cape Pogue Lighthouse tours (1½ hours), where you'll learn about the fascinating history of the light and the keepers who lived there, depart from Mytoi Garden from late May to mid-October. Space is limited, so reserve early. Don't miss it. $$$. 🏖

Mytoi (508-627-7689; thetrustees .org), Dike Road. Open daily, sunrise to sunset. This 14-acre Japanese garden, built by Hugh Jones in 1958, has camellias, irises, a goldfish pond, and a picturesque little bridge.

Poucha Pond Kayak Tour (508-627-3599; thetrustees.org), Dike Bridge. Late May to mid-October. Only members of the Trustees of Reservations may take these self-guided tours; rentals available. Nonmembers must first purchase an introductory family membership. $$$. 🏖

KIM GRANT

YMCA of Martha's Vineyard (508-696-7171; ymcamv.org), off Edgartown–Vineyard Haven Road in Oak Bluffs. This community center has a 25-yard, six-lane pool, a large workout room, and a snack bar. $$$.

FOR FAMILIES There are so many family-friendly activities that I've interspersed them throughout this section.

GOLF **Farm Neck Golf Club** (508-693-3057; farmneck.net), off County Road, Oak Bluffs. Open April through December. Reservations are strongly suggested at this stately 18-hole course, but they're only taken 2 or 3 days in advance. A challenging course, but not long.

❄ **Mink Meadows** (508-693-0600; minkmeadowsgc.com), off Franklin Street, Vineyard Haven. A fairly long but very subtle nine-hole semiprivate course; more challenging than you might think. Just ask President Obama.

HORSEBACK RIDING **White Stone Equestrian** (774-563-0220; whitestonemv.com), 85 Red Pony Farm Road, West Tisbury. Lessons, boarding, winter clinics, and summer camp offered at this professional equestrian school. $$$$+.

❄ ✏ **Nip-n-Tuck Farm** (508-693-1449), 39 Davis Look Road, West Tisbury. Hayrides are offered year-round.

ICE-SKATING **Martha's Vineyard Ice Arena** (508-693-5329; mvarena.com), Edgartown–Vineyard Haven Road, Oak Bluffs. Who brings skates to the Vineyard? No one, but you can rent them here. $.

KAYAKS & PADDLEBOARDS **Long Point Wildlife Refuge** (508-693-7392 summer; 508-693-3678 year-round; thetrustees.org). Kayak and paddleboard rentals available July and August, tours and programs open mid-June to mid-September. Led by the Trustees of Reservations, these 2-hour tours are perfect for beginners who may or may not have strong paddle techniques. Your guide will entertain you with the natural history of Long Point and about local ecology. If your visit is timed right, inquire about their thrilling full moon tours. $$$$+.

Chilmark Pond Preserve (508-627-7141; mvlandbank.com), Land Bank access just before Abel's Hill Cemetery (where, incidentally, John Belushi and Lillian Hellman are buried) on South Road, Chilmark. When you paddle across Chilmark Pond, you'll be rewarded with a small ocean beach on the south shore. This local secret (well worth the effort) is accessed only by canoe or kayak, which you must supply.

Wind's Up (508-693-4252; windsupmv.com), 199 Beach Road at the drawbridge, Vineyard Haven. Open mid-May to late September (and possibly into October). This full-service outfit (on-island since 1962) rents Sunfish and small catamarans in addition to kayaks, stand-up paddleboards, body boards, canoes, wind- and surfboards, and wetsuits. Located on sheltered Lagoon Pond, Wind's Up is a great place for beginner and intermediate lessons. The water is shallow and the instructors are patient. Those more experienced can rent equipment, consult the shop's map, and head out solo. Sailboarding is excellent all over the island, but experienced surfers should head to Menemsha, Aquinnah, and South Beach.

See also **Cape Pogue Wildlife Refuge** in "Chappaquiddick" on page 396.

MINI-GOLF **Island Cove** (508-693-2611; islandcoveadventures.com), 386 State Road across from Cronig's Market, Vineyard Haven. Open mid-May to mid-October. After

VINEYARD HAVEN HARBOR KIM GRANT

golf, try your mountaineering prowess on the rock-climbing wall, then stick around for barbecue and ice cream.

SAILING **Magic Carpet** (508-627-2889; sailmagiccarpet.com), Memorial Wharf, Edgartown. Trips from June through October. This classic 56-foot wooden yawl comfortably accommodates 12 people on 2-hour charters along Cape Pogue. You'll learn some good island history and tales along the way.

Mad Max Sailing Adventures (508-627-7500; madmaxmarina.com), at the Seafood Shanty, Edgartown Harbor. This 60-foot catamaran sets sail on 2-hour voyages from late May to September. $$$$$+.

Sea Witch **Sailing Charters** (508-650-0466; seawitchsailingcharters.com), Vineyard Haven. Trips from June to mid-September. Sail the Vineyard aboard the *Sea Witch*, a luxurious 58-foot LOA Ketch. Choose from 2-, 4-, or 8-hour trips with a highly skilled and knowledgeable captain and crew. In the off-season, the *Sea Witch* enjoys the warmer waters off the Caribbean Islands.

Sail Ena (508-627-0848; sailena.com), Vineyard Haven. This classic 34-foot wooden sloop designed by John Alden sets sail from quiet and beautiful Tashmoo in Vineyard Haven. Choose from half-day sails, full day private trips, or sunset cruises. They also offer instructions for women and family lessons.

SPECIAL PROGRAMS ❄ **Vineyard Conservation Society** (508-693-9588; vineyard conservation.org), Wakeman Conservation Center, 57 David Avenue off Lambert's Cove Road, Tisbury. Since it was established in 1965, this nonprofit group has protected thousands of acres from commercial and residential development by engaging in conservation land acquisition and advocacy. The society also sponsors a wide range of public activities, most of them free, including the Winter Walks program, a summer environmental lecture series, educational seminars and workshops on such topics as alternative wastewater treatment and solar-powered building technology, and the annual Earth Day all-island cleanup.

OPEN SPACE RULES

KIM GRANT

Martha's Vineyard Land Bank (508-627-7141; mvland bank.com), 167 Upper Main Street, Edgartown. The Land Bank was established in 1986 in order to purchase open space with funds raised by a 2 percent tax on real estate transactions. I highly recommend getting this organization's map prior to your visit for a current look at the Vineyard's open land (more than 3,100 acres). Many of the island's conservation areas—ocean beach, moors, meadows, ponds, and woods—are free for all to enjoy. Maps are available at the six town halls, libraries, this office, and online. Don't forget to check out their guided walks. 🐾

❋ 🍃 **Featherstone Center for the Arts** (508-693-1850; featherstoneart.org), 30 Featherstone Lane, Oak Bluffs. On 6 acres donated by the Martha's Vineyard Land Bank, this former horse barn and farm has been transformed into a community art center. **Classes** change seasonally but might include woodworking, stained glass, pottery, papermaking, printmaking, weaving, guitar lessons, and photography. Weekly summer art camps for kids, too. Continuously searching for ways to be more responsive to its community, from late June to late August the center also stages a **flea and fine-arts market**, an **open pottery studio**, an open **darkroom**, and **Musical Monday** evenings (with folk, country, jazz, blues, reggae . . . you name it). About 20 of the surrounding acres are crisscrossed with so-called **Featherstone Trails** for hiking.

🍃 **Farm Institute** (508-627-7007; farminstitute.org), 14 Aero Avenue, off South Beach and Katama Road, Edgartown. By now you hopefully are aware of the Vineyard's deep agricultural roots. Well, this is the place to milk goats, watch baby piglets or calves being born, explore vegetable gardens, or get lost in a multiacre corn maze (when they can pull it off)—for a day or a week or the whole season! This nonprofit educational center offers summer programs for kids, Saturday morning farm chores, adult workshops, tons of fresh produce and meats, and more special events. It's a rare opportunity for most of us to connect to the natural world.

TENNIS Public courts are located at: **Church Street** (clay) near the corner of Franklin Street and Lake Street near the town landing, both in Vineyard Haven; **Niantic Avenue** (hard courts) in Oak Bluffs; **Robinson Road** (hard courts) near Pease's Point Way in Edgartown; **Chilmark Community Center** (508-645-3061) on South Road at Beetlebung Corner in Chilmark (available when members are not using them); and **Old County Road** (two hard) in West Tisbury.

❋ 🏋 **Airport Fitness** (508-696-8000; airportfitnessmv.com), 22 Airport Road, off Edgartown–West Tisbury Road, West Tisbury. When it's raining, this full-service indoor facility arranges matches. Lessons, tennis camps for all ages, and ball machines, too.

❋ **Vineyard Family Tennis** (508-693-7762; vineyardfamilytennis.org), 618 Barnes Road, just west of Edgartown–Vineyard Haven Road in Oak Bluffs. An inflatable bubble over the courts allows youngsters to play for free, year-round.

Farm Neck Golf Club (508-693-9728; 508-693-3057; farmneck.net), off County Road, Oak Bluffs. Tennis from mid-May to mid-October. Outdoor Har-Tru courts are available, reserved a few days in advance.

WALKING TOUR **Ghosts, Gossip, and Downright Scandal** (508-627-8619) is conducted by very knowledgeable folks from Vineyard History Tours. They take people by appointment any time of the year, except perhaps during a nor'easter. $$.

See also Martha's Vineyard Land Bank guided walks at mvlandbank.com; and **Vineyard Conservation Society's** Winter Walks under *Special Programs.*

PLEIN AIR PAINTING, EDGARTOWN   KIM GRANT

WATERSPORTS See **Martha's Vineyard Ocean Sports** under *Boat Excursions & Rentals*; and **Wind's Up** under *Kayaks & Paddleboards.*

❋ Green Space

Manuel E. Corellus State Forest (508-693-2540; mass.gov/eea/agencies/dcr/mass parks), off Edgartown–West Tisbury Road or Barnes Road. Comprising almost 5,400 acres of woodland and meadows in the center of the island, the forest's trails are used regularly by bikers, joggers, picnickers, and hikers. Park near the Barnes Road entrance.

IN AND NEAR EDGARTOWN

✧ **Felix Neck Wildlife Sanctuary** (508-627-4850; massaudubon.org), off Edgartown–Vineyard Haven Road, Edgartown. The Vineyard is populated by many species of birds that flock to the island's forests and wildlife sanctuaries. This 219-acre preserve, affiliated with the Audubon Society, has 4 miles of easy trails that traverse thick woods, open meadows of wildflowers, beaches, and salt marshes. The interpretive exhibit center has turtles, aquariums, a gift shop, and a library. Year-round activities for children and adults include guided nature walks and bird-watching trips for novices and experts alike. Inquire about weeklong children's day camps. $.

See also **Mytoi, Cape Pogue Wildlife Refuge** and **Wasque Reservation,** and **natural history tours** under "Chappaquiddick" on page 396.

IN OAK BLUFFS

Ocean Park, along Ocean Avenue. Fringed with some of Oak Bluffs' best-preserved gingerbread cottages, the park's centerpiece is a large white gazebo that serves as a bandstand for summer evening concerts.

IN WEST TISBURY AND UP-ISLAND

Menemsha Hills Reservation (508-693-3678; thetrustees.org), off North Road, Chilmark. This exceptional Trustees of Reservations property makes for a great two-hour hike. The 3-mile crestline trail, part of which runs along the island's second highest point, leads down to a rocky beach. This point was used during World War II as a military lookout. No swimming allowed.

Cedar Tree Neck Sanctuary (508-693-5207; sheriffsmeadow.org), off Indian Hill Road from State Road, West Tisbury. The 400-acre sanctuary, owned and managed by the Sheriff's Meadow Foundation, has trails through bogs, fields, and forests down to the bluffs overlooking Vineyard Sound.

Long Point Wildlife Refuge (508-693-7392; thetrustees.org), off Edgartown–West Tisbury Road, West Tisbury. A long, bumpy, dirt road leads to a couple of mile-long trails, Long Cove Pond, and a long stretch of the south shore. Parking is limited at this 632-acre preserve, maintained by the Massachusetts Trustees of Reservations, so get there early. $ per person, parking $$ per vehicle.

Peaked Hill Reservation (mvlandbank.com), off Tabor House Road from Middle or North roads, Chilmark. Turn left on the dirt lane opposite (more or less) the town landfill and then keep taking right-hand turns until you reach the trailhead. This 149-acre Land Bank property is the highest point on the island, at a whopping 311 feet above sea level. Good for hiking, picnicking, and mountain biking, this reservation also offers vistas of Noman's Land Island, the Aquinnah peninsula, and Menemsha Bight.

Waskosim's Rock Preservation (mvlandbank.com), North Road, just over the Chilmark town line. At almost 200 acres, this is one of the largest and most diverse of the Land Bank properties, with great hiking, bird-watching, picnicking, and mountain biking. The Waskosim boulder marks the start of a stone wall that ran down to Menemsha Pond, separating the English and Wampanoag lands in the mid-17th century.

Allen Farm Vista (mvlandbank.com), South Road, Chilmark. On the south (or the left side) about 1 mile beyond Beetlebung Corner as you head toward Aquinnah. Practically the entire stretch of South Road in Chilmark once looked like this striking 22-acre field and pastureland, protected as a Land Bank property. Lucy Vincent Beach is just beyond the pond, grazing sheep, and moorlands.

Cranberry Acres, West Tisbury. This cranberry bog, on the southside of Lambert's Cove Road from Vineyard Haven, has walking trails.

❋ **Polly Hill Arboretum** (508-693-9426; pollyhillarboretum.org), 809 State Road, West Tisbury. Grounds open year-round; visitor center open late May to mid-October; tours during the summer and winter walk program during the off-season. This is a magical place. Now totaling 70 acres, this former sheep farm was brought under cultivation by legendary horticulturist Polly Hill in order to preserve it as native woodland. The arboretum, opened to the public in the late 1990s, is a not-for-profit sanctuary devoted to a mix of almost 3,100 native and exotic plants, many threatened by extinction. The arboretum is tranquil and beautiful from early spring well into fall. Wandering visitors will discover an extraordinary range of plants. Lecture series, too. Donations gratefully accepted.

ISLAND MYSTERIES

Vineyard mystery novelist Philip R. Craig writes page-turners that are perfect for beach get-aways. In one of my favorites from this 20-plus-book series, *The Double Minded Men*, we first meet J. W. Jackson, a retired Boston cop, and his future wife, Zee, who tangle with a potentate, stolen necklace, and murder—all of which threaten their idyllic island home.

A big Craig fan who visited the Vineyard frequently, I always looked forward to the next install-ment of J. W.'s escapades, ones that took him to every nook and cranny of the island. When visiting, I'd always know with certainty that I'd just passed a little road that led to one of his char-acter's homes or a favorite fishing beach where he and Zee would catch blues when they were running. I recognized places from every page: street corners, shops, summertime traffic, Alley's General Store, or a specific beach on which we'd search for shells. The Vineyard becomes even more real to anyone who's read Craig's books.

J. W.'s friends and family are sometimes helpful in solving these cozy mysteries, but at other times he must protect them as he becomes involved in schemes by land developers, old-time gangsters, entertainers, environmentalists, and old pals. The characters who pop up become old friends we look forward to meeting in subsequent books. Sprinkled throughout, his love of cooking also becomes apparent through his recipe riffs for smoked bluefish, clam cakes, and striped bass ("delish"). When reading the last sentence of his last book—*Vineyard Chill*, which was completed just before his death—I felt a sadness that I'd not read another J. W. case that would bring Martha's Vineyard even more to life than it already is.

—Martha Grant

Fulling Mill Brook Preserve, off Middle Road, about 1½ miles east of Beetlebung Corner, Chilmark. Biking and foot access from South Road. Hiking trails pass through 49 acres of forests, fields, and streams.

See also **Featherstone Meetinghouse for the Arts** under **To Do**.

BEACHES Unlike Nantucket, many Vineyard beaches are private, open only to home-owners or cottage renters. (By law, though, anyone has the right to fish from any beach between the high- and low-water marks. So if you want to explore where you other-wise aren't allowed, make sure you're carrying a fishing pole!) Many innkeepers, espe-cially those in the up-island establishments, provide walk-on passes to their guests. (A much-coveted Chilmark pass will get you access to Lucy Vincent Beach off South Road, the island's prettiest.) And just to keep you in the loop, two other private beaches in Chilmark—Quansoo and Hancock—require a key to gain entry. It's *always* locked and sometimes guarded. If you don't summer in Chilmark, you might consider pur-chasing a key, which sells for hundreds of thousands of dollars. (File under: if you have to ask the price, you probably can't afford it.) The following are public beaches.

IN EDGARTOWN

Lighthouse Beach, at the end of North Water Street, adjoining Fuller Street Beach. From Lighthouse Beach you can watch boats going in and out of the harbor. Rarely crowded with bathers because of seaweed, but always crowded with picture-takers; gentle waves. No facilities. **Fuller Street Beach** is a short bike ride from town and gen-erally quiet.

Katama (or South) Beach, off Katama Road, is a favorite among college students. A shuttle runs from Edgartown to this popular, 3-mile-long barrier beach, which has medium to heavy surf, a strong undertow, and high dunes. Children can swim in the calm and warm salt water of Katama Bay. There are lifeguards, but not along the entire beach. Facilities at the end of Katama Road and Herring Creek Road. This beach becomes the Trustees of Reservations' **Norton Point Beach** when you are traveling east.

See also **Cape Pogue Wildlife Refuge** and **Wasque Reservation** in "Chappaquiddick" on page 396, and **Long Point Wildlife Refuge**, above.

IN VINEYARD HAVEN

Lake Tashmoo (or Herring Creek), at the end of Herring Creek Road, off Daggett Avenue from Franklin Street. This small beach offers good swimming, surf-fishing, and shellfishing. No facilities; limited parking; lifeguard.

◌ **Owen Park Beach**, on the harbor just north of the ferry. Good for small children and swimming. Public restrooms; lifeguard. Limited parking.

IN OAK BLUFFS

◌ **Oak Bluffs Town Beach**, on both sides of the ferry wharf, Oak Bluffs. This calm, narrow beach is very popular with Oak Bluffs families and seasonal visitors with small children. No facilities. Public restrooms next to the ferry dock.

◌ **Joseph Sylvia State Beach**, along Beach Road between Edgartown and Oak Bluffs. The Edgartown end of this 2-mile-long barrier beach is also called Bend-in-the-Road Beach; this part of the gentle beach has lifeguards but no facilities. Park free along the roadside. Kids will like jumping into the water from Big Bridge, famous from the movie *Jaws*. Good shore fishing and crabbing along the jetties, too.

Aquinnah Beach, just south of the Clay Cliffs of Aquinnah. Take the boardwalk and path through cranberry and beach plum bushes down to the beach, about a 10-minute walk. Resist the temptation to cover yourself with mud from the cliff's clay baths; the cliffs have eroded irreparably over the past century. (If that doesn't dissuade you,

JOSEPH SYLVIA STATE BEACH KIM GRANT

UP-ISLAND KIM GRANT

perhaps the law will: it's illegal to remove or use the clay.) Instead, walk along this 5-mile beach, called, from north to south, **Moshup Public Beach,** Moshup (the shuttle bus drops off here—otherwise, it's a 10-minute walk from paid Aquinnah parking), Philbin, and Zack's Cliffs. The cliffs are to the north, but the beaches are wider to the south. **Philbin** and **Zack's Cliffs** beaches are reserved for residents, but if you stick close to the waterline, you might not have a problem. Zack's fronts Jacqueline Kennedy Onassis's former estate. The farther south you walk, the fewer people you'll see. But those people you do see, you'll see more of—people come here specifically to sunbathe nude. It's not legal, but generally the authorities look the other way. Swimming is very good here; the surf is usually light to moderate, and the shore doesn't drop off as abruptly as it does along the island's south shore. Facilities include restrooms and a few small fast-food shops at the head of the cliff. Parking is plentiful; $$.

✇ **Eastville Beach**, Beach Road (at the drawbridge), Oak Bluffs. This county-owned public beach has gentle surf and good views of the ferries coming and going in Vineyard Haven Harbor. No facilities.

IN WEST TISBURY

✇ **Lambert's Cove Beach**, off Lambert's Cove Road. Although it's restricted to town residents and inn-goers in-season, you can park here off-season to enjoy one of the island's top beaches. The sand is fine and the waters are calm.

UP-ISLAND

Long Point Wildlife Refuge, off Waldron's Bottom Road from Edgartown–West Tisbury Road, West Tisbury. Owned by the Trustees of Reservations, this wide beach is isolated and beautiful, with good surf. From here you can also follow nature trails to **Tisbury Great Pond**. Limited parking. $.

✏ **Menemsha Beach**, Menemsha Harbor. This calm, gentle beach is also pebbly. Nearby restrooms. Sunsets from here can't be beat.

✏ **Lobsterville Beach**, off State and Lobsterville Roads, Aquinnah. This beach is popular with families because of shallow, warm water and gentle surf. Limited parking along the road. Popular for fishing, too.

Lucy Vincent Beach, off South Road, is arguably the island's nicest beach. Although it's open only to residents and Chilmark inn goers (which is reason enough to stay in Chilmark), you can enjoy the wide, cliff-backed beach off-season. The farther east you walk, the less clothing you'll see. The farther west you walk, the more trouble you'll get in, because that stretch of beach is as private as they come.

Squibnocket Beach, also off South Road in Chilmark, has the most reliable surfing on the island.

✏ **Uncle Seth's Pond**, off Lambert's Cove Road. A tiny (but public) freshwater pond on the side of the road. Good for children. Limited parking.

PICNICS **Owen Park**, off Main Street, north of the ferry dock, Vineyard Haven. This thin strip of grass runs from Main Street down to the harbor beach. It's a great vantage point for watching boats sail in and out of the harbor. Swings for the kids. Limited parking.

Mill Pond, West Tisbury. This wonderful place to feed ducks and swans is next to the simple, shingled West Tisbury Police Department.

✳ Lodging

With a few exceptions (primarily smaller bed-and-breakfasts), it is very expensive to stay on the Vineyard. Room rates have soared well beyond the rate of inflation since the late 1990s. Of all the towns, Edgartown is the most expensive by far; Oak Bluffs tends to draw younger visitors; and Vineyard Haven and West Tisbury are the most sensibly priced towns.

Reservations, made well in advance of your visit, are imperative during July and August and on weekends from September to mid-October. The height of high season runs, of course, from late June to early September, but many innkeepers define high season as mid-May to mid-October. In addition, many up-island inns are booked months in advance by hundreds of bridal parties, many with no ties to the island, who want meadows, stone walls, and spectacular ocean views as a backdrop for their photographs.

So many inns require a 2- or 3-night minimum stay in summer (and 2 nights on weekends in autumn) that I have

omitted this information from the individual reviews. Assume it's true. Although there are quite a few year-round lodging choices, the island is incredibly quiet from January to March. Rate ranges listed below are for high season.

RESORTS

IN EDGARTOWN

✏ **Winnetu Oceanside Resort** (508-310-1733; winnetu.com), South Beach, Edgartown. Open mid-April to late October. The Winnetu is easily one of the best family resorts on the Eastern Seaboard. But it also offers plenty of ways for romantics and more active folks to have a stellar holiday, too. It has no rivals on the Vineyard or Cape Cod. (It's rival on Nantucket—the **Nantucket Hotel & Resort**—isn't really a rival; it's their sister property!) Three miles from Edgartown proper, and abutting South Beach (via a private pathway), this 11-acre resort offers tip-top service and plentiful amenities—two heated pools, a kiddie pool, a first-rate tennis club and fitness center with an array of classes

WINNETU OCEANSIDE RESORT   KIM GRANT

and massages, plenty of teen and children's programs (including a complimentary one in the mornings in-season), oversized chess pieces for playful fun, poolside bingo, a little pond with turtles, outdoor table tennis, a putting green, antique fire truck rides, weekly clambakes, a library with fireplace, and a sublime restaurant (see **The Dunes** under *Dining Out*). A variety of accommodations suit a multitude of vacationer configurations: studios; one-bedroom suites with a combo living/dining area and a deck or patio (sleeping a family of five); and larger suites. Full kitchens are available. Furnishings are summery, contemporary, and upscale but not so precious that you can't enjoy the place after the beach. In the end, it's hard to say what's better—the facilities or the services, but they do go hand in hand. Tons of organized trips make it easy to relax here: kayak tours of Poucha Pond, private charters to Nantucket, whale watching, lighthouse and dune trips, and sunset water taxis to Edgartown. Concierges are ready to help with any and all requests and nary a staff member passes without a huge smile on their face and a ready hand. Rooms $$–$$$$$+; off-season packages offer a great value.

BED-AND-BREAKFASTS & INNS

IN EDGARTOWN

🐾 **The Christopher** (508-627-4784; thechristophermv.com), 24 South Water Street. Formerly the Victorian Inn, and now completely renovated, this boutique property is a 2-minute walk from the harbor and a world away when you are sitting by the backyard patio fire pit. The inn manages to walk a casual-chic line straddling contemporary, breezy and comfy. Attention to detail reigns in their 15 rooms, right down to black out shades, iPads for use during your stay, Apple TV for the flat screen TVs, waffle robes, and luxe bedding. Full breakfast and afternoon snacks are included, as you might expect with this level of service. $$–$$$$.

❅ **Hob Knob Inn** (508-627-9510; hobknob.com), 128 Main Street. This boutique property exudes a haughty

HOB NOB INN   KIM GRANT

sense of self and prides itself on attentive services and ecofriendliness. Just a few minutes' walk from the center of town (request a room off Main Street if you like to sleep in—otherwise you'll be awakened by truck traffic), this Gothic Revival house has 17 spacious guest rooms (and two private houses) with down bedding, king-sized beds, fine antiques, and a very soothing and tasteful ambience. Afternoon tea and a full, local, organic breakfast, served at small tables, are included. Or have breakfast in bed. During inclement weather, you'll appreciate the enclosed porch, a private back patio, two sitting rooms, and a front porch with rockers. Exercise hounds will appreciate the fitness room. $$$–$$$$$+.

❄ **The Charlotte Inn** (508-627-4751; thecharlotteinn.com), 27 South Summer Street. The Vineyard's highbrow grande dame is owned by Gery and Paula Conover, ardent Anglophiles who make frequent trips to the United Kingdom to purchase antiques. Without an ounce of hyperbole, it's fair to say that it has few equals in the United States. Equestrian prints, elegant armchairs, and collections of beautifully bound classic novels have turned each of the 17 rooms (and two suites) into a luxuriously inhabitable museum. The Conovers' taste for all things English reveals itself on the inn's grounds, too: ivy-edged brick sidewalks, small croquet-quality lawns, impeccable

CHARLOTTE INN KIM GRANT

flower beds. Continental breakfast included; full breakfast available for an additional charge. $$$–$$$$$+.

❄ 🐾 **The Lightkeepers Inn** (508-627-4600; thelightkeepersinn.com), 25 Simpson's Lane. Within a short walk of Lighthouse Beach and just a block from the harbor, the five suites in the main house each have a separate sitting room and kitchen or kitchenette, and they share a covered patio with a grill. (The East Chop suite boasts its own deck.) None is fancy, but they sure are comfortable. The separate cottage sleeps four. $$–$$$.

IN VINEYARD HAVEN

❄ **Nobnocket Boutique Inn** (508-696-0859; nobnocket.com), 60 Mt. Aldworth Road. No indulgence was spared in this 2016 top-to-bottom renovation; no detail within the Arts & Crafts manor house was too small to overlook. It's the signature work of innkeeper/owners Simon and Annabelle Hunton, who most immediately hail from an extraordinary property on Cape Cod. They tackled this seven-room boutique property with the same aplomb. The result? Just the balance of soulful rejuvenation and visual excitement. Just the right aesthetic for modern travelers with a respectful nod to its historic bones. And of course,

NOBNOCKET BOUTIQUE INN KIM GRANT

CROCKER HOUSE INN KIM GRANT

what truly sets Nobnocket apart is its concierge-level services. $$-$$$$.

🦞 ❄ **Crocker House Inn** (508-693-1151; crockerhouseinn.com), 12 Crocker Avenue. With each return visit, I remain impressed by the value that Jynell and Jeff Kristal offer at their turn-of-the-20th-century bed-and-breakfast on a quiet side street near the center of town. And to boot, they're one of the few inns that takes one-nighters (although I certainly suggest staying longer). Each of the eight guest rooms has a fresh summer charm, retiled bathroom, and an iPod docking station. The primo third-floor loft, tucked under the eaves with a gas fireplace and Jacuzzi, also has harbor views. Room 5 has good cross breezes and a private feeling; Room 7 is larger, with a gas fireplace and strong morning sun; Room 3 is good for three people traveling together and boasts a private entrance. A word of caution: The intimate size of the inn allows sound from the common areas to carry into the downstairs rooms. If you're a light sleeper, opt for a room on the second or third floors. A full breakfast, served daily in the small combination living/dining room, is included. But many guests linger over a second cup of coffee and the newspaper on the front wraparound porch set with rockers. You can't go wrong here. Also check out the first-rate, fabulous "cottage" that Jynell and Jeff offer! $$–$$$$.

IN OAK BLUFFS

✐ **The Oak Bluffs Inn** (508-693-7171; oakbluffsinn.com), 64 Circuit Avenue at Pequot Avenue. Open May through October. You can't miss the inn—it's the marvelously detailed pink building with an enormous third-floor cupola. It also has a great location: at the tip of Circuit Avenue, on the edge of the "campground," three blocks from a beach, and a 10-minute walk to the ferry. And it completely reflects the ethos of Oak Bluffs: laid-back casual. The friendly innkeepers, Erik and Rhonda Albert, have done a great job freshening the place up. All 10 guest rooms have small but

OAK BLUFFS INN KIM GRANT

newly redone baths, air-conditioning, cottage-style bedroom sets, and views of colorful neighboring cottages from every window. Make a beeline for the soothing and contemporary two-bedroom apartment ($$$$) on the third floor; you could easily settle in for a week, especially given the balcony and kitchenette. Families are welcome in the carriage house or the first-floor room. An expanded continental buffet breakfast, enjoyed at individual tables, is included; guests may also eat on the wraparound porch. $$–$$$$$+.

✳ **Isabelle's Beach House** (508-693-3955; isabellesbeachhouse.com), 83 Seaview Avenue. This turn-of-the-20th-century guest house was resurrected in 2008 by the namesake innkeeper, who has been associated with in-town inns for some time. Most of the 11 simply and tastefully decorated rooms have ocean views; all have air-conditioning and refrigerators. Although the house sits on the main drag heading out of town and toward Edgartown, the traffic isn't a problem for city dwellers (who are at the beach and exploring during the day anyway). Two big pluses: It's across the street from the expansive town beach and it's just a five-minute walk to town from here. The wide front porch is also perfect for sunset cocktails. Buffet breakfast included. $$$–$$$$$.

Hotel Ginger (508-338-2804; hotelginger.com), 9 Healey Way. Leighton and Cathy Collis took a bold risk when they embarked on the multimillion dollar renovation of the historic Nashua House Hotel—and it paid off. Hotel Ginger opened its arched French doors in 2019. Designed with "the taste of a personal shopper, the energy of a comic, and the wit of an art-school dropout," expect rooms reminiscent of Parisian-styled apartments inspired by iconic female trendsetters like Audrey Hepburn, Diana Ross, Joan Rivers, Beyoncé, and other political and cultural leaders. All rooms boast lavish vanity bathrooms that "echo Roaring 1920s luxury" with French marble and polished nickel fixtures. Enjoy ocean views from the large airy windows naturally brightening the carefully curated space. King suites include either a private rooftop porch or outdoor verandah. Cocoon yourself in soft ecofriendly bedding tucked into the handsomely handcrafted canopy bedframe. (Note: Hotels are big offenders when it comes to sustainability and reducing carbon emissions. Leighton and Cathy have made a herculean effort not to fall into this category, and one way is by conserving the hotel's water and energy. This means no bleached or heavily ironed sheets, but instead ultra-soft wrinkled linens that beam with green pride.) Those who previously stayed at the Nashua House might miss the original and unique charm, but one thing remains common: the location. Not only is the hotel within walking distance from the ferry, but it's also near a plethora of fine restaurants and shopping. $$–$$$.

🐚 **Attleboro House** (508-693-4346; attleborohousemv.com), 42 Lake Avenue. Open mid-May through September. This authentic gingerbread cottage faces Oak Bluffs Harbor and sits on the outer perimeter of the Methodist Camp Meeting Association. It's been taking in seaside guests since 1874, and it hasn't changed much since then. In Estelle Reagan's family since the 1940s, the guest house has 10 simple but tidy guest rooms that share five bathrooms. (Some rooms have a sink.) Most rooms have a porch, but if yours doesn't, there's a wraparound porch on the first floor. $–$$.

UP-ISLAND

✳ **Lambert's Cove Inn & Restaurant** (800-535-0272; lambertscoveinn.com), 90 Manaquayak Road, West Tisbury. This place is quite something. The secluded country inn has a setting that couldn't be more picturesque. The farmhouse estate once belonged to an ardent horticulturist, and the impressive formal gardens (and ancient rock walls) are nicely preserved. Common rooms, straight out of a magazine shoot, have the feel of a private gentleman's club; everything is just so, right down to the gilded mirrors and hunting prints. That said, service is quite friendly rather than haughty. Fifteen guest rooms are scattered throughout the inn and two outbuildings. They vary considerably, but each is distinctive and highly recommended. The grounds boast a heated outdoor pool and hot tub, around which are plenty of chaises and teak furnishings. Guests also receive parking passes to nearby Lambert's Cove, one of the island's prettiest beaches. In addition, the secluded and beautiful Ice House Pond is within walking distance. Tennis court, too, and a full breakfast featuring farm-fresh eggs laid by 50 hens and goat products from their "future cheese makers." The **restaurant** (see *Dining Out*) is outstanding. $$–$$$$$.

Beach Plum Inn (508-645-9454; beachpluminn.com), 50 Beach Plum Lane (off North Road), Menemsha. Open May through October. Secluded amid 7 wooded acres overlooking Menemsha Harbor in the near distance, the Beach Plum offers 11 luxurious guest rooms with fine bedding, first-class bathrooms (many with deep soaking or whirlpool tubs), stylish but unpretentious furnishings, and high-quality craftsmanship. A few inn rooms have small but private balconies with harbor views, and most rooms have some sort of water view. Practical in-room amenities like umbrellas, beach chairs, playing cards, and flashlights are not overlooked, either. Each of the six cottages are decorated with a simple but fresh style and grace. Facilities include beach access, a croquet court, and a tennis court. Don't be alarmed if you see some alpaca grazing on the grounds; they are gentle and soft creatures. Because this is such a popular place for weddings, you'll find a large white lawn tent between the inn and the harbor in spring and fall. The inn also offers dinner (see *Dining Out*). Full

breakfast and afternoon wine and cheese included. $$–$$$$.

Outermost Inn (508-645-3511; outermostinn.com), Lighthouse Road, Aquinnah. Open early May to mid-October. Hugh and Jeanne Taylor's 20-acre parcel of land has the island's second-best ocean view. (The best view is just up the hill from the Aquinnah Lighthouse, where Jeanne's great-great-grandfather was born.) The inn's seven rooms (one with a whirlpool, two with views of the lighthouse) and one suite feature natural fabrics, wool rugs, and down duvets. Subdued colors and unpainted furniture emphasize the seaside light. Rooms are named for the wood used in each: beech, ash, hickory, oak, and cherry. (Speaking of wood, don't miss the outdoor bar made from one long, impressive hardwood tree.) Inquire about the adjacent lighthouse suite. In keeping with the family's musical tradition, guitars, pianos, and other instruments are placed in the common areas. (You might get lucky and wander into an impromptu living-room concert given by Hugh's brother James.) There's also a full-service restaurant on premises; see *Dining Out*. $$$–$$$$.

❄ 🐾 🦮 **The Duck Inn** (508-645-9018; duckinnonmv.com), 10 Duck Pond Lane, off State Road, Aquinnah. A throwback to the '70s in that it feels like a hippie retreat, The Duck Inn is arguably the most unusual place to stay on the island. It's also only a five-minute walk to Philbin Beach, one of the island's top two or three strands. You may be sleeping in a sleigh bed with a silk, hand-painted, feather duvet (in my favorite room, which also boasts a balcony). Another room has a brass bed, freestanding marble basin, a little balcony, and one French door to the water closet. Ask longtime proprietor Elise LeBovit for a complete description of the eclectic rooms. The whole open first floor is a communal-style gathering space, complete with wax-covered candlesticks on the dining table, a central fireplace and Glenwood stove, and kilims and American Indian carpets. There is a well-used game area and special breakfast table for kids, not to mention a hot tub and masseuse. A full organic breakfast is included. Ask about the sauna in the "Flintstone" room. $–$$.

COTTAGES & EFFICIENCIES

IN EDGARTOWN

✎ **Edgartown Commons** (508-627-4671; edgartowncommons.com), 20 Peases Point Way. Open May to mid-October. These 34 efficiencies—from studios to two-bedroom apartments—are near the center of town and great for families. Most of the individually owned units are in very good condition; these are rented first. Units in the main building have high ceilings and thus feel more spacious. Many units surround the pool, all are comfortably furnished, and most feature newish kitchens. Outside there are grills, picnic tables, and a nice enclosed play area. $$–$$$.

UP-ISLAND

🍴 **Menemsha Inn and Cottages** (508-645-2521; menemshainn.com), North Road, Menemsha. Open May through October. This secluded 25-acre parcel of forest has some lovely views of Vineyard Sound, a 4-minute wooded path to Menemsha Beach, and a friendly atmosphere. Over the years (it was actually opened in

MENEMSHA INN AND COTTAGES KIM GRANT

1923) it has been continuously upgraded and maintained with pride. There's an emphasis on peace and quiet, rather than fussy interior decorating. The complex boasts six luxurious and crisp rooms in the carriage house (with a great room and fieldstone fireplace); nine smaller but first-rate "regular" rooms with freshly retiled bathrooms; 11 tidy seascape cottages; and one elegant, two-bedroom suite. Cottages have a screened-in porch, fully equipped kitchen, outdoor shower, barbecue, and wood-burning fireplace. Walk-on passes to Lucy Vincent and Squibnocket Beaches are provided. Reserve cottages as far ahead as February if you can; this well-manicured place has a loyal, repeat clientele. Facilities include a fitness center, bike rentals, basketball court, table tennis, croquet, and a tennis court. Expanded continental breakfast with smoked salmon quiche and the like included. $$$$–$$$$$+; inquire about weekly cottage rates.

HOTELS

IN EDGARTOWN

❄ ✎ **Harbor View Hotel and Resort** (508-627-7000; harborviewhotel.com), 131 North Water Street. This is one privileged perch. Overlooking a lighthouse, grass-swept beach, and Chappaquiddick, the 1891 Harbor View Hotel is Edgartown's best-situated hostelry. This grande dame boasts 114 rooms and 21 suites. (Suites, by the way, are privately owned condos but available for rent. They feature deep soaking tubs and kitchenettes with granite countertops.) Tranquil harbor views from the hotel's spacious veranda (lined with rocking chairs) are reason enough to patronize the place. Some guest rooms enjoy these views; other rooms have porches overlooking the pool. The upscale guest rooms are generally large and appointed with antique prints and watercolor landscapes by local artists. Facilities include room service, summertime children's programs, a swimming pool, and a concierge. Because of its size, the hotel caters to large groups. $$$$$+.

⚓ **Harborside Inn** (508-627-4321; theharborsideinn.com), 3 South Water Street. Open mid-April to early November. This seven-building place—half time-share and half conventional hotel—is one of the few waterfront (harborfront, no less!) accommodations on the island. And it's the only one on Edgartown Harbor. Practically all rooms have some sort of water view; most have a porch or patio. The 90 rooms and four suites are well appointed with standard hotel-issue furnishings. Facilities include a heated pool overlooking harbor boat slips. $$–$$$$.

IN VINEYARD HAVEN

❋ ⚓ **Mansion House Inn** (508-693-2200; mvmansionhouse.com), 9 Main Street. This professionally operated four-story hotel, located just a few blocks from the ferry, features 40 rooms and suites that range from cozy to spacious—with prices to match. Deluxe rooms have soaking tubs, fireplaces, and balconies that afford views of Vineyard Sound (or Main Street). The basement health club and spa, with a 75-foot mineral spring pool, pampers guests with a wide array of services, including clay cliffs **Moshup Mud Wraps**. The roof deck is a quiet place to escape. Continental breakfast included. $$$–$$$$$.

IN OAK BLUFFS

🦞 ❋ 🏠 **Surfside Motel** (508-693-2500; mvsurfside.com), 7 Oak Bluffs Avenue. One of the few Oak Bluffs places open through the winter (with limited availability), the Surfside has above-average motel-style rooms near the ferry. The area can get a bit boisterous on summer evenings, but room rates reflect that. Each room has a queen, two double beds, or two twin beds, air-conditioning, and a small refrigerator; cribs and roll-away beds are available for a fee. Corner rooms are particularly nice and spacious. $$–$$$$.

RENTAL HOUSES & COTTAGES ⚓ **MV Seacoast Properties** (508-627-9201; mvseacoast.com), 261 Upper Main Street, Edgartown. Dozens of agencies handle thousands of rentals, which vary from tiny cottages to luxe waterfront homes, from dismal and overpriced units to great values. I like this one.

CAMPGROUNDS 🦞 ⚓ **Martha's Vineyard Family Campground** (508-693-3772; campmv.com), 569 Edgartown Road, Vineyard Haven. Open mid-May to mid-October. In addition to shaded tent and trailer sites, the island's only campground also has rustic one- and two-room cabins.

YOUTH HOSTEL 🦞 ⚓ **Hostelling International—Martha's Vineyard** (508-693-2665; 888-901-2087 for in-season reservations; hiusa.org/marthasvineyard), Edgartown–West Tisbury Road, West Tisbury. Open mid-May to mid-October. This saltbox opened in 1955, and it remains an ideal lodging choice for cycling-oriented visitors. The hostel is at the edge of the Manuel E. Correllus State Forest (which is full of bike paths; see *Green Space*) and next to the path that runs from Edgartown to West Tisbury. The large kitchen is fully equipped, and the common room has a fireplace. Reservations strongly recommended, especially from mid-June to early September, when large groups frequent the hostel. Linens, pillows, and blankets provided free of charge. Accommodations are single-sex, dormitory-style bunk beds, with the exception of one private room ($–$$) available.

❋ Where to Eat

DINING OUT

IN EDGARTOWN

⚓ 🍸 **Atria** (508-627-5850; atriamv.com), 137 Upper Main Street. Open D, April through October. Atria specializes in

A FEW WORDS ABOUT THE MV DINING SCENE

Most restaurants are open May to mid-October; some are open through Christmas. Each year more and more operate year-round. Opening and closing days vary considerably from week to week, largely dependent on the weather and number of visitors, so it's impossible to tell you reliably which days any given restaurant will be open. Always call ahead after Labor Day and before Memorial Day.

There are a few more generalizations I can make. Vineyard Haven and up-island towns are "dry," so BYO wine or beer. West Tisbury is now "half wet," so beer and wine are sold in some establishments. (Some/most restaurants charge a nominal corking fee.) I've tried to note when there is a chef/owner because generally these places provide the most reliable food. Many Oak Bluffs establishments are family-oriented and casual, though there are a few sophisticated options. The dress code in Edgartown is a bit more conservative. Dining options are scarcer up-island and require reservations well ahead of time. Otherwise, reservations are highly suggested at all *Dining Out* establishments.

elegant, hip dining with a global flair. It's the kind of quiet and sophisticated place where celebs like to hang out. It's classy but casually romantic; tables are closely spaced and there's a rose garden patio, too. Fish is a big deal here; look for rare ahi tuna tempura as a starter and pan-seared Georges Bank scallops and cauliflower-goat cheese puree. The menu changes daily, but it's always worth asking about a vegetarian risotto. (The burgers with onion rings are also great.) Natural flavors come through loudly and clearly. As for dessert, think along the lines of gooey chocolate molten cake or traditional thin pecan tart. The bar (which hosts live jazz, folk, and blues on many nights) is a great place for solo diners and an even better place for a nightcap—try their martinis. $$$$–$$$$$.

♆ **Alchemy** (508-627-9999; alchemy edgartown.com), 71 Main Street. Open L, D, February through December. Owners Scott and Charlotte Caskey, so successful at Savoir Faire for so many years, have struck gold in this larger and more visible casual American space. Chef Giordano Smiroldo (new to Alchemy in 2015) is their bullion, keeping the inspired food focus loosely on French and Italian. If you're lucky, you'll get one of a few sidewalk tables. Fish and seafood specialties at dinner change

regularly, but with luck you'll find seared salmon with creamed lentils or halibut meunière with lemon. The wine list is quite well chosen. In the evening, the open, rotunda-like, two-story bistro and bar is loud and energetic; it's a great place for singles to nosh at the bar. L $$, D $$$–$$$$$.

l'étoile (508-627-5187; letoile.net), 22 North Water Street. Open D, late April to late November. After all these years (since 1986, to be exact), chef/owner Michael Brisson is still the go-to guy for that singularly spectacular meal. Check out his impressive resume on the website; it's a dishwasher-to-young-prodigy-chef story. There isn't a more elegant

ALCHEMY KIM GRANT

dining room on the island, nor more perfect contemporary French cuisine in New England. Although the garden patio is romantic too, I'm always bowled over by the soothing main dining room. Nothing short of spectacular, dishes like Dover sole, rack of lamb, and étuvée of native lobster are meticulously prepared and artistically presented. Michael uses local fish and produce whenever possible, and you can taste the difference. If your wallet and appetite aren't quite up to the main event, a lighter bar menu has venison burgers, cheese panini with roasted tomato soup, and the like. Look for biweekly wine tastings and tapas on the lawn. Bar menu $$–$$$$, D $$$$–$$$$$, tasting menu $$$$$+.

♈ **Détente** (508-627-8810; detentemv .com), 15 Winter Street. Open D, May through mid-October. This intimate and stylish restaurant, tucked back in Nevin Square, feels like a real find. Especially when you're inside with white linens and dark furniture. Especially when you dine on the summertime terrace. Especially when you grab a bite at the soapstone bar. It doesn't matter where you dine: it's candlelit, refined, romantic, and tickling to a modern palate. Owners Kevin and Suzanna Crowell get my warm thanks for superb New American cuisine. The menu, which features locally procured ingredients, is thankfully limited to about six entrées, all executed with aplomb. Try the harpooned swordfish with sweet pea raviolis on spiced carrot slaw. The wine list is excellent. $$$$–$$$$$+.

❧ **The Dunes** (508-627-3663; winnetu .com), 31 Dunes Road (Katama Road). Open B, L at the pool, D, mid-April through October. The Dunes, emphasizing the freshest of island ingredients, is a centerpiece of the outstanding **Winnetu Oceanside Resort** (see *Resorts* under **Lodging**). It successfully walks the tightrope of feeding regulars multiple times a week and pushing the envelope for foodies. Although I didn't get to dine here on my most recent visit, based on island

contacts I'm comfortable with wholeheartedly endorsing the new (in 2016) chef Noel Middleton. Katama Bay oysters (plucked from waters just a stone's throw away) and sea scallops prepared in any manner of ways remain divine. To give you as many reasons as possible to return, children have their own menu and families have their own dining room. Snag a seat on the second-floor deck and enjoy the sunset during dinner. Snag their free sunset water taxi to the restaurant from Edgartown at 5:30 p.m. in the summertime. It's a lovely way to arrive. L $$–$$$, D $$$–$$$$$.

❄ **Square Rigger** (508-627-9968; squareriggerrestaurant.com), at The Triangle. Open L, D, February through December. You can tell right away that this place is by and for locals: patrons and servers are friendly well into September! It's a meat-and-potatoes kind of place; actually, it's a char-grilled meat, seafood, and lobster kind of place—with an emphasis on lobster. There's nothing surprising—just good and casual, with plenty of parking and a publike atmosphere. $$$–$$$$.

IN VINEYARD HAVEN

❄ ❧ **Black Dog Tavern** (508-693-9223; theblackdog.com), 21 Beach Street Extension. Open B, L, D. Longtime Vineyarder Bob Douglas became frustrated when he couldn't find good chowder within walking distance of the harbor, so he opened this place in 1971, naming it for his dog. These days the restaurant—and its ubiquitous T-shirts—are synonymous with a Vineyard vacation. And although the portions are smaller now that Bob's son is running the establishment, it's a fair place to eat. While you'll have to wait an hour for dinner, lunch won't be much of a problem. Interior décor is simple, with pine floors, old beams, nautical signs, and shellacked wooden tables packed close together. Best of all, this shingled saltbox is cantilevered over the harbor. And you can now sit outside. Fresh

BLACK DOG TAVERN KIM GRANT

island fish and locally grown vegetables dominate the menu. Although staff are often eager to hustle you out the door, don't be shy about finishing your meal. B $, L $–$$, D $$–$$$$.

IN OAK BLUFFS

Sweet Life Café (508-696-0200; sweetlifemv.com), 63 Circuit Avenue. Open D, May through September. What started as a summer romance between a chef and waitress turned into marriage, parenthood, and now business ownership for Erin and Hal Ryerson. Sweet Life retains a classical gourmet menu of fresh island seafood within a restored and airy Victorian house or outside on the twinkling garden patio. The restaurant caters to everyone from presidents to beach bums with equal aplomb. Fun fact: The café was a must for the Obamas when they vacationed on the Vineyard. $$$$.

M.V. Chowder Company (508-696-3000; mvchowder.com), 9 Oak Bluffs Avenue. Open L, D. Stop here for the "best chowder on the island," deemed so by the venerable *Yankee Magazine*, as well as *Cape Cod Life Magazine* and *Martha's Vineyard Magazine*. Needless to say, it rules. Beyond that, come for classic burgers and BLTs or Asian fusion dishes like pork dumplings and tempura nuggets. The ambiance is classy but dark. They also specialize in cocktails, particularly martinis. $–$$$$.

🍸 **Red Cat Kitchen** (508-696-6040; redcatkitchen.com), 14 Kennebec Avenue. Open D, April through September. Don't let burly, tattooed chef and co-owner Ben deForest fool you; he has a delicate way with food. The menu features robust items like buttermilk fried chicken and waffles, "Big-Ass Scallops," and PBR-braised pork shank, but changes daily; the flavors, sides, and desserts are divine and imaginative. $$$–$$$$.

UP-ISLAND

Lambert's Cove Inn & Restaurant (800-535-0272; lambertscoveinn.com), 90 Manaquayak Road, West Tisbury. Open D; call for opening months. Dine on exceptional New American cuisine far from the crowds in a rarefied world that epitomizes genteel elegance. Wall sconces, floor-to-ceiling bookcases, fireplaces, and well-spaced tables set a deeply romantic tone. Tinkling piano music in the summer furthers it. The inn serves beer and wine. $$$–$$$$.

Beach Plum Inn (508-645-9454; beachpluminn.com), 50 Beach Plum Lane, off North Road, Menemsha. Open D, May through October. Although you're probably drawn here for its country location and distant sunset views of Menemsha Harbor, the chef would probably prefer the focus to be their locally caught seafood and locally grown produce from Chilmark's Beetlebung Farm. With good reason. Although the menu at this minimalist dining room changes nightly, portions tend toward nouvelle (read: small). And unless you're allergic to chocolate, you'd be crazy not to order the chocolate quad cake. Service, by the way, is friendly and low-key but professional. BYOB. $$$$$.

Outermost Inn (508-645-3511; outermostinn.com), 81 Lighthouse Road, Aquinnah. Open D; call for opening months. Take the inn on its terms—or don't. It draws patrons because it's exclusive (there are a limited number of tables), because they do things their own funky way out here, and because of dramatic sunsets over the ocean. As for the New American menu, it highlights fresh island ingredients. There are usually four or five appetizer and entrée choices, perhaps including Edgartown oysters and roasted halibut. Two seatings; reservations required. $$$$$+.

❄ ✿ **Home Port** (508-645-2679; homeportmv.com), 512 North Road, Menemsha. Open D. New ownership in 2009 saved this institution by retaining the menu and improving the quality. It's an efficient surf-sun-and-turf kind of place, with long wooden tables and lobster cooked lots of different ways, thick swordfish, jumbo shrimp, and a raw bar. The servings are large and the clientele are a bit older. Dine on the outside deck for the best sunset views of Menemsha Creek. Or get takeout from the back door and sit at the harbor. BYOB. $$$$.

Chilmark Tavern (508-645-9400; chilmarktavern.com), 9 State Road, Chilmark. Open D. If you're stationed up-island, the haul to Edgartown, Vineyard Haven, or Oak Bluffs for dinner can be daunting. Chilmark Tavern is one of the few up-island options, but it's a good one. The food is simply but classily presented, like the establishment itself. Perhaps not surprisingly, crowds can slow down the service in summertime. BYOB. $$$-$$$$$.

EATING OUT

IN EDGARTOWN

🦞 ✿ **Among the Flowers** (508-627-3233), Mayhew Lane, off North Water Street. Open B, L, D, May through October. This small, friendly café has some of the most reasonable prices in Edgartown. It's a good choice for healthier options, and the lunch specials always feature unique flavor combos. There aren't many indoor tables, but there is an outdoor patio, enclosed and heated during inclement weather. Look for excellent omelets, lobster rolls, PB&J for the kids, crêpes, salads, quiches, corn chowder, and clam chowder. L $-$$, D $$-$$$$.

🦞 ❄ ✿ 🍷 **The Newes From America** (508-627-4397; thenewesfromamerica.com), 23 Kelley Street. Open L, D. Occupying the basement of the Kelley House, the food here is surprisingly good for pub grub—renowned burritos and fish-and-chips, as well as burgers and sandwiches. Stick to pub mainstays and don't order anything too fancy. At about $15 per person, lunch here is one of the better island values. The atmosphere is cozy, too: exposed beams, red brick, and a wood floor. Check out the selection of microbrews, or try the beer sampler rack and receive a wooden nickel souvenir (collect at least 500 and you'll get a

AMONG THE FLOWERS KIM GRANT

THE NEWES FROM AMERICA KIM GRANT

named bar stool). When it's cold outside, this place will warm you to the core. $$

🦞 ❄ 🍃 **Edgartown Diner** (508-627-9337; edgartowndinermv.com), 65 Main Street, Old Post Office Square. Open B, L, D. This nostalgic 1950s-style diner is a fun place for kids because there's plenty to look at—from old signs to a jukebox. As for the actual dining, you've got your basic comfort foods: eggs, pancakes, grilled cheese, meat loaf, PB&J, burgers, and some Italian. Parents won't mind the prices either. L $–$$, D $$.

🍃 🍸 **Seafood Shanty** (508-627-8622; theseafoodshanty.com), 31 Dock Street. Open L, D, mid-May through September. So you just want to nibble on something and have drinks on the water? Head here for lobster cakes, something from the raw bar or sushi bar, and a beverage of your choice. If you can't get a table on the rooftop deck, don't bother, though. They also have DJs, reggae nights, and the like in the summer. L $$, D $$$–$$$$.

Right Fork Diner (508-627-5522; rightforkdiner.com), 12 Mettakesett Way. Open B, L, D, mid-May to mid-October. Parked at the edge of the airfield on Katama's right fork, this diner is a fun spot to enjoy a hearty breakfast while watching classic biplanes putter around. $$.

❄ **Dock Street Coffee Shop** (508-627-5232), 2 Dock Street. Open B, L, D.

A hole-in-the-wall with an old-timey breakfast counter, the joint's menu is straightforward, the service is quick, and they stay open late a few nights a week to satisfy those milkshake cravings.

IN VINEYARD HAVEN

🦞 ❄ 🍃 **Art Cliff Diner** (508-693-1224), 39 Beach Road. Open B, L. Great things come from this little package. Although it's not much to look at and the parking is limited in summer, the buzz is resounding and the dishes stellar. Chef/owner Regina Stanley, a whirlwind of energy who was the pastry chef at Blair House, the guest house of the White House, meets and greets patrons. She works alongside Teddy Diggs, who has brought success to island restaurants like Home Port and The Beach Plum. Breakfast is out of this world: fancy frittatas, daily scone and eggs Benedict specials, tofu scramble, almond-crusted French toast, breakfast tacos, and the Bayou Bundle. Anything-but-prosaic meat loaf is a terrific lunch choice. It's also family-friendly, with crayons available for the kids. $$.

❄ 🍃 **Waterside Market** (508-693-8899; watersidemarket.com), 76 Main Street, Vineyard Haven. Open B, L. Stop by these spacious and casual digs for quick but filling lunchtime

ART CLIFF DINER KIM GRANT

THE NET RESULT KIM GRANT

sandwiches and salads, as well as breakfast dishes like hash, croissant sandwiches, and buttermilk pancakes. There's always something appealing on the huge blackboard menu. Watch the street scene through large, street-front picture windows. The sandwiches are huge. You can usually get away with splitting one, but the fresh ciabatta bread will make you want to eat the whole thing. $–$$.

🦞 **Sandy's Fish & Chips** (508-693-1220), 5 Martin Road. Open mid-May to mid-September. Located within John's Fish Market, this family-operated, no-frills place has great fried fish sandwiches and fried clams. The fish market opened in the 1960s and the restaurant started in 1978. $–$$.

❊ **Net Result Fish Market** (508-693-6071; mvseafood.com), 79 Beach Road. Sushi, lobsters, shellfish, smoked fish, and bay scallops (in-season) purchased on the spot or shipped home as a nostalgic reminder. $–$$.

❊ **Rocco's** (508-693-1125; marthas vineyardpizza.com), 79 Beach Road in Tisbury Marketplace. Open L, D. Though hidden in the back corner of a plaza,

Rocco's is a local favorite for pizza and one of the only spots to get a good pie off-season. In addition to New York–style cheese and pepperoni slices, they offer inventive meat and veggie specials daily. Full pizzas come with all the usual toppings. Skip the rest of the offerings—only because the pizza rules. $.

❊ **Little House Café** (508-687-9794; littlehousemv.com), 339 State Road. Open B, L, D. This easy-to-miss, tiny gem next to Cronigs puts a Mediterranean twist on breakfast, lunch entrées, and salads. Regulars and I dive into their fish tacos and shawarma. $$.

IN OAK BLUFFS

Nancy's Restaurant and Snack Bar (508-693-0006; nancysrestaurant.com), 29 Lake Avenue. Open L, D, late May to mid-October. Nancy's is another sought-after spot of the Obama family. Classic lobster rolls, a nice raw bar, and the Dirty Banana mudslides at Donovan's Reef, the downstairs bar, drive the success of this busy location. Not to mention, you can almost pull your boat right up to the window. $$–$$$.

🍴 ❄ 🍷 **Linda Jean's** (508-693-4093; lindajeansrestaurant.com), 25 Circuit Avenue. Open B, L, D. Established in 1976, this is a classic American diner without the chrome. It's a pleasant storefront eatery serving old-fashioned meals at old-fashioned prices. Breakfast is still the best meal of the day here: pancakes are thick but light, for instance. But the fish sandwich is quick and good, and the onion rings are crispy. Kids are happy with burgers and PB&J. And the waitstaff is friendly. What more could you ask for? If you haven't tried that famed New England "delicacy," Grape-Nuts custard, this is the place to do it. Expect a wait for breakfast even in the dead of winter! $$.

🍴 ❄ 🍷 **Offshore Ale Co.** (508-693-2626; offshoreale.com), 30 Kennebec Avenue. Open L, D. Not only is the food good—crispy, wood-fired, brick-oven pizzas, hefty burgers, grilled fish, fried calamari, and beer-batter fish-and-chips—but the place is fun, too. The front door is marked with a big barrel full of peanuts, and patrons toss the shells onto the floor. But freshly fermented beer is reason enough to frequent this dark, two-story barn—as is the homemade root beer. Check the blackboard for what's fresh from the shiny copper vats, and try to come in the afternoon for a brewery tour before eating. Frequent entertainment off-season. L $$, D $$–$$$.

🍷 **Oak Bluffs Harbor Boardwalk**, Circuit Avenue Extension. Among the many eateries that line the boardwalk, two places deserve particular mention:

Coop de Ville (508-693-3420; coopdevillemv.com), 12 Circuit Avenue Extension. Open L, D, late April to late October. This place is the best fry joint and raw bar. The oysters are excellent and fish-and-chips very good. Otherwise, you know the menu: seafood by the pint or quart; steamed lobster with corn; wings. But the wings . . . the hot wings are arguably the best on the island. With picnic tables and counters, this is a great location for fast food and people watching. $$–$$$.

COOPE DE VILLE KIM GRANT

Lobsterville Bar and Grille (508-696-0099; lobstervillemv.com), 8 Circuit Avenue Extension. Open L, D, mid-May to mid-October. The big turquoise tower has run-of-the-mill offerings (lots of seafood and fried appetizers), but you can always get a reliable burger here. The real kicker: sit on the second-story deck for an unbeatable view of the harbor. $$–$$$.

🍴 🍷 **Farm Neck Café** (508-693-3560; farmneck.net), at the golf club off County Road. Open B, L, D, early April to late November. When I ask locals to recommend a great, inexpensive lunch place, this place inevitably pops up. Yes, it's crawling with golfers, but the setting is lovely—with views of long, manicured fairways. While the atmosphere is clubby, it's public and very comfortable. You can get grilled shrimp and other seafood, soups, Cobb salad, sesame chicken wrapped in a flour tortilla, a burger, or a roast beef sandwich Philly style. L $–$$, D $$–$$$$.

🍴 🍷 **Lookout Tavern** (508-696-9844; lookoutmv.com), 8 Seaview Avenue.

Open L, D, April through December. This aptly named pub looks out over the ferry terminal and into Vineyard Sound. Most folks come for super-fresh sushi, but they also offer de rigueur American fare and fried seafood. It's a great place to have a draft while watching a Sox game.

🦞 ❄ 🐾 **Ocean View Restaurant** (508-693-2207; oceanviewmv.com), 16 Chapman Avenue. Open L, D. Sink into a seat and watch TV and nosh from a bar menu, or try the tavern. Wherever you sit, the servers make bustling summer OB feel like a small town where everyone knows your name. The combination of a surf-and-turf-oriented menu and crayons for kids keep all familiy members happy. If you haven't had your fill of fried food for the week, don't miss this guilty pleasure: the hodgepodge of fried wings, ravioli, and mozzarella sticks. $$.

🦞 ❄ **Bangkok Thai Cuisine** (508-696-6322; bkkcapecod.com), 67 Circuit Avenue. This authentic, spicy, and welcome diversion makes a mean peanutty pad thai. Servers are prompt and polite, and the atmosphere is casually romantic, especially outdoors on the brick patio. $$–$$$.

UP-ISLAND

Fella's Take Out (508-693-6924; fella caters.com), 479 State Road, West Tisbury. Open B, L, D, May through October. Stop by this tiny, low-key take-out place for breakfast sandwiches, hearty sandwiches, hot pressed panini, chili, and pizza. You can always count on them when you're hungry and heading up-island. $–$$$.

🐾 **Aquinnah Shop** (508-645-3867, theaquinnahshop.com), 27 Aquinnah Circle, Aquinnah. Open B, L, D, mid-April to mid-October. Come for the island's best sunset views rather than decent food and unbearably slow service. The Vanderhoop and Madison families, native Wampanoag, operate this homey restaurant, located near the Aquinnah Cliffs. Try the Tomahawk Special at breakfast: homemade fish cakes covered with salsa atop poached eggs. Lunch is more prosaic: burgers, sandwiches, and salads. I'd go elsewhere for dinner, but just so you know, they dress up the place with sautéed shrimp, lobster with béarnaise sauce, fresh fish daily, and buffalo short ribs braised in cabernet. L $$, D $$$–$$$$.

❄ **Plane View** (508-693-1886; mvyairport.com), 71 Airport Road, West Tisbury. Open B, L. If you're flying in, this airport diner is a good first stop—especially at breakfast. Lunches revolve around sandwiches and burgers. $.

LIGHT MEALS, SNACKS & SWEETS

IN EDGARTOWN

❄ **Soigne** (508-627-8489), 190 Upper Main Street. A connoisseur's deli just outside town, Soigné has all the makings for a gourmet picnic: the island's best take-out sandwiches, soups, myriad cold salads, and boutique wine from around the world. Owners Ron and Diana, who have been at this since 1986, also sell "designer" pastas, pâtés, pastries, mousses, excellent clam chowder, dried fruits, imported cheeses, sauces, and select wines. It's a bit pricey, but worth every penny. By the way, something like "millions and millions" of brownies have been gobbled up here.

Espresso Love (508-627-9211; espressolove.com), 17 Church Street, Edgartown. Open B, L, March through December. Tucked back off Main Street, these folks make strong cappuccino and sweet pastries. If you're a big breakfast eater, their small egg sandwiches will leave a hole in your stomach. A limited selection of soups and sandwiches is offered at lunch, when you can enjoy the outdoor patio.

See also **Morning Glory Farm** under *Farm Stands* and **Humphrey's** under *In Vineyard Haven*.

IN VINEYARD HAVEN

🦪 ❄ **Humphrey's Bakery** (508-693-6518; humphreysmv.com), 455 State Road, West Tisbury. Pick up homemade soups and enormous sandwiches made with homemade bread, and save room for their jelly- or cream-filled doughnuts, affectionately called "belly bombs." Find two other seasonal operations at Dippin Donuts (508-627-7725; 241 Edgartown-Vineyard Haven Road, Edgartown) and Woodland Center (508-693-6518; 455 State Road, Vineyard Haven).

❄ **Tisberry Frozen Yogurt** (508-687-9314; tisberrymv.com), 29 Main Street. Stop for a real fruit smoothie or a low-fat and no-fat froyo with more than 30 fruit, nut, and candy toppings. They also do soups and salads.

❄ **Not Your Sugar Mamas** (508-338-2130; notyoursugarmamas.com), Tisbury Market Place. Look for Chilmark Coffee and healthier baked goods using cacao and coconut rather than junk ingredients.

IN OAK BLUFFS

❄ **Mocha Mott's** (508-696-1922; mochamotts.com), 10 Circuit Avenue. This tiny, aromatic basement café has rich espresso that keeps me going well into the evening, plump bagels, and newspapers that keep me in touch. In Vineyard Haven they're at 15 Main Street (508-693-3155).

❄ **Tony's Market** (508-693-4799; tonysmarketmv.com), 119 Dukes County Avenue. Doubling as a small grocer, this is a good pit stop for caffeine, baked goods, and sandwiches.

UP-ISLAND

❄ **Scottish Bakehouse** (508-693-6633; scottishbakehousemv.com), 977 State Road, Tisbury. Be prepared for summertime waits that are well worth it. Baking scones, meat pies, sweetbreads, and more since the mid-1960s. Double-egg sandwiches and lunch entrées are just

as good as the sweets. It's also a good choice for vegan or gluten-free options.

🦪 🛥 **The Galley** (508-645-9819; menemshagalley.com), 515 North Road, Menemsha. Open mid-May to mid-October. This tiny place has the best chowder on the island and great lobster rolls. Burgers and soft-serve ice cream, too.

Chilmark Store (508-645-3739; chilmarkgeneralstore.com), 7 State Road, near Beetlebung Corner, Chilmark. Open mid-May through September. This general store offers great pizzas and baked goods (especially the pies) in addition to conventional general-store items. Do some people watching from the front-porch rockers before you leave.

❄ **7a Foods** (508-693-4636; 7afoods.com), 1045 State Road, West Tisbury. Behind Alley's General Store, this busy spot sells killer baked goods, gelato, and filling sandwiches. The Liz Lemon—pastrami, turkey, Swiss, coleslaw, Russian dressing, and potato chips on rye—is a favorite, as are the jalapeño-cheddar biscuits. Lots of ingredients come straight from 7a Farms in Aquinnah.

MOCHA MOTT'S KIM GRANT

Larsen's Fish Market (508-645-2680; larsensfishmarket.com), Dutcher's Dock, Menemsha. Open early May to late October. Down some oysters and cherry-stones at the raw bar while you wait for your lobsters to be boiled. Or pick up some stuffed quahogs and head to the beach.

❋ **Menemsha Fish Market** (508-645-2282; menemshafishmarket.net), 56 Basin Road, Menemsha. This little place smokes its own fish and has a small raw bar, which is convenient for appetizers while you wait for your lobsters-to-go.

AROUND THE ISLAND

Mad Martha's has irresistible homemade ice cream (with island specialties like lobster ice cream!) and many locations in all the right places (near the ferries, on Main Street, and the like).

FARM STANDS

Despite summer traffic, $45 dinner entrées, chichi boutiques, and a building boom, the Vineyard is an agricultural island at heart. With little effort you'll find farms with produce so fresh that you can almost taste the earth. Stop often; it will be one of the things most cherished about a Vineyard holiday.

Morning Glory Farm (508-627-9674; 508-637-9003; morninggloryfarm.com), 120 Meshacket Road, off West Tisbury Road, Edgartown. Open late May through December. Although their business card says "Roadside Stand," this is a full-fledged farm with a large, rustic barn-board building. You'll find farm-fresh eggs, a great salad bar, home-baked pies and breads, and homemade jellies, including especially tasty white grape jelly.

DECIDE BETWEEN TWO MENEMSHA FISH MARKETS   KIM GRANT

❋ Entertainment

ARTS & MUSIC ❋ ♪ **Vineyard Playhouse** (508-693-6450; box office 508-687-2452; 508-696-6300; vineyardplayhouse.org), 24 Church Street, Vineyard Haven. This small, community-based professional theater produces well-done plays and musicals; the main stage is within a former Methodist meetinghouse. They also host many special events; keep your eyes peeled. Summer performances are scheduled most nights. Look for a varied and entertaining lineup at the troupe's Tisbury Amphitheater, Tashmoo Overlook, State Road, Vineyard Haven. The playhouse also offers educational programs, theater for young audiences, summer outdoor productions, and a theater arts camp. $$$$.

The Yard (508-645-9662; dance theyard.org), Middle Road, near Beetlebung Corner, Chilmark. May through October. Founded in 1973, this colony of performing artists in residence is always engaging and appreciated. The choreography and dance are spirited. If you have a chance to go to one of their performances, by all means go. The Yard is one of those special organizations that makes the Vineyard uniquely the Vineyard. Most shows $$$; some are free.

❋ **Martha's Vineyard Chamber Music Society** (508-696-8055; mvcms.org). Mid-July to mid-August. Monday concerts are held at the Old Whaling Church in Edgartown; Tuesday concerts are at the Chilmark Community Center. $$$$.

The Vineyard Sound band concerts (866-846-7686; vineyardsound.org). Check the website for locations, days, and times around the island.

See also **Katharine Cornell Theatre** under **To See**.

♈ NIGHTLIFE

❋ **The Newes From America** (508-627-4397; kelley-house.com), 23 Kelley Street, Edgartown. This colonial-era basement tavern is atmospheric and cozy, with hand-hewn beams. The Newes features microbrews; try the specialty Rack of Beers, a sampler of five brews from the outstanding and unusual beer menu (see *Eating Out*).

Atlantic (508-627-7001; atlanticmv .com), 2 Main Street, Edgartown. Open April through October. The setting at this waterfront restaurant and bar couldn't be better, especially if you get an outdoor table on the porch. It's hip, urban, and loud, with live bands and DJs. It's owned by Charlotte Inn proprietor Gery Conover (see *Bed-and-Breakfasts & Inns* under **Lodging**), who also developed the oh-so exclusive and private Boathouse (above the Atlantic).

❋ **The Ritz** (508-693-9851; theritzmv .com), 4 Circuit Avenue, Oak Bluffs. Mostly middle-aged locals hang out at this funky blues bar, which, according to the *Improper Bostonian*, is: "seedy," "smokin'," "scary," "disgusting," "hilarious," and "a blast."

❋ **The Wharf** (508-627-9966; wharf pub.com), Lower Main Street, Edgartown. A popular pub with a cozy, sports bar feel.

See **20ByNine** and **Offshore Ale Co**. under *Eating Out* in Oak Bluffs, and **Atria** under *Dining Out* in Edgartown.

MOVIES ❋ ♈ **Capawock Movie Theater** (508-696-9369; mvfilmsociety .com), 43 Main Street, Vineyard Haven. Built in 1912, the Capawock was the oldest continuously operating movie theater in Massachusetts until its closure in the mid-2000s for about three years. As entertaining as movies can be, though, you might be just as entertained by conversations before the film begins.

❋ **Martha's Vineyard Film Center** (508-696-9369; mvfilmsociety.com), 79 Beach Road, Tisbury Market Place, Vineyard Haven. Richard Paradise is the man behind this elegant little theater, established by the nonprofit Martha's Vineyard Film Society in 2002. They play some blockbusters, but mostly fine independent and foreign films. Many screenings for the Martha's Vineyard International Film Festival are held here in early September.

♈ **Entertainment Cinemas** (508-627-8008; entertainmentcinemas.com), 65 Main Street, Edgartown.

❋ Selective Shopping

These entries are truly "selective," for they do not begin to scratch the surface of what's available shopping-wise on the Vineyard.

ART GALLERIES For a super-complete listing of artists and galleries, look for the free and excellent *"Arts Directory"* available in many galleries.

Alison Shaw Gallery (508-693-4429 for studio; 508-696-7429; alisonshaw .com), 88 Dukes County Avenue, Oak Bluffs. Open seasonally. This prolific photographer started in abstract black-and-white imagery (for the *Vineyard Gazette*) before moving to highly graphic color imagery. Her work these days is more painterly than postcardy. Alison also leads excellent workshops and mentorship programs.

❀ ✳ **Craftworks** (508-693-7463; craftworksgallery.com), 42 Circuit Avenue, Oak Bluffs. These folks have a mixed but usually affordable selection of contemporary American crafts that's worth a look and always visually interesting. Clay, metal, glass, paper, and wood. Fun and colorful.

Old Sculpin Gallery (508-627-4881; oldsculpingallery.org), 58 Dock Street at corner of Daggett, Edgartown. Open late May to mid-October. Operated by the nonprofit Martha's Vineyard Art Association, the building was originally Dr. Daniel Fisher's granary, then a boatbuilder's workshop. Look for the long, wide depression in the main room where boatbuilder Manuel Swartz Roberts's feet wore down the floor as he moved along his workbench during the early 20th century. Paintings, photographs, and sculpture of varying degrees of quality are exhibited. Classes for all ages are offered throughout the season.

✳ **North Water Gallery** (508-627-6002; northwatergallery.com), 27 North Water Street, Edgartown. Regional and national artists emphasizing Vineyard landscapes, seascapes, maritime scenes, figurative works, photography, and still lifes are represented here.

✳ **Granary Gallery at the Red Barn** (508-693-0455; granarygallery.com), 636 Old County Road, West Tisbury. In addition to folk art and landscape paintings, this gallery carries old and new photography. Look for classic photos by the venerable photographer Alfred Eisenstaedt, who came to the island on assignment for *Life* in 1937 and vacationed here until his death in 1995. Most artists represented here have some affiliation with the island.

Field Gallery (508-693-5595; fieldgallery.com), 1050 State Road, West Tisbury. Open seasonally. Tom Maley's field of joyfully dancing figures, which seem to be celebrating the surrounding beauty, is an icon of the Vineyard's cultural life. Other Vineyard artists are exhibited during summer months; receptions are

OLD SCULPIN GALLERY KIM GRANT

held 5 p.m.–7 p.m. on many Sundays June through August.

See also **Featherstone Center for the Arts** under **To Do**.

ARTISANS ❋ **Tuck & Holand Metal Sculptures** (508-693-3914; tuckand holand.com), 275 State Road, Vineyard Haven. Although Travis Tuck died in 2002, his partner and former apprentice Anthony Holand carries on as the exclusive maker of Tuck's famed weather vanes. Holand also creates wonderful original designs of his own. Given the prices ($12,000 and up) and time required to painstakingly produce one (weeks and weeks), the wait times are long. The client list includes Steven Spielberg, who owns an animated velociraptor, and Bill and Hillary Clinton. You can see examples of their work around the island, too. Check out the weather vanes atop the new Agricultural Hall in West Tisbury (a Holstein cow); Cronig's Market on State Road (a grasshopper, as

A FIELD GALLERY SCULPTURE KIM GRANT

a public market symbol); the Tisbury and Edgartown Town Halls (a whale tail and whaling ship, respectively); and the *Vineyard Gazette* building (a quill pen). A short video with striking images of notable vanes on the website offers a glimpse into this extraordinary enterprise.

❋ **Chilmark Pottery** (508-693-6476; chilmarkpottery.wixsite.com/chilmarkpottery), 145 Field View Lane, off State Road, opposite Nip-n-Tuck Farm, West Tisbury. In 1982 artist Geoffrey Borr established his studio in a weathered shingled barn, where he and his staff transform thoughtfully designed, wheel-thrown creations into hand-painted pottery with distinctive seascape, oxblood, and copper red hues. You'll find functional and sculptural mugs, vases, and plates, as well as more unusual sculptural pieces.

Martha's Vineyard Glass Works (508-693-6026; mvglassworks.com), 683 State Road, West Tisbury. Open April through January. Many designers share this dynamic studio, a colorfully bold visual feast where you can watch the artists and apprentices at work.

BOOKSTORES 🖋 **Edgartown Books** (508-627-8463; edgartownbooks.com), 44 Main Street, Edgartown. Open February through December. This charming independent bookshop has everything from travel and local fiction to books and activities for children.

❋ **Bunch of Grapes Bookstore** (508-693-2291; bunchofgrapes.indielite.org), 35 Main Street, Vineyard Haven. This beloved island establishment continues its 40-plus year tradition as the Vineyard's best year-round, independent, locally owned general bookstore.

CLOTHING **Bryn Walker** (brynwalker.com), 21 Kelly Street, Edgartown (open April through December), and 16 Main Street, Vineyard Haven (open year-round). Upscale but affordable, mix-and-match women's linen and cotton clothing in updated styles and colors.

❋ **The Great Put-On** (508-627-5495; thegreatputonmv.com), 10 Dock Street at Mayhew Lane, Edgartown. One of the island's most fashionable clothing stores stocks an impressive selection of dressy clothing for women, more shoes for women than for men, and unisex accessories like leather backpacks, loose jackets, and sweaters.

Pandora's Box (508-645-9696), 4 Basin Road (off North Road), Menemsha. Open May to mid-October. The emphasis here is on comfortable, contemporary women's clothing.

FARMS **West Tisbury Farmers' Market** (wtfmarket.org). In summer you can find this open airy market at Grange Hall on Saturdays mid-June to mid-October and Wednesdays late June to late August. In fall the market is moved indoors to the New Agricultural Hall on Saturdays mid-October to mid-December.

Allen Farm Sheep & Wool Company (508-645-9064; allenfarm.com), 421 South Road, Chilmark. Call ahead for hours or take your chances. Engaging in sustainable and organic farming practices, the Allen family has been raising black-and-white Corriedale sheep on these rolling fields for more than 200 years. Their wool is custom-spun and hand-dyed and used by islanders to make sweaters, scarves, mittens, and the like.

Island Alpaca (508-693-5554; islandalpaca.com), 1 Head of the Pond Road, off Edgartown–Vineyard Haven Road, Oak Bluffs. These gentle creatures, more than 80 in this herd at last count, are raised for breeding, sales, and for their fleece. It's as soft as cashmere, four times warmer, comes in more than 20 natural colors, and is hypoallergenic. The farm store sells all things alpaca. Inquire about spinning and knitting classes and Alpaca Jr. Discovery Days, on Sunday mornings in the summer, for children ages 8 and up. Follow the alpacas on their very own webcam.

EDGARTOWN BOOKS   KIM GRANT

Seaside Daylily Farm (508-693-3276), Great Plains Road, off Old County Road, West Tisbury. Open seasonally with limited hours; call ahead. These lilies are grown without the use of harmful chemicals that disrupt the ecosystem's natural balance.

See also the **Farm Institute** in *Special Programs* under **To Do**.

HOME FURNISHINGS **LeRoux** (508-693-0030; lerouxkitchen.com), 62 Main Street, Vineyard Haven. This store is devoted to kitchen items, home goods, and furnishings. Their gourmet shop across the street is a foodie's dream.

JEWELRY ❋ **C. B. Stark** (508-693-2284; cbstark.com), 53A Main Street, Vineyard Haven. Goldsmiths Cheryl Stark and Margery Meltzer have designed gold and silver jewelry with island motifs since 1966. Cheryl created the original grape design that has become so popular on the island. The shop also carries locally made wampum from quahog shells. Look for their shop on North Water Street, Edgartown, too.

SPECIALTY SHOPS **Chilmark Chocolates** (508-645-3013), 19 State Road, near Beetlebung Corner, Chilmark. Open in summer and around Christmas and Valentine's Day. Good deeds and good products make an unbeatable combination. Not only will you love the creamy truffles and mouthwatering chocolates, it's nice to know that this chocolatier believes all members of society should be given a chance to be productive. They hire people with disabilities to make and sell the chocolate. Try their Tashmoo Truffles, West Chomps, or Squibnuggets.

✳ **Mosher Photo** (508-693-9430; mosherphoto.com), 25 Main Street, Vineyard Haven.

✳ Special Events

The Vineyard has hundreds and hundreds of charming—great and small—special events throughout the year. A sampling of the larger, predictable, annual events follows. Contact the chamber of commerce (508-693-0085; mvy .com) for specific dates unless an alternative phone number is listed below.

Mid-May through November: **Antiques at the Old Grange Hall.** On most Fridays, but also on some Tuesdays and Saturdays.

Throughout the summer: **Vineyard Artisans Summer Festivals** (508-693-8989; vineyardartisans.com). Shows May to December. Don't have time to pop into two dozen galleries? Then check this out. These excellent shows are held indoors and outdoors, rain or shine, at the Grange Hall in West Tisbury. Look for furniture, ceramics, book arts, fiber arts, glass, jewelry, mixed media,

CB STARK JEWELERS KIM GRANT

painting, photography, printmaking, and sculpture.

Mid-June: **Oak Bluffs Harbor Festival** (508-693-3392). Since 1991.

Fourth of July Weekend: **July Fourth.** One of the busiest weeks of the summer. Edgartown puts on a family-friendly parade followed by fireworks in the harbor.

Late July/Early August: **Possible Dreams Auction** (mvcommunity services.com), Winnetu Oceanside Resort, Edgartown. Given the celebrity involvement, it's not surprising that national publicity surrounds this event. Celebrities offer to fulfill "dreams" that vary from predictable to unusual. High bidders in the past have won a tour of the *60 Minutes* studios with Mike Wallace; a sail with Walter Cronkite on his yacht; a seat at a Knicks game with Spike Lee; a tour of Carnegie Hall with Isaac Stern; a walking tour of the Brooklyn Bridge with David McCullough; a song and a peanut butter sandwich from Carly Simon; and a lesson in chutzpah at the Five Corners intersection in Vineyard Haven with Alan Dershowitz. Longtime island celebrities see the auction as their chance to give back to the

Vineyard—the auction raises hundreds of thousands of dollars for Martha's Vineyard Community Services. That's a far cry from the $1,000 raised in 1979 when it began, and folks bid in $5 increments for the privilege of helping lobstermen set out their pots. More than 1,000 people usually attend the event, and to date it has raised more than $11 million.

July–August: **Community Sing** (508-693-0525). Singing and more at the Tabernacle at the Methodist "campground" in Oak Bluffs every Wednesday at 8 p.m. **Band concerts** every Sunday evening, alternating between Owen Park in Vineyard Haven and Ocean Park in Oak Bluffs.

Mid-July: **Edgartown Regatta** (508-627-4361; edgartownyc.org). Racing since the mid-1920s.

Late July: **Book Sale** (508-693-3366). A benefit since the late '50s for the West Tisbury Library, held at the West Tisbury Elementary School on Old County Road.

Early August: **Edgartown House Tour** (508-627-7077). This event, sponsored by the Federated Church of Martha's Vineyard, opens up five antique houses in downtown Edgartown for tours every year. Tea and refreshments are served in the Old Parsonage at the end of the tour. $$$$.

Mid-August: **Illumination Night.** Usually held the third Wednesday in August, the evening always begins with a community sing and is followed by an Oak Bluffs resident (usually the oldest) lighting a single Japanese lantern after all the electric lights in town are turned off. Then the rest of the "camp" residents illuminate their gingerbread cottages with lanterns and candles.

Fireworks. Usually held the third Friday in August, these fireworks in Ocean Park, set to the music of the Vineyard Sound, are far more spectacular than the Fourth of July display.

Agricultural Fair (508-693-9549; marthasvineyardagriculturalsociety.org). Held at the Ag Hall and Fairgrounds on State Road in West Tisbury, this is arguably the island's most beloved summer event. It's certainly one of the oldest: it began during the Civil War! $.

KIM GRANT

Mid-September: **International Film Festival** (mvfilmsociety.com). A laid-back but passionate 4-day celebration of films.

Early to mid-September–early to mid-October: **Striped Bass and Bluefish Derby** (mvderby.com). When dozens of surf casters begin furiously fishing from your favorite beach, you'll know it's derby time. Prizes are awarded for the largest fish caught each day, with a grand prize for the largest fish caught during the monthlong tournament. Weighing is done in Edgartown Harbor, just as it's been done every year since the mid-1940s.

Mid-September: **Tivoli Day**. A lively street fair on Circuit Avenue in Oak Bluffs.

Mid-October: **Food & Wine Festival** (mvfoodandwine.com), Edgartown. A 3-day fete of food and wine with cocktail parties, chef demonstrations, tastings, seminars, and a Sunday farmer's brunch.

Early–mid-December: **Christmas in Edgartown**. The town and its lighthouse get dressed up for the occasion. There's also a parade, a chowder contest, horse and carriage rides, and more.

Vineyard Artisans Holiday Festival (508-693-8989; vineyardartisans .com), at the Grange Hall, West Tisbury. More than 50 crafters and artists have gathered for this event since the mid-1960s.

NANTUCKET

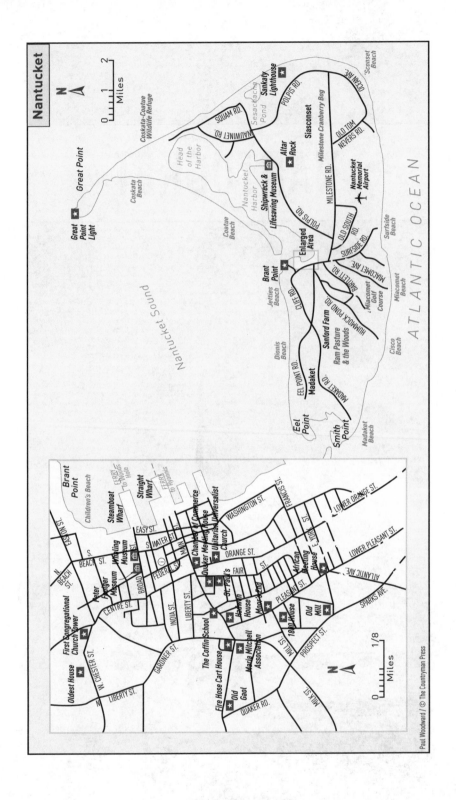

Nantucket

N

Miles
0   1   2

Great Point

Great
Point
Light

Coskata Beach

Coskata-Coatue
Wildlife Refuge

Nantucket Sound

Head
of the
Harbor

SQUAM RD.

Sesachacha
Pond

Sankaty
Lighthouse

NADWINET RD.

POLPIS RD.

Nantucket
Harbor

Shipwreck &
Lifesaving Museum

Altar
Rock

Siasconset

'Sconset
Beach

OCEAN AVE.

OLD TOM NEVERS RD.

Milestone Cranberry Bog

MILESTONE RD.

Nantucket
Memorial
Airport

Coatue
Beach

Enlarged
Area

Jetties Beach

Brant
Point

CLIFF RD.

POLPIS RD.

OLD SOUTH RD.

SURFSIDE RD.

BARTLETT RD.

MIACOMET AVE.

Surfside
Beach

Dionis
Beach

EEL POINT RD.

Sanford Farm
Ram Pasture
& the Woods

HUMMOCK POND RD.

Miacomet
Golf
Course

Miacomet
Beach

Eel
Point

MADAKET RD.

Madaket

Smith
Point

Madaket
Beach

Cisco
Beach

ATLANTIC OCEAN

Brant
Point

Children's Beach

Steamboat
Wharf

FERRY
To Woods Hole

Straight
Wharf

FERRY
To Hyannis

EASTON ST.

N.
BEACH ST.

S.
BEACH ST.

Whaling
Museum

Peter
Foulger
Museum

CENTRE ST.

BROAD ST.

FEDERAL ST.

EASY ST.

S. WATER ST.

MAIN ST.

Chamber of Commerce

Quaker Meeting House

Unitarian Universalist
Church

WASHINGTON ST.

FRANCIS ST.

ORANGE ST.

St. Paul's

FAIR ST.

INDIA ST.

LIBERTY ST.

GARDNER ST.

The Coffin School

First Congregational
Church Tower

W. CHESTER ST.

Oldest House

N.
LIBERTY ST.

Fire Hose Cart House

Old
Gaol

Maria Mitchell
Association

QUAKER RD.

MILK ST.

PLEASANT ST.

Macy
House

African
Meeting
House

1800 House

Old
Mill

PROSPECT ST.

MILL ST.

E. YORK ST.

W. YORK ST.

LOWER ORANGE ST.

LOWER PLEASANT ST.

ATLANTIC AVE.

SPARKS AVE.

N

Miles
0   1/8

Paul Woodward / © The Countryman Press

NANTUCKET

Thirty miles out to sea, Nantucket was called "that far away island" by local American Indians. Just 14 by 3.5 miles in area, Nantucket is the only place in America that is simultaneously an island, a county, and a town. In 1659 Thomas Mayhew, who had purchased Nantucket sight unseen (he was more interested in Martha's Vineyard), sold it to Tristram Coffin and eight of his friends for £30 and "two Beaver Hatts." These "original purchasers" quickly sold half-shares to craftsmen whose skills they would require to build a community.

When Mayhew arrived, there were more than 3,000 indigenous residents, who taught the settlers which crops to farm and how to spear whales from shore. By the early 1700s, the number of settlers had grown to more than 300, and the number of natives had shrunk to less than 800, primarily because of disease. (The last native descendant died on-island in 1854.)

In 1712, when Captain Hussey's sloop was blown out to sea, he harpooned the first sperm whale islanders had ever seen. For the next 150 years, whaling dominated the island's economy. The ensuing prosperity allowed the island's population to climb to 10,000. By comparison, there are also about 10,500 year-rounders today.

Nantucket sea captains traveled the world to catch whales and to trade, and they brought back great fortunes. By the late 1700s, trade was booming with England, and in 1791 the *Beaver*, owned by islander William Rotch, rounded Cape Horn and forged an American trade route to the Pacific Ocean. Fortunes were also made in the Indian Ocean—hence, Nantucket's India Street. Speaking of place names, the nearby village of 'Sconset takes its name from the local language for "near the great whale bone." It was first settled three centuries ago as a whaling outpost, around a lookout tower used for spotting whales.

In its heyday, Nantucket Harbor overflowed with smoke and smells from blacksmith shops, cooperages, shipyards, and candle factories. More than 100 whaling ships sailed in and out of Nantucket. But when ships grew larger to allow for their longer voyages at sea, they couldn't get across the shallow shoals and into Nantucket Harbor. The industry began moving to Martha's Vineyard and New Bedford.

At the height of the whaling industry in 1846, the "Great Fire," which began in a hat shop on Main Street, ignited whale oil

BRANT POINT LIGHTHOUSE KIM GRANT

NANTUCKET HARBOR KIM GRANT

at the harbor. The catastrophic blaze wiped out the harbor and one-third of the town. Although most citizens began to rebuild immediately, other adventurous and energetic souls were enticed to go west in search of gold in 1849. When kerosene replaced whale oil in the 1850s as a less expensive fuel, it was the final blow to the island's maritime economy. By 1861 there were only 2,000 people on-island.

MODERN DAY TOURISM

Although tourism began soon after the Civil War and picked up with the advent of the railroad to 'Sconset, the island lay more or less in undisturbed isolation until the 1950s. Perhaps it was the sleepiness of those 100 years that ultimately preserved the island's architectural integrity and community spirit, paving the way for its resurrection. In the late 1950s and early 1960s, islander and S&H Green Stamp heir Walter Beinecke Jr. organized a revitalization of the waterfront area, replacing decrepit wharf buildings with cottages. He also declared the premise that guides tourism to this day: it is preferable to attract one tourist with $100 than 100 tourists with $1 each. In accordance with the maxim, strict zoning laws were adopted, land-conservation groups were launched, and Nantucket's upscale tourism industry began in earnest.

By the late 1990s, the well-to-do set was foregoing the Hamptons and similar enclaves for Nantucket. By 2000 it had become too popular for its own good and was placed on the list of Most Endangered Historical Places, as decreed by the National Trust for Historic Preservation. In contrast to the Vineyard's showy excess and celebrity allure, Nantucket is a restrained haven for behind-the-scenes power brokers.

In the recent past, mammoth multimillion-dollar trophy houses (and to be fair, some of the more understated ones, too) have belonged to people like the Gambles of Procter & Gamble, the Du Ponts, R. H. Macy, R. J. Reynolds, Bill Blass, David Halberstam, Graham Gund, Jack Welsh, Tommy Hilfiger, John Kerry, and Russell Baker. And now, downtown properties like the former Harbor House Hotel are being converted into one- to three-bedroom residences (a.k.a. condos) with hefty price tags.

It was only a matter of time, I suppose, although many islanders are up in arms with dismay at what their island is fast becoming: a gated theme park for the rich. It's no longer enough to be a millionaire on Nantucket. Billionaires are the new millionaires.

In 1966 Nantucket was declared a **National Historic Landmark**: it boasts more than 800 buildings constructed before 1850—the largest concentration of such buildings in the United States. The historic district is picture-perfect: paved cobblestone streets, brick sidewalks, electrified "gas" street lamps. Gray-shingled houses are nestled close together on narrow lanes, which wind as you amble beyond the downtown grid of streets. Elegant white residences are trimmed with English boxwood hedges, white picket fences, and showcase flower gardens.

With a daily summer population that swells to about 50,000, today's tourist industry is about as well oiled as the whale industry once was. It's difficult to find a grain of sand or a seashell that hasn't been discovered.

Most sites in Nantucket are within a mile of the **historic center**—you might walk more than you're accustomed to. In addition to historic houses and museums, Nantucket prides itself on offering world-class dining. Although there are little pockets of settlements around the island, the only real "destination" is **'Sconset**, an utterly quaint village with rose-covered cottages. Elsewhere on the island, more than 45 percent of the island's 10,000 acres are held by conservation trusts; you'll be able to explore places where most tourists don't venture. The island boasts excellent bicycle paths and almost limitless public beaches.

Nantucket is a year-round destination. Hundreds of thousands of daffodils blanket the island in yellow as the earth reawakens each April. The weather in May and June is slightly less predictable than in fall, but if you hit a nice stretch, you'll probably muse that life just doesn't get any better. Gardens are brightest in May and June. Where once there were whaling ships, yachts now fill the harbor in summer. Warm ocean water and beach barbecues beckon, wild roses trail along picket fences, and many special events are staged. Come September (my favorite month on-island), the crowds recede a bit. You can swim in the still-temperate ocean by day and not have to wait for a table at your

BRANT POINT LIGHTHOUSE AND FERRY KIM GRANT

favorite restaurant at night. Skies turn crisp blue, and cranberry bogs, heathlands, and the moors blaze red, russet, and maroon.

Many restaurants that close in mid-October (at the end of Columbus Day weekend) reopen for the long Thanksgiving weekend. The first three weeks of November are very quiet indeed. Before the monochrome days of winter set in, there is one last burst of activity: Nantucket Noel and Christmas Stroll (see **Special Events**). In January, February, and March you'll discover why whaling captains called the island the "little gray lady"—she is often shrouded in fog. It's a time of reflection and renewal for year-rounders and visitors alike.

GUIDANCE ❋ **Nantucket Visitor Services & Information Bureau** (508-228-0925; nantucket-ma.gov), 25 Federal Street. The bureau also maintains seasonal kiosks at Straight Wharf and Nantucket Memorial Airport.

❋ **Nantucket Island Chamber of Commerce** (508-228-1700; nantucketchamber .org), 0 Main Street. For sure (!), get their glossy book, *The Official Guide: Nantucket*, which is free on-island (and can also easily be downloaded in sections) but costs $ to mail in advance of your visit.

Nantucket Historical Association (NHA) (508-228-1894; nha.org), 15 Broad Street. The NHA owns 23 historic properties, 10 of which are open to the public, representing island life from its farming beginnings to its prosperous whaling days, and is a fabulous source of historical information. Generally, NHA properties have "normalish" hours late May to mid-October and shortened winter hours; they change from year to year. A Historic Sites ticket ($) is valid for admission to Hadwen House, the Oldest House, the Old Mill, and the Quaker Meeting House. Guided tours are available at the Hadwen House, Oldest House, and Old Mill. The combo ticket, which includes the Whaling Museum (see **To See**), is a good deal ($$).

GETTING THERE With high-speed ferry service, day-tripping to Nantucket from Hyannis is more feasible than ever. Although I still recommend spending a few days on Nantucket, you are no longer shut out if you can't.

WHALING MUSEUM KIM GRANT

By bus: **Peter Pan/Bonanza** (800-343-9999; peterpanbus.com) travels from points south to Hyannis, where you can catch the boats. **Plymouth & Brockton** (508-746-0378; p-b.com) runs from Boston to Hyannis.

❄ *By boat from Hyannis:* **The Steamship Authority** (508-477-8600 for information and advance auto reservations; 508-771-4000 for day-of-sailing information—no reservations—in Hyannis; 508-228-0262 for day-of-sailing information—no reservations—on Nantucket; steamship authority.com), South Street Dock, Hyannis. The steamship, established in 1948, carries autos, people, and bikes to Steamship Wharf year-round. Make car reservations in the spring for the summer if

WAITING FOR THE STEAMSHIP AUTHORITY FERRY   KIM GRANT

you can; no reservations are needed for passengers. There are six high-season sailings daily and three off-season. Parking in Hyannis is $$ per calendar day. The voyage takes 2¼ hours. Round-trip fares: $$$$; bicycles $$. Cars cost a whopping $450+ mid-May to late October, about $320 off-season—but you really don't need one. Take it from me, a my-car-is-my-home-when-I-travel nut.

The Steamship Authority's **high-speed passenger boat**, *Iyanough* (508-495-3278 for reservations; 508-477-8600 for information) sails dock-to-dock in one hour, early May through December, and makes four to five trips daily; $$$$$+. Reservations strongly suggested.

❄ **Hy-Line Cruises** (800-492-8082; hylinecruises.com), Ocean Street Dock, Hyannis. Passengers and bicycles to Straight Wharf, late May to mid-October. There are three summertime boats daily, one to three daily off-season. Round-trip fares are $$$$$, bicycles $$. Parking in Hyannis is $$ per calendar day.

❄ **Hy-Line's high-speed passenger boat**, *Grey Lady* (800-492-8082; hylinecruises .com), Ocean Street Dock. This high-speed luxury catamaran costs a bit more, but it operates year-round. Reservations are strongly recommended. There are five to six boats daily.

By boat from Harwich: **Freedom Cruise Line** (508-432-8999; nantucketislandferry .com), Saquatucket Harbor in Harwich Port, provides daily passenger service to Nantucket, early June to late September and during the Christmas Stroll (see **Special Events**). During the summer, two of the three trips are scheduled so that you can explore Nantucket for about 6½ hours and return the same day. In spring and fall, there is only one morning boat daily. Reservations are highly recommended; make them three to four days in advance. Round-trip prices: $$$$$+, bicycles $$. Free parking for day-trippers; $$ daily thereafter. The trip takes 80 minutes each way.

By boat from Martha's Vineyard: **Hy-Line Cruises** (508-778-2600 in Hyannis; 508-228-3949 on Nantucket; 508-693-0112 in Oak Bluffs, Martha's Vineyard; hylinecruises .com). One daily, interisland departure from mid-June to mid-September. The trip takes 75 minutes. (There is no interisland car ferry.) One-way: $$$$, bicycles $.

By air: **Cape Air/Nantucket Airlines** (508-771-6944; flycapeair.com; nantucke tairlines.org) offer dozens of daily flights direct from Boston, Hyannis, New Bedford, Providence (T. F. Green), and Martha's Vineyard. Frequent-flier coupon books for 10 one-way trips are available.

GETTING AROUND *By shuttle:* 🚲 **NRTA Shuttle** (508-228-7025; nrtawave.com). WAVE information aides and other amenities are available at the Greenhound Building at 10 Washington Street. Buses daily, late May to early October. This is an economical, relatively convenient (if you pay attention to departure times), and reliable way to travel to 'Sconset (two routes) and Madaket, but the schedule is too complicated to disseminate here. Pick up a route map on-island. Shuttles have a bike rack, so you can take the bus out to 'Sconset, for instance, and ride back. The Surfside Beach and Jetties Beach buses run on a shorter season, from mid-June to early September. Tickets cost $, depending on the route; exact change required. Ask about multiday passes at the NRTA office at 3 East Chestnut Street.

By car or four-wheel drive: There isn't a single traffic light in Nantucket, and Nantucketers intend to keep it that way. You don't need a car unless you're here for at least a week or unless you plan to spend most of your time in conservation areas or on outlying beaches. Even then, a four-wheel-drive vehicle is the most useful, as many of the stunning natural areas are off sandy paths. Nantucket is also ringed by 80 miles of beaches, most of which are accessible via four-wheel drive. Four-wheel drives are rented faster than the speed of light in summer, so make reservations at least a month in advance. And lastly, parking is severely restricted in the historic center. Rent from my favorite company, **Affordable Rentals** (508-228-3501; affrentals.com), 6 South Beach Street, early April to late December. Expect to pay $125+ for a compact during the summer, $250+ for a four-wheel-drive Jeep. **Nantucket Windmill Auto Rental** (508-228-1227; nantucketautorental.com) is based at the airport but also offers free pickup from the ferry; **Hertz** (800-654-3131; hertz.com) is also based at the airport. Prices drop by almost half off-season.

If you get stuck in the sand, call **Harry's 24-Hour Towing** (508-228-3390). Once you do call him, though, wait with your vehicle so he doesn't make the trek out to fetch you, only to find that you've been helped by a friendly local.

Contact the **Police Department** (508-228-1212), South Water Street, for **overland permits**, which are required for four-wheel, over-sand driving. Expect to pay $100+ off-season and $150+ in season.

The **Coskata-Coatue Wildlife Refuge** (see **Green Space**) requires a separate permit, available from the **Nantucket Conservation Foundation** (508-228-2884 information; 508-228-0006 Wauwinet gatehouse, where permits are purchased; nantucketconservation.com), mid-May through October. Most beaches are open to four-wheel-drive traffic, except when terns are nesting.

By bicycle: Bicycling is the best way to get around (see **To Do**).

By moped: **Nantucket Bike Shop** (508-228-1999; nantucketbikeshop.com), Steamboat Wharf, rents scooters April through October. $$$$$+ daily.

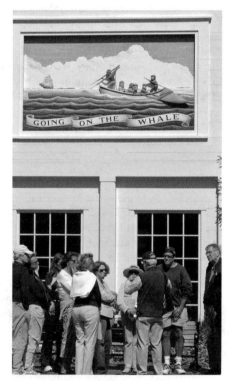

WALKING TOURS KIM GRANT

A DAY TRIP TO NANTUCKET

Morning: Board a high-speed ferry in Hyannis. When you're on the island, head over to the Juice Bar for freshly squeezed concoctions and treats. Take a walking tour with the Nantucket Historical Association or learn about the island's rich history at the Nantucket Whaling Museum.

Afternoon: Split an oversized sandwich from Provisions with your companion, followed by a drive around the island with Nantucket Island Tours. Look for unique gifts as you stroll the cobblestone streets, and pop into the Atheneum.

Evening: Enjoy regional cuisine at the Boarding House or Centre Street Bistro. Take the last high-speed ferry back to Hyannis.

KIM GRANT

On foot: ❧ **Architectural Walking Tours** (508-228-1387; nantucketpreservation.org), 55 Main Street, by the Nantucket Preservation Trust. June through September. $$.

❧ See the Nantucket Whaling Museum for great walking tours sponsored by the **Nantucket Historical Association**.

By van or bus tours: ❋ **Ara's Tours** (508-228-1951; 508-221-6852; arastours.com) offers a 90-minute island tour for $$$ that makes stops for photography. On a clear day you can see all three lighthouses. For those who have more time and money, ask about the 3-hour barrier beach tours of Great Point (see **Green Space**).

🦞 **Trustees of Reservations** (508-921-1944; thetrustees.org) offers excellent 3½-hour natural history tours from mid-May to mid-October. Tours depart from the Nantucket Shipwreck & Lifesaving Museum, where a guided tour of the museum is followed by a tour of the Coskata-Coatue Wildlife Refuge. $$$$$; reservations strongly recommended.

Barrett's Tours (508-228-0174), 20 Federal Street, and **Nantucket Island Tours** (508-228-0334), 34 Straight Wharf, offer 90-minute narrated mini-bus tours May through October. $$$.

MEDIA The venerable *Inquirer and Mirror* (ack.net) has been published on Thursday since 1821 and is also available online.

The free weekly *Yesterday's Island* (yesterdaysisland.com) is useful for entertainment listings.

On-island, tune into **Channel 22** and **Channel 17** to learn more about the island.

WNAN 91.1 (508-548-9600; wgbh.org) is the NPR affiliate.

MORE WEBSITES Mahonabouttown.wordpress.com. You wanna know about this island, you gotta know about this "Mahon About Town" blog.

Artsnantucket.com. Look for their free color guide to the island's visual and performing arts.

Nantucketonline.com. Look for their glossy publication, *Only Nantucket,* which is also viewable online.

Nantucket.net. A complete guide.

PUBLIC RESTROOMS Visitor Services & Information Bureau at 25 Federal Street (open year-round); Children's Beach (see **Green Space**) and Straight Wharf (both open seasonally).

PUBLIC LIBRARY See **Atheneum** under "Quiet Time" on page 445.

ATM Short on greenbacks? In town, look for automatic teller machines at the Pacific National Bank (15 Sparks Avenue), Bank of America (15 Main Street), the Steamship Authority terminal (Steamboat Wharf), and Nantucket Bank (2 Orange Street).

EMERGENCIES **Nantucket Police Department** (508-228-1212; nantucket-ma.gov), 4 Fairgrounds Road, or call **911.**

Medical: **Nantucket Cottage Hospital** (508-825-8100; nantuckethospital.org), 57 Prospect Street. Open 24 hours.

Lyme disease. Ticks carry this disease, which has flulike symptoms and may result in death if left untreated. Immediately and carefully remove any ticks that may have migrated from dune grasses to your body. Better yet, wear long pants, tuck pants into socks, and wear long-sleeved shirts whenever possible when hiking. Avoid hiking in grassy and overgrown areas of dense brush.

✻ To See

ON THE HARBOR **The wharves** (from north to south). The Steamship Authority is now based at **Steamboat Wharf,** but from 1881 to 1917, steam trains, which met the early steam-powered ferries and transported passengers to Surfside and 'Sconset, originated here. **Old North Wharf** is home to privately owned summer cottages. **Straight Wharf,** originally built in 1723 by Richard Macy, is a center of activity. It was completely rebuilt in the 1960s (except for the Thomas Macy Warehouse; see below) as part of a preservation effort. The wharf is home to Hy-Line, a few T-shirt and touristy shops, restaurants, a gallery, a museum, a nice pavilion area, and charter boats and sailboats. Straight Wharf was so named because folks could cart things from here "straight" up Main Street. **Old South Wharf** houses art galleries, crafts shops, and clothing shops in quaint little one-room "shacks" (see **Selective Shopping**). **Commercial Wharf,** also known as Swain's Wharf, was built in the early 1800s by Zenas Coffin.

Thomas Macy Warehouse, Straight Wharf. Built after the Great Fire of 1846, when the wharves were completely destroyed and more than 400 houses burned, the warehouse stored supplies to outfit ships.

MAIN STREET

The lower three blocks of Main Street were paved in 1837 with cobblestones, purchased in Gloucester, which proved quite useful—they kept carts laden with whale oil from sinking into the sand and dirt as they were rolled from wharves to factories. After the Great Fire swept through town, Main Street was widened considerably to prevent

STRAIGHT WHARF KIM GRANT

future fires from jumping from house to house so rapidly. In the mid-1850s Henry and Charles Coffin planted dozens of elm trees along the street, but only a few have survived disease over the years. The former drinking fountain for horses, which today spills over with flowers, has been a landmark on Lower Main since it was moved here in the early 1900s.

Pacific Club, Main Street at South Water Street. This three-story Georgian brick building was built as a warehouse and countinghouse for shipowner William Rotch, owner of the *Beaver* and *Dartmouth*, two ships that took part in the Boston Tea Party. In 1789 it served as a US Customs House. In 1861 a group of retired whaling captains purchased the building for use as a private social club, where they swapped stories and played cribbage. Descendants of these original founders carried on the tradition of the elite club until the 1980s.

Pacific National Bank, 61 Main Street at Fair Street. This 1818, two-story, Federal-style brick building is one of only four to survive the Great Fire. It's no coincidence that the two important buildings anchoring Main Street are named "Pacific" for the fortunes reaped from the Pacific Ocean: This bank almost single-handedly financed the wealthy whaling industry. Step inside to see the handsome main room, original teller cages, and murals of the port and street scenes.

Thomas Macy House, 99 Main Street. Many think this is Nantucket's most attractive doorway, with its silver doorplate, porch railing that curves outward, and wooden fanwork. This Nantucket Historical Association (NHA) property is open to the public on special occasions.

"Three Bricks," 93, 95, and 97 Main Street. These identical Georgian mansions were built in 1836 for the three sons (all under the age of 27) of whaling-ship magnate Joseph Starbuck. Joseph retained the house titles to ensure that his sons would continue the family business. When the sons approached age 40 (firmly entrenched in the business), Joseph deeded the houses to them. One house remains in the Starbuck family; none is open to the public.

OLD SOUTH WHARF KIM GRANT

Hadwen House (508-228-1894; nha.org), 96 Main Street. Taken together, 94 Main (privately owned) and 96 Main are referred to architecturally as the "Two Greeks." Candle merchant William Hadwen married one of Joseph Starbuck's daughters and built the Greek Revival house at No. 96. Starbuck's two other daughters also ended up living across the street from their brothers—at 92 and 100 Main Street, creating a virtual Starbuck compound. Docents point out gas chandeliers, a circular staircase, Italian marble fireplaces, silver doorknobs, and period furnishings. Don't overlook the lovely historic garden in back. The "other" Greek (No. 94) was built in the mid-19th century for Mary G. Swain, Starbuck's niece; note the Corinthian capitals supposedly modeled after the Athenian Temple of the Winds. This is an NHA property (see *Guidance* for hours and fees).

Henry Coffin House and **Charles Coffin House**, 75 and 78 Main Street. The Coffin brothers inherited their fortunes from their father's candle-making and whaling enterprises and general mercantile business. They built their houses across the street from each other, using the same carpenters and masons. Charles was a Quaker, and his Greek Revival house (No. 78) has a simple roof walk and modest brown trim. Henry's late-Federal-style house (No. 75) has fancy trim around the front door and a cupola. Neither is open to the public.

John Wendell Barrett House, 72 Main Street. This elegant Greek Revival house features a front porch with Ionic columns and a raised basement. Barrett was the president of the Pacific National Bank and a wealthy whale oil merchant, but the house is best known for another reason. During the Great Fire, Barrett's wife, Lydia, refused to leave the front porch. Firefighters wanted to blow up the house in order to deprive the fire of fuel. Luckily for her, the winds shifted and further confrontation was averted. Not open to the public.

NORTH OF MAIN STREET

✳ **Whaling Museum** (508-228-1894; nha.org), 13 Broad Street. This 1846 brick building, another NHA property (see *Guidance* for hours), is a must-see on even the shortest

ONE OF "THREE BRICKS" KIM GRANT

itinerary. It began life as Richard Mitchell's spermaceti candle factory, and as such, it now tells the story of the candle factory and preserves Nantucket's whaling history. Spermaceti, by the way, is a substance found in the cavity of a sperm whale's head; it once was a great source of lamp and machine oil. During the restoration of the original candle factory in 2004, the NHA discovered an original beam press and the base of the factory triworks. (It's the only one in the world still in its original location.) So, the story the museum can tell grows even richer. You can also see the lens from the Sankaty Head Lighthouse, as well as an entire exhibit about the *Essex* whaling ship. **Gosnell Hall** houses a 46-foot sperm whale skeleton and a fully rigged whale boat, which will help you envision the treacherous "Nantucket sleigh ride." When the small boat harpooned a mammoth whale and remained connected by a rope, the boat was dragged through the waves until the whale tired. **Peter Foulger Gallery** is named for one of the island's first settlers, who acted as an interpreter when the settlers purchased the island from the local American Indians in 1659. Peter's daughter, Abiah, was Ben Franklin's mother. $$; History Tickets with guided walking tours are additional. Combo pass for the museum, Hadwen

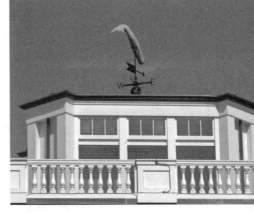

WHALING MUSEUM KIM GRANT

MAIN STREET KIM GRANT

House, the Oldest House, the Old Mill, and the Quaker Meeting House is $$$.

Centre Street was referred to as Petticoat Row during the whaling era, when men went out to sea and women were left to run the shops and businesses. It's still chock-full of fine shops.

First Congregational Church Tower (508-228-0950; nantucketfcc.org), 62 Centre Street. Church open mid-May to mid-October; tower open mid-June to mid-October. This church is known for its 120-foot steeple, from which there are 360-degree panoramic views of the island and ocean. The climb to the top is 94 steps—not that I've counted or anything. On a clear day you can see from Eel Point to Great Point (see **Green Space**) and all the moors in between. Serious photographers shouldn't get too excited, though, because they'll have to shoot through dirty storm windows.

The current steeple was built in 1968; the previous one was dismantled in 1849, when it was deemed too shaky to withstand storms. The church was built with whaling money at the industry's apex in 1834. Note the things money could buy: a 600-pound brass chandelier and trompe l'oeil walls. The rear wing of the church contains the simple vestry, the oldest church building on the island (circa 1720). Donation suggested for climbing the steeple $.

🦈 **Oldest House** (508-228-1894; nha .org), 16 Sunset Hill Lane. Also known as the **Jethro Coffin House**, this 1686 home was built as a wedding present for Jethro Coffin and Mary Gardner by their parents. Peter Coffin cut and shipped timbers from his land in Exeter, New Hampshire, for the house. The marriage joined two prominent island families—the Coffins were "original purchasers," while the Gardners were "half-share men." Features include small, diamond-shaped, leaded windows, sparse period furnishings, and a huge central chimney decorated with an upside-down horseshoe. When lightning struck the house in 1987, the Nantucket Historical Association decided it was time to restore it. To provide visitors with a better understanding of what everyday

FIRST CONGREGATIONAL CHURCH TOWER KIM GRANT

Nantucket Atheneum (508-228-1110; nantucketatheneum.org), 1 India Street. This fine Greek Revival building with Ionic columns was designed by Frederick Coleman, who designed the "Two Greeks" (see Hadwen House under To See). When the library and all its contents were lost in the Great Fire of 1846, donations poured in from around the country and a new building replaced it within six months. The Great Hall on the second floor has hosted such distinguished orators as Frederick Douglass, Daniel Webster, Horace Greeley, Henry David Thoreau, Ralph Waldo Emerson, and John James Audubon. (The hall seats about 100 people; there are numerous free readings and lectures here.) Maria Mitchell (see "Homage to a Local 19th-Century Hero" on page 448) was the first librarian. Since then there have been, amazingly, only seven other librarians in its long history. In addition to comfortable reading rooms on both floors, the Atheneum has an excellent children's wing and a nice garden out back. Some of the more than 50,000 volumes include town newspapers dating from 1816, early New England genealogy, and ships' logs. Portraits of whaling captains grace the space, while display cases are filled with scrimshaw and other historical artifacts. This is one of the island's most special places. It's a quiet refuge from the masses in the height of summer, as well as a delightful place to spend a rainy day. Call for information about special events and story hours. ❄ 🖉 ⊤

life was like three centuries ago, a kitchen garden and a small orchard of old-variety apple trees was planted in 2007.

Brant Point Lighthouse, off Easton Street. In 1746 the island's first "lighthouse" (and the country's second oldest, after Boston Light) guarded the harbor's northern entrance. It was rather primitive, consisting of a lantern hung on rope between two poles. The lighthouse standing today is small in size but large in symbolism. Folklore

BRANT POINT LIGHTHOUSE KIM GRANT

and tradition suggest that throwing two pennies overboard as you round the point at the lighthouse ensures your return. Many throw two pennies, and many return. Don't pass up the chance to catch a sunset from here; it's the reason you came to Nantucket in the first place.

NEAR OR OFF UPPER MAIN STREET

Quaker Meeting House (508-228-1894; nha.org), 7 Fair Street. Open late April to mid-October. This small, simple building with wooden benches and 12-over-12 windows began as a Friends school in 1838. NHA property (see *Guidance* for hours and fees).

❋ **Nantucket Historical Association Research Library** (508-228-1894, ext. 4; nha .org), 7 Fair Street. This library contains Edouard A. Stackpole's collection of manuscripts, photographs, ships' logs, and other items. $.

St. Paul's Episcopal Church (508-228-0916; stpaulschurchnantucket.org), 20 Fair Street. Stop in to admire this granite church's Tiffany windows.

❋ **Unitarian Universalist Church** (508-228-5466; unitarianchurchnantucket.org), 11 Orange Street. Open July and August, or by appointment during the rest of the year. This 1809 church, also called **South Church**, is known for its tall spire (quite visible at sea and a distinct part of the Nantucket "skyline"); a wonderfully illusory trompe l'oeil golden dome; and a mahogany and ivory 1831 Goodrich organ. Orange Street was once home to more than 100 whaling captains, and for years a town crier watched for ships (and fires) from this tower.

🐚 **The Coffin School** (508-228-2505; eganmaritime.org), 4 Winter Street, one block off Main Street. Open for seminars and presentations only. The school was founded in 1827 by Adm. Sir Isaac Coffin, English baronet and a descendant of Tristram Coffin, one of the island's first settlers. It was established to provide a "good English education" for Coffin descendants. (In the early 19th century, more than half of Nantucket's children were Coffin descendants.) The impressive brick Greek Revival building now serves as home for the **Egan Maritime Institute**, displaying special exhibits related to Nantucket history. A fine collection of 19th-century paintings portraying significant Nantucket events is featured, including works by Elizabeth R. Coffin, a student of Thomas Eakins. Historical lectures on the school and maritime subjects are given year-round. Admission $; price also includes admission to the Nantucket Shipwreck and Lifesaving Museum (see *Around the Island*).

See also **Lightship Basket Museum** under "Lightship Baskets" on page 477.

BEYOND UPPER MAIN STREET

Fire Hose Cart House (508-228-1894; nha.org), 8 Gardner Street. This small 1886 neighborhood fire station is the only one of its kind remaining on-island. As you can imagine, lots of stations were built after the Great Fire. On display are leather buckets and an old hand pumper used more than a century ago. NHA property (see *Guidance* for hours); self-guided.

The Old Gaol (508-228-1894; nha.org), 15R Vestal Street. This 1806 penal institution, built of logs bolted together with iron, was used until 1933. It had only four cells. The first incarcerated felon escaped (a 15-year-old climbed out the chimney), but others weren't so lucky. Well, perhaps they were—it's said that the last prisoners got to sleep at home rather than on the planks that served as beds. NHA property (see *Guidance* for hours); self-guided.

Old Mill (508-228-1894; nha.org), 50 Prospect Street. Reputed to be made with salvaged wood, this 1746 Dutch-style windmill has canvas sails and a granite stone that still grinds corn in summer. A reminder of when the island's principal activity was farming, this windmill is the only remaining of the four originals. (It's in its original location, too.) NHA property; tours offered. (See *Guidance* for hours and fees.)

African Meeting House (508-228-9833; afroammuseum.org), 29 York Street. Open June through October. Built as a church and a schoolhouse in the 1820s, when Black children were barred from public school, this house is thought to be the second oldest such building in the country. Boston's Museum of African American History presents cultural programming and interpretive exhibits on the history of African Americans on Nantucket. It also publishes a very good pamphlet with a walking tour of the island's Black heritage sites. The Florence Higginbotham House (at Pleasant Street), also at the center of the thriving 19th-century African American community on the island, has recently been acquired. The pre-Revolutionary War building has a fascinating history. Thanks to federal funding, the meetinghouse is being restored to its 19th-century state. $.

Moor's End, 19 Pleasant Street. This large 1830s Georgian house—the first island house made with brick—belonged to Jared Coffin. Although today it's among the island's finest, Mrs. Coffin was not satisfied with its location. She wanted to be closer to town, so Jared built another at 29 Broad Street (see **Jared Coffin House** under **Lodging**). A beautiful garden lies behind the tall brick wall, but unfortunately for us, like the house, it's private.

AROUND THE ISLAND

Great Point Light, Great Point, is accessible by four-wheel-drive vehicle, by boat, or by a difficult 5-mile (one-way) trek through soft sand. A 70-foot stone structure guarded the island's northeastern tip for 166 years, until a ferocious storm destroyed it in 1984. This new one was built to withstand 20-foot waves and 240 mph winds.

Madaket. When Thomas Macy landed here in 1659, he found poor soil and didn't stay long. Today there is a large summer community and many rental houses. On the

NANTUCKET SHIPWRECK & LIGHTSAVING MUSEUM KIM GRANT

HOMAGE TO A LOCAL 19TH-CENTURY HERO

Maria Mitchell Association (MMA) (508-228-9198; mariamitchell.org), 4 Vestal Street. Founded in 1902, the association owns six properties that celebrate the life and continue the work of Maria (pronounced *mar-EYE-a*) Mitchell, born on-island August 1, 1818. At age 13, she helped whaling captains set their navigational devices with the aid of astronomical projections. At 18, she became the librarian at the Atheneum, where she served for the next 20 years. At 29, Mitchell was the first woman to discover a comet (which was dubbed Mitchell's comet)—from atop the Pacific National Bank, where her father (bank president and an amateur astronomer) had set up an observatory. She was also the first woman admitted to the American Academy of Arts and Sciences and the first woman college professor of astronomy. (She taught at Vassar from 1865 until her death in 1888.) ❄ ✒

The association hosts a number of children's programs that foster an appreciation of the connection between science and "beauty and poetry." Also, look for postings of special lectures and walks sponsored by the group; I've never been to one that was less than excellent. And, in July 2009, the association received the ultimate seal of approval when President Obama announced that the Maria Mitchell Association had been selected to receive the Presidential Award for Excellence in Science, Mathematics, and Engineering Mentoring.

A combination ticket to the birthplace, observatory, and museum (available at any of the properties) costs $$. Tickets may also be purchased separately for the aquarium. To whet your appetite, enjoy free tours of the Vestal Street campus most days during the season, meeting in the Science Library Courtyard.

Maria Mitchell Science Library (508-228-2896; mariamitchell.org), 2 Vestal Street. This library, which has a children's section, houses 19th-century science books, current scientific periodicals, Maria's own papers, and natural history and astronomy books. Maria's father taught navigation by the stars in this former schoolhouse. Appointments available for research. ❄ ✒

western coast, Madaket is a great place to enjoy a sunset, do some bluefishing, or get a boat repaired in the boatyard. The picturesque creek is best viewed from the little bridge to the right of the main road.

✒ ⌂ **Nantucket Shipwreck & Lifesaving Museum** (508-228-1885; eganmaritime.org), 158 Polpis Road on Folger's Marsh. Open late May to mid-October. This building replicates the original 1874 Surfside Lifesaving Service station that survives today as the Nantucket Hostel (see **Lodging**). Instead of being at water's edge, however, it's scenically situated on a salt marsh—perfect for a picnic. Dedicated to humanity's dramatic efforts against the relentless sea—treacherous shoals and inclement weather led to more than 700 shipwrecks in the surrounding waters of Nantucket—this museum houses equipment used for the daring rescues of sailors stranded offshore in their sinking boats. Treasures include one of only three Massachusetts Humane Society lifesaving surfboats and the only surviving beachcart still used for demonstration drills. You'll also find photographs, accounts of rescues, Nantucket's three Fresnel lighthouse lenses, and artifacts from the *Andrea Doria*, which sank off Nantucket almost half a century ago. $.

❄ To Do

BIRD-WATCHING **Maria Mitchell Association** (508-228-9198; mmo.org), 1 Vestal Street, offers birding field trips June to early September. $$; binoculars available for

Maria Mitchell Birthplace (508-228-2896 in summer, 508-228-9219 rest of year; maria mitchell.org), 1 Vestal Street. Open mid-June to mid-October. Built in 1790, Mitchell's birthplace contains family memorabilia and the telescope she used to spot her comet. Tour the house and check out the island's only public roof walk. See above for ticket.

Maria Mitchell Vestal Street Observatory (508-228-9273; mariamitchell.org), 3 Vestal Street. Call for tour times.

Natural Science Museum (508-228-0898; mariamitchell.org), Hinchman House, 7 Milk Street. Open late May to mid-October. See displays of Nantucket's natural history and visit the live animal room to meet frogs, turtles, snakes, spiders, insects, fish, and other island creatures. There's also a popular, well-stocked museum shop; a new high-tech scavenger hunt; and kids can learn how to (theoretically) save Nantucket Harbor with a Jenga-style game and learn more about wider ecological issues. 🐾

Loines Observatory (508-228-9273; mariamitchell.org), 59 Milk Street Extension. Open June through December (see website for dates and times, and call to confirm weather conditions), when lectures and telescope viewings are held. Climb a ladder to the eyepiece of a fine old telescope and sample the sights of the distant heavens. You'll also have the opportunity to see the MMA's new 24-inch research telescope. $$. ❄

Maria Mitchell Aquarium & Museum Shop (508-228-5387; mariamitchell.org), 28 Washington Street. Open early June through August. Once a railroad station ticket office for the Nantucket Railroad, the aquarium has grown into a much-loved island resource. Visitors have the opportunity to learn about Nantucket's marine ecology through firsthand experience with many of the organisms that inhabit our coastal areas. The expanded aquarium complex contains 20 saltwater tanks in three buildings, an orientation area for dry exhibits and small group instruction, and two large "touch tanks" for curious hands. Visitors might count the eyes of a scallop, watch a channeled whelk feeding on a mollusk, or see baby squid hatching. Call about the popular marine ecology walks, whale watches, and seal cruises. $; see combo ticket details above. 🐾

hire. Some people think that Nantucket offers the best wintertime bird-watching on the East Coast. I wouldn't argue.

See also **Eco Guides** under *Outdoor Adventure*.

BOAT EXCURSIONS & RENTALS **Endeavor** (508-228-5585; endeavorsailing.com), Slip 1015, Straight Wharf. May through October. Capt. Jim Genthner and his wife, Sue, operate a 31-foot Friendship sloop that departs on at least three daily 90-minute harbor tours and a sunset cruise. Custom sails may include pirating for children and an on-board fiddler or storyteller. $$$$+.

Island Boat Rentals (508-325-1001; boatnantucket.com), Straight Wharf, Slip 1001. You don't have to be macho to handle one of these little runabouts or powerboats that can take you across the harbor to Coatue, where you can sunbathe and picnic in relative quiet. Leave in the morning when there is less wind. Rentals start at $385.

🛶 **Nantucket Island Community Sailing** (508-228-6600; nantucketcommunity sailing.org), Jetties Beach. Rents Windsurfers, Sunfish, kayaks, and large sailboats, and it holds youth, sailboard, sailing, and racing classes. For a really unique thing to do, take a class in how to sail a replica 19th-century whaleboat. Mid-June to early September.

COOKOUTS Contact the **Fire Department** (508-228-2324), 131 Pleasant Street, for the requisite (nominally-priced) permits for charcoal cookouts.

KIM GRANT

FISHING & SHELLFISHING Permits for digging clams, mussels, and quahogs are obtained from the Marine Department and shellfish warden (508-228-7261), 34 Washington Street. Or try online (mass.gov). Scalloping season opens October 1, after which you'll see fishermen in the harbor and off nearby shoals of Tuckernuck Island; local scallops harvested from mid-October through March are delicious.

Try your luck freshwater fishing at **Long Pond** (see **Green Space**). Nantucket blues, which run in schools from May to October, are caught from the southern shore. Fishing isn't as good in July and August when the waters are warmer, but if that's the only time you're here, toss out a line anyway. No fishing licenses are needed for Nantucket.

Bill Fisher Tackle (508-228-2261; billfishertackle.com), 127 Orange Street, rents a full line of equipment, supplies daily fishing reports, and provides guide service.

Most charter boats in search of striped bass and bluefish are located on Straight Wharf, including *Herbert T* (508-228-6655; fishnantucket.net), Slip 14, and *Just Do It Too* (508-228-7448; justdoittoo.com), Slip 13.

KIM GRANT

FITNESS CLUB ❋ **Nantucket Health Club** (508-228-4750; nantuckethealthclub .com), 10 Young's Way. A full array of machines, free weights, classes, and personalized training sessions.

FOR FAMILIES ⚓ **Strong Wings Summer Camp** (508-228-1769; strongwings .org), late June to late August. Choose from weekly action-filled day and half-day camps for kids. These might include sea kayaking, rock climbing, snorkeling, biking, ghost stories, crafts, and nature exploration.

❋ ⚓ **Nantucket Babysitters Service** (508-228-4970; nantucketbabysitters.com) provides parents a respite. Ronnie Sullivan-Moran assesses your needs, matches

BICYCLING & RENTALS

Excellent paved, two-way bicycle paths lead to most major "destinations." If you're riding on the street, ride in the direction of traffic or you'll be fined. Or walk your bike. ✐
   Madaket Bike Path begins on Upper Main Street. This 6-mile (one-way) road takes you to the western end of Nantucket in 45 minutes. Although the route is a bit hilly and winding, it's beautiful. There are rest areas along the way, a water fountain at the halfway point, picnic tables at Long Pond (see Green Space), and usually elegant swans, too.
   Dionis Bike Path is a 1-mile spur trail off the Madaket Bike Path that runs to Dionis Beach. Getting to the beach has never been easier.
   'Sconset (or Milestone) Bike Path begins at the rotary east of the historic district. This 6.5-mile (one-way) route with slight inclines parallels Milestone Road; it takes about an hour to get to 'Sconset. (Visually, the ride is a bit dull.) There's a water fountain at the rotary.
   Surfside Bike Path. Take Main Street to Pleasant Street, then continue straight and bear right onto Atlantic Avenue to Surfside Road. This flat 2.5-mile (one-way) path is very popular in summer; it takes about 20 minutes to get to the beach.
   Polpis Road Path. The loop from the 'Sconset Bike Path to Polpis Road and back to town is about 16.5 miles. It's definitely worth the detour, especially in springtime, when it's lined with thousands of daffodils.
   Cliff Road Bike Path begins on Cliff Road from North Water Street. This 2.5-mile, slightly hilly road passes large summer homes.
   Rental Shops. With more than 2,500 rental bikes on-island, companies offer competitive rates. Average daily adult prices: $$$; kid's bikes, trailers, zipper strollers, and trail-a-bikes, too. Inquire about discounts for family rentals. The following shops rent bicycles: Young's Bicycle Shop (508-228-1151; youngsbicycleshop.com), 6 Broad Street, Steamboat Wharf, one of the best in town, a third-generation, family-owned bike shop since 1931); Nantucket Bike Shop (508-228-1999; nantucketbikeshop.com), 4 Broad Street, Steamboat Wharf; and Cook's Cycles (508-228-0800; cookscyclesnantucket.com), 6 South Beach. Young's has the longest season, but Cook's is often a bit less expensive.
   See also Eco Guides under *Outdoor Adventure*.

a sitter to your kids (all ages), and then sends the sitter to wherever you're staying. The company also offers grocery shopping services, event planning, and meal preparation assistance.

GOLF **Siasconset Golf Club** (508-257-6596), 260 Milestone Road. Open late May to mid-October. This nine-hole public course, encircled by conservation land, dates to 1894.
   ❋ **Miacomet Golf Course** (508-325-0333; miacometgolf.com), 12 West Miacomet Road. This flat, 18-hole course is the island's only 18-hole public golf facility. It's owned by the Land Bank and has views of Miacomet Pond, heathland, and the coastline.
   Sankaty Head Golf Club (508-257-6655; 508-257-6629; sankatyheadgc.com), 100 Polpis Road, 'Sconset. Although this links-style, 18-hole course is private, the public may play off-season from October to May. There are magnificent lighthouse views. This course operates one of the last remaining caddy camps in the United States (for boys), and it has done so since the early 1930s.
   Nantucket Golf Club (508-257-8500; nantucketgolfclub.org), 250 Milestone Road (there's no sign, nor is entry allowed for tourists). One of the most exclusive clubs anywhere. Many members, like gazillionaire Bill Gates, do not own property on-island, but rather jet in, play golf, and jet out. Memberships cost hundreds of thousands of dollars,

KIM GRANT

plus annual dues. The membership list is closely guarded, of course, but it has its share from the Forbes 400 Wealthiest Americans list. As for the golf, the par-72, links-style course rolls with the naturally undulating landscape, within sight of Sankaty Head Light, on the moors with scrub oak and pitch pine. Generally appreciated by island conservationists, who realize that it could have been developed in less favorable ways, the 350-acre course was designed by Rees Jones.

IN-LINE SKATING Summertime skating is prohibited in town. You can skate on bike paths and at the skateboarding park at Jetties Beach; helmets and pads are required.

OUTDOOR ADVENTURE ❋ ✇ **Strong Wings Eco Guides** (508-228-1769; strongwings .org). Casual, customized adventure instruction and guided group trips, for novices and experts, in birding, climbing, mountain biking, sea kayaking, and natural history. After settling on a trip, price, and meeting time with them, be absolutely sure that you confirm and reconfirm your trip. There is also a large youth organization geared toward year-rounders, but vacationing kids can participate, too.

SCUBA DIVING ❋ **The Sunken Ship** (508-228-9226; sunkenship.com), 12 Broad Street. Perhaps because the *Andrea Doria* sank off Nantucket's treacherous shoals in July 1956, the island attracts Atlantic Ocean divers. This full-service dive shop has the market cornered with charters, lessons, rentals, and even fishing referrals.

SEAL CRUISES ❋ **Shearwater Excursions** (508-228-7037; shearwaterexcursions .com), Straight Wharf, Slip 1011. Daily departures, weather permitting, to see lounging seals on the outer island of Muskeget. Tours are 2½ hours. $$$$$+.

SPECIAL PROGRAMS ❋ ✇ **Nantucket Island School of Design and the Arts** (508-228-9248; nisda.org), 23 Wauwinet Road. Founded in 1973, NISDA presents an extraordinary range of classes and lectures for adults and kids. Summerlong, weeklong, or daylong classes might include drawing, design, textile, folk art, floorcloth painting, puppet making, garden tours, yoga, modern dance, clay and sculpture, painting, and photography. Affiliated with Massachusetts College of Art in Boston, the school offers college graduate and undergraduate summer sessions in a converted dairy barn. Individuals attending classes may rent the school's studios and one-bedroom cottages on the harbor.

✳ ✍ **Artist's Association of Nantucket** (508-228-0722; nantucketarts.org), One Gardner Perry Lane. Offering seasonal workshops and classes in a variety of disciplines for adults and children, the association also maintains a fine art library on Gardner Perry Lane and a gallery at 19 Washington Street (see **Selective Shopping**).

✳ ✍ **Nantucket Community School** (508-228-7285, ext. 1571; nantucketcommu nityschool.org), 10 Surfside Road. Offers adult-education classes and programs and camps for kids.

SURFING **Force 5 Watersports** (508-228-0700), 6 Union Street, a retail surf shop with a knowledgeable staff, is a good source of information, too. Surfing is best on the southern beaches. Open May through December.

SWIMMING POOL ✳ ✍ **Nantucket Community Pool** (508-228-7285, ext. 1578; nan tucketcommunityschool.org), Atlantic and Surfside Avenues. An Olympic-sized pool at the Nantucket High School is open for swimming and offers lessons—both for a fee.

TENNIS Free, public courts are open at **Jetties Beach** (see **Green Space**) from early September to mid-June; from mid-June to late August there is a fee. Sign up at the **Parks and Recreation Building** (508-228-7213), North Beach Street, for one of six courts. Clinics and lessons are offered for adults and children.

WINE, BEER & SPIRITS ✳ **Nantucket Vineyard, Cisco Brewers, and Triple Eight Distillery** (508-325-5929; ciscobrewers.com), 5 Bartlett Farm Road, about 2.5 miles south of town off Hummock Pond Road. Imagine a warm summer afternoon, sitting at an outdoor café in the interior of the island, surrounded by Bartlett farmland, sipping a frosty beer or icy vodka. Well, imagine no longer: it's a fun diversion. Come to sample fresh, traditionally brewed ales, porters, stouts, and seasonal concoctions like Celebration Libation. Look for the excellent Cisco beer at island restaurants and package stores. It's more satisfying (and cheaper) than most bottles of restaurant wine. And look for the clean tastes of 888 vodkas, flavored with vanilla, cranberry, and orange. (In tastings, the pure 888 outscored Ketel One.) I didn't get a chance to sample their boutique Hurricane Rum, Gale Force Gin, or Nor'Easter Bourbon (hey, someone has to be clear-eyed for long research days!), but I encourage you to sip to your heart's content. As for wine, because grapes don't grow particularly well on Nantucket, this vineyard imports grapes for its wines.

✳ Green Space

🐚 **Maria Mitchell Association** (508-228-9198; mmo.org) leads informative field trips around the island (see **To See**). $$.

Coskata-Coatue Wildlife Refuge, at the end of Wauwinet Road, accessible only by four-wheel-drive vehicle and on foot. The narrow strip of very soft sand leading to Great Point is about 5 miles long. Note the "haulover," which separates the head of the harbor from the Atlantic Ocean. This stretch of sand is so narrow that fishermen would haul their boats across it instead of going all the way around the tip of Great Point.

'SCONSET

This charming village on the eastern shore is the island's only real "destination," 7 miles from town. (Well, for the adventuresome, Great Point—see Green Space—is the other "destination.") The village is renowned for its tiny rose-covered cottages, all a few feet from one another. Some of the oldest are clustered on Broadway, Centre, and Shell Streets. You won't have any problem finding them, given that the town consists of only a post office, a liquor store, a market, and a few restaurants. Of course, 'Sconset also has its share of grand summer homes—along Ocean Avenue and Sankaty and Baxter Roads (on the way to Sankaty Head Lighthouse; see below). Recently, the combination of severe winter storms and the absence of offshore shoals to break incoming waves has created extreme beach erosion. Beachfront homes have been moved after several were engulfed by the sea.

TELLING TIME WITH THE SUNDIAL IN 'SCONSET KIM GRANT

Siasconset, which means "land of many bones," was probably named after a right whale was found on the beach. The 17th-century village was settled by and used as a base for fishermen in search of cod and whales. When wives began to join their husbands here in summer, the one-room shanties were expanded with additions called warts. (Perhaps early summer visitors wanted to escape the oil refineries in town, too.) When the narrow-gauge railway was built in 1884, it brought vacationing New York City actors who established a thriving actors' colony. Today 200 hardy souls live here year-round.

KIM GRANT

During severe storms, the ocean breaks through the haulover, effectively creating an island. (Sand is eventually redeposited by the currents.) The spit of sand known as Coatue is a series of concave bays that reaches all the way to the mouth of Nantucket Harbor.

There's a wealth of things to do in this pristine preserve: birding, surf casting, shellfishing, sunbathing, picnicking, and walking. Because the riptides are dangerous, especially near the Great Point Lighthouse (see **To See**), swimming is not recommended. These three adjacent wildlife areas, totaling more than 1,100 acres, are owned by different organizations, but that doesn't impact visitors. The Conservation Foundation owns both Coatue and the haulover. But the world's oldest land trust, the Trustees of Reservations, also manages part of the land. Ara's Tours and the Trustees

A few "sites" in 'Sconset include the 'Sconset Pump, an old wooden water pump dug in 1776, and the 'Sconset Union Chapel, the only place of worship in town. Despite its name, the Siasconset Casino, built in 1899 as a private tennis club, has never been used for gambling. Turn-of-the-20th-century actors used it for summer theater; movies are now shown in summer (see Entertainment).

Sankaty Head Light, 'Sconset. Partially solar powered, this red-and-white-striped light stands on a 90-foot-high bluff about 300 feet from the shoreline—it was relocated in 2007, thanks to community action and should be safe for the foreseeable future. Its light is visible 24 miles out to sea.

KIM GRANT

Nantucket is renowned for the amount of open, protected land on the island. In fact, thanks to the efforts of various conservation groups, about half the island is protected from development. Two organizations deserve much of the credit: Nantucket Conservation Foundation (508-228-2884; nantucketconservation. org), 118 Cliff Road; and the Nantucket Land Bank (508-228-7240; nantucketlandbank.org), 22 Broad Street. The Conservation Foundation was established in 1963 to manage open land— wetlands, moors, and grasslands. It's a private, nonprofit organization that's supported by membership contributions. Because the foundation is constantly acquiring land, call for a map of its current properties, published yearly; free. The Land Bank was created by an act of the state legislature in 1983, granting permission to assess a 2 percent tax for all real estate and land transactions. With the tax receipts, property is purchased and kept as conservation land.

KIM GRANT

of Reservations offer tours of Great Point; see *Getting Around* for tours and for information on getting your own four-wheel-drive permits.

Eel Point, off Eel Point Road from the Madaket Bike Path (see **To Do**), about 6 miles from town. Leave your car or bicycle at the sign that reads 40th Pole Beach and walk the last ½ mile to the beach. There aren't any facilities, just unspoiled nature, good birding, surf-fishing, and a shallow sandbar. Portions of this beach are often closed to protect nesting shorebirds. For in-depth information, pick up a map and self-guided tour from the **Nantucket Conservation Foundation** (see *Getting Around* in Nantucket).

Sanford Farm, **Ram Pasture**, and **the Woods**, off Madaket Road. These 700-plus acres of wetlands, grasslands, and forest are owned and managed by the Conservation

THE MOORS KIM GRANTT

Foundation and the Land Bank. Ram Pasture and the Woods were one of the foundation's first purchases (for $625,000) in 1971. Fourteen years later, Sanford Farm was purchased for $4.4 million from Mrs. Anne Sanford's estate. A 6.5-mile (round-trip) walking and biking trail goes past Hummock Pond to the ocean, affording great views of heathlands along the way. Interpretive markers identify natural and historic sites. There is also a popular 45-minute (1.6-mile) loop trail as well as the Barn Trail (1½ hours, 3 miles), which affords beautiful expansive views of the island's southern coastline.

Milestone Bog, off Milestone Road on a dirt road to the north, about 5 miles from town. When cranberries were first harvested here in 1857, there were 220 acres of bogs. Today, because of depressed prices and a worldwide cranberry glut, very few bogs are still harvested. The land was donated to the Conservation Foundation in 1968. It's not open to the public, but it's interesting to know it's here.

Windswept Cranberry Bog, off Polpis Road to the south. This 40-acre bog is also completely owned by the Conservation Foundation.

BEACHES Nantucket is ringed by 50 miles of sandy shore, much of which is publicly accessible. In general, beaches on the south and east have rough surf and undertow; western and northern beaches have warmer, calmer waters. There is limited parking at most beaches; NRTA (508-228-7025) provides a special beach bus to Jetties Beach and Surfside Beach from mid-June to early September, and regular buses to Madaket and 'Sconset Beaches.

NORTHERN BEACHES

♪ **Children's Beach**, off South Beach Street on the harbor. A few minutes' walk from Steamboat Wharf, this is a great place for children (hence its name). Facilities include a lifeguard, restrooms, a bathhouse, a playground, food, picnic tables, a bandstand, and a grassy play area.

Brant Point, off Easton Street. A 15-minute walk from town and overlooking the entrance to the harbor, this scenic stretch is great for boat-watching and surf-fishing. Swimming conditions aren't great: there's a strong current and a beach that drops off suddenly.

Jetties, off Bathing Beach Road from North Beach Road. Shuttle buses run to this popular beach—otherwise it's a 20-minute walk. (There is also a fairly large parking lot with lots of bike racks.) This is a great place for families because of the facilities (restrooms, lifeguards, showers, changing rooms, a snack bar, chairs for rent) and the activities (volleyball, tennis, swings, concerts, a playground, an assortment of sailboats and kayaks). The July Fourth fireworks celebration is held here. Look for the skateboarding park, for which helmets and pads are required.

Francis Street Beach, a 5-minute walk from Main Street at Washington and Francis Streets. This harbor beach is calm. There are kayak rentals, portable restrooms, and a small jungle gym.

Dionis, off Eel Point Road from the Madaket and Dionis bike paths (see **To Do**). Nantucket's only beach with dunes, Dionis is about 3 miles from town. The beach starts out narrow but becomes more expansive (and less populated) as you walk farther east or west. Facilities include a bathhouse.

SOUTHERN BEACHES

Surfside, off Surfside Road; large parking lot. Three miles from town and accessible by shuttle bus, this wide beach is popular with college students and families with older kids because of its proximity to town and its moderate-to-heavy surf. Kite flying, surf casting, and picnicking are popular. Facilities include restrooms, lifeguards, showers, and a snack bar.

Nobadeer, east of Surfside, near the airport and about 4 miles from town. There are no facilities at Nobadeer, but there is plenty of surf.

Madaket, at the end of the scenic Madaket Bike Path (see **To Do**). About 5 miles west of town (served by shuttle bus), Madaket is perhaps the most popular place to watch

CHILDREN'S BEACH KIM GRANT

sunsets. This long beach has heavy surf and strong currents; there are lifeguards, portable restrooms, and very little parking.

 Cisco, off Hummock Pond Road from Milk Street. About 4 miles from town, this long beach is popular with surfers. There are lifeguards and surfing lessons for kids, but very little parking.

"Nude Beach," an unofficial beach, certainly, is unofficially located between Miacomet and Cisco.

EASTERN BEACHES

'Sconset a.k.a. **Codfish Park**, at the end of the 'Sconset Bike Path; turn right at the rotary. About 7 miles from town and accessible by shuttle bus, this long, narrow beach takes a pounding by heavy surf. Seaweed lines the beach when the surf whips up. Facilities include lifeguards, a playground, and very limited parking.

PONDS **Long Pond**. Take Madaket Road from town and, when you reach the Hither Creek sign, turn left onto a dirt road. This 64-acre Land Bank property is great for birding. A mile-long path around the pond passes meadows and a cranberry bog.

Miacomet Pond, Miacomet Avenue (which turns into a dirt road), off Surfside Road. This long, narrow, freshwater pond next to the ocean has a sandy shore and is surrounded by grasses and heath. This Land Bank property is a pleasant place for a picnic, and the swans and ducks make it more so.

Sesachacha Pond. Take Polpis Road to Quidnet Road. A narrow barrier beach separates the pond and ocean. There's a nice view of the Sankaty Head Lighthouse from here. Makes a nice afternoon with the kids.

WALKS The Moors and Altar Rock, off Polpis Road, to the south, on an unmarked dirt road. When you want to get away from the summertime masses, head to the moors (preferably at dawn or dusk, when they're most magical). From Altar Rock, the third-highest point on the island (rising a whopping 103 feet above sea level), there are expansive views of lowland heath, bogs, and moors. It's stunning in autumn. The moors are also crisscrossed with trails and deeply rutted dirt roads.

Lily Pond Park, North Liberty Street. This 6-acre Land Bank property supports lots of wildlife and plant life, but the trail is often muddy. You may find wild blackberries, grapes, or blueberries.

✳ Lodging

Consider making summertime reservations in February. No kidding. Also keep in mind that the historic district, while convenient, has its share of foot traffic (and boisterous socializers) late into the evening and that houses are also very close together. A 10-minute walk from Straight Wharf will put you in quieter surroundings. Most lodgings require a 2- or 3-night minimum stay in-season; I indicate only minimum-night-stay policies that go beyond that norm.

I also only indicate high season rates (and an abstract range at that!). You can also reasonably deduce that places are relatively lower, relative to one another, off-season.

Much to my chagrin, many places charge more for weekends than weekdays. Lastly, most places are not appropriate for small children. More and more folks are renting houses rather than staying in guest houses. Which means that, even though the number of bed-and-breakfast rooms dwindles every year, it's worth calling at the last minute to check on availability—even at the primo places.

IN A CLASS BY THEMSELVES

ON THE OUTSKIRTS OF TOWN

♫ **Cliffside Beach Club** (508-228-0618; cliffsidebeach.com), 46 Jefferson Avenue. Open late May to mid-October. "Stylish simplicity," "understated elegance," and "breezy beachside living" are the watchwords at this low-key luxe inn. You can't get a bed closer to the beach than this: decks sit on the beach, and a boardwalk over the sand connects the low-slung, weathered-shingle buildings. A private club when it opened in 1924, it has been in Robert Currie's family since 1958. Family pride of ownership knows no bounds here. Improvements are constant. The lobby is large and airy, decorated with white wicker furniture, local art, and quilts hanging from the rafters. The dedicated breakfast room is sunny and window-filled. The 22 contemporary guest rooms (most with ocean views) feature handcrafted woodwork and granite bathrooms. Five newer suites, with outstanding views of dunes and sunsets, offer the most privacy. There is also a luxuriously simple three-bedroom apartment that almost defies description. If it were possible, I'd live in this unit forever. For meals, shuffle to the excellent **Galley Beach** (see

THE WAUWINET KIM GRANT

Dining Out), the rustic-chic **Bob's Bar** (open to resort guests only), or walk 15 minutes into town. For exercise, nothing on-island compares to their impressive health club, an oh-so-private 60-foot lap pool, leisure pool, Jacuzzi, and saunas. If you get the impression that I'm smitten with this place, you are correct. It's pricey but it's worth every penny. $$$$$+ rooms and suites.

AROUND THE ISLAND

& **The Wauwinet** (508-228-0145; 508-426-8718; wauwinet.com), 120 Wauwinet Road. Open mid-May to late October. When privacy and extraordinary service are of utmost concern, this Relais & Châteaux property is *the* place. Nine miles from town, it occupies an unparalleled location between oceanside dunes and a beach-rimmed harbor. The 28 guest rooms and six cottages feature luxe linens and toiletries, pine armoires, Audubon prints, and sophisticated decorating touches. Public rooms are awash in chintz, trompe l'oeil, fresh flowers, and bleached woods. There's practically no reason to leave the enclave. Facilities include tennis courts, a spa, boating, mountain bikes, croquet, a DVD library, lobstering demonstrations, afternoon port and cheese in the inn's library, and Great Point nature trips. All are included in the room rates. **Topper's** (see *Dining Out*) offers truly outstanding dining. In the morning, enjoy as much from the complimentary breakfast menu as you'd like. $$$$$+.

THE NANTUCKET HOTEL AND RESORT KIM GRANT

HOTELS

IN TOWN

❄ ✒ **The Nantucket Hotel & Resort** (508-228-4747; 508-310-1734; thenantuckethotel.com), 77 Easton Street. The owners of the top-notch Winnetu Oceanside Resort on Martha's Vineyard have definitely outdone themselves. To say they have completely rehabbed this former hostelry does not come close to explaining the depths of their efforts and extraordinary execution. The grand, historic property is my new favorite place to stay on-island. It feels authentic and real; it caters to couples as ferociously as families; and it redefines the intersection of luxury and comfort. Oh, and the service—it artfully walks the fine line between attentive and giving guests their space. It almost has too many sweet spots to call out, but I'll at least whet your appetite. In no particular order: two heated swimming pools, a full children's program (free), a spa/fitness center, the excellent **Breeze Restaurant** (see *Dining Out*), an in-town/central location, super-sophisticated but oh-so-relaxed décor, a sense of whimsy throughout, rocking chairs lining the 1891 wraparound porch, and an appealing mix of hotel rooms, suites, and cottages. $$$–$$$$$+.

White Elephant Hotel (508-228-2500; whiteelephanthotel.com), Easton Street. Open late April to early November and during Stroll. After recent total renovations, the sedate White Elephant is more sedate than ever. A 10-minute walk from the center of town and on the edge of the harbor, many of the spacious 65 rooms, suites, and garden cottages have prime water views framed by shuttered white windows. Most have a balcony or deck; many suites have a fireplace. Décor is a sophisticated blend of leather armchairs and white wicker; crisp linens and textured, neutral fabrics; antique prints and contemporary artwork. Bathrooms boast fine toiletries, lots of white tile, and marble counters. Common space includes a handsome library, a fitness room, an extensive spa, and broad lawns that reach a harborside dock. Inquire about their two in-town lofts (three-bedroom places that sleep eight with fully equipped kitchens, one of which includes use of a BMW). $$$$$+.

NEAR THE AIRPORT

Nantucket Inn (508-228-6900; 800-321-8484; nantucketinn.net), 1 Miller Lane. Open mid-May to mid-October. The main reason I'm including this tasteful but undistinguished motor inn near the airport is because it has 100 rooms, which is a lot of rooms for this small island. Other amenities include an indoor pool, tennis courts, and a complimentary full breakfast. $$$.

BED-AND-BREAKFASTS & INNS

IN TOWN

Union Street Inn (508-228-9222; unioninn.com), 7 Union Street. Open April through October. The island's best run bed-and-breakfast, a circa 1770 hostelry, is run by innkeepers Ken and Deb Withrow with a sense of understated hospitality. You want to know perfection? Stay here. There are a variety of rooms, many with fireplace and all with air-conditioning and TV. The two-room suite and Room #3 (with pine-paneled wall and wing chairs in front of the fireplace) are the premier rooms, but smaller chambers aren't slighted in any way. (Value-conscious shoppers should inquire about the inexpensive room with a detached bath.) After a new round of redecorating and renovating, the 12 rooms are more luxurious than ever, with fine linens, plush bathrobes, and fluffy duvets. On my last visit the full breakfast, served on the side patio, was a choice between an omelet with goat cheese and dill or bagel and smoked salmon. (It's the only bed-and-breakfast that's allowed to serve a full "B.") The art of providing attentive service remains a strong suit here. $$$$–$$$$$+.

THE VERANDA HOUSE KIM GRANT

The Veranda House Hotel Collection (508-228-0695; theverandahouse .com), 3 Step Lane. Open mid-May to mid-October. This consortium consists of three properties where concierge and personalized service are hallmarks. The **Veranda House**, with 15 guest rooms and three suites, reflects a "retro chic" vibe—awash in black, white, and neutral tones with a splash of red here or there. No expense seems to have been spared, and it could certainly hold its own in SoHo. Gracious "extras" are the norm here: Balconies overlooking the harbor, goose down comforters, spanking new bathrooms with hip tile, and Frette linens make for a most hospitable stay. Fortunately, the owners kept one of the best features: three wraparound porches that offer spectacular views of Nantucket Harbor. For this reason and more, they're to be seriously applauded. An ultrasophisticated continental breakfast is served on the patio by oversolicitous servers, and the terraced garden is a welcome respite. The three-room **Arbor Cottage** next door is all about a sense of calm, style, and privacy. Rooms have a fresh summery feel, with clean lines, a pale palette of whites, and a liberal dose of sisal and linens; amenities are top notch. You'll long remember tucking into a decadent bed dressed in Frette linens and the epicurean breakfast across the lane at the Veranda. $$–$$$$$+.

❊ **Anchor Inn** (508-228-0072; anchor -inn.net), 66 Centre Street. This friendly bed-and-breakfast, one of the best values in town, has been innkeeper owned and operated since 1983. Charles and Ann Balas and their crackerjack staff offer 11 guest accommodations in a historic 1806 house; the most spacious rooms are corner ones with a queen canopy bed. All have tiled bathrooms, TV, air-conditioning, and comfortable period furnishings. One has a private porch. The less expensive rooms are snug but inviting, tucked under the eaves in the back of the house. A continental breakfast is served on the enclosed porch or carried to the tranquil side garden. Beach towels and ice packs are available in-season. $–$$.

Pineapple Inn (508-257-4577; pine appleinn.com), 10 Hussey Street. Open late April to late October and on Christmas Stroll weekend. This 1838 whaling captain's house led the surge toward luxury bed-and-breakfast renovations in 1997 with a refined and understated elegance. Six years later it was acquired by the Summer House in its march toward the acquisition of fine properties around the island. Historic grace and modern conveniences (like air-conditioning) coexist comfortably in this 12-room inn. Except for the lack of an on-site innkeeper, first-rate touches surround you, including white marble bathrooms and custom-made four-poster beds fitted with Ralph Lauren linens and down comforters. I particularly like the enclosed

THE PINEAPPLE INN KIM GRANT

back patio, complete with trickling water fountain; it makes for a nice respite from the crowds. Complimentary use of the Summer House Beach and Pool Club is included. $$–$$$.

Ship's Inn (508-228-0040; shipsinn nantucket.com), 13 Fair Street. Open May through October. Beyond the bustle of Main Street and a 10-minute walk from Straight Wharf, the Ship's Inn is known for its fine dining (see *Dining Out*) but is a largely unsung, very comfortable choice for lodging. The three-story 1831 whaling captain's house was completely restored in 1991. Its 13 large guest rooms, named for Capt. Obed Starbuck's ships, all have refrigerator, air-conditioning, and TV. Many are bright corner rooms. Like the living room, they're large, airy, and sparsely furnished to create a summery feel. Expanded continental breakfast included. $$–$$$, single with shared bath $.

❄ **Vanessa Noel Hotel** (508-228-5300; vanessanoelhotel.com), 5 Chestnut Street. The VNH—a chic but cozy boutique property by the noted, eponymous shoe designer—is often confused with the Vanessa Noel Green Hotel, which feels to me like overflow for VNH. Because there is so much confusion

when visitors book online through various agencies, please be careful if you book. $$$–$$$$.

❄ **Martin House Inn** (508-228-0678; martinhouseinn.com), 61 Centre Street. A resident innkeeper presides over this 1803 mariner's house, an elegantly comfortable and relaxed place that consistently gets rave reviews. The side porch is decked out in white wicker; on cooler days you can curl up in front of the fire or in a window seat in the large living room. Many of the 13 guest rooms (four with shared bath) have a canopy bed, period antiques, and a fireplace. Some bright third-floor singles are tucked under the eaves. A continental buffet breakfast is served at one long table, or you can take a tray table to the porch or your room. $$–$$$; single rates, too.

Centerboard Guest House (508-228-9696; centerboardinn.com), 8 Chester Street. Open April through December. A five- to 10-minute walk from the ferry, Centerboard is a restored 1886 former whaling captain's home with a generally light Victorian sensibility. You'll find pleasing contemporary touches throughout, including an outdoor fire pit. The second-floor rooms are romantic, with feather beds, luxurious linens, stripped floors and woodwork, and gleaming bathrooms. The two-room master suite

MARTIN HOUSE INN KIM GRANT

features inlaid floors, rich woodwork, a working fireplace, marble bathroom, deep Jacuzzi tub, and pencil-post canopy bed. Two garden rooms are decidedly different. One is reminiscent of a houseboat, with built-in carpentry, a galley kitchen, a matching pair of raised double beds, and a snug twin berth; it can sleep five. Modern amenities include mini-refrigerators and flat-screen TVs. Expanded continental breakfast included. $$–$$$$.

Century House (508-228-0530; centuryhouse.com), 10 Cliff Road. Open mid-May to mid-October. The oldest continuously operating inn on Nantucket, dating to 1835, has 16 rooms and suites that are just far enough from the center of town to be quiet and just close enough for a pleasant walk. Innkeepers Gerry Connick and Jean Ellen Heron, hands-on owners since 1984, have created a homey and luxurious getaway, complete with an abundant Berry Buffet Breakfast enjoyed on the wraparound veranda or garden patio. Beach towels and tote are provided for the nearby sands. $$–$$$$$+.

✳ ♂ **The Chestnut House** (508-228-0049; chestnuthouse.com), 3 Chestnut Street. Not many old-fashioned guest houses remain, and this one has been in the Carl family since the early 1980s. The family-friendly place is busy and eclectic, with local art taking up almost every inch of wall space. (See **Hawthorn House**, below, for more about familial contributions to décor.) Two-room suites can sleep four people if they are good friends, or a family. Otherwise, they are nice and roomy for two people. One suite is particularly quiet, and there is only one "regular" guest room. All have TV, a small refrigerator, air-conditioning; most have a DVD. The freestanding cottage is more like a suite, with a Murphy bed and separate kitchen. You'll find added value in the additional bathrooms, which allow for a final post-beach shower and late departures. Rates include a daily breakfast voucher, valid at two good restaurants. $$–$$$; cottage more.

✳ **The Hawthorn House** (508-228-1468; hawthornhouse.com), 2 Chestnut Street. A guest house since the mid-1940s, this simple bed-and-breakfast was built in 1849, so the rooms are small. Seven of the nine guest rooms and suites are upstairs, off a casual common area; all rooms have a private bath. Because the bed-and-breakfast is in the historic district, the two ground-floor rooms can be a tad noisy in the evening. Innkeepers Mitchell and Diane Carl came to Nantucket on their honeymoon and loved it so much they returned three years later to purchase the inn and have operated it since. Mitchell's father made the hooked rugs; Diane made the needlepoint pillows; and Mitchell's mother did most of the paintings. Mitchell is responsible for the lovely stained-glass panels. Inquire about the efficiency cottage and two-room suite. Rates include a daily breakfast voucher, valid at two good restaurants. $$.

✳ **21 Broad Hotel** (508-228-4749; 21broadhotel.com), 21 Broad Street. This complete overhaul, restoration, and rehab (in 2014) bears zero resemblance to its former incarnation as the Nesbitt. If you're a repeat visitor to Nantucket, you'll probably walk by shaking your head, thinking, hey wait a minute . . . Restoration was painstaking—and worth every second. Modern and almost urban in feel, this lively and breezy 27-room hotel suits travelers to a tee. From Vitamin C-infused showerheads (!) to loaner iPads to blackout shades, they've overhauled the place with a fresh appeal—right down to a flickering fire housed in a concrete vessel in the living room to a back deck where you BYOB to add to their mixers. $$–$$$$$$+.

Jared Coffin House (508-228-2400; jaredcoffinhouse.com), 29 Broad Street. The island's first three-story house, topped with a cupola and slate roof, was built in 1845 by a wealthy ship owner for his wife. Made of brick, it was also one of the few buildings to survive the Great Fire of 1846. One year later, after

JARED COFFIN HOUSE KIM GRANT

Coffin's wife refused to live here, it was converted to an inn. (I simply note it here for its historical value.)

AROUND THE ISLAND

Summer House Cottages (508-257-4577; thesummerhouse.com), 17 Ocean Avenue, 'Sconset. Open late April to late October. The brochure's photograph is almost too idyllic to believe: Honeysuckle vines and roses cover a shingled cottage with tiny windows; the double Dutch door opens to a white, skylit interior that's cozy and simple. But it's true! Dating to the 1840s, these enchanting cottages surround a colorful garden set with Adirondack chairs. The munchkin-like cottages have been updated with marble Jacuzzi bathtubs, English country-pine antiques, and hand-painted borders; some have a fireplace and kitchen. All have off-season heat. Shuffle across the street to the eastern beach or to the inn's pool, nestled in the dunes just below the bluff. Drinks and lunch are served in their dining room, as well as pool- and oceanside. Continental breakfast included. $$$$$+, more for two- and three-bedroom cottages.

COTTAGES

IN TOWN

🐾 **The Cottages** (508-325-1499; thecottagesnantucket.com), 24 Old South Wharf. Open early May through November. These 29 snug cottages are fun for a change, although they'll cost a pretty penny for all that fun! Occupying a unique location—jutting out on wharves in the midst of harbor activity—most have private decks and water views; all have fully equipped kitchens, TVs, and daily maid service. Although the cottages are small and rather rustic by Nantucket standards, they're efficiently designed and crisply decorated in yellows, whites, and blues. It can be noisy on the pier, but that's part of the fun of staying here. Complimentary daily shuttle to Surfside Beach, and guests have access to the new spa at the White Elephant Hotel (see above). Several of the cottages, known as the Woof Cottages, are also pet-friendly. $$$$$+.

See also **The Chestnut House, Hawthorn House,** and **Anchor Inn** under *Bed-and-Breakfasts & Inns.*

AROUND THE ISLAND

🐾 **Wade Cottages** (508-257-1464; wadecottages.com), 37 Shell Street, 'Sconset. Open early May to early October. There's nothing between the property and the ocean here except a broad lawn and an ocean bluff. Parents will appreciate the wide-open lawns and the play area and swings for kids. The five apartments have from one to three bedrooms. A portion of this private estate is still used by Wade family members. Rented weekly.

See also **Summer House 'Sconset** under *Bed-and-Breakfasts & Inns.*

RENTAL HOUSES Many islanders are opposed to the residential building boom that began in earnest in the mid-1990s because the island's infrastructure just can't handle it. But there's no going back. There are thousands of new three- to seven-bedroom rental houses on the market. Expect a nice two-bedroom house to rent for $2,000 to $4,000 weekly in August.

Congdon & Coleman (508-325-5000; congdonandcoleman.com), 57 Main Street.

Jordan Associates (508-228-4449; jordanre.com), 8 Federal Street.

✵ **Barntucket** (508-228-4835; barntucket.com), 73 North Liberty Street. A five-bedroom, three-bath beauty built in the early 1800s, with prices that are actually quite reasonable if you're splitting them among five other couples or individuals.

TimeAndPlace.com. A stellar site with premier homes for rent.

CAMPGROUNDS Camping is not permitted.

HOSTEL ✵ ♫ **Hostelling International Nantucket** (508-228-0433; hiusa.org/hostels), 31 Western Avenue. Open mid-May to early October. Originally built in 1873 as the island's first lifesaving station, and now on the National Register of Historic Places, this hostel is 3 miles from town on Surfside Beach (see **Green Space**) and steps from the NRTA beach shuttle. Facilities include a kitchen, barbecue and picnic area, and volleyball. Dormitory-style, gender-separated rooms accommodate about 50 people; inquire about private rooms. Reservations are essential in July and August and on all weekends. Continental breakfast included.

✵ Where to Eat

The dining scene here is highly evolved. Enough Nantucket diners are so passionate about haute cuisine that the island supports one of the densest concentrations of fine-dining establishments in the country. And one of the most expensive: $50 entrées are commonplace. Some restaurants offer less expensive, bistro-style fare in addition to their regular menu.

Prices aside, many of Nantucket's 60-some restaurants would hold their own in New York or San Francisco. It's rare to be served a bad meal in Nantucket, but some restaurants do offer more value (note the ❧ symbol for value) than others.

A few more details: Unless otherwise noted, reservations are highly recommended at all *Dining Out* establishments. In addition, you might need to reconfirm your reservation on the day of or you'll lose it. There are perhaps 10 restaurants (not all are reviewed here) that serve the year-round community. Generally, you can assume that all places below are open daily late June to early September.

Because dining particulars (which meals are served on which days) change with lightning speed, I simply indicate which meals are served. Never assume a particular meal is offered on any particular day or month. It's best to pick up the phone.

By the way, don't pass up the opportunity to have bay scallops after mid-October (when the scalloping season begins). The experience might explain why Nantucketers are so passionate about food.

DINING OUT

IN TOWN

✵ ⍭ **Boarding House** (508-228-9622; boardinghousenantucket.com), 12 Federal Street. Open D and brunch, May through December. Chef/owners Seth and Angela Raynor's contemporary, sexy, Euro- and Asian-inspired cuisine stands center stage at one of Nantucket's most consistent and superior restaurants. An award-winning wine list and organic ingredients from local farms are featured. As for atmosphere, with brick and plaster arched walls, the main dining room is cozy. At street level, there's a lively bar packed with locals and 30-something visitors; it's a real scene and has an extensive appetizer menu. But in good weather, the patio—surrounded by flowers and a white picket fence—is the place you'll want to be. It's common for folks to line up in summer at 4 p.m. for one of these seats. $$–$$$$.

☙ **The Pearl** (508-228-9701; the pearlnantucket.com), 12 Federal Street. Open D, May through October. From the attitude to the oh-so-trendy-cocktail bar to the whole scene, don't look now: You just might be in Miami's South Beach. Executive chef/owner Seth Raynor (see **Boarding House**, above) has furthered his winning formula of coastal cuisine prepared with an Asian flair. The atmosphere and cuisine here are sophisticated, relaxing, and dramatic. (Note the onyx bar, huge fish tanks filled with brilliant fish and coral, pearl-shaped ceiling, and pale blue lighting.) Although the menu changes frequently, you can always count on creatively prepared native seafood and local fish. Patrons are

COMPANY OF THE CAULDRON KIM GRANT

particularly fond of tuna martinis (non-alcoholic) and Chef Seth's wok-fried lobster. After dinner the pearl transforms into a late-night lounge. $$$$–$$$$$.

Company of the Cauldron (508-228-4016; companyofthecauldron.com), 5 India Street. Open D, late May to mid-October and on Christmas Stroll weekend (see **Special Events**). Peer through ivy-covered, small-paned windows and you'll see what looks like an intimate dinner party. Sure enough, since the tables are so close together, you'll probably end up talking to your neighbors before the night is over. It's a warm and inviting place, with low-beamed ceilings and plaster walls illuminated by candlelight and wall sconces. Classical harp music wafts in the background three evenings of the week. The New American menu is set a week in advance (check on Friday by 5 p.m.), but it might go something like this: a trio of crab, lobster, and salmon cakes with three luxurious sauces; a mesclun salad with caramelized shallot vinaigrette; ginger- and herb-crusted rack of lamb with blackberries and pine nut couscous; and a pear almond tart to top it all off. One or two seatings; prix fixe $$$$$+.

THE PEARL KIM GRANT

American Seasons (508-228-7111; americanseasons.com), 80 Centre Street. Open D, April to mid-December. While inspired by America's regional traditions, Chef Neil Ferguson's menu is both inviting and innovative. The ever-changing menu might feature venison saddle with red cabbage and rutabaga puree or black pearl salmon with an apple-bacon compote, sunchoke puree, and hazelnuts. Portions are balanced with savory and sweet tastes, crunchy and smooth textures. Not up to a full-on meal? Sip a cocktail, dine from the (light) bar menu, and add a fanciful dessert. The candlelit dining room is as tasteful as they come. $$$–$$$$.

⚲ **Cru** (508-228-9278; crunantucket .com), 1 Straight Wharf. Open L, D, mid-May to mid-October. Night or day, try to get a chic outdoor patio table at Nantucket's only harborside (yachtside might be more apt) restaurant. If you can't, though, don't worry; the upscale interior is open to sea breezes and rolling fog banks. Lunchtime is a bit less of a scene than dinner, but no matter the time

of day, drinks are super-pricey. I prefer to come for lobster rolls and oysters from the raw bar; I stay away from the clams. The super-bustling (read loud and buzzy) Cru occupies the former perch of the longtime Ropewalk. Oh, and they take reservations for the best seats; try your luck! $$$–$$$$.

🦞 ❄ ⚓ **Breeze Bar & Café** (508-228-4730; thenantuckethotel.com), 77 Easton Street. Open B, Sunday brunch, L, D. Within the Nantucket Hotel & Resort, this welcome addition to the local dining scene excels in so many important ways: personalized attention, great cuisine at good prices, and a lack of pretense. It's a breath of fresh air and a downright pleasure. (And it doesn't feel like a hotel restaurant.) Start with super-tasty lobster bisque or perfectly light calamari rings and move to utterly satisfying crabcakes (with practically no filler) or a big bowl of clams. Oh yeah, and then there are those incredible truffle fries and that lunchtime lobster-stuffed burger. Desserts are homey: think brownie sundaes and other treats that

THE BREEZE BAR & CAFÉ KIM GRANT

hark back to simpler times. Throughout the deep winter, the café is open for light bar meals most nights and full dinners on weekends. $$$–$$$$.

🍴 ⓨ **Ship's Inn Restaurant** (508-228-0040; shipsinnnantucket.com), 13 Fair Street. Open D, May through October. Longtime chef/owner Mark Gottwald, who graduated from La Varenne in Paris and apprenticed at Le Cirque and Spago, serves California-French-style cuisine in a romantic, subterranean, bistro-style space. He often catches his own seafood, too. I always leave here very satisfied. Many dishes are healthful (that is, sans butter or cream) without sacrificing taste or creativity. I particularly like the signature sautéed halibut with a cognac lobster ragout. Save room for the chocolate soufflé. They have an award-winning wine list; sit at the old dory boat bar and enjoy a glass. $$$–$$$$.

ⓨ **Straight Wharf Restaurant** (508-228-4499; straightwharfrestaurant.com), 6 Harbor Square. Open D, June through October, as well as lunch and brunch in July and August. When given the choice, I prefer the more casual dining, reasonable price points, and first-come, first-served nature of the bar. It's also pleasantly upbeat and zippy (despite no air-conditioning). No matter where and when you dine, though—whether it's on the deck overlooking the harbor or in the lofty main dining room with exposed rafters—the New American dishes are well prepared and elegantly presented. Look for the likes of wood-grilled sirloin or a clambake with buttered lobster, sweet corn, chorizo, and potatoes. Other dishes might overwhelm some palates and totally tantalize others: pumpkin chowder with cranberries, fennel, and shoestring potatoes; dayboat scallops with royal trumpets, kumquats, butternut squash, and vadouvan-cauliflower puree; and chèvre cheesecake with Concord grapes, walnut crust, and quince sorbet. L $$–$$$, D $$$–$$$$$.

❄ ⓨ **Lola 41** (508-325-4001; lola41 .com), 15 South Beach Street. Open L, D. This is one hip eatery. I mean, really. Walk through the doors and you'll forget you're on Nantucket. Along with boasting a "global bistro menu," Lola 41 specializes in sushi, sashimi, and designer rolls. Try the excellent gnocchi Bolognese, or go for one of the house specialties: sesame-crusted calamari with Korean chili dipping sauce or a houseground rib eye served on an English muffin. Bring a fun attitude and live it up. No reservations taken in summer. $$$–$$$$.

ⓨ **Brant Point Grill** (508-325-1320; whiteelephanthotel.com), at the White Elephant Hotel, 50 Easton Street. Open B, L, D, seasonally. There's no more pleasant place to have an alfresco luncheon than this harborside terrace. (Heaters and awnings keep it warm well into autumn.) The handsome grill with attentive service specializes in steamed and grilled lobsters and thick, juicy steaks. Nothing is too fussy or overdone. On Friday afternoons check out the raw bar, too. B $–$$, L $$–$$$, D $$$$–$$$$$, Sunday brunch $$$$.

ⓨ **Club Car** (508-228-1101; theclubcar .com), 1 Main Street. Open L, D, mid-May through October. The kitchen has been churning out the same Continental cuisine since 1972, and its off-season beef Wellington Sunday-evening specials are still classic—best enjoyed in the elegant and haughty dining room, set with linen and silver. I prefer to come simply for a seafood salad and chowder at lunch—and to enjoy the only remaining club car from the narrow-gauge train that used to run between Steamboat Wharf and 'Sconset. Depending on the time of night, be prepared for sing-alongs at the piano bar. L $$, D $$$$–$$$$$.

❋ **Fifty-Six Union** (508-228-6135; fiftysixunion.com), 56 Union Street. Open D. Since they opened in 2003, chef/owners Peter and Wendy Jannelle have succeeded in creating a friendly find away from tourists roaming the more well-known haunts downtown. It's one of the more playful and lighthearted "serious" restaurants in town—to wit, you can't miss the mannequins out front. Seasonal menus reflect what's fresh in the world of global cuisine: Curried mussels and dayboat summer fluke are personal favorites. There are two seatings (at 5:30 p.m. and 8:15 p.m. during peak season; open seating rest of year) at banquettes as well as patio dining. Inquire about the outdoor table "#56." $$$–$$$$$.

ON THE OUTSKIRTS OF TOWN

&. **Galley Beach** (508-228-9641; galley beach.net), 54 Jefferson Avenue. Open L, weekend brunch, D, late April to late October. At the Cliffside Beach Club (but with no relation to it), you'll literally dine beachside, drinking in sunsets along with your cosmos. But this isn't a sand-in-your-shoes kind of place—it's elegant, candlelit dining on Nantucket Sound, thanks to a multimillion-dollar renovation in 2009, complete with a zinc bar. The coastal cuisine menu features sea scallops, other local seafood, and organic greens. A restaurant with this kind of location might be content to pass, but the Galley Beach is absolutely stellar in all ways. $$–$$$$$+.

🍴❄ **Island Kitchen** (508-228-2639; nantucketislandkitchen.com), 1 Chin's Way. Open B, L, D. This super-pleasant place is owned by the former chef of famed Le Languedoc, Patrick, and features locally sourced New American cuisine. It's a great find and value. Even better? It's not "a scene," and it's heavily patronized by old Nantucket folks rather than newcomers. Dress down, appreciate a limited menu (knowing that they concentrate on doing a few things well), and sit back and enjoy. It's across the street from Stop & Shop, so there's plenty of parking. $–$$$.

AROUND THE ISLAND

🍴 **Topper's** (508-228-8768; wauwinet .com), 120 Wauwinet Road, Wauwinet. Open L, D, and Sunday brunch, May through October. You could break the

bank here and Topper's would still be worth every penny. All the superlatives in the dictionary just can't do the place justice. The setting and service are luxurious, indulgent, and sophisticated yet relaxed. Regional dishes are downright sublime: New American cuisine is matched by outstanding pairings from a French and California wine list. (Topper's consistently wins the just-about-impossible-to-win *Wine Spectator* Grand Award.) And to quote myself in *National Geographic Traveler*, "Their wine pairing is unrivaled on the Eastern Seaboard.") On my most recent visit, I splurged on the off-season six-course degustation menu with wine pairing. Each dish and wine comes into its own when paired with the other: one plus one equals three. It's pricey, but it's an uncommonly rare dining experience. Dishes and wines ascend in boldness, telling a story exuberantly, then come back down to earth. For lunch, served on the bayside porch, Topper's offers a two-course menu ($$$). Topper's offers complimentary van service from town, as well as transportation aboard the *Wauwinet Lady*, which takes guests from Straight Wharf to the restaurant's private dock in-season. Kudos to

'SCONSET CAFÉ KIM GRANT

THE CHANTICLEER KIM GRANT

chef Kyle Zachary and the whole staff. $$–$$$$$, multicourse prix fixe, too.

'Sconset Café (508-257-4008; sconsetcafe.com), 8 Main Street, 'Sconset. Open L, D, mid-May to mid-September, breakfast in summer. This tiny place is always great. It's known for its chowder with herbs, but you'll also find creative salads and sandwiches at lunch. Chefowner Rolf Nelson's dinners really shine and tend toward sophisticated New American dishes. The menu changes constantly, but chocolate volcano cake is often the dessert specialty. Reservations accepted for 6 p.m. seating only. No credit cards; BYOB. Rolf owns the wine shop next door, where he recommends wines that go with his menu. Customers typically buy their wine there for dinner. $–$$$$.

The Chanticleer (508-257-4499; thechanticleer.net), 9 New Street, 'Sconset. Open L, D, May through October. This venerated institution features a modern French menu emphasizing New England and artisan ingredients. Meals are served in the courtyard of a rose-covered cottage, in small dining rooms overlooking the courtyard through small-paned windows, or in the more formal main dining room with low ceilings. Local fish, local produce, and game birds are highlighted. I suspect that dining here will live on in your memory for years. The wine list is outstanding. Jackets preferred. $$$–$$$$$.

EATING OUT

IN TOWN

Centre Street Bistro (508-228-8470; nantucketbistro.com), 29 Centre Street. Open B, L, D. Chef/owners Ruth and Tim Pitts, who have been cooking on-island since 1989, have cultivated a deservedly loyal following. Perhaps it's because they serve exceedingly good food at even better prices. Their ever-evolving menu might include dishes like cheeseburger tortilla, but I often revert to their signature smoked salmon taco. Or start your day with their "Nantucket Breakfast"—scrambled eggs, bacon, potato pancake, and blueberry pancake. There are only

BLACK-EYED SUSAN'S   KIM GRANT

Broad Street. Open L, D. The 1840s former whaling tavern feels like an English pub: brick walls, beamed ceilings, and few windows. It's a convivial place—helped along by an extensive coffee and drinks menu—frequented by locals chowing on good chowder, burgers, cheddar cheese soup, shoestring fries (long and curly), and thick sandwiches. Open until late at night. Expect a line in summer; patio dining available until mid-October. $$–$$$.

❦ ❄ ✎ **Fog Island Café** (508-228-1818; fogisland.com), 7 South Water Street. Open B, L, D. Anne and Mark Dawson preside over one of the top two or three breakfast joints on-island. Casual and inviting with wooden tables and booths, they offer food that you can relate to: burgers, quesadillas, and specialty sandwiches at lunchtime, and grilled salmon and roasted pork loin at dinner. I love the thick-cut brioche French toast and Nantucket fishcakes in the morning (as long as I'm skipping lunch). They also do breakfast and lunch to go. $–$$.

❄ **Sushi by Yoshi** (508-228-1801; sushibyyoshi.com), 2 East Chestnut Street. Open L, D. When you tire of eating fancy gourmet preparations, this small place offers fresh sushi and sashimi, Aloha rolls with yellowtail tuna from Japan, dynamite rolls, and noodle dishes. For dessert, consider banana tempura or green tea ice cream. They do a brisk take-out business. BYOB. $–$$$.

❄ ✎ ✧ **Rose & Crown** (508-228-2595; theroseandcrown.com), 23 South Water Street. Open L, D, mid-April through September. This hopping place serves decent American fare—sandwiches, pastas, chicken wings, steak, and seafood—in a traditional pub atmosphere. Formerly a carriage livery, the large, barnlike room is decorated with signs from old Nantucket businesses. $–$$.

❄ ✎ **Starlight Café** (508-228-4479; starlightack.com), 1 North Union Street. Open L, D. I like to come to this low-key spot for live music in the summer, a glass of wine, and their house specialty:

a couple of dozen seats (and a small bar) within this Mediterranean-style space, but that's fine, as people enjoy the summertime patio. BYOB. $–$$$.

Black-Eyed Susan's (508-325-0308; black-eyedsusans.com), 10 India Street. Open brunch, D, seasonally. This small place with no air-conditioning and with pickled walls is part bistro, part glorified lunch counter with open kitchen. Hip, funky (in a good way), mellow, and homey, the downscale décor belies the stylishly presented plates. The global menu changes frequently, but look for complex fish preparations and dishes like North African spiced chicken with seasonal veggies. Breakfasts run the gamut from bagels and grits to Pennsylvania Dutch pancakes and a veggie scramble with pesto (made with eggs or tofu). BYOB. No credit cards. $–$$$.

❦ ❄ ✎ ✧ **Brotherhood of Thieves** (508-228-2551; brotherhoodofthieves.com), 23

BROTHERHOOD OF THIEVES KIM GRANT

lobster macaroni and cheese. The arbor patio is perfect on a warm summer night. Look for Italian Nights and late-night menus, too. $–$$$.

✎ **Nantucket Lobster Trap** (508-228-4200; nantucketlobstertrap.com), 23 Washington Street. Open D, May through September. If you've got a hankering for lobster, plain and simple, head to this casual eatery with barn-board walls and booths. (I recommend only the basic lobster here.) Other pluses include a large patio and outdoor bar; Tuesday "Buck-a-Shuck" with bluegrass and folk music; delivery and takeout packed with dinnerware with beach picnicking in mind; and a food truck parked outside Cisco Brewery, starting at noon. $$$–$$$$.

ON THE OUTSKIRTS OF TOWN

❋ **Sea Grille** (508-325-5700; theseagrille.com), 45 Sparks Avenue. Open L, D. Despite having plenty of parking, this attractive restaurant is overlooked by nonlocals (except in winter, when it's one of a handful open). Every kind of seafood and fish is prepared practically every way: such as bouillabaisse (a specialty),

grilled, blackened, steamed, fried, and raw (there's an extensive raw bar). Light meals at the bar are a good alternative. The wine list is excellent. $$–$$$$.

COFFEE & SWEET TREATS

IN TOWN

Provisions (508-228-3258; provisionsnantucket.com), 3 Straight Wharf at Harbor Square. Open early May to mid-October. Even in the height of summer, when this island institution is cranking, they make excellent sandwiches (big enough to feed two people), salads, and soups. Hot and cold vegetarian dishes, too. Since 1979. $$.

❋ **The Bean** (508-228-6215; nantucketcoffee.com), 4 India Street. This funky little café has strong coffee, specialty teas, and baked goods. Grab a local newspaper, play some board games, and watch this rarefied world go by. $.

✎ **Henry Jr.** (508-228-3035), 129 Orange Street. Open mid-May to mid-October. Downright excellent sandwiches with fast, efficient service. $.

✎ **"The Street."** The first block of Steamboat Wharf is lined with fast-food

THE JUICE BAR KIM GRANT

different items baked daily, including Portuguese breads, desserts, muffins, croissants, quiches, cakes, and pastries. You can take Jay and Magee Detmer's word for it; they've been baking the goodies since 1976. $$.

❋ **Pi Pizzeria** (508-228-1130; pipizze ria.com), 11 West Creek Road. Excellent wood-fired, thin-crust pizza for takeout and dining in. Someone in your group not a pizza fan? Nightly seasonal alternatives include roasted cod, beet salad, chicken piccata, and New York strip. $$–$$$.

AROUND THE ISLAND

Claudette's, (508-257-6622), 10 Main Street at Post Office Square, 'Sconset. Open mid-May to mid-October. Known primarily for catering (perhaps the best catered clambakes on Nantucket), this tiny shop's raisons d'être are box lunches and lemon cake. Although there are a few indoor tables, most people take their sandwiches to the beach or ice cream to the front deck. $$.

❋ Entertainment

MUSIC ♪ **Band concerts** (508-228-7213) at the Children's Beach bandstand off South Beach Street. They're mostly held on Thursday and Sunday early evenings in July and August.

Noonday concerts (508-228-5466), 11 Orange Street at the Unitarian Universalist Church. These concerts, featuring ensembles, soloists, and an 1831 Goodrich pipe organ, are held on Thursday in July and August. Donations.

Nantucket Musical Arts Society (508-228-1287; nantucketmusicalartsso ciety.org), 62 Centre Street at the First Congregational Church. Look for concerts with world-renowned musicians on most Tuesday evenings in July and August. On the night before the concert, there is a meet-the-artist event hosted

shops appreciated by families and those catching ferries. Take-out eateries are generally open May to mid-October. $–$$$.

The Juice Bar (508-228-5799), 12 Broad Street. Open late May to mid-October. Yes, they offer fresh juices like carrot, lemonade, and orange, but they also make their own low-fat ice cream, nonfat yogurts, and baked goods. In fact, they make everything from scratch. $.

ON THE OUTSKIRTS OF TOWN

♪ **Downy Flake** (508-228-4533; the downyflake.com), 18 Sparks Avenue. Open April through February. Order justifiably famous doughnuts (there are only three kinds, but who cares?) and pancakes (but not on the same morning, please) from this island institution. Light lunches, too. $$.

Nantucket Bake Shop (508-228-2797; nantucketbakeshop.com), 17½ Old South Road. Open April through November. Its advertisement claims more than 100

at the Unitarian Universalist Church, 11 Orange Street. $$.

THEATER ✱ **Theatre Workshop of Nantucket** (508-228-4305; theatreworkshop .com), Methodist Church, 2 Centre Street. Since 1956, this community-based group has staged a variety of plays, musicals, and comedy nights.

See also **Dreamland Theater** below.

🎞 🍸 MOVIES & FILMS **Dreamland Theater** (508-332-4822; nantucketdreamland .org), 17 South Water Street. This institution has a long and beloved history. It began as a Quaker meetinghouse, was converted to the Atlantic Straw Company, and was eventually moved to Brant Point to serve as part of a hotel before it was floated back across the harbor in 1905 on a barge. More recently it shuttered its doors to first-run movies in 2005 and was headed for demolition. But thanks to a powerhouse of locals (hedge fund managers, the wife of Google's CEO, the former CEO of Starwood Hotels, and more), it was purchased for almost $10 million in the late 2000s and reopened in fall 2010 after an enormous renovation. It's just another little example of summer folks pitching in to help preserve a little of Nantucket's history. Year-round movies, children's theater, speaker series, and wide-ranging collaborations for visual and performing arts programming.

✱ **Starlight Theatre and Café** (508-228-4435; starlightack.com), 1 North Union Street, shows first-run movies. Drop by the café for a drink before or after the show. See *Eating Out*.

🍸 NIGHTLIFE **Chicken Box** (508-228-9717; thechickenbox.com), 16 Dave Street, off Lower Orange Street. This divey, boxy bar and music club is very laid-back. When things quiet down in town, take a cab out to "The Box" to extend your night—if you're into pool tables, table tennis, and live tunes. No, you can't get chicken here, but you could

in 1948 when it opened as a restaurant-club.

The Muse (508-228-6873; 508-228-1471 for takeout; 44 Surfside Road). This roadhouse has DJs, techno music, live bands (the Dave Matthews Band cut its teeth here), pool tables, table tennis, and a big-screen TV. It's on the shuttle circuit and has take-out pizza, too.

Many *Dining Out* restaurants have bars that, when diners depart for the evening, become happenin' places to socialize. Look for the 🍸 symbol.

✱ Selective Shopping

ANTIQUES **Nina Hellman Antiques** (508-228-3857; nauticalnantucket.com). Nautical items, folk art, Nantucket memorabilia, and work by scrimshander Charles A. Manghis, who gives scrimshaw demonstrations on premises.

The J. Butler Collection (508-228-8429; butlersoffarhills.com), 12 Main Street in rear courtyard. Open June to mid-October. Antiques and reproduction furnishings, collectibles, and dishware in a homey setting.

Antiques Depot (508-228-1287; nantucketantiquesdepot.com), 2 South Beach Street. An interesting collection of furniture and fine decorative arts.

ART GALLERIES **Cecilia Joyce & Seward Johnson Gallery (Artists Association of Nantucket)** (508-228-0294; nantucketarts.org), 19 Washington Street. Open April through December. This association of 200 artists was founded in 1945 to showcase members' work. Changing AAN member exhibits, juried shows, demonstrations, and special events conspire to make this a vital venue for the local arts scene. See *Special Programs*.

Old South Wharf. Generally open mid-May to mid-October. Lined with small galleries, clothing stores, artisans, and a marine chandlery, Old South is located in the boat basin just beyond the Grand Union parking lot. Definitely wander over.

OLD SOUTH WHARF KIM GRANT

Art Cabinet (508-325-0994; artcab inet.com), 18 Dukes Road. Open May to late September. Owner Doerte Neudert showcases European contemporary artists; the relocated studio and sculpture garden are delightful.

Dane Gallery (508-228-7779; dane gallery.com), 28 Centre Street. An outstanding shop with a dazzling array of sophisticated glass sculpture by artists like shop owner Robert Dane.

BOOKSTORES ✎ **Nantucket Bookworks** (508-228-4000; nantucketbookpartners .com), 25 Broad Street. This shop has a very well-chosen selection of travel books, literature, children's books, and biographies—along with an incredibly helpful staff.

Mitchell's Book Corner (508-228-1080; mitchellsbookcorner.com), 54 Main Street. This icon, which has anchored Main Street since the late 1960s, was sold in early 2008 to Wendy Schmidt, a philanthropist, wife of Eric Schmidt (Google CEO), and seasonal visitor to the island. The former owner, Mimi Berman,

a descendant of astronomer Maria Mitchell, vowed to stay on for matchmaking (books to people, that is). There's a great selection of maritime, whaling, and naturalist books. Sit and browse titles in the small "Nantucket Room," which features all things Nantucket.

CLOTHES **Hepburn** (508-228-1458), 3 Salem Street. Open April through January. A chic boutique with designs for women executed in crushed velvet, satin, silk, and wool.

Johnston's Cashmere (508-228-5450), 4 Federal Street. Scottish cashmere, with a nice selection of classic women's sweaters, dresses, and scarves.

Pollack's (508-228-9940; pollack snantucket.com), 5 South Water Street. Open mid-May through December. The personable proprietor, Bob Pollack, stocks comfortable, sophisticated clothing for men and women.

Murray's Toggery Shop (508-228-0437; nantucketreds.com), 62 Main Street. This shop "invented" and owns the rights to Nantucket Reds, all-cotton

LIGHTSHIP BASKETS

Although it is thought that Nantucket's first famed baskets were made in the 1820s, they didn't get their name until a bit later. When the first lightship anchored off the Nantucket coast to aid navigation around the treacherous shallow shoals, crewmembers were stationed on board for months at a time. In the spare daylight hours, sailors created round and oval rattan baskets using lathes and wooden molds. Stiff oak staves were steamed to make them more pliant; the bottoms were wooden. They were made to withstand the test of time. There are perhaps 20 stores and studios that sell authentic lightship baskets, which retail for hundreds to thousands of dollars and require at least 40 hours of work to produce. Among the shops that make them and take custom orders are **Michael Kane Lightship Baskets** (508-228-1548; michaelkaneslightshipbaskets.com), 18A Sparks Avenue, and **Bill and Judy Sayle** (508-228-9876), 112 Washington Street Extension.

Make it a point to visit the **Nantucket Lightship Basket Museum** (508-228-1177; nantucket lightshipbasketmuseum.org), 49 Union Street. Open late May to early October. This informative little museum has re-created a workshop with simple tools that helps visitors understand the simple techniques artisans employed to make exquisite baskets. With baskets from the 1850s to the present, the museum certainly helps promote the art form. $.

If you want to try making lightship baskets on your own, purchase kits and materials from **Peter Finch Basketmaker** (508-332-9803; bracklet.com), 5 Polliwog Pond. Because it's a long walk to the shop, take the South Loop shuttle in summer.

The Golden Basket (508-228-4344; ackgoldenbasket.com), 18 Federal Street, sells miniature gold versions of the renowned baskets.

KIM GRANT

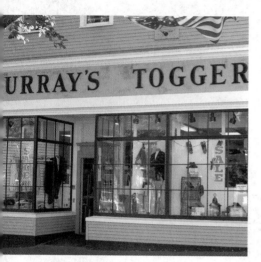

MURRAY'S TOGGERY SHOP KIM GRANT

pants that fade to pink after numerous washings—almost as "Nantucket" as lightship baskets. This is the only shop that sells the real thing, and has since 1945.

Peter Beaton Hat Studio (508-228-8456; peterbeaton.com), 16½ Federal Street and on Straight Wharf. Open April through December. Down a little walkway, this fun little shop has finely woven straw hats. Custom fitting and trimming, of course.

Zero Main (508-228-4401), 34 Centre Street. Formerly located at 0 Main Street, this shop is now known as Zero Main on Centre. It still sells classic and contemporary women's clothes and shoes.

CRAFTS SHOPS **Stephen Swift Furniture** (508-228-0255; stephenswiftfurnituremaker.com), 23 Federal Street. Beautifully handcrafted chairs, benches, stools, beds, dressers, and other furnishings.

Erica Wilson Nantucket (508-228-9881; ericawilson.com), 25-27 Main Street. Wilson, an islander since 1958, is known worldwide for needlework and has taught the art to numerous celebrities. The store also sells jewelry and clothing.

Nantucket Looms (508-228-1908; nantucketlooms.com), 51 Main Street.

Features weavers at work on their looms and their creations. Although customers are not allowed into the work area, they can watch the weavers through a window in the shop.

Claire Murray (508-228-1913; clairemurray.com), 11 South Water Street. Murray came to Nantucket in the late 1970s as an innkeeper and began hooking rugs during the long winter months. She has since given up the bed-and-breakfast business to concentrate on designing and opening more stores; her staff now makes the rugs. She sells finished pieces as well as kits.

Four Winds Craft Guild (fourwindscraftsguild.com), 15 Main Street, off Fair Street. Baskets, lightship purses, scrimshaw, and marine items.

FARM PRODUCE **Main Street at Federal Street**. Local produce is sold from the backs of trucks daily except Sunday, May through October. It doesn't get any fresher than this.

Nantucket Farmers' and Artisans Market (they're always downtown, often at Cambridge and Union Streets, but constantly on the move). From 9 a.m. to noon on Saturdays, June to mid-October, weather permitting. Run by Sustainable Nantucket (sustainablenantucket

NANTUCKET FARMERS' MARKET KIM GRANT

.org), all products offered here are either grown or made on the island.

Bartlett's Farm (508-228-9403; bart lettsfarm.com), 33 Bartlett Farm Road, off Hummock Pond Road. Bartlett's boasts a 100-acre spread run by an eighth-generation islander family. Its market carries thousands of different food and nonfood items for any eating-related occasion, plus a kitchen selling panini, deli items, and all kinds of food to go.

SPECIALTY **Sweet Inspirations** (508-228-5814; nantucketchocolate.com), 0 India Street. Purveyor of Nantucket Clipper Chocolates, displayed in luscious mounds in the glass cases. Of particular note are cranberry-based confections such as cranberry cheesecake truffles and chocolate-covered cranberries.

Nantucket Natural Oils (508-325-4740; nantucketnaturaloils.com), 12 Straight Wharf. A treat for the senses, this shop deals in essential oils and perfumes and looks like an old apothecary. Take a seat at the bar and let master perfumer John Harding custom-mix you an original fragrance. Gorgeous handblown glass perfume bottles, too.

Vanderbilt Gallery (508-325-4454; vanderbiltgallery.com), 18 Federal Street #B. Open April through December. An eclectic assemblage of paintings, sculpture, and classic custom jewelry.

✑ **The Toy Boat** (508-228-4552; thetoyboat.com), Straight Wharf 41. An old-fashioned children's toy store selling great wooden boats, a wooden ferryboat and dock system, rocking boats, cradles, handmade toys and puzzles, marbles, and books.

✳ Special Events

Contact the chamber of commerce (508-228-1700; nantucketchamber.org) for specific dates unless an alternative phone number is listed below. Also, remember that this is just a sampling of the larger, predictable annual events. The chamber produces an excellent events calendar.

Late April: **Daffodil Festival** (daffodilfestival.com). In 1974 an islander donated more than a million daffodil bulbs to be planted along Nantucket's main roads. It is estimated that after years of naturalization, there are now more than 3 million of these beauties. The official kickoff weekend to celebrate spring includes a vintage-car parade to 'Sconset, a tailgate picnic in 'Sconset, and a garden-club show. This is a Very Big Weekend.

May: **Historic Preservation Month** (508-228-1387; nantucketpreservation .org). This celebration of Nantucket's rich local history and heritage includes discussions about preservation and education efforts. **Wine Festival** (617-527-9473; nantucketwinefestival.com). Look for Grand Tastings at the Nantucket Yacht Club, as well as winery dinners at local restaurants.

Late May: **Figawi Sailboat Race** (508-221-6891; figawi.com). A famed race over Memorial Day weekend that goes from Hyannis to Nantucket; since 1972.

Mid-June: **Nantucket Film Festival** (646-480-1900; nantucketfilmfestival .org). It's been an intimate and important venue for new independent films and filmmakers since 1996. Screenings, Q&A seminars, staged readings, as well as panel discussions on how screenplays become movies and the art of writing screenplays. The festival has attracted the Farrelly brothers and Natalie Portman and included readings by Rosie Perez and Jerry Stiller.

July 4: **Independence Day** (508-228-0925). Main Street is closed off in the morning for pie- and watermelon-eating contests, a 5K run, a dunk tank, puppets, face painting, fire-hose battles, and more. Festivities are capped off with fireworks from Jetties Beach off Norton Beach Road.

Late July–early August: **Billfish Tournament** (508-228-2299; nantucketangler sclub.com). A weeklong event on Straight Wharf since 1969.

Mid-August: **House Tour** (508-325-5239; nantucketgardenclub.org). Sponsored by the Nantucket Garden Club since 1955 and featuring a different neighborhood every year; preregistration is required. **Sandcastle & Sculpture Day**. Jetties Beach off Norton Beach Road, since 1974.

Mid-September: **Island Fair** (508-228-7213). At the Tom Nevers Recreation Area, a two-day event with puppet show, flea market, music, food, pumpkin weighing contest, and more.

Late November–December: **Nantucket Noel** begins the day after Thanksgiving with a Christmas tree–lighting ceremony. Live Christmas trees decorated by island schoolchildren line Main Street, and special concerts and theatrical performances heighten the holiday cheer and merriment.

Early December: **Christmas Stroll**. Begun in 1973 and taking place on the first Saturday of December, the Stroll includes vintage-costumed carolers, festive store-window decorations, wreath exhibits, open houses, and a historic house tour. Marking the official "end" of tourist season, like the Daffodil Festival this is a Very Big Event. Make lodging reservations months in advance.

INDEX

Page numbers in *italics* refer to illustrations.

A

Abel's Hill Cemetery, 391, 398
Academy Playhouse, 251
Acadia National Park, 329
Adams, John, 105–6
Addison Art Gallery, 253
Adult Field School, 284
Adventure Rentals, 383
African American Heritage Trail, 385
African Meeting House, 447
AIDS Support Group's Annual Silent and
    Live Auction, 369
Airport Fitness, 395, 400
Albert Merola Gallery, 365
Alden Gallery, 365
Algonquian, 120
Alison Shaw Gallery, 424
Allard Farm, 188, *189*
All Cape Boat Rentals, 125
Allen Farm Sheep & Wool Company,
    427
Allen Farm Vista, 402
Allen Harbor, 194
Alley's General Store, 391
Alvin, 69
American History Museum, 51
American Lobster Mart, 45
American Revolution, 280, 373
"America the Beautiful," 68, 74
AMP Gallery, 365
Andrea Doria, 448, 452
Annual Antiques Show, 90
Annual Chatham Antiques Show & Sale,
    232
Annual Figawi Sailboat Race Weekend,
    134
Annual Jazz Festival, 204
Annual Rhododendron Festival, 63
Antique Automobile Museum, 51
Antiques at the Old Grange Hall, 428
Antiques Center of Cape Cod, 168
Antiques Depot, 475
Aptucxet Trading Post and Museum, 35,
    35

Aquinnah, 377, 385, 391–93, *393*, 395,
    404, 421
Ara's Tours, 439, 454
Arbor Cottage, 462
Architectural Walking Tours, 439
Arey's Pond, 240, 242
Aries East Gallery, 188
Armstrong-Kelley Park, 112
Art Cabinet, 476
Artful Hand Gallery, 231, *231*
Art House, The, 360
ARTichoke, 273, *273*
Artist's Association of Nantucket, 453,
    475
Artist Shanties, 127
Arts and Crafts Street Fair, 90
Art's Dune Tours, 334, *335*
Ashumet Holly Wildlife Sanctuary, 76,
    76
Atlantic (restaurant), 424
Atlantic House, 362
Atlantic Spice Co., 315, *315*
Atlantic White Cedar Swamp Trail, 278,
    286
Atwood Higgins House, 277, *277*
Atwood House Museum, 211, *211*
Audubon Society, 76, 401

B

Bagel Heaven, 100
Baker, Susan, 302
Bakker Gallery, 366
Ballston Beach, 308
Bank Beach, 197
Barb's Bike Shop, 155
Barclay Pond, 219
Barnstable, 103–17
Barnstable Harbor, 28, 29, 108, 109, 110
Barnum, P.T., 302
Barrett's Tours, 439
Bartlett's Farm, 479
baskets, 23, 477, *477*
Bas Relief Park, 328
Bass Hole Beach, 143, 144

Bass Hole Boardwalk, 143, *143*
Bass River Beach, 140, 143
Bass River Bridge, 140, 157
Bass River Charters, 140
Bass River Farmers' Market, 149
Bass River Golf Course, 141
Bass River Historic District, 142
Bates, Katharine Lee, 68, 74
Baxter Grist Mill, 139
Bayberry Hill, 288
Bayberry Hills Golf Course, 141
Bay End Farm, 46
Bay Lady II, 331, 334
Bay View Trail, 284
Beach Bar Grille, 221
Beach Bum Surf Co., 230
Beachcomber (boat excursion), 214
Beach Point Beach, 308
Beaver, 433, 441
Beebe Woods, 78
Beech Forest Trail, 341, *343*
Beetlebung Corner, 390
Beinecke, Walter, 434
bells: Chatham School Bells, 211; First
    Congregational Church, 68; St.
    Joseph's Bell Tower, 70; Wellfleet,
    278; West Parish Meetinghouse, 104
Bells Neck, 199
Belmont, Augustus, 36
Belushi, John, 377, 391, 398
Benjamin Nye Homestead and Museum,
    47, 52
Berta Walker Gallery, 296, 364
Beston, Henry, 29, 218, 257, 259, 264, 266
Beth Ann Charters, 335
Bike Zone, 125, 140
Bill and Judy Sayle, 477
Bill Fisher Tackle, 450
Billfish Tournament, 479
Bird Watcher's General Store, 26, 253
Black Crow Gallery, 62
Black Whale Gallery, 133
Blueberry Bog, The, 53
blueberry picking, 53
Blue Claw Boat Tours, 239
Bluefin Charters, 71
Blue Heron Gallery, 296
Blue Rock Resort, 141, 144
Blue Water Resort, 144
Board Stiff, 363
Boat Shop Museum, 107

Boatslip Resort & Beach Club, 362, *363,*
    337
Bob's Bar, 460
bonfires, 117, 258, 263, 364
Book Sale, 429
Books by the Sea, 116
Boston Tea Party, 441
Botanical Trails of the Historical Society
    of Old Yarmouth, 143–44
Botanique of Cape Cod, 149
Bourne, 33–46
Bourne, Richard, 93
Bournedale, 33
Bournedale Herring Run, 35, *37,* 38
Bourne Farm, 78
Box Turtle Woods, 288
Brant Point Beach, 457
Brant Point Lighthouse, *433, 435,* 445,
    445
Breakwater Beach, 173, 178
Breakwater Landing, 180
Breakwater/Long Point Dike, 342, *342*
Breeze Restaurant, 461
Brewster, 173–90
Briggs McDermott House & Blacksmith
    Shop, 37
British Beer Company, 80
Brooks Academy Museum, 193
Bryn Walker, 426
B-Strong, 395
Bucks Pond, 198
Bucktail Fishing Charters, 95
Buddha & Beads, 272
Bud's Go-Karts, 197
Bunch of Grapes Bookstore, 426
buoy tree, *257*
Burgess, Thornton W., 56, 62
Burton Baker Beach, 287
Butterflies of Cape Cod, 42
Buttermilk Bay, 33
Buttonbush Trail, 265
Buzzards Bay, 33
Buzzard's Bay Bikes, 38
Buzzards Bay Farmers' Market, 46
Buzzards Bay Recreation Area, 36

C

Cahoon Hollow Beach, 285, 291
Cahoon Hollow Lifesaving Station, 287
Cahoon Museum of American Art, 106
Caleb Nickerson House, 211

Callery-Darling Trail, 143
Cammett House, 107
Camp Edwards, 37
Campground Beach, 263
Canal Bait and Tackle, 40, 54, 95
Canal Cruisers, 38
Cannot Live Without Books, 169
canoeing & kayaking, 27
Capawock Movie Theater, 424
Cape Cinema, 166
Cape Cod Ahoy! (Tarbell), 93
Cape Cod Airfield, 107
Cape Cod Art Association, 116
Cape Cod Beer, 124, 133
Cape Cod Beer Farmers' Market, 133
Cape Cod Canal, 36, *38*, 43
Cape Cod Canal Bikeway, 37, 39, 53
Cape Cod Canal Company, 36
Cape Cod Canal Cruises, 38
Cape Cod Canal Vertical Lift Railroad
    Bridge, 36
Cape Cod Canal Visitor Center, The, 41
Cape Cod Catamaran, 282, *281*
Cape Cod Central Railroad, 38, 54, 123,
    123
Cape Cod Charter Guys, 39
Cape Cod Children's Museum, 96
Cape Cod Country Club, 73
Cape Cod Inflatable Park, 141, *141*
Cape Cod Kayak, 41, 74, *75*
Cape Cod Lavender Farm, 204, *205*
Cape Cod Light, 300
Cape Cod Mall, 134
Cape Cod Marathon, 90
Cape Cod Maritime Museum, 124
Cape Cod Melody Tent, 133, *133*
Cape Cod Museum of Art, 155, *155*
Cape Cod Museum of Natural History,
    174, 177, 178
Cape Cod National Golf Course, 200
Cape Cod National Seashore (CCNS), 27,
    257, 258, 291, 320
Cape Cod observation platform, 278
Cape Cod Parasail and Jet Ski, 142
Cape Cod Photo, Art & Framing, 254
Cape Cod Rail Trail, 26
Cape Cod Rail Trail Bike & Kayak, 176
Cape Cod Scallop Fest, 90
Cape Cod School of Art, 320
Cape Cod Theatre Project, The, 88
Cape Cod Waterways, 157

Cape Cod Windsurfing, 41
Cape Cod Windsurfing & Paddleboards,
    75
Cape Cod Winery, 69
Cape Cod YMCA, 109
Cape Cycle, 194
Cape Escape, 240
Cape Fishermen's Supply Inc., 216
Cape Playhouse, 167
Cape Pogue Lighthouse, 396, *396*, 397
Cape Pogue Wildlife Refuge, 395–98
Cape repertory Theatre, 183, 186
Cape Sail, 178
Capeshores Charters, 215
Cape Symphony Orchestra, 117, 132
Cape Tip'N Charter Fishing, 335
Cape Tip Seafood Market, *312*, 313, 314
Captain Bangs Hallet House, 139
Captain Joe P Charters, 54
Captain Jonathan Parker House, 107
Captain's Daughters, The, 367
Captain's Golf Course, The, 177
Captain's Mile, 144
Carnival, 368, 370
carousel, 51, 127, 128, 389
Carpenter Gothic, 390
Cartland of Cape Cod, 40
Cartwheels, 157
Castle Hill, 302
Cataumet Arts Center, 41, 46
Cataumet Marina, *42*
Cataumet Pier, 33
Catch of the Day, 293
Cayuga, 107
C. B. Stark, 427, *428*
Cecilia Joyce & Seward Johnson Gallery,
    475
Cedar Tree Neck Sanctuary, 402
Cee-Jay, 335
Cellar Leather, 134
Center for Coastal Studies, 329
Centerville, 103
Centerville Historical Museum, 107
Centerville Old Home Week, 117
Chameleon, 363
Champlain, Samuel de, 208, 233, 265
Chapin Memorial Beach, 153, 159, 163
Chappaquiddick, 395, 396
Charles Coffin House, 442
Charles Moore Arena, 239
Chase Park, 218

Chas'n Tails Charter Fishing, 335
Chatham, 206–33
Chequessett Neck Road, 278
Chequessett Yacht & Country Club,
    281–283
Cherry Stone Gallery, 294
Chicken Box, 475
Children's Beach, 456, *457*
Chilmark, 373–74, *376*, 377
Chilmark Chocolates, 428
Chilmark Pond Preserve, 398
Chilmark Pottery, 426
Chilmark Store, 422
Christina's Jewelry, 367
Christmas by the Sea, 90, 232
Christmas in Edgartown, 430
Christmas Stroll, 232, 436, 480
Christmas Tree Shop, 46
Christmas Weekend in the Harwiches,
    205
Church of the Messiah, 70
Cisco Beach, 458
Cisco Brewers, 453
cisgender, 321, 368
Claire Murray, 478
clam trees, 238, *238*
Clapps Pond, 343
Classic Aviators, 394
Clay Cliffs Aquinnah, 377, 383, 392, *393*
Cleveland, Grover, 33, 35, 37, 96, 179
Clifford, Barry, 327
Cliff Pond, 178
Cliff Road Bike Path, 451
Clinton, Kate, 337, 359
Club, The, 359
Coast Guard Beach, 257, 259, 262–64,
    264, 308
Coast Guard Heritage Museum (Old
    Customs House), 106, *106*
Cockle Cove Beach, 213, 216, 217
Codfish Park, 458
Coffin, Tristram, 433
Coffin School, The, 446
Cold Storage Beach, 308
Coleman, Frederick, 445
Collections Unlimited, 62
Collector's World, 273
College Light Opera Company, 87
'Comber, 291
Commercial Wharf, 440
Community Sing, 429

Conant House, The, 68
Connamessett Pond, 73
Cook's Brook Beach, 263
Cook's Cycles, 451
Cook Shop, 189
Coope De Ville, 420, *420*
Coop's Bait & Tackle, 395
Corner Cycle, 71, 108
Corn Hill Beach, 307
Corporation Beach, 157, 159
Coskata-Coatue Wildlife Refuge, 438,
    439, 453
Cottage Grove, 268
Cottage Museum, 390
Cottages, The, 465
Cotuit, 103
Cotuit Antiques, 116
Cotuit Fresh Market, 115
Cotuit Highground Country Club, 109
Cotuit Kettleers, 107
Cove Burying Grounds, 260
Cove Gallery, 296
Craftworks, 425
Craig, Philip R., 403
Craigville Beach, 103, 108, 110, 125
cranberries, 25, 56, 151, 196, 456
Cranberry Acres, 402
Cranberry Bog Tours, 196
Cranberry Harvest Festival, 25, 191
Cranberry Highway, 33, 40, 45, 54, 95,
    252
Cranberry Valley Golf Course, 197
Creative Arts Center, 213, 232
Crocker Pond, 79
Crosby Landing Beach, 178
Crosby Mansion, 176
Crowell, A. E., 107
Crowell, Elmer, 51
Crowes Pasture Conservation, 160
Crow Farm, 62
Crown & Anchor, 358
Crush Pad Food Truck, 301
Crystal Lake, 239, 242
Cultured Clam Corp., 159
Cycle Works, 394

D

Daffodil Festival, 479
Daily Brew Coffee House, 45
Dairy Bar & Grill, 293
Dallin, Cyrus Edward, 328

Dane Gallery, 476
Dangerfield, 297
Danville, 65
Dartmouth, 441
David Oliver's Cape Tip Sportswear, 363
Days Cottages, 310, *310*
Day's Market, 313, *313*
Dennis, 151–70
Dennis Pond, 140
Design Works, 149
Dexter, Charles O., 51
Dexter Grist Mill, 49, *50*
Dick's Bait & Tackle, 395
Dillard, Annie, 337
Dionis Beach, 451, 457
Dionis Bike Path, 451, 457
distillery, 301, 453
Doane Homestead Site, 260
dockworkers, 33
Dog Gone Sailing Charters, 336
Dog Runs, The, 219
Dolphin Fleet Whale Watch, 338
Dome, The, 71
Dowd, John, 310, 365
Down Cape Charters and Boat Rentals, 194
down-island, 373, 385
Dowses Beach, 108
Dr. Daniel Fisher House, 386, *387*
Dreamland Theater, 475
Dr. Gravity's Kite Shop, 204
Dry Line Gin, 301
Duck Harbor, 281, 287
Duck Inn Pub, 132
dune shacks, 259, 332, *332*, 343

E
Earle Road Beach, 198
Earth House, 254
East Beach at Cape Pogue Wildlife
    Refuge, 395
East Chop Lighthouse, 389, *389*
East Falmouth, 65
Eastham, *12*, 257–73
Eastman's Sport & Tackle, 73, 95
Eastville Beach, 405
Eastward Ho, *218*
Eben House, 345
ecosystem, 27
Ecotourz, 53, 54
Eddy Elementary School, 177
Eden Hand Arts, 169

Edgartown, 373–74, 379; artisans, 426;
    bookstores, 426; clothing, 426; to
    do, 394–95, 398–401; entertainment,
    424; farm stands, 423; galleries, 425;
    green space, 401–3; lodging, 406–7,
    412–13; to see, 386–88; special
    events, 428–29; where to eat, 413–15,
    417–18, 421
Edward A. Bigelow Gallery, 213
Edward Gorey House, 138, *138*
Edward Penniman House, 259, *259, 260*,
    267
Edward VII, 278
Eel Point, 455
Eel Pond, 73, 78, *79*
Egan Maritime Institute, 446
Egg Island, 125
Eight Cousins Children's Books, 88
1869 Schoolhouse and Museum, 259
Elburne, 170
Eldred's Auctions, 168
Emma Jack Charters, 140
Endeavor, 449
Entertainment Cinemas, 167, 424
Erica Wilson Nantucket, 478
Eriksson, Leif, 153, 373
Eriksson, Thorvald, 320
Esther Underwood Johnson Nature
    Center, 284
Evaul Studios & Gallery, 366
Expedition Whydah, 327
Exuma, 366

F
Fall for Harwich, 205, *205*
Falmouth, 65–90
Family Week, 368
Fancy's Market, 115
Fantasia Fair, 369
Farland by the Beach, 341
Farm Institute, 400
Farm Neck Golf Club, 398, 401
Featherstone Center for the Arts, 400
Felix Neck Wildlife Sanctuary, 401
Ferretti's Market, 185
ferries, 18
Festival of Arts, 232
Field Gallery, 425, *426*
Figawi Sailboat Race, 134, 479
Fine Arts Work Center, 321, 336, 368
Fire Hose Cart House, 446

First Church of Christ, 50
First Congregational Church, 68, 104, 193, 278
First Congregational Church Tower (Nantucket), 444, *444*
First Encounter Beach, 260, 263
First Encounter Coffee House, 272
First Light, 370
First Night Celebration, 232
First Parish Church, 176
Fisher Beach, 308
Fisherman's Daughter, 230, *231*
Fishermen's View, 61
fishing, 28
Flax Pond, 142, 177, 178
Florence Higginbotham House, 447
Flyer's Boat Rental, 334, *334*, 336
Flying Horses Carousel, 389
Food & Wine Festival, 430
Fooding Around Harwich, 205
Force 5 Watersports, 453
Fort Hill, *12*, 257, 266, *266*, 267, *267*
fountain, 49
Four Ponds Conservation Area, 40
Four Seas Ice Cream, 115
Four Winds Craft Guild, 478
Fox & Kit, 100
Fox Island Marsh, 288
Francis Street Beach, 457
Fred Thatcher Playground, 141
French Cable Station Museum, 235, *236*
Fresnel Light, *387*, 448
Friends Marketplace, 250
Friends Meeting House, 52, *53*
Fritz Glass, 169
Frost Fish Creek, 219
Frying Pan Gallery, The, 296
Fuller, Buckminster, 71
Fuller Street Beach, 403
Fulling Mill Brook Preserve, 403
Fun Seekers, 281

G
Gaa Gallery, 296, 365
Gale Force Bikes, 331
Galeria Cubana, 366
Gallagher, Russell, 291
Gallery 31 Fine Art, 253
Gannon and Benjamin Boatbuilders, 376
Gary Marotta Fine Art, 366
Gay Head Lighthouse, 392, *393*

Gay Head Sightseeing, 383
genealogy, 216
Ghosts, Gossip, and Downright Scandal, 401
gingerbread cottages, *376*, 390, 402, 410, 429
Girl Splash, 368
Glass Studio on Cape Cod, The, 62
Golden Basket, The, 477
Goombay Smash, 292
Goose Hummock, 27, 28, 215, 239, *240*, 241, 262
Goose Hummock Seasonal Shop, 157
Goose Pond, 215, 284
Gorey, Edward, 138, *138*
Gorham Cobbler Shop, 139
Gosnell Hall, 443
Gosnold, Bartholomew, 65, 120, 233, 373
Governor Bradford, 359
Granary Gallery at the Red Barn, 425
Grand Slam Entertainment, 196
Grange Hall, 390, 428
Gray Gables, 33, 45
Gray's Beach, 143–44
Grazing Fields Farm, 41
Great Cape Herbs, 188
Great Flat Pond Trail, 76, 97
Great Hollow Beach, 308
Great Island Tavern, 288
Great Island Trail, 287
Great Marsh Kayak Tours, 141
Great Neck South/Route 151 Path, 94
Great Point Light, 447, 454
Great Pond, 262, 263, 281, 287, 305
Great Provincetown Schooner Regatta, The, 369
Great Put-On, The, 427
Green Briar Nature Center, 47, 56, *56*
Greenough, Thomas, 142
Grews Pond, 78
gristmill, 47, 49, 55, 174, 236
Gristmill Park, 218
Grotta Bar, 359
Guild of Harwich Artist, 205
Gull Pond, 281, 282, 287
Gustare Oils & Vinegars, 232
Guyer Art Barn, 134

H
Hadwen House, 436, 442, 443
Hallet Barn, 68

Hallet's, 138
Halloween, 369
Hamblin Pond, 108, 111
HandCraft House, 189
Hangar B Eatery, 226
Harbor Beach, 341
Harbor Hotel Provincetown, 337
Harbor Lighting and Boat Parade, 134
Harbor Stage Company, 294
Harden Studios, 116
Harding Beach, 217
Harris-Black House, 175
Harwich, 191–205
Hatches Harbor, 340
Hatch's Fish Market, 293, *294*
Hathaway's Pond, 111, 127
Hawthorne, Charles W., 320, 327–28, 337
Hay, John, 174, 178
Head of the Meadow Beach, 307, *307*
Head of the Meadow Bike Trail, 304
Heart Pottery, 186
Helen H Deep Sea Fishing, 125
Henry Coffin House, 442
Hepburn, 476
Heraclitus, 12
Heritage Museums & Gardens, 51, *51*, 55, 63
heron, blue, 38, 52, 160, 199, 279
Herridge Books, 294
Herring Cove Beach, 329, 331, 335, 341, *341*
Herring Pond, 263
Herring River, 199
Herring Run, 190
Hidden Gem, 254
Higgins Farm Windmill, 175
Higgins Pond, 177
Highfield Hall and Gardens, 78, *78*, 87
Highland Golf Links, 302, 305
Highland House Museum, 300, *302*, 305
Highland Light, 297, 300, *304*, 305
high season, 18
High Tea at the Captain's House Inn, 227, *227*
Hill, Polly, 402
Hinckley's Pond, 198
Hindu Charters, 331, *331*, 334
Historic Preservation Month, 479
Historic Walking Tour of Provincetown, 337
HMS *Newcastle*, 237

HMS *Nimrod*, 68
Hog Island Beer Company, 246, *246*
Holiday Hill, 158
Holly Days, 63
Holly Folly Festival, 370
Holly Ridge Golf Club, 54
Home for the Holidays, 63
Homegrown Boutique, 252
Home of the Big Red Rooster, 89
Honey Candle Co., 254
Honeysuckle Lane, 219
Hook Charters, 335
Hopkins, Constance, 267
Hopkins, Stephen, 135
Hopkins Blacksmith Shop, 175
Hopper, Edward, 297
horseback riding, 28
Horton, Isaiah, 267
Hot Diggity, 100
House Tour, 480
Howes Street Beach, 159
Hoxie House, 50, *50*
Huntington, Cynthia, 29, 333
Hussey (captain), 433
Hyannis, 119–34
Hyannis Village Parade, 117
Hyannis Whale Watcher Cruises, 109
Hyannis Youth & Community Center, 109, 127
Hydrangea Walk, 217, *217*
Hy-Line Fishing Trips, 126

I
ice–skating, 41
Idle Times Bike Shop, 239, 279
Illumination Night, 429
Impulse, 367
Independence Day, 232, 296, 368, 479
Indian burial ground, 390
Indian Lands Conservation Area, 160
Indian Neck Beach, 287
Indigenous Museum of the Aquinnah Wampanoag, 393
Instant Karma, 134
International Film Festival, 358, 368, 424, 429
Island Alpaca, 427
Island Boat Rentals, 449
Island Carousel, 127
Island Cove, 398
Islander Sportfishing, 71

Island Fair, 480
Island Queen, 66, 380
Island Time Charters, 394
itineraries, 16

J
Jackknife Beach, 217
Jack's Boat Rentals, 281
Jail Break Fishing Charters, 195
Jailhouse Tavern, 246
Jam Kitchen, 56
Jams, 313
Janine B. Sportfishing, 157
Jarves, Deming, 46, 47, 52
Jaws, 377, 404
JazzFest, 90
J. Butler Collection, The, 475
Jean Finch Skateboard Park, 240
Jehu Pond Conservation Area, 97
Jenny Lind Tower, 302
Jericho House and Barn Museum, 155
Jethro Coffin House, 444
Jetties Beach, 449, 452, 453, 456, 479, 480
JFK Memorial, 122, *122*
Jigged-Up Sportfishing, 305
Jirah Luce House, 388
Jobi Pottery & Gallery, 315
Joey's Joint, 270, *270*
John F. Kennedy Hyannis Museum, 122
John Gallo Ice Arena, 41
Johnson, Joyce, 332
Johnston's Cashmere, 476
John Wendell Barrett House, 442
Jonathan Young Windmill, 236, *236*
Joseph Sylvia State Beach, 404, *404*
Josiah Dennis Manse Museum, 154, *154*
Josiah Mayo House, 210
Jules Besch Stationers, 315
Julia Wood House, 68
Julie Heller, 364
Junior, 107
junior ranger programs, 41

K
Kalmus Park Beach, 127
Kandy Korner, 134
Katama (or South) Beach, 403
Kate Gould Park, 228, *228*
Katharine Cornell Theatre/Tisbury Town Hall, 388

kayaks & paddleboards, 41
Kelley, David, 142
Kelley Chapel, 144
Kemp, Harry, 105, 332
Kemp pottery, 252, *252*
Kennedy, Joe, Jr., 65, 124
Kennedy, John F., 120, 122, 258, 291
Kennedy Compound, 122
Kent, Rockwell, 166
Kent's Point, 242
Kerouac, Jack, 332
Kescayogansett Pond, 242
Kiley Court Gallery, 366
King's Way Golf Club, 141
Knob, 73
Kobalt Gallery, 366

L
labor strike, 33, 47
labyrinth, 51
Lady J. Sportfishing, 108
Lady's Slipper, 78, 144, 160, 286
Lagoon Pond, 394, 398
Lake Tashmoo, 404
Lambert's Cove Beach, 405
Lambert's Farm Market, 61
Lands End Marine Supply, 367
Larkin Gallery, 315
Laura Jay Charters, 54
Lea's Boat Rentals, 178
Lecount Hollow Beach, 281, 285
Left Bank Gallery, 253, 296
Lemon Tree Village Shops, 189, *189*
LeRoux, 427
Lewis, David, 122, 124
Lewis Bay, 117, 119, 124, 125
LGBTQ, 319, 321–22, 359, 362, 368, 370
Liam Maguire's Irish Pub & Restaurant, 87, *87*
Liam's, 185
LiBAYtion, 201
Liberté, The, 75
Liberty Fishing Charters, 176–77
Liberty House, 89
Lighthouse Beach, 209, 218, 403
lighthouses: Brant Point, 445, *445*; Cape Cod Light, 300; Cape Pogue, *396*, 397; Chatham, 209; East Chop, 389, *389*; Edgartown Lighthouse, 388; Fresnel Light, 387; Gay Head, 392, *393*; Great Point, 447, 454; Highland

Light, 300, *304*, 305; Long Point, 338; Nauset, 261; Nobska, 73; Race Point, 338; Sankaty Head, 455; Stage Harbor, 209; tours, 300; West Chop Lighthouse, 388; Wood End, 338, *339*
Lighting of the Lobster Pot Tree, 370
Lighting of the Monument, 369
Lighting the Trail, 385
Lightship Basket Museum, 477
Lilly, Eli, 51
Lilly, Josiah K., 51, 76
Lily Pond Park, 459
Lincoln Brothers Fishing, 39
Lind, Jenny, 302
Lindbergh, Charles, 235
Linnell Landing, 178
Little Capistrano Bike Shop, 262, 279
Little Cliff Pond, 177
Lobsterville Beach, 406
Logan, 287
Loines Observatory, 449
Long Beach, 110
Longnook Beach, 308
Long Pasture Wildlife Sanctuary, 112
Long Point, *319*, 338, 398, 402, 405
Long Pond, 140, 178, 198, 281, 284, 287, 450, 458
Lothrop, John, 103, 104, 106
Lothrop Bible, 105
Lothrop Hill Cemetery, 106
Lou Lou's Leasing, 108
Lovell's Pond, 111
Lowell, Abbott Lawrence, 96
Lowell Holly Reservation, 96
Lucy Vincent Beach, 406
Luke's Love Boundless Playground, 109

M

MacMillan, Donald B., 328, 360
MacMillan Wharf, 326
Maco's Bait and Tackle, 40
Mac's on the Pier, 292
Macy, Thomas, 447
Madaket, 447, 451, 455, 457
Mad Max Sailing Adventures, 399
Magellan Deep Sea Fishing Charters, 195
Magic Carpet, 399
Mailer, Norman, 332
Main Street Antique Center, 168
Main Street at Federal Street, 478
Main Street Books, 252, *252*

Main Street Pottery, 229
Malcolm Cottage, 122–23
Manuel E. Correllus State Forest, 401, 413
Maps of Antiquity, 232
Maquire Landing, 287
Marchant House, 123
Marconi Beach, 263, *285*, 287, 288, 327
Marconi Wireless Station, 277
Margo's, 116
Maria Mitchell Aquarium & Museum Shop, 449
Maria Mitchell Association, 448, 453
Maria Mitchell Science Library, 448
Maria Mitchell Vestal Street Observatory, 449
Marine Biological Laboratory, 65, 69
Marine Debris and Plastics Program, 329
Marine Specialties, 360, 363, 367, *367*
Mark August, 232
Market Street Bookshop, 100
Marrinan Gallery, 296
Marstons Mills, 103, 107–9, 111
Martha's Vineyard, *16*, 373–430
Mashnee Island, 41, *41*
Mashpee (Massapee, Massipee), 91–100
Mashpee pond, 96
Mashpee River Woodlands, 96
Mashpee–Wakeby Ponds, 57, 95, 96
Massachusetts Maritime Academy, 33, 35
Massachusetts Military Reservation (Otis Air National Guard Base), 33, 35, 37
Mattakeese, 103, 124
Mattaquason (Chief), 208
Mauclere, Florence, 363
Maushop, 160
Mayflower, 135, 257, 260, 267, 299, 328
Mayflower, The, 232
Mayflower Beach, 159
Mayflower Café, 355
Mayflower Compact, 328, 329
Mayflower Trolley, *324*
Mayhew, Thomas, 433
Mayhew Chapel, 390
Mayo Beach, 287
maze garden, 51
Meadowbrook Road Conservation Area, 144
Meeting House Museum, 235
Memorial Wharf, 388
Memories of Provincetown, 366

Menauhant Beach, 77
Menemsha, 377, *377*, 392, 394, 402, 406, 412, *412*, 423, *423*
Menemsha Pond, 391, 402
Mermaids on Cape Cod, 169
Mermaids on Main, 232
Methodist Campground, 373
Mews at Brewster Antiques, 186
Meyerowitz, Joel, 310
Miacomet Golf Course, 451
Miacomet Pond, 459
Michael Kane Lightship Baskets, 477
Middle Pond, 108
Mielziner, Jo, 166
Mike's Bike Trail Rentals, 239
Milestone Bog, 456
Mill Pond, 139, 215, 406
Millway Beach, 110
Mink Meadows, 398
Mitchell, Maria, 453, 448, 449
Mitchell's Book Corner, 476
Moccasin Flower, 286
Mocean Cape Cod, 94, 96
Modern Vintage Design Studio, 63
Moffett, Ross, 328
Monomoy, 206, *206*, 212, 214, 229
Monument Beach, 33, 38, 43
Moors and Altar Rock, The, 459
Moor's End, 447
mopeds, 383
Morning Glory Farm, 423
Morris Island, 213, 215
Mosher Photo, 428
Moshup Beach Overlook, 393
Moshup Public Beach, 405
Mourt's Relation (Winslow), 329
Movies Under the Stars, 87
Mrs. Mugs, 63
Munson Gallery, 230
Murray's Toggery Shop, 476, *478*
Muse, The, 475
Museums on the Green, 68
Mussel Beach Health Club, 335
Mytoi, 396, 397

N
Nantucket, 433–80
Nantucket Vineyard, 453
Narrow Land Pottery, 294
National Marine Fisheries Service, 65
National Marine Life Center, 37

National Seashore trail on Great Island, 275
Native Plant Protection Act, 286
Natural History Day Camps, 284
Natural Science Museum, 449
nature preserves, 28
Naukabout Beer Co., 100
Nauset Beach, 218, 233, 241, *243*
Nauset Bike Trail, 261, 279
Nauset Lantern Shop, 252
Nauset Light, 261
Nauset Light Beach, 29, 262, 263
Nauset Marsh, 141, 233, 257, 265, 267
Nauset Model Railroad Club, 240
Nauset Surf, 240
Nauset tribe, 257
Newcomb Hollow Beach, 283, 285, *285*
New Seabury, 91
Nickerson, Edmond, 156
Nickerson, William, 208, 211, 216
Nickerson State Park, 27, 173, 176–79, *177*
Nicky's Park, 343
Night at the Chef's Table, A, 368
Nina Hellman Antiques, 475
Nip-n-Tuck Farm, 398
Nobadeer Beach, 457
Nobel Prize winners, 70
Nobscusset Pier Corporation, 159
Nobska Farms, 89
Nobska Light, 72, 73, 75, *75*
Noon's Landing, 308
North Beach (Chatham), 218
North Chatham Outfitters, 216
North Falmouth, 65
North Shore Charters, 395
North Trail, 178, 181
North Truro Air Force Base, 302
North Water Gallery, 425
North Water Street, 388
"Nude Beach," 458

O
Oak Bluffs, 373, 376
Odell Studios and Gallery, 230
Off Main Gallery, 296
Oils by the Sea/Roccapriore Gallery, 366
Old Cobb Library, 303, *303*
Old Colony, 359
Old Colony Bikes, 194
Old Colony Railroad, 26, 320

Olde Barnstable Fairgrounds Golf
    Course, 109
Olde Colonial Courthouse, 107
Oldest House, 436, 444
Oldest Windmill, 260, *261*
Old Gaol, The, 446
Old Harbor Lifesaving Station, 328
Old Indian Meetinghouse, 104
Old King's Highway Historic District, 173
Old Mill, 447
Old North Wharf, 440
Old Schoolhouse, 388
Old Sculpin Gallery, 425, *425*
Old Silver Beach, 71, 75, 77
Old South Wharf, 440, *442*, 475, *476*
Old Town House Road Park, 141
Old Whaling Church, 387, *388*, 424
Oliver's Red Clay Tennis Courts, 283
On Center Gallery, 366
O'Neill, Eugene, 320, 332
On the Fringe, 170
Open Air Antiques Fair, 190
Orleans, 233–54
O'Shea's Olde Inne, 167
Osterville, 23, 103–4, 107–9, 112, 114–16
Otis, James, Jr., 105
Otis Air National Guard Base, 37
Outer Bar & Grille, 201
Outermost Adventures, 214, *214*
Outermost Home, 364, *365*
Outermost House, The (Beston), 218, 257,
    264
Owen Park Beach, 404, 406
Oyster Pond, 218, 232
Oyster River, 215
oysters: Barnstable Harbor, 130; Brew-
    ster, 180; Chatham, 203; Cotuit, 98;
    Edgartown, 417; Katama Bay, 415;
    Nobscussett, 162; Quivet Neck, 163;
    Wellfleet, 276, 280, 290; Wellfleet
    Oyster Fest, 295; wood fired, 223
Oysterville, 103

P
Pacific Club, 441
Pacific National Bank, 441, 448
Packard Gallery, 365
Paine's Creek Beach, 178
Pamet, 297, 299, 304, 306, *306*, 309
Pamet Harbor Yacht and Tennis Club,
    305

Pamet River, 306
P&D Fruit, 169
Pandora's Box, 427
Paramount, 358
Parnassus Book Service, 150, *150*
Pastoral Fort Hill, 267
Patriot Party Boats, 71
Paul Harney Golf Club, 74
PAVE PAWS, 37
Pawkannawkut tribe, 142
Paw Wah Point Conservation Area, 242
Payomet, 297
Payomet Performing Arts Center, 315
Peaked Hill Reservation, 402
Peaked Hill Trust, 332
Peary, Robert, 328
Pedal Ptown Bike Tours, 331
Pedego Electric Bikes, 140
Pelo Mar, 187
Peregrine Theatre Ensemble, 361
Peter Beaton Hat Studio, 478
Peter Finch Basketmaker, 477
Peter Foulger Gallery, 443
Philbin, 405
Pier 37 Boathouse, 87
Pilgrim Heights Area, 308
Pilgrim Lake, 242, 297, *297*, 303
Pilgrim Monument and Provincetown
    Museum, 328
Pilgrims, 257, 260, 278, 299, 307–8, 320,
    328–29
Pilgrims' First Landing Park, 329
Pilgrim Spring Trail, 308
Pilgrim Spring Woodlands, 288
Pine Island Cove, 125
pipe organ, 155, 278, 474
Pip's Rip, 54
Pirate Adventures, 125, 395
Pirate's Cove Adventure Golf, 142
Plan Sea, 95
Playground by the Bay, 177
Pleasant Bay, 194, 197, 213, 233, 239, 241,
    242
Pleasant Bay Beach, 217, 222, 242
Pleasant Bay Community Sailing, 197
Pleasant Lake General Store, 203
Pleasant Road Beach, 197
Plush & Plunder, 132
Pocasset, 33
Pocasset Naturals, 46
Pocasset River Marina, 38

Pollock, Jackson, 332
Pollack's, 476
Polly Hill Arboretum, 402
Polpis Road Path, 451
Pond Road, 305
Popponesset Marketplace, 100
Pops by the Sea, 134
Porchside Bar, 355
Portuguese Festival, 368, *370*
Portuguese matriarchs, 330, *330*
Portuguese sailors, 320
Possible Dreams Auction, 428
Postcard Harbor Tours, 283
Post Office Cabaret, 359
Post Office Gallery, 315
Poucha Pond Kayak Tour, 397
Powers Landing, 287
powwow, 89
Predatuna Sportfishing, 126
Prence, Thomas, 257
Preservation Hall, 278
Princess Beach, 160
Province Lands, 320, 331
Provincetown, 319–70
P-Town Airs, 331
Ptown Bikes, 331
Ptown Pedicab, 324, *324*
Puma Park Playground, 305
Pump House Surf & Paddle, 240
Punch Bowl, 78
Punkhorn Parklands, 173, 181
Pure Vita, 272, *272*
Putnam, Ida, 56

Q

quahogs, 238, 276, 280, 450
Quaker Meeting House, 446
Quarterdeck Lounge, 132
Quashnet River, 73, 76
Quashnet Valley Country Club, 96
Quissett Harbor, 73
Quitsa Overlook, 391
Quitsa Pond, 391
Quivett Neck, 151

R

Race Point Beach, 328, 340, *340*
Race Point Lighthouse, 338, 340
Ragg Time Ltd., 253
Ram Pasture, 455–56
recommended reading, 29–30

Recreation and Beach Department, 307
Red Brook Pond, 43
Red Fish Blue Fish, 133
Red Maple Swamp, 267
Red River Beach, 197
Reed Books, 204
Reel Deal Fishing Charters, 304
Regal Cape Cod Mall, 132
Regal Mashpee Commons, 100
Regatta (Hyannis), 134
Revere, Paul, 68, 104, 302, 328
Rhododendron Display Garden, 242
rhododendrons, 51, 76, 96, 144
Rice Polak Gallery, 365
Richard G. Luce House, 388
Riddle Escape Room, 95
Rideaway Adventures, 53, 54, 94, 96
Ridgevale Beach, 217
Ripley's Believe It or Not, 278
Ritz, The, 424
Riverview Bait & Tackle, 140
Riviera, 144
Rock Harbor, 233, 236, *237*, 238
Rock Harbor Charter Fleet, 239
Roosevelt, Franklin D., 36
Roosevelt, Theodore, 278, 328
Roots, 367
Ross Coppelman and Kate Nelson, 169
Ross' Grill, 350
Rotch, William, 433, 441
Route 6A's antiques and galleries, 187
Rubel Bike Maps, 26, 394
R. W. Cutler Bikes, 394
Ryan Family Amusements, 41, 141
Ryder Beach, 308

S

Sacco and Vanzetti trial, 166
Sacred Cod, The, 221
Sagamore, 33, 38, 42, 44
Sail Ena, 399
Sailworld, 38
Salt House, The (Huntington), 333
Salt Pond Areas Bird Sanctuaries, Inc., 78
Salt Pond Visitor Center, 257, 258, 263, *263*
Salt Yarn Studio, 170
Salty Crown Boutique, 252, *253*
Salty Market, 313
Samuel B. Dottridge House, 107
Sandcastle & Sculpture Day, 480

Sandcastle Contest, 170
Sand Pond, 198–99
Sandwich, 47–63
Sandy Neck Beach, 26, 47, 108, 110, *110*
Sandy Neck Great Salt Marsh Conserva-
  tion Area, 47, 54, 111, *111*, 123
Sandy Pond, 142
Sanford Farm, 455, 456
Sankaty Head Golf Club, 451
Sankaty Head Light, 443, 454–55
Santuit Pond, 73
Saquatucket Harbor, 178, 191, 194–95, *198*
Sarah (catboat), 124
Sativa, 204
Scargo Beach, 160
Scargo Lake, 154, 157, 160
Scargo Pottery, 168, *168*
Scargo Tower, 153, 154, *154*
Schoolhouse Gallery, 364
Schoolhouse Pond, 215, 218
Schubael's Pond, 108
'Sconset, 433–45, 454–58, 465, 471, 474,
  479
Scusset Beach State Reserve, 39, 54, 55
Scusset State Park, 38
Sea Bird and Seal Cruise, 284
Sea Call Farm, 242
Sea Captains Church, 155
Sea Dog Fishing Team & Charters, 156
Sea Gull Beach, 142
Sea Gypsy, 395
Seaside Daylily Farm, 427
Seaside Festival, 150
Sea Sports, 125
Sea Street Beach, 159
Sea Witch Sailing Charters, 399
Secret Garden Tour, 368
Sesachacha Pond, 459
Sesuit Harbor, 151
Seymour Pond, 198
S-4 Crash Site, 336
Shaker Round Barn, 51
sharks, 195, 239, 282–83, 305, 340
Shark Shark Tuna, 140
Shawme-Crowell State Forest, 55
Shawme Duck Pond, 47, 55, *55*
Shearwater Excursions, 452
Sheep Pond, 177, 178
shellfishing, 29
Shining Sea Bike Path, 71, *72*, 74
Ship Shops Inc., 140

Shop Therapy, 363, 367
Shore Road, 303, *303*
Shuckers, 87
Siasconset, 451, 454, 455
Sickday, 294
Simie Maryles Gallery, 365
Single Women's Weekend, 368
Sippewissett, 65, 81
1641 Wing Fort House, 52
Skaket Beach, 241
Skiff Hill, 267
Skipper, The, 395
Skull Island Adventure Golf & Sports
  World, 141
smallpox, 68, 142
Small Swamp Trail, 308
Smith, John, 93
Smuggler's Beach, 140, 143
Smuggler's Beach Fishing Pier, 140
Solis, 205
Soul to Sole, 88
South Beach (Chatham), 218
South Cape Beach State Park, 76, 91,
  94–97
South Church, 446
South Dennis Historic District, 156
South Hollow Spirits, 301
South Trail, 178
Sovereign Bank, 388
Sow's Ear Antiques, 116
Sparks Jewelry, 367
Spinnaker (whale), 329
Spohr Gardens, 72, *72*
Sports Port Bait & Tackle, 127
Spruce Hill Conservation Area, 181
square dancing, 294
Squeteague Harbor, 73
Squibnocket Beach, 406
Stage Harbor, 215
Stage Harbor lighthouse, 209
Stage Harbor Marine, 210
Stage Stop Candy, 170
Standish, Myles, 36, 257, 260, 299
Starbuck, Joseph, 441, 442
Starlight Theatre and Café, 472, 475
State Army Aviation complex, 37
Stellwagen Bank National Marine
  Sanctuary, 338
Stephen Swift Furniture, 478
Steve Lyons Gallery, 231
St. Francis Xavier Church, 124

Stick'n Rudder Aero Tours, 213
St. Joseph's Bell Tower, 70
St. Mary's Church Gardens, 112, *112*
St. Mary's Garden, 70
Stonebridge Marina, 38
Stonewall Pond, 391
Stony Brook Grist Mill, 174, *175*
St. Paul's Episcopal Church, 446
Straight Wharf, 440, *441*
Strawberry Festival, 232
Striped Bass and Bluefish Derby, 430
Strong Wings Eco Guides, 452
Strong Wings Summer Camp, 450
Sturgis Library, 105
submarine, 69, 96, 233
Sugar Surf Cape Cod, 241
summer camp, 109, 177, 398, 450
Summer Concerts on the Green, 314
"Summer White House," 33
sundial, *454*
Sunken Ship, The, 452
Sunrise Bait & Tackle, 196
Superfund site, 37
SUPfari Adventures, 178, 240, *241*
Surf Drive Beach, 77
surfing & sailboarding, 29
Surfside Beach, 438, 456, 457, 465, 466
Surfside Bike Path, 451
Susan Baker Memorial Museum, 302
Susan Jean, 71
Sushi by Yoshi, 472
Swan Pond Overlook, 160
Swan River, 153
Swan River Fish Market, 167
Sweet Inspirations, 479
Swift-Daley House and Tool Museum,
    259, *260*
Swiss Family Robinson, 141
Sydenstricker Galeries, 187

T
Talbot's Point Salt Marsh Wildlife
    Reservation, 57
Tales of Cape Cod, 107
Tao Water Art Gallery, 116
Tarbell, Arthur Wilson, 93
Taylor-Bray Farm, 144
Taylor Point Marina, 38
Teichman Gallery, 188
Tennessee Williams Theater Festival,
    369

Thacher, Mary, 139
Theatre Workshop of Nantucket, 475
They Also Faced the Sea, 327, 330, *330*
Thomas A. D. Watson Studio, 315
Thomas Macy House, 441
Thomas Macy Warehouse, 440
Thompson, Ben, 119
Thompson's Field, 199
Thoreau, Henry David, 26, 29, 173, 300,
    339, 445
Thoreau's, 201
Thornton W, Burgess Society, 56
"Three Bricks," 441, *443*
Three Sisters Gifts, 273
Three Sisters Lighthouses, 261, *261*
tidal flats, 112
Time and the Town (Vorse), 336
Tim's Used Books, 363
Tisbury Great Pond, 405
Titanic, 69
Titcomb's Book Shop, 62, *62*
Tivoli Day, 430
Toad Hall, 124
Toast of Harwich, 205
Tony Kent Arena, 158
Touch of Glass, A, 169
Toy Boat, The, 479
Trading Company, The, 230
Trampoline Center, 196
Tree's Place Gallery, 253
Trinity Park Tabernacle, 389
Triple Eight Distillery, 453
Trolley Tour Taste of Yarmouth, 150
Truro, 297–316
Tuck & Holand Metal Sculptures, 426
Turner, Naomi, 228
Twenty Boat Rums, 301
Twenty-Eight Atlantic, 201
Twigs, 90
Twin Brooks Golf Course, 127

U
Uncle Seth's Pond, 406
Uncle Tim's Bridge, *287*, 288
Underground, The, 359
Underground Art Gallery, 188
Underground Railroad, 243
Under the Sun, 88
Union Chapel, 390, *390*
Unitarian Universalist Church, 446, 474
Universalist Meetinghouse, 329

up-island, 373
Upper Mill Pond, 177, 178
USCG *Paulding*, 336
US Coast Guard Air Station, 37
USS *Squalus*, 336
Utilities, 367

V

Vanderbilt Gallery, 479
Vault, The, 359
Veteran's Field Playground, 216
Veterans Beach, 127
Veterans Memorial Park, 127
Victor Powell's Workshop, 362
Village Toy Store, 189
Vincent House Museum, 387
Vineyard Artisans Holiday Festival, 430
Vineyard Artisans Summer Festivals,
    428
Vineyard Conservation Society, 399, 401
Vineyard Family Tennis, 401
Vineyard Haven, 374, *374*, 380, 404
Vineyard Haven Harbor, 373, *374*, 399
Vineyard Playhouse, 423
Vineyard Sound band concerts, The, 424
vintage-cars, 51, 479
Viv's Kitchen & Juice Bar, 249, *249*
Vorse, Mary Heaton, 336

W

Wakeby Pond, 57, 96
Walkway to the Sea, 119
Wampanoag: Aptucxet Trading Post and
    Museum, 35; Aquinnah Commu-
    nity Baptist Church, 391; Aquinnah
    Cultural Center, 393; Aquinnah
    Cultural Trail, 385; Aquinnah Shop,
    421; Aquinnah Tribal Adminis-
    trative Building, 392; Aquinnah,
    377; Clay Cliffs of Aquinnah, 392,
    393; Edgartown, 373; Indian Burial
    Ground, 390; Mashpee Indian Meet-
    inghouse, 94; Mashpee Wampanoag
    Museum, 94; Mashpee, 91, 93, 100;
    Mayflower, 91; Mayhew Chapel, 390;
    New Seabury, 91; Pilgrim Monument
    and Provincetown Museum, 328;
    powwows, 89; Provincetown, 320;
    Wampanoag Indian Museum, *95*;
    Yarmouth, 142
wampum, 35, 428

Waquoit Bay National Estuarine
    Research Reserve, 76
Waquoit Jetty, 95
War of 1812, 233, 237
Warren, Mercy Otis, 106
Washburn Island, 76, 77
Washington George, 36
Waskosim's Rock Preservation, 402
Wasque Point, 395, 396
Wasque Reservation, 396
Waterfront Park, 78
Water's Edge Cinema, 358
Water Wizz Park, 40
Wave, 358
Wayne's Antiques, 186
Weather Store, The, 63
Webster, Daniel, 96, 445
Weeping Beach Trees, 124, *124*, 139
Wellfleet, 275–96
Wellfleet Bay Wildlife Sanctuary, 275;
    Chatham, 214; Eastham, 262; Orle-
    ans, 239; Wellfleet, 282
Wendte, Carl, 329
Wequaquet Lake, 108, *109*, 111
Wequassett Resort and Golf Club, 194,
    200, 201, 204, 205, 216
Werner, Hazel Hawthorne, 333
Wesleyan Grove, 376, 390
West, Dorothy, 376, 385
West Barnstable Cemetery, 105
West Barnstable Conservation Area, 112
West Barnstable Tables, 116, *117*
West Chop Lighthouse, 388, *389*
West Dennis Beach, 153, 158, 159
West End, The, 131
West Falmouth, 65, 73, 74, 76, 78, 86
West Parish Meetinghouse, 104, *105*
West Tisbury, 376–77
whale oil, 70, 300, 443
Whaler's Wharf, 350, 360–61, 368
whales, 299, 329
whale-watching, 29, *111*; Barnstable Har-
    bor, 108; Beth Ann Charters, 335; Dog
    Gone Sailing Charters, 336; Dolphin
    Fleet Whale Watch, 338; Falmouth, 71;
    Hyannis, 109; MacMillan Wharf, 326;
    Maria Mitchell Aquarium & Museum
    Shop, 449; Provincetown, 337–38,
    337, 368; Race Point Beach, 340; Tree-
    house Lodge, 82; Winnetu Oceanside
    Resort, 407; Woods Hole, 71

whaling, 299, 433–34, 436, 442, 443, *443*, 449

Whaling Museum, 436, 442, *443*

Wharf, The, 424

Wheeler, Wilfred, 76

Wheel Happy, 394

Wheelhouse Bike Co., 214

Where the Sidewalk Ends, 230, *230*

Whimsy, 204, *204*

White Crest Beach, 285

White Stone Equestrian, 398

Whydah, 327

Whydah Pirate Museum, 139, 327

Wianno Senior, 107

Wicked Thrift, 149, *149*

Wicks, Francis, 68

Wild Animal Lagoon, 142

Wildflower Pottery, 187, *187*

Wild Rice, 363

Wiley Park, 262, 263

William-Scott Gallery, 365

William Street, 388

Willy's Gym, 262

Windfall Market, 86

Windmill Park, 139

windmills: Aptucxet Trading Post and Museum, 35; Brewster, 173, 175–76; Christmas Tree Shop, 46; Jonathan Young Windmill, 236, *236*; Old Mill, 447; Oldest windmill, 260, *261*; Sandwich Art Museum, 51; Swan River fish Market, 167; Yarmouth Windmill Park, 139

Windmill Weekend, 273

Wind's Up, 398, 401

windsurfing, 41, 75, 281

Windswept Cranberry Bog, 456

Wine Festival, 430, 479

Wing's Island Trail, 174, 178

Winslow, Edward, 329

Winslow Crocker House, 139

Wish Gift Co., 63

Wisteria Antiques, 186

Wizard of Oz, The, 166

Women of Color Weekend, 368

Women's Week, 369

Wood End Light Lookout Station, 338, *339*

Woods, the, 455–56

Woodshed, The, 186

Woods Hole, 65–90

Woodworks Gallery, 189

Writs of Assistance, 105

Wychmere Harbor, 191, *191*, 194

Y

Yankee Doodle Shop, 205

Yankee Ingenuity, 232

Yankee II Deep Sea Fishing, 195

Yanno, 120

Yard, The, 423

Yarmouth, 135–150

Yellow Umbrella Books, 229

YMCA of Martha's Vineyard, 398

Young's Bicycle Shop, 451

Young's Fish Market, 251, *251*

Z

Zack's Cliffs, 405

Zero Main, 478

zip line, 55, 196

zoo, 42